Labor Guide
to Labor Law

Labor Guide to Labor Law

Bruce S. Feldacker, J.D., LL.M.

Reston Publishing Co., Inc.
A Prentice-Hall Company
Reston, Virginia

To Barbara

Library of Congress Cataloging in Publication Data

Feldacker, Bruce S
  Labor guide to labor law.

  Includes bibliographies and index.
   1. Labor laws and legislation—United States.
2. Trade-unions—United States.   I. Title.
KF3369.F44   344.73'01   79-29694
ISBN 0-8359-3921-9

10 9 8 7 6 5 4 3 2 1

Printed in the United States

Contents

Preface

Labor Studies programs, in which Union members study labor relations from the perspective of labor, are growing rapidly throughout the United States. Labor Law is an important course in these programs. During the past six years, I have served as an instructor of Labor Law at the Labor Studies Center, St. Louis Community College at Forest Park. I have found the students to be interested and hard working. Still, teaching a labor law course has been hampered by the lack of a suitable text. Law school labor law texts are too technical, and emphasize many procedural points that are of no interest to a lay person. Most graduate labor law texts are intended for business school use. They are written from management's perspective, and they tend to emphasize issues of interest to management rather than labor.

This book is intended to fill the gap. It is a comprehensive survey of labor law in the private sector, written from the labor perspective for labor relations students and for unions and their members. Thus, issues of greatest importance to unions are emphasized, just as a text intended for management would emphasize issues of importance to management. Where the law permits a union to make certain tactical choices, those choices are pointed out. Included is material on internal union matters, which tend to be either ignored or noted only briefly in management texts; examples are drawn from the workplace.

Labor Guide to Labor Law is intended for use in either a one- or two-semester course in labor law. I generally cover the basic material included in the first seven chapters thoroughly in a single thirty-hour course, and include an introductory survey on selected subjects covered in Chapters 8, 9, and 10. The material included in Chapters 8 through 14 is covered in detail in a second thirty-hour course. Other instructors may prefer a different order or pace, or they may choose to select portions for seminars.

Labor Guide to Labor Law is also a useful reference and review for full-time union officers and representatives who have a working knowledge of labor law but wish to brush up on certain points. A union faced with a particular legal problem will find that reading the material included here on that issue will help the union to understand the issue and take appropriate action. However, this book is not intended to take the place of an attorney. Labor Law is a changing field. Although this book is as accurate as possible, a few principles will undoubtedly change. Thus, the book cannot take the place of up-to-the-minute advice based on the latest developments and the specific facts of a case.

The chapters are arranged in progression from initial Union attempts at organizing, through representation elections, collective bargaining, strikes and picketing; then the internal relationship between a Union and its members is discussed. The book thus covers labor law from the beginning of the collective bargaining process through the mature bargaining relationship. Each chapter contains a summary and review questions, with answers at the back of the book. Each chapter also includes a review section of "Basic Legal Principles" where key cases on the points discussed in the text, including each case referred to in the chapter, are fully cited for the reader who wishes to read the full opinions or do additional research. The cases cited expand on the basic legal points. Each chapter also contains a list of recommended reading on the subjects covered.

Many thanks are due to those who helped in the preparation of this book. Special thanks go to my associate Attorney Joan Garden and St. Louis Attorney/Arbitrator Lesley Guttenberg for their assistance. Dan Wille, a former student, provided valuable assistance in reviewing the manuscript from the student's perspective. The many hours my secretarial staff has put in on this project are greatly appreciated. Special thanks are also due to my students at Forest Park Community College, whose interest in labor law encouraged me to undertake this project.

Explanation of Legal Citations

Each chapter in this book concludes with a section of Basic Legal Principles citing leading cases of the National Labor Relations Board, the United States Supreme Court, the United States Courts of Appeals, and the United States Federal District Courts discussed in the chapter.

There are eleven United States Courts of Appeals. Each of ten of these courts serves a separate geographic area (called a circuit) composed of a number of states. These Courts are referred to as the First through Tenth Circuits. There is an eleventh Court of Appeals for the District of Columbia only, which is known as the District of Columbia Circuit. Each state is served by one or more United States Federal District Courts. The number of districts per state is generally based on the state's population. There is also a separate District Court for the District of Columbia.

Decisions of the United States Supreme Court are published in bound volumes called the United States Reports, abbreviated U.S., or the Supreme Court Reporter, abbreviated S.Ct. Decisions of the United States Courts of Appeals are reported in the Federal Reporter, Second Series, abbreviated F.2d. Decisions of the United States District Courts are reported in the Federal Supplement, abbreviated F. Supp. Decisions of the National Labor Relations Board are reported in the National Labor Relations Board Decisions and Orders, abbreviated NLRB.

Citations to the United States Reports (U.S.), the Federal Reporter Second Series (F.2d), and the Federal Supplement (F. Supp.) follow a uniform numbering system. The first number, before the name of the reporter, indicates the volume of the reporter in which a decision is published. The second number, following the reporter's name, indicates the page in the volume where the decision begins. This number is followed by a citation in parentheses to the court and year of the decision. Thus, the citation "*Smith v. Jones*, 178 F.2d 220 (4th Cir., 1949)" means that the case decision is found in Volume 178 of the Federal Reporter, Second Series, beginning at page 220. The decision was rendered by the United States Court of Appeals for the Fourth Circuit in 1949. The opposing parties were Smith versus Jones. A decision such as "410 F. Supp. 948 (E.D. Mo., 1976)" means that the decision is found in Volume 410 of the Federal Supplement beginning at page 948, and that the decision was rendered by the United States District Court for the Eastern District of Missouri in 1976.

Citations to National Labor Relations Board decisions use the same basic numbering sequence: the volume followed by either a case number or a volume page number. Thus, a reference to 234 NLRB No. 162 means that the decision is found in Volume 234 of the National Labor Relations Board Decisions and Orders, and is Case Number 162

Several reporting services report federal and state court decisions on labor law issues and the decisions of the National Labor Relations Board in the same volumes. The Bureau of National Affairs (BNA), Washington, D.C., publishes two widely used reporting services: the Labor Relations Reference Manual (abbreviated LRRM), which reports Federal and State court labor decisions and NLRB decisions; and the Fair Employment Practice Cases Reporter (F.E.P. Cases), which reports civil rights cases. As a convenience to readers, citations in *Labor Guide to Labor Law* are to both the official reporters and to the appropriate BNA reporter. These reporters are also cited first by volume and then by page number. Thus, a case reference such as "429 U.S. 1037, 94 LRRM 2202" means that the decision is found in Volume 429 of the United States Reporter at page 1037, and that the same case is reprinted in Volume 94 of the Labor Relations Reference Manual beginning at page 2202.

Some cases discussed in this book were decided so close to the book's publication date that the complete case citations were not yet available. These cases are cited only to the appropriate BNA Reporter. A reference such as _____ F. 2d _____ or _____ U.S. _____ indicates the citation to these volumes was not available at the time of printing.

Citations to legal periodicals and law journals are also given by volume number, periodical name, and page number. Thus, the citation "25 *Lab. L.J.* 418" means that the particular article can be found in Volume 25 of the *Labor Law Journal* beginning at page 418. The abbreviation *"L. Rev."* refers to a law review published by a law school. Law review articles are written either by law professors, practicing lawyers, or by students under a professor's direction.

The case reporters and legal journals cited in this book can be found in virtually any law school library, most of which are open to the public. Most bar associations in larger cities and counties also maintain complete libraries; and the Regional Offices of the National Labor Relations Board maintain libraries containing most of the cited material as well.

Chapter One

Federal Regulation of Labor Management Relations: A Statutory and Structural Overview

This book is a practical guide to labor law in the private sector. The first ten chapters present a discussion of legal principles primarily based on the Labor Management Relations Act (LMRA), 1947, as amended, commonly referred to as the Act. The remaining chapters discuss principles based on the Labor Management Reporting and Disclosure Act and the Civil Rights Act of 1964, as well as on the LMRA. The Appendix contains pertinent sections of these statutes, and it should be referred to as these sections are discussed in the text.

Because of the LMRA's importance, this chapter will begin with a brief historical survey of federal labor legislation leading to the passage of the LMRA in the current form studied in this book. This survey is followed by an introductory overview of the major provisions of the LMRA that will be considered in detail in subsequent chapters. The chapter concludes with an explanation of the structure and procedures of the National Labor Relations Board, the agency administering the Act.

PART I: THE HISTORICAL DEVELOPMENT OF THE LABOR MANAGEMENT RELATIONS ACT

A. The Railway Labor Act

The Railway Labor Act, passed by Congress in 1926, was the first comprehensive federal statutory regulation of labor management relations. It originally covered only railroad employees, but was amended in 1936 to cover airlines as well. The Railway Labor Act is important to all employees because it was the first comprehensive federal legislation and it specifically recognized the right of em-ployees to form unions and engage in collective bargaining.

B. The Norris-LaGuardia Act

In 1932, Congress passed the Norris-LaGuardia Act, a fundamental turning point in federal statutory regulation. The Act prohibited federal courts from issuing injunctions in any labor dispute regardless of the strike's purpose. The law prevented judges from engaging in the previously common practice of enjoining a strike because the judge did not approve of the strike's goals or methods. However, the law did not guarantee the employees any collective bargaining rights. Bargaining rights, except in the railroads, were still won in a test of economic strength between an employer and a union. But with the Norris-LaGuardia Act, the federal courts' injunctive power was removed as a weapon against labor.

C. The National Labor Relations Act

In 1935, Congress passed the National Labor Relations Act (NLRA), frequently referred to as the Wagner Act after the New York Senator who sponsored the legislation. The Supreme Court upheld the NLRA's constitutionality in 1937.

The NLRA established employee rights to organize, join unions, and engage in collective bargaining. The NLRA established employer unfair labor practices, making it unlawful for an employer to interfere with an employee's rights to join a union and engage in concerted (union) activities. Employers were required to bargain in good faith with the union and were prohibited from discharging or otherwise discriminating against employees because they engaged in union activities.

The NLRA also established procedures by which employees may elect their bargaining agent. Before passage of the NLRA, employees could secure bargaining rights only if their employer voluntarily agreed to recognize the union or if the employees struck and forced recognition. The NLRA thus dramatically paved the way for peaceful unionization, especially of industrial workers whose employers had consistently opposed organizing efforts until then. The provisions first enacted in the NLRA remain the basic franchise of American workers.

Employees now take the right to have a union for granted, but consider the case of farm workers who are not covered by federal law. They engaged in a nationwide boycott for recognition until California passed a bargaining law covering them. Public employees are still struggling for collective bargaining rights, and must frequently strike (even unlawfully) just for recognition.

Beyond establishing employee rights and employer unfair labor practices, the NLRA established the National Labor Relations Board to enforce its provisions. Today it is common for federal laws to be enforced by administrative agencies, as the NLRB was established to enforce the NLRA. But until the 1930s, it was far more common for the courts to enforce all laws. Congress established the NLRB because it mistrusted the manner in which the courts, which were historically associated with employer interests, might enforce the law. Congress also felt the need for a specialized agency to develop and apply expertise in the unique field of labor relations.

D. The Taft-Hartley Act (The Labor Management Relations Act)

In 1947, Congress passed the Taft-Hartley Act, named after Senator Taft and Congressman Hartley, who co-sponsored the legislation. The Taft-Hartley Act extensively revised the NLRA, renamed it the Labor Management Relations Act (LMRA), 1947. The LMRA, incorporating the original NLRA as amended by the Taft-Hartley Act in 1947, is the basic statute studied in this book. The term NLRA is still used sometimes to refer to the provisions of the original NLRA that were continued as part of the LMRA [basically the employer unfair labor practices now found in LMRA Section 8(a)].

The original NLRA was pro-labor, establishing employee rights and restricting employer acts. Congress intended for the Taft-

Hartley Act to embody what it regarded as a better balance between labor and management. For example, the NLRA established the right of employees to engage in collective bargaining and other mutual aid and protection; the Taft-Hartley Act added a provision that employees also have the right to refrain from any or all such activities. The NLRA established employer unfair labor practices now contained in LMRA Section 8(a); the Taft-Hartley Act added Section 8(b), union unfair labor practices, which prohibits unions from interfering with employee rights, prohibits unions from coercing or discriminating against employees because of their union activities, and requires unions to bargain in good faith—provisions that place the same restrictions on unions as the NLRA placed on employers. The restrictions on secondary boycotts and on picketing (see Chapter 7) are all an outgrowth of the Taft-Hartley Act.

E. The Landrum-Griffin Act

In 1959, Congress passed the Landrum-Griffin Act, named after the Congressional co-sponsors, formally entitled the Labor Management Reporting and Disclosure Act (LMRDA). The LMRDA primarily regulates internal union matters. It established the so-called "Bill of Rights" for union members; internal union election procedures; and reporting and disclosure requirements for unions, union officers, and employers (see Chapter 11).

The LMRDA also amended the LMRA by adding additional restrictions on picketing, closing certain "loopholes" in Taft-Hartley; and by adding Section 8(e) of the LMRA, prohibiting "hot cargo" clauses (clauses prohibiting one employer from dealing with other employers who are nonunion or who are on strike; see Chapter 8). After 1959, the

formal name of the LMRA was changed to the "Labor Management Relations Act, 1947, as amended," the present formal title.

F. The Health Care Amendments

The last amendments to the LMRA, enacted in 1974, pertain to health care institutions. Profit-making hospitals were always covered by the Act, but the 1974 amendment brought all health care institutions, profit and nonprofit, under the Act. Thus, profit institutions are covered by the special provisions for health care institutions, where applicable, rather than the general provisions to which they were previously subject.

PART II: AN OVERVIEW OF THE LABOR MANAGEMENT RELATIONS ACT IN CURRENT FORM

A word of caution and encouragement is in order before reviewing the LMRA in its present form. This is an introductory overview providing a general understanding of the structure and coverage of the Act. Do not expect to understand all of the statute at first reading. The statute is complex. Some of it is of interest only to lawyers, and other parts are understandable only in the light of subsequent court decisions interpreting the language discussed in later chapters. Sections briefly highlighted here are discussed in detail in subsequent chapters.

A. Basic Structure and Definitions: Sections 1 Through 6

Section 1 of the Act contains basic findings and policies stating the background reasons for which Congress originally passed the

NLRA. Section 2 of the Act includes the definitions used throughout the Act. Note the definition of employer in Section 2 (2). Federal and state government agencies are excluded from coverage under the Act. Labor organizations are covered by the Act when acting as an employer for their own employees. For example, the secretaries of a labor union have the rights of employees. Note the definition of employee in Section 2 (3). An employee who is on strike is still entitled to the protection of the Act. Agricultural and domestic employees are excluded from the act as are people employed by their own parent or spouse, independent contractors, and supervisors. (See Chapter 2.)

Section 2 (11) defines the term "supervisor" and Section 2 (12) defines the term "professional employees." Supervisors are exlcuded from coverage under the Act, and professional employees have the right to a bargaining unit of their own. (See Chapter 2.)

Sections 3, 4, 5, and 6 of the Act all pertain to the establishment and structure of the National Labor Relations Board. (See Part III of this chapter.)

B. Sections 7 and 8: The Unfair Labor Practice Sections

Section 7 of the Act establishes the basic right of employees to bargain collectively. Section 8 is the heart of the Act. Section 8(a) establishes employer unfair labor practices, and Section 8(b) establishes union unfair labor practices. Sections 8(a)(1) through 8(a)(5) and Sections 8(b)(1) through 8(b)(3) generally prohibit either employers or unions from taking certain actions against each other or against employees. Thus, Section 8(a)(1) and Section 8(b)(1)(A) respectively prohibit an employer and a union from interfering with employee rights under Section 7. Section

8(a)(3) prohibits an employer from discriminating against an employee because of union membership, but permits mandatory union membership ("union security agreements") under certain circumstances (See Chapter 10). Section 8(b)(2) prohibits a union from causing the employer to violate Section 8(a)(3). Section 8(a)(5) and Section 8(b)(3) require both an employer and a union to engage in good faith bargaining. (See Chapters 3 through 6.)

Section 8(b)(4) contains the secondary boycott provisions of the Act. Section 8(b)(5) prohibits excessive or discriminatory union initiation fees. Section 8(b)(6) attempts to prohibit "featherbedding." Section 8(b)(7) regulates union picketing for recognition or organizational purposes. (See Chapters 7 and 8.)

Section 8(c) is the so-called "free speech" provision under which employers are permitted to express their opinion about union representation for their employees. (See Chapter 3.) Section 8(d) defines good faith bargaining and establishes notice requirements before a contract can be terminated or modified. (See Chapter 5.)

Section 8(e) prohibits hot cargo provisions. (See Chapter 8.) Section 8(f) permits certain prehire contracts in the construction industry and shortens the period after which an employee may be required to join a union to seven days after hiring in the construction industry, in contrast to the 30 day requirement in other industries. Section 8(g) contains the special notice requirements for a strike or for picketing in the health care industry.

C. Section 9: Election Procedures

Section 9 governs union election procedures leading to the certification of a union as the employees' bargaining representative. (See Chapter 2.) Under Section 9(a), the certified representative is the exclusive representative of the employees. (See Chapter 4.) Under Section 9(b), the Board has very broad discretion in determining the appropriate bargaining unit. However, Section 9(b)(1) gives professional employees the right to a separate vote before they can be included in a unit that includes non-professionals; Section 9(b)(2) places certain restrictions on the Board's right to include craft employees in a broader unit; and Section 9(b)(3) requires that guards be certified separately in a unit composed only of guard employees.

Sections 9(c)(1) through 9(c)(5) regulate the election process. Section 9(c)(3) prohibits a valid election from being held more than once a year, establishes the right of economic strikers to vote in an election, and establishes the procedure for run-off elections if no choice initially receives a majority of the valid votes counted. Section 9(e)(1) permits employees whose contract contains a union security clause to hold a deauthorization election rescinding the clause.

D. Section 10: Enforcement of the Unfair Labor Practice Provisions

Under Section 10(a) the NLRB is established as the authority for enforcing the unfair labor practice provisions found in Section 8.

Under Section 10(b) an unfair labor practice charge must be filed within six months after an unfair labor practice has occurred. Sections 10(b), (c), and (d) establish trial procedures in unfair labor practice cases. Sections 10(e) and (f) of the Act set the procedures that the Board follows in enforcing its decisions or that a party may follow to appeal a Board decision to the courts.

Contrast Sections 10(j) and Section 10(1) of the Act. Under Section 10(j), the Board has discretionary authority to request a federal district court to issue an injunction prohibiting certain unfair labor practices after the Board has issued a complaint alleging that the conduct violates the Act. In contrast, under Section 10(1), the Board is required to seek an injunction even before a complaint is issued if the regional director has reasonable cause to believe that a charge alleging violations of Sections 8(b)(4), 8(b)(7) or 8(e) of the act is true. Note that the mandatory provisions of Section 10(1) apply only to union unfair labor practices. Unions have frequently complained that there are no employer unfair labor practices for which the Board must seek an injunction.

Section 10(k) is a unique provision giving the Board authority to determine the merits of a work assignment dispute if any party to the dispute threatens to strike, picket, or engage in other concerted activities in order to force a work assignment. (See Chapter 8.) Section 11 sets the investigatory powers of the Board, the manner in which Board documents are served, and other procedural matters. Section 12 makes it a criminal act to interfere with the Board's processes.

E. Protection of the Right to Strike: Section 13

Section 13 preserves the right to strike. Two other important sections deal with the right to strike. Section 8(b)(4) provides that "nothing contained in this subsection (b) shall be construed to make unlawful a refusal by any person to enter upon the premises of any employer (other than his own employer), if the employees of such employer are engaged in a strike ratified or approved by a representative of such employees whom such employer is required to recognize under this Act. . . ." Under the provisions of Section 502 an individual employee cannot be required to work without his consent, and employees who quit in good faith because of abnormally dangerous conditions are not considered to be on strike. (See Chapter 6.)

Section 14(a) permits supervisors to be members of a labor organization. However, employers are not required to bargain about the working conditions of supervisors or to recognize a supervisor's union.

Section 14(b) permits individual states to pass so called "Right to Work" laws. Section 19 is a special provision enacted as one of the 1974 amendments for compulsory union membership applicable to employees of health care institutions. (See Chapter 10.)

F. Titles II and III of the Act

Title II of the Act establishes the Federal Mediation and Conciliation Service and defines its authority.[1]

Section 301 authorizes the enforcement of collective bargaining agreements. Section 301 has encouraged the growth of arbitration rather than the courts or strikes as the primary method of resolving contractural disputes. (See Chapter 9.)

Section 302 restricts employer payments to union representatives. This section prohibits union representative from receiving gifts from employers and prohibits an employer from giving financial support to a union. (See Chapter 4.) Important subsections include Section 302 (c)(4), which permits an employer to deduct union dues from an employee's wages; and Section 302 (c)(5), which establishes the basic structure and purposes of

jointly administered fringe benefit trust funds. The establishment and operation of employee fringe benefit funds are extensively regulated by the Employee Retirement Income Security Act (ERISA), effective Labor Day 1974.

Section 303 permits a court to award damages against a union engaging in unfair labor practices in violation of Section 8 (b)(4) (the secondary boycott provisions). Sections 301, 302, and Section 303 are all enforced by the courts rather than the NLRB.[2]

PART III: STRUCTURE AND PROCEDURE OF THE NATIONAL LABOR RELATIONS BOARD

The NLRB administers the LMRA following set procedures in unfair labor practice and representation cases established by the statute and by regulations issued by the board. Most of the principles discussed in this book were developed by the NLRB in decisions made through the procedures outlined here. This outline gives the basic information needed to understand the process should you or your union be involved in Board proceedings. Do not expect to remember the details of these procedures at first reading. Read this part now to get a general understanding of the Board's structure and procedures. Then review this material as you study the following chapters.

A. The National Labor Relations Board and the General Counsel

The National Labor Relations Board, located in Washington, D.C., has five members. The members who serve for five-year terms, are appointed by the President and approved

---

[1] This book does not discuss the Federal Mediation and Conciliation Service in detail except as the agency's activities relate to statutory matters such as bargaining notice requirements. Most of the agency's activities relate to the bargaining process beyond the scope of this text.

[2] The relationship between the NLRB and federal courts in administering the act is discussed in Chapter 14.

by a vote of the Senate. One of the five is appointed as Board Chairman by the President with Senate confirmation. Usually the Board decides cases using three-member panels, but important cases can be decided by all five members (en banc).

In addition to the Board, the Labor Management Relations Act established a separate, independent general counsel, also appointed by the President and approved by the Senate for a four-year term. Figure 1 is an organizational chart of the National Labor Relations Board and of the Office of the General Counsel.[3]

To understand the functions of the five-member Board and the general counsel, think of the relationship between a prosecutor and a judge. In unfair labor practice cases (Section 8), the Board acts as the judge and it decides whether the charged party (the defendant) has violated the Act. Judges do not decide cases unless a prosecutor brings a charge alleging a violation of the law. The Board functions in a similar way, hearing only cases in which a complaint has been filed alleging an unfair labor practice. The general counsel fills the prosecutor function. Anyone may file a charge with the general counsel alleging that the Act has been violated.[4] The general counsel investigates and decides whether a charge has merit. If it does, the general counsel issues a complaint charging that the act has been violated, just as a prosecutor might file a complaint in a criminal case. The case is then tried and the Board decides whether there has been a violation, just as a judge (or jury) might in a criminal case.

[3] The Charts and other documents reproduced in Figures 1 through 9 are publications of the National Labor Relations Board reprinted with the agency's permission.

[4] People frequently refer to filing a charge with the Board but a charge is actually filed with the general counsel.

The division of authority between the Board and the general counsel applies only to unfair labor practice cases under Section 8. The general counsel has nothing to do with election procedures under Section 9; those are handled solely by the Board.

B. The Regional Offices

Although the headquarters for both the Board and general counsel are in Washington, D.C., the work load is far too heavy to handle from Washington. Thus, the Board has regional offices that administer the Act. Figure 2 shows the location of each regional office and the area it serves.

Each region is headed by a regional director appointed by the Board who serves two functions. The regional director is the local representative of the general counsel in processing unfair labor practice charges and, pursuant to authority delegated by the Board, he renders decisions in representation cases under Section 9.

This book frequently refers to the Board, the general counsel, or the regional director as taking certain action. That is because they are ultimately responsible for certain decisions. Remember, however, that the Board, the general counsel and the regional director all have large staffs to support them. As indicated in the organizational chart (Figure 1), each Board member has a personal staff to assist him and the Board has an executive secretary who administers a large office staff to assist the Board in its overall functions. The general counsel has a number of associate and assistant general counsel in charge of the various functions of the office. The regional offices have a large staff of attorneys and field examiners under the supervision of the regional director. Field examiners are career civil servant employees performing primarily

NATIONAL LABOR RELATIONS BOARD

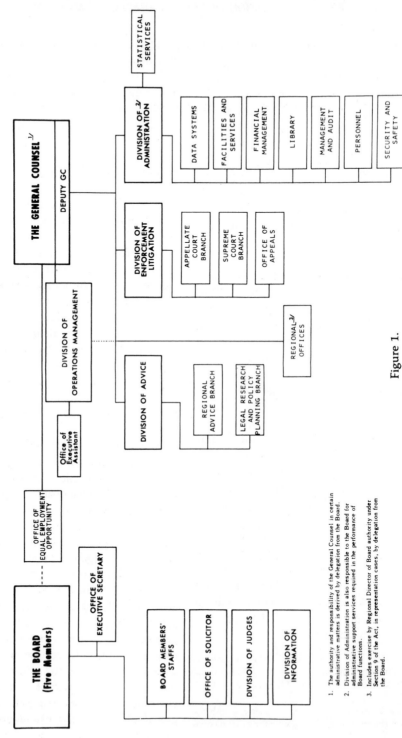

Figure 1.

1. The authority and responsibility of the General Counsel in certain administrative matters is derived by delegation from the Board.

2. Division of Administration is also responsible to the Board for administrative support services required in the performance of Board functions.

3. Includes exercise by Regional Director of Board authority under Section 9 of the Act, in representation cases, by delegation from the Board.

investigatory functions in unfair labor practice and representation matters.

C. Jurisdiction of the NLRB

It is important to understand the limited jurisdiction of the Board's authority. Some employees go to the NLRB every time they are dissatisfied with an action of their employer or union. But the Board was not established to regulate the entire relationship between employers, unions, and employees. The Board enforces only Section 8 (unfair labor practices) and Section 9 (elections) of the Act. All the other provisions of the LMRA provide the framework within which the Board enforces these two sections.

The Board's authority is even more limited because some employers and some employees are not covered. State and federal agencies are excluded from coverage under Section 2 (2). Agricultural workers, domestic employees in a private home, independent contractors, and supervisors are excluded by the definition of covered employees under Section 2 (3). The Board has ruled that it will assert jurisdiction over nonprofit service organizations such as head start programs, child care, and medical clinics, etc., that are supported by state and/or federal funds. Some of these organizations have argued that they were excluded from the Act by the exemption for governmental agencies. The Board held that such agencies are covered by the Act, even though governmentally funded, if they retain independence in labor-management matters, such as establishing wages, hours, and working conditions of their employees.

1. The Commerce Standard

Further, the Board's jurisdiction only covers employers whose operations affect commerce as defined in Section 2 (6) and (7) of the Act. Section 9(c)(1) empowers the Board to hold elections only if it determines that there is a question concerning representation *affecting commerce*. Section 10(a) empowers the Board "to prevent any person from engaging in any unfair labor practice [listed in Section 8] *affecting commerce*" (emphasis added). Why does the statute have these restrictions and what do they mean?

The federal government has limited constitutional authority. Some conduct is not subject to federal regulation. Congress, for example, amended the wage and hour law (the Fair Labor Standards Act) to cover state employees. The Supreme Court held that the amendment was unconstitutional as beyond the power of federal regulation.

The broadest scope of Congress's constitutional authority is that Congress, under the commerce clause of the Constitution (Article 1 Section 8), can regulate any activity that affects commerce among the states. This is the clause under which most federal legislation in the fields of labor, education, and social welfare is upheld. The Labor Management Relations Act was originally upheld on the legal theory that labor unrest disrupts commerce. Goods will not flow in commerce between states if there is a strike. Thus, Congress can regulate labor relations to maintain industrial peace and prevent disruption of commerce.

Since the LMRA applies to any employer or unfair labor practice affecting commerce, the statute has the broadest possible constitutional reach, covering most small employers. For example, the operation of a small business whose customers are all located within the same state as the business would still "affect commerce" if the business purchases supplies produced in another state. A business that purchases all of its supplies within the state would still affect commerce if it has customers in or if its products are sold in another state. A business that operates solely

■ RESIDENT OFFICES

ALBANY, NEW YORK
ALBUQUERQUE, NEW MEXICO
ANCHORAGE, ALASKA
BIRMINGHAM, ALABAMA
CORAL GABLES, FLORIDA
EL PASO, TEXAS
JACKSONVILLE, FLORIDA
LAS VEGAS, NEVADA
LITTLE ROCK, ARKANSAS
NASHVILLE, TENNESSEE
SAN ANTONIO, TEXAS
SAN DIEGO, CALIFORNIA
TULSA, OKLAHOMA
WASHINGTON, DISTRICT OF COLUMBIA

Figure 2.

PUERTO RICO

24

BOUNDARY LINES
——— REGIONAL
▰▰▰▰ SUB-REGIONAL
——— STATE

◆ SUBREGIONAL OFFICES
36. PORTLAND
37. HONOLULU

● REGIONAL OFFICES

1. BOSTON	9. CINCINNATI	17. KANSAS CITY	25. INDIANAPOLIS
2. NEW YORK CITY	10. ATLANTA	18. MINNEAPOLIS	26. MEMPHIS
3. BUFFALO	11. WINSTON-SALEM	19. SEATTLE	27. DENVER
4. PHILADELPHIA	12. TAMPA	20. SAN FRANCISCO	28. PHOENIX
5. BALTIMORE	13. CHICAGO	21. LOS ANGELES	29. BROOKLYN
6. PITTSBURGH	14. ST LOUIS	22. NEWARK	30. MILWAUKEE
7. DETROIT	15. NEW ORLEANS	23. HOUSTON	31. LOS ANGELES
8. CLEVELAND	16. FT WORTH	24. HATO REY	32. OAKLAND
			33. PEORIA

within a state may still affect commerce if a labor dispute at the business would affect the operations of another employer that does engage in interstate commerce. For example, a small manufacturer may supply a part to another manufacturer in the same state for a product shipped to other states. If the manufacturer of the part is shut down by a labor dispute, the interstate manufacturer will not be able to produce the product, and the flow of goods in interstate commerce will be disrupted. The operations of the parts manufacturer, therefore, affect commerce under the Act. However, some employers' operations may be so small that they might not affect commerce. Thus, although the operations of almost all employers would affect commerce as the courts have interpreted this term, employees must be aware that some employers may not meet the standard.

2. The Board's Jurisdictional Standards

In addition to the constitutional and statutory requirement that an unfair labor practice or representation matter affect commerce under Sections 8 or 9, the Board has set certain monetary jurisdictional standards that an employer must meet before the Board will assert jurisdiction. Because so many small employers meet the constitutional and statutory requirement of affecting commerce, the Board established these jurisdictional standards to avoid being engulfed with more cases than it can possibly handle. These standards apply to both unfair labor practice and representation cases.

The monetary standards that an employer must meet before the Board will assert jurisdiction vary by industry, and may be based either on the amount of sales or on gross revenue. Nonretail businesses must either have $50,000 in direct or indirect sales outside their state, or make direct or indirect purchases of

supplies from businesses in other states in that amount. Direct sale or purchase means that the transaction is directly with the out-of-state consumer or supplier. Indirect sale or purchase means that the employer sells to or buys from another company within the same state that meets one of the Board's direct jurisdictional standards. A nonretail business must meet either the sales or supply standard. Costs of sales and supplies cannot be combined to meet the $50,000 standard.

The general retail enterprise standard is at least $500,000 annual volume of business. Hotels and taxicab companies must also meet the $500,000 standard. Other industries have different annual volume of business jurisdictional requirements: $250,000 for public utilities and transportation companies; $200,000 for newspapers; $100,000 for communication companies; $100,000 for nursing homes; $250,000 for all other health care institutions; and $1,000,000 for private colleges and symphony orchestras.

Interstate transportation companies must meet a $50,000 annual income requirement. The Board will assert jurisdiction over defense contractors that affect commerce and have a substantial defense impact, regardless of the monetary amount.

Thus, if an employer commits an act that you believe may violate the LMRA or if you are about to organize a new employer, first consider whether the employer meets the definition of an employer covered by the Act and whether the employees meet the definition of an employee under the Act. Be sure alleged employer misconduct is the type covered by the Act; not, for example, just a contract violation. Then consider whether the employer meets both the statutory standard of affecting commerce and the appropriate Board monetary jurisdictional standard. Proceed to the Board only after reasonably satisfying yourself on all these matters.

D. Processing an Unfair Labor Practice Charge

1. Filing the Charge

The procedures followed in unfair labor practice cases are outlined in Figure 3. The first step is filing a document called a "charge." The Board has a standard form for filing a charge (Figure 4) that is used in all regional offices. The person filing a charge, called the charging party, states the facts constituting a violation of the Act. Anyone, an employer, an employee, or a union, can file a charge. Usually the facts alleged in a charge are set forth in general terms rather than in great detail. The regional office will assist the charging party in filing the charge. A charge must be filed within six months of the date of the alleged unfair labor practice or else it will be barred as untimely under Section 10(b).

A charge is filed in the regional office in the region in which the unfair labor practice occurred. A copy of the charge must be served, usually by mail, on the charged party. The regional director cannot refuse to accept a charge even though the facts alleged are clearly outside the Board's jurisdiction. A charge is simply an allegation; the fact that a charge is filed is not an indication that the facts alleged are true or that they constitute a violation of the Act.

All regional offices use a standard case numbering system. The first two numbers indicate the region in which the charge is filed; the next two letters indicate whether the charge is against an employer or a union and the provision of Section 8 allegedly violated. The final numbers are the numerical sequence of the charge within the region. For example, in the number 14–CA–1085, 14 indicates that the charge was filed in the fourteenth region, C indicates that the case is an unfair labor practice charge, and A indicates that the charge alleged a violation of Section 8 (a), a charge against an employer. The 1085 is the sequence number within the region. Figure 5 is an NLRB chart of the types of cases and the lettering system that the Board uses in both unfair labor practice and representation cases. Unfair labor practice cases begin with a C. For this reason, unfair labor practice charges are frequently referred to by labor practitioners as "C cases."

2. Regional Determination and Appeal

After a charge is filed in the regional office, it is referred either to an attorney or to a field examiner within the office for investigation. The investigator reviews the facts, researches the law, and takes formal statements (affidavits) from witnesses. He asks the charged party for a statement of its position and any evidence it wishes to offer in its defense. The charged party must decide whether and to what extent it will cooperate with the investigation.

Sometimes a charge filed with a regional office involves a unique question or a legal area in which the Board's position is unclear. In that case, the regional director may refer the charge to the Advice Section of the Office of General Counsel. This office advises the regional directors on difficult or unique cases. Occasionally the Advice Section issues memorandums or directives to the regional directors on how to handle cases raising certain issues. Sometimes the general counsel requires that all cases raising a certain issue be forwarded to the Advice Section for consideration. This insures that similar problems arising throughout the country are handled uniformly.

If a case is referred to the general counsel for a decision, the local Board agent assigned the case informs the charging party that the case is "on advice." Even after a complaint has been issued, the Board will still try to settle the case if possible.

BASIC PROCEDURES IN CASES INVOLVING
CHARGES OF UNFAIR LABOR PRACTICES

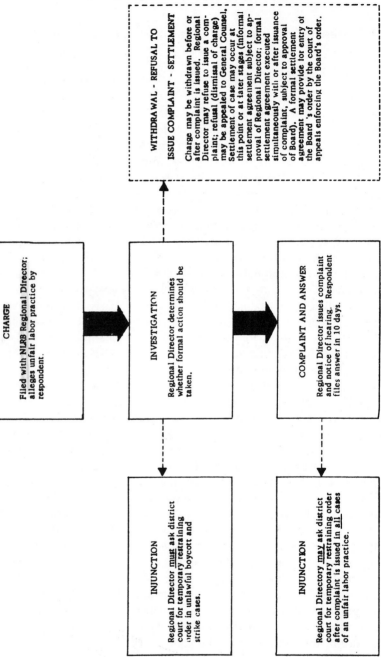

CHARGE

Filed with NLRB Regional Director; alleges unfair labor practice by respondent.

INVESTIGATION

Regional Director determines whether formal action should be taken.

COMPLAINT AND ANSWER

Regional Director issues complaint and notice of hearing. Respondent files answer in 10 days.

INJUNCTION

Regional Director _must_ ask district court for temporary restraining order in unlawful boycott and strike cases.

INJUNCTION

Regional Directory _may_ ask district court for temporary restraining order after complaint is issued in _all cases_ of an unfair labor practice.

WITHDRAWAL - REFUSAL TO ISSUE COMPLAINT - SETTLEMENT

Charge may be withdrawn before or after complaint is issued. Regional Director may refuse to issue a complaint; refusal (dismissal of charge) may be appealed to General Counsel. Settlement of case may occur at this point or at later stages (informal settlement agreement subject to approval of Regional Director; formal settlement agreement executed simultaneously with or after issuance of complaint, subject to approval of Board). A formal settlement agreement may provide for entry of the Board 's order by the court of appeals enforcing the Board's order.

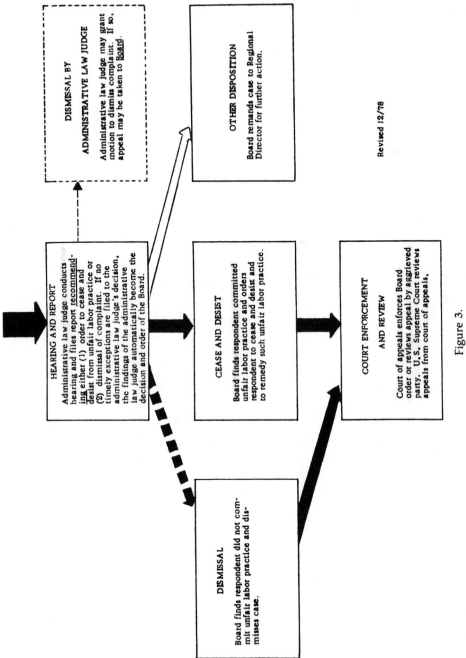

HEARING AND REPORT

Administrative law judge conducts hearing and files report recommending either (1) order to cease and desist from unfair labor practice or (2) dismissal of complaint. If no timely exceptions are filed to the administrative law judge's decision, the findings of the administrative law judge automatically become the decision and order of the Board.

DISMISSAL BY ADMINISTRATIVE LAW JUDGE

Administrative law judge may grant motion to dismiss complaint. If so, appeal may be taken to Board.

OTHER DISPOSITION

Board remands case to Regional Director for further action.

CEASE AND DESIST

Board finds respondent committed unfair labor practice and orders respondent to cease and desist and to remedy such unfair labor practice.

DISMISSAL

Board finds respondent did not commit unfair labor practice and dismisses case.

COURT ENFORCEMENT AND REVIEW

Court of appeals enforces Board order or reviews appeal by aggrieved party. U.S. Supreme Court reviews appeals from court of appeals.

Revised 12/78

Figure 3.

FORM NLRB-501
(2-67)

FORM EXEMPT UNDER
44 U.S.C. 3512

UNITED STATES OF AMERICA
NATIONAL LABOR RELATIONS BOARD

CHARGE AGAINST EMPLOYER

INSTRUCTIONS: *File an original and 4 copies of this charge with NLRB regional director for the region in which the alleged unfair labor practice occurred or is occurring.*

DO NOT WRITE IN THIS SPACE
Case No.
Date Filed

1. EMPLOYER AGAINST WHOM CHARGE IS BROUGHT

a. Name of Employer

b. Number of Workers Employed

c. Address of Establishment (Street and number, city, State, and ZIP code)

d. Employer Representative to Contact

e. Phone No.

f. Type of Establishment (Factory, mine, wholesaler, etc.)

g. Identify Principal Product or Service

h. The above-named employer has engaged in and is engaging in unfair labor practices within the meaning of section 8(a), subsections (1) and _____ of the National Labor Relations Act,

(List subsections)

and these unfair labor practices are unfair labor practices affecting commerce within the meaning of the Act.

2. Basic of the Charge (Be specific as to facts, names, addresses, plants involved, dates, places, etc.)

By the above and other acts, the above-named employer has interfered with, restrained, and coerced employees in the exercise of the rights guaranteed in Section 7 of the Act.

3. Full Name of Party Filing Charge (If labor organization, give full name, including local name and number)

4a. Address (Street and number, city, State, and ZIP code)

4b. Telephone No.

5. Full Name of National or International Labor Organization of Which It Is an Affiliate or Constituent Unit (To be filled in when charge is filed by a labor organization)

6. DECLARATION

I declare that I have read the above charge and that the statements therein are true to the best of my knowledge and belief.

By ———————————————————— ————————————————
    (Signature of representative or person filing charge) (Title, if any)

Address ———————————————————— ————————————————
    (Telephone number) (Date)

WILLFULLY FALSE STATEMENTS ON THIS CHARGE CAN BE PUNISHED BY FINE AND IMPRISONMENT (U.S. CODE, TITLE 18, SECTION 1001)

Figure 4.

TYPES OF CASES

1. CHARGES OF UNFAIR LABOR PRACTICES (C CASES)

Charge Against Employer		Charge Against Labor Organization	
Section of the Act <u>CA</u>	**Section of the Act** <u>CB</u>	**Section of the Act** <u>CC</u>	**Section of the Act** <u>CD</u>

Section of the Act   <u>CA</u>

8(a)(1) To interfere with, restrain or coerce employees in exercise of their rights under Section 7 (to join or assist a labor organization or to refrain).

8(a)(2) To dominate or interfere with the formation or administration of a labor organization or contribute financial or other support to it.

8(a)(3) By discrimination in regard to hire or tenure of employment or any term or condition of employment to encourage or discourage membership in any labor organization.

8(a)(4) To discharge or otherwise discriminate against employees because they have given testimony under the Act.

8(a)(5) To refuse to bargain collectively with representatives of its employees.

Section of the Act   <u>CB</u>

8(b)(1)(A) To restrain or coerce employees in exercise of their rights under Section 7 (to join or assist a labor organization or to refrain).

8(b)(1)(B) To restrain or coerce an employer in the selection of its representatives for collective bargaining or adjustment of grievances.

8(b)(2) To cause or attempt to cause an employer to discriminate against an employee.

8(b)(3) To refuse to bargain collectively with employer.

8(b)(5) To require of employees the payment of excessive or discriminatory fees for membership.

8(b)(6) To cause or attempt to cause an employer to pay or agree to pay money or other thing of value for services which are not performed or not to be performed.

Section of the Act   <u>CC</u>

8(b)(4)(i) To engage in, or induce or encourage any individual employed by any person engaged in commerce or in an industry affecting commerce, to engage in a strike, work stoppage, or boycott, or (ii) to threaten, coerce, or restrain any person engaged in commerce or in an industry affecting commerce, where in either case an object is:

(A) To force or require any employer or self-employed person to join any labor or employer organization or to enter into any agreement prohibited by Sec. 8(e).

(B) To force or require any person to cease using, selling, handling, transporting, or otherwise dealing in the products of any other producer, processor, or manufacturer, or to cease doing business with any other person, or force or require any other employer to recognize or bargain with a labor organization as the representative of its employees unless such labor organization has been so certified.

Section of the Act   <u>CD</u>

(C) To force or require any employer to recognize or bargain with a particular labor organization as the representative of its employees if another labor organization has been certified as the representative.

(D) To force or require any employer to assign particular work to employees in a particular labor organization or in a particular trade, craft, or class rather than to employees in another trade, craft, or class, unless such employer is failing to conform to an appropriate Board order or certification.

2. PETITIONS FOR CERTIFICATION OR DECERTIFICATION OF REPRESENTATIVES (R CASES)

By or in Behalf of Employees		By an Employer
Section of the Act <u>RC</u>	**Section of the Act** <u>RD</u>	**Section of the Act** <u>RM</u>

Section of the Act   <u>RC</u>

9(c)(1)(A)(i) Alleging that a substantial number of employees wish to be represented for collective bargaining and their employer declines to recognize their representative.*

Section of the Act   <u>RD</u>

9(c)(1)(A)(ii) Alleging that a substantial number of employees assert that the certified or currently recognized bargaining representative is no longer their representative.*

Section of the Act   <u>RM</u>

9(c)(1)(B) Alleging that one or more claims for recognition as exclusive bargaining representative have been received by the employer.*

* If an 8(b)(7) charge has been filed involving the same employer, these statements in RC, RD, and RM petitions are not required.

Charges filed with the National Labor Relations Board are letter-coded and numbered. Unfair labor practice charges are classified as "C" cases and petitions for certification or decertification of representatives as "R" cases. This chart indicates the letter codes used for "C" cases and "R" cases, and also presents a summary of each section involved.

Figure 5.

Section of the Act **CG**	Section of the Act **CP**	Section of the Act **CE**
8(g) To strike, picket, or otherwise concertedly refuse to work at any health care institution without notifying the institution and the Federal Mediation and Conciliation Service in writing 10 days prior to such action.	8(b)(7) To picket, cause, or threaten the picketing of any employer where an object is to force or require an employer to recognize or bargain with a labor organization as the representative of its employees, or to force or require the employees of an employer to select such labor organization as their collective-bargaining representative, unless such labor organization is currently certified as the representative of such employees: (A) where the employer has lawfully recognized any other labor organization and a question concerning representation may not appropriately be raised under Section 9(c). (B) where within the preceding 12 months a valid election under Section 9(c) has been conducted, or (C) where picketing has been conducted without a petition under 9(c) being filed within a reasonable period of time not to exceed 30 days from the commencement of the picketing; except where the picketing is for the purpose of truthfully advising the public (including consumers) that an employer does not employ members of, or have a contract with, a labor organization, and it does not have an effect of interference with deliveries or services.	8(e) To enter into any contract or agreement (any labor organization and any employer) whereby such employer ceases or refrains or agrees to cease or refrain from handling or dealing in any product of any other employer, or to cease doing business with any other person.

3. OTHER PETITIONS

By or in Behalf of Employees	By a Labor Organization or an Employer	
Section of the Act **UD**	Board Rules **UC**	Board Rules **AC**
9(e)(1) Alleging that employees (30 percent or more of an appropriate unit) wish to rescind an existing union-security agreement.	Subpart C Seeking clarification of an existing bargaining unit.	Subpart C Seeking amendment of an outstanding certification of bargaining representative.

Revised 12/78

The regional director is required by Section 10 (1) to seek a federal court injunction against certain union unfair labor practices if, after investigation, the regional director has reasonable cause to believe the charge is true. These are primarily cases in which the union is alleged to be engaged in unlawful picketing, secondary boycotts, or unlawful hot cargo agreements. Cases in which the Board is required to seek an injunction have priority for investigation. Sometimes a union voluntarily ceases the alleged unlawful conduct after such a charge is filed. In that case, the regional director does not have to seek an injunction.

If the regional director, after investigation, or consultation with advice, determines that the charge lacks merit, the Board agent conducting the investigation will contact the charging party and suggest that the charge be withdrawn. This is basically a face-saving gesture to avoid a formal dismissal. If the charging party will not withdraw the charge, and the regional director has determined that it lacks merit, the regional director dismisses the charge. If the charge is dismissed, the charging party can appeal the dismissal to the General Counsel Office of Appeals.

If the charging party is not planning to appeal, it is best in most cases to withdraw the charge rather than having it formally dismissed. The only exception might be if the charging party wants detailed reasons for the regional director's decision. A union, for example, might want to present its members with the regional director's detailed reasons if the regional director dismisses a union charge on issues the members consider to be very significant.

The regional director uses one of two dismissal formats, a short or long form. The short form dismissal briefly states that the charge has been dismissed and can be appealed, without giving any detailed reasons for the dismissal. The long form gives a detailed explanation of the reasons. The charging party's choice is again a tactical one. The charging party is allowed to choose the format the regional director uses. The long form gives the charging party a more detailed statement of the regional director's reasons, and may make the appeal slightly more effective. On the other hand, the long form frequently contains strong statements supporting the charged party. A union might not want a strong statement upholding the employer's position on the record, and should therefore request the short form. Less than ten percent of the regional directors' decisions which are appealed to the general counsel are reversed. The general counsel's decision is final. There is no further appeal to the Board.

A general counsel's decision upholding the regional director's dismissal is not binding on either an arbitrator or a court should there be proceedings before either on the same issue giving rise to the unfair labor practice charge. Still, there may be an adverse psychological effect if the general counsel refuses to proceed. Thus, the decision to appeal the regional director's determination must be carefully considered. An appeal should be taken only if the case is sufficiently important and there is a reasonable likelihood of success.

3. Settlement or Issuance of a Complaint

If the regional director determines, based upon the investigation, that a charge has merit, the director will usually advise the charged party of this determination and propose a settlement. A settlement is an agreement in which the violator, whether an employer or a union, agrees to cease the particular unfair labor practice and take whatever action may be necessary to correct the wrong, including back pay if appropriate.

A written settlement may either be informal or formal. An informal settlement is approved by the regional director. A formal settlement is approved by the Board, usually in conjunction with the issuance of a complaint. Formal settlements are usually used only in aggravated or extensive unfair labor practice cases. If the charged party is unwilling to enter into such a settlement, the regional director issues a complaint. A complaint is a detailed legal document, drafted with the same care and precision as when a suit is filed in court. It contains detailed allegations to show that the Board's jurisdictional standards are met, summarizes the facts giving rise to the violation, and lists the provisions of the Act that have been violated.

A charge can be filed by **anyone** and does not indicate that the facts are true or that the charge has merit. In contrast, a complaint is issued only if the regional director determines that the charge has merit. Basically, a complaint describes in greater detail the facts generally alleged in the charge. However, a complaint may allege acts that were not even mentioned in the charge, and that the charged party might not even have known of. The Board is permitted to base its complaint on the charges alleged, and also on any additional violations that the Board investigator discovers during the course of the investigation that are reasonably related to the charge. Sometimes, to avoid any question of the relationship, the regional director will ask that a charging party file an amended charge alleging additional violations discovered during the course of the investigation.

A charge must be filed within six months of the date of the alleged unfair labor practice. However, there is no maximum time limit between when a charge is filed and a complaint is issued. Sometimes many months may elapse between the filing of a charge and the issuance of a complaint, especially in complex cases that have been referred to Advice for a decision or in which a complaint is issued pursuant to successful appeal to the Office of Appeals.

4. Trial Procedures and Board Decision

After a complaint is issued, there is a hearing before an administrative law judge, commonly referred to as an "ALJ" (previously known as Trial Examiners). The administrative law judge, a civil service appointee, is independent of the Board and hears the case independently. Unfair labor practice cases are tried in the region where the case arose. Administrative law judges are permanently stationed in New York, Washington, D.C., and San Francisco but travel to the region for hearings.

The trial of an unfair labor practice case is similar to a typical civil trial, except there is no jury. The ALJ functions very much like a federal judge. An unfair labor practice trial is a formal proceeding, very different from typically informal arbitration hearings. Section 10(b) of the act provides that the federal rules of evidence apply in an unfair labor practice case hearing.

At the trial, the general counsel has the burden of proving that the act has been violated as alleged in the complaint. An attorney from the regional office representing the general counsel tries the case. The charging party is not required to have its own attorney, although it is permitted to have one at its own expense. Even if the charging party has an attorney, the general counsel's attorney has the primary responsibility for trying the case. The charging party's attorney can, however, give valuable assistance to the Board's attorney because of his familiarity with the case. At trial, the charged party, termed the respondent, is entitled to an attorney at its own cost.

There is one important difference between the role of an ALJ and a federal judge. District court judges enter binding decisions that can be appealed. However, an administrative law judge simply makes a *recommended* report and order for the Board. This report is not binding unless approved by the Board.

The ALJ's report contains recommended findings of fact and conclusions of law as to whether the facts constitute a violation of the Act. If the ALJ finds a violation, he issues a recommended order listing the actions the respondent must undertake to cure the effects of its unlawful actions, such as requiring back pay for a discharged employee. Either the charging party, the general counsel, or the respondent has an absolute right to appeal the ALJ's report to the Board. The Board then makes a binding decision.

A party files an appeal of the ALJ's report by filing "exceptions" to the ALJ's decision. This is a formal document listing the alleged errors the ALJ made in factual conclusions, legal conclusions, or in the proposed remedy. Briefs and counter-briefs are filed. The Board makes the final decision and order based on the transcript of the hearing and exhibits and the briefs. There is not another full trial before the Board. The Board's decision is a binding, enforceable order. (See Chapter 10 for the complete text of a typical Board decision.)

5. Appeal Procedures

After the Board's decision, the case can be appealed to a United States Court of Appeals. Figure 6 illustrates the enforcement process. There are ten courts of appeal, each serving an appellate circuit composed of a number of states, and one appellate court for the District of Columbia. The party losing before the Board can appeal the decision to the court of appeals covering the state where the alleged

unfair labor practice occurred, where the appealing party resides or transacts business, or in the United States Court of Appeals for the District of Columbia.

On the other hand, the respondent can simply refuse to obey the Board's decision. In that case, the general counsel can file a petition in the appropriate court of appeals to enforce the Board's decision.

There is no new trial before the court of appeals. The court bases its decision upon the transcript and exhibits of the hearing before the ALJ and the Board's decision. The Supreme Court has held that a court of appeals must uphold the Board's decision if it is based on substantial evidence on the record as a whole. This means that if there is substantial evidence to support the Board's decision, the court of appeals cannot reverse the Board even though the court might have reached a different conclusion on the same evidence. This standard is applied because Congress, in establishing the NLRB, intended for the Board, not the courts, to be the primary agency to interpret and apply the act.

The court of appeals can enforce the Board's decision and order in full, modify the Board's decision in some aspect and enforce the decision as modified, or vacate the Board's entire decision. Sometimes the court may remand a case to the Board for reconsideration in light of some point raised by the court of appeals that the court feels the Board should consider before further action is taken. Overall, most of the Board's decisions are upheld on appeal. Practically, there is little chance of reversing the Board on appeal if the only issue is one of fact, such as whether an employee was discharged for cause or for union activity. There is a greater likelihood of success on appeal if the issue pertains to the law's meaning. The substantial evidence rule

NLRB ORDER ENFORCEMENT CHART

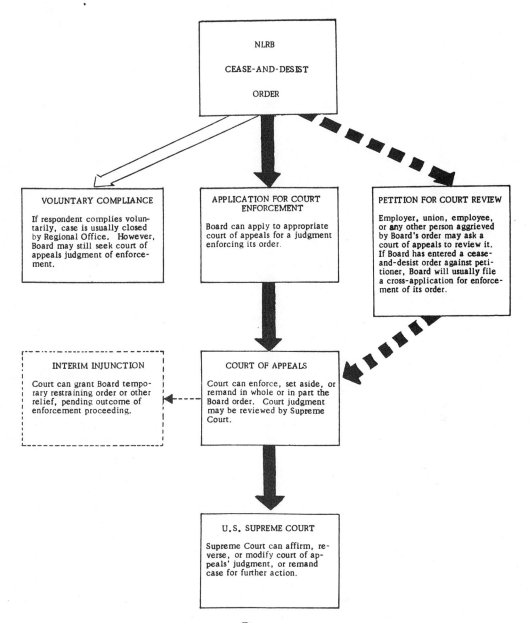

Figure 6.

discourages the courts from substituting their judgment for the Board's on fact issues.

There is a unique relationship between the NLRB and the courts of appeals that is sometimes difficult for laymen to understand. The Board is bound only by Supreme Court interpretations. The Board is bound by a court of appeals decision in a particular case affirming, denying, modifying, or remanding the Board's decision. However, the Board is not bound by any general interpretations of the Labor Management Relations Act that a court of appeals may make. Sometimes a particular court of appeals interpretation will differ from the Board's on a specific point. The Board may continue to issue decisions applying one view of the law that the court of appeals consistently reverses because the court has a different interpretation. Sometimes some courts of appeals may agree with the Board's interpretation while other courts of appeals may not. This means that some courts of appeals will affirm the Board's decision on a given point while other courts of appeals will refuse to enforce the Board's decision on the same issue. That conflict may continue until such time as the Board changes its view, the courts of appeals finally reach agreement with the Board, or the Supreme Court issues a binding decision.

A party appealing a Board's decision usually has a choice as to where to appeal; and because courts of appeals may disagree with the Board or among themselves, a party may maneuver to file its appeal in a court of appeals that would interpret the law favorably. This is called *forum shopping*. Generally, the court of appeals in which an appeal is first filed has jurisdiction over the case. Sometimes parties engage in a "race to the courthouse" attempting to file their respective appeals as quickly as possible in a court of appeals favorable to their position. Although forum shopping or courthouse races do occur in

important or unique cases, appeals in most cases are routinely filed in the court of appeals where the unfair labor practice occurred.

Appeal to the Supreme Court. Following a court of appeals decision, it is possible to appeal to the Supreme Court. In contrast to the court of appeals, which must consider every case appealed to it, the Supreme Court has discretion as to whether it will consider a case. The technical term for requesting the Supreme Court to hear a case is a Petition for Writ of Certiorari (abbreviated "Cert"). A petition for Cert describes the basic facts of the case and the reasons why the Supreme Court should consider it. The petition is reviewed by the Court, and if at least four of the justices agree to hear the case, the petition is granted. The case is then placed on the Court's appeal calendar. There is no trial before the Supreme Court; the appeal is based on the trial transcript, the Board's decision, and the parties' briefs.

The Supreme Court usually does not hear a case just because the facts are complicated. Normally, the Supreme Court only considers a case involving a unique issue of law or if the courts of appeals have reached conflicting decisions on the same issue and the Court wants to resolve the uncertainty that the conflict creates. Sometimes, however, an issue may be so controversial that the Court will simply prefer not to consider the matter at that time until the ramifications are clearer. Denial of a Writ of Certiorari does not indicate that the Court agrees or disagrees with the lower court decision; it simply means that the Court, for whatever reason, chose not to hear that particular case.

Supreme Court action either in denying a Writ of Certiorari, or in affirming or reversing the decision of the court of appeals on the merits, is the final step in the judicial process.

Of course, sometimes the same case may be before a court of appeals or the Supreme Court more than once. A court of appeals, for example, may modify or remand a Board decision, and the case may come back to a court of appeals for a second time. Similarly, the Supreme Court may remand a case to the court of appeals for reconsideration in light of a principle stated by the Supreme Court. The decision on remand may be reappealed to the Supreme Court after the court of appeals issues its second opinion.

6. Compliance Proceedings

After an unfair labor practice charge is finally resolved, either by settlement, by a Board decision, or by a final appellate court decision, the case goes to the compliance stage. Each regional office has a compliance officer who insures that the Board's order or the terms of a settlement agreement are complied with. That includes making sure that required notices have been posted, that any back pay has been paid, or that any other actions required have been taken.

An unlawfully discharged employee is entitled to back pay based on the difference between what would have been earned and what was earned, on a quarterly basis, after discharge. If there is a disagreement on the amount of back pay under a Board decision that the parties cannot settle, the matter is resolved in a back pay specification hearing. The regional director issues a back pay specification alleging the amount of back pay the regional director has determined the employee should receive. The employer has the burden of proving that the amount claimed is erroneous and that a lesser amount is due. These cases usually involve issues such as whether the employee was actively looking for work while unemployed, as the law re-

quires; or whether the employee would have been legitimately terminated before the date the Board ordered the reinstatement (such as by a legitimate economic layoff), so that the back pay period should end prior to the date the Board ordered reinstatement. Back pay specification hearings follow the same procedures followed in an unfair labor practice case and are heard by an ALJ. There is again an absolute right to appeal the ALJ's decision to the Board and ultimately to a court of appeals.

Usually, the compliance officer simply checks with the charging party about 60 days after the Board's decision has been rendered or a case has been settled to make sure that the Board's decision or settlement is being complied with. If so, the case is routinely closed. If a settlement is not being complied with, the settlement can be set aside and the case will be resumed as a formal proceeding. If an employer fails to follow a Board decision, the matter can be appealed to a court of appeals by the Board. If there has been a court decision enforcing the Board's award, and the respondent is not complying with the court decision, the Board can request the court of appeals to find the respondent in contempt of court.

The Board decides whether or not a respondent is complying with a Board order and what action to take if it is not. Suppose that an employer has been ordered to bargain in good faith with a union. The compliance officer will contact the union about the employer's compliance. If the union believes that the employer is not bargaining in good faith, the compliance officer will investigate the facts. The regional director, acting for the general counsel, determines whether the employer is complying.

If the regional director decides that the employer is complying, notwithstanding the union's assertion that it is not, what can the union do? Can the union seek court enforcement or contempt of court if the employer is failing to comply? No, it is the general counsel's decision; he controls the case. If the general counsel does not act, the union cannot go to court on its own. There have been several cases involving flagrant employer violations, in which the general counsel has settled pending court actions over the union's objection that the general counsel accepted a settlement that was too lenient. The unions involved could protest, but they could not prevent the general counsel from taking the action he did.

7. Unfair Labor Practice Processing Time

A charge has to be filed within six months of the unfair labor practice, although there is an exception for what is called a "continuing violation." For example, an employer's pattern of bad faith bargaining may continue for a long time. The time limit for filing a charge over a continuing violation is six months from the last unlawful act, which might be the last bargaining session. A discharge is not a continuing violation, so a charge must be filed within six months from the date of the discharge. It is best, however, to file a charge within six months of the first violation. Do not rely upon the Board concluding that the violation is a continuing one.

The regional director's processing in the typical unfair labor practice charge case usually takes approximately forty-five days from the filing of a charge to issuance of a complaint. In that time, the regional director either dismisses a charge that lacks merit or attempts to settle a meritorious case. More time is taken in a complicated case or cases sent to the general counsel for advice. If the regional director is unable to settle a meritorious case, and a formal complaint and trial are

necessary, the case is usually set for trial a minimum of two or three months from the date the original charge was filed. Because of a shortage of ALJs, the delay before trial is even longer in some cases. Allowing time for all parties to file briefs with the administrative law judge, and for the ALJ to consider the case, the ALJ decision is usually issued three to four months after the hearing.

If the ALJ's decision is appealed to the Board, another four to six months will elapse before the Board issues its decision. Thus, the typical Board case can take close to a year to process from the day the charge is issued to the date the Board issues its decision.

These time limits are the minimum for the simpler cases. If a case is complicated or if the Board members are divided over it, the Board may hold a case for a year or more before deciding. If a case raises an issue that the Board is reconsidering, cases raising that issue may be held up for a long period while the Board decides the point.

If a case is appealed to a court of appeals, it takes close to a year after the appeal is filed before the court's decision is rendered. That time includes time for filing the Board's case record with the appellate court, filing briefs, oral argument, and court consideration. The courts of appeals also, of course, have a backlog of cases to consider. If a case is appealed to the Supreme Court and the Court agrees to hear the case, it takes at least another year before the Court may reach a decision.

Thus, some labor cases may take three years to resolve: one year to process the case through the Board, a second year to go through the court of appeals, and a third year if the case reaches the Supreme Court.

In some cases, employers will take advantage of the time lag and attempt to destroy employee rights by illegally delaying the process even longer. Some employers will risk a court of appeals contempt citation because it is cheaper for them to pay fines than to pay the higher wages a union may have won for its employees. Most cases, however, do not go through this entire process. In fiscal year 1978, 82.5 percent of all meritorious unfair labor practice charges were settled. Contested Board decisions were issued in only 9.8 percent of the cases. Only one percent of all charges filed go all the way to a court of appeals decision.[5]

E. Procedure in Representation Cases

The form filed to start a representation proceeding is a petition (see Figure 7). Figure 8 is a chart of the representation proceedings process. Just as unfair labor practice cases have a "C" letter designation, representation cases also have letter designations. A petition filed by a union to represent employees has the designation "RC." Figure 5 shows the types of representation petitions and the designations used. Representation petitions use the same numbering system as used in unfair labor practice cases: the regional number, the letter code, and the case number. Representation cases are commonly referred to as "R" cases.

1. Administrative Investigation

Representation matters are governed by Section 9 of the Act. A representation petition filed by a union must be supported by a "showing of interest" that at least 30 percent of the employees in the proposed unit want an election. This rule prevents the Board from getting bogged down in elections that the union has no chance of winning. Why have an election when less than 30 percent of the employees are willing to express their sup-

port for the union? Usually a union showing of interest is made by authorization cards signed by 30 percent of the employees in the bargaining unit stating that they wish union representation. However, cards are not the only method that can be used. Employees can simply sign a petition circulated by the union. However, cards are undoubtedly the preferred method. Cards must be dated to be accepted by the Board and as a matter of good practice, they should also be initialed by the person getting the signatures. In that way, if there is ever any question about the authenticity of the card, a witness can verify it.

The Board makes an "administrative investigation" to determine whether the petition is supported by the 30 percent showing. Someone from the regional director's office conducts the investigation usually by verifying the number of cards against a payroll list submitted by the employer to the regional office. The Board has consistently held that the question of a "showing of interest" is an internal matter for the Board to resolve. That means that there is no hearing on the question of showing of interest. Rather, if showing of interest is disputed, either side may informally submit evidence on the question to the regional director for consideration.

2. Consent Elections

If, after preliminary investigation, the regional director determines that the petition raises a question concerning representation, the regional director will normally hold an informal conference between the employer and the union to decide whether the parties can agree to the terms of an election.[6] If so, the parties may enter into a consent election

[5] *Source:* Annual Report, National Labor Relations Board (Fiscal Year Ended September 30, 1978).

[6] Sometimes another union may also be seeking to represent the employees in a question. If so, the other union may be permitted to intervene, participate in the proceedings, and appear on the ballot.

Form NLRB-502
(11-64)

FORM EXEMPT UNDER
44 U.S.C. 3512

UNITED STATES OF AMERICA
NATIONAL LABOR RELATIONS BOARD

PETITION

DO NOT WRITE IN THIS SPACE
CASE NO.
DATE FILED

INSTRUCTIONS.—Submit an original and four (4) copies of this Petition to the NLRB Regional Office in the Region in which the employer concerned is located.
If more space is required for any one item, attach additional sheets, numbering item accordingly.

The Petitioner alleges that the following circumstances exist and requests that the National Labor Relations Board proceed under its proper authority pursuant to Section 9 of the National Labor Relations Act.

1. Purpose of this Petition *(If box RC, RM, or RD is checked and a charge under Section 8(b)(7) of the Act has been filed involving the Employer named herein, the statement following the description of the type of petition shall not be deemed made.)*

(Check one)

☐ **RC—CERTIFICATION OF REPRESENTATIVE** —A substantial number of employees wish to be represented for purposes of collective bargaining by Petitioner and Petitioner desires to be certified as representative of the employees.

☐ **RM—REPRESENTATION (EMPLOYER PETITION)** —One or more individuals or labor organizations have presented a claim to Petitioner to be recognized as the representative of employees of Petitioner.

☐ **RD—DECERTIFICATION** —A substantial number of employees assert that the certified or currently recognized bargaining representative is no longer their representative.

☐ **UD—WITHDRAWAL OF UNION SHOP AUTHORITY** —Thirty percent (30%) or more of employees in a bargaining unit covered by an agreement between their employer and a labor organization desire that such authority be rescinded.

☐ **UC—UNIT CLARIFICATION** —A labor organization is currently recognized by employer, but petitioner seeks clarification of placement of certain employees: *(Check one)* ☐ In unit not previously certified ☐ In unit previously certified in Case No. _____

☐ **AC—AMENDMENT OF CERTIFICATION** —Petitioner seeks amendment of certification issued in Case No. _____
Attach statement describing the specific amendment sought.

2. NAME OF EMPLOYER	EMPLOYER REPRESENTATIVE TO CONTACT	PHONE NO

3. ADDRESS(ES) OF ESTABLISHMENT(S) INVOLVED *(Street and number, city, State, and ZIP Code)*

4a. TYPE OF ESTABLISHMENT *(Factory, mine, wholesaler, etc.)*	4b. IDENTIFY PRINCIPAL PRODUCT OR SERVICE

5. Unit Involved *(In UC petition, describe PRESENT bargaining unit and attach description of proposed clarification.)*

Included

Excluded

6a. NUMBER OF EMPLOYEES IN UNIT
PRESENT
PROPOSED (BY UC/AC)

6b. IS THIS PETITION SUPPORTED BY 30% OR MORE OF THE EMPLOYEES IN THE UNIT?*
☐ YES ☐ NO
*Not applicable in RM, UC, and AC.

(If you have checked box RC in 1 above, check and complete EITHER item "a or "b. whichever is applicable)

7a. ☐ Request for recognition as Bargaining Representative was made on .... and Employer
(Month, day, year)
declined recognition on or about .... (If no reply received, so state)
(Month, day, year)

7b. ☐ Petitioner is currently recognized as Bargaining Representative and desires certification under the act.

8. Recognized or Certified Bargaining Agent (If there is none, so state)

NAME | AFFILIATION

ADDRESS | DATE OF RECOGNITION OR CERTIFICATION

9. DATE OF EXPIRATION OF CURRENT CONTRACT, IF ANY (Show month, day, and year) | 10. IF YOU HAVE CHECKED BOX UD IN 1 ABOVE, SHOW HERE THE DATE OF EXECUTION OF AGREEMENT GRANTING UNION SHOP (Month, day, and year)

11a. IS THERE NOW A STRIKE OR PICKETING AT THE EMPLOYER'S ESTABLISHMENT(S) INVOLVED? YES .... NO .... | 11b. IF SO, APPROXIMATELY HOW MANY EMPLOYEES ARE PARTICIPATING?

11c. THE EMPLOYER HAS BEEN PICKETED BY OR ON BEHALF OF .... A LABOR
(Insert name)

ORGANIZATION, OF .... SINCE ....
(Insert address) (Month, day, year)

12. ORGANIZATIONS OR INDIVIDUALS OTHER THAN PETITIONER (AND OTHER THAN THOSE NAMED IN ITEMS 8 AND 11c,) WHICH HAVE CLAIMED RECOGNITION AS REPRESENTATIVES AND OTHER ORGANIZATIONS AND INDIVIDUALS KNOWN TO HAVE A REPRESENTATIVE INTEREST IN ANY EMPLOYEES IN THE UNIT DESCRIBED IN ITEM 5 ABOVE. (IF NONE, SO STATE.)

NAME	AFFILIATION	ADDRESS	DATE OF CLAIM (Required only if Petition is filed by Employer)

I declare that I have read the above petition and that the statements therein are true to the best of my knowledge and belief

....
(Petitioner and affiliation, if any)

By ....
(Signature of representative or person filing petition) (Title, if any)

Address ....
(Street and number, city, State, and ZIP Code) (Telephone number)

WILLFULLY FALSE STATEMENT ON THIS PETITION CAN BE PUNISHED BY FINE AND IMPRISONMENT (U.S. CODE, TITLE 18, SECTION 1001)

GPO 923-758

Figure 7.

29

OUTLINE OF REPRESENTATION PROCEDURES UNDER SECTION 9(c)

Revised 12/'78

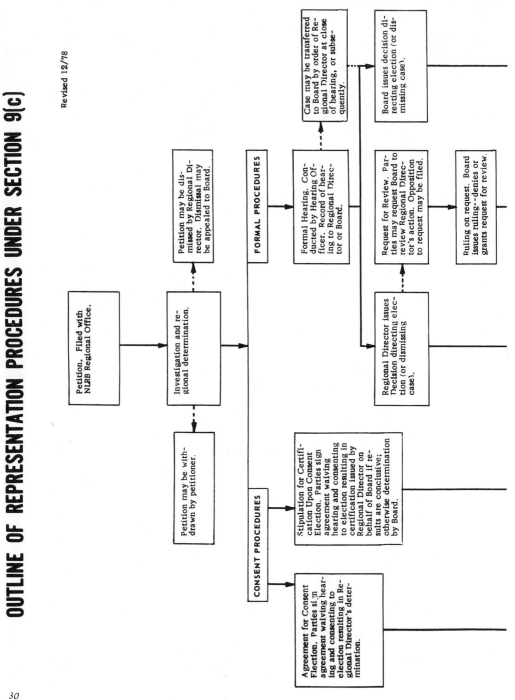

Petition. Filed with NLRB Regional Office.

Petition may be withdrawn by petitioner.

Investigation and regional determination.

Petition may be dismissed by Regional Director. Dismissal may be appealed to Board.

CONSENT PROCEDURES

Agreement for Consent Election. Parties sign agreement waiving hearing and consenting to election resulting in Regional Director's determination.

Stipulation for Certification Upon Consent Election. Parties sign agreement waiving hearing and consenting to election resulting in certification issued by Regional Director on behalf of Board if results are conclusive; otherwise determination by Board.

FORMAL PROCEDURES

Formal Hearing. Conducted by Hearing Officer. Record of hearing to Regional Director or Board.

Case may be transferred to Board by order of Regional Director at close of hearing, or subsequently.

Board issues decision directing election (or dismissing case).

Regional Director issues Decision directing election (or dismissing case).

Request for Review. Parties may request Board to review Regional Director's action. Opposition to request may be filed.

Ruling on request. Board issues ruling--denies or grants request for review.

30

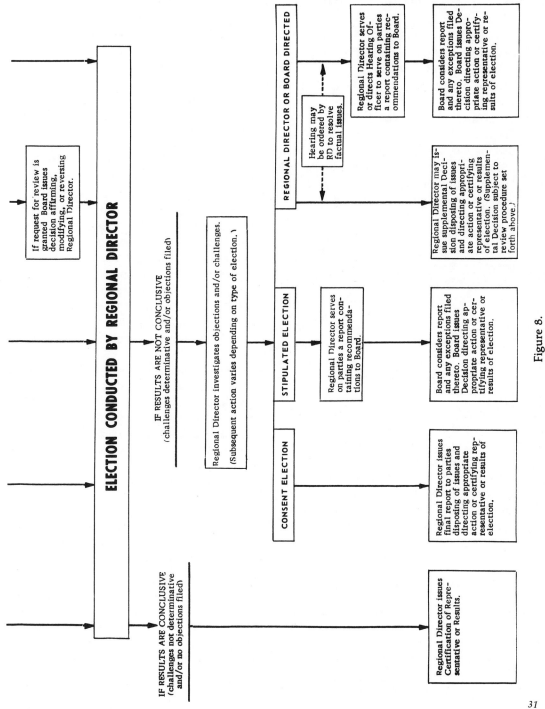

Figure 8.

31

agreement that includes a description of the appropriate unit, the time and place of the election, and the payroll eligibility date (the date by which a person must be employed in order to vote).

If, for example, a union has filed for a production and maintenance unit (P & M unit) and the employer agrees that the unit is appropriate, a consent election can be held. However, the employer may be unable or unwilling to reach agreement as to the unit. The employer may employ clerical employees. Plant clerical employees are generally included in a P & M unit, but office clerical employees are not. If the employer and the union agree which employees are plant clerical or office clerical, they can enter into a consent agreement. But if there is disagreement, if the union says that clericals are in the unit and the employer says they are not, or if—as frequently occurs—there is a dispute as to which employees are supervisors, a hearing must be held.

Sometimes an informal conference is handled by phone. The Board agent will call the parties to find out whether there is agreement as to the unit, or other issues. If there is agreement, the agent may arrange a time for everybody to sign a consent agreement or may simply mail copies to the parties. If there is no agreement, the regional director will send out a notice of hearing.

3. Representation Hearings and Decisions

The representation hearing is intended to resolve any disputed issue on to the appropriateness of the unit, the employees to be included or excluded, and election procedures. A hearing in a representation case is held before a hearing officer rather than an ALJ, who hears unfair labor practice charges. Hearing officers are members of the local re-

gional director's staff. The senior attorneys and field examiners rotate as hearing officers.

Although the federal rules of evidence apply to unfair labor practice trials, the Board's rules provide that the rules of evidence shall not apply to representational matters.

Technically, a representation hearing is "nonadversary"—its purpose is simply to bring out all the facts on the disputed issues. Theoretically, one side is not against the other. In fact, however, representation hearings are sometimes more strongly contested than unfair labor practice cases because they involve basic issues of the union's representation rights. Generally, a representation hearing is less formal than an unfair labor practice case, although it is more formal in fact than the Board's rules might lead someone to believe. A person observing a representation case hearing would probably consider it a trial.

The regional director usually decides the disputed issues in a representation case based on the hearing record. The hearing officer does not make or even recommend a decision. His duty is to make sure all relevant evidence is brought out at the hearing for the regional director to consider. This is in contrast to the ALJ, who makes a recommended decision.

Although the regional director formally issues the decision, a member of the staff, called the decision writer, actually writes the decision. This function is rotated among the senior attorneys. The decision writer reads the hearing transcript, reads the briefs, and writes a draft decision, after which the regional director reads the decision and makes sure that he agrees with it before it is issued. It is the regional director who bears the ultimate responsibility. However, in exceptional cases involving some unique issue, the regional director can transfer a case directly to the Board for immediate decision.

The regional director's decision can be appealed to the Board through a "Request for Review." In an unfair labor practice case, the parties have an absolute right to appeal the ALJ's decision to the Board. In contrast, the Board will consider an appeal from the regional director's decision in a representation case on only four limited grounds: if the case raises a substantial question of law or policy; if the regional director committed clear error on a substantial factual issue; if prejudicial error was committed in the conduct of the hearing; or if there are compelling reasons to reconsider an important Board rule or policy. If the Board grants the request for review, the parties can submit supplemental briefs to the Board. The Board will thereafter decide the disputed issues based on the hearing record and the briefs.

In order to expedite election procedures, the Board proceeds with an election even though a request for review is pending or has been granted. Under this procedure, the ballots are impounded pending the outcome of the request. If the request for review is denied or the regional director's decision upheld on review, the ballots are counted and the result is certified as in any other election. If the Board overrules the regional director's decision upon review, the ballots are not counted.

The general counsel does not have a role in representation proceedings. In an unfair labor practice case, the charging party files the charge. If the regional director, acting for the general counsel, finds merit in the charge, the general counsel issues a complaint and prosecutes the case. In a representation case, however, the petitioner is on his own. The regional director will investigate a petition to make sure it raises a question of representation, may suggest changes in the unit description, and will try to work out a consent election between the parties if they are agreeable. But if there is a hearing on disputed issues, the petitioner presents his own case. The hearing officer is required to make a complete record, but the Board does not act on behalf of either party. The decision of the regional director or the Board resolves the disputed issues, and either dismisses the petition or directs an election in the appropriate unit.

4. Post-Election Proceedings

At the time of the election, whether pursuant to a consent agreement or an order after hearing, either party can challenge the ballot of an employee who the party believes is ineligible to vote. If there is any unlawful conduct during the election campaign, either party can file objections to the election within five days after the election.[7] If there are no challenges or objections, the regional director certifies the results, and the matter is closed.

If there are objections or challenges, the regional director can investigate them administratively without a hearing. In that case, the parties simply submit their evidence to the regional director and he issues a decision based on the evidence as submitted. If the evidence is conflicting or there are issues of witness credibility, the regional director will order a hearing on the challenges or objections to the election. The regional director has discretion to choose between an administrative investigation or hearing.

If there is a hearing on post-election challenges or objections, it is held before a hearing officer following the same procedures used in a pre-election hearing. The action the regional director takes following the hearing depends upon whether the election was by consent or was directed by a regional director or Board order after a hearing.

There are two types of consent agree-

[7] See Chapter 2 for a discussion of the grounds for challenging a voter and for setting aside an election because of campaign misconduct.

ments. Under one type, the parties agree that the regional director's decision on post-election matters is final with no appeal to the Board. Under the other type of consent agreement, called a stipulation, the regional director issues a report on challenges and objections, which summarizes the facts and recommends a decision. This report can be appealed to the Board. Most parties who agree to a consent election execute the stipulation agreement since they retain the right to appeal.

In a directed election the regional director can either issue a recommended report on the challenges or objections, as in a consent election, or can direct the hearing officer to issue such a report. In that case, the report can be appealed to the Board. The regional director can also issue a formal decision from which there is no automatic right to appeal. Rather, the parties can request review, as in the case of a regional director's decision in a pre-election hearing.

The final step in the representation process is certification of the election results. Certification is made by the regional director or the Board following resolution of any post-election objections or challenges. When employees refer to a union as being certified, they are referring to a union that has won an election. Actually, though, the results are certified whether the union wins or loses.

5. Appellate Review of Representation Decisions

Although the Board's decision in an unfair labor practice case may be appealed to the court of appeals, there is no direct right of judicial review in representation cases. What can an employer do if a union wins an election, but he feels that the Board's decision on the unit, election challenges, or election procedures was in error? An elaborate ritual ensues.

The only way the employer can challenge the representation proceedings is by refusing to bargain with the union on the grounds it was improperly certified due to the Board's erroneous decision in the representation case. The union must then file an unfair labor practice charge alleging a violation of Section 8(a)(5) of the act (refusal to bargain). The case is processed through the unfair labor practice procedures discussed above. The case is handled more quickly, though, because the Board does not permit an employer to relitigate the issues that were raised previously in the representation case. The Board normally reaffirms its prior rulings in the disputed representation case and orders the employer to bargain.

The employer can then appeal the Board's decision in the unfair labor practice case to the court of appeals. The court of appeals can review the Board's ruling on the representation issues as part of its review of the unfair labor practice case. The court can either rule that the employer properly refused to bargain because the union was improperly certified or it can affirm the Board's decision and order the employer to bargain.

This appeal procedure may seem to be a cumbersome process, as it allows an employer to drag things out for a long time. On the other hand, because the process is cumbersome and expensive, most employers, even if dissatisfied with the result, simply accept the NLRB's decision in representation case and forego an appeal. Thus, in most cases, the employer and union bargain sooner than if there were a direct appeal of a representation case decision.

6. Representation Case Processing Time

If the parties do not enter into a consent agreement, a hearing is usually scheduled within 30 days from the date a petition was filed. In that time the regional director must make an administrative investigation into the union's showing of interest, explore the possibility of a consent agreement, and then arrange a hearing date if consent is not possible. The regional director's decision after a hearing, allowing time for briefs, is usually issued quickly in representation cases, frequently within two or three weeks after the hearing. Thus, even in a contested election, the regional director's determination is usually made within two months from the date the petition was filed.

The processing is quicker in a consent election. The realistic minimum for an election would be about four weeks after a petition is filed. A consent agreement might be entered into within a week or two after a petition is filed. An employer has to submit a list of the employees who are in the proposed unit to the union (see Chapter 2) and has seven days after a consent agreement is executed, or after an election is directed following a hearing, to file the list of names with the Board. The election cannot be scheduled for less than ten days after the list is due. Thus, seventeen days from the date of a consent agreement is the absolute minimum amount of time. As a practical matter, a certain week or day of the week may be the best time to hold the election for all parties so the election may be scheduled three or four weeks after consent date. If there is a hearing, and the employer requests review of the regional director's decision, the process takes longer. It might take the Board 30 days to rule on the request for review. If the Board grants review, a Board decision may take four to six months or more if the case is unusually complex or novel.

If, after an election is held, challenges and/or objections are filed, the process takes more time, depending upon whether the post-election disputes are resolved by the Board or re-

gional director. Post-election processing takes about as long as the pre-election procedures discussed above—four to six weeks in simple cases, but a minimum four to six months in complicated ones. In a strongly contested representation case the entire process may take close to a year, after which the employer can seek judicial review by refusing to bargain after the union is certified. That will easily add another year to the process.

But most representation cases, even those with disputed issues, are handled expeditiously. According to the Board's *Annual Report*, 13,609 representation and related petitions were filed in 1978. Formal hearings by a regional director were held in only 1,497 of these cases and only 603 cases reached the Board for a full decision. On average, it took 40 days to process a petition from the date of filing to the issuance of the regional director's decision. Although most election cases are handled informally and quickly, the procedures can be abused by employers who use every delaying tactic to gain time to undermine the union.

7. Other Types of Representation Petitions

The procedures outlined above are used when a union files a representation petition for an election. Employees may also file a petition either for a union to represent them or to decertify (revoke the representation rights) their existing union. Employees may file a petition to revoke the union security clause of their collective bargaining agreement (see Chapter 10). An employer can also file a petition for an election (an "RM" petition), but only if the employer has a good faith doubt, based on objective considerations, that the union no longer represents a majority of the unit's employees. (See Chapter 5.) The procedures discussed above are used in processing all types of representation petitions. However, a showing of interest is not required for an employer petition.

A union may also file a petition to amend its certification (an "AC" petition). This petition may be filed if there has been a change in the name of the employer or the union, but no change in the bargaining unit. For example, if the local number of a union has been changed, the union can file a petition to amend its certification to the new number.

A unit clarification (UC) petition may be filed if the employer and the union disagree about whether certain employee classifications should be included within an existing unit. This situation occurs most frequently when an employer adds new jobs after a unit has been certified and the parties are unable to agree whether the new classifications are within the existing unit or are entitled to separate representation.

If there is a question of representation, rather than just a simple change of name, a unit amendment petition cannot be used. If a union wants to represent additional employees, it must file either a unit clarification petition or a representation petition, as appropriate (see Chapter 2). The procedures followed in unit amendment or clarification cases are basically the same as in election cases except that no showing of interest is required.

F. Consolidated Unfair Labor Practice and Representation Proceedings

Frequently, improper conduct during an election campaign may be grounds both for setting aside the election in a representation case and an unfair labor practice charge. For example, an employer might discharge an employee during an election campaign be-

cause the employee favored the union. In such a case the union would file an objection to the election and an unfair labor practice charge against the employer. The cases would be consolidated for hearing. Consolidated cases are heard before an ALJ, and are processed the same as unfair labor practice cases, using the procedures discussed above.

G. Other Agencies Administering Labor Law

Although this chapter has emphasized the role of the National Labor Relations Board, a number of other agencies are also important in labor law. The Department of Labor administers portions of the Labor Management Reporting and Disclosure Act (see Chapter 11), as well as the Fair Labor Standards Act, the Occupational Safety and Health Act, and portions of the Employee Retirement Income Security Act. The Equal Employment Opportunity Commission (see Chapter 13) administers Title VII of the Civil Rights Act. Under a new federal reorganization, the EEOC also administers the Equal Pay and the Age Discrimination In Employment Acts, acts formerly administered by the Department of Labor.

Finally, despite the emphasis on federal law in this text, the states still play an important role in labor relations. State courts have retained their traditional jurisdiction to prevent violent conduct during a labor dispute and have concurrent jurisdiction with the federal courts, applying federal law, to enforce the terms of collective bargaining agreements. The states also have authority to enforce state labor laws over employers not covered by federal law. (See Chapter 14.)

Summary

The Railway Labor Act, passed in 1926, was the first comprehensive federal statutory regulation of labor-management relations. It specifically recognized the right of employees to engage in collective bargaining. This act was followed by the Norris-LaGuardia Act, passed in 1932, prohibiting federal courts from issuing injunctions in labor disputes.

The National Labor Relations Act (NLRA), passed in 1935, established the basic legislative framework protecting employee collective bargaining rights. The Act protected the right of employees to join unions and engage in collective bargaining, prohibited employer unfair labor practices, provided election procedures for determining the employees bargaining agent, and created the National Labor Relations Board that enforces the Act.

In 1947, Congress passed the Taft-Hartley Act to counterbalance the strength of unions under the NLRA. The entire Act was renamed the Labor Management Relations Act (LMRA).

The Taft-Hartley Act established union unfair labor practices to match the employer unfair labor practices prohibited by the NLRA. Among other provisions, Taft-Hartley extensively regulated union picketing and secondary activity. The Taft-Hartley Act also amended Section 7, giving employees the right to refrain from, as well as engage in, union activities.

Section 8 is the heart of the LMRA. It established employer and union unfair labor practices. Section 9 established election procedures. Section 10 established NLRB jurisdiction and procedures in unfair labor practice cases. In addition to the Board, the Labor Management Relations Act established a separate independent general counsel who functions like a prosecutor in unfair labor practice cases.

The first step in an unfair labor practice case is the filing of a charge. If the general counsel finds merit in a charge, a complaint is issued. There may be a trial before an administrative law judge with an appeal to the Board and, ultimately, to the courts, but most cases are settled without going through the entire process.

A representation proceeding is started by filing a petition. Most representation proceedings are handled by consent. However, there may be formal proceedings before the regional director with the right to appeal to the Board. There is no right to appeal a Board's decision on a representation matter directly to court. An employer may refuse to bargain following a Board's decision in a representation case and ultimately obtain judicial review of the decision in the representation proceeding by appealing the unfair labor practice case.

The Board, general counsel, and regional director all have sizable staffs. Thus, when they take a certain action, it is usually taken by a staff member acting in their behalf, even though the Board, general counsel or regional director can review the action and does bear ultimate responsibility.

Finally, the National Labor Relations Board has limited jurisdiction. It has authority only to prevent unfair labor practices under Section 8 and administer elections under Section 9. These are very important functions, but they are not all of labor law. Further, the Board has jurisdiction only over employers and employees covered by the Act. It has further limited its own jurisdiction by establishing monetary standards that an employer must meet before the Board will assert jurisdiction over a dispute within its statutory authority.

Review Questions

1. What was the importance of the Norris-LaGuardia Act?
2. What was the purpose of the Taft-Hartley Act?
3. How does the function of the five-member Board differ from the function of the general counsel?
4. Does the Board assert jurisdiction in every case in which the employer's operations affect commerce as defined in the Act?
5. What is the first step in an unfair labor practice case?
6. Who can file a charge with the NLRB?
7. What is the time limit for filing a charge?
8. What is the purpose of a representation hearing?
9. What is a "showing of interest"?
10. How is a regional director's decision in a representation case appealed to the Board?

(Answers to review questions appear at end of book.)

Basic Legal Principles

1. The first step in an unfair labor practice proceeding is to file a charge with a regional office of the Board alleging a violation of the LMRA by an employer or a labor organization. *NLRB Rules and Regulations* §102.9.

2. A charging party can appeal a regional director's dismissal of an unfair practice charge to the Office of the General Counsel in Washington, D.C. If the appeal to the general counsel is denied, there is no further appeal to the Board. The general counsel's decision dismissing a charge is final and not reviewable by the courts. *United Electrical Contractors Assn. v. Ordman*, 366 F.2d 776, 63 LRRM 2223 (2nd Cir. 1966), *cert. denied*, 385 U.S. 1026, 64 LRRM 2158 (1967).

3. Either the charging party, the general counsel, or the respondent has an absolute right to file exceptions with the Board to an administrative

law judge's decision in an unfair labor practice case. Only the Board makes a binding decision. *NLRB Rules* §102.46.

4. Only final orders of the NLRB in unfair labor practice cases are subject to review by the courts of appeals. Decisions in representation cases are not final orders and can only be reviewed in an appeal in an unfair labor practice proceeding. *AFL v. NLRB,* 308 U.S. 401, 5 LRRM 670 (1940). However, federal district courts can set aside NLRB certification orders if the Board has plainly exceeded its statutory authority. *Leedom v. Kyne,* 358 U.S. 184, 43 LRRM 2222 (1958); *Physicians National House Staff Ass'n v. Murphy,* 100 LRRM 3055 (D.C. Cir. 1979).

5. A court of appeals must uphold the Board's decision on appeal if the decision is based on substantial evidence on the record as a whole, including the evidence opposed to the Board's conclusions. A court of appeals cannot reverse the Board even though the court might have reached a different conclusion on the same evidence. *Universal Camera Corp. v. NLRB,* 340 U.S. 474, 27 LRRM 2373 (1951); *NLRB v. Jack August Enterprises, Inc.,* 583 F 2d 575, 99 LRRM 2582 (1st Cir. 1978).

6. If the regional director has ordered a representation election, a party may request that the Board review the decision. There are only four limited grounds on which the Board will accept review: if the case raises a substantial question of law or policy, if the regional director committed clear error on a substantial factual issue, if prejudicial error was committed in the conduct of the hearing, or if there are compelling reasons to reconsider an important Board rule or policy. *NLRB Rules* §102.67 (c).

7. Either the Board agent or an employer or union observer may, for good cause, challenge the eligibility of any voter. Persons challenged are allowed to vote, but their ballots are impounded by the Board agent. The challenged ballots are not resolved unless there are enough to affect the results of an election. *NLRB Rules* §102.69.

8. If a representation election is conducted pursuant to a stipulation for certification and there are post-election objections or challenges, the regional director merely issues a recommended report on objections and challenged ballots. The Board makes the final ruling. If the parties hold an election pursuant to a consent agreement, the regional director's decision on post-election matters is absolutely final with no appeal to the Board. *NLRB Rules* §102.62 (a) & (b).

9. A trial in an unfair labor practice case is an adversary proceeding governed by the federal rules of evidence. A representation case proceeding is technically nonadversary, and the rules of evidence do not apply. *NLRB Rules* §§102.38–39 & §102.66.

10. The Board statutory jurisdiction applies to covered employers whose activities affect commerce, the broadest possible constitutional ju-

risdiction. *American Gypsum Co.*, 231 NLRB No. 152, 97 LRRM 1069 (1977); *Ogden Food Service Corp.*, 234 NLRB No. 69, 97 LRRM 1190 (1978). Also, United Services, 239 NLRB No. 140, 100 LRRM 1057 (1978) (jurisdiction over private employers providing services for exempt governmental agencies).

Suggested Reading   Fanning, "National Labor Relations Act and the Role of the NLRB," 29 *Lab. L.J.* 683 (1978).

Gregory, *Labor and the Law*, (2nd Ed. 1958).

McGuiness, *How to Take a Case Before the National Labor Relations Board*, (4th Ed., 1975).

L. Modjesk, "Commentaries on the National Labor Relations Board," 39 *Ohio S.L.J.* 35 (1978).

Chapter Two

The Collective Bargaining Unit

*U*nions represent and bargain for employees in appropriate bargaining units. To understand the bargaining process, it is necessary to understand the appropriate bargaining unit concept. This chapter discusses how the appropriate bargaining unit is determined, which employees may be part of a unit, and election rules and procedures.

The rules applying to appropriate bargaining units in certain industries or occupations can be very detailed. Entire books have been written on collective bargaining units and representation issues. This chapter is necessarily limited to general principles and the issues most frequently faced by unions. If you understand these general principles, you should be able to handle most specific situations as well. Remember, the principles discussed in this chapter assume that the employer is subject to the Board's jurisdiction as discussed in Chapter 1.

A. DETERMINING THE APPROPRIATE BARGAINING UNIT

An employer may voluntarily agree to recognize and bargain with a union, in which case the parties mutually determine the bargaining unit. Generally, the Board permits a union to bargain for the employees in any unit the employer and union voluntarily agree or consent to, provided the unit does not violate basic Board policies and statutory requirements covering an appropriate unit, discussed below.

1. The Community of Interest Principle

The most important factor used in determining an appropriate unit is the existence of a community of interest among the employees. A community of interest refers to what the employees have in common. The more the employees have in common, the more likely it is that the Board will find that they have a community of interest and are thus an appropriate unit for bargaining. Several factors are considered in determining the existence of a community of interest. Do the employees: (1) perform similar types of work, such as craft work, clerical work, or production and maintenance work; (2) work in the same location and/or interchange with each other; (3) perform integrated production activities; (4) enjoy similar working conditions such as being on the same shift or using the same locker room and cafeteria facilities; (5)

have the same wage and benefit schedule; and (6) have common supervision?

The Board also considers the scope of any existing bargaining unit that represents the employees, the organizational structure of the employer, and the bargaining history in the industry. No one factor is controlling—any evidence showing common interest will be considered by the Board in determining community of interest. While the factors listed above are frequently considered, they are by no means all-inclusive.

Suppose, for example, a plant has had no union. Both salaried and hourly employees work on an assembly line. Obviously the salaried employees and the hourly workers have different wage conditions. If, however, they are all performing similar work, are at the same location, and work the same shift schedule, they may still have a sufficient community of interest so that both the salaried and hourly employees would be in the same appropriate unit.

What if employees at one company plant produce part of a product and employees at the company's second plant across town finish the product? There may be a sufficient community of interest, based on such factors as working conditions or wage and benefit structure to form one appropriate unit although the employees are at two separate locations. The employees at each plant may also both have a separate community of interest among themselves so that each plant would constitute an appropriate unit for bargaining.

2. Multiple Appropriate Units

It is possible for one union to represent all the employees in a plant in one unit. Production employees in one department may share a community of interest with those in other departments, and with the maintenance and craft employees, based on the factors discussed above, to make a plant-wide unit appropriate. All employees, for example, might work the same hours, have similar working conditions, and have common supervision. Frequently, however, there is more than one union representing employees in a plant because there is more than one appropriate unit. Craft employees, production and maintenance employees, technical employees, or employees in a particular department may each have a separate distinct community of interest among themselves. Under these conditions each employee group would be an appropriate unit.

Generally, the Board allows employees to bargain in any appropriate unit even though other units may also be appropriate. A unit does not have to be the "best" or most appropriate in terms of employer efficiency or bargaining convenience. A bargaining unit can be compared to a pie that can be cut up in many different ways. The employees can be divided up any way so long as the individual piece is an appropriate unit.

Extent of Organization

Section 9 (c) (5) of the LMRA provides that in determining the appropriateness of a unit for collective bargaining , the extent to which the employees have organized shall not be controlling. This means that the Board cannot decide that a unit is appropriate just because a group of employees have joined a union and wish to be represented by it. Rather, the Board must consider whether these employees have a separate community of interest among themselves. The Board has held that as long as the Board does not treat extent of organization as the controlling factor, it can consider extent of organization in determining community of interest along with the other factors discussed above.

3. Unit Segments

There may be a number of possible bargaining units, but the union cannot represent a segment of an appropriate unit; it must represent all the employees in the unit. Assume that a union sought a unit consisting only of craft employees in one of the two departments. However, the craft employees regularly work interchangeably in both departments, have common supervision, and share a common wage structure. The Board would probably conclude that the craft employees in the two departments were so interrelated that the appropriate unit would have to include the craft employees in both departments.

The Board would not permit an election in only one of the departments, even if all the craft employees in the department wanted the union to represent them because a union cannot represent only a segment of an appropriate unit. If the Board permitted the union to represent only the craft employees in the one department in this example, the Board would be giving controlling weight to the extent of organization contrary to Section 9 (c) (5). Similarly, a union seeking to represent production employees at a plant would probably have to represent all of them, not just those on a single production line, as a single line would represent only a segment of the appropriate production employee unit.

Single Employee Units

Because one person cannot engage in collective bargaining by himself, the Board has held that a bargaining unit must have a minimum of two employees and will not certify a one-employee unit. However, this rule does not prevent an employer from voluntarily recognizing a union as a representative for a single employee. Single employee contracts are most frequently found in the construction industry, where a craft union may have contracts with a number of small employers.

4. Commonly Accepted Bargaining Units

Over the years, the Board has recognized that certain groups of employees, because of their distinct community of interest, almost always comprise a separate appropriate unit. These are called *presumptively appropriate units.* Office clerical employees' units and a single unit for production and maintenance employees are presumptively appropriate. In some industries, certain departments are traditionally recognized as presumptively appropriate for separate bargaining. In the printing trades, for example, the printing and bindery departments are traditionally in separate units.

The Board has also determined that the structure of some industries makes certain units presumptively appropriate. The appropriate unit for public utilities is usually system-wide in contrast to retail chains where a single store is presumptively appropriate. If a union seeks a system-wide unit for utility employees or a single-store unit in a retail chain, it will have little difficulty getting Board approval. But if a union seeks less than a system-wide utility unit, such as a single division, it must show that the structure of the particular company is unique. Or the union must prove that there is some special factor in the employees' community of interest setting them apart from the usual industry pattern so that the employees the union seeks to represent have a separate community of interest.

If a union seeks a grocery employee unit composed of all company stores in a metropolitan area, even though a single store would be appropriate, the Board would probably permit the broader unit. Why? Because all the employees would probably have enough common interests, such as similar working conditions and pay and fringe benefits, to have a community of interest on a company-wide basis even though each store would also have a separate community of interest because each store had separate supervision, etc. In that case, there would be more than one appropriate unit. Since the Board permits employees to be represented in any appropriate unit, not just "the best unit," the union would have a choice.

The Board's decisions on appropriate units in health care institutions are an excellent example of the application of community of interest factors. When Congress passed the health care amendments covering nonprofit hospitals, the legislative history, but not the statute itself, contained a statement that the Board should guard against a proliferation of bargaining units in the health care field.

Hospitals argued that this meant that hospital-wide units were preferred for bargaining. The Board disagreed. It held that the Congressional statement against proliferation meant that there should not be separate representation for each craft, as in the construction industry. However, the Board held that it should follow the same community of interest standards applied to industrial plants. Thus, the Board has held that appropriate health care institution bargaining units are (1) all service and maintenance employees, (2) office clerical employees, (3) technical employees, and (4) professional employees. Nurses and doctors are entitled to separate representation as professionals. However, the Board has approved separate units of service and maintenance employees if the union can

prove a distinct community of interest. In that case, an overall service and maintenance unit is also appropriate.

5. Multi-Union and Globe Elections

If more than one union wants to represent a particular unit, each union is on the ballot along with the choice of no union. One of the choices (the competing unions or no union) must receive a majority of all valid votes cast in the election. If there is no majority, a run-off election is held between the top two choices.

Suppose that there are 100 employees in the unit and that 70 employees cast valid ballots in the election. The election results are 35 votes for Union A, 33 votes for union B, and two votes for no union. There is no winner because none of the choices on the ballot received the necessary majority of 36 votes or more. A run-off election would have to be held between the top two choices, Union A and Union B. There would not be a no union choice. Everyone is eligible to vote in the re-run election. The union receiving a majority of the valid votes cast in the second election is the winner. If the top two choices in the first election had been union A and no union, the second election would have been only between those two choices, and union B would not have been on the ballot at all.

Globe Elections

Suppose there are two departments, A and B, which are both separate appropriate units but that could also comprise a single appropriate unit. For example, a print shop might have printing and bindery departments, each with a separate community of interest, but both having sufficient common interests to make a plant-wide unit appropriate as well. Suppose union X wants to represent only the employees in department A while union Y wants to represent the employees in both departments. Union Y, of course, would need a 30 percent employee showing of interest overall in the two departments. Union Y would not need a 30 percent interest in each of the two departments. That means it can have proportionately more recognition cards from one department than the other. In such a case, there would be a so-called "globe election," named after the case (Globe Machine & Stamping Co.)[1] setting down this procedure.

In a *Globe* election, the employees in department A would receive a ballot listing union X, union Y, and no union because both unions want to represent those employees. The employees in department B would have a choice between union Y or no union. Union X would not appear on the department B ballot because it does not seek to represent those employees. The votes of each department are tallied separately. If a majority of the employees in department A vote to be represented separately by union X, which sought to represent them separately, then union X will be certified as the representative of those employees, regardless of the vote of the employees in department B.

Suppose there are ten employees voting in department A and the result of the election is six votes for union X, three for union Y, and one vote for no union. There are also 30 employees voting in department B, and they vote 14 for union Y and 16 for no union. Union X would be certified as the representative of department A. Department B would be unrepresented because union Y did not receive a majority of the votes cast by employees in that department. If the vote in department B were reversed, and union Y did receive a majority, there would be two units. Department A would be represented by union X,

while department B would be represented by union Y.

If union X does not receive a majority of the votes in department A, the votes in departments A and B will be counted together to determine whether union Y will represent both departments as a single unit. Thus, what if the vote in department A had been four for union X, four for union Y, and two for no union; and the vote in department B had remained 14 for union Y and 16 for no union? Since union X failed to receive the majority in Unit A that it sought to represent separately, Department A would not have separate representation. Therefore, the votes in department A would be counted in the overall unit of department A and B. The final tally in the combined voting group would be four votes for union X, 18 for union Y (the combined tally of 4 Y votes in department A and 14 Y votes in department B), and 18 for no union. Since there is a tie between Y and no union there would be a run-off election between these two top choices.

Employees in department A would be able to vote in the run-off election, but they would no longer be able to vote for union X. If union Y received the majority of votes cast in the overall unit during the run-off election, it would be certified as the representative of a unit consisting of departments A and B.

Sometimes two unions will seek joint certification. That may happen if two unions representing employees in the same industry begin an organizing drive among the same employees. The two unions may decide that it is better for them to seek joint certification as the bargaining agent rather than fight between themselves, which might result in neither union being certified. The Board permits unions to be jointly certified; however, if two unions are jointly certified, they are not permitted to divide the employee group between themselves after the election. Instead,

[1] See legal principle 6.

both unions have an obligation to represent the entire work force. It is an unfair labor practice for one jointly certified union to refuse to represent a segment of the jointly certified bargaining unit. Such a refusal can lead to the revocation of a joint certification.

6. Accretions to Bargaining Units

Once a union is certified as the representative of the bargaining unit, other employees may be added to the unit without being entitled to vote for union representation. Employees added in this manner are called an accretion to the bargaining unit. This occurs when an employer expands operations and the new employees have the same community of interest as those already in the unit. For example, if a union is a certified representative of employees on assembly lines A, B, and C, and the employer adds assembly line D, the new employees working on Line D would have the same community of interest as the employees already working on the other production lines. The employees on line D would be added to the bargaining unit as an accretion without a vote on union representation. Sometimes employees working at a new plant can be added as an accretion to an existing plant bargaining unit if the employees at the old and new facility have a common community of interest and the two plants have interrelated production. It is common for employees at a new separate warehouse to be added as an accretion to an existing production and maintenance unit at the plant.

If the employer disputes the inclusion of new employees, the union may file a clarification petition (a "UC" petition) with the Board, requesting the Board to decide whether the union's certification should include the new employees. If the Board determines that the new employees have the same community of interest as those employees already in the unit, the new employees are automatically added as an accretion without a vote. If, however, the Board concludes that the employees should not be added as an accretion, the Board will require that the union obtain a showing of interest from the employees in the new operation and file an election petition.

Elections are the preferred way of determining representation. The Board has ruled, therefore, that a unit will not be clarified to include additional employees if there is doubt about the employees' community of interest. Also, as a general principle, the Board will not allow employees to be added to a unit through the clarification method if the disputed employee classifications existed at the time of the union's original certification and could have been included in the original unit. Such employees are entitled to an election before being added to the unit.

7. Craft and Departmental Severance Elections

After a unit has been established, employees sometimes subsequently seek a different bargaining unit structure. The craft employees included in an overall production and maintenance unit might decide they preferred separate representation. It is difficult to sever employees out of an existing unit because the longer employees stay in a unit together, the closer their community of interest with other employees in the unit becomes. For example, the longer hourly and salaried employees work together on an assembly line, the more likely it is that they will have common supervision, work the same hours, and have other factors in common that establish a community of interest.

Until 1966, it was fairly easy for craft employees included in a larger department to sever themselves and establish their own unit. As a general rule, the Board permitted craft units to be severed from a larger unit if the proposed unit was a true craft unit (meaning the employees in the unit exercised craft level skills rather than routine work) and the union seeking to represent the craft unit traditionally represented craft employees. Similarly, the Board permitted severance of a department under the same factors if the department traditionally had separate representation, such as printers or maintenance shop departments. The only exceptions were in a few industries, such as aluminum, where craft severance was not permitted because of the integrated nature of the operations and the bargaining history of plant-wide units.

The Board's decision in the *Mallinckrodt Chemical* case[2] changed this approach. In *Mallinckrodt*, a group of craft mechanics petitioned to be severed from a larger production and maintenance unit. The Board denied the petition and ruled that it would no longer grant automatic craft severance. The Board stated that although the mechanics had a separate community of interest, this interest was overshadowed by a broader community of interest they shared with the other employees because of their long-standing association in the existing bargaining unit. It also noted that the employer's production processes were integrated with the maintenance work. The continued normal operation of the production processes depended upon the performance of the mechanics' assigned tasks.

In *Mallinckrodt*, the Board listed six illustrative factors it would apply in determining whether a craft unit or a departmental unit would be severed from a broader unit. Those six factors are:

2 See legal principle 2.

1. Whether or not the proposed unit consists of a distinct and homogeneous group of skilled journeymen craftsmen performing the functions of their craft on a nonrepetitive basis or of employees constituting a functionally distinct department, working in trades or occupations for which a tradition of separate representation exists.

2. The history of collective bargaining among the employees and at the plant involved, and at other plants of the employer, with emphasis on whether the existing patterns of bargaining produce stability in labor relations, and whether such stability will be unduly disrupted by the destruction of the existing pattern of representation.

3. The extent to which the employees in the proposed unit have established and maintained their separate identity during the period of inclusion in a broader unit, and the extent of their participation or lack of participation in the establishment and maintenance of the existing pattern of representation, and prior opportunities, if any, afforded them in obtaining separate representation.

4. The history and pattern of collective bargaining in the industry involved.

5. The degree of integration of the employer's production processes, including the extent to which the continued normal operation of the production processes depends upon the performance of the assigned functions of the employees in the proposed unit.

6. The qualifications of a union seeking to carve out a separate unit, including that union's experience in representing employees like those involved in the severance action.

Since the adoption of the *Mallinckrodt* principles, the Board has usually denied petitions seeking to sever craft and departmental employees from an existing unit. Unions have been successful in severing craft or depart-ment al units only if there is clear evidence that the employees have maintained a sepa-rate identity. Such evidence of separate iden-tity might be shown by the retention of special rights, such as the right to select spe-cial representatives on a bargaining commit-tee or the right to vote separately on a contract. The Board also considers whether the interests of the group are adequately rep-resented by the broader unit. For example, if the grievances of the craft employees do not get processed while those of the production and maintenance employees do, the Board might hold that the craft employees are enti-tled to separate representation.

Unions have been far more successful in obtaining separate craft or departmental units if the employees to be severed are not already included in a broader bargaining unit. Under those circumstances, there is, of course, no history of bargaining in a broader unit. The petitioning union is usually able to prove that the craft or departmental employees have not lost their separate identity. Also, the Board is more likely to find a separate unit appropriate if the only alternative to separate representa-tion is no representation at all.

8. Multi-Plant and Multi-Employer Units

If an employer has more than one plant, the Board generally considers each plant as a separate appropriate unit. When an employer has more than one plant and a union seeks to represent only the employees at one, it will have little trouble getting Board approval for the unit. If either the employer or the union wants a unit consisting of employees in a multi-plant unit, the burden is on that party, applying the community of interest factors, to prove that employees in the two plants share a community of interest.

If the Board finds that both a single plant or a multi-plant unit are appropriate, the union can choose which unit to represent, provided, of course, the union has a 30 per-cent showing of interest in the combined unit if it seeks the broader representation. Re-member, so long as the union is seeking to represent an appropriate unit, it cannot be compelled to represent a different one. Thus, the union could not be required to represent employees on a multi-plant basis except in the unique situation where only a multi-plant unit is appropriate. A multi-employer unit is an association of separate employers who have come together to bargain with a union. Multi-employer units are established volun-tarily between the employers and the union. Multi-employer bargaining is discussed fur-ther in Chapter 5.

B. EXCLUSION OF EMPLOYEES FROM THE BARGAINING UNIT

In addition to determining the appropriate bargaining unit, the parties, or the Board in a contested case, must determine whether cer-tain persons are to be included or excluded from the unit. There are four general catego-ries of persons who are excluded from a bar-gaining unit: (1) employees whom the LMRA requires or permits to have separate repre-sentation; (2) individuals excluded from the LMRA definition of employee (Section 2(3)) and thus not entitled to representation at all; (3) employees excluded from the unit because they do not regularly perform bargaining unit work; and (4) employees the Board excludes as a matter of policy because their interests are more closely aligned with management than with the bargaining unit.

A word of caution for bargaining purposes. There is a distinction between whether certain employees are in the bargaining unit and whether they may do bargaining unit work. The fact that the Board finds that a particular individual should be excluded from the unit does not prevent that person from performing bargaining unit work. As many unions have learned the hard way, Board certification only establishes that the union represents a particular group of employees in an appropriate unit for bargaining. The Board has held in many cases that certification is not a guarantee that employees will perform any particular work or that the work may not be subcontracted. The bargaining unit's work is a matter of negotiations. If the Union wants to prevent nonbargaining unit employees from performing its work, or prevent subcontracting, it must negotiate contract clauses providing this protection—certification alone is insufficient.

1. Employees Entitled to or Required to Have Separate Representation

a. Professional Employees and Technical Employees

Professional employees are not excluded from collective bargaining rights, but special rules do apply to them. Section 9(b)(1) provides that the Board shall not find a unit containing both professional and nonprofessional employees appropriate unless a majority of the professional employees vote for inclusion in the broader unit. This prevents a small group of professionals from being swallowed up in a larger unit without the professionals' approval.

The term professional employee generally refers to someone who performs work of a predominantly intellectual, nonstandardized nature. The work must require the use of discretion and independent judgment, and

knowledge of an advanced type in a field of science or learning customarily acquired in an institution of higher learning. Lawyers, doctors, teachers, and certified public accountants (CPAs) are examples of professional employees.

A person who has a professional degree is classified as a professional under the Act only if he is functioning in a position requiring the use of professional training. A person trained as a teacher who is working as a clerk would not be considered a professional. A CPA doing routine bookkeeping rather than skilled accounting work would not be a professional.

Professional Election Procedures. The voting procedures in an election involving professional employees are similar to those in a *Globe* election. Professionals vote by ballot first on whether they wish to be included in an overall unit, and second whether they wish to be represented by the petitioning union. If a majority vote for inclusion in the larger unit, their votes are counted with the votes of the other employees in determining whether the union has won the election. If a majority of the professional employees vote for separate representation and also for the union, the union can represent the professional employees separately if it desires. The union can also represent the other employees separately if a majority of them vote for representation. Thus, the union can end up separately representing two units of employees

Technical Employees. A distinction must be made between professional and technical employees. Technical employees do not meet the qualifications for a professional, but perform work of a technical nature requiring the use of independent discretion and special training acquired in college or technical schools.

Technical employees are not entitled to vote separately on representation. At one time the Board permitted technical employees to be represented separately, just as craft employees were. The Board also routinely excluded technical employees from a production and maintenance unit if either party requested it. The Board no longer follows this rule, but applies traditional community of interest factors to technical employees to determine whether their community of interest is with the production and maintenance employees or separate.

b. Guards

Section 9(b)(3) provides that the Board shall not find a unit appropriate if it includes, together with other employees, anyone employed as a guard. A guard is someone who enforces rules to protect the property of the employer or protects the safety of persons on the employer's premises against employees and others. The section also requires that a guard's union not be affiliated with a union that admits employees other than guards. Congress included these provisions because it believed that guards, whose job is to protect employers' property in part from other employees, and to enforce rules or take action against their fellow employees, might be reluctant to do so if both groups were in the same union. Security guards employed by an outside firm to protect the property of another employer are classified as guards under the Act even though they do not protect their own employer's property.

Employees falling within the exclusion for guards can have their own bargaining unit, provided that the labor organization representing them neither represents nor is affiliated with any organization that represents employees other than guards. Note, however, that a unit consisting of guards and nonguards is not illegal. The Board has held that it cannot certify a unit composed of guards and nonguards because of the statutory restrictions. But an employer and a union may voluntarily agree to a unit containing both groups.

2. Individuals Excluded from the Definition of Employee

Only employees are entitled to be members of a bargaining unit. Section 2(3) excludes certain employees from coverage by the Act: (1) agricultural laborers or people in the domestic service of a family or person in a home, (2) persons employed by a parent or spouse, (3) independent contractors, and (4) supervisors.

A person who is excluded from the definition of employee is not subject to the various protections the Act gives employees. Such individuals, for example, may be fired for attempting to form a union. There is a narrow exception if a person is fired in order to discourage or frighten employees from organizing or supporting a union. For example, if an employer fired a supervisor who supported a union as a lesson to employees that the same thing might happen to them, the Board could order the supervisor reinstated. The supervisor would be reinstated not because he has any statutory rights (he does not), but in order to eliminate the chilling effect the discharge would have on employees whose rights are statutorily protected.

a. Agricultural Laborers and Domestics

An agricultural laborer is one who works with an agricultural or horticultural product in its natural state. A person who changes a raw product in some way, such as processing wheat into flour or canning vegetables, is classified as a manufacturing employee and is covered by the Act. Domestic employees (such as housekeepers) are excluded from the

Act if they are employed by a family or person at his home. Individuals doing domestic type work but employed by an outside contractor, such as a cleaning service, are classified as employees under the Act.

b. Individuals Employed By a Parent or Spouse

The wife or child of an employer is not classified as an employee under Section 2(3) and is therefore excluded from the bargaining unit.

Individuals such as mothers, brothers, or daughters-in-law of the employer are not specifically excluded from the definition of employee under Section 2(3). However, the Board has held that these other relatives may be excluded if it finds that their interests are more closely aligned with the employer than with the other employees. They are then classified as managerial employees, (discussed below). Exclusion is not automatic. The Board determines whether these relatives have a special relationship with the employer other than being related. For example, if the brother of an employer performed the same work on the same schedule as other employees and received no special consideration from his employer-brother, he would be included in the bargaining unit. In contrast, the son of the employer, even if he worked under the same conditions, would automatically be excluded under Section 2(3). If the brother could come and go as he liked, was invited to attend management meetings or enjoyed other special privileges, he would be excluded as a managerial employee because of his special status.

The Closely Held Corporation. Corporations raise different issues. Because a corporation is not a natural person and it cannot have children or a spouse, the statutory exclusion for individuals employed by a parent or spouse does not apply. What if all the corporate stock is owned by one person whose children work in the business? Is it right that the son of a person who owns a business outright is excluded from the bargaining unit, but the son of a stockholder who owns 100 percent of a corporation is included? To deal with this situation, the Board has held that the spouse or children of the principal stockholders of a closely held corporation must be excluded from a bargaining unit as managerial employees, just as if the employer were an individual. This rule usually applies only to persons owning 50 percent or more of the stock. Other relatives, such as the mother, brother, or daughter-in-law of the stockholder, are not automatically excluded. The same test is applied to these relatives as to those of an individual owner. They will be in the unit unless they have a special relationship with management, as shown by special privileges, etc., making their interests more closely aligned with management than with their coworkers.

Similarly, relatives of a corporate officer who is not a principal stockholder or of a supervisor are included in a bargaining unit unless they have special privileges. It does not matter that they would almost certainly vote against the union so long as they work within the unit without special privileges.

c. Independent Contractors

Independent contractors are excluded from the definition of employee under Section 2(3). Independent contractors are generally distinguished from employees based on the amount of control the employer exercises over how a person does his work. The more an employer controls how the work is done, the more likely it is that the individual will be classified as an employee. On the other hand, if the employer specifies only the result, but not the method of work, the person is an independent contractor.

Suppose there are two cab drivers, each of whom rents the cab and uniforms from a cab company. The operator of cab A, assigned to work in a certain area of the city from 8:30 A.M. to 5:30 P.M., must wear a uniform, take all paging calls, and turn over a percentage of the fares to the cab company. The operator of cab B is told neither when nor where to work; he is only required to pay the company a flat fee for use of the cab and the paging service. Cab A driver would probably be classified as an employee because the company controls both the driver's method and the results. The operator of cab B would probably be classified as an independent contractor because the company only controls the end result, but not the method.

A distinction must be made between an independent contractor and an employee who—because of experience, skill, and ability—is given greater working freedom. Such an employee is not an independent contractor, as the employee remains subject to the same wages, hours, and working conditions as the other employees in the bargain unit. The employer still controls the method of operation as well as the result, even though the senior employee knows the procedures well and thus requires little or no supervision.

d. Supervisors

Many employees believe that a supervisor is someone who has authority to hire or fire; however, the statutory definition is much broader. Section 2(11) of the LMRA defines a supervisor as "any individual having authority, in the interest of the employer, to hire, transfer, suspend, lay off, recall, promote, discharge, assign, reward, or discipline other employees, or responsibly to direct them, or to adjust their grievances, or effectively to recommend such action, if in connection with the foregoing the exercise of such authority is not of a merely routine or clerical nature, but requires the use of independent judgment."

The statute lists 12 different factors that make an employee a supervisor. A person with the authority to perform even one of those functions, even if it is not exercised, is classified as a supervisor.

Effective Authority to Recommend Action. Section 2(11) does not require that a person have the independent authority to take any of the actions listed above in order to be a supervisor. An employee who cannot take action alone, but has effective authority to recommend supervisory action, is also classified as a supervisor. Effective authority means that an employer acts on the employee's recommendations without making an independent investigation and determination.

For example, an employee with 30 years of service tells the employer that a probationary employee is not performing satisfactorily and should be let go. If the employer fires the probationary employee based on the recommendation without making a further investigation of the facts, the employee making the recommendation is a supervisor because he or she has effective authority to recommend a supervisory act—the power to fire.

If the employer asks other employees or the foreman about the new employee's performance and then decides to fire him based on all the facts, however, then the employee making the recommendation is not a supervisor because the employer made a separate investigation and did not as a matter of course follow the employee's recommendation.

Exercise of Independent Judgment. An employee is not a supervisor if the authority exercised does not require independent judgment, but is routine or clerical. A supervisor must use independent judgment in at least one of the factors listed in section 2(11). An employee who fires another employee because of instructions from higher management is not a supervisor because no discretion is exercised. But, if the same employee was instructed to discipline another employee and was given discretion as to the penalty, the employee would be a supervisor because of that discretion.

Imagine a department with five typists and a senior typist who has the authority to assign work to the others. If the senior typist assigns work merely on the basis of which typist is busy or on a rotating basis, her assignment authority is only routine or clerical and not supervisory. If, however, she decides which typist is particularly capable of doing a certain kind of work and assigns the work on that basis, she is exercising independent judgment and is considered a supervisor.

An employee who has authority to give employees time off from work may or may not be a supervisor. An employee who is told by higher management that he may allow employees to go home early if their work is finished or they are ill is not a supervisor because he is simply carrying out rules established by higher authority. He lacks the discretionary judgment to be a supervisor. On the other hand, if the employee is simply told he may allow employees to go home early at his discretion, he is a supervisor.

An experienced senior employee who assists or directs a less skilled junior employee is not a supervisor. The Board holds that an employee whose authority is based on a knowledge of how certain work is to be performed and that does not involve the exercise of independent judgment is not a supervisor. This situation frequently arises in skilled crafts in which highly skilled journeymen direct apprentices or even younger journeymen. Since the senior journeyman's authority is based on superior knowledge and ability

rather than any discretionary supervisory control, the employee would not be classified as a supervisor.

An employee's duties, not his title, control whether he is classified as a supervisor. An employee may be called a supervisor or foreman by the employer, but may not be classified as supervisor by the Board if he does not exercise supervisory control. Most leadmen, for example, lack the discretionary judgment to be classified as a supervisor. But if a leadman does have discretionary authority, he will be classified as a supervisor regardless of his title.

Sometimes the Board looks at the ratio of alleged supervisors to employees in a unit to determine which employees are supervisors. If classifying an employee as a supervisor results in an unusually low supervisor-employee ratio and the employee's supervisory status is questionable, the Board might conclude that the employee is not a supervisor.

Remember that a person must have discretionary control over employees to be classified as a supervisor. Thus, a person working in a department by himself with no employees under his control (such as a stockroom supervisor in a one-room stockroom) would not be classified as a supervisor regardless of his title. As discussed below, however, he might be classified as a managerial employee.

e. Employees Not Regularly Employed in the Bargaining Unit

1. *Part-Time Employees.* A part-time employee, as the name implies, is an individual who only works part-time for an employer. Part-time sales clerks in retail stores are a typical example.

Whether a part-time employee is included in a bargaining unit and entitled to vote in an election depends upon whether the employee is classified as a regular part-time employee and thus shares a community of interest with the full time workers. At one time the Board held that an employee had to work a certain percentage of the work week to be classified as regular part-time, but that rule is no longer followed.

Currently an employee's regular part-time status is based on the regularity of the work rather than the number of hours. An employee is included in a unit if he works a sufficient number of hours on a regular basis to have a substantial interest in the wages, hours, and working conditions in the unit. Thus, an employee who works only one day a week every week, as a weekend relief, is included in the bargaining unit. On the other hand, an employee who works only as needed and who has no regular schedule is not included in the unit, but classified as an irregular or casual employee. An on-call employee could be included in a bargaining unit if the employee worked regularly, which might be the case if a person worked for a large employer where there were absences every week to be filled.

There are Board cases in which an employee has worked for 10 percent or less of the work week, but was included in the unit because the work was on a regular schedule. In addition to regularity, the Board considers whether the employee performs the same duties and receives the same benefits as full-time employees.

2. Dual Status Employees. Employees who work part-time in the bargaining unit and part-time for the employer out of the unit are classified as dual status employees. An example would be an employee who works three days a week in the office doing clerical work and two days a week as a production worker. The determining factors for a dual status employee are the same as those applied to part-time employees. A dual status employee who works regularly in a bargaining unit is included in it. This means, for example, that an employee may actually be included in two or more bargaining units because he regularly works in them.

3. Seasonal Employees. Seasonal workers (e.g., people hired for the summer at a resort) may be included in a bargaining unit of regular full-time employees if the seasonal employees have a reasonable expectation of returning each season. On the other hand, if the employees are hired only for one season, with no expectation of returning the next year, they are not included in the unit. Since these employees have no expectation of future employment and have no great interest in the wages, hours, or working conditions, they lack a community of interest with the full-time and returning seasonal employees.

4. Students, Retirees, Trainees, and Probationary Employees. Students may be included in a bargaining unit depending upon their community of interest. A student working after school on a regular schedule can be included in the unit as a regular part-time employee. But a student who works one season at a summer resort or in a factory with no reasonable expectation of returning the next summer is excluded from the bargaining unit.

At one time the Board held that retirees who work part-time in a unit would be excluded if they limited the number of hours they worked in order to make maximum social security benefits. This rule has now been changed. A retiree who works regularly will be in the bargaining unit even if working a limited number of hours. A retiree's unit eligibility is determined the same as any other part-time employee.

The eligibility of employees hired as management trainees is determined by their reasonable expectations of becoming managers. If trainees have a reasonable expectation of becoming part of management within a reasonably short period, they will be excluded from the unit. On the other hand, if promotion to management is uncertain or far in the future, the Board looks to the current status of the trainee and may include him in the bargaining unit. Probationary employees with a reasonable expectation of completing their probationary period and being permanently hired are included in a bargaining unit.

3. Individuals Excluded Because of their Relationship to Management

a. Managerial Employees

The Board has long recognized that there are employees who do not meet the definition of supervisor, but whose interests are far different from rank-and-file employees. A company treasurer, for example, might not supervise, but would have interests obviously aligned with management and not with the bargaining unit. To cover these types of employees, the Board developed the concept of the managerial employee.

There are two types of managerial employees: (1) those whose interests, based on community of interest factors, are closely aligned with management and (2) those who are involved in the formulation or effectuation of management policy. The Board has held that these individuals, although not specifically excluded from the definition of employees in the Act, should be excluded from a unit. The Supreme Court has held that managerial employees are not entitled to separate representation. Thus, the status of managerial employees differs from that of guards or professional employees who may be excluded from an overall unit, but are still entitled to representation in their own right.

Enjoyment of Special Privileges. The first type of managerial employee, those with special privileges that align them with management rather than fellow employees, was discussed above in regard to the exclusion of an employer's relatives from a unit. The key to this determination is whether an individual has a special relationship with management as evidenced by the receipt of special privileges not usually afforded other employees, or different terms or conditions of employment.

Participation in Company Policies. The second type of managerial employee is involved in making company policy or exercises discretion and independent judgment in carrying out such policy. An employee meeting either test will be excluded from the bargaining unit. For example, a head buyer determining the goods his company will purchase is a managerial employee because he helps formulate company policy. Even if the buyer did not help choose the goods, he may still be classified as managerial if he exercises discretion and independent judgment in carrying out policies. For example, if the buyer is told which goods to buy, but has discretion in selecting the supplier and negotiating the contract price, he would be classified as managerial. In general, an employee who has discretionary control over more than a minimal amount of purchases is considered managerial.

Is the buyer a managerial employee if he is told what goods are required, and also directed to place the order with a particular supplier at a particular price? No, because even though the buyer is formally making the purchase, the buyer would be performing a routine function that does not require the use of independent judgment.

b. Confidential Employees

Confidential employees are also excluded from the bargaining unit because of their relationship with management. A confidential employee acts in a confidential capacity to a person who formulates, determines, or effectuates *labor policy*. The person who formulates the policy might be a supervisor or a managerial employee. Under this definition, many personal secretaries, who commonly have confidential company information, are not classified as confidential for bargaining purposes if their information does not pertain to labor policy. In the prior example of the head buyer, the buyer would undoubtedly have confidential information about the company's future purchases and be classified as managerial. If the buyer, however, did not formulate, determine, or effectuate labor policy, the buyer's secretary would not be a confidential employee, even though the secretary might have access to important trade secrets. The confidential employee exclusion only applies to a person having confidential information about labor matters.

Working in the personnel department does not mean that an employee is automatically excluded from a unit. Payroll clerks, for example, may not have any confidential information. A secretary who simply types routine notices to employees would probably not be classified as confidential, but a secretary who types letters from the company's personnel director to the company's labor attorney or types minutes of personnel policy meetings, would be confidential.

Finally, to be classified as confidential, an employee must be regularly engaged in confidential work. Thus, if an employer had a secretarial pool of ten employees, each of whom might in turn type a confidential letter on labor relations, none of the ten would be classified as confidential. All would be eligible for union representation. On the other hand, if the employer regularly used only one of the ten employees for all labor relations matters,

that one employee probably would be excluded as confidential.

C. ELECTION TIMING AND PROCEDURES

In addition to determining the appropriate unit and the placement of employees within the unit, the time when an election may be held is another important issue in representation proceedings.

1. New or Expanding Units

Unions frequently seek to organize newly opened plants. How long must a union wait after a new plant is opened before an election can be held? What if a union files a petition when only 100 employees out of a potential work force of 1,000 are present? Is it fair that 100 employees determine whether the plant will be unionized? But, what if it will take five years for the new plant to reach the full work force? Is it right that the current employees should be denied representation when they may need it most only because more employees may be hired in the future?

The Board has had to develop a principle balancing the respective rights of present and future employees. The Board has ruled that an election may be held if the existing work force is a substantial and representative employee complement. The Board considers the relationship between the duties and functions of the current employees and of the work force after the contemplated expansion to determine whether the current employees will adequately represent future employees as well. The employer's prediction about the total number of employees and job classifications that the plant will eventually have must be based on a reasonable period of time. The employer cannot consider a potential expansion five years in the future to set figures. Also, the expansion plans cannot be speculative. Usually the Board will consider evidence of expansion only within the year.

2. The 12 Month Election Rule

Section 9(c)(3) provides that "no election shall be directed in any bargaining unit or in any subdivision within which, in the preceding twelve-month period, a valid election shall have been held." This provision, commonly known as the 12 month rule, has some exceptions.

First, the provision applies only if there has been a *valid* election. If an election has been set aside because of some irregularity, the union involved or another union can seek another election within the year.

Second, the 12 month rule applies only to elections held in a particular bargaining unit or subdivision of the unit. If a union seeks to represent a different unit that is not merely a subdivision of the first, then an election could be held within 12 months. If a union lost an election in a proposed craft unit, could a second union seeking to represent all employees have an election within 12 months of the first? Yes, because the unit that the second union sought to represent is neither the same nor a subdivision of the bargaining unit involved in the previous election. On the other hand, if the first election was in a bargaining unit of all production and maintenance employees, a second union seeking to represent only craft employees could not have an election within 12 months. The craft unit would be considered a subdivision of the first unit.

Because the 12 month rule applies only to an election, it has no effect on union organizing. A union may begin soliciting cards again the day after it loses an election. A petition for an election may be filed as early as 60 days before the end of the 12 month period, and the Board will begin processing the petition so long as the election is not held before the year is up.

The 12 month rule also does not prohibit an employer from voluntarily recognizing a union within 12 months of an election. For example, if union A loses an election and six months later union B obtains cards from a majority of the employees and requests recognition, no election can be held because of the 12 month rule, but union B can still voluntarily be recognized. Also, the law does not prohibit the union from striking for recognition. (For some general restrictions on recognition picketing that would apply, see Chapter 7.)

3. Certification Bar and Recognition Bar

The 12 month election rule is a statutory requirement. As a matter of policy, the Board has established a similar rule if a union wins an election. The Board will not permit another election in the bargaining unit, or its subdivision, within 12 months of a union's certification. This is called certification bar. The purpose of this rule is to promote stability in the bargaining relationship by giving the parties a reasonable bargaining period without the interference of an election campaign. As a related rule, an employer is required to bargain with a union in good faith for a full year after a union is certified. The union's majority status is irrebuttable for that period (see Chapter 5).

The Board also prohibits an election in a unit for a reasonable period of time (anywhere up to 12 months) after an employer voluntarily recognizes a union as the bargaining agent. This prohibition is called recognition bar. Again, the employer is also required to bargain with the union in good faith for this period.

4. The Contract Bar Doctrine

The certification and recognition bar periods of up to a year apply to the time before a company and union enter into a contract. Once a contract is executed, the Board usually does not permit an election in a unit covered by the contract until that contract expires, up to a maximum period of three years. This rule, called the contract bar doctrine, applies to a petition filed by another union to represent the employees (an RC petition), a petition filed by the employees to decertify the union (an RD petition), or a petition filed by the employer (an RM petition). The contract bar rules do not apply to a petition to clarify or amend the unit's certification (UC and UA petitions), as those petitions do not require elections. The purpose of the contract bar doctrine, as for the recognition and certification bar, is to promote stability in the bargaining relationship by prohibiting an election during the contract duration. The Board strikes a balance between the employee's right to free choice and bargaining stability.

a. Basic Requirements for Contract Bar

There are three basic requirements for a contract to be a bar. First, the contract must contain substantial terms and conditions of employment. A contract, for example, which simply recognizes the union as the bargaining agent but does not contain provisions on wages, hours, and working conditions might be a recognition bar for its first year, but would not be sufficient for a contract bar.

Second, a contract must be of a definite duration. If the contract does not contain a termination date, an election may be held at any time as long as 12 months have elapsed since the last election. This is because a bargaining agreement without a set period would not promote bargaining stability.

Third, as mentioned above, a contract is only a bar for up to a three year period. A longer period would unduly deprive employees of a free choice in their bargaining unit. This means, for example, that if the union and the employer negotiate a five year contract, another union could seek an election after three years even though two years remain on the first contract. A contract for longer than three years is lawful. The length does not completely remove the contract as a bar. It would still be a bar for the first three years. If no election is held or if the contracting (incumbent) union wins an election, the parties are still bound by the contract until it expires.

If a collective bargaining contract is not a bar to an election and another union wins an election that is held, the Board has held that the newly certified union has the choice of keeping the old contract or negotiating a new one. The Board permits renegotiation in this situation because it reasons that a new union was not a party to the old agreement and it would not promote stable labor relations to bind employees to a contract negotiated by a union they have repudiated.

By combining a certification or recognition bar with a contract bar no election might be held for up to four years. That could happen if a union and employer did not negotiate their first contract until the recognition bar period was nearly up and then entered into a three year agreement.

b. The Insulated and Open Periods

The Board has established time limits within which a representation petition may be filed at the end of a contract that has been a bar.

Under Section 8(d), the parties to a contract must serve a notice of their desire to terminate or amend the agreement 60 days before the end of their contract. By statute, a 90-day notice is required in the health care industry (see Chapter 5). The Board has ruled that no representation petition can be filed in the 60 days before a contract expires so that this period may be devoted exclusively to bargaining rather than election campaigning. This 60-day period is called the insulated or closed period because it is insulated from a petition being filed. The Board has further ruled that a petition may not be filed more than 90 days before a contract expires.

Why have these restrictions? Why shouldn't a petition, for example, be filed six months before the end of a collective bargaining agreement? The Board reasons that the existence of a pending petition causes instability as the bargaining unit employees divide over campaign issues and the competing unions jockey for position. The Board wants to limit this instability. Thus a petition can be filed only in the 60 to 90 days before the contract expires. This is referred to as the open period in contrast to the 60 day insulated period.

These time rules for filing a petition apply only if a contract is a bar. If a contract is of an indefinite duration, a petition can be filed at any time. If a contract is for more than three years, a petition can be filed at any time after three years.

A rival union may seek recognition cards during the period of the incumbent's contract. It does not have to wait until the open period to begin solicitation. However, the cards must be less than a year old to be valid as a showing of interest.

If a petition is filed within an open period and supported by a showing of interest, the employer and incumbent union cannot negotiate for a new contract until the election is held and the results certified, or the representation case proceeding is terminated. It is an unfair labor practice for the parties to negotiate a new contract while a petition is pending because the terms of a new agreement may unduly favor the existing incumbent union. However, the parties may continue to administer the old contract.

If no representation petition is filed during the 90-to-60-day open period and the parties execute a new contract during the 60-day closed period, no petition can be filed. The new contract is once again a bar. If, however, the parties fail to execute a new agreement during the closed period and the contract expires, a petition may be filed at any time until a new agreement is executed. The filing period is open again after the contract expires. This is often a strong incentive for an incumbent union to agree to a contract if it sees another union collecting cards and getting ready to file a petition as soon as the contract expires. If a contract is executed before a petition is filed, the contract is once again a bar for its duration up to three years. If the contract has expired, and a timely petition is filed before a new contract is agreed to, negotiations must cease, just as they must cease if a petition is filed in the 90-to-60-day open period.

Ratification and Contract Bar. Is the contract a bar if a union and an employer sign a new contract on the day after their old contract expired, before a rival petition is filed, but a petition is filed before the contract is ratified? The answer depends on whether the contract itself expressly requires ratification by the employees before it can take effect. If the effectiveness of a contract is not expressly contingent on ratification, then signing the contract is sufficient to make it a bar. This rule applies so long as effectiveness is not expressly contingent on ratification, even though the parties understand that the contract is subject to ratification by the members. If a contract is rejected by the union members and the incumbent union is forced to return to the bargaining table, the period would once again be open for the filing of a petition until another contract is signed.

Premature Contract Extensions. What if an incumbent union anticipates that another union may challenge it either at the time its contract expires or at the end of the three year contract bar period? Can it prevent the filing of a rival petition by prematurely negotiating a new contract before the old contract expires in order to extend the bar? No. If a contract is prematurely extended, a petition is still timely if it is filed during the open period based on the original contract's expiration date.

For example, a union in the second year of a three year contract may enter into a new three year contract at that time while the old contract still has a year to run. The new contract would be valid between the employer and the incumbent union. However, another union could still file a timely petition in the open period as determined by the end of the original three year contract. Naturally, the same rule applies if the parties in good faith decide to enter into a new contract after two years, rather than at the original expiration date. A timely petition could still be filed in the 90-to-60-day period before the original expiration date.

C. Exceptions to Contract Bar

1. Unlawful Contract Clauses. In some instances the Board may permit an election before three years are up even though the contract is in effect. First, a contract will not be a bar if the contract contains a union security clause or a check-off provision that is unlawful on its face. An example would be a union security clause requiring employees to join the union on their first day of work (see Chapter 10). What if the language of a contract union security clause appears to be lawful but, in fact, a union unlawfully requires employees to join on the first day of employment? The Board will not consider evidence that a union security clause is being unlawfully applied in a representation case hearing. It will only consider the express language and the contract will therefore still be a bar. If the clause is being unlawfully enforced, an unfair labor practice charge must be filed because the Board does not permit unfair labor practice issues to be resolved in representation cases, due to the different procedures and rules of evidence that apply.

What if a contract contains no unlawful clauses, but was entered into unlawfully, such as an employer and union entering into a contract at a time when the union did not represent a majority of the employees? What if an employer favored a particular union and pressured employees into ratification in the hopes that the contract would be a bar to a petition filed by another union that the employer did not want? Should that contract be a bar? It should not be as a matter of policy. However, the contract will not be set aside as a bar in a representation proceeding. The challenging party must file an unfair labor practice charge that the contract was unlawfully executed. If the challenger prevails on the unfair practice case, the contract will be set aside. Until then, it would remain as a bar.

2. Schisms and Defunct Unions. A contract is also not a bar if there is a schism in the union. A schism is a basic split over fundamental policy within the union that results in the presentation of conflicting representation claims to the employer. There must be a basic split—the formation of a dissident group within a union is not sufficient.

Another exception to the contract bar rule

is if a union is defunct, if it has ceased to function as a bargaining agent. The Board will not set aside a contract, however, if the union is attempting to function even though it is weak and ineffective.

3. *Expanding Units.* A contract does not bar an election if there has been a substantial expansion in the plant since the contract was executed. Also a contract will not be a bar if it was executed prematurely. To be a bar, at least 30 percent of the employees who will eventually work in the bargaining unit in 50 percent of the total job classifications must have been employed in the unit at the time a contract was executed. If a plant was to eventually have 100 employees in 20 job classifications, a contract would not be a bar unless there were at least 30 employees in 10 of the job classifications working at the time of execution. The 30 percent requirement only applies to the total number of employees in the unit. There is no requirement that each classification be at least 30 percent filled, only that the overall percentage be met.

d. *Contract Bar Following a Merger, Consolidation, or Sale.*

Contract bar problems frequently arise following a merger or consolidation of two or more plants. The Board has ruled that a contract is not a bar to an election following a merger or consolidation of one contracting employer with another employer, or of two plants with the same employer, if the nature of the enterprise changes because of the merger. The Board reasons that a merger that changes the nature of the operation creates an unstable bargaining situation. The contract is not a stabilizing factor and the purpose of the contract bar doctrine, to preserve a stable relationship, is not served. In that case, if a rival union tries to represent the employees, an election to determine the bargaining representative may lead to greater stability than preserving the existing contract.

Whether a merger has the effect of changing the nature of a business is a question of fact. Sometimes two companies merge, but each plant continues to operate independently. In that case, each contract remains as a bar. Sometimes one plant closes and employees are transferred to the remaining facility and covered by its contract. A newly purchased plant may simply be added as an accretion to an older plant's bargaining unit covered by an existing contract because of the close community of interest between the new and old facilities.

In some cases, however, substantial numbers of employees previously represented by different unions at different locations may be relocated to the same facility. Which union's contract should control? The Board has an easy solution: The Board reasons that since neither union clearly represents the employees, neither contract promotes stability and neither contract should be a bar. Thus, the two competing unions (or any other unions wishing to intervene) are free to file a representation petition to determine majority status.

As discussed in Chapter 5, an employer purchasing a company, called a successor employer, normally is not obligated to assume the existing collective bargaining agreement between the old employer and existing union. The successor employer's only obligation is to bargain in good faith with the prior union if it still represents a majority of the employees.

Since a successor employer is normally not obligated to assume the existing collective bargaining agreement, the Board has held that an existing agreement is not a contract bar if there is a successor employer. The only exception is that the contract will be a bar if the successor expressly assumes it. This distinction arises because of the underlying contract bar policy of promoting stability in the bargaining relationship. If a successor employer is not obligated to assume an existing collective bargaining agreement, and does not do so, the contract is not a stabilizing factor. On the other hand, if the successor employer expressly assumes the agreement, applying the contract bar doctrine promotes stability.

D. VOTER ELIGIBILITY

Voter eligibility is another important issue. After a representation election is directed, the Board establishes a payroll eligibility date, the date by which an employee must be on the employer's payroll in order to be eligible to vote. Normally, the payroll eligibility date is the payroll period immediately preceding the direction of election or the execution of a consent election agreement. To be eligible, an employee must be employed on the payroll eligibility date and also on the date of the election—both dates must be met. An employee hired after the payroll eligibility date, but working by the election date, cannot vote. An employee who is on the payroll as of the payroll eligibility date, but quits before the election, is also ineligible.

The employer is required to give the union a list of the names and addresses of all employees who are eligible to vote as of the payroll eligibility date. This list must be furnished within seven days after the Board directs an election. The list is called the Excelsior list, after the case (Excelsior Underwear, Inc.) in which the Board first adopted this requirement.[3] Normally, the union must possess the list ten days before an election. The Excelsior list gives a union the opportunity to contact the employees before the election. Failure of the employer to provide the list or the presence of so many inaccuracies that the

[3] See legal principle 10.

list cannot reasonably be used may be grounds for setting aside an election.

1. Voting Rights of Striking and Replacement Employees

Elections may be held while employees are on strike. This occurs most frequently when employees who are not striking file a petition to decertify the union while other employees continue to strike. An election can also be held during a strike if, after a contract has expired, the employer has a good faith doubt that a striking union continues to represent a majority of the employees and files a representation (RM) petition (see Chapter 5). Another union may obtain recognition cards while the employees are on strike and seek an election. Some employees may have continued to work during a strike, and the employer may have hired replacements for those who struck. In any of these situations, where there are both striking and nonstriking employees, the question is, who votes in the election: the striking employees, their replacements, or both the strikers and replacements? The answer depends on the type of strike and the length of the strike.

a. Unfair Labor Practice vs. Economic Strikers

There are two types of strikers, unfair labor practice strikers and economic strikers (see Chapter 6). An unfair labor practice striker is on strike protesting an employer's unfair labor practices. An economic striker is on strike over an economic issue such as grievances or a new collective bargaining agreement.

The Board has held that unfair labor practice strikers are entitled to reinstatement at work at any time if they unconditionally offer to return. Although an employer can continue to operate during an unfair labor practice strike, unfair labor practice strikers cannot be permanently replaced. The Board has reasoned that since unfair labor practice strikers may return to work at any time and cannot be permanently replaced, they are entitled to vote in any election held during the strike. Further, their replacements are ineligible to vote.

Replaced Economic Strikers and Their Replacements. In contrast to unfair labor practice strikers, economic strikers may be replaced permanently. An employee hired by an employer to replace an economic striker, provided the employer intends to retain the employee after the strike is over, is called a permanent replacement. Temporary replacements are employees who do the strikers' work only while the strike lasts, such as a supervisor or a non-bargaining unit employee or a student. A permanently replaced economic striker is not entitled to reinstatement at the end of a strike, but is placed on a recall list, to be reinstated as jobs become available. (See Chapter 6.)

An economic striker's right to vote is determined by whether he has been permanently replaced by another employee. An economic striker who has *not* been permanently replaced has the right to vote in any election, as does an unfair labor practice striker. However, under Section 9(c)(3), economic strikers who have been permanently replaced, and are thus not entitled to reinstatement, are eligible to vote only in elections held within 12 months after a strike begins. This means that the permanently replaced economic striker can vote in an election held within 12 months, but not after 12 months, even though he still has recall rights.

Permanent replacements for economic strikers are eligible to vote from their date of hire. Temporary replacements are not eligible to vote regardless of the election date. Thus, during the first 12 months of an economic strike, both economic strikers and permanent replacements may vote. After 12 months, only permanent replacements and economic strikers who have not been permanently replaced are eligible.

If a representation petition is filed before 12 months are up, the Board generally expedites an election so that permanently replaced economic strikers will be eligible to vote.

b. Strikers Obtaining Permanent Employment Elsewhere

Either an economic or unfair labor practice striker who is eligible to vote in an election may lose his eligibility if he has obtained permanent employment elsewhere and abandoned his prior job. This does not mean that an employee loses the right to vote if he obtains temporary work to get by while striking. He will be excluded only if he has obtained permanent employment elsewhere. There is a presumption that employment during a strike is temporary and that the employee intends to return to his former job at the end of the strike. That is true even though the temporary position is equivalent work and pays as well or better. The person challenging a striker's right to vote has to prove that the employee does not intend to return. For example, a striking electrician who places an ad in a newspaper that he is available for home electrical repairs does not lose his status as an employee because the work is obviously temporary. If, however, the electrician went to a bank and financed his own electrical contracting firm with a long-term loan and built an electrical shop, the Board would probably conclude that the employee had no intent to return.

While there is a presumption that temporarily employed strikers intend to return to their former employment at the end of the strike, it is also presumed that replacements hired during the strike are permanent. The union has the burden of proving that the replacements were hired only for the period of the strike. For example, students obviously planning to return to school at the end of the summer or a supervisor who is working as a production worker during the strike would not be permanent replacements.

c. Discontinuance of a Job or Strike Misconduct

A striker may also lose eligibility if his job is permanently discontinued during the strike. An employer who has two departments operating before a strike began can decide to close permanently one of the departments during the strike. Only the employees who worked in the remaining department could vote.

Obviously, an employer may simply claim to have permanently closed down a department in order to limit the number of strikers eligible to vote. For that reason, the employer has the burden of proving to the Board that discontinuance is permanent before the Board will find an employee ineligible to vote. The Board looks closely to make sure that an employer has just not shut down a department during a strike because a strike has been effective in reducing the employer's business, or that the employer is not manipulating his departmental structure in an attempt to deprive employees of the right to vote.

Employees can lose their eligibility through strike misconduct. An employee discharged for strike misconduct is not eligible for reemployment or to vote. However, the misconduct must be serious. The Board recognizes that tempers may flare during a strike and will not deprive employees of their employee status or the right to vote because of

minor wrongdoing. Employees unlawfully discharged during a strike may vote subject to challenge. Whether their discharge was lawful is decided in an unfair labor practice proceeding, which is usually consolidated with the pending representation case. If the discharge is unlawful, then the employee's ballot will be counted. If the Board decides that the employee was lawfully discharged, the ballot will not be counted (see Chapter 6).

2. Employees on Layoff or Sick Leave

The voting eligibility of an employee on layoff is determined by the reasonable likelihood of the employee returning to work with his employer. Each case of a laid off employee is based on the specific facts. An employee placed on indefinite layoff under a contract that preserves the employee's seniority rights for one year would be able to vote in any election held within the year. After that, if the employee no longer had recall rights, he would not be eligible to vote because he would not have a reasonable likelihood of returning.

An employee placed on layoff with the understanding that he would be recalled if a large order scheduled the following month came in would most likely be permitted to vote since his recall is fairly definite. An employee whose department was permanently closed and who was told only that someday, if the company expanded he would be recalled, would probably not be eligible because the expansion might never occur and he would have no reasonable likelihood of returning to work.

The voting status of an employee on an indefinite leave of absence would also basically be determined by whether that employee has a reasonable likelihood of returning to work.

Employees on sick leave can vote if they

have a reasonable likelihood of returning to work. An employee with a broken arm recuperating at home would be eligible to vote. An employee with a heart condition, who would probably never return, would not be eligible. The eligibility decision basically involves comparing the nature of the employee's work with the disability and determining whether there is an expectation of returning within a reasonable period.

Employees on military leave can vote if they appear in person at the poll. No absentee ballots are permitted.

3. Voter Challenge Procedure

The Board prefers that voter eligibility issues be resolved at a representation hearing prior to the election if the parties know such issues exist. Then the Board can rule on both eligibility issues and the appropriate unit at the same time. However, an employee's right to vote on the grounds that he is not properly in the unit or ineligible for one of the reasons discussed above may be challenged at the time the employee votes, by either party or the Board agent. It is the parties' responsibility to make their challenges at the time an employee votes; he cannot be challenged after he votes.

When an employee is challenged, he is allowed to vote subject to challenge. His ballot is set aside in a sealed envelope rather than placed in the ballot box. After all employees have voted, the unchallenged ballots are counted first. If the results of the election would not be effected by the number of challenged ballots, the Board will not even rule on the challenges. If a union wins by ten votes and there are only four challenged ballots, those four ballots could not make a difference and the Board will not resolve the eligibility of these voters. What, then, is the status of these employees? Are they in the unit or not? The unit status would be left to collective bargaining between the parties. If no agreement is reached, then the union might file a unit clarification petition with the Board to determine their status.

Summary

The appropriate bargaining unit concept is fundamental to understanding the bargaining process as unions represent and bargain for employees through appropriate bargaining units. The most important factor in determining the appropriate unit is the community of interest among the employees. A bargaining unit is appropriate if it has a separate community of interest. Generally, the Board allows employees to bargain in any unit that is appropriate even though other units may also be appropriate. The unit does not have to be the best or most appropriate.

Because of their distinct community of interest certain groups of employees, called presumptively appropriate units, almost always comprise a separate appropriate unit. An office clerical employees unit and a production and maintenance employees unit are typical examples. Craft employees and departmental employees were at one time entitled to separate representation, but they are now entitled only under specific circumstances. Generally, if an employer has more than one plant, each plant is a separate appropriate unit. However, if either the employer or the union wants a multi-plant unit, the burden is on the party requesting it to prove that the employees in the two plants shared a community of interest. In some cases both a single or multi-plant unit might be appropriate.

Multi-employer units are established voluntarily between the employers and the union. However, once an employer has voluntarily joined a multi-employer group, he cannot withdraw from the group after negotiations have begun.

An employer and a union have some discretion in determining the employees included in a unit. However, certain categories are excluded because the LMRA specifically prohibits them from being included in a unit with other employees. They may be excluded from the definition of employees and therefore not entitled to union representation; they may not regularly work in the bargaining unit; or they may have a special relationship with management and thus lack a community of interest with their fellow employees. Persons falling within these categories are not included in a bargaining unit and are not permitted to vote in a Board election. These categories include supervisors; managerial employees; casual, part-time, and temporary employees; confidential employees; the children or spouse of the owner; independent contractors; and agricultural laborers.

The 12 month election rule (Section 9(c)(3)) prohibits an election in any bargaining unit or subdivision if a valid election has been held within the preceding 12 months. The rule applies only to an election. It does not prohibit union organizing or voluntary employer recognition during the period.

In addition to an election bar, the Board, as a matter of policy, has established similar rules if a union is voluntarily recognized. The Board will not permit another election in a bargaining unit within 12 months of the union's certification or for a reasonable period of time after an employer voluntarily recognizes a union.

Once a contract is executed, the Board, applying the contract bar doctrine, usually does not permit an election in the unit covered by the contract until it expires up to a maximum of three years. This rule applies to a petition filed by another union to represent the employees, a petition filed by the employees to decertify the union, or a petition filed by the employer.

To be eligible to vote in an election, an employee must be on the payroll on the payroll eligibility date and also on the date of the election. The employer is required to provide the union with a list of the names and addresses of all employees who are eligible to vote as of the payroll eligibility date.

Elections may be held while employees are on strike. The basic rules are that an unfair labor practice striker can vote in a Board election regardless of how long he has been on strike. An economic striker who has been replaced can only vote in an election held within the first year of the strike.

Unreplaced economic strikers can vote indefinitely. Permanent replacements for economic strikers can vote, but temporary replacements or replacements for unfair labor practice strikers cannot vote.

An employee on layoff or on sick leave is eligible to vote if there is a reasonable likelihood he will return to work with his employer. If so, he has a community of interest with the other employees and can vote.

An employee's right to vote may be challenged at the time he votes by either party or the Board agent. The Board will only rule on the challenged ballots if the number of challenged ballots affects the outcome of the election.

Review Questions

1. What is a community of interest?
2. Will the Board allow an election in a unit that is appropriate for bargaining though other units are more appropriate?
3. Will the Board certify a one-employee unit?
4. Who is a professional employee under the LMRA?
5. If an employee is called a guard by his employer, will he automatically be excluded from a unit that includes nonguard employees?
6. What persons are excluded from the definition of employee under Section 2(3) of the Act?
7. How is an independent contractor distinguished from an employee under the Act?
8. Can a person be a supervisor under the Act even though he does not have authority to hire or fire employees?
9. Can seasonal workers (for example, persons hired for the summer season at a resort) be included in a bargaining unit of regular full time employees?
10. What is the contract bar doctrine?
11. How long is an unfair labor practice striker eligible to vote in a representation election?
12. What are the insulated and open periods for filing a representation petition?

(Answers to review questions appear at end of book.)

Basic Legal Principles

1. The primary factors in determining community of interest are: (1) the distinctiveness or integration of the emloyees into the overall work force; (2) bargaining history in the industry and of the parties before the Board; (3) common supervision and similarity of duties, skills, interests, wages, and working conditions; (4) organization structure of the company,

and (5) desires of the employees. *Capital Bakers, Inc.,* 168 NLRB No. 119, 66 LRRM 1385 (1967). *Phillips Products Co. Inc.,* 234 NLRB No. 71, 97 LRRM 1195 (1978). *Sears Roebuck & Co.,* 235 NLRB No. 96, 98 LRRM 1009 (1978).

2. In determining whether craft or departmental employees are entitled to separate representation, the Board considers: (1) the distinctness and homogeneity of a group, (2) the collective bargaining history, (3) the crafts' or department's separate identity from the larger employee groups, (4) the industry's bargaining practice, (5) the integration of production and craft functions, and (6) the qualifications of the union seeking representation. *Mallinckrodt Chemical Works,* 162 NLRB No. 48 (1966), 64 LRRM 1011 (1966). *International Foundation of Employee Plans, Inc.,* 234 NLRB No. 51, 97 LRRM 1144 (1978).

3. The Board relies on its traditional community of interest criteria in making unit determinations in the health care industry. To avoid proliferation, the Board has established four basic health care units: service and maintenance employees, office clerical employees, technical employees, and professional employees. *Allegheny General Hospital,* 239 NLRB No. 104, 100 LRRM 1030 (1978).

4. Part-time employees who are regularly employed in the unit have a substantial community of interest with the unit's full-time employees and are included in the unit. Regularity of employment rather than the number of hours is controlling. *Sears, Roebuck and Co.,* 172 NLRB No. 132, 68 LRRM 1469 (1968); *Leaders-Nameoki, Inc.,* 237 NLRB No. 202, 99 LRRM 1132 (1978).

5. Whether employees who are not actively at work, but who retain employee status (e.g. laid-off employees or employees on sick leave) are included in a bargaining unit depends upon whether they have a reasonable expectation of returning to work. *Sullivan Surplus Sales, Inc.,* 152 NLRB No. 12, 59 LRRM 1041 (1965); *East Bay Newspapers, Inc.,* 225 NLRB No. 128, 93 LRRM 1102 (1976).

6. If one union seeks to represent an overall production and maintenance unit and another union seeks to represent a separate craft group, both of which are appropriate, the Board will hold a self-determination election for the employees to decide their preference. *Globe Machine and Stamping Co.,* 3 NLRB No. 25, 1 LRRM 122 (1937); *Columbia Transit Corp.,* 237 NLRB No. 201, 99 LRRM 1114 (1978).

7. To serve as a contract bar, a contract must contain substantial terms and conditions of employment sufficient to stabilize the bargaining relationship. A fixed duration must be stated in the contract to be a bar for any period. *Appalachian Shale Products Co.,* 121 NLRB 1160, 42 LRRM 1506 (1958). *T. E. Connelly, Inc.* 239 NLRB No. 197, 100 LRRM 1138 (1979).

8. A person is classified as a supervisor if he can exercise any of the

twelve powers listed in LMRA Section 2(11), or effectively recommend such action, provided that he is exercising independent judgment. *Thayer Dairy Co., Inc.* 233 NLRB No. 205, 97 LRRM 1102 (1977); *Barnes & Noble Book Stores, Inc.*, 233 NLRB No. 198, 97 LRRM 1176 (1977).

9. Both replaced economic strikers and their permanent replacements may vote in an NLRB election held during the first year of a strike. Thereafter employees who are permanently replaced are ineligible to vote. Unfair labor practice strikers remain eligible to vote regardless of the strike's length. *Pacific Tile & Porcelain Co.*, 137 NLRB No. 169, 50 LRRM 1394 (1962); *W. Wilton Wood, Inc.*, 127 NLRB No. 185, 46 LRRM 1240 (1960); *Larand Leisurelies, Inc.*, 222 NLRB No. 131, 91 LRRM 1305 (1976).

10. Within seven days after the Board directs a representation election the employer is required to give the union a list of the names and addresses of all employees who are eligible to vote in the election. *Excelsior Underwear Inc.*, 156 NLRB No. 111, 61 LRRM 1217 (1966).

Bogano, Suntrup, "Graduate Assistants' Response to Unionization: The Minnesota Experience," 29 *Lab. L.J.* 39 (1976).

Suggested Readings

"Collective Bargaining and the Professional Employee," 69 *Colum. L. Rev.* 277 (1969).

"Development of the Craft Severance Doctrine," 11 *St. Louis U.L.J.* 615 (1967).

Chapter Three

Union Organizing Rights and Employer Response

*T*his chapter describes permissible union and employer tactics in organizing employees and conducting an election campaign. It also discusses the unique blend of Section 8 unfair labor practices and Section 9 acts that may interfere with an election, which together govern union organizing rights and employer responses.

The rights and obligations of unions, employees, and employers in organizing and in election campaigns are regulated by Sections 8 and 9 of the LMRA. Some of the actions discussed below are either protected or prohibited as unfair labor prac-

tices under Section 8. However, in addition to the unfair labor practice restrictions, the Board, under its authority to administer elections pursuant to Section 9, has determined that an election must be conducted under "laboratory conditions." The Board prohibits an employer or union from engaging in misconduct that destroys the laboratory conditions and interferes with the employees' right to a free-choice election. An election may be set aside for acts that the Board concludes interfere with an election under Section 9, even though those acts may not constitute an unfair labor practice under Section 8.

A. OBTAINING RECOGNITION CARDS

Union organizational drives usually begin by having employees sign recognition cards authorizing the union to represent them; these cards are submitted to the NLRB for an election. Cards are not the only method of obtaining an NLRB election. The Union can circulate a petition asking for an election. The Board will hold an election if 30 percent of the employees in the appropriate unit sign cards or a petition. Cards are far more common and convenient and cause fewer legal problems that could disrupt the election process.

In representation campaigns, the union usually obtains recognition cards from a majority of the employees in the proposed unit and then seeks voluntary recognition from the employer. Frequently, the union proposes that the employer verify the cards against the payroll records or have them verified by an independent person such as a local minister. However, a union need not request recognition before filing a representation petition at the Board, but may go directly to the Board.

The Supreme Court has held that an employer has an absolute right to an election. An employer does not have to recognize a union voluntarily even if the union has obtained cards from a majority of the employees, but can simply decline recognition. In that case the union has no choice but to file a representation petition using the cards as a showing of interest except in the rare case of a recognition strike.

1. Single Purpose vs. Dual Purpose Cards: Bargaining Orders

There are two types of recognition cards: single purpose and dual purpose cards. The single purpose card expressly authorizes the union to represent the employee signing the card. Its sole purpose is recognition. The single purpose card customarily states: "I hereby authorize Local _____ to represent me for the purpose of collective bargaining with my employer."

The dual purpose card is for recognition and an election. These cards typically state: "I want an NLRB election, and I authorize Local _____ to represent me for purposes of collective bargaining."

The Board accepts both single and dual purpose cards for a showing of interest. Most cards now are single purpose recognition cards only, because of the Supreme Court's decision in *Gissel Packing Company*.[1] In *Gissel*, the union had single purpose recognition cards signed by a majority of the employees in the unit. The union alleged that it lost an election because the employer engaged in unfair labor practices that undermined the union's support. The Supreme Court, upholding the Board's position, held that if a union has the support of a majority of the employees in the unit before an election, as shown by single purpose authorization cards signed by a majority of the unit employees, but loses the election because of employer unfair labor

practices that · undermined the union's strength, the employer can be ordered to bargain with the union even though the union lost the election.

The Board will not base a bargaining order on dual purpose cards. This is because a bargaining order requires proof that a majority of the employees wanted the union to represent them at one point. With a single purpose card, which expressly authorizes the union to represent the employee, there is no question of the employee's intent. But the Board reasons that an employee who has signed a dual purpose card may have signed the card just to get an election, although the card refers to both recognition and an election. The clear intent of a single purpose card is lacking. The Board requires clear intent before it will order an employer to bargain with a union that has lost an election. So that the union will have an opportunity for a bargaining order if it should lose an election, most unions have abandoned the dual purpose card and use only single purpose cards.

2. Employee Intent in Signing a Recognition Card

What if a union organizer hands an employee a single purpose card, but tells the employee that the card will be filed with the NLRB to get an election? Can that card be used to prove the union represented a majority of the employees at one time? The employee might not have paid attention to the wording of the card as it related to recognition. The employee might have signed the card only because he thought his fellow employees deserved an election if they wanted it. Is the employee's intent that he wanted union representation clear?

The Board rejects the approach of reading an employee's mind. The express wording of

[1] See legal principle 11.

the card controls. The employee's subjective understanding, or even misunderstanding, of what the card means, or what the card could be used for, does not matter.

The only exception to this rule is that a single purpose card will not be counted in determining the union's majority status if the employee is told that the *only* purpose is an election. Then the card would not indicate the employee wanted the union to represent him. Thus, the Supreme Court held in *Gissel* that a union organizer can tell an employee who signs a single purpose card that the union will first seek voluntary recognition from the employer, but will seek an NLRB election if the employer declines. The card will count in determining the union's majority status because the employee was not told the card's only purpose is an election. On the other hand, what if an employee tells an organizer that he does not want a union himself, but he is willing to sign a card so that other employees can have an election? The organizer replies: "Don't worry about it, the only purpose of this card is to get an election." In that case, the Board would not count the card for bargaining order purposes because the employee was misled into believing the card would be used only for an election, even though the card referred to recognition. Remember, the card is still valid for determining whether the union has a 30 percent showing of interest in the appropriate unit.

The Board is sometimes very technical in applying the doctrine that a single purpose card will be counted unless an employee has been told that the only purpose is an election. There are a number of Board cases in which it appears that an employee did not understand the significance of the card, but the union organizer did not specifically say that the only purpose was an election. The Board has upheld the cards in such cases.

Also, the Board generally prohibits testimony from an employee as to what he thought the card meant. The Board is concerned that employees who testify about what they thought a card meant months after they signed it might be intimidated by their employer into testifying that they either did not understand what the card meant or that they were misled. Or an employee may have simply forgotten what he was told at the time. The Board feels that the wording of the card itself, if it clearly states the purpose is recognition, should control. The wording of the card, not the employee's subjective interpretation, is a better indication of the employee's intent at the time of signing.

3. Recognition Card Procedures

Employees frequently ask the union if their employer will see the signed recognition cards. This question should be answered forthrightly. Yes, the employer may see the card under some circumstances. The employer does not see the cards when they are filed with the Board or during the course of representation election proceedings. However, if the union loses the election and files an unfair labor practice charge seeking a bargaining order, the union must prove that it represented a majority of the employees at one time. That is done by introducing the cards at the trial where the employer can examine them. If the union wins the election or does not file unfair labor practice charges after a defeat, the cards will not be revealed to the employer. Thus, if questioned, a union organizer may answer that the employer might possibly see the cards at a later date. The organizer could emphasize, however, that seeing the cards is an unlikely possibility and that the LMRA protects an employee's right to sign a recognition card without retaliation by an employer.

The Board requires that recognition cards be dated. A card over a year old is not counted in determining a union's showing of interest. Although not required, it is a good idea to have each card witnessed and initialed by the witness. Suppose you have 50 or even 500 signed cards. The union loses the election and unfair labor practice charges are filed. At the trial, the union may have to prove that each card was validly executed. If the union does not know who solicited each card, it may be impossible to verify the card. On the other hand, if each person collecting cards initials them, each solicitor can be called as a witness if necessary.

Also, each solicitor should be given detailed instructions on what to tell employees about the card's purpose when it is signed. In that way the union can be sure that employees are not improperly told that the only purpose of a card is an election, which, as discussed above, would invalidate the card for purposes of a bargaining order.

B. UNION SOLICITATION AND DISTRIBUTION OF CAMPAIGN LITERATURE

Where can a union solicit employee support? The work place is the logical choice, but there are restrictions on where and when this may be done. A distinction is made between oral solicitation and the distribution of written literature in support of a union. The rules covering solicitation and distribution of literature are based on Section 8(a)(1), which protects an employee's right to engage in concerted activities under Section 7. Concerted activity includes the right to organize. Handing an employee a recognition card and talking to him about the union is considered solicitation, which is governed by the rules

for solicitation although the card is obviously literature.

It is an unfair labor practice under Section 8(a)(1) for an employer to impose an unlawfully broad rule against solicitation or distribution, to discipline, or to threaten to discipline employees who engage in lawfully protected solicitation or distribution in violation of the rule. Also, the imposition of an unlawful rule or discipline or the threat of discipline to employees for violating such a rule interferes with the laboratory conditions that the Board insists must be maintained during an election. Such a rule would be grounds for setting aside an election.

1. Oral Solicitation of Union Support

As a general rule an employee can orally solicit in working and non-working areas, but only on his own non-work time. An employee can talk to fellow employees on the production line about union matters, and can solicit recognition cards, if the employees have a break with no work to do. The employee is not limited to formal breaks such as a coffee break or lunch time. If employees have idle time where they stand around and talk about sports, etc., they can stand around and talk about union activities instead. An employee's own time means time when the employee is not working, so-called "free time," even though it is paid company time.

If an employer allows the employees to engage in casual conversation while they are actually working, the employees could discuss union matters as long as production is not interrupted. An employer who allows the employees to talk about anything but union activities is interfering in the employees' rights to engage in concerted (union) activities.

2. Distribution of Literature

As with oral solicitations, union literature can be distributed only on an employee's own time. While oral solicitation can take place in work areas, employers can limit the distribution of literature to nonwork areas. There is this distinction between the two because the distribution of literature is more likely to create litter, disrupt operations, and cause accidents. The employer has a right to keep the work area free of these hazards. A nonwork area is any area not related to production, such as a break area, locker room, coffee machine area, or company parking lot.

Sometimes employers have general rules governing all types of solicitation or distribution of literature in the plant including solicitation for charities or sports pools. These general rules, however, cannot override an employee's statutory rights. A rule prohibiting the distribution of literature in the plant, even in nonwork areas, is valid for nonunion literature. But employees still have the statutory right to distribute union literature on company time in nonwork areas.

Although an employer cannot restrict an employee's right to distribute union literature, an employer's rules may expand that right. If an employer has always permitted distribution of literature in production areas he cannot suddenly prohibit the distribution of literature after a union organizing campaign begins. That would be unlawful discrimination. If an employer's rules are more permissive than the statute requires, they must be evenly applied.

3. Exceptions to the General Distribution and Solicitation Rules

There are a few exceptions to the general rule that an employee, on his or her own time, may solicit union literature in work areas and distribute literature in nonwork areas. In un-usual circumstances, an employer might prove the existence of unique conditions justifying a broader "no distribution" or "no solicitation" rule than otherwise permitted. Department stores may establish rules prohibiting employees from soliciting on the sales floor, even on an employee's own time, provided that employees are generally prohibited from casual conversation in that area because customers waiting for service may take offense at seeing employees talking to each other.

Exceptions approved by the Board are very rare and the general rules apply in almost every case. Many hospitals argue that they should be permitted to establish broader rules prohibiting solicitation in any areas where patients may be, including cafeteria areas that both employees and patients share. Hospitals want employee union activities limited to exclusive nonpatient areas such as locker rooms. The Supreme Court has upheld the Board's position that health care employees should be permitted to engage in union solicitation in areas other than the immediate patient care areas, such as lobbies, lounges and cafeterias, even though patients may use those areas as well. Solicitation may be prohibited in patient care areas such as patient rooms, operating rooms, treatment areas, and adjoining corridors and sitting rooms where solicitation could disturb patient care.

Any rule that an employer establishes limiting employees' rights to solicit and distribute literature must be clear. The Board has consistently held that ambiguous rules, which an employee might interpret to prohibit statutorily protected rights, are unlawful.

4. Organizing Rights of Outside Organizers and Off-Duty Employees

The rights to solicit and distribute union literature on company property are employee rights only. Normally, an employer can prohibit outside union organizers from entering its premises for these purposes. If an organizer wants to distribute literature and is willing to do it during breaks in nonwork areas, does the union organizer have a right to come into the plant and talk to the employees? No, he must find an employee to do it for him. The rights to solicit and distribute are employee, not union rights. As an exception, if an employer permits other solicitors to enter the plant, he cannot exclude union organizers.

Some unions have one of their professional organizers hire on as an employee. The organizer, provided he does his job, has the same right as any other employee to solicit and distribute union literature.

Does an off-duty employee have the right to enter the plant while on off-duty time to engage in union organizing? The Board has held that if employees are prohibited from entering the interior or other work areas while off duty, they may be prohibited from re-entering for union activity. However, if an employer permits off-duty employees to re-enter the plant before a union began its organizing effort, the employer cannot prevent re-entry after the union campaign begins. The employees must be aware of any rule prohibiting re-entry in advance. Further, if employees are permitted back into the plant for any reasons, they cannot be prohibited from returning for union activity.

Although the employer can validly prohibit off-duty employees from re-entering the plant or other work areas, off-duty employees cannot be prohibited from union activity on company property outside the plant in nonwork areas unless there are special circumstances justifying a total prohibition. Thus, off-duty employees can engage in union activities in company parking lots or at the plant gates. Finally, employees cannot be prohib-

ited from remaining after the end of their shift to engage in union activity if they are allowed to remain after their shift for other reasons.

Inaccessible Employees

The principal, but narrow, exception to the employer's right to prohibit outside union organizers from entering the plant is that a union has the right to enter the company's property to talk to employees if there is no other way to reach the employees. This exception is restricted primarily to company towns where employees live on company premises or to the maritime industry where a union may not be able to reach employees except on the ship where they work. If the gate to an enclosed plant is far from the employees' parking lot, employees can speed through the gate at 50 m.p.h. Union organizers, standing on the edge of the property trying to hand out cards to the employees, have little chance of success. Still, these organizers generally would not have the right to enter the company's property and go to the parking lot area because the organizers probably have other ways to reach the employees. They can take down license plates and find out the owners, follow employees home, go to nearby taverns, or even put ads in local newspapers. These other methods are certainly not easy or convenient, but they are sufficient alternatives so that organizers would not have the right to enter the property.

The right of union organizers to enter company property involves balancing the employer's right of private property against the employee's right to union activity. Except in rare cases, the employer's private property rights outweigh the organizing rights of the employees to have a union organizer on the premises.

5. Post-Recognition Solicitation and Distribution Rights

The employees' rights to solicit for the union and distribute literature apply not only to initial organizing, but after union recognition as well. Employees have a continuing right to discuss union matters in their work areas on company time and distribute literature in nonwork areas. These are employee as well as union rights.

In the *Magnavox* case an employer and union negotiated a provision that restricted the right to distribute literature to certain bulletin boards.[2] The employer prohibited employees from distributing literature in nonwork areas, relying on the contract provision that restricted notices to the bulletin board. The Supreme Court upheld the Board's decision that the contract provision was unlawful and that the union could not contractually waive the employees' rights to distribute literature.

The right to discuss union matters and distribute union literature pertains to all collective bargaining activities and subjects, including related political activity. Thus, the Supreme Court has held that a union may circulate literature in the plant against right-to-work laws because the abolishment of such laws is a political act designed to further the union's collective bargaining goals. Can an employer prohibit employee political activity unrelated to the union's collective bargaining activities? Yes, because the employer has a statutory obligation to permit employee solicitation and distribution pertaining to collective bargaining activities on the company's premises, but the employer has no statutory or constitutional obligation to permit any other political activity. The constitution provisions protecting free speech apply only to governmental bodies, not to a private employer.

Can an incumbent union and an employer agree to prohibit a rival union from posting notices about meetings? The Supreme Court has held that employers cannot allow an incumbent union to post notices and at the same time prohibit other unions or employee groups from doing so. Bulletin boards may be reserved for the incumbent union's notices. If bulletin boards are reserved, however, other space has to be made available for notices by other employee groups.

6. Organizing in Shopping Centers

Questions frequently arise about a union's right to enter a shopping center to organize employees. Unions have argued that shopping centers should be treated as public places and that union organizers should be able to enter them to organize employees as a matter of constitutional free speech. The Supreme Court rejected this argument in the *Central Hardware* case, holding that a shopping center is private property and not to be treated as a public block.[3]

The Court said that the rules applied to organizing employees working in a shopping center should be the same as those applied to outside organizers entering any other plant. This means that if a union has other methods of reaching employees who work in a shopping center besides entering the center, it must use those methods. On the other hand, if there is no other reasonable method of reaching the employees, then the union has the right to enter the shopping center just as it could enter into private plant property under similar circumstances. As emphasized above, a union's right to enter a plant is very limited and a union would undoubtedly have a diffi-

---

[2] See legal principle 5.

[3] See legal principle 6.

cult time proving that it did not have an alternative way to reach shopping center employees. Problems also frequently arise about picketing within shopping centers, either for organizational or other purposes (See Chapter 7).

C. EMPLOYER ANTI-UNION SPEECHES ON COMPANY TIME

1. The Captive Audience Doctrine

Although unions are limited in how campaigns may be conducted on company property, employers are not. Under the *Peerless Plywood* rule, an employer has the right to speak to employees against the union on company time and require employees to attend the meeting.[3] This is the so-called "captive audience" doctrine. A union does not have the right to reply on company time. The union must limit its activities to the employees' own time off premises or to the employees' own solicitation and distribution of literature. The only exception under which a union might be able to give a speech on company premises is in the rare situation (such as a retail store) in which an employer can enforce a broad no solicitation-no distribution rule. In that limited situation, if an employer gives a speech on company time the union can be permitted to reply on premises because otherwise the union has no effective way to reply. Usually, however, the employer may give a speech and the union has no right to reply on company time.

2. The Twenty-Four Hour Rule

The one general exception to the captive audience doctrince is the "24-hour Rule." The Board sets aside an election if an employer gives a speech on company time to a

[3] See legal principle 7.

mass employee audience in the last 24 hours before an election.

The twenty-four hour rule applies only to a speech before a mass group. It is lawful for a foreman to go around during the last 24 hours before an election and talk to the employees individually or in small groups against the union. The 24-hour rule does not prohibit all compaigning against a union, only an employer's speech to a mass audience. Similarly, the employer can have a picnic after work within the 24 hours before the election. The picnic can be on paid time as long as no mass speech is given. If attendance at the picnic is voluntary and not on company time, the employer can give a speech to the employees present without violating the 24-hour rule.

The Board strictly enforces the 24-hour rule. Even if an employer's speech before a mass audience on company time starts before the beginning of the 24-hour period and runs for only five or ten minutes into the 24-hour period, the Board will set aside the election. The Board reasons that if it makes exceptions for short violations, the rule gradually will be undermined with exceptions. On the other hand, the Board has held that the 24-hour rule is not violated if an employer ends his speech before the 24-hour period begins, but answers questions from employees who voluntarily remain afterwards causing the meeting to end less than 24 hours before the election.

3. Speeches in Management Authority Areas

One other exception to the employer's right to speak to employees is that an employer cannot at any time speak to small groups of employees about the union in an area of management authority. A management authority area is an area where employees normally do not go except on management matters, such as a supervisor's office or a board room. The Board feels that an employee may be intimidated in an area of management authority. The employee might couple the employer's anti-union remarks with the surroundings, which would remind the employee of the employer's authority to hire or fire. The small group rule applies even if the employer's remarks are perfectly legal and noncoercive. The setting itself is regarded as coercive regardless of what is said.

D. FREE UNION MEMBERSHIP AS A CAMPAIGN TECHNIQUE

Unions used to offer free union membership during election campaigns to employees who signed recognition cards before the election. This helped a union get a show of interest and majority support for a bargaining order. An employee who waited until after the election to join the union had to pay, so there was a strong incentive to join early.

In the *Savior* case, the Supreme Court limited this union practice.[4] The Court held that a union cannot limit free membership offers to those signing before the election date. That would be an employer ground for an objection setting aside an election. However, the Court did not invalidate free membership as an organizing technique altogether. A union can still offer free membership if it is allowed both before and for a reasonable time after an election. The most common practice now, which the Board has upheld, is to offer free membership to anyone who joins the union up to the time the first contract is executed.

What the Supreme Court feared in *Savior* was that an employee who had to sign a recognition card before the election in order to get free membership might feel compelled to vote for the union. By offering free member-

 ship up to the time of the contract, the union avoids that misunderstanding. An employee then realizes that his vote has no effect on his right to free membership.

Can membership be contingent on the outcome of the vote? Can the union say that membership is free only if the union wins the election? In a sense, that gives the employees an incentive to vote for the union. That offer, provided it remains open until the first contract, is legal because the employees know they can be out of the union if they vote against it. That is different than telling an employee he can only join the union up until the election. Thus, signing the card does not put pressure on the employee to vote for the union, as the Supreme Court hoped to eliminate in *Savior*.

E. INCENTIVES TO ATTEND CAMPAIGN MEETINGS

Unions want to get large employee turnouts at meetings during organizing drives. Can a union offer attendance prizes to employees attending a campaign rally? Can the union, for example, offer a television set as a door prize with eligibility limited to those meeting and remaining for the drawing (naturally at the end of the meeting)? Employers would argue that this technique is an attempt to buy votes for the union.

The Board has held that attendance prizes are lawful techniques as long as the prizes are not excessive, amounting to a bribe. There is nothing wrong with using incentives to encourage employees to attend union meetings. Of course, this rule works both ways. An employer can also have a meeting with door prizes, as long as they are not excessive. Obviously, outright payments of money or something of value to influence a vote is not permitted. If everybody who attended a

4 See legal principle 1.

meeting was paid $25, that would be grounds for setting aside the election.

If employees miss work time and lose pay to assist in a union organizing drive or to attend a Board hearing, it is lawful for the union to reimburse the employees for lost time. However, if a union pays an employee not only for lost time, but for his inconvenience, that can be construed as an unlawful bribe and therefore grounds for setting aside the election. Payments should be limited to an employee's lost time and out-of-pocket expenses only.

F. BOARD REGULATION OF CAMPAIGN STATEMENTS

The Board's goal in elections is to maintain laboratory conditions in order to maintain the employee's free choice. Nonetheless, the Board recognizes that both the employer and the union need a broad range of permissible campaign promises and propaganda, as in any political election. Both sides in an election may puff their positions. The employer may paint an extra bright picture of how good employee conditions are without a union. The union can say how much better things would be with it. Such talk is election propaganda that the Board feels employees can recognize and judge for truthfulness.

If employees are making $3 an hour and the union promises to double the wages, that's a lot of puffing. It is unlikely that wages will be doubled. But, the Board has held that such promises are permissible campaign propaganda because employees are able to recognize such statements for what they are.

1. Substantial Misrepresentations: The Hollywood Ceramics Doctrine

What sorts of campaign propaganda, by either an employer or a union, exceed per-

missible limits? Under the *Hollywood Ceramics* rule, an election is set aside if (1) there is substantial misrepresentation (2) on a material fact (3) made at a time when the other party has inadequate time to respond and correct the misrepresentation.[5] All three of these factors must be present for an election to be set aside.

Honest Mistakes of Facts

Suppose an employer tells employees that a union lost a strike at another plant and that all the employees the union represented lost their jobs and were replaced permanently. This accusation would almost certainly be a material campaign issue. If the accusation is false, and made at a time when the union does not have time to reply, the election would be set aside. But what if the employer honestly, but mistakenly, believes that the union lost a strike at another plant that was actually lost by another union? The employer's good faith does not matter. As long as the statement is a substantial misrepresentation on a material issue made at a time when the union has inadequate time to reply, the election can be set aside.

Time to Reply

A week is almost certainly sufficient time for the union to reply. Thus, even if the accusation is a flagrant misrepresentation, made in bad faith, the election will still not be set aside. There is no hard and fast rule as to how long before an election a false accusation must be made. It depends upon factors such as the size of the bargaining unit, the communications available to reply, the nature of the accusation, or how long it could take the union to uncover and communicate the true facts. A false statement made in the last 24

[5] See legal principle 9.

hours before an election probably would leave inadequate time to reply. Obviously, the more time the union has, the greater its burden to prove it had inadequate time.

The error must be substantial to be grounds for setting aside the election. For example, if an employer states that a union has 4,000 members although it has only 500 members, and the employees will lose their identity if they join the union, that is a substantial error. But, if the union has 3,500 members, the error is not substantial because the basis of the statement is true even though the exact figures are erroneous.

For nearly a year, in 1977–78, the Board abandoned the *Hollywood Ceramics* rule, reasoning that employees are mature enough to evaluate last minute misrepresentations. The Board also felt that the *Hollywood Ceramics* doctrine could be used as a tool to delay certification by employers who raised claims of union false misrepresentation. In place of *Hollywood Ceramics*, the Board adopted the *Shopping Kart* doctrine, under which an election is set aside only for abuse of Board processes (explained more fully below) or if a party uses fraudulent documents, preventing an employee from recognizing a misrepresentation as false campaign propaganda.[6]

The Board's abandonment of the *Hollywood Ceramics* doctrine was heavily criticized by both employers and unions. In late 1978, following a change in Board membership, the Board reversed itself and went back to the *Hollywood Ceramics* doctrine. However, the Board's opinion stressed that, to avoid abuse, *Hollywood Ceramics* would be strictly applied to cases of serious misrepresentation. Also, regional directors should expedite their investigation of election objections based on *Hollywood Ceramics*, so that employers could

[6] See legal principle 9.

not raise questions of campaign misrepresentation as a delaying tactic.

2. Abuse of Board Processes

Another ground for setting aside an election is abuse of Board processes by either party by making it appear that the Board favors one side over the other. This issue most frequently arises in the use of sample ballots. Both sides may send out sample ballots with an "X" in a box favoring them. But the parties cannot send out a sample ballot that looks like an official Board ballot with an "X" in it. That makes it appear that the Board backs one side over the other.

The parties may not make statements in an election campaign that make it appear the Board backs one side or the other. The union cannot make statements, for example, that make it appear the Board prefers that employees be organized. Technically, the Board takes no position on whether employees should or should not be represented by a union. The Board's only function is to insure a free and fair election so the employees can make their own choice.

But, the union can truthfully state the Board's role to protect employee rights. The union can tell employees that the law protects their right to join a union and that it is unlawful for an employer to discriminate against an employee for union activity. Also, if the employer has been a party in an NLRB proceeding, the union can truthfully state the results of the proceeding. However, the union cannot mislead the employees into believing the Board; rather than protecting the employee's rights to a free election, this actually favors the union's effort to represent them.

Both the employer and the union can have an observer at the election to verify the vote, make challenges, and ensure fair procedures.

However, no campaigning is permitted in the polling area. The union can stand outside the plant the morning of the election and the employer can go around and talk to employees in small groups (provided it is not in an area of management authority), but neither party can pass out literature or solicit where the election is being held.

3. Employer Free Speech

A recurring issue in election campaigns is the right of employers to express their views on the union's campaign. In theory, it can be argued that an employer should not be able to express any views at all during an election campaign, as the election is the employees' concern only. However, that is not the law. Congress has recognized that employers have a legitimate right to express their opinion as to whether their employees should be unionized.

a. Employer Threats

Section 8(c) of the Labor Management Relations Act states that the "expressing of any views, arguments or opinions or the dissemination thereof, whether in written, printed, graphic or visual form, shall not constitute or be evidence of an unfair labor practice under any provision of this Act, if such expression contains no *threat of reprisal or force or promises of benefits*" (emphasis added).

This amendment, known as the free speech amendment, was added in 1948 as part of the Taft-Hartley Act. The amendment nullified prior Board cases that set aside elections based on statements employers had made. Section 8(c) was intended to make it clear that an employer has the right to speak against the union.

The most important part of Section 8(c) is the last phrase (emphasized above), that the employer's remarks can contain neither threats of reprisal or force nor promises of benefit. Some threats are obvious such as if an employer blatantly says he will close the plant if the union wins an election.

Most employers are more sophisticated than that. What if the employer says:

> Listen, if this union comes in, there will be problems. We deal with a lot of nonunion customers. They are going to be concerned if the plant goes union that we are going to be shut down with strikes. I'm not telling you how to vote but I think that if you vote for the union that we are going to lose customers. They will go to other companies that they can depend on. I'll try my best, but that means that there might be a layoff here.

Are these statements a threat of reprisal or simply a statement of fact, which the employer has a right to make under Section 8(c)? The key is whether a statement is a prediction of something within the employer's control. An employer's prediction of an adverse effect outside its control is a permissible expression of opinion under Section 8(c). But, a prediction about an adverse effect within the employer's control, something the employer can carry out or not, is an unlawful threat under Section 8(c).

For example, the possible loss of customers is not within the employer's control, it is simply a matter of opinion. But the employer can control whether employees are laid off. If the employer states that there might be layoffs if the union wins, that is a threat, a statement of something that can be controlled. The statement violates Section 8(a)(1) because it is a threat of retaliation (a layoff) if the employees exercise their rights under the Act to join a union.

Threatening or coercive remarks, which are not protected by Section 8(c), are both an unfair labor practice under Section 8 and grounds for setting aside the election under

Section 9. Remember that the Board's decision on whether an election should be set aside is based upon the totality of conduct. The Board determines, based on the totality of conduct, whether the laboratory conditions to insure employee free choice have been interfered with. The determination of whether a specific coercive statement justifies setting aside an election might depend upon the employer's overall conduct of the election campaign. If an employer who conducted a fair campaign gave a speech that was generally noncoercive but contained an isolated threatening remark, the election would probably not be set aside. One the other hand, if an employer who had engaged in other unlawful conduct such as discharging union supporters gave the same speech containing the isolated threat, the Board would probably find the speech coercive in its overall context. The Board reasons that employees will tend to discount an isolated threat made by an employer who has otherwise conducted a fair campaign, but could be intimidated by a threat in a speech made by an employer engaging in other unlawful conduct.

c. The Futility Doctrine

Another important limitation on employer speech is the futility doctrine. An employer cannot indicate that voting for a union is a futile act, that it will lead inevitably to strikes, that collective bargaining will not bring any benefits, or that even with a union nothing is going to improve. For example, an employer might state: "I am already paying you a good wage. If the union comes in you should understand that I don't have to pay any more than that. All I have to do is bargain in good faith with the union. You might end up with a contract that pays you less than you now get." Perhaps the employer, to reinforce his point, will add: "All I have to do is bargain. I don't

have to reach any agreement at all. And after one year, if there's no contract, many of you may be gone and the union may be out altogether."

All these statements are legally correct, but why, then, should they be a basis for setting aside an election? Because the employer is trying to convey the impression to the employees that it is futile for them to have a union, that no matter what the employees do they are not going to be any better off with the union than without it. Such remarks interfere with the employee's free choice.

The hypothetical employer statements discussed above might not be unfair labor practices. The statements do not contain any threat of retaliation or promise of benefit violating Section 8(c). However, by conveying the impression of futility, they undermine the employee's free choice and interfere with laboratory conditions. The statements would therefore be grounds for setting aside the election.

Section 8(c) only provides that certain statements cannot be unfair labor practices under the Act. The section does not deal with election procedures governed by Section 9. The Board holds that although a statement may not be an unfair labor practice under Section 8(a), because of the exceptions contained in Section 8(c), it may still be grounds for setting aside an election under the Board's responsibility under Section 9 to ensure a fair election.

Substantial factual misrepresentations violating the *Hollywood Ceramics* doctrine discussed above are another example of elections being set aside based on statements that are not unfair labor practices but that may still interfere with required election conditions. There are many kinds of statements that can interfere with laboratory conditions, but not be unfair labor practices.

c. Racial Appeals

Appeals to racial prejudice can be grounds for setting aside an election. An employer might try to play black and white workers off against each other by saying that a union would benefit one race at the expense of the other. Such statements are probably not unfair labor practices because there is no promise of benefit or threat of reprisal. But the statements could be grounds for setting aside an election because by playing upon racial hostility, the employer has destroyed employee free choice.

In contrast, the Board has held that union may appeal to racial pride. If a work force has a high percentage of blacks, women, or chicanos, a union can appeal to their pride as a group and their goals of group improvement as a reason for favoring the union. These are considered bona fide campaign arguments. Thus, appeals to racial pride are permissible, but appeals to racial prejudice are not.

d. Employer Promises of Benefits

Although threats are a common union busting technique, Section 8(c) also prohibits employers from promising benefits if the union loses the election. The Supreme Court has referred to such promises as "a velvet glove over an iron fist". That is because the employees understand that although the employer has promised benefits if the union loses (the velvet glove) the employer can take those benefits away if the union wins (the iron fist). Promises of benefits and threats of reprisal are frequently coupled together. An employer may state that he has been thinking about increasing vacation weeks, but he is not sure that he can afford the increase if there is a union. Such a statement promises a benefit (to increase vacations) if the union loses and a threat if the union wins. Also, since vacation benefits are within the employer's control, the

statement is not merely a prediction protected by Section 8(c), but also constitutes an unfair labor practice.

Sometimes employers faced with an organizing drive call a meeting of their employees to ask them what conditions led them to form a union. The Board has held that it is objectionable conduct for an employer to solicit grievances from employees during an election campaign with either an express or implied promise to correct the unsatisfactory conditions without a union. The solicitation is like promising a benefit to the employees if the union is defeated. If an employer regularly held meetings with its employees before a union began organizing, the employer would not be prohibited from holding meetings during the campaign. The burden would be on the employer, however, to show that the meetings held during the union's election campaign and the promises the employer made were no different than those made before the organizing drive began.

The whipsaw effect, coupling promises of benefits if the union loses with coercive acts during the campaign, is a technique frequently used by employers who wish to defeat a union. It is effective because it brings home sharply the overall force of management to the employees. Such conduct, if proven, is both an unfair labor practice and grounds for setting aside an election. Unfortunately, however, because of the weakness in the Board's remedies, some employers willingly run the risk of purposely engaging in unlawful conduct in order to defeat a union.

G. BENEFIT INCREASES DURING AN ELECTION CAMPAIGN

Is it unlawful for an employer to give all employees a $1 per hour raise during an election campaign? Isn't the increase designed to win employee support and decrease union support? The Board holds that an employer may give benefit increases during an election campaign only if the benefit increase was planned before the election. An employer cannot give increases that were not planned or regularly scheduled. The employer must prove that the increased benefit was preplanned. For example, if the employer can show that it traditionally gives raises on January 1, the employer has the right to give a raise on January 1 even though a union election campaign is in progress.

It is unlawful retaliation for an employer to fail or refuse to give employees a scheduled increase in benefits, or rescind existing benefits, simply because a union is seeking to represent the employees. In the prior example, if the employer refused to give its normal January increase during an election campaign, the refusal would violate Section 8(a)(1) because the employer would be retaliating against the employees for exercising their right to engage in union activities. The refusal would also be grounds for setting aside the election. The Board also holds that it is unlawful for an employer to condition participation in a pension plan on the employees agreeing to remain unorganized.

H.   SURVEILLANCE, THE IMPRESSION OF SURVEILLANCE, AND INTERROGATION

Surveillance—keeping track of the employee's union activities—is also unlawful. It is an implied threat that there will be retaliation against employees for joining or supporting the union.

Giving employees the impression of surveillance violates the Act, even though the employer actually may not be checking up on

union activity at all. An employer might intentionally give the impression of surveillance in order to intimidate employees into refraining from union activity. Thus, an employer may tell an employee: "I heard that you were at the union meeting last night," while only guessing that the employee was at the meeting. But by making the statement, the employer is giving the employee the impression that the employer is keeping track of those who favor the union.

Polling Employees. An employer has no right to question employees about union activity even though there are no threats or the employee willingly answers the questions. One exception is that if a union requests recognition, an employer may poll its employees to determine if they do support the union. There are strict rules on such polls. The poll must be conducted for the purpose of determining the truth of a union's claim of majority status; the employer must tell the employees that the purpose is to determine the union's majority status; the employer must give assurances against reprisals; and the employees must be polled by secret ballot. Also, the poll must be conducted in an atmosphere free from employer coercion. If an employer polls its employees and determines that a majority favor the union, the employer is bound by the result of the poll and must recognize and bargain with the union without an election.

Sometimes a foreman, who is a supervisor, has friends in the bargaining unit. Is it unlawful if such a foreman innocently asks questions about union activity out of interest rather than for surveillance or retaliation? The answer depends upon all the surrounding circumstances. If the foreman's questioning was an isolated event, the questioning would not be unlawful. On the other hand, recurring questioning about union activity, even though there is no other unlawful conduct, might be grounds for setting aside the election because of the chilling effect of the impression of surveillance. Remember, in election campaigns the totality of the employer's conduct must be considered.

I. CONDUCT OF OUTSIDE PARTIES

Although it does not occur often, an election can be set aside because of the conduct of an outside person (commonly called a third party) not connected with either an employer or union. For example, in a small rural area, the town newspaper may carry an editorial against the union's election campaign. The newspaper article may contain a substantial misrepresentation about the union or threaten that the plant will probably close if the union wins. Such a threat would be an unfair labor practice if the employer had made it. But unless there is proof that the employer instigated the newspaper article, the employer probably will not be held responsible for the paper's remarks in an unfair labor practice case. On the other hand, if the third party's statement contains a serious threat or a substantial misrepresentation, the Board might still rule that the comments could interfere with the employees' free choice. The election can be set aside even though the employer is not in any way responsible for the statement.

J. PROCEDURES FOR CHALLENGING AN ELECTION

An election is challenged by filing objections to the conduct of the election within five days after the tally of ballots is furnished to the parties. The tally is usually furnished immediately after the ballots are counted on the election day. The objections list the acts that occurred during the campaign that interfered with the employees' right to a free election. The Board has held that only acts occurring between the date the union filed its petition and the election are grounds for setting aside the election.

The objections are processed by the regional director (see Chapter 1). As previously discussed in this chapter, many of the grounds for setting aside an election under Section 9 are also unfair labor practices under Section 8. However, the board sets aside an election only if timely objections are filed. Unions frequently file both objections and unfair labor practice charges based on the same conduct although filing an unfair labor practice charge alone is insufficient to have the election set aside.

K. REMEDIES FOR EMPLOYER UNFAIR LABOR PRACTICES: THE BARGAINING ORDER

What happens if an election is set aside for employer misconduct? Will there simply be another election or should a union be entitled to bargaining rights without going through another election?

The Board has a number of specific remedies for unlawful employer acts. It can issue a cease and desist order requiring the employer to cease an unlawful tactic or to assure employees that their rights are protected. The Board can remedy specific unfair labor practices by ordering employees reinstated or ordering the reinstitution and back payment of benefits unlawfully denied. In cases in which an employer has committed outrageous and pervasive unfair labor practices to undermine the union's organizing efforts (by engaging in multiple unlawful acts as discussed in this Chapter and Chapter 4), the Board can order so-called extraordinary remedies requiring an employer to: allow the union to post notices on employee bulletin boards and to meet with employees in nonwork areas of the plant on their nonwork time; give the union notice of and the right to respond to any employer speeches to its employees about union representation; allow the union to give a speech on working time prior to any scheduled NLRB election; and supply the union upon request with an up-to-date list of employee names and addresses.

The Board has long taken the view that even though a union loses an election, the Board can order an employer to bargain with the union if the employer's unfair labor practices undermined the union's majority status as proved by single purpose authorization cards signed by a majority of the employees. The Board is not limited to remedying the specific violations and ordering a new election.

Employers opposing the Board's view argued that, if a union loses an election, the only appropriate redress is for the Board to remedy the specific violations and then hold a rerun election. The employers argued that they should not be required to bargain with a union that loses an election because there was no way to prove that the union represented a majority of the employees. Also, to require an employer to bargain with a union that loses forces the union upon the employees. Employers further argued that recognition cards are inherently unreliable for proving that a union ever had a majority.

The Gissel Decision

In the landmark 1969 *Gissel* case, the Supreme Court upheld the Board's approach in favor of bargaining orders under some circumstances.[7] The Court held that, although signed recognition cards are not preferable to

[7] See legal principle 11.

an uncoerced election, single purpose cards can adequately reflect a Union's majority status.

1. Misconduct Justifying a Bargaining Order

Once the Supreme Court decided that an employer could be ordered to bargain with a union based on a card majority, it determined what type of misconduct warranted a bargaining order. First, the Court emphasized that absent unfair labor practices undermining the union, an employer has an absolute right to an election. No bargaining order should be issued, even if the union has cards from all the employees, if the employer simply refuses recognition. As previously discussed, the only exception would be if the employer verifies the union's majority status, thus waiving its right to an election.

The Court went on to divide employer misconduct into three categories. The first category consists of pervasive unfair labor practices of such a nature that the coercive effect cannot be eliminated by lesser remedies and a fair election cannot be held. In such cases a bargaining order is an appropriate remedy.

The second category of employer misconduct is that of less pervasive unfair labor practices that still have a tendency to undermine the union's majority strength and impede the election process. The Board in such cases must weigh the seriousness of the misconduct against the effectiveness of its remedies to ensure a fair rerun. The Board considers the extensiveness of the employer's unfair labor practices in terms of their past effect on election conditions and the likelihood of the recurrence in the future. The Court stated:

If the Board finds that the possibility of erasing the effects of past practices and of ensuring a fair election (or a fair rerun) by the use of traditional remedies, though present, is slight and that employee sentiment once expressed through cards would, on balance, be better protected by a bargaining order, then such an order should be issued.

The Supreme Court emphasized, however, that "there is a third category of minor or less extensive unfair labor practices which, because of their minimal impact on the election machinery, will not sustain a bargaining order." An employer's isolated threat to discharge an employee for union activity, which is not carried out, is an example of this third category.

The Board's decisions applying *Gissel* follow the Supreme Court's pattern. First, the Board decides whether an employer's conduct falls into the first (pervasive), second (serious), or third (minor) category. If a case falls within the first category and the union has a valid card majority, the Board issues a bargaining order. If a case falls into the second category, the Board analyzes the impact of the unfair labor practices versus the possibility of a free election through lesser remedies. If a case falls into the third misconduct category, the Board issues an order remedying the specific violations.

Hard and fast rules are not possible in determining the situations in which the Board will issue a bargaining order. Each case is based on the specific facts of the employer violations. Generally, cases involving discharges or reprisals, plant closings, or major changes in employee benefits fall into the first or second category, justifying a bargaining order depending upon their extent. However, cases involving only threats or promises, but no action, generally fall into the third minor misconduct category.

A bargaining order is based on the commission of unfair labor practices. If acts occurring during the election campaign interfere with employee free choice (i.e., substantial misrepresentations), but are not unfair labor practices, the election is set aside. There is not a bargaining order; the only remedy is a rerun.

2. Procedures for Obtaining a Bargaining Order

Generally, a bargaining order dates from the date the employer began to engage in unfair labor practices, provided the union can demonstrate a card majority by that date. If an employer engaged in unfair labor practices before the union obtained majority status, the bargaining order starts from the date the union obtained majority status.

Although unions frequently request voluntary recognition from an employer before filing a representation petition with the Board, a request for recognition is not necessary to get a bargaining order. If an employer engages in unfair labor practices warranting a bargaining order under the *Gissel* criteria, the Board issues a bargaining order even if the union never requested voluntary recognition, provided the union had a card majority. This means that a union that does not bother with requesting voluntary recognition because it realizes the futility of such a request does not forfeit its right to a bargaining order. The advantage to requesting recognition is that a union has greater certainty as to the date it achieved majority status. This is important in determining the date of an employer's bargaining obligation under a bargaining order.

Procedurally, to obtain a bargaining order, a union that has lost an election must file timely objections to the election and also file unfair labor practice charges against the employer's misconduct. The representation and unfair labor practice cases are consolidated for hearing (see Chapter 1). If the Board finds that the objections have merit, the Board sets aside the election. If the Board also finds that the unfair labor practices are serious enough under the *Gissel* criteria, the Board issues a bargaining order. If the unfair labor practices are not sufficient, the Board simply orders a rerun election and issues an order remedying the specific violations. No bargaining order is issued unless the Board sets aside the election based on the objections.

Choice of Proceeding with an Election

A union does not have to go ahead with an election in the face of serious unfair labor practices that the union feels make an election futile. Instead, the union can file unfair labor practice charges against the employer before the election is held. The representation election does not proceed while the unfair labor practice charges are pending. A charge filed while a representation case is pending is called a "blocking charge." The board can issue a bargaining order, even though an election was never held, if the employer's unfair labor practices warrant a bargaining order under the *Gissel* criteria.

In most cases, a union goes ahead with a pending election although the employer has committed serious unfair labor practices during the election campaign. A union can file charges and then sign a "request to proceed," permitting the representation case to proceed even though there are unfair labor practice charges pending. Why would a union want to proceed? Unions proceed because they hope to win the election even though the employer has comitted serious unfair labor practice. If the union wins despite the employer's unlawful acts, there is no need for a bargaining order. If, however, the union loses the election, it can still file objections to the election, pro-

ceed with the unfair labor practice charges, and seek a bargaining order.

Weakness of the Bargaining Order Remedy

There are weaknesses in bargaining orders as a remedy. The bargaining order is just that, an order that the employer bargain with the union. Even if the employer is ordered to bargain, the union may have been permanently weakened by the employer's misconduct. Many union supporters might have left the company before the bargaining order was issued. Thus, the time needed to process a case through the Board might result in a practical victory for the employer although the union wins the legal battle. An employer who is determined to defeat the union can drag out bargaining after the bargaining order is issued, further frustrating the employees' rights.

Bargaining Orders if the Union Lacks Majority Status

Since the *Gissel* decision, the Board has only issued bargaining orders in cases in which unions have a card majority as the unions did in *Gissel*. However, the Board is divided over whether it can issue a bargaining order in an appropriate case even if the union never had a majority. Two of the five Board members have stated their opinion that the Board can issue a bargaining order even if a union never obtains a card majority if the employer engages in extremely flagrant and pervasive unfair labor practices which prevent the union from obtaining majority support. One Board member is of the opinion that the Board lacks the authority. The two other Board members have stated that the Board "may" have the authority but have refused to render a definite opinion until faced with what they regard as an appropriate case. These members favor using the Board's "extraordinary remedies" (such as giving union organizers access to the plant etc. . . .) short of a bargaining order to reinstate an atmosphere in which the employees are given a meaningful opportunity for an election. Even if the Board should ultimately decide it can issue a bargaining order if a union does not have majority status, such cases will be extremely rare. A union should thus attempt to obtain majority support and not rely on this remote possibility.

Summary

The rights and obligations of unions, employees, and employers in organizing and elections are regulated by both Sections 8 and 9 of the Act. Some tactics by an employer or a union may be protected or prohibited as unfair labor practices under Section 8. In addition to the unfair labor practice restrictions, an employer and a union are prohibited from engaging in certain misconduct that destroys the "laboratory conditions" necessary to protect the employees' right to a free choice election under Section 9. An election may be set aside for election misconduct even if there was no unfair labor practice.

Section 8(c) allows employers to express their views on whether their employees should be unionized, as long as the employer's remarks do not contain a threat of reprisal or force, or promise of benefit. Threatening or coercive remarks are both an unfair labor practice and grounds for setting aside the election. However, the Board's decision on setting aside an election is based upon the totality of an employer's or union's conduct. Thus, a single remark may not be grounds for setting aside an election, even though it was an unfair labor practice.

To be grounds for setting aside an election, objectionable conduct must occur after the union has filed its representation petition. Objectionable conduct may include: (1) certain company restrictions on employees distributing union literature and soliciting for the union; (2) interrogation or surveillance of employees' union activities; (3) a company speech within the 24-hour period preceding the election to a mass assembly of employees on company time or to small groups of employees in an area of management authority at any time during the campaign; (4) substantial misrepresentations on a material fact to which the other party has inadequate time to reply; (5) threats of adverse consequences if the union wins; (6) granting new or additional benefits during the election campaign; (7) coercion or denial of benefits during the campaign; and (8) interference with the Board's conduct of the election.

The employer may sometimes, however, commit unfair labor practices during a campaign that are serious enough that a rerun election is an insufficient remedy. In such cases, the Board can order the employer to bargain with the union even though it lost the election. The union must be able to prove through single purpose recognition cards that it had majority status at one time. The card is a valid indication of an employee's support unless an employee was told that the card's only purpose was for an election. The Supreme Court held in the *Gissel* decision that a bargaining order was an appropriate remedy for two types of employer's misconduct: first, pervasive unfair labor practices of such a nature that the coercive effect could not be eliminated by lesser remedies, so that a fair election could not be held; and, second, less pervasive unfair labor practices that still had a tendency to undermine the union's majority strength and impede the election process.

Review Questions

1. Is an employer obligated to recognize a union that can prove its majority support without an election?

2. What are the two types of recognition cards?

3. Will the Board base a *Gissel* bargaining order on a majority proven through dual purpose cards?

4. Should recognition cards be dated?

5. When will the Board reject a single purpose recognition card as a basis for proving majority support?

6. Can an employee hand out recognition cards and talk to other employees during his free time in working areas?

7. Can a union offer free membership in the union as a campaign technique?

8. Is there a First Amendment right of free speech to engage in political campaigning at work?

9. Is an employer's statement that there might be layoffs if the union wins an election grounds for setting aside the election?

10. Can an employer give employees benefit increases during the election campaign?

11. Can an unfair labor practice be committed during an election campaign, but not be grounds for setting aside an election?

12. If a union loses an election, how many days after the election does it have to file objections to the employer's alleged misconduct?

(Answers to review questions appear at end of book.)

Basic Legal Principles

1. An employer and a union are prohibited from engaging in election misconduct that destroys laboratory conditions and undermines the employee's right to a free choice election. An election may be set aside for such acts even though they may not constitute an unfair labor practice. *General Shoe Corp.*, 77 NLRB 124, 21 LRRM 1337 (1948); *Newport News Shipbuilding*, 239 NLRB No. 14, 99 LRRM 1518 (1978); *Kurz-Kasch, Inc.*, 239

NLRB No. 107, 100 LRRM 1118 (1978); *NLRB v. Savair Mfg. Co.*, 414 U.S. 270, 84 LRRM 2929 (1973).

2. Generally an employee can solicit for the union in working areas on his own time. Literature can be distributed on an employee's own time, but only in nonworking areas. *Republic Aviation Corp. v. NLRB*, 324 U.S. 793 16 LRRM 620 (1945); *Stoddard-Quirk Mfg. Co.*, 138 NLRB 615, 51 LRRM 1110 (1962); *Norris K. W. Printing Co.*, 231 NLRB No. 156, 97 LRRM 1080 (1977); *United Parcel Service, Inc.*, 234 NLRB No. 11, 97 LRRM 1212 (1978); *NLRB v. Baptist Hospital, Inc*, 99 S. Ct. 2598, 101 LRRM 2556 (1979); (discussing hospital rules on solicitation and distribution of literature).

3. Rules that an employer establishes limiting employees' rights to solicit and distribute literature must be clear. Ambiguous rules, which an employee might interpret to prohibit statutorily protected rights, are unlawful. *G.C. Murphy*, 171 NLRB No. 45, 68 LRRM 1108 (1968); *NLRB v. Charles Miller & Co.*, 341 F.2d 870, 58 LRRM 2507 (2nd Cir. 1965); *Tri-County Medical Center*, 222 NLRB No. 174, 91 LRRM 1323 (1976).

4. Normally outside union organizers are not allowed into an employer's premises to solicit and distribute literature even though other means of reaching employees may not be as easy or convenient. *NLRB v. Babcock & Wilcox Co.*, 351 U.S. 105, 38 LRRM 2001 (1956).

5. The right to discuss union matters and distribute union literature pertains to all legitimate collective bargaining activities and subjects, including related political activity such as distributing literature against right-to-work laws. *Eastex Inc. v. NLRB*, 437 US 556, 98 LRRM 2717 (1978). A union cannot contractually waive the employees' statutory right to distribute union literature. *NLRB v. Magnavox*, 415 US 322, 85 LRRM 2475 (1974).

6. A shopping center is private property. Union organizers do not have a constitutional free speech right to enter shopping centers to organize employees. The rules on entering a shopping center to organize employees working there are the same as those applied to entering the private property of any other employer. *Central Hardware Co. v. NLRB*, 407 U.S. 539, 80 LRRM 2769 (1972).

7. An employer cannot give a speech to a mass employee audience on company time in the last 24 hours before an election. Talking to employees individually, in small groups, or at a voluntary meeting is not prohibited. *Peerless Plywood Co.*, 107 NLRB No. 106, 33 LRRM 1151 (1953); *Associated Milk Producers*, 237 NLRB No. 120, 99 LRRM 1212 (1978).

8. An employer cannot speak to small groups of employees in an area of management authority against the union at any time during an election campaign. The atmosphere is considered coercive even if the

statements made are not. *The Hurley Co.*, 130 NLRB No. 43, 47 LRRM 1293 (1961); *Han-Dee-Pak, Inc.*, 232 NLRB No. 71, 97 LRRM 1054 (1977).

9. An election is set aside if either party makes substantial misrepresentation on a material fact at a time when the other party has inadequate time to respond and correct the misrepresentation. All three factors must be present. *Hollywood Ceramics*, 140 NLRB No. 36, 51 LRRM 1600 (1962); *General Knit of California, Inc.*, 239 NLRB No. 101, 99 LRRM 1687 (1978). See also *Shopping Kart Food Market*, 228 NLRB No. 190, 94 LRRM 1705 (1977).

10. Abuse of the Board's processes by either party, by making it appear that the Board favors one side over the other, is grounds for setting aside an election. *Allied Electric, Inc.*, 109 NLRB 1270, 34 LRRM 1538 (1954); *Gulton Industries*, 240 NLRB No. 73, 100 LRRM 1321 (1979).

11. An employer can be ordered to bargain with a union that had majority support in the unit before the election as shown by sole purpose authorization cards, but lost the election, if the employer engaged in pervasive unfair labor practices or extensive unfair labor practices that tended to undermine majority strength and impede the election. *NLRB v. Gissel Packing Co.*, 395 U.S. 575, 71 LRRM 2481 (1969); *Drug Package Inc.*, 228 NLRB No. 17, 94 LRRM 1570 (1977). See also *United Dairy Farmers Coop. Assn*, 242 NLRB No. 179, 101 LRRM 1278 (1979); (discussing scope of Board's remedial power and bargaining orders without union majority status).

12. An employer's threat of adverse consequences within the employer's control if a union wins an election is an unfair labor practice not protected by the free speech exception. *NLRB v. Gissel Packing Co., supra.*; *Tendico, Inc.*, 232 NLRB No. 118, 97 LRRM 1107 (1977).

Suggested Readings

Bok, "The Deregulation of Campaign Tactics in Representation Elections," 78 *Harv. L. Rev.* 38 (1969).

"Disclosure of Union Authorization Cards Under the Freedom of Information Act —Interpreting the Personal Privacy Exemptions," 62 *Minn L. Rev.* 949 (1978).

Golub, "Propriety of Issuing Gissel Bargaining Orders Where The Union Has Never Attained a Majority," 29 *Lab. L.J.* 639 (1978).

Chapter Four

Protection of the Employee's Right to Union Representation

What are the union's rights as the bargaining representative? What are the employee's rights to engage in collective bargaining activities through his union, and how are those rights protected? This chapter examines what happens after a union has obtained bargaining rights, either through a Board-conducted election, voluntary recognition, or perhaps a bargaining order.

The principles discussed in this chapter are primarily based on Sections 7, 8(a)(1), 8(a)(2), and 8(a)(3) of the Act, which should be referred to while reading this material. Section 7 grants employees the right to engage in concerted activity (collective bargaining) or to refrain from such activity. Section 8(a)(1) makes it an employer unfair labor practice to interfere with the employees' rights under Section 7. Section 8(a)(2) prohibits an employer from dominating or interfering in the activities of the employees' labor organization. Section 8(a)(3) prevents the employer from discriminating against employees either because of their union activities or because they choose not to engage in union activities.

Although this chapter emphasizes restrictions on employer conduct, remember that there are similar restrictions on unions. Section 8(b)(1) prohibits a union from interfering with the employees' Section 7 rights. A union cannot force an employee to engage in union activities or to refrain from them. Also, Section 8(b)(2) prevents a union from causing an employer to discriminate against an employee in violation of Section 8(a)(3). The limitations these sections place on union activities are discussed in Chapters 10, 11, and 12.

Although employees have a right to engage in concerted activities through a union, the Act protects concerted activity whether through a union or through a less formal employee group. Thus, employees without a union who informally protest unsafe working conditions are also engaged in concerted activities and enjoy the same statutory protection as union members discussed in this chapter. Remember, therefore, that although this chapter covers employees' rights to engage in union activities, the broader right of concerted activity belongs to all employees whether or not they belong to a labor organization.

A. THE DOCTRINE OF EXCLUSIVE REPRESENTATION

Once a union is either properly recognized voluntarily or certified as the bargaining agent by the NLRB, the union has the right of exclusive representation. This means that the employer cannot deal with any other employee representative about wages, hours, or other terms and conditions of employment. This concept of exclusive representation is fundamental to our system of democratic collective bargaining under which the union, as a representative of the majority, speaks for all employees in the unit.

Exclusive representation prevents an employer from playing the employees off against each other. By preventing an employer from dealing directly with employees, the doctrine of exclusive representation prevents an employer from taking advantage of some bargaining unit employees who might otherwise be subject to employer domination. Because of this doctrine, an employer cannot hire an employee on the condition that he accept working conditions less than those provided in the contract. Also, an employer cannot condition an individual employee's continued employment on his willingness to accept different conditions. An employer, for example, cannot tell an employee that because his work is slower he must accept lower pay. Under the doctrine of exclusive representation, an employer cannot enter into individual contracts with employees containing different provisions than the collective bargaining agreement. An individual employee cannot be forced to waive his contract rights. However, a contract may expressly permit individual bargaining on some subjects. Theatrical or sports collective bargaining agreements, for example, frequently provide only base pay rates and the employees may bargain individually for higher rates. In the absence of such exceptions, however, the contract determines the wages, hours, and working conditions for all employees.

The doctrine of exclusive representation is based on Section 9(a)(1), which provides that:

> Representatives designated or selected for the purposes of collective bargaining by a majority of the employees in a unit appro-priate for such purposes, shall be the exclusive representatives of all the employees in such unit for the purposes of collective bargaining in respect to rates of pay, wages, hours of employment, or other conditions of employment. . . .

Note that Section 9(a) says "designated or selected," not just elected. Thus, a union that is voluntarily recognized is also entitled to exclusive representation.

1. Individual Adjustment of Grievances

There is an exception to Section 9(a) under which any employee or group of employees has the right at any time "to present grievances to their employer and to have such grievances adjusted, without the intervention of the bargaining representative. . . ." However, this exception also provides that the adjustment cannot be inconsistent with the terms of a collective bargaining agreement in effect and that the bargaining representative must be given the opportunity to be present at such an adjustment.

The Supreme Court has interpreted the Section 9(a) exception for direct employee adjustments with an employer very narrowly. The Court has held that employees are permitted to deal directly with their employer outside the grievance procedure, as an exception to the doctrine of exclusive representation. However, the employer is not obligated to meet directly with the employees. The employer can refuse to meet and can require the employee to use the grievance procedure. Also, talking to the employer directly, even if the employer is willing, may not satisfy the time requirements of the grievance procedure. Thus, if a contract allows only three days to file a grievance and an employee spends five days attempting to resolve the problem directly with the employer, the employee may have lost the right to file a grievance.

2. Direct Employer/Employee Dealings on Civil Rights Issues

The Supreme Court's decision in *Emporium Capwell Co.* is an important case demonstrating the scope of the union's authority as the exclusive bargaining representative.[1] In that case, black employees formed an alliance within the unit. They demanded that the employer deal directly with them rather than the union on issues of black minority rights. The employer refused to deal with the black employees, taking the position that the employees should work through the union. The black employees picketed the employer, in violation of the contract's no-strike clause, and they were discharged. The employees argued in part that the employer improperly refused to meet directly with them and that they could not lawfully be discharged for protesting the employer's alleged civil rights violations.

The Supreme Court upheld the discharges, holding that under the doctrine of exclusive representation the black employees had to go through the union. Otherwise, the Court reasoned, every employee group could go directly to the employer with their own special problems. That would undermine the entire concept of majority rule, under which one of the union's functions is to consider the conflicting demands of its members, make a decision, and then present a united approach to the employer.

In *Emporium Capwell*, the union was trying to correct the conditions about which the black employees were complaining. The Supreme Court left open the possibility that if the union had been unwilling to represent the

black employees or had violated its duty of fair representation, then the employees might have been able to deal directly with the employer. But, ordinarily, under the doctrine of exclusive representation, if employees have a grievance they must proceed through the union; they cannot seek to supplant the union by dealing directly with the employer.

B. EMPLOYER DOMINATION OR INTERFERENCE WITH A UNION

In order for the doctrine of exclusive representation to function as it should, a union must independently represent the views of the employees. Primarily for this reason, Section 8(a)(2) makes it an unfair labor practice for an employer to dominate or interfere with the formation or administration of a union or to contribute financial or other support.

1. Employer Domination

The Board has held that an employer has dominant control if the union has no independence. Domination is a throwback to the company unions that existed back in the 1920s and early 1930s before passage of the Wagner Act. Section 8(a)(2) is intended to make sure that a union represents the interests of the employees, not the employer. For example, an employer might believe that an outside union was trying to organize. To avoid this, the employer calls a meeting of its employees, tells them they need a union, suggests the officers, and remains while an election is held. Then the employer helps draft the union's by-laws and quickly enters into a sweetheart contract with the union to bar the outside union from having an election. Section 8(a)(2) prevents an employer from dominating a union in this fashion. Such conduct,

---

[1] See legal principle 4.

which was common in the pre-Wagner Act days, is seldom seen today.

If the Board does find that an employer dominates a union, the union is disestablished (dissolved) and its rights to engage in collective bargaining are taken away.

2. Employer Assistance

It is more common for an employer to assist a union than to dominate it. This may occur if an employer realizes that he is unable to dominate a union, but still prefers one union over another. An employer has the free speech right under Section 8(c) to state a preference for one union over another. However, if an employer couples a statement of preference with a threat as to the consequences if the other union wins, the statement constitutes unlawful assistance under Section 8(a)(2) and an unlawful threat under Section 8(a)(1). Another example of unlawful assistance is a supervisor who obtains recognition cards for a union.

If an employer simply assists a union, but does not dominate it, the union is decertified and the employer ordered to cease the conduct that constituted unlawful assistance. However, the union will not be disestablished, as an employer-dominated union is. Instead, if the employer ceases its unlawful assistance, the union will be allowed to obtain new recognition cards and seek certification once again through a Board election.

Assistance vs. Normal Courtesies

The Board has held that accepting normal social courtesy or amenities is not prohibited by Section 8(a)(2). If the employer and union are meeting at lunch and the employer pays the bill, the company technically might have assisted the union. But this is normal social courtesy between persons, of which the Board approves. If the employer, however, had provided the union leaders with a lavish meal out of all proportion to the meeting occasion, there might be a violation. The purpose of the Section 8(a)(2) restriction against financial assistance is twofold: first, to maintain arm's-length bargaining between an employer and a union; and, second, to prevent a union from becoming dependent on the employer's assistance so that the employer cannot influence union decisions by threatening to withdraw his aid. With these purposes in mind, the distinction between acts that are normal social courtesies and those that are unlawful assistance is fairly clear.

The Board has upheld contract clauses that provide that grievance meetings are to be held on company time. Such clauses assist a union because stewards are paid by the employer although engaged in union business. But, the clauses have a legitimate collective bargaining function and are the result of arm's-length bargaining.

Suppose an employer wants to introduce a new piece of labor saving equipment already being used in another city. The union opposes the new equipment because it cuts down on manpower. The employer offers to pay the union's air fare and hotel expenses to the city to see how the equipment actually works. That kind of assistance to the union is unlawful under Section 8(a)(2) because it interferes in the union's administration and is financial support. It does not matter even that the union might not be able to afford the trip and the employees might benefit from the employer's offer. Congress, in passing Section 8(a)(2), decided it was better for a union to be poor but independent of the employer.

3. Section 302 Restrictions on Employer Assistance

Section 8(a)(2) is similar to Section 302, which prohibits a union officer or agent from accepting anything of value from an employer. There is an exception that permits the sale or purchase of an article or commodity at the prevailing market value in the course of regular business. That means, for example, that an employer could sell the union supplies at the prevailing rate. Also, a union officer or agent who is a full-time employee can accept regular compensation for work.

Section 302 is a criminal provision that is enforced by the Department of Justice rather than by the NLRB. However, Sections 8(a)(2) and 302 are generally interpreted the same. For example, accepting social amenities is not a violation of either provision.

4. Improper Employer Recognition

Aside from financial assistance, improper employer recognition of a union is a violation of Section 8(a)(2). An employer is prohibited from prematurely recognizing a union. That happens if an employer recognizes a union without proof of the union's majority standing or if an employer recognizes a union before the employer has a representative work force. If an employer signs a collective bargaining agreement that would not be a contract bar because it was executed prematurely (see Chapter 2), signing it also violates Section 8(a)(2) because the employer is giving unlawful assistance to the union by recognizing it prematurely. The contract can be set aside in an unfair labor practice proceeding, and it would thereafter not bar an election.

a. Competing Union Recognition Claims

A recurring issue under Section 8(a)(2) involves an employer who signs a contract or recognizes a union at the same time that another union is also seeking to represent the employees. Obviously, signing a contract with one union at the same time another union is in the process of an organizing effort assists the contracting union. Does that mean that an employer can never recognize, bargain with, or execute a contract with one union if another union is also organizing?

Under the *Midwest Piping* doctrine, an employer may violate Section 8(a)(2) if he voluntarily recognizes one of two or more competing unions at a time when there is a "real question of representation in the unit."[2] An example of unlawful recognition, related to the contract bar doctrine, would be if an employer signed a new contract with the incumbent union even though an outside union had filed a timely representation petition during the open period for filing at the end of the prior contract (see Chapter 2). Such a contract signed during the open period, does not bar an election. The Board has held that signing a contract with one union after a representation petition has been properly filed by another union also violates Section 8(a)(2), because signing assists the incumbent union against the rival.

In contrast, an employer might bargain harder with the incumbent union, thus producing a poor contract and assist the rival. To avoid employer assistance either way, the Board prohibits all bargaining for a new contract when there is a real question of representation in the bargaining unit. Of course, employees should not be left totally unprotected because two unions claim to represent them. For that reason, the Board has also held that the incumbent union may continue to administer the existing contract and to adjust grievances even though the employer and the incumbent cannot negotiate a new contract.

[2] See legal principle 2.

b. Real Questions of Representation

There must be a "real question of representation" before an employer violates Section 8(a)(2) by recognizing or signing a contract with one competing union. A real question of representation is a question presented at a time and in a method that raises substantial question about which union represents the employees. For example, a timely petition filed with the Board supported by a 30 percent showing of interest raises a question of representation. What if a union files a petition with the Board during the contract's 60 day closed period at the end of the contract? There is no real question of representation because a representation petition cannot be filed then. Thus, the employer is free to negotiate and execute a contract. Also, an employer may sign a contract the same day a rival union files a timely petition with the Board as long as the employer does not have knowledge that the petition was filed before the contract is signed.

If two unions both contact the employer and demand recognition, the employer cannot recognize either union unless one claim is unsubstantiated. But, if, as sometimes happens, both unions claim majority status and both have card majorities (because some employees may have signed cards with both unions), the employer cannot recognize either union. The employer cannot pick and choose, but must sit back and let a Board-conducted election settle the matter.

The fact that the employer knows that one union is organizing does not prevent the employer from recognizing another union that proves its majority. The Board has held that a real question concerning representation does not exist if the claim of the rival union is clearly unsupportable, is specious, or otherwise not a colorable claim. A claim is not colorable if it is filed during one of the contract's insulated (closed) periods under the contract bar rule.

Remember that an employer is normally not obligated to recognize a union voluntarily. Thus, although an employer might conclude that it could voluntarily recognize one of two competing unions without violating the *Midwest Piping* doctrine, it might choose to deny recognition. The employer might prefer the certainty of an election over the uncertainties that can arise if it accords voluntary recognition to one of two competing unions.

c. Construction Industry Exceptions

There is one statutory exception to the rule against entering into premature or pre-hire agreements with a union. Section 8(f) expressly allows pre-hire agreements in the construction industry. This means that a construction union does not have to prove its majority status to obtain voluntary employer recognition. This exception was made because construction jobs are frequently of short duration and employers look to the construction unions as a source of employees. However, Section 8(f) also provides that a pre-hire agreement is not a bar to an election petition filed by another union. This means that an election can be held during the term of a pre-hire contract. Further, the Board has held that an employer may lawfully withdraw from a Section 8(f) agreement at any time until the construction union represents a majority of the employees covered by the agreement.

C. PROTECTION OF THE RIGHT OF CONCERTED ACTIVITY

Exclusive representation is the most fundamental protection that employees have to engage in concerted activities. How effective is a union if the employer deals with other organizations, or even directly with the employees, to undermine on an individual basis what the union has obtained through collective bargaining? However, the Labor Management Relations Act does more than protect the union as an entity through the doctrine of exclusive representation. The Act also protects the right of each individual employee to engage in concerted activity or to refrain from that activity.

Section 7 protects the right of employees to engage in concerted activities or to refrain from such activity. Section 8(a)(1) makes it an unfair labor practice for an employer to interfere with, restrain, or coerce employees in these rights. Section 8(b)(1)(A) makes it an unfair labor practice for a union to restrain or coerce an employee in the exercise of these rights. It is not possible to list all the actions that might consititute employer interference with employee rights in violation of Section 8(a)(1). Union rights to solicit and distribute literature are rights guaranteed by Section 7 and protected by Section 8(a)(1). Employer threats or promises of benefits; granting or withholding benefits; and coercion, such as discipline or harder working conditions in retaliation for supporting a union, are all prohibited by Section 8(a)(1) because they interfere with the employees' rights. Interrogation of employees about their union activities, surveillance of an employee's union activities, or transferring an employee to an isolated area of the plant to prevent him from engaging in union activities are other common examples of employer conduct that interfere with an employee's right to engage in concerted activity.

1. Concerted vs. Individual Activity

The rights to protest working conditions, including safety matters; to protest contract violations; or to file grievances are all activities protected by Sections 7 and 8(a)(1). However, Section 7 only protects concerted activity. What if an employee protests that an employer's contract violation denied him a certain right? If the employee is protesting only for himself, is he engaged in concerted activity? The Board has held that the employee is engaged in concerted activity because the contract applies to all employees. An employee protesting a contract violation is protecting the right of all employees to have the contract followed, even though the particular violation may only affect him. Similarly, a single employee's protest of an employer's violation of a contractually established safety standard is considered concerted activity to protect all employees. It does not matter whether the employee is right or wrong on the merits of the dispute—the employee's right to protest is protected. If, however, an employee is protesting a matter outside the contract, which applies only to the individual employee, the protest is not protected under Section 7 because it is not concerted activity.

2. Right to a Shop Steward In Disciplinary Proceedings

One of the fundamental rights of collective bargaining is that an employee upon request may have a shop steward present if the employee is called to a meeting with his employer for disciplinary purposes. The Board considers the right to a steward as a Section 7 right of concerted activity protected by Section 8(a)(1). However, the employee must ask for the steward. The employer has no obligation to tell an employee that he has a right to have the shop steward present. Therefore, it is important that unions educate their members about this right.

The Board distinguishes between an employer meeting with an employee for the purpose of general investigation and for possible discipline. An employee does not have a right to a steward if the employer is simply investigating the circumstances of an event that may lead to discipline. If the employee is definitely to be disciplined or if the employer is contemplating such discipline, the employee is entitled to the steward upon request.

How does the employee know the purpose of the meeting? Basically, the employee is entitled to the steward if the investigation is focused on the employee and the employee reasonably believes that he may be facing discipline. For example, if an employee has been absent many days during the year and the employer calls the employee into a meeting for the purpose of discussing his attendance, the employee can reasonably conclude that the meeting might lead to discipline for poor attendance. The employee would then be entitled to his steward upon request. But if some tools have been stolen and the employer is questioning every employee in the bargaining unit to see what they know, the investigation is not focused on one person and no employee has the right to a shop steward. Of course, at a given point, the investigation may be focused on a few employees who might be disciplined. They would be entitled to a steward upon request.

Because an innocent employee might be the focus of an investigation, the request of a shop steward is certainly not an admission of guilt. Even an innocent employee would be well advised to request his steward. The employee may not be able to express himself well or might make innocent mistakes of fact that erroneously lead the employer to believe that the employee has committed a disciplinary offense. Having the steward present might avoid this.

a. Employer Choice If an Employee Requests His Steward

If an employee requests his steward based on a reasonable belief that he faces discipline, the employer has three choices. The employer can either stop the meeting, call in the shop steward and continue the investigation in the steward's presence, or tell the employee that the meeting will be terminated unless the employee voluntarily agrees to proceed without a steward. Some employees incorrectly believe that if the employer stops the meeting, the employee cannot be disciplined at all. That is not true. The employer cannot discipline the employee for requesting his steward and cannot question the employee in the steward's absence without the employee's consent. However, the employer can discipline the employee for the alleged misconduct based on the information the employer already has. In the case of an employee who has been absent many times, the employer may ask the employee for his reasons. The employee may reply that he will not discuss his record without his shop steward being present. If the employer wishes, he can stop the interview, consider the evidence, and base discipline upon that evidence if it is sufficient. There is no statutory requirement that the employer question an employee before he is disciplined. Of course, if the employee's discipline is arbitrated, the employer has the burden of proving just cause for the discipline taken. If the employer chooses not to interview the disciplined employee with the steward present, the employer might not have sufficient evidence to prove just cause.

b. Steward Opportunity to Meet With the Employee

The Board has recently expanded the employee's right to a steward by holding that the employee is entitled to meet in private with his steward before a disciplinary meeting is held. The Board reasons that, to be an effective advocate, the steward needs time to find out the facts ahead of time from the employee. In that way the steward can advise the employee of his rights and prepare the employee's defense. The steward has the right to meet with the employee privately for a reasonable period of time before the meeting, but not to call in other employees or make a full investigation of the facts.

If no steward is reasonably available at the time an employer calls in an employee, the employer does not have to postpone the investigation until someone is available. It is the union's responsibility to have a steward present. The employer is not obligated to offer time for the steward to meet with the employee in private. The steward must request it. If the employee requests a steward and the steward is called into a room with the employer present, the steward should immediately request a recess to meet with the employee in private. Again, if the employer does not wish to give the steward time he may refuse, stop the interview, and base his decision on the information he already has if it is sufficient. The right to meet privately with an employee beforehand may be very important in protecting an employee's job and stewards should take full advantage of it.

Finally, the right to have a steward present applies only if the employee is to be questioned. If the employer has already made the decision to discipline an employee and simply hands the employee the disciplinary notice without asking any questions, there is no right to a steward.

Although the Board requires that an employee ask for his steward, nothing prevents the union from negotiating stronger contractual protection. Thus, the contract may require the employer, rather than the employee, to call in the steward whenever an employee is to be questioned or disciplined.

3. Steward's Right to Free Expression

An important right for stewards under Section 8(a)(1) is protection against employer retaliation for statements made during the course of grievance meetings. Ordinarily, an employee can be disciplined for disrespect to a supervisor. Disrespect may be insubordination. However, the Board has generally held that a steward cannot be disciplined for abusive remarks made to a supervisor or management officials during a grievance meeting or in a bargaining session. The steward may use profanity or even accuse the employer of lying without fear of discipline. The Board applies this rule so that a steward may speak freely without having to weigh every word said or hold back arguments for fear of overstepping the line.

There are, however, a few exceptions to the steward's very broad rights. The steward cannot threaten an employer representative with physical violence. Also, a steward may be disciplined in extremely aggravated situations if the steward is disrespectful to the employer in the presence of rank-and-file employees to the point that an employer is no longer able to exercise proper control over the work force.

4. Exceptions to the Protected Concerted Activity Doctrine

Some employees incorrectly believe that all concerted activity is protected from employer retaliation. That is not true. Employee conduct basically falls into three categories under the LMRA. First, there is conduct protected under Sections 7 and 8(a)(1), such as the right to form a union and to solicit and distribute literature in appropriate places. An employer cannot discipline an employee for engaging in such protected activities. Second, there is conduct prohibited by Section 8(b), such as unlawful secondary boycotts (see Chapter 7). Third, there is conduct that is neither prohibited nor protected by the Act.

An employee engages in conduct in the third category at his own risk. It is not an unfair labor practice to engage in such conduct; but, since the activity is not protected, the employer can take disciplinary action in retaliation without commiting an unfair labor practice. For example, a union, as a lever in bargaining, might engage in petty harrassment against the employer. Employees might engage in quickie strikes or slowdowns. That is lawful concerted activity as long as there is no contractual no-strike clause in effect. However, although this conduct is lawful, it is not protected. This means that an employee who takes part in quickie strikes or slowdowns is subject to discipline.

The LMRA does not prohibit strikes in breach of a contractual no-strike clause, but such conduct is unprotected and is subject to employer discipline.

D. DISCRIMINATION AS TO HIRE, TENURE, OR TERMS AND CONDITIONS OF EMPLOYMENT

Section 8(a)(3) prohibits discrimination regarding hiring, tenure of employment, or conditions of employment. This section applies to such conduct as discharging an employee, denying a promotion, denying or reducing an employee's benefits, giving an employee more difficult work, or having an employee work under less favorable conditions than other employees. Section 8(b)(2) prohibits a union from causing or attempting

to cause an employer to discriminate against an employee in violation of Section 8(a)(3).

One of the most common mistaken beliefs is that the Board has jurisdiction over any unjust discharge. That is not so. The Board only has jurisdiction over a discharge, or other discrimination, which violates Section 8(a)(3). The discrimination must be with the intent to encourage or discourage membership in a labor organization.

1. Section 8(a)(1) Versus 8(a)(3) Violations: The Intent Requirement

The acts prohibited by Section 8(a)(3) are narrower than those prohibited by Section 8(a)(1), discussed above. Section 8(a)(1) applies to any type of employer coercion. Section 8(a)(3) applies only to discrimination in employment or terms of employment. Also, Section 8(a)(3) requires that discrimination be with the *intent* of encouraging or discouraging union membership. The intent to encourage or discourage membership has been interpreted broadly to include intent to encourage or discourage union activity in general. In contrast, Section 8(a)(1) does not expressly require that conduct have an anti-union intent as Section 8(a)(3) does. The courts and the Board, in comparing the language of Sections 8(a)(1) and (3), have held that there does not have to be an anti-union intent in order for an employer to violate Section 8(a)(1). When the courts or Board speak of anti-union intent, they use the term "anti-union animus."

2. Inherently Destructive Conduct

An act may violate Section 8(a)(1), regardless of its anti-union animus, if the employer's actions are inherently destructive of employee rights. For example, an employer may have a rule barring all solicitation of any kind in the plant (see Chapter 3). That rule is valid except as applied to union solicitation. The rule may have been in effect long before there was any union activity and might not have any anti-union intent. Once a union begins an organizing drive, however, the employer violates Section 8(a)(1) by enforcing the rule, because the rule infringes on the employees' rights to engage in concerted activity.

Cases involving the discharge of economic strikers are another example of the application of Section 8(a)(1). The Supreme Court has held that, even if the employer does not have an anti-union animus, the discharge of an economic striker is inherently destructive of employee rights, and thus a violation of Section 8(a)(1). On the other hand, the Court holds that it is not inherently destructive to replace strikers with permanent replacements to maintain operations during a strike. Thus, replacement does not violate Section 8(a)(1) (see Chapter 6).

Board and court decisions applying Section 8(a)(1) sometimes distinguish between acts that are inherently destructive regardless of the employer's motive and those that have a lesser impact. If an action is inherently destructive, it is unlawful regardless of the employer's business justification. Economic strikers cannot be discharged regardless of the employer's good faith business reasons. However, there is a second category of conduct that has an adverse impact on a union, but is not inherently destructive. In such cases, the employer's business justification for an act is weighed against the adverse impact. If the business justification outweighs the impact, the employer's actions are lawful. The right of an employer to replace (rather than discharge) an economic striker falls into this category. The courts have reasoned that the employer's business justification for hiring permanent replacements (i.e., to remain open during a strike) outweighs the adverse impact upon the employee.

It is frequently difficult to forecast those acts the Board or a court may regard as inherently destructive, and those they may regard as of lesser impact. It appears that the courts first decide whether they approve or disapprove of a given employer tactic. If they approve, they classify the act as having minor impact. If they disapprove of the tactic, they classify the act as inherently destructive.

Note that every violation of Section 8(a)(3) also necessarily violates Section 8(a)(1). Any discrimination with intent to encourage or discourage union activity infringes upon the employee's Section 7 rights. On the other hand, every violation of Section 8(a)(1) does not violate Section 8(a)(3). An act might violate Section 8(a)(1) because it is inherently destructive of organizing rights, but it might not violate Section 8(a)(3) unless there is discriminatory intent.

3. Proving Anti-Union Intent

How do you prove the anti-union animus (intent) required to prove a Section 8(a)(3) violation? Few, if any, employers are going to admit their motive. Section 10(c) provides that the Board cannot order the reinstatement or back pay for an employee discharged or suspended for cause. Usually an employer charged with violating Section 8(a)(3) tries to show cause for his actions. If an employer fires the chief union supporter for alleged drunkenness, how does the union prove the employee was, in fact, discharged for union activities? First, the union should check whether the employee actually engaged in the alleged conduct justifying discharge. If not, and the employer has no other valid reason, the Board may well conclude that the employee was actually discharged for union activity. Even if the conduct allegedly justifying discharge did occur, the union should determine how other employees who have done the same thing have been treated. If the union supporter has been given a more severe penalty than other employees, the Board may conclude that a greater penalty was imposed because of the employee's union activities.

The Board will also consider whether the reasons given by the employer are a pretext. For example, what if the employer has put up with an employee's alleged poor conduct for a long time and other employees who have engaged in the same misconduct have not been disciplined? The Board may conclude that the employee was, in fact, discharged because of union activities. A reason for discharge which might otherwise be valid may be unlawful under Section 8(a)(3) if it was, in fact, in retaliation for an employee's union activities.

The Board will examine the alleged discrimination in the context of the employer's overall anti-union animus and conduct. An employer may have made anti-union statements or engaged in other unlawful conduct so that an anti-union animus for a specific act may be inferred from the employer's overall conduct.

The Board has also held that an employer's intent can be inferred from the natural consequences of an employer's actions. The leading case in applying the natural consequences test is the *Radio Officers* decision.[3] There, the employer, at the union's request, discharged certain employees who had not joined the union or who were disfavored by the union. The employer was charged with violating Section 8(a)(3) by discharging the employees. The union also violated Section 8(b)(2) by causing the employer to engage in the dis-

[3] See legal principle 8.

crimination. The employer argued that it was simply following the union's orders and did not have any anti-union intent to encourage or discourage union membership. The Board rejected this argument. It reasoned that Section 8(a)(3) not only prohibits discrimination to encourage union membership, but also discrimination to encourage an employee to be a "good member" who, for example, does not oppose the union's policies. The Board stated the natural consequences of firing an employee improperly at the union's request is to encourage union membership or good membership in violation of Section 8(a)(3), because employees may fear that they will be discharged at the union's request if they incur the union's disfavor.

The Board's view is that an employee's discharge does not have to be based solely on union activities in order to violate Section 8(a)(3). A discharge based even in part on union activities is unlawful. Some appellate courts have used a slightly narrower "but for" test, under which a discharge is unlawful if an employee would not have been discharged "but for" union activity. In most cases, the test applied by the Board and by the courts reaches the same result.

4. Proving Employer's Knowledge of Union Activity

In order to prove an 8(a)(3) violation, it is necessary to prove that the employer had knowledge of union activity. An employer cannot possibly take an act to discourage or encourage union activity if he does not even know that union activity is taking place. Thus, employers frequently allege as a defense that they were unaware of the union's activity. Usually, however, it is not difficult to prove the employer's knowledge. The employer's knowledge can, for example, be shown through supervisors' statements about the union indicating their knowledge of union activity. Some unions purposely notify an employer when they undertake an organizing drive so there can be no question about the employer's knowledge in case union supporters are later discharged or discriminated against.

The Board also applies the so-called "Small Shop Rule," in which the Board presumes that employers in a small shop (usually employing 10 or fewer employees) know if a union organizing campaign is underway. The basis of this rule is the presumption that an employer in a small shop knows what is going on. A union organizing drive is usually open enough that a small shop owner is bound to know about it just as he knows about other employee matters.

5. Constructive Discharges

Most 8(a)(3) discharge cases involve situations in which an employee is fired. However, in some cases, an employer may not discharge a union supporter, but make his working conditions so miserable that the employee resigns. Such conduct, called a constructive discharge, violates Section 8(a)(3) just as if the employer had discharged the employee outright. Consider an employee who has worked for a company for many years without a problem, but as soon as the employee becomes active in the union's organizing campaign he finds that he can no longer do anything right. The employer begins to watch the employee's work closely whereas he previously was rarely watched. The employee's work is constantly corrected; when anything goes wrong, the employee is blamed; he is forbidden to talk to other employees. Finally, after being severely rebuked for a minor mistake, the employee quits in disgust. Forcing

the employee to the point of resignation in this manner is a constructive discharge violating 8(a)(3), the same as discharging the employee.

6. Back Pay Remedies for 8(a)(3) Violations

An employee who has been discharged or otherwise discriminated against in violation of Section 8(a)(3) (such as the discriminatory denial of overtime or transfer to a lower paying job) is entitled to back pay for the monetary loss. In the case of a discharged employee, the Board uses a quarterly system to determine the amount owed the employee. An employee's earnings each quarter after the discharge are subtracted from the amount the employee would have earned in that quarter had he not been discharged. The back pay owed per quarter is the difference between what the employee actually earned and what he would have earned if not discharged.

The Board uses the quarterly system rather than basing back pay on the total difference between what an employee earned the entire time after his discharge and what he would have earned but for his discharge, so that an employee fortunate enough to obtain a higher paying job toward the end of a long unemployment period does not end up with little or no back pay. The large amount received toward the end might balance the total amount the employee would have earned. Yet, the amount earned after months of unemployment realistically cannot make up for the employee's struggle to get by with no income. The Board has determined that the quarter system is a better measure of the employee's true loss than simply subtracting total interim earnings from what the employee would have earned during the same period if he had not been discharged.

The Board also awards interest on back pay owed. At one time interest was fixed at 6 percent. However, the Board now uses the current Internal Revenue Service interest rate as the interest rate on a Board award. The IRS interest rate fluctuates with the prevailing rate of interest in the economy and thus better reflects inflationary costs than the Board's old 6 percent rule.

A discharged employee cannot sit back without looking for work, counting on quarterly back pay. The Board requires that employees actively look for and be available for work. An employee who goes back to school full-time and is not looking for work, or an employee who goes on an extended vacation, does not receive back pay for those periods. The amount of back pay due under a Board's decision, if disputed, is determined in compliance procedures (see Chapter 2).

7. Super Seniority for Shop Stewards and Union Officers

Questions have been raised about whether granting super seniority to shop stewards violates Sections 8(a)(3) and 8(b)(1) of the Act. Super seniority means that a shop steward has first seniority preference for certain purposes based on his steward position rather than his actual years of service. It has been argued that granting stewards super seniority encourages union members to be "good union members" so that they will be appointed or elected stewards and that granting stewards super seniority is therefore unlawful discrimination against other employees.

Job Selection Preference

In considering this issue, the Board has concluded that super seniority clauses are lawful if their purpose is to ensure that stewards are retained at work or on a job to en-

force the contract and represent employees. Such job retention super seniority clauses can include super seniority to stewards for purposes of layoff, recall, shift assignment, or retention of the same job or same job category while a steward. The Board has upheld super seniority clauses that grant stewards preference for overtime on the grounds that a steward must be present to ensure compliance with the contract during overtime work.

The Board has also approved construction industry contract clauses under which unions have the right to appoint a shop steward to work as an employee on a given job. Some employers argued that such clauses permit the union to send union favorites out on the best jobs. The employers argued that the union should be required to appoint a steward from among the employees the contractor has hired and not be permitted to select a steward sent directly from the union. The Board rejected the employer's arguments, reasoning that a union is entitled to ensure the presence of a steward who will enforce the contract and not be concerned with employer retaliation.

The Board has also upheld super seniority clauses granting privileges to other union officers involved in bargaining, grievance administration, or the effective administration of the contract. That includes executive board members who take no direct part in bargaining, but who are involved in overall administration and the determination of union policies.

Other Contract Benefits

The Board has held that it is presumptively unlawful to grant super seniority for contractual benefits unrelated to keeping a steward on the job, such as shop steward preference for vacations or promotions. Granting super seniority for these benefits does not aid the shop steward or other union officers in performing their contractual duties. Giving stewards this type of preference might unlawfully encourage employees to be "good union members" so that they will be selected as stewards. These broader super seniority clauses are only presumptively unlawful. If a union can prove a valid reason for granting additional special privileges to a steward, the Board might uphold them. If a contract gives vacation preference to stewards, a union might be able to argue that the stewards needed vacation preference to ensure that a steward was always at work during the vacation period. Although this type of clause would presumptively be unlawful under the Board's reasoning, the union might be able to overcome the presumption by proving the need. On the other hand, a very broad super seniority clause granting super seniority "for all purposes" undoubtedly would be invalid.

8. Plant Closings as a Section 8(a)(1) or 8(a)(3) Violation

One of the most important cases applying Sections 8(a)(1) and 8(a)(3) is the Supreme Court decision in *Darlington Mfg. Co.*[4] The Darlington Company, a single factory, was a subsidiary of a company that operated many other mills. The Textile Workers Union won an organizing election, and, six days later, the board of directors voted to close the plant permanently. The plant ceased operations soon thereafter. The Supreme Court upheld the NLRB's decision that the shutdown violated Section 8(a)(3) of the Act.

The *Darlington* decision contains a number of important principles. First, the Supreme Court emphasized that Darlington was part of a larger corporate structure. The Court held that a single employer can go out of business

[4] See legal principle 1.

for any reason, including a desire not to be unionized. The Court said that this was an absolute right. However, the decision to close must be permanent. The Court stated that an employer cannot threaten in advance to shut down if a union wins an election or state that it will reopen the plant if the employees abandon the union. Leaving open the possibility that the plant will remain open would put pressure on the employees in violation of Section 8(a)(1).

Is closing a plant a violation of Sections 8(a)(1), 8(a)(3), or both? The Supreme Court held that a plant closing could violate the Act only if the closing was intended to discourage union activities at another one of the employer's plants that remained open. The Court reasoned that closing a plant is such a basic employer right that discriminatory intent must be proven. Closing a plant cannot be unlawful just because the natural consequence is to undermine a union. As discussed above, an act may violate Section 8(a)(1) if it is inherently destructive of employee rights regardless of intent. Section 8(a)(3) violations require proof of discriminatory intent. Since the Court requires a finding of intent for a plant closure to be unlawful, a closing is unlawful only if it violates Section 8(a)(3).

The Darlington Company violated Section 8(a)(3) only because it was part of a larger corporation and the employees at the other plants might be discouraged from union activity because of the discriminatory closure. Even though Darlington was part of a larger company, the plant could still have been closed down permanently except for the discriminatory intent. Otherwise, even the right to shut down a single plant in a multi-plant chain is absolute. The Court said in this regard:

The closing of an entire business, even though discriminatory, ends the employer-employee relationship; the force of such a closing is entirely spent as to that business when termination of the enterprise takes place. On the other hand, a discriminatory partial closing may have repercussions on what remains of the business, affording the employer leverage for discouraging the free exercise of Section 7 rights among remaining employees of much the same kind as that found to exist in the 'run-away shop' and 'temporary closing' cases.

The Court also set down the test for determining when a partial closing violates Section 8(a)(3), stating:

> While we have spoken in terms of a "partial closing" in the context of the Board's finding that Darlington was part of a larger single enterprise controlled by the Milliken family, we do not mean to suggest that an organizational integration of plants or corporations is a necessary prerequisite to the establishment of such a violation of Section 8(a)(3). If the persons exercising control over a plant that is being closed for anti-union reasons (1) have an interest in another business, whether or not affiliated with or engaged in the same line of commercial activity as the closed plant, of sufficient substantiality to give a promise of their reaping a benefit from the discouragement of unionization in that business; (2) act to close their plant with the purpose of producing such a result; and (3) occupy a relationship to the other business which makes it realistically foreseeable that its employees will fear that such business will also be closed down if they persist in organization activities, we think that an unfair labor practice has been made out.

Note that the Supreme Court does not require a formal tie between two businesses. If the same person were the majority stockholder in two independent corporations, closing one of the two corporations for anti-union reasons might violate Section 8(a)(3), if it could be proven that the majority stockholder could reap a benefit at the remaining plant by

closing the other. If the employees at the remaining plant have no knowledge of the common ownership, closing one plant does not violate Section 8(a)(3) under *Darlington*, because it is not realistically foreseeable that closing one plant will affect the employees at the remaining plant.

Remedies for Plant Closings or Transfers

An employer violates both Sections 8(a)(1) and (3) by transferring a plant to a new location in retaliation for the employees' exercise of their right to collective bargaining. A common example is that of an employer who closes a plant and reopens at a new location after its employees vote in a union. A plant transfer for discriminatory reasons is similar to the partial plant closing prohibited by the *Darlington* decision, and the remedies are similar.

The Board has broad power to remedy either the unlawful closing or transfer of a plant. It can require back pay for the employees and can order a plant reopened at its first location. However, if the costs of reopening are too excessive, the Board does not require reopening. The Board may order the employer to offer the terminated employees employment at the remaining plant or, in the case of a run-away shop, at the new location.

The employer may be required to pay employees their travel and relocation expenses and grant the employees seniority rights at their new location based on their original date of employment at the prior location. If relocation is not practical, the Board may require the employer to pay employees until the date they obtain substantially equivalent employment. If an employer can prove that it would have legitimately closed down by a certain date, the Board may limit the employees' back pay to the date the plant would have lawfully closed. The Board may also order the employer to recognize and bargain with the old union at the new location.

E. PROTECTION FOR TESTIFYING IN BOARD PROCEEDINGS

One other important employee protection is afforded by Section 8(a)(4) that prohibits an employer from discharging or otherwise discriminating against an employee because he has filed charges or given testimony under the Act. The Board has broadly applied this section to include protection for giving an affidavit in the course of a Board investigation even if the employee does not actually testify. No specific section of the Act prohibits a union from disciplining employees who testify, but the Board has held that a union violates Section 8(b)(1)(A) if it disciplines an employee for filing charges or testifying at a Board proceeding (see Chapter 11). The Board reasons that this conduct interferes with an employee's right to engage in or refrain from concerted activity, protected under Section 7.

Recall the discussion of Board bargaining orders based upon employer unfair labor practices under the *Gissel* case (see Chapter 3). Violations of Sections 8(a)(1) and 8(a)(3), if occurring during an election campaign, are the types of unlawful conduct upon which the Board may base a bargaining order, provided the total impact is sufficient under the *Gissel* criteria.

Summary

This chapter considered a union's authority as the bargaining representative after it obtains bargaining rights, either through a Board-conducted election, voluntary recognition, or a bargaining order. It also considered the employees' rights to engage in collective bargaining activities through their union and how those rights are protected.

Once a union either is recognized voluntarily or certified as the bargaining agent by the NLRB, it has the right of exclusive representation. This means that the employer cannot deal with any other employee representative on wages, hours, or other terms and conditions of employment. There is an exception under which any employee or group of employees has the right at any time "to present grievances to their employer and to have such grievances adjusted without intervention of the bargaining representative." However, the Supreme Court has interpreted this exception very narrowly, ruling that employees may contact their employer outside the grievance procedure, but the employer is not obligated to deal directly with them.

A union must independently represent the views of the employees. It is an unfair labor practice for an employer to dominate or interfere with the formation or administration of a union or to contribute financial or other support to it. If an employer dominates a union, the union will be disestablished. If an employer simply assists a union, but does not dominate it, the union will be decertified and the employer will be ordered to cease the conduct constituting unlawful assistance.

Under the *Midwest Piping Doctrine*, an employer cannot recognize one union when a real question of representation exists in the bargaining unit unless the rival union's claim is clearly unsupported and lacking in substance.

The Labor Management Relations Act not only protects the union as an entity, through the doctrine of exclusive representation, but also protects the right of each employee under Section 7 to engage in concerted activity or to refrain from such activity. It is an unfair labor practice for either an employer or a union to interfere with, restrain, or coerce employees in their rights.

One of the basic employee rights under Section 7, protected by Section 8(a)(1), is that an employee, upon request, may have the shop steward present if called to meet with the employer for the purpose of discipline. The rights to protest working conditions, including safety matters; protest contract violations; or file grievances are also protected by Sections 7 and 8(a)(1).

Section 8(a)(3) prohibits discrimination because of union activity in hiring, tenure, or conditions of employment. This prohibits conduct such as discharging an employee because of union activity, denying a promotion, denying or reducing an employee's benefits, giving an employee more difficult work to do, or working an employee under less favorable conditions than other employees.

In contrast, an employer's actions may violate Section 8(a)(1), regardless of the intent, if the employer's actions are inherently destructive of employee rights. The discharge of an economic striker, rather than his replacement, is an example of a Section 8(a)(1) violation regardless of intent.

An employee's discharge, based even in part on union activities, is unlawful. Also, a reason for discharge that would otherwise be valid may be unlawful under Section 8(a)(3) if it is used as a pretext to discharge an employee for union activities.

The Supreme Court decision in *Darlington Mfg. Co.* is one of the most important cases on the application of Sections 8(a)(1) and 8(a)(3). The Court held that a plant closing violates the Act only if it is closed with the intent of discouraging union activities at another one of the employer's plants that remains open. The Court reasoned that closing a plant is such a basic employer right that intent has to be proven. Thus, in order for a plant closure to be unlawful, it must violate Section 8(a)(3).

Another important employee protection is afforded by Section 8(a)(4), which prohibits an employer from discharging or otherwise discriminating against an employee because he has filed charges or given testimony under the Act. The Board has broadly applied this section to include protection covering affidavits given during a Board investigation even if the employee does not actually testify.

Review
Questions

1. What rights do employees who are not in a union have to engage in concerted activity?

2. What is the right of exclusive representation?

3. What evidence is needed to prove an employer's intent to discriminate in violation of Section 8(a)(3)?

4. Can an employer express an opinion favoring one union over another?

5. What is the purpose of the Section 8(a)(2) restrictions against employer financial assistance?

6. Can a shop steward be disciplined for insubordinate remarks to the employer during a grievance meeting?

7. Can a contract provide super seniority for shop stewards for purposes of layoff and overtime preference?

8. What is the statutory exception to the rule against an employer entering into a premature or pre-hire agreement with a union?

9. Is an employee protesting an employer's contract violation by himself engaged in concerted activity?

10. When can an employee request to have his shop steward present at a meeting with the employer?

11. What options does an employer have if an employee requests a steward based on a reasonable belief that he faces discipline?

12. Under what circumstances may a discharge be unlawful under Section 8(a)(3) although the employer presents an apparently bona fide reason for his action?

(Answers to review questions appear at end of book.)

Basic Legal
Principles

1. An inherently destructive act, such as discharging economic strikers, violates Section 8(a)(1) of the Act, regardless of the employer's motive. *NLRB v. Erie Resister Corp.*, 373 U.S. 221, 53 LRRM 2121 (1963); compare *Textile Workers v. Darlington Mfg. Co.*, 380 U.S. 263, 58 LRRM 2657 (1965) (specific intent violating Section 8(a)(3) required in case of plant closing).

2. An employer violates Section 8(a)(2) if it voluntarily recognizes one of two competing unions at a time when there is a "real question of representation in the unit." A rival claim that is clearly unsupportable or specious does not raise a real question of representation. *Midwest Piping and Supply Co.*, 63 NLRB 1060, 17 LRRM 40 (1945); *Buck Knives, Inc.*, 223 NLRB No. 144, 92 LRRM 1017 (1976).

3. If an employer unlawfully assists a union, the Board will order the employer to cease recognizing the assisted union and to cease giving effect to any contract between the employer and the union until the union is certified through an election. *Spiegel Trucking Co.*, 225 NLRB No. 26, 92 LRRM 1604 (1976); *Wintex Knitting Mill, Inc., Newport Division*, 223 NLRB No. 195, 92 LRRM 1113 (1976).

4. Discipline of employees for engaging in unprotected concerted activity does not violate Section 8(a)(3). Concerted efforts by minority groups to bargain directly with their employer are not protected activity if the employees are represented by an exclusive bargaining representative. *Emporium Capwell Co. v. WACO*, 420 U.S. 50, 88 LRRM 2660 (1975).

5. Protesting working conditions, unsafe conditions, contract violations or filing grievances are all concerted activities protected by Section 7 and 8(a)(1). An employee protesting a contract violation that affects only himself is still engaged in concerted activity because the employee is upholding the right of all employees to have their contract followed. *Roadway Express, Inc.*, 217 NLRB No. 49, 88 LRRM 1503 (1975); *Alleluia Cushion*, 221 NLRB No. 162, 91 LRRM 1131 (1975).

6. An employee, upon request, is entitled to have a shop steward present at a meeting with the employer if the investigation is focused on the employee and the employee reasonably believes that he may be facing discipline. *NLRB v. J. Weingarten, Inc.*, 420 U.S. 251, 88 LRRM 2689 (1975); *Amoco Oil Co.*, 238 NLRB No. 84, 99 LRRM 1250 (1978). See also *Union Fork & Hoe Co.*, 241 NLRB No. 140, 101 LRRM 1014 (1979); (protection of steward in processing grievances).

7. The employee and the steward are entitled to meet in private for a reasonable period before the disciplinary meeting with the employer. *Amax, Inc.*, 227 NLRB No. 154, 94 LRRM 1177 (1977); *Coca Cola Bottling Co.*, 227 NLRB No. 173, 94 LRRM 1200 (1977).

8. Section 8(a)(3) requires that discrimination be with the intent to encourage or discourage union membership. The intent can be inferred if an act has the foreseeable consequences of either encouraging or discouraging union membership or being a "good" union member. *Radio Officers Union v. NLRB*, 347 U.S. 1733 LRRM 2417 (1954); *Universal Mobile Homes*, 210 NLRB No. 115, 86 LRRM 1417 (1974); *Rogers Furniture Sale, Inc.*, 207 NLRB No. 7, 84 LRRM 1643 (1973).

9. A discharge is unlawful under Section 8(a)(3) if it is in part for union activity or if a bona fide reason is a pretext for discharging the employee because of union activities. *Coca-Cola Bottling Co.*, 232 NLRB No. 125, 97 LRRM 1290 (1977); *Tuscola Truckers' Home, Inc.*, 233 NLRB No. 97, 97 LRRM 1302 (1977).

10. Contract clauses granting super seniority to shop stewards or for other union officers are lawful if their purpose is to ensure that union officials are retained at work or in a job to enforce a contract and represent employees. Granting super seniority for all contractual benefits, including those unrelated to job security, would be unlawful discrimination. *Dairylea Cooperative, Inc.*, 219 NLRB No. 107, 89 LRRM 1737 (1975); *Auto Warehouses, Inc.*, 227 NLRB No. 100, 94 LRRM 1445 (1976); *Painters Dist. Council 2*, 239 NLRB No. 192, 100 LRRM 1152 (1979); *Painters Local 1555*, 241 NLRB No. 112, 100 LRRM 1578 (1979); *A.P.A. Transport Corp.*, 239 NLRB No. 165, 100 LRRM 1165 (1979).

Cabot, Jarin, "Third Circuit's New Standard for Strike Misconduct Discharges: NLRB v. W. C. McQuaide, Inc," 23 *Vill. L. Rev.* 645 (1978).

"Intent, Effect, Purpose, and Motive as Applicable Elements to Section 8(a)(1) and Section 8(a)(3) Violations of the National Labor Relations Act," 7 *Wake Forest L. Rev.* 616 (1971).

Schatzki, "Majority Rule, Exclusive Representation, and the Interest of Individual Workers: Should Exclusivity Be Abolished," 123 *U. Pa. L. Rev.* 897 (1975).

Suggested Readings

Chapter Five

The Duty to Bargain

The ultimate purpose of a union is the successful negotiation and administration of a collective bargaining agreement. This chapter discusses the legal principles governing the collective bargaining process.

The duty to bargain is governed by Sections 8(a)(5), 8(b)(3), and 8(d). It is an unfair labor practice under Section 8(a)(5) for an employer to refuse to bargain collectively with the representative of its employees. Section 8(b)(3) makes it an unfair labor practice for a union to refuse to bargain collectively with an employer whose employees it represents.

Section 8(d) defines the duty to bargain, described as the mutual obligation of the employer and the union to meet at reasonable times and confer in good faith over wages, hours, and other terms and conditions of employment. The duty includes the negotiation of an agreement or any question arising under the agreement. The parties are required to execute a written contract incorporating any agreement reached if requested by either party. Section 8(d) further provides, however, that the duty to bargain does not compel either party to agree to a proposal or make a concession. The duty to bargain exists before and during the negotiation of a collective bargaining agreement, during the administration of the agreement, and upon expiration.

A. INCEPTION AND DURATION OF THE BARGAINING OBLIGATION

1. Bargaining Before a Contract is Negotiated

An employer's obligation to recognize and bargain with a union under Section 8(a)(5) may result from certification of a union by the Board following a representation election, a bargaining order issued under *Gissel* principles (see Chapter 3), or voluntary recognition.

Sometimes an employer and union with an established bargaining relationship contractually agree that the employer will voluntarily recognize the union as the collective bargaining representative at any new facility the employer opens. This agreement is binding on the employer. However, the Board has held that the union must produce evidence of its majority status at the new facility through signed recognition cards before the employer can extend voluntary recognition. The duration of an employer's bargaining duty depends upon whether the union has been certified by the Board or voluntarily recognized.

a. The Effect of Board Certification

If the union has been certified by the National Labor Relations Board, the employer is obligated under Section 8(a)(5) to bargain with it for a full year following certification. The Board says that there is an irrebuttable presumption that a union has majority status for the year. The one year rule also applies to bargaining pursuant to a *Gissel* bargaining order (see Chapter 3). A union is entitled to a full year of good faith bargaining. If an employer fails to bargain in good faith during the certification year, and the Board issues an order requiring the employer to bargain, the employer must bargain in good faith with the union for a full year after the order is entered, even though more than one year has passed since certification.

After one year, there is a rebuttable presumption that the certified union still represents a majority of the employees. However, if the parties have not negotiated a contract after one year of good faith bargaining, the employer may withdraw recognition if he has a good faith doubt based on objective considerations that the union no longer has majority status.

b. Effect of Voluntary Recognition

If the employer has voluntarily recognized a union, he is obligated to bargain with the union for "a reasonable period of time." If no contract is agreed to after a reasonable period, the employer may withdraw recognition if he has a good faith doubt based on objective considerations that the union no longer represents a majority.

There is no definite period during which an employer must bargain with a union that has been voluntarily recognized. In some cases, the Board has held that a reasonable period is the twelve months required for bargaining with a certified union. However, the Board has upheld the right of an employer to terminate recognition after bargaining with a union for only three months.

2. The Basis For Withdrawing Recognition

a. Effect of a Decertification Petition

The Board has held that if employees file a timely decertification petition (see Chapter 2), the employer may cease bargaining for a contract with the incumbent union until the decertification issues are resolved. This is similar to the rule that an employer and union must cease bargaining if another union files a timely representation petition raising a question of representation (see Chapter 4).

The filing of a decertification petition does not relieve an employer of its bargaining obligation if the employer supports or instigates the decertification petition, or if the employer's unfair labor practices or bad faith bargaining undermined the union's majority status. An employee's decision to file a decertification petition cannot be coerced or supported by unlawful employer action. Such employer conduct violates Sections 8(a)(1) and (5).

Although the filing of a lawful decertification petition terminates the duty to bargain for a new agreement, the incumbent union and employer can continue to administer the existing contract, if any, and adjust grievances. The status quo bargaining relationship can be maintained even though no new agreement can be executed until the decertification petition issues are resolved.

The Board has voted three to two that a decertification petition is grounds for an employer to refuse to bargain. The dissenters argue that a decertification petition is only evidence that at least 30 percent of the employees no longer wish the union to represent them, not that the union has lost majority support. The dissenters would require other evidence of lost support besides the petition before an employer can refuse to bargain. Otherwise, the dissenters would require the employer to continue bargaining until the union is, in fact, decertified. Because of the narrow split on this question and possible changes in Board membership, the law is subject to change in this area.

b. Employer's Good Faith Doubt of Majority Status

An employer may also withdraw recognition at the end of the certification year or after a reasonable period of voluntary recognition if he has a good faith doubt that the union represents a majority of the employees. Again, the employer cannot withdraw recognition if the employer's own unlawful acts lead to the union's loss of majority support. An uncoerced petition signed by a majority of the employees and given to the employer stating that the employees no longer wish to be represented by the union is one example of evidence that the union has lost majority status.

Evidence that employees are dissatisfied with the union is not sufficient proof that the union no longer represents a majority of the work force. That employees cease paying union dues and cancel their check-off authorizations is not sufficient proof of lost majority status because the union represents all employees whether they are members or not. A large turnover in the employee work force does not constitute loss of majority status because the new employees are presumed to support the union in the same ratio as the former employees. Similarly, because an employer replaces striking employees who are union members with nonunion replacements does not indicate a loss in the union's majority status. It is again presumed that the union represents the replacement employees as well as the strikers. A deauthorization election in which the employees revoke the union security clause of their contract is not evidence of lost majority status, only an indication that the employees do not wish union membership to be compulsory. That a majority of the employees abandon a strike and return to work also is not necessarily evidence that the employees do not want the union to represent them. Although none of the factors listed above conclusively establishes that the union has lost its majority status, combined they can be the basis of an employer's good faith doubt to withdraw recognition. The Board considers each case on its specific facts.

A decertification petition only relieves the employer of an obligation to bargain with the union for a new agreement. The employer may still be required to bargain with the union over routine matters and grievances to maintain the status quo relationship. If the employer has a good faith doubt based on objective consideration that the union has lost majority support the employer may withdraw recognition completely provided no contract is in effect.

3. Withdrawal of Recognition During The Contract's Term

There is a presumption that a union continues to represent a majority of the employees for the duration of a contract. Except in very rare circumstances, an employer cannot withdraw recognition during the contract term. That is true even if a majority of the employees were to sign a petition that they no longer wanted the union to represent them.

Mailing a notice is sufficient if the notice is mailed in time to be received on the required date in the normal course of the mails.

b. The Strike/Lockout Ban During the Notice Period

Section 8(d) prohibits either party from engaging in a strike or lockout until the expiration of the notice periods or the expiration of the contract, whichever comes later. If either party gives the proper notices, both parties are free to engage in a strike or lockout at the termination of the notice period. Thus, if a union gives a 60 and 30 days notice, the employer can engage in a lockout. If the employer gives proper notices, the union can strike at the end of the notice period even though it has not given notice.

The notice requirements apply to midterm modification of a contract, such as a wage reopener, as well as to the contract's expiration. However, the Supreme Court has held that the notice requirements do not apply to unfair labor practice strikes. Thus, a union can strike immediately, even during the term of a collective bargaining agreement, if an employer has committed serious unfair labor practices (see Chapter 6).

Section 8(d) carries severe penalties for failure to comply with the notice requirements. An employee who strikes before the expiration of the notice periods loses his status as an employee of the employer under the Act unless he is rehired. What does this mean? Normally, an economic striker can be replaced by another employee, but not discharged. If a strike occurs before the expiration of either the 60 or 30 day notice period, the employee can be discharged and lose his reinstatement rights. The employer can lawfully discharge union supporters, while keeping other employees, because the strikers are not considered employees protected by the Act.

c. Consequences of Late Notice

A union does not forfeit the right to strike forever by failing to meet the notice requirements. It can give the notice late and strike after waiting the appropriate period. For instance, suppose a union gives proper notice to the employer by the sixtieth day, but forgets to give 30 days notice to the FMCS. If the union strikes without giving notice to the FMCS, it violates Section 8(d) and the striking employees will lose their employee status. However, if the union realizes its mistake and gives late notice to the FMCS, the union can strike 30 days after giving the notice.

d. Statutory Versus Contractual Notice Requirements

The Section 8(d) notice requirements must be distinguished from contractual notice requirements. Contracts frequently provide for automatic renewal for another year unless either party serves notice on the other to modify or terminate the agreement. If a union fails to give the contractual notice on time, the contract renews itself and remains in effect in accordance with its terms. The employer has no duty to bargain for a new agreement during the renewal period. For example, what if a contract provides for automatic renewal unless a termination notice is sent at least 60 days before the expiration date? A union sends the employer a notice to terminate the contract on the fifty-ninth day. Technically, the union can still meet the requirements of Section 8(d) by waiting the full 60 days to strike after giving the late notice. However, because of the lateness of the notice, the contract renews itself for another year and the employer has no obligation to bargain. If the contract contains a no-strike clause, the union cannot strike even though the statutory notices have been given.

Failure to give the statutory notices has no effect on the contract's expiration—only upon the right to strike. Thus, if a contract has a fixed termination date and no provision for automatic renewal, the contract expires by its terms even if the statutory notices are not given.

2. Selection of the Bargaining Committee

Both the union and the employer have the absolute right to choose their respective bargaining committees. Neither party can refuse to bargain because they disapprove of someone on the other's bargaining committee.

Coordinated and Coalition Bargaining

The union's right to choose its own bargaining committee is used by unions to engage in coordinated or coalition bargaining among several unions representing separate bargaining units of the same employer. Since unions can select their own bargaining committees, one union can have representatives from other unions sitting in on the bargaining as part of the contracting union's bargaining committtee. Under Section 8(a)(5), it is unlawful for an employer to refuse to meet with a bargaining committee that includes members from another bargaining unit.

There is, however, one limitation. An employer can insist that bargaining be limited to the bargaining issues between the employer and the contracting union. The employer can refuse to discuss any issues pertaining to the other bargaining units even though the employer cannot prevent other unions from being present. The employer has the right to negotiate each contract separately. Thus, if one of the other unions raises an issue pertaining to its contract, the employer can break off bargaining or refuse to discuss the issue. The employer can, of course, voluntarily agree to true coalition bargaining in which all the unions simultaneously negotiate with the employer.

3. The Good Faith Concept

a. Intent to Reach an Agreement

The LMRA does not require an employer and union to agree to the terms of a collective bargaining agreement. A party's only obligation is to bargain in good faith with an intent to reach an agreement. If an agreement is reached, either party may require that it be written and executed.

The law does not regulate the contents of an agreement, only the bargaining process. Each side in the bargaining process naturally wants to get the best contract it can for itself. The law does not require either party to be "fair" or to compromise its position to reach an agreement. Section 8(d) specifically states that neither party can be required to agree to a proposal or make a concession. A party may lawfully bargain for the most favorable agreement possible. An employer whose bargaining power is stronger than the union's can use that power to get a better agreement, so long as the employer intends to reach an agreement. Similarly, a union whose bargaining power is greater than the employer's can use its power to negotiate an agreement more favorable to it.

b. The Bargaining Impasse

Although both the employer and the union may bargain in good faith and intend to reach an agreement, they may eventually reach a good faith deadlock on an issue. A good faith deadlock is a bargaining impasse. The parties may move on to other issues or break off bargaining altogether at that point. The duty to bargain includes the duty to meet at reasonable times and places. But either an employer or a union can refuse to meet if a bargaining impasse has been reached and neither side is willing to change its position. That is not bad faith bargaining.

However, if an impasse is broken by a change in the position of either party, or by a change in circumstances, the parties are once again obligated to meet at the request of either side. The Board frequently regards a strike following an impasse as a changed circumstance. Thus, if an employer breaks off negotiations before a strike begins, the employer may be required to begin bargaining again if the the employees strike.

There is no set amount of time before the parties can reach an impasse. In theory, the parties could reach an impasse after a few minutes of bargaining on a particular matter. That, however, would be unusual. If the parties bargained with the intent to reach an agreement and they are deadlocked, there is an impasse regardless of the time taken to reach that point.

c. Surface Bargaining: The Totality of Conduct Doctrine

If an employer simply refuses to meet with a union to negotiate an agreement, the employer is obviously not bargaining in good faith as required by Section 8(a)(5). Most employers, however, are more sophisticated than that. An employer who meets with the union, but only goes through the motions of bargaining with no intent to reach an agreement is using the tactic called "surface bargaining."

How does the Board distinguish an employer who is engaging in hard bargaining, which is legal, from one that is bargaining in bad faith? No single factor determines whether an employer or a union are bargaining in good faith with an intent to reach an agreement. Good faith is judged on the totality of a party's conduct. There are, however, certain acts that are usually considered evidence of bad faith bargaining. These include: agreeing on minor bargaining issues, but refusing to give in on any major point (such as agreeing to general contract language but maintaining a fixed position on all major economic issues); refusing to agree to provisions found in most collective bargaining agreements (such as a just cause clause or seniority provision); proposing wages and benefits that are no better than those under the prior contract or before the union was certified; rejecting union proposals without making any counter proposals or indicating why the union's proposals are unacceptable; and delaying meetings.

No one factor is controlling. An employer, for example, may have perfectly legitimate reasons for refusing to have any seniority provisions in a contract or for not offering any wage increase. Whether an employer is engaged in surface bargaining is a matter of overall intent. All factors are considered, including whether the employer has displayed hostility toward the union or engaged in coercive activities.

Some employees erroneously believe that an employer's refusal to agree to a union security clause requiring union membership after 30 days of employment (see Chapter 10) is bad faith bargaining. That is not so. An employer may legitimately reject proposals for a union security clause or engage in hard bargaining to require that a union make some major concession to obtain a union security clause. However, failure to agree to a union security clause may be one factor among the others in judging the totality of the employer's conduct.

d. Circumventing the Union

An employer violates the duty to bargain under Section 8(a)(5) if he attempts to go around the union during bargaining and deal directly with the employees on their terms and conditions of employment. An employer can lawfully keep its employees informed concerning the employer's bargaining position, the reason for its positions, and bargaining progress. The employer cannot, however, make an offer to the employees that it has not made to the union or attempt to undermine the union's bargaining position.

e. Take It or Leave It Bargaining: Boulwareism

Can an employer adopt a "take it or leave it" attitude on its bargaining proposals, a technique frequently referred to as "Boulwareism"? Boulware was the personnel director for General Electric and developed the technique bearing his name. Under this approach, the company did extensive preliminary research on its bargaining position. Based upon all its research and the union's proposals, the Company devised what it regarded as a "fair but firm offer," which it then presented to the union. The company listened to whatever counter proposals the union made, explained its reasons for rejecting them, but would not change its position.

The Board held that this technique was unlawful, but for a very narrow reason. The company not only held to a rigid position at the bargaining table, but also circumvented the union through a widespread publicity campaign to convince the employees that the company's offer was best. The company disparaged the union in its literature. The Board held that it was unlawful for the company to

make it appear that union representation was futile by acting as if there were no union at all. Thus, the company's conduct was in bad faith because the totality of its conduct, not just the one technique, indicated that it had no true intent to bargain.

Section 8(d) provides that neither party can be required to reach an agreement or make a concession. Therefore, bargaining techniques close to Boulwareism are lawful, as long as the employer's other conduct does not indicate he has no intention of reaching an agreement.

f. Tentative Agreements

During bargaining, either side has the right to keep all agreements tentative until a complete agreement is reached. It is not necessarily bad faith bargaining for either an employer or a union to change position on an item previously agreed to. The Board permits the parties to retract tentative agreements because it understands that a party may agree to particular contract language or certain benefits during bargaining on the assumption that the overall agreement will be acceptable or that it will win some concession from the other side. If the entire agreement falls short of expectations, a party has the right to revise its total proposal. However, it may be evidence of bad faith if a party puts issues already agreed to back on the bargaining table at the last moment without any reason.

g. Ratification Procedures

Both the employer and the union may condition agreements reached at the bargaining table on higher approval. Thus, the union negotiators can reach an agreement contingent on membership ratification. The employer negotiators can make their agreement contingent on approval by higher management or the board of directors. However the employer's representative must have sufficient authority to conduct meaningful negotiations for a tentative agreement. It is bad faith bargaining if the negotiator has to check continually with someone else who is not present on every major point.

It is assumed that both the employer and the union negotiators have full authority to reach a binding agreement on their own. If a negotiator's agreements are subject to approval, he must advise the other party of this restriction at the beginning of negotiations. If a negotiator does not indicate the limits of his authority, a party may be bound by an agreement the negotiator reaches even though he exceeded his authority. Neither the employer nor the union is bound by the internal ratification procedures of the other unless it has notice of them or there is a past practice of ratification. For example, if a union's by-laws require that contracts be ratified, but the union's bargaining committee does not tell the employer about this requirement, the union is bound by an agreement the committee reached even though it went beyond its authority.

h. Economic Force During Bargaining

The Supreme Court held in the *Insurance Agents*[1] case that economic pressure is not inconsistent with good faith bargaining. In *Insurance Agents*, the union engaged in a work slowdown. The members refused to fill out paper work, reported to work late and left early, and engaged in other harassing tactics to pressure the employer into accepting the union's bargaining position. The Court held that it was not bad faith bargaining for the union to use economic pressure to force the other party to concede. It stated that economic power has a legitimate role in the bargaining process, that:

[1] See legal principle 1–B.

It must be realized that collective bargaining, under a system where the Government does not attempt to control the results of negotiations cannot be equated with an academic collective search for truth—or even with what might be thought to be the ideal of one. The parties—even granting the modification of views that may come from a realization of economic interdependence—still proceed from contrary and to an extent antagonistic viewpoints and concepts of self-interest. The system has not reached the ideal of the philosophic notion that perfect understanding among people would lead to perfect agreement among them on values. The presence of economic weapons in reserve, and their actual exercise on occasion by the parties, is part and parcel of the system that the Wagner and Taft-Hartley Acts have recognized. . . . [A]t the present statutory stage of our national labor relations policy, the two factors— necessity for good-faith bargaining between parties, and the availability of economic pressure devices to each to make the other party inclined to agree on one's terms—exist side by side.

Thus, a union has the right to strike or engage in other concerted activity to support its bargaining position. Similarly, the employer has the right to lock out employees in support of its position.

There is a common misunderstanding that a union can only strike if negotiations have reached an impasse following good faith bargaining. That is not so. As long as a no-strike clause is not in effect, a union has the right to strike at any time to force an agreement, even though bargaining is still going on and the parties are not deadlocked. Under the *Insurance Agents'* decision, economic force is not inconsistent with a good faith intent to reach an agreement, although the agreement sought is one favorable to the union.

i. Union Bad Faith Bargaining

Although the emphasis has been on employer conduct constituting bad faith bargaining, a union can also be guilty of bad faith bargaining. Suppose a union has a master contract with a multi-employer association that the union wants other smaller independent employers in the same industry to sign. An independent employer suggests a change in the master agreement, but the union insists that all employers sign the same agreement without the change. That may be bad faith bargaining because the union has no intention of engaging in the give and take of bargaining with the employer, just as an employer using Boulwareism tactics has no intention of engaging in true bargaining with a union.

C. SUBJECTS FOR BARGAINING

1. Classification of Bargaining Subjects

The Board has divided the subjects for bargaining into three categories: mandatory, permissive, and unlawful subjects for bargaining. Each category has a different bargaining obligation.

The mandatory subjects for bargaining are those listed in Section 8(d) of the Act: wages, hours, and other terms and conditions of employment. The parties have a duty to bargain over mandatory subjects at the request of either party. The parties may bargain to impasse and engage in a strike or lockout over mandatory subjects.

Permissive subjects do not relate directly to wages, hours, and working conditions, but are discussed voluntarily. One party may request bargaining on a permissive subject, but the other party may lawfully refuse to bargain over it. The party may bargain about a permissive subject at first, then unilaterally decide to stop. That is lawful because there is no duty to bargain over permissive subjects. The parties may not bargain to impasse,

strike, or lockout over a permissive subject. Thus, if the parties have reached an agreement on all mandatory subjects on which they are bargaining, they must sign a contract incorporating their agreement. A party cannot refuse to sign because agreement was not reached on a permissive subject. If agreement is reached on a permissive subject and incorporated into the contract, the agreement is binding and enforceable. However, a party may retract an agreement on a permissive subject of bargaining at any time until the contract is signed.

Bargaining is prohibited on illegal subjects. An agreement reached on an illegal subject is void and unenforceable. Illegal subjects include such matters as a clause requiring union membership as soon as an employee is hired rather than after 30 days of employment as required by Section 8(a)(3); a clause discriminating between employees on the basis of race or sex; or a clause containing an unlawful hot cargo agreement (see Chapter 8).

2. Typical Mandatory Subjects

Since a bonus or an incentive plan is a form of wages, bonuses are therefore mandatory subjects of bargaining. Issues such as seniority, job assignments and promotions are all conditions of employment, and therefore are mandatory subjects.

Fringe Benefits

Vacations, holiday pay, and fringe benefits, such as pension and health and welfare plans are all mandatory subjects of bargaining because they pertain to wages. However, the Supreme Court has held that the subject of increased pension benefits for employees who are already retired is a permissive subject of bargaining. The Court reasons that retired persons are no longer employees under the Act.

Conditions of Employment

The Supreme Court has held that vending machine food prices in a company cafeteria used by employees are a mandatory subject of bargaining. The Court said that the availability of food during working hours and the conditions under which it is consumed is a term and condition of employment. Even if the prices are set by an outside vending company, the employer can negotiate prices with the supplier or else subsidize the vending machine prices.

A union security clause (see Chapter 10) is a mandatory subject of bargaining as a condition of employment, as is permitting a discharge only for just cause. Is a proposal that an employer post a bond guaranteeing the employees' wages or payment of fringe benefits a mandatory subject of bargaining? Although a bond relates to the mandatory subject of wages, the Board has held that bonds are a permissive subject because the relationship to wages is too remote.

Arbitration Provisions

Grievance and arbitration provisions are mandatory subjects of bargaining because they are considered conditions of employment. However, a provision for interest arbitration (arbitration of new contract terms) is classified as a permissive subject of bargaining. The Board has reasoned that interest arbitration has only a remote impact upon contractual wages, hours, and working conditions.

3. Permissive Subjects of Bargaining

Ratification Procedures

The procedures either party uses to approve a contract are a permissive subject of bargaining. The employer can lawfully propose that the union submit the employer's final offer to a full union membership vote. However, the union has the right to decide on its own ratification process and can lawfully refuse to bargain over the employer's proposal. In contrast, the employer cannot condition a wage offer on the union's agreement to subject the offer to ratification or to have a secret ballot. That is improperly conditioning a mandatory subject (wages) on the union's agreement on a permissive subject (the ratification process). As previously discussed, the composition of each side's bargaining committee is a permissive subject of bargaining.

Changes in the Bargaining Unit

Attempts to expand, narrow, or modify the bargaining unit are permissive subjects. Suppose a union certified to represent the production and maintenance employees proposes that the contract cover clerical employees as well. The employer could refuse to bargain over expanding the unit and the union could not insist to impasse on expansion. But if the employer and union signed a contract expanding the unit and the employer reneged on the agreement, the employer's agreement expanding the unit would be enforceable.

If a bargaining unit is certified in the name of an international union, but the international assigns the employees to a local; can the international insist that only the local's name appear on a contract? No, because any attempt to modify the international's certification to the local is a permissive subject of bargaining. Similarly, if the certification is only in the local's name, an employer's proposal to include the international as a contractual party is a permissive subject.

Transcripts of Bargaining Sessions

The Board has held that neither party can insist that there be a stenographic transcript of bargaining sessions. The presence of a stenographer is a permissive subject of bargaining because it does not have a material or significant effect or impact upon a term or condition of employment. Presumably, this same rule applies to the presence of a stenographer at a grievance meeting.

Strike Settlement Agreements

A strike settlement agreement on the rights of returning strikers is a permissive subject of bargaining. A union can lawfully propose that the employer take back all strikers including those who have been permanently replaced and not discipline any employees for strike misconduct. But the employer can refuse to bargain on these subjects. Sometimes, there are unfair labor practice charges and suits pending at the end of a strike. Again, proposals to withdraw charges or suits are permissive subjects. Thus, if an employer and union have agreed on all mandatory bargaining subjects, a union cannot refuse to sign a contract unless the employer agrees to drop pending charges or a suit.

4. Bargaining Tactics in Light of the Mandatory/Permissive Subject Distinction

Sometimes a subject is very important to a union although it is classified as a permissive

subject. If a strike has been marked by violence, the union may need a clause forgiving strike misconduct and dropping pending litigation. What if a union resolves all mandatory subjects of bargaining, but these permissive subjects remain open? Or what if a union does not bring up these matters until all mandatory subjects are resolved? Then the union is in a helpless position, as the employer can refuse to discuss the permissive subjects. Since all mandatory items are already agreed to, the union could be forced to sign the agreement and return to work.

Thus, as a tactic, a union must keep both mandatory and permissive subjects of bargaining open on the bargaining table and resolve the permissive subjects at the same time that agreement is reached on the mandatory items. That way the union can preserve its right to a bargaining impasse, strike, or both. The union must be skillful in using this approach; otherwise, the Board might conclude that the union is keeping its position on a mandatory subject open to force the employer to agree to a permissive subject. That is bad faith bargaining.

What if a party submits a package proposal that includes both mandatory and permissive bargaining subjects, such as coupling a wage offer with a proposal for interest arbitration on a midterm wage reopener, and the other side accepts the mandatory subject proposal, but rejects the permissive subject proposal? The party is not bound by its proposals on the mandatory subject. Even though part of the overall package was accepted, the Board has held that a party can properly change its position on a mandatory subject proposal if the other side rejects its permissive subject proposal. The Board has reasoned that the mandatory subject proposal is conditional on acceptance of the total package, including the permissive subjects.

D. THE EMPLOYER'S DUTY TO BARGAIN BEFORE CHANGING CONDITIONS OF EMPLOYMENT

When does an employer have a duty to bargain with a union? An employer has the duty to negotiate a collective bargaining agreement covering the employees the union represents. Beyond that, however, an employer has a continuing duty to notify and bargain with the union before making any changes in the employee's wages, hours, or working conditions on a mandatory subject of bargaining. A change an employer makes without the union's consent is called a unilateral change. It is the employer's duty to bargain before making unilateral changes in conditions of employment. This duty may arise before the parties have negotiated a contract, during a contract's term, or after a contract's expiration.

1. Unilateral Action Before a Contract

The duty to bargain arises as soon as a union is certified by the Board or recognized voluntarily by the employer—even before formal contract negotiations begin. The employer must bargain to impasse before making a change in any mandatory subject of bargaining. (Remember, an impasse is a deadlock reached after good faith bargaining.) After an impasse has been reached, the employer can unilaterally implement its changes. But the employer cannot put any changes into effect except those discussed in the bargaining. Thus, an employer cannot offer employees better conditions than those contained in its last offer to the union.

In general, an employer must bargain over both the decision it proposes to make and the effect of the decision on the employees. As an exception, the Board has held that an employer does not have to bargain on basic capital decisions on the direction of the business. However, an employer must still bargain over the effect of such a decision. This exception arises most frequently in cases pertaining to subcontracting, plant shutdowns, or plant transfers (discussed below).

2. Unilateral Changes During Bargaining

Even after contract bargaining has begun, under certain circumstances an employer can still make unilateral changes in working conditions. If the parties have reached a bargaining impasse, the employer can put its last offer into effect without the union's approval. Although the employer cannot offer employees better terms and conditions of employment than those offered to the union, he can implement any increase up to the amount offered to the union.

After an impasse has been reached, an employer can unilaterally impose more restricted working conditions. For example, what if an employer proposes doing away with certain equipment manning requirements, the union opposes the proposal, and the parties bargain to impasse? If there is no contract in effect, the employer can unilaterally put the changes into effect after impasse. The union's choice at that time might be to accept the changes or strike.

An employer has a right to hire replacements and continue operations during a strike (see Chapter 6). If an employer hires replacements, they can be hired at the terms and conditions contained in the last offer to the union.

3. Bargaining During the Contract's Term

a. Items Not Covered by the Contract

After the parties execute a contract, the employer's right to make unilateral changes in working conditions during the contract's term depends upon whether the contract covers the subject of the change. The employer cannot take unilateral action contrary to the agreement. The contract establishes the terms and conditions of employment and they cannot be changed unilaterally. Thus, if a contract provides for promotions based on strict seniority, the employer cannot unilaterally decide to consider skill and ability as well. Such an action both violates the contract and is a unilateral change in a working condition violating Section 8(a)(5).

Also, the employer must bargain with the union before instituting new plant rules during the term of a contract or new production standards if the rules are enforced through disciplinary action.

An employer can unilaterally take any action the contract permits it to take without notice to and bargaining with the union. If a contract gives an employer the right to lay off employees for lack of work, the employer can unilaterally layoff in accordance with the contract without any further bargaining. In contrast, if there is no contract, the employer must bargain with the union before laying off employees. After bargaining to impasse in the absence of a contract, the employer can layoff employees unilaterally.

If the contract is silent on a particular condition of employment, the employer has a duty to bargain with the union before making any unilateral change on that condition as if there were no contract in effect. If the contract does not cover the employer's right to layoff, the employer must notify the union and bar-

gain with it before laying off any employees. If the contract is silent, the employer's only obligation is to bargain. After bargaining in good faith to an impasse, the employer can take unilateral action. In contrast, if the issue is covered by the contract, the employer cannot unilaterally change the terms, even after bargaining.

b. The Board's Authority to Interpret the Contract

Frequently it is difficult to determine whether or not a contract permits unilateral action without bargaining on a particular matter. The contract language may be ambiguous. Interpreted one way, the employer may have authority to act unilaterally, but interpreted another, the contract may prohibit the employer's actions altogether. A contract may be silent, but past practice between the parties or the bargaining history may establish that the employer is prohibited from taking action or that the union had waived its bargaining rights. Thus, the Board must interpret the contract to determine whether unilateral employer action is permitted or not.

In *C & C Plywood*, the employer unilaterally established a production bonus for an entire work crew.[2] The contract permitted premium rates to reward individual employees for special fitness. The employer argued that this clause permitted it to give premium pay to an entire crew across the board. The union argued that premium pay to an entire crew, rather than for individual achievement, was a unilateral change in conditions. The Board, reviewing the contract language and the negotiating history, concluded that the contract did not permit the unilateral adoption of the bonus system. Thus, the employer's unilateral action violated Section 8(a)(5).

The case was appealed to the Supreme

---

[2] See legal principle 10.

Court. The employer argued that the Board had no right to interpret the contract or to determine whether the employer or union had correctly interpreted it. The Court upheld the Board's authority, stating that the Board has jurisdiction to interpret an agreement necessary to determining whether an unfair labor practice has occurred. The Board can interpret a contract to determine whether it permits an employer to take unilateral action on a given matter. If the Board concludes that the contract does not permit unilateral action, an employer's unilateral change without bargaining violates Section 8(a)(5). The employer has not violated Section 8(a)(5) if the Board concludes that the contract permits unilateral action.

c. Waiver of Bargaining Rights

Although an employer is usually obligated to bargain over mandatory subjects of bargaining not covered by the contract, the union can waive that right.

(1) Waiver Through Bargaining. The most common form of waiver occurs during bargaining if the union proposes a clause limiting the employer's authority, but fails to obtain the desired provision. What if a contract has no clause prohibiting subcontracting and the union proposes a contractual restriction? The matter is negotiated thoroughly but the employer refuses to agree to any contractual restriction, maintaining it has a management right to subcontract. The contract is signed without any subcontracting restrictions and the employer subsequently subcontracts work without bargaining with the union. Since the contract is silent, the employer ordinarily has a duty to bargain with the union before subcontracting. However, the Board would probably conclude that the union waived its right to bargain by proposing, but failing, to obtain a contractual restriction.

The Board has stated that a waiver of the right to bargain over matters not covered by the contract must be "clear and unmistakable." This rule follows the general Board principle that a waiver of a statutory right (e.g., the right to bargain over a change in working conditions) must be clear and unmistakable. The Board will not find a waiver unless a subject is fully discussed during bargaining and consciously waived by the union. For example, what if a union simply proposes a limit on subcontracting in its written proposals, but does not discuss the matter or drops it after only a brief discussion. By making the proposal, the union probably does not waive its right to bargain over subcontracting during the contract's term. But if the proposal is discussed fully and then dropped, the union probably has waived its right to bargain on the subject during the contract.

Withdrawal of a proposal does not necessarily waive a union's bargaining rights. But if a union withdraws a proposal, the better procedure in most cases is for the union to state expressly it is not waiving its right to bargain on the subject if the employer should take unilateral action. In that way, the union may avoid inadvertently waiving its rights.

(2) Waiver by Union Inaction. A union may also waive its rights by inaction. If an employer takes unilateral action and the union fails to protest and request bargaining, the union may have waived its rights.

(3) Contractual Zipper Clauses. A union may also waive its right to bargain over a unilateral change by agreeing to a so-called contractual "zipper clause." This is a clause that "zips up" the agreement by stating that the parties have had the right and opportunity to bargain over all mandatory subjects of bargaining and that they waive their right to bargain over any matters during the term of the agreement. If such a clause is applied literally, the employer

can take unilateral action on any matter not expressly covered in the contract. However, the Board has usually refused to apply zipper clauses literally. The Board holds that a union cannot waive the right to bargain on new matters following the execution of a contract despite broad zipper clause language. The Board examines all the facts and circumstances of the negotiations to determine what bargaining rights the union gave up. But the clause will not be applied to bar all bargaining across the board. Thus, employer unilateral action may violate Section 8(a)(5) even though there is a zipper clause.

4. The Duty to Bargain Over Subcontracting, Plant Shutdowns, and Plant Transfers

One of the most controversial issues pertaining to the duty to bargain is the employer's obligation to bargain over changes in business operations, such as subcontracting, plant transfers, or closing the business.

If the contract either permits or prohibits unilateral action, both the employer and the union are bound by their agreement, as they are to any other term in the contract. If, for example, the contract permits unilateral subcontracting, the employer could subcontract without bargaining with the union. But what if the contract is silent? Must the employer bargain with the union before subcontracting work, transferring the plant to a new location, or even closing the facility?

a. The Fibreboard Decision

In virtually every case, an employer must bargain with the union about the effect on employees of a decision to change the nature of the operations. The controversial area is the employer's duty to notify the union and bargain over the *decision itself* before it is made rather than just bargain over the effect.

In *Fibreboard Paper Products Corp.*, an employer hired an outside contractor to do plant maintenance work formerly done by bargaining unit employees.[3] The employer notified the union of the decision after it had been made and offered to bargain on the effect on the employees. The Supreme Court upheld the NLRB's decision that the employer had to bargain over the decision itself, not just the effect. The Court, however, limited its decision to the specific facts of the case. It said that the employer must bargain over the decision to subcontract, rather than just the effect, if the subcontracting replaces bargaining unit employees with employees of an independent contractor to do the same work under similar conditions of employment.

The Board further limited *Fibreboard* by holding that subcontracting must have a demonstrable adverse impact on employees in the unit before the employer is obligated to bargain over it. There is no need to bargain over subcontracting of small amounts of bargaining unit work repeatedly subcontracted on a regular basis because of the minimal impact. However, the employer must bargain if the subcontracting varies from past practice, or has a significant impact on job tenure, employment security, or anticipated work opportunity.

b. Basic Capital Decisions

The *General Motors* case further restricted the employer's duty to bargain over certain basic decisions.[4] General Motors decided to sell a retail service center. The Board held that the company had no duty to bargain over its decision to sell because it was a basic capital

[3] See legal principle 13.
[4] See legal principle 14.

decision on the scope and ultimate direction of the enterprise. The Board said:

> [D]ecisions such as this, in which a significant investment or withdrawal of capital will affect the scope and ultimate direction of an enterprise, are matters essentially financial and managerial in nature. They thus lie at the very core of entreprenurial control, and are not the types of subjects which Congress intended to encompass within rates of pay, wages, hours of employment, or other conditions of employment.

c. Board Decisions Since Fibreboard

Since *Fibreboard* and the *General Motors* decision, the Board's cases applying to an employer's duty to bargain over subcontracting have been narrowly decided on the particular facts. However, in many cases the Board requires bargaining on both the decision and the effect, depending upon whether the subcontracting is to be done on premises, if there is significant adverse impact on the employees, and if the subcontracting affects the basic nature of the enterprise.

Because it is frequently difficult to predict whether the Board will classify an employer's actions as a basic capital decision, a union should request bargaining immediately over both the decision and the effect if an employer subcontracts or takes other action unilaterally. In that way, the union does not waive its right to bargain over the decision by failure to act. Since the employer may also be uncertain whether a particular unilateral action is a basic capital decision, he may, upon the union's request, agree to bargain over the decision itself. If the employer rejects the union's request, the union can proceed to the Board.

Plant Closures and Shutdowns. The Board has held that there is no duty to bargain over a decision to close a business entirely, but there is a duty to bargain over the effect such as severance pay or retraining programs.[5] However, the Board has also held that an employer must usually bargain over a decision to shut down one facility if others remain open, as partial shutdown is not regarded as a basic capital decision.

The only exception to the bargaining rules on partial shutdowns is if the employer is totally revamping its operations. This is considered a basic capital decision. What if an employer who operates two unrelated businesses, food processing and clothing, decides to close down the food processing business altogether? The employer would not have to bargain over the decision to close the food processing plant although the clothing plant remained open. The employer still has a duty to bargain over the effect of its decision. If the employer has two food processing plants and only closes one, the employer must bargain over both the decision and the effect.

Ordinarily, a decision to transfer a facility from one location to another is not a basic capital decision and the employer must bargain over both the decision and the effect.

d. Board Remedies for Unilateral Actions

The Board has strong remedies against an employer who refuses to bargain over a decision that does not fall within the exception for basic capital decisions. A company can be ordered to bargain with the union over both the decision and the effect. The Board can order the employer to resume the prior operations if that is at all feasible. Whether the prior operation is resumed or not, the Board can also order the company to pay its adversely affected employees back pay from the date of

---

[5] Remember, the employer's only obligation is to bargain in good faith. It does not have to agree with any union proposal and can act unilaterally after bargaining to impasse.

the company's unilateral action until the employer and union reach a mutual agreement on the decision and effect, a bona fide impasse is reached, or the union fails to request bargaining.

e. Arbitration and the NLRB's Role in Unilateral Change Cases: The Collyer Doctrine

As the *C & C Plywood* case points out, it is possible for an employer's unilateral change to be both an unfair labor practice and a contract violation. The Board may have to interpret the contract to see if there is a violation. If the contract contains an arbitration clause, should the arbitrator or the Board interpret the contract? *C & C Plywood* establishes that the Board has the authority to interpret the contract to determine whether an unfair labor practice has been committed. However, national labor policy also strongly favors arbitration as a means of resolving contractual disputes. How should the respective roles of the arbitrator and the Board be accommodated?

The Board resolved these issues in *Collyer Insulated Wire*, holding that if a collective bargaining agreement provides for arbitration, the Board will defer unfair labor practice charges alleging a unilateral change in violation of Section 8(a)(5), which might also be a contract violation, to arbitration.[6] The Board defers to arbitration even though it has the statutory authority to resolve the issue. This policy is known as the "Collyer Doctrine."

The Board defers these cases to arbitration because resolution of the contract interpretation issue will also resolve the unfair labor practice charge. Thus, if the employer's action violates the contract, the employer cannot take unilateral action. The arbitrator's award requiring the employer to rescind the action and restore the prior conditions also

remedies any possible unfair labor practice. If the arbitrator decides that the contract permits the employer's action, there is no need for bargaining and no Section 8(a)(5) violation because an employer does not have to bargain if the contract permits unilateral action. Thus, the arbitrator's decision, either way, resolves the unfair labor practice issues as well.

The procedures the Board follows in deferring cases to arbitration and the standards it applies in determining whether to accept an arbitrator's decision on a matter that may also be an unfair labor practice, are discussed in Chapter 9.

5. The Duty to Bargain Upon the Contract's Expiration

When a contract expires, the contractual wages, hours, and other terms and conditions of employment remain in effect as established conditions. Conditions that are mandatory bargaining subjects cannot be changed unilaterally by the employer although the agreement has expired. The employer must bargain to impasse before making a change. For instance, an employer cannot unilaterally change the employees' contractual wages or the seniority system after the contract has expired before bargaining to impasse. The employer's bargaining obligation before changing the conditions of employment after a contract expires is basically the same as its bargaining obligation before a contract is executed. A unilateral change without bargaining violates Section 8(a)(5).

As an exception, a contractual union security clause expires automatically; employees cannot be required to be union members or pay union dues after the contract expires (see Chapter 10).

The Board formerly held that there is no

---

[6] See legal principle 12.

duty to arbitrate grievances arising after a contract expires because the duty to arbitrate expires with the contract. The Board recently reversed this position, and now holds that an employer may be required to arbitrate a grievance arising after a contract expires if the grievance is arguably based on a contractual right. Thus, an employer may be required to arbitrate whether an employee's discharge after the contract expires is for just cause. (See Chapter 9 for further discussion of the duty to arbitrate grievances arising under an expired contract.)

To prevent the employer from making unilateral changes after a contract expires, a union can propose short-term extensions of the contract while bargaining on a new agreement takes place. If the employer agrees, the entire agreement remains in effect and cannot be changed unilaterally. An extension preserves the union security provisions.

Of course, the contractual no-strike clause also remains in effect if the contract is extended. Thus, before striking, the union must wait until the end of an extension period or serve a cancellation notice if the contract is extended indefinitely.

E. THE DUTY TO PROVIDE INFORMATION FOR BARGAINING

1. The Right to Relevant Information

Unions have a broad right to information relevant to the negotiation and administration of the collective bargaining agreement. This obligation is based on the principle that the employer's duty to bargain includes the duty to provide the union with the information it needs to engage in informed bargaining.

The employer need not give assistance voluntarily so the union must request the information it wants. The information requested must be relevant to the formulation of the union's bargaining position, contract negotiations, or contract administration. Also, the union is entitled to information needed to evaluate and process a grievance through the grievance procedure to arbitration. If a union is considering a proposal limiting subcontracting, it can request data on company subcontracts. If the union is considering a proposal on overtime, the union can request data on the number and distribution of overtime hours. If the union believes a contractual provision has been violated, such as improper work assignments or overtime distribution, it can request information and inspect company records to check out the matter. If there is a dispute as to production line speed, the union is entitled to the company's time study data, and may even make its own time study. If an employee is discharged, the union can request information about the basis of the discharge and the evidence supporting it.

The union is entitled to information on the employer's hiring and promotion of minority group bargaining unit employees. The Board has held, however, that a union usually is not entitled to a copy of an employer's affirmative action program, if any. A union is entitled to the names of each employee in the bargaining unit, their job classifications, wage rate, and seniority date. This basic data is necessary to begin bargaining. The union can also request the name of each new employee, as hired, in order to enforce the union security provisions of a contract. Technically, a union represents strike replacements; thus, a striking union can request the names of the replacements. However, the Board has held that an employer does not have to release the names if the employer has a reasonable basis for believing that the union will use the list to harass the replacements.

This list of possible information is far from exhaustive. Basically, the scope of the union's right to information is as broad as the union's need for information on any matter relevant to the bargaining process.

Although it does not occur often, employers are also entitled to relevant data from the union. If a contract requires that an employer obtain his employees from a union hiring hall, the employer can request data as to the union's ability to refer enough qualified employees to meet the employer's needs.

2. Limits on the Employer's Duty

There are some limits on the employer's obligation to provide information. The union's request cannot unduly burden the employer. Unions may have to pay for the employer's administrative expenses (such as clerical and copying costs) when gathering large amounts of information. In some cases, the employer's only obligation may be to allow the union access to information that the union examines on its own. Also, the employer can require the union to state why the requested information is relevant. Usually the employer does not have to interpret the data provided to the union or put it in the precise form the union requests. It need only make the information available. However, if the information requested is computerized or needs explanation to be understood, the employer must put the data in a useable form and give the necessary explanation.

a. Right to Profit Information

The union is entitled to financial information about company profits only if the employer pleads he is financially unable to pay a requested increase. This is called "pleading poverty." The union is not entitled to financial data just because it would assist it in preparing wage demands for bargaining.

b. Confidential Data

The Supreme Court has indicated that an employer's legitimate interest in the confidentiality of certain information may prevail over the union's need. In *Detroit Edison*, the union requested that the company provide it with a copy of an aptitude test used to determine eligibility for promotions and copies of the test results for those taking the test.[7] The data was needed to prepare a grievance the union was arbitrating over the denial of promotions to certain senior employees. The company denied the union's request for the test on the grounds that the test had to be kept secret. The company did offer to allow a psychologist, selected by the union, to evaluate the test in confidence, but the union rejected this proposal. The employer also denied the union's request for the test results of individual employees because the company had promised employees that it would keep the results confidential. The company did offer to release the test results of any employee who signed a waiver permitting the release.

The Board held that the union was entitled to a copy of the test and the individual employees' test scores. The Supreme Court reversed the Board, holding that the employer did not have to turn over the test directly to the union. The Supreme Court also said that the employer's requirement that the individual employees agree to the release of their scores was reasonable. The employer's interest in maintaining the confidence of the material was greater than the union's need for the data. The Court stated that the burden on the union in getting the releases was minimal.

[7] See legal principle 4.

F. THE BARGAINING DUTY OF SUCCESSOR EMPLOYERS

Generally, an employer is a successor employer if he takes over the business of another employer, the predecessor's employees are retained as a majority of the new employer's work force, and the new employer continues operations in the same industry. The takeover may be through a merger or consolidation of two companies, a stock transfer, transfer of assets, or any other business combination.

At one time unions argued that a successor employer should be required to assume the collective bargaining agreement between the predecessor employer and the incumbent (existing) union. However, in *Burns International Security Services, Inc.*, the Supreme Court held that a successor employer is not bound by the predecessor's collective bargaining agreement and is free to bargain for its own contract.[8] The Court said that ordering a successor employer to adopt the predecessor's contract is contrary to the principle of Section 8(d), which states an employer cannot be compelled to agree to specific contract terms. The successor may, however, be required to recognize and bargain with the incumbent union under the conditions discussed below.

1. Retaining the Prior Work Force

Under *Burns*, a new employer has no obligation to hire the prior employees. The new employer can hire or bring in all new employees if he wishes. However, the employer cannot discriminatorily refuse to retain prior employees because they are represented by a union.

When is a new employer obligated to bargain with the incumbent union? Under *Burns*,

the employer is obligated to bargain when the employees represented by the incumbent union comprise a majority of the new work force. The new employer becomes a successor at that point. What if the employer hires all the predecessor's employees? The employer becomes a successor employer obligated to bargain with the incumbent union from the date it retains the prior employees. If the employer hires six of ten prior employees and five new employees, the Board presumes that the union continues to represent the six employees. The successor will be required to bargain with the union from the time it is clear that the six employees are a majority of the new work force. If the new employer retains all ten of the prior employees and brings in 12 new employees as well, the employer is not legally a successor. He has no obligation to bargain with the prior union even though all the old employees are retained because the prior employees are not a majority of the new work force. If the employer does not retain any of the prior employees, he has no bargaining obligation with the incumbent union provided his decision to hire all new employees is not motivated discriminatorily.

2. Remaining in the Same Industry

The principal requirement for successorship is that the prior employees comprise a majority of the new work force. There is also a secondary requirement that there be substantial continuity of the employing industry. Basically, this requirement is met if the new employer uses the same facilities and equipment, produces the same or a similar product, or performs the same services. The Board also considers whether the employer serves the same customers and geographic area.

[8] See legal principle 16.

3. The Successor's Right to Establish Initial Terms of Employment

An employer is usually obligated to bargain with a union before making unilateral changes in wages, hours, or working conditions. Assume that an employer purchases a plant and plans to continue production of the same product at the same location. The employer rehires the prior work force. Under *Burns*, the employer is not obligated to assume the existing contract, but can establish new contract terms. But is the employer at least obligated to bargain with the incumbent union before making the changes? Under *Burns*, the Supreme Court held that there is no such obligation. A successor employer is not obligated to bargain with the incumbent union until it is clear that the union still represents a majority. Whether the union still represents a majority cannot be determined until after the work force is hired. Thus, the employer can unilaterally set the initial terms of employment and offer each employee presently working the right to continue under the new terms.

For example, if the employees were making $6 an hour, the new employer can unilaterally announce it will retain employees willing to work for $5 per hour. The employer is classified as a successor employer obligated to bargain with the incumbent union only if the prior employees are a majority of the work force hired at the new rate. The employer cannot make further unilateral changes from then on and must bargain with the incumbent union for a new contract.

There is one situation under which an employer is obligated to bargain with the incumbent union immediately. If an employer announces at the time of a takeover that he is keeping the entire work force, it is immediately clear that the incumbent union will continue to represent the employees. In that case,

the employer must bargain with the union from the beginning and cannot unilaterally set the initial terms of employment. Thus, the Supreme Court stated in *Burns*:

> Although a successor employer is ordinarily free to set initial terms on which it will hire the employees of a predecessor, there will be instances in which it is perfectly clear that the new employer plans to retain all of the employees in the unit and in which it will be appropriate to have him initially consult with the employees' bargaining representative before he fixes terms. In other situations, however, it may not be clear until the successor employer has hired his full complement of employees that he has a duty to bargain with a union, since it will not be evident until then that the bargaining representative represents a majority of the employees in the unit.

Note, however, that even if the employer announces he will keep all employees, his only obligation is to negotiate the initial terms of employment. He is still not obligated to assume the existing bargaining agreement. This exception is narrowly applied. For example, if an employer announces he will retain any of the prior employees who agree to his terms, the employer will be able to establish initial terms because the union's majority status is not determined until the employees have hired on at the new rate. Sophisticated employers, even if they want to keep the present work force, will go through the motions of rehiring the employees individually to preserve their right to establish initial terms.

4. The Effect of Successorship Clauses

Before the *Burns* case, contracts frequently contained a successorship clause generally stating that the contract was binding on the employer and any successor. Under *Burns*, general successorship language in a collective bargaining agreement is ineffective and does not bind the successor. The new employer still has the right to employ his own work force and establish the terms and conditions of employment notwithstanding the clause.

While a general successorship clause is ineffective, a union may bargain for specific protection. The union can negotiate a contract clause under which the predecessor employer agrees that he will not sell or otherwise transfer the business to another employer unless the new employer agrees to assume the existing collective bargaining agreement as part of the transfer agreement. The Board has held that such restrictions are lawful and that a union's demand for such a clause is a mandatory subject of bargaining.

What if the predecessor employer violates the agreement and sells the business without requiring the predecessor to assume the collective bargaining agreement? The union can seek an injunction prohibiting the transfer until the contractual provision is fulfilled. Unions can also sue the predecessor employer for damages for breach of its contract. Finally, the Board has held that the union has the right to picket both the old and new employer to require that they fulfill the terms of the contract.

5. The Alter Ego Employer

A successor employer must be distinguished from an alter ego employer. An alter ego employer is, in fact, the same employer as before even though the outward appearance or name may have changed. The alter ego employer is bound by the existing contract. In one case, an employer liquidated a company that sold and installed garage doors. The prior owners opened another company engaged in the same business. The old and new companies were wholly owned by members of the same family. Both companies had common business purposes, management, equipment, customers, and supervision. The Board held that the new company was the alter ego of the predecessor because the ownership and control of both companies were substantially identical. The new company, as the alter ego of the old, was bound by the terms of the contract between the liquidated company and the union that represented the employees.

6. The Double Breasted Operation

Sometimes an employer will operate two closely related companies, one with a union contract and one without. This is often referred to as the "double breasted" operation. Double breasted employers are most common in the construction industry. An employer may attempt to establish two companies, one to work on union construction projects and the other to do nonunion work. Should the union contract cover the nonunion operation as well? The union and nonunion companies are considered a single employer bound by the union contract if the Board finds that they are a "single integrated enterprise." The Board considers whether there is common ownership and financial control, common management and supervision, common faciles and equipment, interrelationship of operations, and common control of labor relation policy. The more factors that are present, especially common control of labor relations, the more likely the Board will conclude that the nonunion company is the alter ego of the union employer and is thus bound by the collective bargaining agreement.

G. THE DUTY TO BARGAIN AND SUCCESSOR UNIONS

1. The Bargaining Rights of Successor Unions

Sometimes two locals of the same international merge during the term of their respective collective bargaining agreements. Or an international union may reassign employees from one local to another. An independent union may vote to affiliate with an international. Or two international unions may merge and the names and numbers of the preexisting locals may be changed to reflect the new designation.

If a local union's internal structure changes, is the employer still obligated to recognize and bargain with it? The employer is so obligated if the union is a continuation of the prior union and there is substantial continuity in the representation for bargaining unit employees. The successor union also automatically assumes any existing collective bargaining agreement.

The Board normally requires that union members affected by a new affiliation have an opportunity to approve the affiliation by a secret ballot vote before the new union succeeds to the prior union's collective bargaining rights and contract. Bargaining unit employees who are not union members are not entitled to vote. An affirmative employee vote in favor of the new affiliation is evidence that there is continuity in representation. The Board requires that there be adequate due process in the election, including notice of the right to vote, an orderly voting procedure, and reasonable precautions to maintain secrecy. However, the election, as an internal union matter, need not meet the high standards that the Board sets for its own elections.

2. The Successor Union's Right to Assume an Existing Contract

An existing collective bargaining agreement (e.g., one for four years) may not bar a representation election in some cases (see Chapter 2). If an election is held and a new union certified, what is the effect on the existing contract?

The Board has held that, following an election, the successor union has a choice. The union can assume the contract for its remaining term and the employer is obligated to keep the agreement in effect. Or, the union may choose to cancel the existing agreement and negotiate a new agreement. The employer cannot hold the new union to the existing contract, and is obligated to bargain for a new agreement at the union's request.

H. REMEDIES FOR REFUSAL TO BARGAIN

The Board can adequately remedy some bargaining violations. For example, if a party refuses to sign an agreed-to contract, the Board can order the party to sign the agreement and pay back pay for the period the party failed to abide by the contract's terms. If an employer makes unilateral changes, he can be ordered to reinstate the prior conditions and pay back pay equal to any unilateral reduction in benefits. However, what remedy can the Board provide if an employer has engaged in surface bargaining with the purpose of delaying the bargaining process and undermining the union? Unfortunately, the Board's only remedy is to order the employer to bargain in good faith. If an employer is determined to defeat the union, he can appeal the Board's decision to the court of appeals, perhaps delaying bargaining for several years. Even if the employer is eventually forced to the bargaining table, the union may have been defeated through delay. Many of the union's original supporters may have quit or been discharged in the meantime. The union may lack the bargaining power to negotiate a successful agreement.

At one time, the Board tried to remedy bad faith surface bargaining by requiring an employer to sign an agreement incorporating the provisions the employer would have agreed to if the employer had bargained in good faith. In *H. K. Porter*, the Board ordered a company to agree to a dues check-off provision.[9] The company, in bad faith, had refused to agree to a check-off because it was "not going to aid and comfort the union." However, the Supreme Court held that the Board does not have authority to order an employer to accept any specific clause not agreed to. The Court said that Congress intended that the Board regulate the bargaining process, but it could not compel agreement to any specific terms.

After *H. K. Porter*, unions continued to argue that the Board should require an employer who bargains in bad faith to pay employees back pay equal to the difference between what the employees would have earned if the employer had bargained in good faith for a contract and the amount the employees actually earned during that period. Under this approach, if employees are earning $5 an hour and the Board determines that the employer would have agreed to a $6 per hour rate if he had bargained in good faith, the employees receive back pay in the amount of $1 per hour for each hour worked. However, the Board has held that this remedy is beyond its jurisdiction. The Board said that basing a remedy on what the employer would have agreed to would be like dictating the terms of the agreement, which *H. K. Porter* prohibited. The proposed Labor Reform Act, which was narrowly defeated in Congress, would have permitted the Board to give financial remedies in refusal to bargain cases.

The Board imposes additional remedies within its power in extreme cases of flagrant refusal to bargain, or if the employer raises frivolous defenses to a refusal to bargain charge, such as ordering the employer to pay the union's legal expenses for the litigation. In *J. P. Stevens*, for example, the Board required the employer to reimburse the union for the additional organizational costs the union incurred because of the employer's flagrant unlawful opposition to its employees' organizational rights.[10] The Board also ordered the employer to pay the union's legal fees and expenses in the litigation before the Board because of the company's deliberate violations of the law and the serious and sustained nature of the violations.

In some cases where bargaining orders have been enforced by a court of appeals, employers have been held in contempt by the court for failure to comply with the court's enforcement order. These remedies are effective in many cases, but not in those instances where an employer is willing to pay the price to defeat the union.

[9] See legal principle 17.

[10] See legal principle 17.

Summary

This chapter considered bargaining rights and responsibilities, focusing on the meaning of good faith bargaining required by Sections 8(a)(5), 8(b)(3), and 8(d) of the Act. Although good faith means bargaining with an intention to reach an agreement, neither party is compelled to agree to a proposal or required to make a concession. Going through the formalities of bargaining with no intention of reaching an agreement is unlawful "surface bargaining." No one factor determines whether a party is engaged in surface bargaining. Good faith is judged by the "totality of conduct."

Bargaining items are either mandatory, permissive, or illegal subjects of bargaining. Both parties are obligated to bargain over mandatory subjects and may strike over them. A party may choose, but is not required, to bargain over a permissive subject. A party cannot strike to compel the other party to reach agreement on a permissive subject. Wages, hours, and working conditions are mandatory subjects. Permissive subjects are legal, but not directly related to wages, hours, or working conditions.

The duty to bargain arises before, during, and after the negotiation of a contract. In the absence of a contract, an employer must bargain before unilaterally changing any mandatory bargaining condition of employment. There is generally no duty to bargain during the term of a contract over items covered by the contract. But an employer has the duty to bargain before making unilateral changes in conditions not covered by the agreement unless the union has waived that right. After an impasse is reached, an employer can make unilateral changes. An employer cannot give the employees better benefits than were offered the union during bargaining. Under the *Collyer Doctrine*, the Board defers to arbitration most Section 8(a)(5) charges, alleging the unilateral change in wages, hours, or working conditions that are also contract violations. The Board defers because the arbitrator's resolution of the contract interpretation issue also resolves the unfair labor practice issue.

The employer also has a duty to bargain with the union after the contract expires. Most contract terms under the expired agreement remain in effect as established conditions of employment. The employer cannot change them unilaterally until bargaining to impasse.

An employer has a duty to bargain over changes in business operations, such as subcontracting, plant transfers, or partial closures. In most cases, the employer must bargain with the union over both the decision to change and its effect on employees. But an employer is only obligated to bargain over the effect of a basic capital decision on the basic scope and ultimate direction of the enterprise. An employer may have a financial risk if it only bargains over the effect of a decision. There is often no clear dividing line between what is or is not a basic capital decision. If the employer only bargains over the effect, and the Board concludes it should have bargained over the decision itself, the employer may incur substantial back pay liability or even be required to resume operations.

Although the Board has effective remedies against unilateral changes in working conditions, its remedies are inadequate against the employer who intentionally drags out negotiations to undermine the union. Legislative changes are needed to permit financial remedies against these employers.

The union has a broad right to information from the employer relevant to the negotiation and administration of a collective bargaining agreement and to the processing of grievances to arbitration. The information must be relevant and must be requested, and the data must not be unduly burdensome. An employer need not provide information about its profits unless it pleads financial inability to pay (pleading poverty).

A successor employer is not required to accept the predecessor's collective bargaining agreement. It is, however, obligated to bargain with the incumbent union if the prior employees comprise a majority of the new work force. In most cases, the successor is able to set the employees' initial terms or conditions of employement even if it subsequently must recognize the union.

1. What are the statutory notice requirements under Section 8(d) if a party desires to terminate or modify a collective bargaining contract? *Review Questions*

2. Is it surface bargaining for an employer to reject a union's proposal for a union security clause?

3. Does the union forfeit the right to strike "forever" by failing to meet the statutory notice requirements?

4. How may the consequences of giving late statutory notice differ from giving a late contractual termination notice?

5. Must an employer continue to bargain with the incumbent union after the expiration date of their contract?

6. When is an employer regarded as a successor for purposes of the duty to bargain?

7. Is a successor employer bound by the predecessor's contract?

8. Can a successor employer unilaterally set the employees' initial wages and working conditions even if it keeps the prior work force?

9. Can the Board require an employer to sign a contract incorporating a specific term as a remedy for refusing to bargain?

10. Does an employer have to bargain over increased retirement benefits for employees who have already retired?

11. Must an employer bargain over pay for employees on the union's negotiating committee?

12. What information may the union request from the employer in administering the contract?

(Answers to review questions appear at end of book)

Basic Legal   1. A. Bargaining items are either mandatory, permissive, or illegal
Principles   subjects of bargaining. Both parties are obligated to bargain over
mandatory subjects and may strike over them. A party may choose to, but
need not, bargain over a permissive subject. A party cannot strike to compel the other party to agree to a permissive subject. *Pistoresi and Son, Inc.*,
230 NLRB 905, 83 LRRM 1212 (1973); *Allied Chemical and Alkali Workers v.
Pittsburgh Plate Glass*, 404 US 157, 78 LRRM 2974 (1971); *Sheet Metal Workers, Local 493*, 234 NLRB No. 162, 97 LRRM 1476 (1978).

B. The use of economic force to compel agreement is not inconsistent with good faith bargaining. *NLRB V. Insurance Agents International
Union*, 361 U.S. 477, 45 LRRM 2705 (1960).

2. Withdrawal of pending unfair labor practice charges at the end
of a strike is a permissive subject of bargaining. Thus, the parties cannot
condition the execution of a contract on such agreement. *Griffin Inns*, 229
NLRB No. 26, 95 LRRM 1072 (1977).

3. A proposal for interest arbitration, in contrast to grievance arbitration, is a permissive subject of bargaining. *Sheet Metal Workers Local 59*,
227 NLRB No. 90, 94 LRRM 1602 (1976).

4. Unions have a very broad right to information relevant to the
negotiation and administration of a collective bargaining agreement. The
information must be relevant and it must be requested. The data must not
be unduly burdensome and, under certain circumstances, must not be
confidential. *NLRB v. Truitt Mfg. Co.*, 351 U.S. 149, 38 LRRM 2042 (1956);
NLRB vs. Acme Industrial Co., 385 U.S. 432, 64 LRRM 2069 (1967), *NLRB v.
Detroit Edison*, 99 S.Ct., 1123, 100 LRRM 2728 (1979); *Westinghouse Electric
Corp*, 239 NLRB No. 19, 99 LRRM 1482 (1978) (civil rights data).

5. An employer need not provide information about profits unless
he pleads financial inability to pay a requested increase (pleading poverty).
NLRB v. Truitt Mfg. Co., supra.

6. An employer is also entitled to relevant data from a union, such
as the union's ability to furnish employees to meet manning requirements.
Oakland Press Inc., 233 NLRB No. 144, 97 LRRM 1047 (1977).

7. Going through the formalities of bargaining without the intention of reaching an agreement, is "surface bargaining" violating Section
8(a)(5) of the Act. No one factor determines whether a party is engaged in
surface bargaining. Good faith is based on the "totality of conduct." *Byrd's
Terrazzo and Tile Co.*, 227 NLRB No. 122, 94 LRRM 1412 (1977); *Neon Sign
Corp.*, 229 NLRB No. 125, 95 LRRM 1161 (1977); *General Electric Co.*, 150
NLRB No. 36, 57 LRRM 1491 (1964); *Winn Dixie Stores*, 243 NLRB No. 151,
101 LRRM 1534 (1979).

8. Internal union matters are permissive subjects of bargaining.
Thus, an employer cannot insist that the execution of a contract be contingent upon ratification by the union's membership. *NLRB v. Corsicana Cot-*

ton Mills, 178 F2d 344, 24 LRRM 2494 (5th Cir. 1949); Houchens Market, 155 NLRB No. 59, 60 LRRM 1384 (1965); NLRB v. Cheese Barn, Inc., 558 F2d 526, 95 LRRM 3096 (9th Cir. 1977).

9. Within limits, employers are permitted to communicate directly with employees during negotiations on the status of bargaining, but cannot bypass the union in an attempt to undermine it. Safeway Trails Inc., 233 NLRB No. 171, 96 LRRM 1614 (1977).

10. There is no duty to bargain during a contract's term over subjects covered by it, but there is a duty to bargain before making unilateral changes in mandatory subjects of bargaining not covered by the agreement unless that right has been waived. NLRB v. C&C Plywood Corp., 385 US 421, 64 LRRM 2065 (1967); Keystone Consolidated Industries, 237 NLRB No. 91, 99 LRRM 1036 (1978); Brown Co., 243 NLRB No. 100, 101 LRRM 1608 (1979).

11. Waiver of the right to bargain over matters not covered by a contract must be clear, but is based on all the facts and circumstances of bargaining that took place. Clarkwood Corp., 233 NLRB No. 167, 97 LRRM 1034 (1977); Pine Manor Nursing Home Inc., 230 NLRB No. 40, 95 LRRM 1356 (1977); GTE Automatic Elec. Inc., 240 NLRB No. 30, 100 LRRM 1204 (1979).

12. The Board defers to arbitration most Section 8(a)(5) charges alleging a unilateral change in wages, hours, or working conditions that may also be contract violations. Collyer Insulated Wire, 192 NLRB No. 150, 77 LRRM 1931; (1971), Roy Robinson Chevrolet, 228 NLRB No. 103, 94 LRRM 1474 (1977).

13. An employer must bargain over the decision and effect of subcontracting bargaining unit work if the work is still to be done on the company's premises under similar conditions. Fibreboard Paper Products Corp. v. NLRB, 379 US 203, 57 LRRM 2609 (1964). However, the subcontracting must also have demonstrable adverse impact on unit employees. Westinghouse Electric Corp., 150 NLRB No. 136, 58 LRRM 1257 (1965). The obligation to bargain exists even though there may be a legitimate economic reason for a decision. ACF Indus., 231 NLRB No. 20, 96 LRRM 1291 (1977); Donn Products Inc., 229 NLRB No. 9, 95 LRRM 1033 (1977).

14. An employer has the absolute right to close his business entirely without any bargaining over the decision itself, but is required to bargain over the effect. Textile Workers Union v. Darlington Mfg. Co., 380 US 263, 58 LRRM 2657 (1965). The employer may be required to bargain over both the decision and the effect of a partial plant closing. Ozark Trailers Inc., 161 NLRB No. 48, 63 LRRM 1264 (1966); Midland-Ross Corp., 239 NLRB No. 47, 100 LRRM 1020 (1978). An employer need bargain only over the effect of a basic capital decision on the basic scope and ultimate direction of the enterprise. General Motors Corp., 191 NLRB No. 149, 77 LRRM 1537 (1971).

15. On termination, a contract's wages, hours, and other terms and

conditions of employment are regarded as established conditions that cannot be changed unilaterally even though the agreement has expired. A union security clause expires automatically. *Industrial Union of Marine Workers v. NLRB*, 320 F2d 615, 53 LRRM 2878 (3rd Cir., 1963); *Trico Products Corp.*, 238 NLRB No. 184, 99 LRRM 1473 (1978); *American Sink Top & Cabinet Co.*, 242 NLRB No. 53, 101 LRRM 1166 (1979). Compare as to the effect of a decertification petition on an employer's bargaining obligation. *Telautograph Corp.*, 199 NLRB No. 117, 81 LRRM 1337 (1972) and *Lammert Industrial, Inc.*, 229 NLRB No. 128, 96 LRRM 1557 (1977).

16. A successor employer is not obligated to assume the collective bargaining agreement of the predecessor. Its only obligation is to bargain with the incumbent union if and when the prior employees comprise a majority of the new work force. *NLRB v. Burns International Security Services, Inc.*, 406 US 272, 80 LRRM 2225 (1972); *Pre-Engineered Building Products, Inc.*, 228 NLRB No. 70, 96 LRRM 1170 (1977). Compare: *South Prairie Construction Co. v. Operating Engineers Local 627*, 425 US 800, 92 LRRM 2507 (1976); *Edward J. White*, 237 NLRB No. 152, 99 LRRM 1126 (1978) (alter ego). See also *Amoco Production Co.*, 239 NLRB No. 182, 100 LRRM 1127 (1979), (change in union affiliation).

17. The Board cannot require an employer or a union to agree to contractual terms to which the party has not agreed as a remedy for bad faith bargaining. *H. K. Porter Co. v. NLRB*, 397 U.S. 99, 73 LRRM 2561 (1970); *Ex-Cell-O Corp.*, 185 NLRB No. 20, 74 LRRM 1740 (1970). The Board can, however, impose "extraordinary" remedies such as requiring the employer to reimburse the union for its litigation expenses and extra organizing costs caused by the employer's unlawful misconduct, *J. P. Stevens*, 244 NLRB No. 82, 102 LRRM 1039 (1979).

18. A union or individual employer can withdraw from a duly established multi-employer bargaining unit by giving written notice of an intention to withdraw before the date set by the contract for modification or the date agreed upon for the beginning of multi-employer negotiations. The notice must be both timely and unequivocal. Once bargaining has begun, withdrawal is not permitted except by mutual consent or in unusual circumstances. *Bonanno Linen Service, Inc.*, 243 NLRB No. 140, 102 LRRM 1001 (1979).

Recommended Reading   "A Union's Duty to Furnish Information to an Employer for Purposes of Collective Bargaining," 4 *U. Day. L. Rev.* 257 (1979).

Morales, "Presumption of Union's Majority Status in NLRB Cases," 29 *Lab. L.J.* 309 (1978).

Murphy, "Successorship and the Forgotten Employee: A Suggested Approach," 35 *N.Y.U. Conf. Lab.* 75 (1978).

Chapter Six

Strikes, Striker Rights, and Lockouts

The vast majority of all collective bargaining disputes are peacefully resolved. Yet, there are times when bargaining breaks down. On such occasions, employees may resort to their basic traditional right to strike. It is no exaggeration that the freedom of workers to strike, legally exercised, is one of the fundamental distinctions between democratic and totalitarian societies. A lockout is the employer's economic equivalent to a strike. The right to lockout is governed by many of the same principles covering the employee's right to strike.

A. STATUTORY PROTECTION OF THE RIGHT TO STRIKE

A strike is a concerted stoppage of work. While there is a constitutional right of free speech and constitutional protection against involuntary servitude, there is no absolute constitutional right to strike. The right to strike is subject to the legislative regulation embodied in the Labor Management Relations Act.

The Supreme Court has repeatedly stated that there is no federal antistrike policy. The law recognizes the right of both employers and unions to exercise their economic strength except as limited by statute or their collective bargaining agreement. The Norris-LaGuardia Act, by prohibiting issuance of injunctions in labor disputes, recognizes the legitimacy of the strike weapon.

Five sections of the LMRA deal with the right to strike: Section 8(b)(4)(B), 13, 502, 8(d), and 8(g).

Section 8(b)(4)(B) regulates secondary picketing and boycotts (see Chapter 7). A proviso to Section 8(b)(4)(B) states: "Nothing contained in this clause (B) shall be construed to make unlawful, where not otherwise unlawful, any primary strike or any primary picketing."

A primary strike is a strike against the employer with whom a union has its dispute. For example, if the employees of company A are on strike because of a dispute with A, perhaps for a new collective bargaining agreement, the employees are engaged in a primary strike. On the other hand, if the employees of company B stop work in support of the strike at A, the employees of B are engaged in a secondary strike, which is prohibited by Section 8(b)(4)(B). The employees of Company A are engaged in a primary strike protected by the

Section 8(b)(4)(B) proviso, but the employees of Company B are not. The circumstances under which employees of one employer may lawfully stop working in support of a labor dispute elsewhere are discussed in the next chapter.

The second statutory protection of the right to strike is Section 13, which provides:

> Nothing in this Act, except as specifically provided for herein, shall be construed so as either to interfere with or impede or diminish in any way the right to strike, or to affect the limitations or qualifications on that right.

The third statutory recognition of the right to strike is Section 502, which states:

> "Nothing in this Act shall be construed to require an individual employee to render labor or service without his consent, nor shall anything in this Act be construed to make the quitting of his labor by an individual employee an illegal act; nor shall any court issue any process to compel the performance by an individual employee of such labor or service, without his consent; nor shall the quitting of labor by any employee or employees in good faith because of abnormally dangerous conditions for work at the place of employment of such employee or employees be deemed a strike under this Act."

The final sections of the Act dealing with the right to strike are the provisions of Section 8(d), requiring that a party serve notice of its intention to terminate or modify a collective bargaining agreement and prohibiting a strike for the notice period (see Chapter 5), and Section 8(g), requiring that a labor organization give ten days notice of its intent to engage in a strike, picket, or other concerted activity at a health care facility. Section 8(g) is unique, because it applies whether or not the union has a collective bargaining agreement with the health care facility.

B. ECONOMIC VS. UNFAIR LABOR PRACTICE STRIKES

1. Basic Definitions Applied by the NLRB

Strikes are generally either an unfair labor practice or an economic strike. The distinction between an unfair labor practice or economic strike is very important because reemployment, voting (see Chapter 2), and other rights of strikers are determined by the type of strike.

Unfair Labor Practice Strikes

An unfair labor practice strike is a strike over an employer's unfair labor practices. A strike protesting an employer's discharge of a union supporter because of union activity is a typical example. However, a strike can be over virtually any type of employer unfair labor practice. A strike protesting the employer's refusal to bargain in good faith is an unfair labor practice strike.

Economic Strikes

An economic strike is a strike over an economic issue, such as wages, hours, or working conditions. A strike for a contract is an economic strike so long as an employer is bargaining in good faith. Normally, a strike for recognition is an economic strike except if the employer not only refuses to recognize the union, but also engages in extensive unfair labor practices that undermine the union's majority status. In those cases in which a Board bargaining order is appropriate (see Chapter 3), a strike for recognition may be considered an unfair labor practice strike.

What if a strike is over both an employer's unfair labor practices and an economic dispute? The Board has held that a strike is an unfair practice strike if it is in part caused by an unfair labor practice. One exception is if the unfair labor practice occurs some time before the strike begins. In that case, the Board will conclude that the economic dispute is the sole reason for the strike.

2. Recall vs. Reinstatement Rights

a. The Right to Replace Economic Strikers

The reinstatement right of the striking employees depends upon whether they are economic or unfair labor practice strikers.

During a strike, an employer is entitled to maintain operations and free to hire permanent replacements for economic strikers. Also, the employer may lawfully refuse to reinstate an economic striker who is permanently replaced by the time the strike has ended. (The distinction between temporary and permanent replacements was discussed in Chapter 2.) However, the striker must be placed on a recall list and reinstated as vacancies occur. Once reinstated, an employee is not considered a newly hired employee and retains his prior seniority status.

If the economic striker is not replaced by a permanent replacement, he is entitled to reemployment when the strike ends. Employees must offer to return to work before the employer has any obligation to reinstate them. If an employer and union agree to a contract, the employees offer to return in accordance with the contract's terms. However, if a union simply abandons an unsuccessful strike, the employees' offer to return must be unconditional before the employees have reinstatement rights. For example, what if employees, making $6.00 per hour, struck to obtain a wage rate of $6.50 per hour, which the employer refused. If the union offers to return on the condition that the employer agrees to pay $6.25 per hour, the offer is not unconditional. The employees must be willing to return at the previously existing conditions.

If the employer has permanently abolished a striker's job during a strike, he must place the striker on a recall list. Unless the employer can show a legitimate and substantial reason for failing to do so, he must reinstate the employee when a job for which the employee is qualified is available.

b. Contractual Recall Rights of Economic Strikers

After a strike is over, permanent replacements who are working usually have less seniority than the replaced strikers awaiting reinstatement. If a contract has a provision that layoffs and recalls are in seniority order, should the replaced striker be able to exercise his seniority and return to work? Unfortunately, no. The Board has held that unreinstated economic strikers do not have any contractual right to recall in accordance with provisions governing recall from layoff. Of course, the parties can agree to apply the layoff clause to the reinstatement of economic strikers. However, the Board has concluded that a typical layoff-recall clause does not apply to the reinstatement of economic strikers because replaced employees are not in a layoff status.

c. Reinstatement of Unfair Labor Practice Strikers

An employer can also continue operations during an unfair labor practice strike. But, in contrast to an economic striker, an unfair labor practice striker cannot be permanently replaced. An unfair labor practice striker who unconditionally applies for reinstatement when a strike ends is entitled to reinstatement with full seniority and other benefits to his former job. If his former position no longer exists, he is entitled to reinstatement to a substantially equivalent position.

Any replacements are temporary only. If the employer wants to keep people hired during the strike, the employer may do so, but he cannot retain them in place of the strikers. If necessary, the employer will be required to discharge the replacements to restore the unfair labor practice strikers to their former or equivalent positions.

The Five Day Rule. Normally, the Board allows an employer five days to re-employ strikers after they offer to return to work. This period gives the employer time to make the necessary administrative arrangements. Back pay begins immediately when the strikers offer to return if the employer rejects the offer, unduly delays or ignores the reinstatement offer, or places unlawful conditions on reemployment, such as telling employees they can return to work if they disclaim their union.

3. Conversion to an Unfair Labor Practice Strike

A strike that begins as an economic strike can be converted into an unfair labor practice strike if an employer commits serious unfair labor practices during the strike that prolong it, such as unlawfully discharging the strikers. The strikers become unfair labor practice strikers when the unfair labor practices occur. Strikers who are permanently replaced before the strike becomes unfair labor practice strike are not entitled to reinstatement. However, no additional strikers can be permanently replaced after that time.

C. LOSS OF RECALL OR REINSTATEMENT RIGHTS

1. Permanent Employment Elsewhere or Cessation of Employer Operations

There are certain situations in which either economic or unfair labor practice strikers lose their recall rights. A strikers' recall rights end if the employee finds permanent employment elsewhere. An employee who does not intend to return to work at the end of the strike has no recall rights. Also, a striker may lose recall rights if his job is permanently abolished during the strike. (see Chapter 2.)

2. Strike Misconduct

Employees who engage in serious misconduct during a strike may be discharged and thereby lose their right to recall or reinstatement. This rule applies to both economic and unfair labor practice strikers.

The Board's position is that a striker can be lawfully discharged only if the misconduct was serious because some violence or other misconduct is to be anticipated during a strike. The Board considers the severity and frequency of the behavior. For example, pickets who use vulgar language when the plant manager or replacements cross the picket line do not lose their right to recall. Physically blocking others from entering the plant is usually considered minor misconduct. In some cases, even a physical assault on another person is insufficient to justify a discharge if no one was hurt, if the attack was provoked, or even if a striker became momentarily carried away by the heat of strike emotions. The Board refers to such behavior as "anticipated animal exhuberance."

The Board requires evidence of serious misconduct because it is reluctant to terminate the recall rights of a good employee because of a momentary lapse.

The misconduct must render the employee unfit for further employment. Thus, unprovoked assaults causing harm to another or other actions jeopardizing the life of another person are grounds for discharge. Driving dangerously close behind another car that the strikers are trailing or attempting to force a car driven by a striker replacement off the road are examples of such major misconduct.

In almost every case, the Board upholds the discharge of employees who engage in an economic strike in violation of a contractual no strike clause so long as all striking employees are treated equally, and the employer does not single out the union leaders for greater discipline.

a. Shop Steward Conduct During a Strike

At one time, it was an accepted industrial relations doctrine that a shop steward could be held to a higher standard of conduct during a strike because of his position. Employers argued that other employees looked up to the steward for guidance and would engage in misconduct if the steward did. Thus, it was argued, a steward could be discharged for misconduct that would not be serious enough to terminate other employees. The Board now rejects this approach, holding that stewards can only be held to the same standards as other employees during a strike. Thus, if a steward leads a wildcat strike, he can be discharged as could any other wildcat strike leader. But if a shop steward simply participates in the strike without instigating it, he cannot be subjected to greater discipline than the other participating employees. One court of appeals has denied enforcement to a Board decision applying the new rule, and the issue of shop steward discipline may ultimately have to be decided by the Supreme Court.

b. Employer Provocation

As an exception to the general rule permitting discharge for serious strike misconduct, an employer cannot discharge an employee if the employer provokes the employee. If the employer instructs replacements to drive through the picket line at high speed, and the pickets retaliate by throwing rocks, breaking car windows, and slashing tires, the employer's actions provoked this serious strike misconduct. Thus, the Board will probably hold that strikers cannot be discharged for their violent reaction.

D. DISCRIMINATION AGAINST STRIKERS

An employer violates Section 8(a)(3) if he unlawfully discriminates against strikers on account of their union activities. An employer may not discriminatorily refuse to reinstate or re-employ strikers merely because of union membership or strike activity.

Super Seniority for Replacements

An employer cannot discriminate against returning strikers in their wages, hours, or working conditions under the Supreme Court's decision in *Erie Resistor*.[1] Here, the employees struck when negotiations for a new contract broke down. The employer notified the union that he would begin hiring replacements and that strikers would retain their jobs until replaced. This was a lawful tactic because the employees were engaged in an economic strike. Subsequently, the employer announced that it would award 20 additional years of seniority (termed super seniority) to strike replacements and strikers who returned to work by a certain date. The employer argued that this incentive was nec-

[1] See legal principle 3.

essary to get replacements to work. After an increasing number of strikers returned to work, in part because of the fear of losing seniority, the union gave up and signed a contract with the employer. The union then filed an unfair labor practice charge that the granting of super seniority during the strike was discrimination against the strikers because of their union activities in violation of Section 8(a)(3).

The Supreme Court affirmed the Board's decision that the employer had violated the Act. The Court stated that the employer's actions were inherently discriminatory or destructive of the employees' rights to engage in concerted activities.

Based on *Erie Resistor,* an employer cannot grant greater seniority or other benefits to striker replacements. A striker who returns to work retains his prestrike seniority and cannot be made to start over as a new employee. Also, an employer cannot disqualify an employee for benefits because of strike activity. Time lost because of a strike must be treated the same as any other period of unemployment for purposes of contractual benefits. If employees have certain benefits that accrued before a strike and are payable on a certain day, an employer cannot refuse to pay the benefits because the employees are on strike at the time. Thus, if an employee is entitled to vacation pay when a strike begins, the employer cannot withhold the vacation payment until the strike is over.

E. RIGHT TO PAY WHILE ON STRIKE

Employees engaged in an economic strike understand that they are not entitled to pay during the strike. However, employees sometimes erroneously believe that they are entitled to pay if they are engaged in an unfair labor practice strike. That is not so. Because they are withholding their services, employees are not entitled to pay while engaged in either an unfair labor practice or economic strike. As an exception, unfair labor practice strikers and economic strikers who have not been replaced are entitled to back pay if their employer unlawfully rejects an unconditional offer to return to work.

Back Pay for Discharged Unfair Labor Practice Strikers

The Board has held that an unfair labor practice striker who is unlawfully discharged is entitled to back pay from the date of his discharge even though he does not offer to return to work. Instead, the burden is upon the employer to offer reinstatement. The Board reasons that if an employee has been discharged, it is senseless to require that he request reinstatement to be eligible for back pay. However, if an employer offers reinstatment without attaching any unlawful conditions and the employee refuses and continues to strike, the employee is ineligible for back pay. Also, as is true for any unlawfully discharged employee, the discharged unfair labor practice striker must attempt to reduce his losses by seeking employment elsewhere. If the employee spends all his time on the picket line and does not look for work, he is not eligible for back pay.

F. STRIKE SETTLEMENT AGREEMENTS

Many strikes end with the execution of a strike settlement agreement covering such matters as re-employment of strikers and payment of fringe benefits for the strike period. It is a good idea to have an express agreement in which the employer waives the right to discipline employees for strike misconduct. Otherwise, the employer can still discharge employees for misconduct occuring during the strike. An employer and union can also negotiate an agreement limiting the period during which replaced economic strikers are subject to recall. However, replaced strikers must retain recall rights for a reasonable period. The issues of recall rights for replaced economic strikers and waiving discipline for strike misconduct are permissive subjects of bargaining (see Chapter 5).

G.   SYMPATHY STRIKERS

A sympathy strike is a strike in which employees (whether in a union or not) who have no dispute with their employer, honor a union's picket line. Sympathy strikes usually occur in one of two ways. First, employees with the same employer may respect a picket line established by their fellow employees who are in another bargaining unit. For example, clerical employees may respect the picket line established by striking production employees. The clerical employees are sympathy strikers. Second, employees of one employer may honor a picket line established by a union representing employees of another employer. For example, truck drivers employed by one company may refuse to make deliveries to another company across a picket line established by the other company's striking employees.

1. The Protected Status of Sympathy Strikers

Sympathy strikers have the same rights as the employees whose picket line they respect. Thus, employees who honor a picket line established to protest an employer's unfair labor practices have the status of unfair labor

practice strikers and they cannot be replaced. Employees who honor an unlawful secondary picket line (see Chapter 7) are unprotected and are subject to discharge. Employees who honor a picket line established in an economic dispute are considered economic sympathy strikers. They can be temporarily or permanently replaced, as is necessary for their employer to continue operations. However, the economic sympathy striker cannot be discharged for engaging in a lawful sympathy strike.

Suppose an employee of company A refuses to make deliveries across an economic picket line established by company B's employees at B's plant. Company A uses one of its supervisors or another employee to drive across the picket line and make deliveries. Has the sympathy striker been permanently replaced? No. The supervisor or other employee is only a temporary replacement for the employee. The employee cannot be discharged, but he is not entitled to receive pay for the time he refused to cross the picket line.

What if company A's driver is willing to make deliveries to A's customers who were not on strike? Can Company A send the employee home for the entire day because he refused to make the one delivery? No, because the employee has not been permanently replaced and is willing to work, it is unlawful retaliation in violation of Section 8(a)(3) to discipline the employee in any way for exercising his right to engage in a sympathy strike.

Suppose the company has to hire another employee to make the delivery the first employee refuses to make. The employer can hire the new employee as a permanent replacement for the sympathy striker, if that is necessary to maintain operations, just as an employer can hire permanent replacements for economic strikers.

2. Concerted Activity vs. Fearful Acts

A sympathy striker frequently acts alone, but is considered to be engaged in concerted activity because he supports the concerted strike effort. In contrast, an employee who refuses to cross a picket line out of fear of physical harm is acting as an individual and is not considered to be engaging in concerted activities. Whether the employee can be disciplined for refusing to cross a picket line because of fear is primarily a contractual issue based on whether the discipline is for just cause. If the employee has valid reasons for fearing to cross the picket line, an arbitrator will probably conclude that the discipline is not for just cause. In some cases, an employee's refusal to cross a picket line out of fear is protected by Section 502, which protects an employee's right to quit work in good faith because of an abnormally dangerous working condition at his place of employment. (Section 502 is discussed fully later in the chapter.)

3. Refusal to Handle Struck Goods

An employee who refuses to handle struck work (i.e., work produced by an employer whose employees are on strike) is in effect engaged in a sympathy strike. As in the case of an employee who honors an economic picket line, employees who refuse to handle struck work can be replaced, but cannot be discharged.

There is a major restriction on refusing to handle struck work. Two employers have the legal right to maintain their normal business relationship even though one of them is on strike. Thus, the Board has held that employees are not protected if, out of sympathy for strikers at another plant, they refuse to do their normal work on the product of a struck

employer. Employees can be disciplined for refusing to do their normal work, but they can refuse to do work on a product that they would not be doing but for the strike.

For example, suppose a product consists of two components, one produced by company A and one produced by company B. The product is assembled at B's plant. Company A is struck, but continues to operate with replacement employees. Company B's employees cannot refuse to assemble the components produced by company A during the strike. Companies A and B are simply maintaining their normal business relationship and the employees are doing their normal work. But if company B orders its employees to assemble the part Company A would have made except for the strike, they can refuse to do that work because they are being asked to do work they would not do but for the strike.

Some contracts contain clauses specifically protecting the right of employees to respect the picket line of other employees or refuse to handle struck work. (The legal restrictions on such clauses are discussed in Chapter 7.)

H. CONTRACTUAL RESTRICTIONS ON THE RIGHT TO STRIKE

1. Scope of the No-Strike Obligation

It is well established that a union can be sued for damages by the employer if the union strikes in violation of a no-strike clause.

As a general rule, the courts interpret a no-strike clause as having the same scope as the contractual arbitration clause. This means that a union cannot strike over an arbitrable issue. The reason for this rule is that the union's no-strike pledge is considered an exchange for the employer's agreement to arbitrate. Thus, logically, the scope of a no-strike clause and an arbitration clause should be the same. Technically, however, the parties can expressly negotiate a no-strike clause that either permits the union to strike over certain arbitrable issues or broadly prohibits a union from striking even over non-arbitrable issues. Such agreements are rare, but courts will enforce the contract according to its terms. For example, some contracts permit a union to strike if an employer fails to make payments to fringe benefit funds. The employer's failure to pay the contractual amounts owed is certainly arbitrable, but the union can strike because of the express authority. It takes clear language before a court interprets a contract to permit a strike over an arbitrable issue or prohibit a strike over an issue that is not arbitrable.

2. Injunctions to Enforce an Express No-Strike Obligation (The *Boys Market* Decision)

Although a union's liability for damages for a strike in breach of contract is well established, the question of whether a court can issue an injunction prohibiting a strike in breach of contract was not finally resolved until the Supreme Court's 1970 *Boys Market Decision*.[2] Prior to this decision, the Supreme Court had held that Section 4 of the Norris-LaGuardia Act prohibited an injunction against a strike and that damages were the only remedy. Section 4 provided:

> No Court of the United States shall have jurisdiction to issue any restraining order or temporary or permanent injunction in any case involving or growing out of any labor dispute to prohibit any person or persons . . . from doing whether singly or in concert, any of the following acts: (a) Ceasing or re-

fusing to perform any work or to remain in any relation of employment; . . . (i) Advising, urging, or otherwise causing or inducing without fraud or violence the acts heretofore specified. . . .

In *Boys Market*, the Court expressly overruled its prior decision. It held that an injunction can be issued against a work stoppage in violation of a no-strike pledge if the strike is over an issue the parties are contractually bound to arbitrate. The Court stated that it was making an exception to Norris-LaGuardia in order to implement the strong Congressional preference for resolving industrial disputes through arbitration. The Court stated:

> Our holding in the present case is a narrow one. We do not undermine the vitality of the Norris-LaGuardia Act. We deal only with the situation in which the collective bargaining agreement contains a mandatory grievance adjustment or arbitration procedure.

The Court also set down the other requirements that must be met before an injunction can be issued, stating:

> A District Court entertaining an action . . . may not grant injunctive relief against concerted activity unless and until it decides that the case is one in which an injunction would be appropriate despite the Norris-LaGuardia Act. When a strike is sought to be enjoined because it is over a grievance which both parties are contractually bound to arbitrate, the District Court may issue no injunctive order until it first holds that the contract does have that effect; and the employer should be ordered to arbitrate, as a condition of his obtaining an injunction against the strike. Beyond this, the District Court must, of course, consider whether issuance of an injunction would be warranted under ordinary principles of equity—whether breaches are occurring and will continue, or have been threatened and will be committed; whether they have caused or will cause irreparable injury to the employer; and whether the employer will suffer

[2] See legal principle 6.

more from the denial of an injunction than will the union from its issuance.

Suppose a union misses the contractual time limit for filing a grievance and the union strikes over the dispute despite a contractual no-strike clause. If the employer files suit for an injunction, he must be willing to arbitrate the dispute, even though the grievance was filed late. If not, the court will not issue an injunction against the strike because the purpose of the injunction is to uphold the arbitration process.

A suit to enforce a collective bargaining agreement, including the no-strike clause, is usually brought in Federal court under Section 301 of the Labor Management Relations Act (see Chapter 9).

Remember, an employer has remedies besides an injunction for the union's breach of its no-strike obligation. An employer can lawfully discharge the strikers or can just file a damage suit and not seek an injunction at all. That may put greater pressure on the union than an injunction because the employer's damages increase each day the strike continues.

3. Enforcement of an Implied No-Strike Clause

A union with a contract containing an arbitration clause, but that does not contain a no-strike clause, might believe that it is free to strike as it wishes. That is not so. The Supreme Court has held that there is an implied obligation not to strike over any issue arbitrable under the arbitration clause. A union that strikes over an arbitrable issue is subject to a damage suit and a court may issue an injunction against the strike as if there were an express no-strike agreement. The union would, of course, be free to strike over any issue that is not subject to arbitration.

I. EXCEPTIONS TO NO-STRIKE CLAUSES

1. Sympathy Strikes

The Supreme Court expressly stated in *Buffalo Forge* that a restriction on sympathy strikes cannot be implied from an agreement to arbitrate.[3] The implied no-strike obligation doctrine applies only to disputes arising under the contract. Since *Buffalo Forge*, the federal courts have generally ruled that restrictions on the right to engage in sympathy strikes cannot even be implied from an express no-strike agreement. The courts have reasoned that a general no-strike clause only applies to disputes between the contracting employer and union subject to arbitration under the parties' contract. Sympathy strikes do not involve a dispute between the contracting employer and union. Under this view, an employer is not even entitled to damages if a union engages in a sympathy strike. The NLRB has also ruled that a general no-strike clause does not prohibit a sympathy strike.

Of course, a no-strike clause can expressly prohibit sympathy strikes. Also, the bargaining history between an employer and a union might demonstrate that the union waived its statutory right to engage in sympathy strikes and the parties intended that the general no-strike clause prohibit sympathy strikes as well. For example, what if a union proposes an express provision giving it the right to engage in sympathy strikes? The proposal is discussed extensively during negotiations, but ultimately the employer rejects the proposal. Based on this bargaining history, a court or the Board could conclude that the general no-strike clause prohibits a sympathy strike as well. Therefore, a union should be

[3] See legal principle 6.

very cautious before even proposing an express contractual provision permitting a sympathy strike. If the union makes such a proposal, but fails to obtain the contractual language, it may have waived its statutory right.

If the express language of a no-strike clause bars a sympathy strike or if the union's waiver of its right to engage in a sympathy strike is clear from the bargaining history, an employer can obtain damages against the union for engaging in a sympathy strike and discipline the employees who participated. But, under the *Buffalo Forge* decision, the employer still cannot get an injunction against a sympathy strike because the strike is not over an arbitrable issue even though it violates the contract.

2. Unfair Labor Practice Strikes

The Supreme Court has held that a no-strike clause does not apply to a strike in protest over an employer's unfair labor practices. The Court reasoned that a no-strike clause is intended to apply to economic disputes between employer and a union arising under the terms of their collective bargaining agreement and not to waive the union's statutory right to protest employer unfair labor practices. Thus, an employer cannot discharge an employee for engaging in an unfair labor practice strike even though the contract contains a no-strike clause.

However, the Board has limited the impact of the Court's decision by holding that an employer must commit a serious unfair labor practice before a union can strike notwithstanding a contractual no-strike clause. The Board adopted this policy to prevent a union from seizing upon a minor infraction to justify a strike primarily motivated by economic reasons. As is true for a sympathy strike, a union can expressly waive the right to engage in an unfair labor practice strike. Because the union has a statutory right to strike over an employer's unfair labor practice, such a waiver must be expressly stated in the contract or unmistakenly clear from the bargaining history.

3. Safety Dispute Strikes

Section 502 of the Labor Management Relations Act provides:

> . . . nor shall the quitting of labor by an employee or employees in good faith because of abnormally dangerous conditions for work at the place of employment of such employee or employees be deemed a strike under this Act.

The Supreme Court held in *Gateway Coal* that, based on Section 502, employees refusing to work cannot be disciplined so long as there is ascertainable objective evidence supporting the employees' conclusion that the work is abnormally dangerous.[4] A no-strike clause does not prohibit a strike protected by Section 502. The courts and the Board have held that a strike or other concerted activity over abnormally dangerous conditions is protected even though the employees are wrong about the danger or there is a good faith disagreement between the employer and the employees as to the danger. The employees' decision must only be reasonably based on ascertainable objective evidence.

J. LOCKOUTS

1. Offensive vs. Defensive Lockouts

A lockout refers to an employer's action prohibiting its employees from working as a

[4] See legal principle 8.

tactic in a labor dispute. A defensive lockout occurs when an employer fears that the employees will strike at a time when the employer is particularly vulnerable, and so locks out the employees instead at a time that strengthens his bargaining position. For example, the employer, engaged in contract negotiations during the slow season, may believe that the union is delaying bargaining in order to strike during the busy season. He may lock out the employees during the slow season when he has the economic advantage.

In an offensive lockout, the employer locks out employees in order to put greater economic pressure on a union to adopt the employer's bargaining demands, just as unions strike to put greater pressure on employers.

At one time, the Board permitted lockouts for defensive purposes only. It permitted employers who were members of a multiemployer bargaining association to lock out all the employees if a union struck one member of the association. That was considered a lawful employer defensive tactic to prevent a union from undermining the association and pressuring each employer to sign an agreement favorable to the union.

The Supreme Court rejected the Board's distinction between offensive and defensive lockouts in the *American Ship Building Co.* case.[5] There the Court upheld the employer's right to use a lockout offensively to secure more favorable contract terms. The Board had argued that an offensive lockout inherently destroyed employee rights in violation of Section 8(a)(1) and 8(a)(3) (see Chapter 4). However, the Court basically equated an employer's right to lockout with a union's right to strike, holding that a lockout is permissible unless the Board can prove that there is specific intent to discriminate against employees because of their union activities.

[5] See legal principle 9.

Since *American Ship Building Co.*, the Board has generally upheld the right of employers to engage in an offensive lockout. A union can strike at anytime after its contract has expired provided that the proper statutory notices have been given, even though no bargaining impasse has been reached. Similarly, an employer can lock out its employees after a contract has expired even before a bargaining impasse has been reached, in support of its bargaining position.

2. Replacement of Locked Out Employees

The employer's right to continue operations with replacements during a lockout remains a major unresolved issue.

Both the Board and the courts agree that an employer can lock out employees and continue operations using supervisors, temporary replacements, or both. The open issue is whether an employer can permanently replace employees whom the employer has locked out. The Supreme Court held in *American Ship Building* that a lockout as such is not destructive of employee rights. Similarly, use of temporary replacements does not place undue pressure on employees to submit to the employer's proposals. But, an employer obviously would have very strong bargaining power if it could lock out its employees and then permanently replace them. That places the employees' continued employment totally in the employer's hands. The impact is similar to an employer granting replacements super seniority, which the Supreme Court held unlawful in the *Erie Resistor* case discussed above. For these reasons, unions have argued that employers should not be permitted to permanently replace locked out employees.

So far, there have been very few reported

cases of the permanent replacement of locked out employees. Apparently most employers avoid the tactic because of its questionable legality. In one case the Board held that an employer violated Section 8(a)(1) and (3) by permanently locking out employees without giving the union prior notice and bargaining with it first. It is not clear if there might be situations where the Board would uphold the permanent replacement of locked out employees.

Summary

This chapter covered strikes and strikers' rights, focusing on the re-employment rights of strikers under the LMRA. While there is no constitutional right to strike, the LMRA affords a statutory basis for the right to engage in a primary strike.

Strikes are generally classified as either an unfair labor practice strike (a strike over an employer's unfair labor practice) or an economic strike (a strike over an economic issue). Whether a union is engaged in an unfair labor practice or economic strike is important because it determines the striker's re-employment rights. In an economic strike, the employer is free to hire permanent replacements for the strikers. Replaced strikers have the right to reinstatement as vacancies occur. In contrast, an unfair labor practice striker cannot be replaced. An unfair labor practice striker who unconditionally offers to return to work is entitled to reinstatement. Both economic and unfair labor practice strikers may lose their reinstatement or recall rights if they engage in serious strike misconduct.

An employer may violate Section 8(a)(3) if he unlawfully discriminates against strikers because they engaged in a strike. After the termination of a strike, an employer may not discriminatorily refuse to reinstate or re-employ the strikers because of their union membership or concerted activity. Also, the employer cannot discriminate between strikers and non-strikers on wages, hours, or working conditions such as granting replacements super-seniority after the strikers' return to work.

A contractual no-strike clause only restricts the right to engage in an economic strike. In the absence of express wording, a no-strike clause does not prohibit an unfair labor practice strike over an employer's serious unfair labor practices. Similarly, a no-strike clause usually does not prohibit sympathy strikes. Sympathy strikers have the same statutory protection as the employees whose strike they respect. Thus, a sympathy striker who refuses to cross a picket line established by economic strikers can be replaced, but not discharged. However, a no-strike obligation will be implied in the absence of any express provision if the contract provides for arbitration. A union cannot then strike over an arbitrable issue.

In *Boys Market*, the Supreme Court held that the federal courts have jurisdiction to enjoin a strike in violation of an express or implied no-strike clause over an arbitrable issue. In addition to injunctive relief, an employer can lawfully discharge employees who strike in breach of contract and file suit for damages against the union under Section 301 of the Labor Management Relations Act.

In *Buffalo Forge*, the Supreme Court held that the *Boys Market* doctrine did not apply to a sympathy strike because a sympathy strike is not over an arbitrable issue under the parties' contract. Although a sympathy strike cannot be enjoined, an employer might be able to collect damages growing out of such a strike if the court or arbitrator should find that the no-strike clause prohibits a sympathy strike based on either the clause's express wording or the parties' bargaining history.

An employer lockout is the counterpart to a union strike. Generally, an employer may engage in either a defensive or offensive lockout in support of its bargaining position. The Board has held that an employer can lawfully continue operating with temporary replacements. It may be unlawful for an employer to lock out its employees and then permanently replace them, but there is no clear case on the point.

Review Questions

1. Is there a constitutional right to strike?

2. What is the statutory basis of the right to strike?

3. What is an unfair labor practice strike?

4. What is an economic strike?

5. What is the difference in reinstatement rights for economic and unfair labor practice strikers?

6. How do the voting rights of economic and unfair labor practice strikers differ in an NLRB election?

7. How can economic or unfair labor practice strikers lose their reinstatement or recall rights?

8. Are unfair labor practice strikers entitled to lost wages during the term of the strike?

9. What is a sympathy strike?

10. Can a sympathy striker be discharged for engaging in a sympathy strike if the contract contains an express no-strike clause?

11. Can a sympathy striker be permanently replaced?

12. Does a no-strike clause prohibit all strikes during a contract?

13. Under what circumstances will a court imply a contractual obligation not to strike in the absence of an express no-strike clause?

14. What are an employer's judicial remedies against a union's breach of a no-strike clause?

15. Will a federal court enjoin a sympathy strike under Section 301 of the Labor Management Relations Act?

(Answers to review questions appear at end of book).

1. Unfair labor practice strikers are entitled to reinstatement to their former jobs even if the employer has hired replacements. *Tarlas Meat Co.,* 239 NLRB No. 200, 100 LRRM 1210 (1979). However, strikers found guilty of serious strike misconduct are not entitled to reinstatement. *Advance Pattern & Machine Corp.,* 241 NLRB No. 70, 100 LRRM 1537 (1979). *Basic Legal Principles*

2. An employer is entitled to hire permanent replacements for economic strikers and may lawfully refuse to reinstate them. Economic strikers are entitled to recall as vacancies occur. An economic striker who has not been replaced is usually entitled to reinstatement upon an unconditional offer to return to work. *NLRB v. Fleetwood Trailer Co.,* 389 US 375, 66 LRRM 2737 (1967); *NLRB v. Mackay Radio and Telegraph Co.,* 304 US 333, 2 LRRM 610 (1938); *Laidlaw Corp.,* 171 NLRB No. 175, 68 LRRM 1252 (1968).

3. An employer cannot discriminate against strikers or hold out inducements, such as super seniority, favoring nonstrikers or replacements over the strikers in order to destroy the right to strike. *NLRB v. Erie Resistor Corp.,* 373 US 221, 53 LRRM 2121 (1963); *NLRB v. Great Dane Trailers Inc.,* 388 US 26, 65 LRRM 2465 (1967).

4. A sympathy striker is engaging in protected activity and cannot be discharged. However, the employer may permanently replace an economic sympathy striker if necessary to the employer's continued operations. *Redwing Carriers Inc.,* 137 NLRB No. 162, 50 LRRM 1440 (1962), *Newberry Energy Corp.,* 227 NLRB No. 58, 94 LRRM 1307 (1976).

5. The refusal of an employee to cross a picket line because of physical fear is not a protected activity. *NLRB v. Union Carbine Corp.,* 440 F2d 54, 76 LRRM 2181 (4th Cir. 1971).

6. A court can enjoin a strike in violation of a no-strike clause over an arbitrable dispute between the employer and the union. *Boys Markets Inc. v. Retail Clerks, Local 770,* 398 US 235, 74 LRRM 2257 (1970). A sympathy strike cannot be enjoined because it is not over an arbitrable issue. *Buffalo Forge Co., v. Steelworkers,* 428 US 397, 92 LRRM 3032 (1976).

7. A no-strike obligation is implied if a contract provides for arbitration and the strike is over an arbitrable issue. *Teamsters Local 174 v. Lucas Flower Co.,* 369 US 95, 49 LRRM 2717 (1962); *Gateway Coal Co., United Mine Workers,* 414 US 368, 85 LRRM 2049 (1974).

8. An employee who strikes in violation of a no-strike clause is not engaged in protected concerted activities and can be discharged. *NLRB v. Rockaway New Supply Co.,* 345 US 71, 31 LRRM 2432 (1953). However, the usual standard form no-strike clause does not prohibit an unfair labor practice strike, a sympathy strike, or refusal to work under abnormally

dangerous conditions. *Mastro Plastics Corp. v. NLRB*, 350 US 270, 37 LRRM 2587 (1956); *Gateway Coal Co. v. United Mine Workers, supra; Gary Hobart Water Corp.*, 210 NLRB No. 81, 86 LRRM 1210 (1974) *enforced*, 511 F2d 284, 88 LRRM 2830 (7th Cir. 1975).

9. Generally, both defensive and offensive employer lockouts are lawful. An employer can engage in an offensive lockout in support of its bargaining position. *American Shipbuilding Co., v. NLRB*, 380 US 300, 58 LRRM 2672 (1965). However, an offensive lockout, initiated in part to compel the union to accept the employer's position on a permissive subject of bargaining, is unlawful. *Movers and Warehousemen Association*, 224 NLRB No. 64, 92 LRRM 1236 (1976), *enforced*, 550 F2d 1962, 94 LRRM 2795 (4th Cir. 1977).

10. An employer can continue to operate with temporary replacements during an offensive lockout. The hiring of permanent replacements for lockout employees is probably prohibited, at least without prior notice to, and bargaining with, the union. *NLRB v. Brown*, 380 US 278, 58 LRRM 2663 (1965); *Johns-Manville Products Corp.*, 223 NLRB No. 189, 92 LRRM 1103 (1976), *enforcement denied on other grounds*, 557 F2d 1126, 96 LRRM 2010 (5 Cir. 1977).

11. An employer cannot impose greater discipline on union officers or stewards than on other employees who participate in, but do not instigate wildcat strike. *Precision Casting Co.*, 233 NLRB No. 35, 96 LRRM 1540 (1977); but see, *Indiana & Michigan Electric Co. v. NLRB* ———F2d.———, 101 LRRM 2475 (7 Cir. 1979) (upholding greater discipline of stewards contrary to NLRB position).

Recommended Reading

Bartlett, Newman, Mauro, "Strikes In Violation of the Contract: A Management View. A Union View.," 31 *N.Y.U. Conf. Lab.* 64 (1978).

"Employer Counter Measures to Union Activity—Sabotage By Unidentified Employees Characterized as an In-Plant Strike by the Union, An Employer Could Respond by Permanently Replacing Union Employees Without Violating the NLRA," 46 *Geo Wash. L. Rev.* 638 (1978).

"Union May Be Liable for Sympathy Strike Damages When It Has Failed to Use Reasonable Care to Prevent Spread of Wildcat Strike," 31 *Vand. L. Rev.* 15 (1978).

Chapter Seven

Picketing and Related Activity

Effective picketing is a key to an effective strike. Although most employees associate picketing with a strike against their own employer, picketing occurs in other situations as well. Picketing may be to protest substandard wages that undercut union wage goals or it may be directed against an employer who is selling a product produced by another employer whose employees are on strike.

The statutory restrictions on the right to engage in picketing are contained in Sections 8(b)(4) and

8(b)(7). There is a limited constitutional right to picket as a matter of free speech. The courts have held that picketing is a form of action, not just speech, and can be regulated. The right to engage in picketing on a labor matter is comprehensively regulated by the LMRA. The Supreme Court has upheld the constitutionality of these provisions. It has further held that a union's right to picket is determined by the LMRA rather than based on constitutional grounds.

A. AN OVERVIEW OF SECTION 8(b)(4)

Section 8(b)(4) is one of the most complex provisions in the LMRA. Its express meaning is so unclear at points that the Supreme Court has held that on some issues, the intent of the provision, rather than the actual wording, must be applied to achieve the statutory purpose. The Board and court decisions emphasize the statutory intent rather than the Act's wording in determining the legality of certain union actions. This chapter concentrates on the restrictions developed by the Supreme Court and Board decisions interpreting the Act rather than analyzing the express wording in detail.

Subsections (A), (B), (C), and (D) of Section 8(b)(4) prohibit different union conduct. Subsection (A) applies to forcing or requiring an employer to become a union member. It also prohibits a union from forcing or requiring an employer to enter into an agreement prohibited by Section 8(e). Section 8(e) pertains to hot cargo agreements (see Chapter 8). Subsection (B), the so-called secondary boycott or secondary activity provision, prevents a union from forcing or requiring a person to cease dealing with any other person because of the union's dispute with the other person. Subsection (C) prohibits forcing or requiring an employer to recognize or bargain with one union if another union has been certified as the bargaining representative. Subsection

(D), which governs jurisdictional disputes, also prohibits forcing or requiring an employer to assign work to one union rather than another (see also Chapter 8).

Section 8(b)(4) contains certain protections for primary picketing. Subsection (B) contains a proviso that "nothing contained in this clause (B) shall be construed to make unlawful, where not otherwise unlawful, any primary strike or primary picketing." Primary picketing, as discussed later in this chapter, is picketing directed against the employer against whom a union has a dispute. There is also a proviso following Subsection (D) that states: "nothing contained in this subsection 8(b)(4) shall be construed to make unlawful a refusal by any person to enter upon the premises of any employer (other than his own employer), if the employees of such employer are engaged in a strike ratified or approved by a representative of such employees whom such employer is required to recognize under this Act." This section recognizes the right of employees of one employer to honor a primary picket line established by other striking employees.

The first paragraph of Section 8(b)(4) has two clauses. Clause (i) prohibits a union from engaging in a strike or inducing an employee to strike or otherwise refuse to work in order to force an employer into one of the acts prohibited by Subsections (A), (B), (C), or (D). Clause (ii) prohibits a union from threatening, restraining, or coercing any person to engage in conduct prohibited by (A), (B), (C), and (D). The principal difference between (i) and (ii) is that (ii) prohibits threats, etc., against any person, not just employees. This section prohibits union threats, etc., directly against an employer in order to obtain one of the objects prohibited by Subsections (A), (B), (C), or (D).

B. THE PRIMARY/SECONDARY PICKETING DISTINCTION

If Section 8(b)(4)(B) were applied literally, it could prevent any picketing. If employees strike and picket their own employer, forcing him to close down, that undoubtedly forces an employer to cease using, selling or handling the products of another employer or to cease doing business with another employer. However, the last sentence of Section 8(b)(4)(B) contains the proviso protecting the right to engage in primary picketing or a primary strike "not otherwise unlawful." In *Rice Milling* (1951), the Supreme Court had to determine what this proviso meant in relationship to Section 8(b)(4)(B).[1]

1. Traditional Primary Picketing

In *Rice Milling*, the union was picketing an employer for recognition. The Act now contains restrictions on recognition picketing, added in 1959 long after the *Rice Milling* decision (see below), but in 1951 the picketing was lawful. Picketing an employer with whom a union has a direct dispute, as in *Rice Milling*, is traditional primary picketing. As a customer's truck came up to the Rice Milling picket line, the union's pickets approached the truck and asked that the occupants not cross the picket line. Applied literally word-for-word, the pickets' request violated 8(b)(4)(i), which prohibits employees from inducing or encouraging any employee or any person in the course of his employment to refuse to transport or otherwise handle the goods of any other person. Did this mean that 8(b)(4)(B) prevented the pickets from asking other employees to respect their picket line?

The Supreme Court examined the structure of Section 8(b)(4) and acknowledged that

---

[1] See legal principle 1.

awful. For example, if the
es of employer A went to the
plier (employer B) and en-
mployees not to cross their
nat would violate Section
though the striking employ-
nary object of shutting down
yer A, the pickets also had the
ect of enlisting employer B's
their support. That entangles
in employer A's primary labor
lation of Section 8(b)(4)(B).

g dealt with the right of primary
ake direct appeals to customers
the primary picket line. Subse-
have held that primary pickets
e right, at the primary location, to
uppliers of the primary employer
heir picket line. Pickets may also
employees of the primary em-
d to strike replacements, not to
ine.

cketing in *Rice Milling* was violent at
he Supreme Court held, however,
eting does not lose its primary status
it is violent. Although violence does
late 8(b)(4)(B), violence directed
employees who refuse to honor the
line does violate Section 8(b)(1)(A).
n employer can obtain an injunction in
te courts against violence.

keting employees have only the moral
th of their picket signs and their power
aceful persuasion to prevent people
crossing their picket line. An employer
thus obtain a state court injunction
st so-called mass picketing in which
e numbers of employees patrol a picket
at one time. Also, state trespass laws and
e court injunctions can prevent employees
m engaging in nonviolent acts, such as
wding around or laying in front of vehicles
empting to cross the line, to prevent people
om crossing their picket line.

C. COMMON SITUS PICKETING

Rice Milling establishes the basic ground
rules of a union's right to picket a primary
employer and to appeal to those approaching
the picket line at the primary employer's
place of business. This is called primary situs
picketing. These principles govern picketing
at industrial plants, retail stores, etc.

What if striking employees normally work
alongside other employees of another employer at the same location, called a common
situs? Can the striking employees appeal to
the other employees on the common situs to
honor their picket line, just as the picketing
union in *Rice Milling* could appeal to another
employer's driver?

The Supreme Court faced this issue in the
Denver Building Trades case.[2] That case involved a construction project situs where different construction trades employed by
various subcontractors worked. The Construction Trade's Council struck the project to
protest the use of a nonunion subcontractor.
A picket line was established and all the construction trades honored the picket line, shutting down the entire project.

The construction unions argued that the
contractors and subcontractors on a construction situs should be treated as a single primary employer because they all perform
related work. Therefore, the unions argued,
any one union should be permitted to picket
the entire project. All employees of a single
employer may honor a strike by any of their
fellow employees, except where this right
may be waived by a contractual no-strike
clause (see Chapter 6). The right of fellow
employees to honor each other's picket lines
is considered mutual aid and protection. The
construction unions argued in *Denver Building
Trades* that all employees on a construction

[2] See legal principle 2.

applied literally, the Act prohibited this type of direct appeal. But the Court went on to conclude that Congress had not intended this result. The Court said that the intent of the Act was to preserve the traditional union right of primary picketing. It said the Act's intent was to distinguish between primary and secondary picketing. A union's right to appeal to other employees to honor their picket line is a traditional primary tool. The court concluded in *Rice Milling* that Congress had not intended to take away that right, therefore upholding the union's right to encourage other employees who approached the primary picket line to honor the line.

In *Rice Milling*, the picketing was primary even though the mill's employees were not on strike. Some employees mistakenly believe that the only kind of primary picket line is that established by employees on strike against their own employer. That is one kind of primary picket line, but it is not the only kind. A primary picket line is any picket line directed against the employer with whom the union has a dispute, even if the employees of that employer are not on strike. Thus, the union in *Rice Milling* had a primary dispute with the mill in attempting to achieve recognition even though the employees were not striking.

A secondary picket line is a line established against an employer other than the employer with whom the union has a dispute. The purpose is to pressure the secondary employer into taking some action, such as terminating its business relationship with the primary employer, which will in turn pressure the primary employer to resolve its dispute with the picketing union. The *Rice Milling* principle on the right of primary pickets to appeal to persons crossing their picket line applies to any primary picket line.

The union in *Rice Milling* appealed to the customer's employees as they approached the

2. The Pri
   Effect

Another
8(b)(4) is the d
ject and a *second*
8(b)(4) refers to
on this wording,
distinction betwe
and the effect. S
mary, picketing is
may be a secondary
ing, the primary obj
picketed employer.
effect because the tru
ployed by the custom
ployer) refused to cro
the secondary employe
terfered with. However,
the picketing was primar
fect did not matter.

To be protected, prima
have only a primary objec
both a primary and secon

picketing is unl
striking employe
facility of a su
couraged B's e
picket line, t
8(b)(4)(B). Ever
ees have a pri
primary emplo
secondary ob
employees in
employer B
dispute in vi

Rice Millin
pickets to m
approaching
quent cases
also have th
appeal to s
to honor t
appeal to
ployer, ar
cross the

The pi
times. T
that pick
because
not vi
against
picket
Also, a
the sta

Pic
streng
of pe
from
can
agai
larg
line
stat
fro
cro
att
fr

project, even though separately employed, should also be permitted to engage in mutual aid and protection. Thus, one striking construction union should be permitted to appeal to other employees for support.

The Supreme Court rejected the unions' arguments. It held that each employer on a construction situs should be treated as a separate employer. Therefore, a union picketing an entire project violates Section 8(b)(4)(B) because the object is to induce employees of other contractors to quit work and involve those secondary employers in another primary employer's dispute. The Court emphasized that shutting down an entire project is a secondary object, not just a secondary effect. The situation was different from *Rice Milling,* because any effect on the customer in *Rice Milling* was a secondary effect of a primary object. The Court stressed that a secondary object need not be the only object of picketing as long as it is an object.

D. RESERVED GATES—THE *MOORE DRY DOCK* STANDARDS

The *Denver Building Trades* case is the basis for the system of reserve gates now commonplace in construction industry strikes. If there were only one gate to a construction project, a striking union would have the right to picket it. In that case, the striking union would have only a primary object, publicizing its dispute. If other unions honor the line, that would simply be a secondary effect of the primary object and the picketing would be lawful.

But what if a general contractor puts up separate gates, one for the employees in the striking union and one for all other employees? The striking union cannot put up a picket on both gates, but is limited to the gate marked for the primary employer's use. If the

union pickets at other gates, it is obviously appealing to other employees with the object of encouraging those employees to quit work for their employers. That, in turn, puts pressure on those secondary employers. Section 8(b)(4)(B) is designed to prevent just this type of pressure. Thus, establishing a separate gate effectively limits a labor dispute to the primary employer.

The rules for picketing at a common situs were set forth by the Board in the *Moore Dry Dock* case in 1950.[3] In the field of labor law, in which change is common, it is unusual, but true, that the rules established in *Moore Dry Dock* remain the governing principles.

In *Moore Dry Dock,* a ship owned by the primary employer was at a dry dock owned by another employer for repairs. The union had a primary dispute with the ship owner about the ship's crew. The ship did not regularly dock at the dry dock, but was there only for repairs. The ship owner had an office that the union could have picketed. This office was the primary situs for picketing, but instead of picketing only at the office, the union picketed at the entrance to the dry dock ship yard, a secondary situs. The issue in *Moore Dry Dock* was whether the union could picket at this secondary situs. The secondary employer argued that picketing at the dry dock secondary situs had a secondary object of having the dry docks' employees honor the picket line and thus embroil the secondary employer in the union's dispute with the ship owner.

The Board upheld the union's picketing. In doing so, the Board set down the rules unions must follow in order to picket lawfully at a secondary situs. If a union follows these guidelines, the picketing has only a primary object of publicizing the union's dispute with the primary employer. If the secondary em-

[3] See legal principle 3.

ployer's employees should honor the picket line, that is considered as only the secondary effect of the lawful picketing. If, however, a union fails to follow the guidelines, and the employees of a secondary employer honor the picket line, the picketing has a secondary object and is thus in violation of Section 8(b)(4)(B). The Board set down four requirements necessary for picketing to be lawful at a secondary location. They are:

1. The primary employer must be engaged in its normal business at the common situs.

2. The picket signs of the picketing union must clearly identify the struck employer who is the subject of the dispute.

3. The pickets must be as reasonably close as possible to the situs of the primary employer, and

4. The primary employer must be "present" when the picketing occurs.

These rules covering secondary or common situs picketing apply to both industrial and construction unions. They also apply to so-called roving situs cases in which an employer moves from one location to another during the work day, such as a struck employer making deliveries. The rules also apply when the primary employer shares a facility away from his main plant with other employers, such as a common warehouse used by a number of employers. Each of the four *Moore Dry Dock* requirements will be discussed in turn.

1. Normal Business Operations at the Common Situs

This requirement is easily met, as most employers engage in their normal business operations at a secondary situs. It is normal operations for an employer to purchase supplies or make deliveries at a secondary location. Thus, a picketing union can follow an employer around from supplier to supplier or customer to customer and picket at the secondary premises as long as the other *Moore Dry Dock* standards are met. Having repairs made is also part of an employer's normal operations, so a union may picket a repair facility, as in the *Moore Dry Dock* case.

2. Identifying the Struck Employer

To meet *Moore Dry Dock* standards, picket signs cannot just say the union is on strike. They must identify the struck employer. The purpose of this requirement is obvious; it prevents an innocent secondary employer from being involved in a dispute because the picket signs are unclear. Note that this requirement does not apply to a striking union picketing at its own primary situs. A union picketing at its own plant can have signs that simply say "on strike"; they do not have to identify the picketed employer. But, in a *Moore Dry Dock* situation, where there is picketing at a secondary situs, the union must identify the employer with whom it has its dispute.

3. Picketing Reasonably Close to the Primary Employer

This requirement is again designed to limit the scope of the dispute and the picketing impact to employees of the primary employer. If an access road leads to many factories, one of which is the situs of a dispute, the union cannot picket at the entrance to the road under *Moore Dry Dock*. That would be an attempt to interfere with deliveries to other employers and involve them in the dispute. Instead, the union must picket at the entrance to the specific plant.

Further, if striking employees follow a struck employer making deliveries, the employees must picket the gate through which the truck enters the secondary employer's premises in order to be reasonably close to the situs. They cannot picket the entire plant that the struck employer enters because the object of such picketing would be to encourage the secondary employer's employees to cease work, thus entangling the secondary employer in the dispute.

What if the secondary employer's employees on their own cease working, even though the picketing union properly limits its picketing to the one gate? The picketing is still lawful, even though the result is a total shutdown of the secondary employer because the shutdown is the effect, but not the object, of the proper primary picketing.

Remotely Located Gates

If an employer purposely establishes a separate gate for the primary employer in a remote area of a common situs, such as at the end of a back alley or other area where the public will not see the pickets, must the picketing union limit its picketing to such a location? There is no easy answer. The primary employer does have the right to establish a gate away from that used by other employers to keep neutral employees from being involved in the dispute. If a picketing union ignores the reserve gate and neutral employees honored the picket sign, there would certainly be an 8(b)(4)(B) violation. On the other hand, in several recent cases the Board has held that a picketing union has a legitimate right to publicize its dispute to the public and the union can properly refuse to limit picketing to the reserve gate area where the union could not legitimately publicize its dispute. Thus, the Board essentially balances the right of the secondary employers to isolate the dispute against the legitimate right of the striking union to publicize the dispute. Certainly, a union should not decide lightly to ignore a reserve gate. If a union makes the wrong decision it is not only subject to Board charges, but also, as discussed below, to a damage suit by a secondary employer.

The Board has held that a picketing union trailing the truck of a primary employer may pass through a reserve gate established for the picketed employer, enter the common situs location with the truck, and picket "between the headlights" of the truck. The Board held that this picketing complied with the *Moore Dry Dock's* standards, even though picketing at this location brought the picketing employees into much closer contact with the secondary employer's employees than if the picket had stopped at the reserve gate entrance. Although the Board concluded that this picketing does not violate *Moore Dry Dock*, it indicated that the employer might be able to obtain a state court injunction against the picketing if it occurs on private property in violation of state trespass laws.

Mixed Use Gates

One well recognized exception to the reserve gate doctrine is that the gate must in fact be reserved solely for the employees of the primary employer and its suppliers. If the primary employer uses other gates, if the reserve gate is used to divert the union while the employer enters elsewhere, or if secondary employers use the gate as well, the union is entitled to picket all entrances to the common situs, not just the reserve gate.

Signal Picketing

A word of caution. The *Moore Dry Dock* standards are not to be applied mechanically. A union may technically meet all the *Moore Dry Dock* standards, but its picketing may still violate Section 8(b)(4)(B) if the picketing actually has a secondary object. The most common example of this is so-called "signal picketing." If a striking union informs a union representing secondary employees that it will be picketing a struck truck making deliveries and would appreciate the other union's "cooperation," that is a signal to the other union to stop working when the pickets arrive. If picketing is, in fact, a signal for other employees to stop working, the picketing violates Section 8(b)(4)(B) even though the picket signs are properly worded and the picketing is conducted reasonably close to the primary employer's location on the common situs because it would have a secondary object.

The possibility of a signal picketing violation is one reason why union officers and members engaged in picketing should be extremely cautious in any public statements they make. If a striking union about to engage in *Moore Dry Dock* type picketing makes public statements about expecting other unions to honor its picket line, the union has probably doomed its picket to failure. If other employees walk out, the Board may conclude, based on the statements, that the picketing was a signal although there has been technical compliance with the *Moore Dry Dock* standards.

4. Presence of the Primary Employer

The final requirement under *Moore Dry Dock* is that the primary employer must be present at the secondary situs when the picketing occurs. If an employer works continually at one location, there is no difficulty. A maintenance contractor may work continually doing routine maintenance in a factory. A union in dispute with the contractor can picket continually at the factory. Picketing can take place even if no one from the primary employer's work force is present if the primary employer still has supplies and equipment at the situs. These supplies and equipment constitute the employer's presence for *Moore Dry Dock* purposes.

a. Roving Employers

But what if the employer roves around to five or six different locations during the work day, such as maintenance services that move from location to location or a supply truck? If the union knows when and where the employer will be, the pickets can simply move from location to location with the primary employer. In that case, picketing must be limited to the time the primary employer is actually present at the secondary situs.

What if the employer tries to evade the pickets or if the union does not know when and where the employer will be next? In that case, the union has the right to picket continuously at each location where the primary employer regularly engages in its normal business operations.

If the picketed employer gives the union a schedule of where and when the primary employer will be working, can the union picket at each secondary situs all the time, even if the primary employer is not present? No, the union can picket only when the employer is present according to his schedule, even if the primary employer is scheduled to work at odd hours when no other employees will be present.

Why have this restriction? Once again, recall the distinction between the primary object and a secondary effect. The Board reasons that if a union only pickets when the employer is present, the union has the primary object of publicizing its dispute. If the union knows that the primary employer will be present at certain times, but pickets even though the employer is not present, the Board reasons that the union has a secondary object applied literally, the Act prohibited this type of direct appeal. But the Court went on to conclude that Congress had not intended this result. The Court said that the intent of the Act was to preserve the traditional union right of primary picketing. It said the Act's intent was to distinguish between primary and secondary picketing. A union's right to appeal to other employees to honor their picket line is a traditional primary tool. The court concluded in *Rice Milling* that Congress had not intended to take away that right, therefore upholding the union's right to encourage other employees who approached the primary picket line to honor the line.

In *Rice Milling*, the picketing was primary even though the mill's employees were not on strike. Some employees mistakenly believe that the only kind of primary picket line is that established by employees on strike against their own employer. That is one kind of primary picket line, but it is not the only kind. A primary picket line is any picket line directed against the employer with whom the union has a dispute, even if the employees of that employer are not on strike. Thus, the union in *Rice Milling* had a primary dispute with the mill in attempting to achieve recognition even though the employees were not striking.

A secondary picket line is a line established against an employer other than the employer with whom the union has a dispute. The purpose is to pressure the secondary employer into taking some action, such as terminating its business relationship with the primary employer, which will in turn pressure the primary employer to resolve its dispute with the picketing union. The *Rice Milling* principle on the right of primary pickets to appeal to persons crossing their picket line applies to any primary picket line.

The union in *Rice Milling* appealed to the customer's employees as they approached the primary line. What if the union had gone directly to the customer's plant, instead of waiting for the customer to approach the picket line, and had asked the customer's employees not to deliver any goods to the struck plant? At that point, the union would have stepped over the line into prohibited secondary picketing. The union would then be putting direct pressure on the secondary employer, involving the secondary employer in a labor dispute that is not its own. Section 8(b)(4)(B) is intended to prevent such direct pressure on secondary employers. Section 8(b)(4)(B) prevents a union from entangling a so-called "neutral employer" in another employer's labor dispute. The section seeks to isolate a labor dispute to the primary employer and union directly involved.

2. The Primary Object vs. Secondary Effect

Another important distinction under 8(b)(4) is the difference between a *primary object* and a *secondary effect.* The first paragraph of 8(b)(4) refers to the object of a dispute. Based on this wording, the courts have developed a distinction between the object of picketing and the effect. So long as the object is primary, picketing is lawful even though there may be a secondary effect. Thus, in *Rice Milling,* the primary object was to shutdown the picketed employer. There was a secondary effect because the truck driver who was employed by the customer (the secondary employer) refused to cross the picket line and the secondary employer's operations were interfered with. However, since the purpose of the picketing was primary, this secondary effect did not matter.

To be protected, primary picketing must have only a primary object. If picketing has both a primary and secondary object, the picketing is unlawful. For example, if the striking employees of employer A went to the facility of a supplier (employer B) and encouraged B's employees not to cross their picket line, that would violate Section 8(b)(4)(B). Even though the striking employees have a primary object of shutting down primary employer A, the pickets also had the secondary object of enlisting employer B's employees in their support. That entangles employer B in employer A's primary labor dispute in violation of Section 8(b)(4)(B).

Rice Milling dealt with the right of primary pickets to make direct appeals to customers approaching the primary picket line. Subsequent cases have held that primary pickets also have the right, at the primary location, to appeal to suppliers of the primary employer to honor their picket line. Pickets may also appeal to employees of the primary employer, and to strike replacements, not to cross the line.

The picketing in *Rice Milling* was violent at times. The Supreme Court held, however, that picketing does not lose its primary status because it is violent. Although violence does not violate 8(b)(4)(B), violence directed against employees who refuse to honor the picket line does violate Section 8(b)(1)(A). Also, an employer can obtain an injunction in the state courts against violence.

Picketing employees have only the moral strength of their picket signs and their power of peaceful persuasion to prevent people from crossing their picket line. An employer can thus obtain a state court injunction against so-called mass picketing in which large numbers of employees patrol a picket line at one time. Also, state trespass laws and state court injunctions can prevent employees from engaging in nonviolent acts, such as crowding around or laying in front of vehicles attempting to cross the line, to prevent people from crossing their picket line.

C. COMMON SITUS PICKETING

Rice Milling establishes the basic ground rules of a union's right to picket a primary employer and to appeal to those approaching the picket line at the primary employer's place of business. This is called primary situs picketing. These principles govern picketing at industrial plants, retail stores, etc.

What if striking employees normally work alongside other employees of another employer at the same location, called a common situs? Can the striking employees appeal to the other employees on the common situs to honor their picket line, just as the picketing union in *Rice Milling* could appeal to another employer's driver?

The Supreme Court faced this issue in the *Denver Building Trades* case.[2] That case involved a construction project situs where different construction trades employed by various subcontractors worked. The Construction Trade's Council struck the project to protest the use of a nonunion subcontractor. A picket line was established and all the construction trades honored the picket line, shutting down the entire project.

The construction unions argued that the contractors and subcontractors on a construction situs should be treated as a single primary employer because they all perform related work. Therefore, the unions argued, any one union should be permitted to picket the entire project. All employees of a single employer may honor a strike by any of their fellow employees, except where this right may be waived by a contractual no-strike clause (see Chapter 6). The right of fellow employees to honor each other's picket lines is considered mutual aid and protection. The construction unions argued in *Denver Building Trades* that all employees on a construction

2 See legal principle 2.

project, even though separately employed, should also be permitted to engage in mutual aid and protection. Thus, one striking construction union should be permitted to appeal to other employees for support.

The Supreme Court rejected the unions' arguments. It held that each employer on a construction situs should be treated as a separate employer. Therefore, a union picketing an entire project violates Section 8(b)(4)(B) because the object is to induce employees of other contractors to quit work and involve those secondary employers in another primary employer's dispute. The Court emphasized that shutting down an entire project is a secondary object, not just a secondary effect. The situation was different from *Rice Milling,* because any effect on the customer in *Rice Milling* was a secondary effect of a primary object. The Court stressed that a secondary object need not be the only object of picketing as long as it is an object.

D. RESERVED GATES—THE *MOORE DRY DOCK* STANDARDS

The *Denver Building Trades* case is the basis for the system of reserve gates now commonplace in construction industry strikes. If there were only one gate to a construction project, a striking union would have the right to picket it. In that case, the striking union would have only a primary object, publicizing its dispute. If other unions honor the line, that would simply be a secondary effect of the primary object and the picketing would be lawful.

But what if a general contractor puts up separate gates, one for the employees in the striking union and one for all other employees? The striking union cannot put up a picket on both gates, but is limited to the gate marked for the primary employer's use. If the

union pickets at other gates, it is obviously appealing to other employees with the object of encouraging those employees to quit work for their employers. That, in turn, puts pressure on those secondary employers. Section 8(b)(4)(B) is designed to prevent just this type of pressure. Thus, establishing a separate gate effectively limits a labor dispute to the primary employer.

The rules for picketing at a common situs were set forth by the Board in the *Moore Dry Dock* case in 1950.[3] In the field of labor law, in which change is common, it is unusual, but true, that the rules established in *Moore Dry Dock* remain the governing principles.

In *Moore Dry Dock,* a ship owned by the primary employer was at a dry dock owned by another employer for repairs. The union had a primary dispute with the ship owner about the ship's crew. The ship did not regularly dock at the dry dock, but was there only for repairs. The ship owner had an office that the union could have picketed. This office was the primary situs for picketing, but instead of picketing only at the office, the union picketed at the entrance to the dry dock ship yard, a secondary situs. The issue in *Moore Dry Dock* was whether the union could picket at this secondary situs. The secondary employer argued that picketing at the dry dock secondary situs had a secondary object of having the dry docks' employees honor the picket line and thus embroil the secondary employer in the union's dispute with the ship owner.

The Board upheld the union's picketing. In doing so, the Board set down the rules unions must follow in order to picket lawfully at a secondary situs. If a union follows these guidelines, the picketing has only a primary object of publicizing the union's dispute with the primary employer. If the secondary em-

[3] See legal principle 3.

ployer's employees should honor the picket line, that is considered as only the secondary effect of the lawful picketing. If, however, a union fails to follow the guidelines, and the employees of a secondary employer honor the picket line, the picketing has a secondary object and is thus in violation of Section 8(b)(4)(B). The Board set down four requirements necessary for picketing to be lawful at a secondary location. They are:

1. The primary employer must be engaged in its normal business at the common situs.

2. The picket signs of the picketing union must clearly identify the struck employer who is the subject of the dispute.

3. The pickets must be as reasonably close as possible to the situs of the primary employer, and

4. The primary employer must be "present" when the picketing occurs.

These rules covering secondary or common situs picketing apply to both industrial and construction unions. They also apply to so-called roving situs cases in which an employer moves from one location to another during the work day, such as a struck employer making deliveries. The rules also apply when the primary employer shares a facility away from his main plant with other employers, such as a common warehouse used by a number of employers. Each of the four *Moore Dry Dock* requirements will be discussed in turn.

1. Normal Business Operations at the Common Situs

This requirement is easily met, as most employers engage in their normal business operations at a secondary situs. It is normal operations for an employer to purchase supplies or make deliveries at a secondary location. Thus, a picketing union can follow an employer around from supplier to supplier or customer to customer and picket at the secondary premises as long as the other *Moore Dry Dock* standards are met. Having repairs made is also part of an employer's normal operations, so a union may picket a repair facility, as in the *Moore Dry Dock* case.

2. Identifying the Struck Employer

To meet *Moore Dry Dock* standards, picket signs cannot just say the union is on strike. They must identify the struck employer. The purpose of this requirement is obvious; it prevents an innocent secondary employer from being involved in a dispute because the picket signs are unclear. Note that this requirement does not apply to a striking union picketing at its own primary situs. A union picketing at its own plant can have signs that simply say "on strike"; they do not have to identify the picketed employer. But, in a *Moore Dry Dock* situation, where there is picketing at a secondary situs, the union must identify the employer with whom it has its dispute.

3. Picketing Reasonably Close to the Primary Employer

This requirement is again designed to limit the scope of the dispute and the picketing impact to employees of the primary employer. If an access road leads to many factories, one of which is the situs of a dispute, the union cannot picket at the entrance to the road under *Moore Dry Dock*. That would be an attempt to interfere with deliveries to other employers and involve them in the dispute. Instead, the union must picket at the entrance to the specific plant.

Further, if striking employees follow a struck employer making deliveries, the employees must picket the gate through which the truck enters the secondary employer's premises in order to be reasonably close to the situs. They cannot picket the entire plant that the struck employer enters because the object of such picketing would be to encourage the secondary employer's employees to cease work, thus entangling the secondary employer in the dispute.

What if the secondary employer's employees on their own cease working, even though the picketing union properly limits its picketing to the one gate? The picketing is still lawful, even though the result is a total shutdown of the secondary employer because the shutdown is the effect, but not the object, of the proper primary picketing.

Remotely Located Gates

If an employer purposely establishes a separate gate for the primary employer in a remote area of a common situs, such as at the end of a back alley or other area where the public will not see the pickets, must the picketing union limit its picketing to such a location? There is no easy answer. The primary employer does have the right to establish a gate away from that used by other employers to keep neutral employees from being involved in the dispute. If a picketing union ignores the reserve gate and neutral employees honored the picket sign, there would certainly be an 8(b)(4)(B) violation. On the other hand, in several recent cases the Board has held that a picketing union has a legitimate right to publicize its dispute to the public and the union can properly refuse to limit picketing to the reserve gate area where the union could not legitimately publicize its dispute. Thus, the Board essentially balances the right of the secondary employers to isolate the dispute against the legitimate right of the striking union to publicize the dispute. Certainly, a union should not decide lightly to ignore a reserve gate. If a union makes the wrong decision it is not only subject to Board charges, but also, as discussed below, to a damage suit by a secondary employer.

The Board has held that a picketing union trailing the truck of a primary employer may pass through a reserve gate established for the picketed employer, enter the common situs location with the truck, and picket "between the headlights" of the truck. The Board held that this picketing complied with the *Moore Dry Dock's* standards, even though picketing at this location brought the picketing employees into much closer contact with the secondary employer's employees than if the picket had stopped at the reserve gate entrance. Although the Board concluded that this picketing does not violate *Moore Dry Dock*, it indicated that the employer might be able to obtain a state court injunction against the picketing if it occurs on private property in violation of state trespass laws.

Mixed Use Gates

One well recognized exception to the reserve gate doctrine is that the gate must in fact be reserved solely for the employees of the primary employer and its suppliers. If the primary employer uses other gates, if the reserve gate is used to divert the union while the employer enters elsewhere, or if secondary employers use the gate as well, the union is entitled to picket all entrances to the common situs, not just the reserve gate.

Signal Picketing

A word of caution. The *Moore Dry Dock* standards are not to be applied mechanically. A union may technically meet all the *Moore Dry Dock* standards, but its picketing may still violate Section 8(b)(4)(B) if the picketing actually has a secondary object. The most common example of this is so-called "signal picketing." If a striking union informs a union representing secondary employees that it will be picketing a struck truck making deliveries and would appreciate the other union's "cooperation," that is a signal to the other union to stop working when the pickets arrive. If picketing is, in fact, a signal for other employees to stop working, the picketing violates Section 8(b)(4)(B) even though the picket signs are properly worded and the picketing is conducted reasonably close to the primary employer's location on the common situs because it would have a secondary object.

The possibility of a signal picketing violation is one reason why union officers and members engaged in picketing should be extremely cautious in any public statements they make. If a striking union about to engage in *Moore Dry Dock* type picketing makes public statements about expecting other unions to honor its picket line, the union has probably doomed its picket to failure. If other employees walk out, the Board may conclude, based on the statements, that the picketing was a signal although there has been technical compliance with the *Moore Dry Dock* standards.

4. Presence of the Primary Employer

The final requirement under *Moore Dry Dock* is that the primary employer must be present at the secondary situs when the picketing occurs. If an employer works continually at one location, there is no difficulty. A maintenance contractor may work continually doing routine maintenance in a factory. A union in dispute with the contractor can picket continually at the factory. Picketing can take place even if no one from the primary employer's work force is present if the pri-

mary employer still has supplies and equipment at the situs. These supplies and equipment constitute the employer's presence for *Moore Dry Dock* purposes.

a. Roving Employers

But what if the employer roves around to five or six different locations during the work day, such as maintenance services that move from location to location or a supply truck? If the union knows when and where the employer will be, the pickets can simply move from location to location with the primary employer. In that case, picketing must be limited to the time the primary employer is actually present at the secondary situs.

What if the employer tries to evade the pickets or if the union does not know when and where the employer will be next? In that case, the union has the right to picket continuously at each location where the primary employer regularly engages in its normal business operations.

If the picketed employer gives the union a schedule of where and when the primary employer will be working, can the union picket at each secondary situs all the time, even if the primary employer is not present? No, the union can picket only when the employer is present according to his schedule, even if the primary employer is scheduled to work at odd hours when no other employees will be present.

Why have this restriction? Once again, recall the distinction between the primary object and a secondary effect. The Board reasons that if a union only pickets when the employer is present, the union has the primary object of publicizing its dispute. If the union knows that the primary employer will be present at certain times, but pickets even though the employer is not present, the Board reasons that the union has a secondary object of entangling the secondary employer's employees in the dispute.

If an employer provides a union with a schedule, but does not follow it, or tries to evade the union pickets and leave before the pickets can arrive, the union is no longer required to picket only when the employer is at a location. The union can then picket permanently at all the places where the employer works.

As an exception to the requirement that the employer be present, a union can continue picketing if the primary employer is briefly gone from the situs. If the primary employees are working at a construction site in the morning, leave for lunch, and come back in the afternoon, a union can continue to picket during the lunch break.

b. Employers Ceasing Operations During Picketing

An employer is also considered present if he would be working at the situs, except that the picketing is effectively stopping operations at the situs. Assume there are maintenance employees working for an outside contractor at a manufacturing plant who are permanently stationed at the plant. Since the maintenance contractor has an office elsewhere, the plant is a secondary situs. After maintenance employees strike and establish a picket line at the plant where they regularly work, the maintenance employer shuts down completely because of the strike. If the maintenance contractor ceases all operations at the plant, the employer technically is no longer present at the secondary situs. Still, the Board has upheld the right of employees in such a situation to continue picketing at the plant. The Board reasons that the employer would be present, but for the fact that the picketing has effectively closed down operations. The union has a right to continue picketing to as-

sure the continued effectiveness of its strike and also to publicize its dispute.

Similarly, if the employer is working at a number of locations when a strike begins but stops operations because of the strike, the union can picket each location where the employer was working when the strike began if the employer would be working there but for the strike.

Frequently, the struck employer continues to operate, but leaves each location as soon as the pickets arrive. The employer would not leave but for the pickets' arrival that forces the employer to cease operations at the location. In cases where the union's pickets prevent the primary employer from working or the primary employer keeps his employees off a job because the picketing might be effective, the Board has held that the union can continue to picket during the period the primary employer would have been present, but for the effective picketing.

5. Trailing Trucks of the Struck Employer

Although many common situs problems involve construction unions, the same principles also apply to industrial unions. If an industrial plant is on strike, the striking employees can follow the struck employer's trucks and picket in accordance with *Moore Dry Dock* as the trucks make deliveries. The Board has held that if the truck enters private property, the pickets must request permission to enter and picket next to the truck. If the secondary employer refuses permission to follow the truck onto the property, the union can picket at the gate. Once the truck leaves, the pickets must leave with it.

What if the secondary employees refuse to unload the truck that is being picketed? That is a legal result of picketing that can properly have the object of forcing the struck employer to cease operations entirely. The picketing would be lawful even if the secondary employees refuse to do any work for their employer as long as the truck is present, because the secondary employees' refusal to work is a secondary effect of a valid primary object, so long as the picketing employees follow the *Moore Dry Dock* standards and there is no "signal picketing."

E. SECONDARY EMPLOYERS AT THE PRIMARY SITUS: THE *GENERAL ELECTRIC* RULES

What happens when employees are on strike against their own employer, but the employees of other employers work at the same location? As discussed above, maintenance employees employed by an outside contractor at a factory can picket at the factory provided they follow the *Moore Dry Dock* rules. They cannot picket a gate reserved for the factory employees. What about the reverse situation, in which the factory employees strike and establish a picket line? Can they appeal to the outside maintenance employees as they approach the factory as in *Rice Milling?* Can a reserve gate be established for the maintenance employees so that picketing directed at the maintenance employees is thereby prohibited under *Denver Building Trades* and *Moore Dry Dock?* If outside construction employees are building an addition to the plant at the time the factory employees strike, can the factory employees direct their picketing at these outside contractor employees?

The Supreme Court set down the rules under which striking employees can direct their picketing at secondary employees working on the primary situs in the *General Electric*

case.[4] In *General Electric,* while production employees were on strike, General Electric had certain maintenance work and new construction work done by outside contractors. The Company established separate gates for the outside employees to use to enter the plant and other gates were established for General Electric's own employees. The issue was whether the striking employees could picket the gates reserved for the outside contractors. The employer wanted to apply the principles of *Denver Building Trades* and *Moore Dry Dock* to the industrial plant situation, which would have meant that the striking production union could not picket the gate reserved for the outside contractors.

The Supreme Court refused to apply *Moore Dry Dock* and *Denver Building Trades* to the industrial plant situation. The Court noted that the General Electric plant employees were picketing their own plant, which was the primary situs of the dispute. *Moore Dry Dock* and *Denver Building Trades* both involve picketing at secondary locations. So, rather than applying these cases, the Court looked to *Rice Milling,* in which the picketing had occurred at the primary situs, for the controlling principles. However, the Court held that even an industrial union does not have an unlimited right to picket outside employees working at the primary location. The Court held that a union cannot picket a separate gate if:

1. There is a separate gate for the outside employees identified as such.

2. The work of the outside employees is unrelated to normal operations.

3. The work being done by the outside contractors is not work that could only be done during a strike or plant shutdown.

If all *three* requirements are met, the striking union can not picket at the gate reserved

---

[4] See legal principle 4.

for the outside employees. Such picketing is secondary picketing in violation of Section 8(b)(4)(B). On the other hand, if there is not a separate gate, if the work of the outside employees is related to normal operations, or if the company is taking advantage of the strike to do work that could only be done while the plant is shut down, the union can picket the gates used by the employees doing that work. The picketing would then be primary activity outside the scope of Section 8(b)(4)(B).

These rules limiting picketing apply only to employees of outside contractors. Striking employees have the right to appeal to their own fellow employees to support a strike for mutual aid and protection even though those employees are not in the bargaining unit (see Chapter 6). Thus, regardless of the work the primary employer's other employees may be doing, the striking employees can picket the gates used by them.

Construction Work by Outside Contractors

What if an employer building an addition to the plant during a strike established a separate gate for the construction contractor's employees? New construction is usually considered unrelated to normal operations. If the work could have been done with the plant open, so that the employer is not taking advantage of a strike to do work that requires a shutdown, a reserve gate established for the construction employees cannot be picketed. But what if a factory has three production lines and during the strike, the employer uses an outside contractor to renovate one of the lines? The employer cannot establish a reserve gate for the employees doing the renovation work because renovating a line is work related to normal operations and the em-

ployer would have had to shutdown the line to renovate it but for the strike. Therefore, the striking union can picket a gate established for the employers doing the renovation work.

What if the striking employees would have been unable to do the renovation work for which the outside employees were hired because it was beyond their skills? That does not matter. The union can picket a gate reserved for the renovation employees even if the striking employees would not have done the work. So long as the work is either related to normal production or would have required the employer to shutdown in order to do it, picketing is legal.

As in *Moore Dry Dock*, the rules established in the *General Electric* case are not applied mechanically. Thus, if construction employees perform unrelated work, but the striking employees engage in signal picketing so that the construction employees leave although the production employees do not picket their reserve gate, the picketing violates 8(b)(4)(B). On the other hand, if there is no prearrangement, and the striking employees properly picket, the picketing is lawful even if the construction employees leave the plant as their own decision—that is a secondary effect of a lawful primary object.

What if a struck employer normally does its own construction work with its own employees? Usually construction work is considered unrelated to normal operations, but if the striking employees actually do construction work like that being done by the outside contractor, the work is considered related to normal operations. So, if an employer's own construction employees who normally would do or have the capability to do the contracted work, are striking, the union can picket a gate reserved for outside employees doing the work during a strike.

Mixed Use Construction Gates

A separate gate for an outside contractor must be strictly limited to the employees of the outside contractor. If a struck employer tries to bring in his own employees or strike replacements through the reserve gate, the gate loses its protected status. The gate can then be picketed continually the same as any other gate.

Striking employees have the right to appeal to their employer's suppliers and customers not to cross their primary picket line. Company supplies, even office supplies, are related to normal operations and separate gates cannot be established for their delivery. However, suppliers of outside contractors are protected to the same extent as the contractor. Thus, if a contractor is doing work unrelated to normal operations, the contractor's suppliers may use the contractor's reserve gate and cannot be picketed.

F. PICKETING IN A SHOPPING CENTER

A recurring issue in picketing is a union's right to picket an employer located in a shopping center. Shopping center owners argued that a center is private property and has the right to keep pickets out of the center and on public property. Of course, this limits the effectiveness of picketing. Customers drive by the pickets without paying attention to the signs. Unions argue that a large shopping center should be treated the same as public property. Since a center is generally open to the public, unions argue that they should be able to enter a center to picket the store with which they have their dispute. This issue was resolved by the Supreme Court in *Hudgens v. NLRB*.[5] In *Hudgens*, striking warehouse em-

[5] See legal principle 10.

ployees sought to picket their employer's retail outlet in a shopping center mall. The mall owner threatened the pickets with arrest for trespass and the union filed a Section 8(a)(1) unfair labor practice charge against the shopping center owner.

The NLRB held that the pickets had a First Amendment freedom of speech right to picket in the shopping center because the center was generally open to the public. The decision was appealed. The Supreme Court held that the Board erred in applying the constitutional free speech standard because that standard applies to the government, not to private parties such as a shopping center. The Court stated that a union's right to picket in a shopping center is to be determined solely under the LMRA by applying the general statutory principles on the right to enter private property during a labor dispute (see Chapter 3). That entails balancing the employees' rights to picket and publicize their dispute against the center's private property rights "with as little destruction of one as is consistent with the maintenance of the other." The Court noted that in *Hudgens*, the employees were engaged in a lawful economic strike, rather than organizational activities, and the pickets were employees of an employer in the center rather than outsiders. The Court remanded the case back to the Board for reconsideration in light of the Court's decision.

In accordance with the Supreme Court decision, the NLRB reconsidered its prior decision in light of the general statutory principles. The Board weighed the shopping center's private property rights against the union's rights. The Board held that the striking employees had the right to enter the center and picket in front of their employer's establishment. The Board reasoned that picketing directly in front of the store is a reasonable way for the pickets to reach customers of the struck store and the store's employees.

The Board said picketing on the edges of the center is ineffective because many people do not pay attention as they do to a sign directly in front of the store. Picketing on the edge of the center is also dangerous because of the traffic. Also, picketing on the edge runs the risk that truck drivers will refuse to make deliveries to other employers in the shopping center, not just the struck employer. Picketing directly in front of the struck employer avoids these possibilities. The Board held that these considerations outweigh the private property rights of the center owner.

It is probable, based upon the Supreme Court and Board decisions in the *Hudgens* cases, that most unions will be able to justify their right to picket directly in front of a struck employer in a shopping center. The Board has applied the same reasoning it used in *Hudgens* to uphold the right of a union to engage in substandards picketing within a shopping center even though there are only two stores in the center.

G. HANDBILLING AND PRODUCT PICKETING

1. Consumer Handbilling

The right to handbill is protected by the second proviso following Section 8(b)(4)(D) that states:

That for the purposes of this paragraph (4) only, nothing contained in such paragraph shall be construed to prohibit publicity, other than picketing, for the purpose of truthfully advising the public, including consumers and members of a labor organization, that a product or products are produced by an employer with whom the labor organization has a primary dispute and are distributed by another employer, as long as such publicity does not have an effect of inducing any individual employed by any person other than the primary employer in the

course of his employment to refuse to pick up, deliver, or transport any goods, or not to perform any services, at the establishment of the employer engaged in such distribution.

This provision means that a union may pass out a handbill addressed to the public stating that the union has a dispute with primary employer A, that employer B (the secondary neutral employer) is continuing to distribute or sell A's products, and that the public should not deal with employer B while B continues to distribute or sell A's products.

Although the proviso expressly refers only to "products" produced by the primary employer, the Board has held that the proviso applies to the performance of services as well as to the processing or distribution of physical products. Thus a union can urge a consumer boycott of a neutral employer who continues to use the services of the primary employer in a labor dispute such as a boycott of a neutral employer who uses a struck trucking company to make deliveries, or the boycott of an advertiser who continues to advertise in a struck newspaper or on a struck television station.

Handbills may be used to support any primary dispute. Frequently, the primary dispute involves a strike in which a company continues to sell the products or use the services of the struck employer, but handbilling is not limited to that situation. For example, if a product is produced by a primary employer who pays substandard wages, a union may distribute a handbill urging the public not to patronize a store so long as it sells the product.

A handbill may request consumers to stop all dealings with the secondary employer, not just refuse to buy the struck product. The union can request a total boycott as long as the secondary employer continues to deal with the primary. Handbilling is a legal secondary boycott. Recent handbilling campaigns asking customers not to shop at stores distributing the products of anti-labor companies are examples of activity permitted by the handbilling proviso.

The Board has held that a union which has a primary dispute with a corporation which is part of a larger diversified parent corporation (commonly called a conglomerate) can engage in a total consumer boycott of all products produced by the entire diversified corporation, not just products produced by the corporate division with which the union has its dispute.

Handbills are the most frequent type of publicity under the proviso, but the language protects any publicity including newspaper ads and radio or TV commercials.

Secondary Effect of Handbilling

Protected publicity can be aimed only at the public including consumers and labor organization members. This means that the handbills cannot be distributed to employees or suppliers of the secondary employer. Primary picketing is lawful even if it has a secondary effect. But the Section 8(b)(4) publicity proviso permits handbilling only if the publicity does not have an *effect* of inducing any individual (other than a primary employee) to refuse to work. The effect alone is sufficient. Congress wanted this provision for consumer activity only and thus prohibited even a secondary effect on the secondary employer's employees or suppliers. If a handbill is properly worded and distributed only to customers, but the store's employees refuse to work in support of the handbilling union, or suppliers refuse to make deliveries, the handbilling loses its protection and violates Section 8(b)(4).

1. Product Picketing

The Section 8(b)(4) publicity proviso excludes picketing from coverage. The Supreme Court dealt with the issue of prohibiting publicity picketing at a secondary location in the *Tree Fruits* case.[6] In *Tree Fruits*, the employees of companies packing Washington State apples were on strike. When groceries continued to sell the apples, the employees picketed and handbilled at groceries urging consumers not to buy Washington State apples. Neither the picket signs nor the leaflets requested a total boycott of the stores, only that consumers not buy the apples.

The Supreme Court upheld the union's right to picket the product on the grounds that Section 8(b)(4) did not intend to take away this traditional employee right. The Court established the basic principles that handbills may urge a total consumer boycott and that picketing may urge consumers not to buy the specific struck product. Of course, handbills can be limited to the product if that is all the union wants.

Product picketing and a handbill urging a total boycott cannot be used together even though both the picket signs and the handbills are properly worded. The Board would conclude that the handbills were intended to aid the picketing; and the object of the picketing, used in conjunction with the handbills urging a total boycott, was a total consumer boycott in violation of the proviso.

Remember that the publicity proviso applies only to secondary activities in aid of a dispute with another employer. The proviso restrictions do not apply if a union has a direct dispute with a store. In that case, the same picketing rules that apply to any other primary dispute, as discussed above, apply.

[6] See legal principle 7.

2. Single and Merged Products

What happens if a secondary employer's entire stock consists only of the struck product, so that if a union pickets the struck product, the union is in effect urging a total boycott of the secondary employer? What if in *Tree Fruits*, for example, the union had picketed an apple stand rather than a grocery store selling many items? The Board has held that a union cannot picket a product if the net effect of the picketing is a total boycott. The union, of course, can handbill in that situation, because handbills can urge a total boycott. For example, in one case, refinery workers picketed a gas station that sold only the struck brand of gas. The Board concluded the picketing was unlawful because the product picketing amounted to a call for a total boycott of the station.

One court of appeals, disagreeing with the Board, has held that a union may picket a struck product even though the product is substantially the only product the secondary employer sells. Other courts of appeals, however, have upheld the Board's interpretation. Because of this conflict, this issue may ultimately be decided by the Supreme Court.

What if the struck product is so interwoven with the secondary employer's other products that a consumer can stop using the struck product only by engaging in total boycott of the secondary employer? The Board applies the merged product doctrine. For example, if a striking bakery union pickets a hamburger stand urging customers not to eat struck buns, the employees are, in fact, urging a total boycott. Under the merged product doctrine, the union cannot picket the secondary hamburger stand, although it can handbill since handbills may request a total consumer boycott.

The merged product doctrine has been applied to construction unions picketing to urge consumers not to buy newly constructed homes containing fixtures made by companies with which the union has a dispute. Several courts have held that since fixtures are merged into a home, picketing of the fixtures is actually a request for a total boycott of the home contractors. The courts have accordingly held that the picketing violated Section 8(b)(4). Again, handbills urging a boycott would have been lawful.

3. Direct Appeals to Management

Section 8(b)(4)(i) prohibits a union from inducing or encouraging employees to cease work for their secondary employer and Section 8(b)(4)(ii) prohibits a union from threatening, coercing, or restraining any other person in aid of a prohibited object. Section 8(b)(4)(ii) was intended to protect employers from union pressure. However, this section does not prohibit a union from inducing or encouraging employers to assist the union. It only protects against threats, etc. In comparing (i) and (ii), the Supreme Court has held that a union can appeal to an employer's discretion not to stock or sell goods involved in a primary labor dispute so long as no threats, etc. are made. The union can even tell the secondary employer that unless certain products are removed the union will handbill the store or picket the product. Those are legal tactics and it is not a threat to tell an employer that the union will take lawful action unless the employer removes the product.

H. SUBSTANDARD WAGES PICKETING

Unions have the right to picket an employer who pays its employees substandard wages even though the union does not represent the employees. The Board has held that a union has a legitimate right to oppose substandard wages because they tend to undercut the conditions that the union has negotiated for its members. The Board recognizes that a union may have absolutely no interest in representing the employees of the picketed employer because the employer is too marginal or the employees are uninterested.

A union that is picketing an employer because of its substandard wages has a primary dispute with that employer. What if a union is engaged in substandard picketing against an employer and suppliers refuse to deliver to that employer? That does not violate Section 8(b)(4)(B). Substandard picketing is governed by the same principles that apply to the other forms of primary picketing. It *can* have the effect of inducing other employees to honor the picket line. Thus, if a union is engaged in substandard picketing of an employer working on a common situs, the picketing is lawful provided it conforms to the *Moore Dry Dock* standards.

Substandard wage picketing runs afoul of the Act when the object of the picketing, in fact, is to require the picketed employer to recognize the union and sign a contract. Picketing for recognition is limited by Section 8(b)(7) of the Act. That section's relationship to substandard wages picketing is discussed more fully below.

I. THE ALLY DOCTRINE

The principle of the restrictions on secondary picketing is that a neutral secondary employer should not become embroiled in a dispute not of his own making. If the secondary employer is, however, the ally of a primary employer who continues to operate during a strike, the other employer is not neu-

tral. The union may picket a secondary, allied employer to the same extent as it can picket the primary employer.

1. Commonly Owned Companies

The mere fact that two companies are owned by the same persons or parent corporation does not automatically make the two companies allies. A union on strike against one corporate subsidiary cannot picket another subsidiary unless there is central management and control over labor relations. For example, employees were on strike against a newspaper in Detroit that also owned a paper in Miami. The Detroit employees established a picket line at the Miami paper. The Board held that the picketing at Miami was unlawful secondary activity in violation of Section 8(b)(4)(B) because each paper had separate control over labor relations at its facility even though they had the same higher ownership.

The situation of separate subsidiaries of the same company must be contrasted to multi-plants of the same employer. A union on strike against an employer at one plant can picket all other plants as well. That is simply a primary appeal to fellow employees for mutual aid.

2. Performance of Struck Work

The most common ally situation is that in which one company does the struck work of another. The key to whether one employer has become the ally of another is whether the two are maintaining their normal business relationship or whether the struck employer has shifted work to the other during the strike. Two employers who had a business relationship before a strike are entitled to maintain it during a strike. An employer does not become an ally by maintaining the same business relationship as before.

Suppose employer A manufactured a product for which employer B manufactures a part. The companies had been dealing with each other before a strike. Employer A's employees strike, and A tries to continue operations during the strike. B continues to supply the part. Can union A picket at employer B's plant? No, because all B is doing is maintaining the existing business relationship, which does not make B the ally of A. But what if employer B, to assist employer A, makes an additional part during the strike that A's employees would have made, but for their strike? Then B would become A's ally because B is not just maintaining its normal business relationship; it has crossed that point and is assisting A to resist the strike. That makes B an ally of A subject to the same picketing as A.

Although an employer who simply maintains a normal business relationship with a struck employer is not an ally, the employer is not totally immune from picketing. Such am employer can be picketed under the same restricted conditions (Moore Dry Dock) as any other secondary employer. For example, employer A's striking employees could picket employer A's truck when it picked up parts at employer B's plant.

3. Need for an Arrangement

The fact that one employer takes over work previously performed by a struck employer before a strike does not make the employers allies unless there has been an agreement or arrangement to shift the work from one struck employer to the other. Suppose employers A and B are competing companies. A is struck so that customers of A, on their own, go to B for the same product. B is doing A's work, but the companies are not allies. There is no agreement between employers A and B for B to help out during the strike. It is simply the customer's choice. On the other hand, what if employer A arranged to have B take care of A's customer needs during the strike? Then there is an arrangement between A and B and they are allies.

Two employers are not necessarily allies just because they first begin dealing with each other during a strike. It is possible for a normal business relationship to start during the strike. For example, a struck employer might obtain a new supplier for a production part during a strike. If the supplier is furnishing a part that would have been furnished by an outside supplier before the strike began, the struck employer and the supplier have a normal business relationship and they are not allies. But if the supplier is furnishing a part that the striking employees would have produced, but for the strike, the two companies may be considered allies.

Although the principle is not altogether clear, some Board cases seem to indicate that an outside employer doing struck work must have notice that a strike is going on in order to be an ally. In most cases the secondary employer's knowledge of the strike can be implied from all the facts, such as if he is seen crossing the union's picket line. To avoid any question, however, if a striking union believes that another employer may not know he is doing struck work, the union should consider sending the employer a notice informing him of the strike and giving a chance to stop doing business with the struck employer before picketing begins.

J. ORGANIZATIONAL AND RECOGNITION PICKETING

Organizational or recognition picketing in which a union pickets for recognition from the employer or to organize the employees, is regulated by Section 8(b)(7). This section only applies to picketing or threats of picketing—it does not prohibit any other conduct. For example, Section 8(b)(7)(B) prohibits organizational or recognitional picketing if a valid Board election has been conducted within the preceding twelve months. The Board has held that even though a union has lost an election, it can still get voluntary recognition from an employer within a year. Voluntary recognition through peaceful persuasion does not violate Section 8(b)(7).

Section 8(b)(7)(A) prohibits recognition picketing where the employer has lawfully recognized any other labor organization in accordance with the Act and a question concerning representation (see Chapter 2) may not appropriately be raised. An employer may lawfully recognize a union under the Act voluntarily or following Board certification (see Chapter 5). Thus, Section 8(b)(7)(A) may prohibit recognition picketing if the union is recognized in either manner.

If a union loses a Board election, but the election is set aside based on union objections, can the union then picket for recognition according to Section 8(b)(7)(B)? Yes, because Section 8(b)(7)(B) only applies if there has been a valid election. An election that is set aside is not a valid election.

The third type of picketing prohibited under 8(b)(7)(C) is picketing that has been conducted without an election petition being filed within a reasonable period of time not to exceed 30 days from the beginning of the picketing. Remember that this provision applies only to picketing for recognition or organizational purposes under 8(b)(7).

Picketing for any other purpose may continue indefinitely.

1. Expedited Elections Under Section 8(b)(7)(C)

Section 8(b)(7)(C) contains an expedited election procedure. The employer who is being picketed for more than 30 days may file an election petition. If he does, the Board must direct an election in such unit as the Board finds appropriate and certify the results. No showing of interest is required. The purpose of this section is to enable an employer to get a quick election determining whether a picketing union, in fact, represents a majority of its employees.

This expedited election procedure is rarely used. In most cases, the picketing union realizes that it has no chance of winning an expedited election held under 8(b)(7). Rather than proceed, most unions will enter into a settlement of the charge with the Board, under which the union agrees to cease the picketing and disclaim any interest in representing the employees.

2. The Publicity Proviso to Section 8(b)(7)(C)

a. Secondary Effect of Consumer Picketing

Section 8(b)(7)(C) contains a proviso that:

Nothing in this subparagraph (C) shall be construed to prohibit any picketing or other publicity for the purpose of truthfully advising the public (including consumers) that an employer does not employ members of, or have a contract with, a labor organization, unless an effect of such picketing is to induce any individual employed by any other person in the course of his employment, not to pick up, deliver or transport any goods or not perform any services.

This proviso permits recognitional picketing directed at customers to continue beyond 30 days so long as it does not have an *effect* on any other employees. A union can lawfully picket to encourage customers not to deal with the employer so long as it does not have a contract with the union. As in the publicity proviso to Section 8(b)(4), permitting consumer boycotts, consumer recognitional picketing is not protected if it has a secondary effect on employees. A secondary object is not necessary.

The Board takes the view that a few isolated instances of employees refusing to cross a properly established recognition picket line directed at consumers does not violate Section 8(b)(7). There must be a pattern to establish the effect. Thus, if a picketed employer receives 50 deliveries a day, and one truck refuses to cross the line, that single incident does not invalidate the picketing. On the other hand, if all 50 truck drivers refuse to cross the picket line, even though the union tells them to cross, the unlawful effect is clear. There is no hard and fast cutoff. Obviously, the more times employees refuse to cross the picket line, the more likely the Board will hold that there is an unlawful effect.

b. Recognitional vs. Substandard Wages Picketing

In applying the Section 8(b)(7)(C) proviso, it is important to distinguish between recognition picketing and substandard wages picketing (discussed above) to protest wages and working conditions below those the union has established. Some employers argued that the Section 8(b)(7)(C) proviso should prohibit substandard wages picketing that has the *effect* of causing employees other than those employed by the picketed employer to quit work

or even interrupt deliveries by suppliers to the picketed employer. The Board rejected this argument. The Board's view, which the Courts have upheld, is that the proviso only applies if the union has a recognitional object prohibited by Section 8(b)(7). Substandard wages picketing, which does not have a recognitional object, can continue indefinitely. Also, as for all other protected primary picketing, it can have the effect (but not the object) of interrupting delivery of supplies etc.

c. Pitfalls in Substandard Wages Picketing

Although unions, primarily in the construction field, which engage in substandard wages picketing know the rules, they sometimes fall into innocent traps. Suppose a union establishes a substandard wages picket line. The picketed employer, or perhaps the manager of a construction project where the picketing is occurring, asks one of the pickets what can be done to get the picket line removed. The picket answers that the line would be removed if the picketed employees join the union. This picket has made it appear that the purpose of the picket line is not to protest substandard wages, but to seek recognition. That places the picketing under Section 8(b)(7).

On the other hand, if the picket replies that the union would not be picketing if the employer paid the prevailing wages and benefit level, the picketing could go on indefinitely. The best answer the picket could have given, however, is no answer at all. As a general rule, pickets should be instructed, if questioned, to reply that their picket sign speaks for itself and they should refer all questions to the union office. This approach is true for any type of picketing.

Another mistake unions make is to tell a prime contractor, in response to questions, that a valid substandard wages picket line will be taken down if the offending employer is removed from a project. This statement makes it appear that one object of the picket line is to put pressure on a prime contractor to remove the offending subcontractor from a project. That is unlawful secondary activity in violation of Section 8(b)(4). The union should tell the inquiring employer that the dispute is not with it and there is nothing for it to do. Of course, that is not a very satisfactory answer, but it is the best way for the union to avoid having an innocent remark be the basis of an 8(b)(4) charge.

Does the picketing become unlawful if a prime contractor decides on his own to remove the picketed employer from a project? No, because that is the secondary effect of a primary object. But if, rather than the primary contractor reaching that conclusion on his own, the union suggests removing the subcontractor, that might be considered a secondary object rather than a secondary effect and thus a violation of Section 8(b)(4).

Another requirement for successful substandard wages picketing is that the union must have evidence that an employer is not paying the prevailing wages and benefits before picketing. If the union does not have any evidence that the employer is actually paying less than the standard wage, then the Board will probably conclude that the picketing's true object is recognition and Section 8(b)(7) will apply. Also, substandard wages picketing can have the object of requiring an employer to pay a total wage and fringe benefit package equal in value to that contained in the union's contract. However, the picketing cannot have the object of requiring the picketed employer to pay the same wages and pay into the same fringe benefit funds. The employer has the right to divide the total economic package any way he wishes. The Board reasons that picketing to require the em-

ployer to pay the exact same union wages and benefits (rather than just requiring the same total figure) is, in fact, picketing for recognition to which 8(b)(7) would apply.

3. Picketing to Enforce a Pre-Hire Contract

Section 8(f) of the Act permits a construction union to execute a collective bargaining agreement with a construction employer even though the union does not represent a majority of the employees at the time. This is a statutory exception to the general rule that an employer may not sign a contract unless the union represents a majority of the employees. The exception was made because of the unique nature of the construction industry in which employment is often short-term and the employer looks to the union to furnish skilled labor.

The Board, in applying Section 8(f), has held that it is not an unfair labor practice for an employer to refuse to give effect to an agreement entered into under Section 8(f) until the union represents a majority of the employees. Once a union represents a majority, the employer is bound by the agreement the same as any other contract. The union can obtain majority status through the enforcement of a union security clause in the contract requiring union membership after seven days of employment as permitted by Section 8(f).

What remedies does a construction union have if the employer reneges on a pre-hire agreement before the union attains majority status? Should the union be permitted to picket in protest over the employer's actions? Generally, a union cannot picket to enforce the agreement. The Supreme Court has upheld the Board's position that a union that is picketing to enforce a Section 8(f) pre-hire agreement is, in fact, picketing to obtain recognition. That means that the picketing may violate either Section 8(b)(7)(A), (B), or (C), as appropriate. Of course, under 8(b)(7)(C) the union could indefinitely engage in consumer picketing, but that is hardly satisfactory to the union. Thus, if the contract does not contain a union security clause, the union should obtain recognition cards from a majority of the employees covered by a pre-hire agreement as quickly as possible so that the agreement is enforceable.

K. REMEDIES FOR SECTION 8(b)(4) AND 8(b)(7) VIOLATIONS

1. NLRB Remedies

Under Section 10(1), the regional director is required to give priority to charges alleging violations of Section 8(b)(4) or 8(b)(7) over all other charges. In practice, if an 8(b)(4) or 8(b)(7) charge is filed against a union, the regional director will immediately take an affidavit from the charging party. The regional director will then telegraph the charged union requesting it to produce any information it wishes immediately. If the regional director finds reasonable cause to believe that 8(b)(4) or 8(b)(7) have been violated, the regional director will seek an injunction against the picketing until the Board proceedings are completed. Some unions, to avoid an injunction, simply cease their picketing voluntarily and give the regional director a letter with assurances that the picketing will not resume. The regional director usually will not seek an injunction so long as the union abides by the letter.

2. Section 303 Damage Suits

The other means of enforcing Section 8(b)(4) is for the injured party to bring a suit under LMRA Section 303, which provides for a private damage suit for violation of Section 8(b)(4). Section 303 is the only section of the Act that allows private damage suits to remedy an unfair labor practice. Note that this section does not apply to 8(b)(7) violations.

Section 303 does not allow an injunction against a violation of Section 8(b)(4); injunctions can only be sought by the regional director under Section 10(1). The employer is entitled to recover actual damages resulting from the unlawful secondary activity. Damages might include items such as loss of customer orders, the overhead cost of maintaining a plant that has shut down because of secondary picketing, or the cost of delayed completion of goods or new construction. Some large judgments have been assessed against unions under Section 303.

Section 8(b)(4) and Section 303 are concurrent remedies. That means that the injured employer can both go to the Board under Section 8(b)(4) and file a civil suit under Section 303. The board and the court independently decide the case before them. A union can win before the Board, but lose in court, or vice versa. Some courts have held, however, that if a union loses an 8(b)(4) case before the Board, the court will accept the Board's decision about a violation and the union will not be permitted to relitigate the issue in court. Technically, this is called the doctrine of collateral estoppel. In such cases, the only issue in court is the amount of damages. That is one reason why there is a strong incentive for unions to settle Section 8(b)(4) charges without a formal Board decision. However, a union should be cautious to request a nonadmission clause if it agrees to a Board settlement. Otherwise, the settlement might be used as an admission in court that the union engaged in secondary picketing in violation of Section 8(b)(4).

L. SPECIAL REQUIREMENTS FOR PRIMARY PICKETING IN THE HEALTH CARE INDUSTRY

Section 8(g) imposes special restrictions on picketing at any health care institution. A union must give ten days prior written notice to the health care institution and the Federal Mediation and Conciliation Service before engaging in any strike, picketing, or other concerted refusal to work at a health care institution.

At first the Board applied Section 8(g) literally to all picketing by any union occurring at a health care institution. Thus, if a hospital was building an addition and an outside construction union picketed at the construction situs because of a dispute with one of the contractors, the Board held that the construction union must give ten days notice of its picketing. Several courts of appeals disagreed with the Board's interpretation, holding that Section 8(g) only applies to strikes, picketing, or concerted activity by the hospital's own employees. The Board subsequently modified its position, and now interprets Section 8(g) as requiring ten days notice if the union either represents the health care institution's employees or has a direct dispute against the institution. Thus, if a construction union is picketing to protest hospital employees doing certain construction type work at a substandard wage (e.g., repainting the hospital's walls), the union must give notice. If the union's dispute is with an outside contractor working at the hospital, the union need not give notice.

Summary   This chapter considered picketing and boycotts, focusing on the union's right to picket and the restrictions imposed by LMRA, Section 8(b)(4). The important distinctions under Section 8(b)(4) are between primary and secondary objectives and between a secondary object and a secondary effect. A primary object is an action directed against the employer with whom the union has its dispute, even if the employees of that employer are not on strike. A secondary object is directed against an employer other than the one with whom the union has its dispute.

In *Rice Milling*, the Supreme Court held that pickets in a primary dispute can seek to persuade people appearing at the primary line not to cross the line in support of the picket. If any employees of another employer honor the line, that is a secondary effect of a primary object. So long as the object is primary, picketing is lawful even though there may be a secondary effect.

The policy of Section 8(b)(4) is to prevent innocent employers from becoming embroiled in a labor dispute that is not their own. An employer who assists a struck employer to resist a strike becomes an ally, has embroiled himself in the dispute, and may be picketed the same as any other primary employer. However, two employers who maintain a normal business relationship are not allies.

In *Denver Building Trades*, the Supreme Court held that each contractor on a construction situs is a separate entity. Therefore, a union cannot picket an entire project because the picketing would have the secondary object of embroiling the employees of other contractors in the dispute.

Moore Dry Dock establishes the criteria for lawful picketing at a secondary location. Remember, the factors are not always rigidly applied. Thus, a union may violate Section 8(b)(4) if it is engaging in signal picketing even though it is technically meeting the *Moore Dry Dock* standards.

The *General Electric* decision governs picketing at a primary situs (such as an industrial plant) where other employers also work. A union may not picket at a gate reserved for outside employees if: (a) there is a separate gate for the outside employees identified as such, (b) the work of the outside employees is unrelated to normal operations, and (c) the work being done by the outside contractors is not work that can be done only during a strike or plant shutdown.

The right to picket in a shopping center is not determined on constitutional free speech grounds. Instead, the Board applies the statutory test of balancing private property rights against the union's right of reasonable access to the employees it seeks to organize or striking employees' rights to publicize a labor dispute.

The right to handbill is protected by the publicity proviso following Section 8(b)(4)(D). However, the publicity proviso does not cover picketing. In *Tree Fruits*, the Supreme Court held that a union can picket at a secondary situs to persuade consumers not to purchase a struck product. The union also has the broader right to handbill at the secondary situs to persuade consumers not to deal with an employer continuing to handle the struck product. However, a union cannot picket a "merged" product because that amounts to a total boycott of the secondary employer. A merged product can only be handbilled.

Organizational or recognition picketing is regulated by Section 8(b)(7). Section 8(b)(7) does not apply to substandard wages picketing. Thus, substandard picketing may have the object of stopping deliveries to the picketed employer and may continue indefinitely the same as other primary picketing.

1. Is there a constitutional right to picket?

2. What is the difference between a primary and secondary picket line?

3. Can a union engage in mass picketing in which a large number of employees patrol the picket line at one time?

4. What is the difference between a primary object and a secondary effect under Section 8(b)(4)?

5. Can picketing lawfully have a mixed primary-secondary object?

6. Would a picket sign that was simply worded "on strike" meet *Moore Dry Dock* standards?

Review
Questions

7. Can a union picket during the regular workday if a prime contractor schedules a picketed employer to work only in the evenings when no other employees are present?

8. Can a striking union appeal to fellow employees of the same employer to join a strike even though they are not in a bargaining unit?

9. Can a union picket at a secondary situs to persuade customers not to buy a specific struck product?

10. Is substandard picketing unlawful if it has the effect of inducing other employees to honor the picket line?

11. When may "informational picketing" violate the Act?

12. What remedies does an employer have against unlawful secondary activity under Section 8(b)(4)?

(Answers to review questions appear at end of book.)

Basic Legal
Principles

1. Primary pickets have the right at the primary location to appeal directly to customers, suppliers, fellow employees, and striker replacements not to cross the picket line. *NLRB v. International Rice Milling Co.*, 341 U.S. 665, 28 LRRM 2105 (1951); *United Steelworkers v. NLRB*, 376 U.S. 492, 55 LRRM 2698 (1964).

2. A union having a dispute with one construction contractor cannot picket the entire project, because the picketing would have the secondary object of embroiling other employers in the dispute. *NLRB v. Denver Building and Construction Trades Council*, 341 U.S. 675, 28 LRRM 2108 (1951); *Building Trades Council (Markwell & Hartz, Inc.)* 155 NLRB No. 42, 60 LRRM 1296 (1965); *Sheet Metal Workers, Local 80*, 236 NLRB No. 6, 98 LRRM 1223 (1978).

3. Primary picketing at a secondary location is lawful if: (a) the primary employer is engaged in its normal business at the situs, (b) the picket signs identify the primary employer, (c) the picket is as reasonably close to the situs as possible, and (d) the primary employer is "present" when the picketing is occurring. *Sailor's Union of the Pacific (Moore Dry Dock)*, 92 NLRB No. 93, 27 LRRM 1108 (1950); *Linbeck Construction Co. v. NLRB*, 550 F.2d 311, 94 LRRM 3230 (5th Cir. 1977); *Wire Service Guild Local 221*, 218 NLRB No. 186, 89 LRRM 1397 (1975); *Local 453 IBEW (Southern Sun Electric Corp.)*, 237 NLRB No. 104, 99 LRRM 1076 (1978).

4. A striking industrial plant union may not picket a gate reserved for outside contractor's employees if: (a) there is a separate gate identified as such, (b) the work of the outside employer is unrelated to normal operations, and (c) the work being done by outside contractors is not work that could only be done during a strike or plant shutdown. *Electrical Workers Local 761 v. NLRB (General Electric)*, 366 U.S. 667, 48 LRRM 2210 (1961);

NLRB v. Electrical Workers, Local 369, 528 F.2d 317, 91 LRRM 3006 (6th Cir. 1976).

5. Secondary employers who are allied with the primary employer because they are performing farmed out struck work because of common ownership and control or integration of operations are not neutrals. They can be picketed the same as the struck employer. *Graphic Arts Union, Local 277,* 225 NLRB No. 186, 93 LRRM 1113 (1976); *Los Angeles Newspaper Guild (Hearst Corp.);*185 NLRB 303, 75 LRRM 1014 (1970), *enforced* 443 F.2d 1173, 77 LRRM 2895 (9th Cir. 1971); *Television and Radio Artists,* 185 NLRB 593, 75 LRRM 1018 (1970) *enforced* 462 F.2d 887, 80 LRRM 2001 (D.C. Cir. 1972); *Teamsters, Local 743,* 231 NLRB No. 156, 97 LRRM 1169 (1977).

6. Two employers do not become allies if they maintain a normal business relationship during a strike. (Cases cited, note 5.)

7. Usually a union can handbill at a secondary situs to persuade consumers not to deal with an employer continuing to handle a struck product. The union cannot picket a product that is merged into the employer's business, so that a consumer must boycott the employer in order to stop using the product. *NLRB v. Fruit and Vegetable Packers Local 760 (Tree Fruits),* 377 U.S. 58, *NLRB v. Servette, Inc.,* 377 U.S. 46, 55 LRRM 2961 (1964); *Steelworkers (Pet Inc.),* 244 NLRB No. 6, 102 LRRM 1046 (1979) (consumer boycott of conglomerate); *American Bread Co., v. NLRB,* 411 F.2d 147, 71 LRRM 2243 (6th Cir. 1969); *K & K Const. Co. v. NLRB,* 592 F.2d 1228, 100 LRRM 2416 (3rd Cir. 1979), *denying enforcement* to 233 NLRB No. 99, 96 LRRM 1575 (1977). But see *Retail Clerks Local 1001 v. NLRB* ———F.2———, 101 LRRM 3084 (D.C. Cir. 1979) (upholding product picketing of sole product of secondary employer.)

8. Section 8(b)(7) does not apply to substandard wages picketing that attempts to induce an employer to observe area wage standards. Such picketing may have the object of stopping deliveries to the picketed employer since it is primary picketing. *Claude Everett Construction Co.,* 136 NLRB 321, 49 LRRM 1757 (1962); *Local 399, Carpenters (K & K Construction Co.), supra.*

9. A striking union can appeal to a store manager's discretion not to stock a struck product, but cannot appeal to the manager to cease work in support of the strike. *NLRB v. Servette, Inc., supra.*

10. Unions may lawfully picket within the private property of a shopping center if, on balance, the union's right to picket and publicize its dispute outweighs the private property interests of the employer. *Hudgens v. NLRB,* 424 U.S. 507, 91 LRRM 2489 (1976); *Scott Hudgens,* 230 NLRB 414, 95 LRRM 1351 (1977); *Giant Food Markets,* 241 NLRB No. 105, 100 LRRM 1598 (1979). Compare *Seattle-First Nat'l Bank,* 243 NLRB No. 145, 101

LRRM 1537 (1979); (upholding primary picketing in front of a restaurant on 46th floor of office building).

Recommended Reading

Brinker, Taylor, "Secondary Boycott Maze," 25 *Lab. L.J.* 418 (1974).

"Recognitional Picketing in the Garment Industry—Garment Unions Granted Protected Status Under Section 8(b)(7)(C) of the National Labor Relations Act," 50 *N.Y.U.L. Rev.* 57 (1975).

"Secondary Boycotts—The Construction Industry and the Status of the Right to Control Test," 24 *Wayne L. Rev.* 1495 (1978).

Chapter Eight

Union Regulation of Work and the Antitrust Laws

(Hot Cargo Agreements, Jurisdictional Disputes, and Featherbedding)

Unions have many legitimate reasons for attempting to regulate work. The historical claim of a fair day's pay for a fair day's work symbolizes labor's claim to negotiate limits on job content and effort. Union efforts to regulate job content and protect work jurisdiction raise issues as to hot cargo clauses, restrictions on subcontracting, jurisdictional disputes, and featherbedding.

Work restrictions affect competition and trade between employers. If a union negotiates a clause with its employer limiting the companies to whom the employer may subcontract work, some companies may be denied business they might otherwise have received. Thus, union efforts to restrict work raise questions about the application of the antitrust laws, which are designed to encourage free competition and prohibit restraint on trade.

PART I. HOT CARGO CLAUSES

A. The Purpose and General Coverage of Section 8(e)

Section 8(e), commonly called the "Hot Cargo" provision, prohibits agreements between employers and unions "whereby such employer ceases or refrains or agrees to cease or refrain from handling, using, selling, transporting or otherwise dealing in any of the products of any other employer, or to cease doing business with any other person." The section provides that such agreements are void and unenforceable. Section 8(e) was enacted in 1959 as part of the Landrum-Griffin Amendments to the Labor Management Relations Act. Prior to Section 8(e), it was common for employers and unions to enter into agreements under which employees, such as truck drivers, would not have to pick up or handle goods of any employer whose employees were on strike. The struck work was considered "hot cargo." These hot cargo clauses were, in effect, agreements in which the contracting employer agreed to cease doing business with another employer. Section 8(e) now broadly prohibits such agreements.

Prior to the 1959 amendments, the original Taft–Hartley version of Section 8(b)(4)(A) prohibited a union from coercing an employer into entering into agreements under which the employer agreed to cease dealing with any other person. However, the Act did not prohibit an employer from voluntarily agreeing to cease dealing with another employer who was struck. The Board held that a union could not coerce an employer into keeping such an agreement, but that the Act did not prohibit an employer's voluntary compliance. Section 8(e) closed this gap by prohibiting even voluntary agreements or voluntary compliance.

Section 8(e) follows the general policy of Section 8(b)(4), limiting a labor dispute to the primary employer and the striking union. Hot cargo clauses were a lawful means of secondary activity that Section 8(e) now prohibits.

Section 8(e) contains a limited exception for the construction industry (discussed more fully below). The garment industry is totally excluded from the provision, based on a Congressional concern that the garment industry has many small employers and that hot cargo type agreements have a legitimate function of maintaining wage standards in the industry.

Section 8(e) prohibits hot cargo agreements whether they are express or implied. That means that oral agreements, informal understandings, or vague contractual language that could be applied in an unlawful manner are prohibited.

Section 8(b)(4)(A), as amended in 1959, makes it unlawful to coerce or restrain an employer into entering into an agreement prohibited by Section 8(e). But remember that Section 8(e) voids and even prohibits agreements that an employer makes voluntarily. The Board will seek injunctive relief under Section 10(1) for a violation of Section 8(b)(4)(A) (see Chapter 7). The employer may also sue for damages under Section 303.

B. Scope of the Section 8(e) Restrictions

Section 8(e) had a specific purpose. Unfortunately the language of the section, as is frequently true in labor legislation, goes much beyond the purpose. There are many types of contract clauses in which an employer agrees not to deal with another employer. For example, an employer's agreement not to subcontract bargaining unit work is an agreement to cease doing business with someone else. Does Section 8(e) prohibit any agreement limiting subcontracting? The Board and the courts, by looking at the intent of Section 8(e), determined what type of agreements are lawful and which are not.

1. Picket Line Clauses

What about a contract clause that protects the right of employees to honor a picket line established at the plant of another employer? A typical clause might provide that the contracting employer's employees may not be disciplined for refusing to pick up or deliver the goods of a struck employer. In effect, the contracting employer has agreed to a provision under which he will not deal with another employer who is on strike. Literally, that agreement is prohibited by Section 8(e). But did Congress, in enacting Section 8(e), intend to prohibit this traditional form of union mutual assistance? The Board, in determining the legality of picket line clauses, has followed the primary-secondary object distinction (see Chapter 7). The Board has reasoned that Section 8(e) is intended to prohibit secondary activity. An employee's right to honor another union's primary picket line is a traditional primary right. Thus, the Board has held that a picket line clause that permits employees to honor a primary picket line established at another location is lawful under Section 8(e). However, a clause that permits a union to honor a secondary picket line is unlawful.

What if a contract gave construction union employees the right to walk off a construction job situs whenever pickets appeared? That clause would be unlawful because it might sanction secondary activity such as walking off a job although picketing did not meet the *Moore Dry Dock* standards (see Chapter 7). A picket line clause permitting employees to honor *any* picket line would be prohibited under Section 8(e) because it might permit employees to honor a secondary picket line. To be lawful, the picket line clause, through appropriate wording, must be expressly limited to primary picketing.

2. Struck Goods Clauses

A struck goods clause protects the right of employees not to handle goods produced by a struck employer. However, Section 8(e) imposes limits on these clauses similar to those on a picket line clause.

What if a struck goods clause states that the employees of the contracting employer cannot be disciplined for refusing to handle goods that are produced by a struck employer? A clause worded that broadly would be unlawful under Section 8(e) because it is not limited to a primary strike. As in the case of a picket line clause, a clause permitting employees to refuse to handle struck goods must be limited to goods produced by an employer struck in a primary dispute.

There is one additional limitation on a struck goods clause. Two employers have the right to continue their normal business relations during a strike (see Chapter 7). The Board, applying this policy, has held that a struck goods clause cannot protect an employee's right to refuse to handle work produced by a struck employer that the employee handled before the strike began. A struck goods clause can only protect an employee's right to refuse to handle or work on goods that the striking employees would have produced, but for the strike. This means that a union can negotiate a clause under which employees may refuse to work on struck goods if doing the work would make the two employers allies rather than simply maintain their normal business relationship.

Thus, a union can have a struck goods clause in its contract providing that employees may not be required to do work that, but for the existence of a primary labor dispute, would have been done by the employees of the struck employer. But the clause cannot allow employees to refuse to handle all goods produced by a struck employer because such a broad clause might sanction secondary activity in violation of Section 8(e).

3. Subcontracting Clauses

a. Work Preservation Clauses. Any restrictions on subcontracting bargaining unit work are literally an agreement with the contracting employer to cease or refrain from dealing with another employer in violation of Section 8(e). The courts and the Board recognize that Congress did not intend to prohibit all restrictions on subcontracting, but the scope of permissible clauses was not established until the Supreme Court's decision in *National Woodwork.*[1]

In *National Woodwork,* the Carpenters' Union collective bargaining agreement prohibited the use of pre-hung doors. The contract required that all hanging be done on the job site. The purpose of the clause was to preserve this work for the job site carpenters rather than using prefabricated materials produced elsewhere. The company, despite its contractual agreement, decided to use pre-hung doors and the union refused to install them. The issue was whether the clause prohibiting the use of pre-hung doors violated Section 8(e). If the clause violated Section 8(e), then the union's refusal to hang the pre-hung doors in order to force the employer to live up to his agreement, violated Section 8(b)(4)(A), which prohibits coercion

[1] See legal principle 1.

to enforce an agreement prohibited by Section 8(e).

In *National Woodwork*, the Court relied on the primary–secondary distinction under Section 8(b)(4). The Court stated that Section 8(e) was intended to prohibit agreements having the object of controlling labor relations of another employer. That would be a secondary object. But the Court stated that section 8(e) does not prohibit clauses that have the primary object of regulating the labor relations between the contracting employer and the union. The purpose of the carpenters pre-hung door clause was to preserve bargaining unit work. The Court stated that preserving bargaining unit work was a primary object, therefore, the clause was not prohibited by Section 8(e). Also it was not unlawful under Section 8(b)(4)(A) for the union to refuse to do work that violated its contract. The pre-hung door clause could possibly cause the pre-hung door manufacturer to lose business, but that would not make the clause unlawful because the manufacturer's lost business would simply be the secondary effect (not object) of a valid primary restriction.

b. Union Standards and Union Signatory Clauses. Under *National Woodwork*, subcontracting clauses that have the sole object of preserving bargaining unit work do not violate Section 8(e), but subcontracting clauses that go beyond a primary object are void. What if a contract clause prohibited all subcontracting of bargaining unit work? That would be a valid primary work preservation clause permitted under Section 8(e).

What if the clause permitted subcontracting only to an employer who maintains wages, hours, and fringe benefits equivalent to the economic provisions in the union's contract, referred to as a union standards clause? Union standards clauses are also a lawful work preservation method. They take

the economic incentive out of subcontracting by requiring the subcontractor to pay wages and benefits equivalent to those required under the union's contract. Of course, a potential subcontractor might be affected by a union standard clause. A subcontractor might have to increase employees' wages to be eligible for a subcontract. However, that result is considered to be a secondary effect of the union's primary object of preserving unit work.

What if a contract permits subcontracting only to employers whose own employees are represented by a union, a so-called union-signatory clause? Such clauses are unlawful under Section 8(e) except for work done on a construction project (discussed below). The union-signatory clause goes beyond the valid object of preserving unit work. By limiting subcontracts only to union contractors, the clause has a secondary object of influencing the labor relations of the secondary employer. That is the type of secondary object Section 8(e) is intended to prohibit.

c. Requiring Payment of Identical Benefits. Union standards clauses requiring that a subcontractor pay the cash equivalent of union wages and benefits are lawful. What if a union goes beyond that, and negotiates a subcontracting clause requiring that an employer pay exactly the same benefits, prohibiting the payment of a cash equivalent? The Board has held that a union cannot require that subcontracting be limited to employers who maintain exactly the same wages, hours, or working conditions. A union cannot dictate the manner in which a subcontractor cuts up the economic pie for its own employees. The Board reasons that requiring the same benefits goes beyond the primary object of taking away the employer's economic incentive for subcontracting. Such a clause also has the secondary object of dictating the terms of the secondary employer's relationship with its own employees. That violates Section 8(e).

The Supreme Court has held that a union may have a subcontracting clause in its contract providing that, if work is subcontracted, contributions must be paid into the union's pension and health and welfare funds for the employees doing the work as if the work had been done by the bargaining unit employees. Employers argued that the clause violates Section 8(e) because the subcontractor's employees who do the work are not members of the union, are not covered by the pension and health and welfare plans, and will never get any benefits from the contributions. But the Supreme Court upheld the requirements, reasoning that the clause is a legitimate work preservation provision designed to take away the economic incentive of subcontracting.

d. Work Expansion Clauses. National Woodwork covered a situation in which a union was attempting to preserve bargaining unit work it was performing. What if a union, through technological change, finds that its traditional work is declining? As a matter of preservation, the union negotiates an agreement under which the bargaining unit employees perform work that has previously been subcontracted and that the unit employees have not done before. The Board has held that an agreement expanding the unit's work by prohibiting the subcontracting of work the unit has not previously performed violates Section 8(e). The Board reasons that such a clause is not limited to the primary object of preserving work, but also has the secondary object (not just secondary effect) of removing work from another employer. As an exception, unions have the right to reclaim work they are not currently doing, but used to perform.

Suppose a production union used to do factory maintenance work, but permitted the work to be subcontracted out without objection. The union could lawfully seek a contract clause requiring bargaining unit employees to do the maintenance work although they are not currently doing it. The union would simply be seeking to reclaim lost bargaining unit work, which the Board regards as solely a primary object.

The Board's application of the distinction between preserving work versus claiming new work is sometimes questionable. For example, a series of cases have involved the Longshoremen Union's right to limit the use of containerized cargo, cargo taken directly off a ship into a waiting truck or train, cutting out the longshoremen's unloading function. The longshoremen have tried to restrict containerized cargo through clauses in their collective bargaining agreements requiring that the containers be unloaded and reloaded. The Board has held that these clauses are not legitimate work preservation clauses. The Board's theory is that containerized cargo is an entirely new process. Therefore, restrictions on container cargo do not preserve work, but are rather an attempt to expand the union's jurisdiction.

The Section 8(e) limitations on protecting bargaining unit work only apply to subcontracting restrictions affecting other employers. Section 8(e) does not regulate clauses on the division of work among the primary employer's employees. Thus, a union can have a clause prohibiting the performance of bargaining unit work by supervisors or the employer's nonunit employees. The union can seek a clause transferring new work from other employees to the bargaining unit. These clauses are outside the scope of Section 8(e) because they only regulate the primary employer's operations and have no secondary object.

e. The Right of Control Test. The principal limitation on work preservation clauses is the so-called right to control test. What if a union's contract prohibits use of a certain process, but the contracting employer does not control the work assignment on a project? What if, in *National Woodwork*, for example, the carpenter's contractor had been told by the project developer to use pre-hung doors and had no choice of material? Could the carpenters, relying on their contract, refuse to hang pre-hung doors even though their employer had no control over the work? The Board has held that a union cannot refuse to perform work if their employer has no control over the assignment, even though the process used violates the union's collective bargaining agreement. The Board reasons that if the contracting employer has no control over the material or process used, the union's actual dispute is with the party, such as the project developer, who does have control. If the union refuses to do the work for its own employer, the contracting employer at that point becomes the innocent secondary employer in the union's dispute with the employer who has control. The union's refusal to work is coercion on its own employer to pressure the employer who has control. Thus, the Board has concluded that the refusal to do work, if the contracting union's employer has no control over the assignment, is unlawful secondary activity under Section 8(b)(4)(B).

Unions, of course, argue that a contracting employer is hardly an innocent secondary employer if the employer enters into a contract requiring it to do work in a way that would violate its own collective bargaining agreement. Unions argue that a contractor should either not accept work that violates the collective bargaining agreement or else should be prepared to face the consequence that the union might refuse to do the work. Also, the right to control test allows the con-tracting employer to circumvent his own collective bargaining agreement by simply accepting a contract requiring it to do work or use a process that its own collective bargaining agreement would otherwise prohibit. These arguments have been unavailing and the Board has held to the right to control doctrine.

The Supreme Court, in *Pipefitters Local 638,* upheld the Board's right of control test.[2] In that case, the union's collective bargaining agreement required that certain internal piping work on climate control equipment be done on the job site. This restriction is a valid work preservation clause. The prime contractor required the use of prefabricated material in violation of the union's contract. The pipefitters' subcontractor agreed to the building contract even though the contract violated the pipefitter's collective bargaining agreement. The employees refused to install the prefabricated pipe, just as the carpenters had refused to install the pre-hung doors in *National Woodwork.* However, the Supreme Court upheld the Board's position by applying the right to control test. The Supreme Court agreed with the Board that the union's refusal to install the pipe was unlawful secondary activity in violation of Section 8(b)(4)(B) because the union's dispute was with the general contractor who had required the use of prefabricated materials. The union's refusal to install the prefabricated material, even though its use violated the collective bargaining agreement, constituted secondary pressure on the union's own employer directed at the general contractor. Thus, since the pipefitter's employer did not have the right to control the work, the union was prohibited from enforcing the contractual restriction by refusing to do the work.

[2] See legal principle 3.

1. *Employer Option to Abide by the Subcontracting Restrictions.* Although the Board's right to control test has been upheld, the Board has indicated that the test will not be applied mechanically. The Supreme Court quoted approvingly from the Board's decision in *George Koch Sons, Inc.*[3] In that case the Board stated:

> Specifically, of late, the Board has characterized its approach simply in terms of a right-of-control test. The test as stated would seem to imply that the Board looked solely at the pressured employer's "contract right to control" the work at issue at the time of the pressure to determine whether that pressure was primary or secondary. In fact, this is not now the Board's approach nor was it ever.
>
> Rather, the Board has always proceeded with an analysis of (1) whether under all the surrounding circumstances the union's objective was work preservation and then (2) whether the pressures exerted were directed at the right person, i.e., at the primary in the dispute . . . . In following this approach, however, our analysis has not nor will it ever be a mechanical one, and, in addition to determining under all the surrounding circumstances whether the union's objective is truly work preservation, we have studied and shall continue to study not only the situation the pressured employer finds himself in but also how he came to be in that situation. *And if we find the employer is not truly an "unoffending employer" who merits the Act's protections, we shall find no violation in a union's pressures such as occurred here, even though a purely mechanical or surface look at the case might present an appearance of a parallel situation.* [emphasis added]

When the Board says it will determine whether the employer is truly unoffending, this means that the Board will determine whether the employer did or did not truly have an option of living up to its collective bargaining agreement. What if the subcontractor tells the prime contractor that it has a clause in its collective bargaining agreement

prohibiting prefabricated goods and the subcontractor suggests that the prime contractor specify the use of prefabricated goods in order to get around the collective bargaining restrictions? The subcontractor is not truly unoffending. Rather, the primary and subcontractor have engaged in collusion to avoid the subcontractor's collective bargaining agreement. If collusion is proven, the union can lawfully refuse to do the work. But if there is a good faith arm's-length business transaction in which the primary contractor insists that the subcontractor use materials violating the subcontractor's collective bargaining agreement, the right to control test will undoubtedly apply. The union cannot lawfully refuse to do the work.

It is clear that a subcontractor does not have to give up a job because the specifications require that the subcontractor violate its own collective bargaining agreement. Given a choice between living up to its collective bargaining agreement or doing the work as a prime contractor requires, the subcontractor can accept the job and the employees will be required to do the work.

2. *Lawful Means of Enforcing the Restrictions.* Although a union cannot refuse to do the work over which its employer has no control so long as its employer is unoffending, the union may be able to file a grievance or sue to enforce subcontracting restrictions. Refusing to install equipment is a form of coercion that violates Section 8(b)(4)(B). But the Board has held that filing a grievance to enforce a contract right is not coercion. Although a union can be required to do the work, it may still be able to get damages for the violation of its collective bargaining agreement. The union might be able to prove that fewer employees were used on a project because of the contract violation and win back pay for the employees who would have been employed.

[3] See legal principle 3.

Of course, an arbitrator cannot order an employer to abide by an agreement that would violate Section 8(e). Remember, Section 8(e) prohibits all hot cargo agreements whether entered into voluntarily or through coercion. An arbitrator's decision is not coercion, but an employer's actions in abiding by an arbitrator's decision enforcing an unlawful clause in itself violates Section 8(e).

f. Conditioning Sale of a Business on Union Recognition. Under the Supreme Court's *Burns Detective* decision (see Chapter 5), a successor employer who purchases a business is not obligated to accept the predecessor employer's collective bargaining agreement. The successor's only obligation is to bargain with the incumbent union if it represents a majority of the new work force. Can a union contractually require its employer to condition sale of the business on the successor employer's agreement to assume the existing collective bargaining agreement even though the law does not require it? Would such a clause require one employer to cease doing business with another employer in violation of Section 8(e)? The Board has upheld clauses in which an employer agrees not to sell its business except to someone who assumes the collective bargaining contract. It has held that such restrictions have a legitimate work preservation object. The clause can be enforced by picketing or by an injunction against selling the business in violation of the assumption agreement. If the predecessor employer fails to include the required assumption clause in the sale agreement, the union might also be able to sue the predecessor employer for damages. The damages can be the monetary loss the employees suffered, such as lost jobs or reduced wages, as a result of the successor employer's failure to accept the existing collective bargaining agreement.

g. The Construction Industry Exception to Section 8(e). Section 8(e) contains a proviso that:

> Nothing in this subsection (e) shall apply to an agreement between a labor organization and an employer in the construction industry relating to the contracting or subcontracting of work to be done at the site of the construction, alteration, painting, or repair of a building, structure, or other work.

As discussed above, subcontracting clauses generally cannot limit subcontracting to union employers. Such a clause goes beyond preserving unit work and is an attempt to dictate the labor relations policies of another employer. However, the proviso to Section 8(e), as an exception, permits a construction union to negotiate a clause limiting contracts and subcontracts for work to be done at a construction site to union contractors. Congress agreed to this exception for the construction industry because the traditional pattern on construction projects is for all contractors to be union. Congress concluded that retention of this practice was necessary to preserve harmony on the job site.

1. *Applicability to Job Site Work Only.* The construction industry proviso only applies to work done on the job site. The *National Woodwork* case pertained to a contract clause prohibiting prefabricated doors, but that clause was not covered by the construction industry proviso because the prefabrication was done off the construction site. On work done off the situs, construction unions are subject to the same restrictions as other unions. Thus, construction unions, as in *National Woodwork*, can have a clause limiting or prohibiting off situs subcontracting as a means of preserving bargaining unit work, but they cannot have a clause limiting off situs subcontracting to union employers.

A construction union cannot limit use of prefabricated materials to those made by union subcontractors because that would violate Section 8(e). But, a construction union can have a clause requiring that prefabricated materials be installed by a union contractor on the construction situs. That restriction would apply to work done on the construction situs and thus would be within the construction industry exception. An industrial union cannot have a clause requiring that any subcontracted maintenance work in the plant be done by union contractors. That restriction would violate Section 8(e) and there is no exception for industrial unions.

2. *The Connell Construction Limitation on the Construction Industry Exception.* In the *Connell Construction* case, the Supreme Court placed an additional limitation on the Section 8(e) construction industry proviso.[4] In *Connell*, a pipefitter's local picketed a general contractor to require that the general contractor sign an agreement that all work within the union's jurisdiction would be subcontracted to contractors whose employees were represented by the union. The union did not represent any employees directly employed by the general contractor. The general contractor signed the agreement under protest. It then filed suit against the union under the antitrust laws to invalidate the agreement.

The primary issue in *Connell* was whether the union's attempt to force this agreement on the general contractor violated the antitrust laws (see below). However, one of the union's defenses was that the agreement was valid under the construction industry exception to Section 8(e) because it regulated subcontracting on a construction situs. The union argued that the construction industry proviso controlled over any possible antitrust violation.

The Supreme Court held that Section 8(e) did not protect the union's agreement. First,

[4] See legal principle 9.

the Court noted that the union did not seek to represent any of the employees hired by the general contractor. Instead, the union attempted to engage in "top-down organizing" by requiring the general contractor to deal only with subcontractors who recognized the union. The Court said Section 8(e) was intended to prevent this type of top-down activity. Second, the Court noted that the proposed clause was intended to apply to all jobs of the general contractor, even those on which no pipefitters were working. Thus, to the extent that the construction industry exception was intended to prevent hostility on the job site between union and nonunion workers, that purpose was not served by the pipefitters' proposal. The Court held that the Section 8(e) construction industry proviso permitted subcontracts limited to union contractors only as part of an overall collective bargaining agreement, which the union was not seeking in *Connell*, and "possibly to common situs relationships on particular job sites. . . ."

Post-Connell Board Decisions. In cases since *Connell*, the Board has affirmed the court's basic ruling that a union may seek construction industry agreements limiting job situs subcontracts to union contractors only if the union has a collective bargaining relationship with the signatory employer. The Board has also held that a union seeking to represent an employer's employees may propose such a construction industry agreement as part of its initial contract. The union need not be recognized before making the proposal. Finally, the Board has held that a Section 8(e) construction agreement may be sought as part of a pre-hire agreement permitted under Section 8(e) in the construction industry.

The Board has indicated that it might uphold a construction industry agreement even if there is no collective bargaining relationship between the union and the signatory employer, if the clause is limited to jobs on which employees represented by the union will be working. The purpose is then to prevent the disharmony that results when union and nonunion employees work on the same project. The construction industry proviso was intended to preserve this union right. However, the restrictions must be limited to the specific jobs on which the union's membership is working. The clause cannot apply generally to all projects as a means of top-down organizing. The Board indicated that the clause would probably have to prohibit all nonunion subcontractors, not just those doing work within the union's jurisdiction. Otherwise, the clause would not prevent disharmony, but could be used for top-down organizing that the Supreme Court indicated was impermissible in *Connell*.

3. *Enforcement of Construction Industry Proviso Clauses*

a. *Striking to Enforce a Clause.* Assume that a construction union obtains a clause limiting subcontracting on the construction situs to union contractors; but the contractor violates the agreement by hiring a nonunion subcontractor. May the union stop work on the project until the nonunion contractor leaves the job in accordance with the contract?

The key to understanding the rules on enforcing a construction industry proviso clause is to remember that such a clause has a secondary object to require that contractors be union. The clause would be unlawful under Section 8(e), as in all other industries, except for the express proviso.

Section 8(b)(4)(B) prohibits picketing or other coercive acts with the object of requiring one employer to cease doing business with any other person. Although Section 8(e) contains an exception for the construction industry, it has no exceptions for Section 8(b)(4)(B) violations. From this, the Board and

the courts have reasoned that, since a construction industry clause has a secondary object, it cannot be enforced through picketing, refusal to work, or other self-help measures. Self-help to enforce the clause, requiring that a nonunion subcontractor be removed from a project, would be coercion, forcing the contractor to cease dealing with a nonunion subcontractor. Although the clause would not violate Section 8(e), enforcement in this manner would still violate Section 8(b)(4)(B). Thus, a valid construction industry clause can only be enforced through peaceful means such as a court injunction to force compliance or through arbitration. Enforcement through court procedures or through arbitration is not considered coercion.

Under the same principles, a construction industry clause limiting subcontracts to union contractors is void under Section 8(e) if the clause permits any form of self-help for enforcement. Thus, the clause cannot permit the union to cancel the entire collective bargaining agreement, including the no-strike clause, if the employer violates the subcontracting clause or fails to follow an arbitrator's decision. That would permit self-help to enforce the clause. Enforcement of construction industry subcontracting clauses must be strictly through voluntary compliance, the courts, or arbitration.

In contrast to the restrictions on enforcing a construction industry clause, a primary work preservation clause under *National Woodwork* may be enforced through self-help provided, of course, the collective bargaining agreement does not contain a no-strike clause. This self-help would not violate Section 8(e), because enforcing the valid work preservation clause is a primary object, although there may be a secondary effect on a subcontractor. The garment industry, of course, has a total exemption from Section 8(e).

b. *Striking to Obtain a Clause.* A union can strike for a valid work preservation clause because the clause has a valid primary object. At one time, the Board held that a union could not strike to obtain a construction industry clause, reasoning that a strike to obtain the clause had a secondary object. The courts of appeals, however, disagreed with the Board's interpretation. Eventually, the Board adopted the courts' view that a construction union can strike to *obtain* a valid construction industry clause, but may not strike to *enforce* the clause because that would violate Section 8(b)(4)(B).

The legal reasoning for the distinction between obtaining a clause and enforcing it rests on the argument that if a construction union uses self-help to enforce a clause to remove a subcontractor from a job, it has a secondary object directed against the specific subcontractor. On the other hand, if a union strikes to obtain a clause, and there is no subcontractor working at the time, the union's acts are directed solely against its own employer to obtain the clause. So the dispute is primary only.

What if a subcontractor is already working on a project at the time a union strikes to obtain a construction industry clause? The Board's position is that a strike to obtain a clause that would require the contracting employer to terminate or change his relationship with an existing subcontractor on a project violates Section 8(b)(4)(B). One object of the strike is to remove the subcontractor or require that the subcontractor become unionized. If there is an existing nonunion contractor, the union can still strike for a construction industry clause if the clause excluded existing subcontractors from the provision.

PART II. WORK ASSIGNMENT DISPUTES

The Board's role in work assignment disputes, sometimes referred to as jurisdictional disputes, arises under Sections 8(b)(4)(D) and 10(k). Section 8(b)(4)(D) makes it an unfair labor practice to engage in a strike or other coercive activities with an object of "forcing or requiring any employer to assign particular work to employees in a particular labor organization or in a particular trade, craft, or class, rather than to employees in another labor organization or in another trade, craft, or class, unless the employer is failing to conform to an order or certification of the Board determining the bargaining representative for employees performing their work." Section 10(k) empowers the Board to resolve a work assignment dispute under certain circumstances.

A. Voluntary Agreements to Resolve Jurisdictional Disputes

Jurisdictional disputes occur in both craft and industrial union settings. One craft union on a project may assert that work belongs to it rather than to another craft. Each of two industrial unions representing competing bargaining units in a plant may each claim that certain work should be assigned to it rather than the other unit. Under Section 10(k), if the Board has reasonable cause to believe that Section 8(b)(4)(D) is being violated, the Board determines the merits of the dispute and assigns the work unless the parties have a voluntary means of adjusting the matter. The Board will not determine the dispute if the parties produce evidence within ten days after an 8(b)(4)(D) charge has been filed that they have either resolved the dispute themselves or have agreed upon a method for voluntarily resolving it. A contractual agreement to arbitrate the dispute is an agreed-upon method. Some craft unions are parties to national or local agreements establishing joint boards to resolve jurisdictional disputes. These agreements may constitute an agreed upon method under Section 8(b)(4)(D). The parties do not actually have to resolve the dispute within ten days, but need only agree upon the method of resolution.

All parties must be bound by a voluntary means of adjustment for the Board to defer to it. For example, if two craft unions are bound to a national agreement to resolve jurisdictional disputes between them, but the employer is not a party to the agreement, there is no agreed-upon method. The Board will proceed under Section 10(k). If an employer has a contract containing an arbitration clause with one competing union, but not with the other, there is no agreed-upon method. Even if the employer has separate contracts with both unions that contain arbitration clauses, the contracts probably do not provide for tripartite arbitration (two unions and the employer taking part in the same arbitration proceedings). The Board has held that separate agreements to arbitrate with each union are not an agreed-upon method of resolving a dispute unless the parties agree to a tripartite procedure in which they are all bound by the result.

If the Board has notice of an agreed-upon method of resolving the dispute within ten days, the Board will hold the case until the proceedings are completed. If the parties comply with the award, the Section 8(b)(4)(D) charge will be dismissed.

B. Coercive Activity to Trigger a Section 10(k) Proceeding

Unions sometimes erroneously believe that the Board can resolve every jurisdictional dispute. The Board has jurisdiction to resolve a dispute under Section 10(k) only if one of the competing unions is charged with violating Section 8(b)(4)(D). That means that one of the competing unions must engage in a strike, the threat of a strike, or other coercive activity to have the work assigned to it. If a union exerts peaceful persuasion on the employer, or requests arbitration under its own contract, Section 8(b)(4)(D) is not violated and Section 10(k) does not apply.

The Board does not have to find an actual violation of Section 8(b)(4)(D) in order to assert jurisdiction under Section 10(k). The Board will proceed under Section 10(k) if it has reasonable cause to believe that Section 8(b)(4)(D) has been violated. That standard is not difficult to meet. Although a contract may contain a no-strike clause, a union may still tell an employer that it will strike if the employer assigns certain work to another union. Although the union may not intend to carry out the threat, the strike threat is sufficient for the Board to find reasonable cause to believe that Section 8(b)(4)(D) has been violated.

Suppose an employer testifies that a union has threatened to strike to have certain work assigned to it and union witnesses deny the accusation. Can the Board make a 10(k) determination when the testimony as to the threat is in direct conflict? Yes, because the Board only has to find reasonable cause to believe that Section 8(b)(4)(D) has been violated in order to proceed under Section 10(k). The Board does not have to make credibility findings in a Section 10(k) hearing. Thus, if the employer testifies about a threat, even though the union denies it, there may still be reasonable cause to believe Section 8(b)(4)(D) has been violated.

C. The need for Two Competing Employee Groups

The Board has held that Section 8(b)(4)(D) applies only if there are at least two competing groups for the disputed work. The section is intended to protect an employer from conflicting pressure, not just pressure from one union, regardless of how strong the pressure may be. Assume that one union represents production employees in a plant and another union represents maintenance employees. The employer assigns certain work to the production employees that the maintenance union regards as its work. The maintenance employees threaten to strike unless the employer reassigns the work to it. Is that threat a possible violation of Section 8(b)(4)(D) to which Section 10(k) will apply? Not necessarily. If the production union does not claim the work, then there are not two competing claims. The dispute is only between the employer and the maintenance union. Thus, Section 8(b)(4)(D) is not violated. If the production union, however, claims the work and if either of the competing unions threatens to strike or engage in other coercive conduct if the work is not assigned to it, Section 8(b)(4)(D) has been violated. The threat may be made by either union, the one doing the work or the one claiming it. A jurisdictional dispute can involve only one union if the employer assigns disputed work to unorganized employees. The Board assumes that these employees want the work and the employer represents their interests.

Section 10(k) proceedings are intended to resolve work assignment disputes, not issues about which union should represent the employees doing the work. If the Board concludes that, rather than seeking certain work for its bargaining unit, a union is actually attempting to add additional employees to the unit as an organizing method, the Board will not proceed under 10(k). The union must follow representation case procedures by petitioning for an election or filing a clarification petition to add the additional employees to the existing unit.

D. Factors Used in Assigning Disputed Work

The Supreme Court, in the *CBS* case, held that Section 10(k) requires that the Board make a positive award of disputed work in cases falling under Section 8(b)(4)(D).[5] The Board usually considers certain factors in awarding work: (1) the skills and work involved; (2) certifications by the Board; (3) company and industry practice; (4) agreements between unions and between employers and unions; (5) awards of arbitrators, joint boards, and the AFL-CIO in the same or related cases; (6) the assignment made by the employer; and (7) the efficient operation of the employer's business.

E. The Critical Importance of the Employer's Assignment

Although the Board states that it considers all factors, the controlling factor in almost every case is the employer's assignment. In well over 90% of all cases, the Board awards disputed work to the union to which the employer had assigned the work. The employer's own estimate of efficient operations is the next most significant factor. The other factors seldom turn out to be controlling. The only time the employer's assignment might not control is if the assignment clearly violates a collective bargaining agreement, but that is rare. Frequently, both unions have a contractual claim to work based upon the ju-

[5] See legal principle 6.

risdictional clauses of their respective collective bargaining agreements. In that case, neither contract controls. But if one union clearly has a contractual right to the work, which the employer's assignment violates, the Board will probably enforce the contract. Remember, however, that the Board is not bound by the contract. If the other factors considered have greater weight in the particular case, the Board can assign the work to another union, despite what appears to be a clear contractual right.

The great weight the Board places on the employer's assignment has important tactical consequences. First, if an employer is about to make an assignment of disputed work, it is important for the union to approach the employer before the assignment is made and convince the employer to assign the work to it. If the employer makes the initial assignment to the other union, the union that did not receive the assignment has little chance of success at the Board. Second, a union that did not receive the assignment, but still claims the work, should do its utmost to avoid Section 10(k) proceedings. The union should avoid any statements that can be considered a threat in violation of Section 8(b)(4)(D). A union that believes it has a strong contractual claim to work that an employer has assigned to another union has a far better chance in arbitration than before the Board. If there is no threat in violation of Section 8(b)(4)(D), the union can proceed with arbitration and hope to attain a favorable award. If a threat is made, however, the Board will assert jurisdiction under Section 10(k). As discussed above, the Board does not defer to arbitration unless the employer and both unions are bound to arbitrate in the same proceeding, a situation that seldom exists. In contrast, what if a union, which has been assigned the work, believes that an employer might give in to peaceful pressure from the rival union? The

union with the assignment might purposely threaten to strike if the work is reassigned. In that way, the Board can assert jurisdiction and affirm the employer's assignment in a 10(k) hearing.

PART III.   FEATHERBEDDING

Section 8(b)(6) makes it an unfair labor practice for a union "to cause or attempt to cause an employer to pay or deliver or agree to pay or deliver any money or other things of value, in the nature of an exaction, for services which are not performed or not to be performed." This provision is referred to as the antifeatherbedding provision of the Act.

A. Requiring Unnecessary Work

Suppose a piece of equipment can be maintained by one employee, but a union insists that two employees be used. That would commonly be regarded as featherbedding because two employees are doing the work that one could do. But insisting that more employees be used than are necessary does not violate Section 8(b)(6). That issue was resolved by the Supreme Court in *American Newspaper Publishers Assn.*[6] In that case, the printers insisted on doing so-called bogus type work if advertisements were prepared by an outside advertising agency. Ads produced by outside agencies came to the newspaper ready to print, but the printers insisted that they make a copy of the same work, called bogus work. This was a way of preserving bargaining unit work. The copy prepared by the outside agency, not the bogus copy, was used in the advertisement.

The Supreme Court held that the union's demand to do the unnecessary bogus type

[6] See legal principle 8.

work did not violate Section 8(b)(6). The bogus type requirement was featherbedding in
the sense that the work was clearly unnecessary. But the Supreme Court held that the
union's insistence on doing the bogus type
work did not violate Section 8(b)(6) because
the work was actually done, even though it
was unnecessary. The section makes it a violation to cause an employer to pay money for
services that are not performed or not to be
performed. The Court reasoned that the section did not make it unlawful to require payment for services rendered even though they
are unnecessary. It only prohibited pay for
work that employees did not do or were not
going to do. The Court noted that the original
statutory proposal leading to Section 8(b)(6)
had broadly prohibited featherbedding, but
the actual language agreed to was much narrower. In light of the legislative history, the
Court refused to apply the section beyond the
express wording.

B. Employees' Willingness to Do Unnecessary Work

The Court's narrow application of Section
8(b)(6) was reaffirmed in *Gamble Enterprises,
Inc.*[7] In that case, the musicians' union refused
to permit out-of-town orchestras to appear in
a theater unless the theater agreed to employ
local musicians for a number of independent
performances, depending upon the number
of traveling band appearances. The theater
signed an agreement to use the local bands.
The local bands were available to play, however, the theater had no need for the local
bands and did not use them. The Supreme
Court held that this agreement did not violate
Section 8(b)(6) because the local musicians
were willing to play even though the employer decided not to use them.

[7] See legal principle 8.

What if the employer paid the local musicians without the musicians having any obligation at all to play? That type of agreement
would violate Section 8(b)(6) because musicians would be paid for work not performed
or not to be performed. However, so long as
the employees were willing to work, but the
employer simply chose not to use them, the
agreement was valid.

PART IV. UNIONS AND THE ANTITRUST LAWS

Limits on subcontracting, work preservation clauses, jurisdictional claims, and restric-
tive work rules lessen or prevent competition
between employers. For example, a subcontracting clause or a union's insistence on its
jurisdictional rights may prevent an employer
from bidding on a job or force two employers
to terminate their business relationship. That
reduces competition. As a union organizes
more employees in an industry and achieves
uniformity in wages and benefits, wages are
removed as a means of competition. These
are legitimate goals of collective bargaining,
but they conflict with the goals of the antitrust
laws to prevent restraint on trade and encourage competition. The history of Congress
and the Supreme Court in reconciling the
conflicting policies of the antitrust laws and
collective bargaining is long and intricate, as
described below.

A. The Sherman Antitrust Act

In 1890 Congress passed the Sherman Act,
which was designed to curtail the monopolis-
tic practices of certain businesses. Section 1 of
the Act makes illegal every contract, combination or conspiracy to restrain trade, fix
prices, or limit competition. Section 2 provides that every person who monopolizes or

conspires with others to monopolize trade or commerce is guilty of a misdemeanor and could be punished by fine or imprisonment. A person injured by activity illegal under the Sherman Act is entitled to monetary damages up to three times the amount of the actual damages.

The early federal court decisions took the position that the Sherman Act applied to all classes of people and all types of combinations, including labor unions. The courts held that union activities that physically interrupted the free flow of trade or tended to create business monopolies were illegal. They also held that a combination of employees to obtain a raise in wages was itself a prohibited monopoly. Injunctions were often issued to stop union activity even if no violation of the Sherman Act was charged.

B. The Clayton Act

Congress enacted the Clayton Act in 1914. The Act expanded the coverage of the antitrust laws; however, it also limited the application of the antitrust laws to unions. It states, in part, that the labor of human beings is not a commodity or an article of commerce. It provides that nothing contained in the anti-trust laws should be interpreted to forbid the existence and operation of labor organizations instituted for the purpose of mutual help, or to forbid or restrain individual members of such organizations from lawfully carrying out their legitimate objectives. The Act also provides that neither unions nor their members should be held or construed to be illegal combinations or conspiracies in restraint of trade under the antitrust laws. The Clayton Act recognizes a union's right to remove wages as a competitive factor.

The Supreme Court did not interpret the Clayton Act as a total exemption of labor un-

ions from the antitrust laws. In several cases, it decided that secondary boycotts against dealers who sold goods manufactured by employers with whom a union had a labor dispute violated the antitrust laws. The Court stated that the Clayton Act exemption applied only to union activities directed against the employees' immediate employer.

C. The Norris–LaGuardia Act

Congress did not agree with the Supreme Court interpretation of the Clayton Act. In 1932, Congress enacted the Norris–LaGuardia Act, which greatly broadened the meaning of the term "labor dispute." The Act defines labor dispute to include "any controversy concerning terms or conditions of employment, or concerning the association or representation of persons in negotiating, fixing, maintaining, changing, or seeking to arrange terms or conditions of employment, regardless of whether or not the disputants stand in the proximate relation of employer and employee." This meant that a secondary boycott could still be a labor dispute contrary to the Supreme Court decisions interpreting the Clayton Act. The Act further restricted the use of injunctions against labor activities.

Norris–LaGuardia specifically provides that the following acts are not considered unlawful combinations or conspiracies: (1) ceasing or refusing to perform any work or to remain in any relation of employment, (2) becoming or remaining a member of any labor organization, (3) giving publicity to any labor dispute by any method not involving fraud or violence, and (4) assembling peaceably to act or to organize to act in promotion of their interests in a labor dispute.

The Sherman, Clayton, and Norris–LaGuardia Acts are still in effect. The best way to understand labor's current coverage under the antitrust laws is to examine some of the major cases decided by the Supreme Court since the Norris–LaGuardia Act was enacted.

D. The Current Basic Rule: Unions Acting Along In Their Own Self-Interest

1. The Hutcheson Decision

In the *United States v. Hutcheson*, (1941), the Court first considered the interrelationship of the Sherman, Clayton, and Norris–LaGuardia Acts.[8] In that case, the carpenters and machinists unions at an Anheuser-Busch plant had a jurisdictional dispute over certain work. After Anheuser-Busch awarded the work to the machinists, the carpenters struck against Anheuser-Busch and against two construction companies who were building facilities for Anheuser-Busch and a tenant on land adjacent to the plant. The union also picketed Anheuser-Busch and the tenant and urged that its members and others boycott Anheuser-Busch beer.

The federal government filed criminal charges against the leaders of the carpenters union alleging that the union's actions consituted a combination and conspiracy in restraint of trade in violation of the Sherman Act. The Supreme Court held that the acts did not violate the antitrust laws. It ruled that the jurisdictional dispute was a "labor dispute" as defined by the Norris–LaGuardia Act. The Court stated that the union could picket the contractors and the tenant, even though they were not directly involved in the dispute. The Court also ruled that the carpenters' actions, including the members' refusal to work, the peaceful picketing, and the boycott were protected by the Clayton and Norris–LaGuardia Acts. The Court stated that, as long as a union

engages in such activities only to promote its own self-interest and does not combine with nonlabor groups, it is exempt from the Sherman Act.

Hutcheson was decided before the Taft-Hartley Act enacted Section 8(b)(4) abolishing most secondary boycotts (see Chapter 7). Thus, although the union conduct in *Hutcheson* would still not violate the antitrust laws, at least part of the tactics would be unlawful under Section 8(b)(4)(B).

2. The Allen–Bradley Decision

The principle that a union loses its antitrust exemption if it combines with a nonlabor group was applied several years later by the Supreme Court in *Allen–Bradley*.[9] In *Allen–Bradley*, a local union representing both production and construction electrical workers in New York City decided that the best way to increase the wages and employment opportunities of its members was to promote the sales of goods produced by local manufacturers who employed its members. To accomplish this, the union waged an aggressive campaign, using strikes and boycotts, to obtain closed shop agreements with all local electrical equipment manufacturers and contractors. Under these agreements, construction contractors were obligated to purchase equipment only from those manufacturers who also had closed shop agreements with the local. Manufacturers, in turn, were obligated to confine their New York City sales to contractors employing local union members. Over time these individual agreements expanded into industry-wide understandings that concerned not only conditions of employment, but also the price of goods and market control. Agencies were set up composed of representatives of the union, the manufacturers, and the contractors to boycott

[8] See legal principle 11.

[9] See legal principle 11.

local manufacturers who did not abide by the terms of the understanding and to bar outside equipment manufactured from the New York City market.

A lawsuit seeking to enjoin these activities as anti-trust violations was filed by manufacturers of electrical equipment who produced their goods outside New York City. These manufacturers could not bargain with the union because the local's jurisdiction was limited to the city. As a result of the understandings between the local and the electrical contractors, these manufacturers were excluded from the New York City market. The Supreme Court ruled that the union had violated the antitrust laws. It stated that the union, acting alone, would not have violated the antitrust laws by entering into bargaining agreements in which the employer agrees not to buy goods manufactured by companies that do not employ union members. However, the Court held that the union lost its exemption in this case because it did not act alone. Instead, it participated in a combination with business interests. The Court stated:

> We may assume that such an agreement standing alone would not have violated the Sherman Act. But it did not stand alone. It was but one element in a far larger program in which contractors and manufacturers united with one another to monopolize all the business in New York City, to bar all other businessmen from the area, and to charge the public prices above a competitive level. It is true that victory of the union in its disputes, even had the union acted alone, might have added to the costs of the goods, or might have resulted in individual refusals of all of their employers to buy electrical equipment not made by Local No. 3. So far as the union might have achieved this result acting alone, it would have been the natural consequence of labor union activities exempted by the Clayton Act from the coverage of the Sherman Act. But when the unions participated with a combination of

businessmen who had complete power to eliminate all competition among themselves and to prevent all competition from others, a situation was created not included within the exemptions of the Clayton and Norris–LaGuardia Acts.

E. Multi-Employer Agreements and the Antitrust Laws (The Pennington and Jewel Tea Decisions)

The *Allen–Bradley* decision establishes that the same labor union activities may or may not violate the antitrust laws, depending upon whether the union acts alone or in combination with business groups. This principle was further illustrated in two later cases decided by the Supreme Court on the same day. *United Mine Workers v. Pennington* and *Meatcutters v. Jewel Tea.*

In the *Pennington* case, the United Mine Workers negotiated a collective bargaining agreement with a multi-employer association of large coal operators in which these operators agreed to pay union members increased wages and fringe benefits.[10] The union then sought to have smaller coal companies sign the same agreement. One of the small operators signed the agreement, but then failed to make required payments into the pension fund. The fund's trustees sued for the delinquent contributions. The small operator then filed a countersuit against the union alleging that the union and the large coal operators had conspired to restrain trade in violation of the Sherman Act. The company alleged that the union had agreed with the multi-employer association to demand the same wage and benefit package from the smaller coal companies, regardless of their ability to pay. The company further alleged that the purpose of the agreement was to drive the small

---

[10] See legal principle 11.

operators out of business. The jury awarded damages to the small operator against the union and the union appealed.

In *Jewel Tea*, the butchers union contract in Chicago for many years had contained a provision restricting the marketing hours for fresh meat from 9:00 A.M. through 6:00 P.M., when the union's members were present.[11] The union wanted this restriction to limit the working hours of its members.

During negotiations, a number of employers, including Jewel Tea, proposed changes in the restriction. The union rejected the changes. Finally, a number of employers, including a multi-employer association, agreed to the contract provision; however, Jewel Tea continued to resist. It finally signed the contract containing the restriction only after being threatened with a strike if it refused. Jewel Tea then filed suit against the union and the multi-employer association seeking to invalidate the marketing hour restriction on the grounds that it violated the antitrust laws. It contended that the union and the association had conspired to restrain the sale of meat.

In *Pennington*, the Supreme Court reversed the judgment against the union because of certain erroneous trial court instructions to the jury. The Court, however, stated that the union would have violated the antitrust law if the union had *agreed* with the large coal operators to impose the contractual terms on the smaller operators in order to eliminate the smaller operators as competition. The Court again emphasized that the union might legally be able to obtain the same result if, on its own, it sought to require the smaller employers to sign the same contract. The Court also stated that multi-employer contracts in themselves do not violate the antitrust laws. Unions act unlawfully only if they attempt to impose the multi-employer association con-

tract on other employers in accordance with an agreement with the multi-employers.

In *Jewel Tea*, the Court found that there was no evidence of any agreement between the union and the multi-employer association to impose the hours restriction on all other employers. The union acted alone following its own long-standing policy concerning the working hours of its members. The Court noted that the hours provision was a restraint on trade, but further stated that working hours are a legitimate subject for collective bargaining. The prohibition on selling meat when no butchers were present was a means of enforcing the hours restriction and protecting bargaining unit work when the butchers were not present. Thus, the restricted marketing hours provision was exempt from the antitrust laws.

F. Union Antitrust Violations in the Absence of a Bargaining Relationship (the Connell Construction Case)

The latest Supreme Court case concerning labor's exemption from the antitrust laws is the *Connell Construction* case (previously discussed in this chapter under hot cargo clauses). In *Connell*, the plumbers union sought an agreement from Connell that it would only subcontract plumbing work to firms whose employees were represented by the union. The clause was a means of putting pressure on nonunion plumbing contractors to recognize the union. It was also a restraint on trade to the extent that it limited Connell's choice of subcontractors. The union contended that the agreement was exempt from the antitrust laws because it acted solely on its own behalf and not in combination with any employer.

The Supreme Court held that the union's attempt to impose the clause on Connell was

[11] See legal principle 11.

not exempt from the antitrust laws. The Court noted that labor's antitrust exemption came from two sources: (1) the statutory exemptions of the Clayton and Norris–LaGuardia Acts that protect specific union activities such as secondary boycotts and picketing from the antitrust laws and (2) the nonstatutory exemption derived from the Congressional policy favoring collective bargaining on wages, hours, and other terms and conditions of employment even though competition may be reduced. The Court said that *Jewel Tea* was an example of the nonstatutory exemption applied to collective bargaining.

The Court stressed in *Connell* that the contractor and the union did not have a collective bargaining relationship. The union did not represent or seek to represent Connell's own employees. Thus the nonstatutory exemption, derived from the policy favoring collective bargaining, did not apply. Further, the Court said that the construction industry proviso to Section 8(e) did not apply in the absence of a collective bargaining relationship and that Section 8(e) did not sanction the top-down organizing the union was attempting.

The Supreme Court then analyzed the effect the agreement between Connell and the union would have on the construction industry in the area. It found that the agreement had the potential of reducing competition for mechanical subcontracting work by excluding nonunion subcontractors from the market. Also, the union's contract with its multiemployer association contained a "most favored nation" clause. This meant that no other subcontractor could enter into a collective bargaining agreement with the union that contained more competitive terms. Taking all these factors into consideration, the Court concluded that the union's proposed clause, in the absence of a bargaining relationship between the union and Connell, was not exempt from the antitrust laws.

The *Connell* decision is significant because there was no evidence of any conspiracy or improper agreement between the union and any employers. The union was acting solely in its own behalf. Prior cases had exempted unions acting solely on their own from the antitrust laws. The Court indicated, however, that the agreement the union sought would not have violated the antitrust laws if the union and Connell had a bargaining relationship.

The *Connell* case created a great stir in labor at the time because it applied the antitrust laws to a union acting solely in its own behalf. There have, however, been very few subsequent cases applying Connell. It is probable that, in the long run, the case will not have great impact, but will be applied only in rare situations in which a union attempts to place direct restraints on the business operations of an employer whose employees the union does not represent nor seek to represent. The basic exemption for a union acting on its own, in the context of a collective bargaining agreement, will remain. For example, the principles set forth in *Connell* would not have changed the decision in either the *Jewel Tea* or *Pennington* cases because, in both those cases the union had a bargaining relationship with the concerned employers.

Summary   This chapter covered a union's right to regulate work content and the application of the antitrust laws to such attempts. Besides the antitrust laws, union efforts to regulate work are subject to LMRA Section 8(e) prohibiting hot cargo agreements, Section 8(b)(4)(D) pertaining to jurisdictional disputes, and Section 8(b)(6) pertaining to "featherbedding" practices.

The courts and the Board recognize that Section 8(e) was not intended to prohibit all restrictions on subcontracting. There are two general categories of subcontracting clauses: work preservation clauses and union signatory clauses. Work preservation clauses are lawful in both the construction field and industry. Work preservation clauses can lawfully prohibit all subcontracts or impose restrictions that remove the economic incentive for subcontracting. Work preservation clauses cannot go beyond the objective of preserving work and seek to control the labor relations of another employer. A work preservation clause may seek to reclaim work, but not to acquire new work. A union can strike to obtain a work preservation clause and to enforce the contract absent a no-strike clause.

A union signatory clause is lawful only in the construction industry for work done on the construction situs. A construction union can usually strike to obtain a construction industry union signatory clause unless there is a subcontractor already working on a project who would be forced to leave if the clause were applied. However, once a clause is adopted, the union cannot use self-help to enforce it. The clause can be enforced only through peaceful means, which might be either arbitration or court action. The primary limitation on enforcing work preservation clauses is the right of control test, under which a contractor may avoid compliance with a valid clause because the contractor does not have control over the work.

Section 10(k) empowers the Board to determine the merits of a jurisdictional dispute if the Board has reasonable cause to believe that Section 8(b)(4)(D) has been violated. Although the Board supposedly considers a number of factors in its determination, the work assignment made by the employer is the controlling factor in almost every case.

The Supreme Court has narrowly applied Section 8(b)(6) by holding that a union's insistence on doing unnecessary work does not violate the section if the work is actually done, or if employees are willing to do the work, but the employer chooses not to have it done.

Although union efforts to control wages and working conditions may limit and/or restrict competition, Congress partially exempted unions from the antitrust laws in the Clayton Act and prevented injunctions against alleged secondary boycotts in the Norris–LaGuardia Act. Based on these statutes and the policy favoring collective bargaining, the Supreme Court has held that a union's collective bargaining activities are exempt from the antitrust laws as long as the union acts to promote its own self-interest and does not combine with nonlabor groups. In *Connell Construction*, however, the Court applied the antitrust laws to a union acting in its own behalf. There the union sought a clause requiring the contractor to restrict subcontractors to employers that recognize the union. This clause was not exempt from the antitrust laws because there was no collective bargaining relationship between the contractor and the union and was an attempt at "top-down organizing."

Review Questions

1. What is the statutory intent of Section 8(e)?

2. Would a picket line clause permitting employees to honor *any* picket line be lawful under Section 8(e)?

3. Is a clause stating that employees cannot be disciplined for refusing to handle goods produced by a struck employer lawful under Section 8(e)?

4. Is a union signatory clause (permitting subcontracting only to employers whose own employees are represented by a union) lawful?

5. Is a clause limiting subcontracts to employers who pay the same benefits as the contracting employer lawful?

6. Can a union contractually require a successor employer to assume an existing collective bargaining agreement even though the law does not require it?

7. What is the construction industry exception to Section 8(e)?

8. Can a primary work preservation clause be enforced through self-help?

9. Does the NLRB have authority to resolve all jurisdictional disputes under Section 10(k)?

10. What is the most important factor the Board applies in making work assignments?

11. Can a union bargain to impasse for a manning requirement that would result in make work?

12. Can a labor union negotiate a contract prohibiting a store from engaging in Sunday sales?

13. Does multi-employer bargaining violate the antitrust laws?

(Answers to review questions appear at end of book.)

Basic Legal Principles

1. A subcontracting clause preserving bargaining unit work has a primary object and does not violate Section 8(e). *National Woodwork Manufacturers Assn. v. NLRB*, 386 U.S. 612, 64 LRRM 2801 (1967); *International Longshoremen's Association v. NLRB*, 537 F.2d 706, 92 LRRM 3260 (2nd Cir. 1976); *Hughes Markets, Inc.*, 218 NLRB No. 84, 89 LRRM 1407 (1975).

2. Picket line clauses broad enough to protect employees from discipline for refusing to cross *any* picket line, whether primary or secondary, are unlawful under Section 8(e). *Bricklayers, Local 2,* 224 NLRB 1021, 92 LRRM 1347 (1976).

3. A union cannot use self-help to enforce a work preservation clause if the primary employer does not have the legal right to control the disputed work. *NLRB v. Plumbers, Local 638,* 429 U.S. 507, 94 LRRM 2628 (1977); *IBEW, Local 501 v. NLRB,* 487 F.2d 159, 96 LRRM 2940 (D.C.Cir. 1977) *enfg. IBEW, Local 501,* 216 NLRB 417, 88 LRRM 1220 (1974); *George Koch Sons, Inc.* 201 NLRB No. 7, 82 LRRM 1113 (1973).

4. Except in the construction or garment industries, an employer cannot expressly or by implication agree to subcontract only to union employers. *Machinists District 9,* 134 NLRB 1354, 49 LRRM 1321 (1961); *Bakery Wagon Drivers and Salesmen, Local 484,* 137 NLRB 987, 50 LRRM 1289 (1962).

5. Union standards subcontracting clauses are lawful under Section 8(e). *Teamsters Local 107,* 159 NLRB 84, 62 LRRM 1224 (1966); *Orange Belt District Council of Painters, No. 48 v. NLRB,* 328 F.2d 534, 55 LRRM 2293 (D.C.Cir. 1964). *But see Associated General Contractors,* 227 NLRB No. 27, 94 LRRM 121 (1976) (clause cannot require payment of identical benefits).

6. Section 10(k) requires the Board to make an affirmative assignment of disputed work in cases falling within the provision. *NLRB v. Radio & Television and Broadcast Engineers, Local 1212 (Columbia Broadcasting System),* 364 U.S. 573, 47 LRRM 2332 (1961).

7. The determination of jurisdictional disputes under Section 10(k) is based upon a balancing of "all relevant factors" including: (1) certifications and collective bargaining agreements, (2) efficiency and economy of operation, (3) skills and work involved, (4) area and industry practice and (5) employer's practice and preference. *Machinists, Lodge No. 1743,* 135 NLRB No. 139, 49 LRRM 1684 (1962); *Typographical Union 48,* 230 NLRB No. 113, 95 LRRM 1361 (1977); *Stage Employees Locals 27 and 48,* 227 NLRB No. 8, 94 LRRM 1050 (1976); *Hanford Trades Council,* 227 NLRB No. 145, 95 LRRM 1007 (1977).

8. A union can insist upon make work for its members, provided some actual work is performed, without violating Section 8(b)(6) even though the work may neither be necessary nor desired by the employer. *American Newspaper Publishers Assn. v. NLRB,* 345 U.S. 100, 31 LRRM 2422 (1953); *NLRB v. Gamble Enterprises,* 345 U.S. 117, 31 LRRM 2428 (1953).

9. A construction industry proviso clause limiting subcontracting on a construction situs to union contractors is lawful if the agreement is made in the context of a collective bargaining relationship between the employer and the union or is to prevent the union members from having

to work with nonunion employees on the same project. *Connell Construction Co. v. Plumbers and Steamfitters, Local 100,* 421 U.S. 616, 89 LRRM 2401 (1975); *Carpenters Local 944,* 235 NLRB No. 40, 99 LRRM 1580 (1978).

10. A union may usually strike or picket to compel an employer in the construction industry to execute a construction industry proviso subcontracting clause. However, such a clause cannot be enforced by self-help, but only through peaceful persuasion, arbitration, or court action. *Los Angeles Building and Construction Trades Council,* 214 NLRB No. 86, 87 LRRM 1424 (1974); *Operating Engineers Local 701,* 239 NLRB No. 43, 99 LRRM 1589 (1978).

11. A union is generally exempt from the antitrust laws if it is acting alone on a collective bargaining matter in its own self-interest. *United States v. Hutcheson,* 312 U.S. 219, 7 LRRM 267 (1941); *Allen Bradley Co. v. IBEW Local 3,* 325 U.S. 797, 16 LRRM 798 (1945); *United Mine Workers v. Pennington,* 381 U.S. 657, 59 LRRM 2369 (1965); *Amalgamated Meat Cutters Local 189 v. Jewel Tea Co.,* 381 U.S. 676, 59 LRRM 2376 (1965). The antitrust exemption does not apply if a union seeks an anticompetitive restriction from an employer with whom the union does not have or seek a collective bargaining relationship. *Connell Construction Co. v. Plumbers, supra.*

Recommended Reading

Antoine, *Connell (Connell Constr. Co. v. Plumbers Local 100),* Anti-Trust Law at the Expense of Labor Law, 62 *Va. L. Rev.* 603 (1976).

Leslie, "Role of the NLRB and the Courts in Resolving Union Jurisdictional Disputes," 75 *Colum. L. Rev.* 1470 (1975).

Roberts, Powers, "Defining the Relationship Between Anti-Trust Law and Labor Law: Professional Sports The Current Legal Battleground," 19 *W.M.L. Rev.* 467 (1978).

Chapter Nine

Enforcement of Collective Bargaining Agreements and the Duty to Arbitrate

Section 301(a) of the Labor Management Relations Act provides that suits for violation of contracts between an employer and a union or between unions may be brought in any district court of the United States. Section 301 permits either an employer or a union to enforce the terms of a collective bargaining agreement. Suits to enjoin a strike in violation of a collective bargaining agreement and for damages are brought under Section 301 (see Chapter 6). Suits brought by a union to enforce an employer's agreement to pay fringe benefit contributions, or to collect union dues that have not been forwarded to the union under a dues check-off clause, are other common examples of Section 301 suits.

Today, everyone accepts the idea that a collective bargaining agreement is an enforceable agreement in federal court. But before Section 301 was enacted as

part of the Taft–Hartley Act, the only law governing collective bargaining agreements was state common law enforced by the state courts. There were many difficulties in enforcing collective bargaining agreements under state law. Section 301 has ended these problems by establishing uniform federal requirements for the enforcement of agreements.

Section 301 applies not only to contracts between an employer and a union, but also to agreements between unions. This provision permits the enforcement of no-raiding agreements between unions.

Most collective bargaining agreements contain provisions for final and binding arbitration of contract disputes. Federal law developed under Section 301 has established that agreements to arbitrate are binding and that both the employer and the union are bound by an arbitrator's decision.

A. UNION AND EMPLOYEE RIGHTS TO FILE SECTION 301 ACTIONS

Although Section 301 authorizes suits for the enforcement of a contract, the section does not state who can bring such a suit. For a long time, it was unclear whether suits to enforce a contract were to be brought by the union or individual union members. Initially,

the Supreme Court took the position that a union could file suit under Section 301 only to enforce "union rights" such as the contract's arbitration, check-off, or union security clauses. The Court indicated a union could not sue to enforce rights that were "uniquely personal" to individual employees, such as seniority rights or pay matters. The Court later changed its position. Currently, a union can bring suit to enforce all terms of a collective bargaining agreement, whether a particular dispute pertains to a union right or an individual employee's rights.

Although the union may bring suit to enforce the contract, individual employees may also bring suit under some circumstances. If a contract is one of those few that do not contain grievance procedures, either the union or the employee whose contractual rights have been violated can bring suit to enforce its terms. If a contract has a grievance procedure, but does not provide for final and binding arbitration, either the affected employee or the union can bring suit to enforce a contractual right after the available grievance procedures have been exhausted. The employee's right to sue, however, is restricted. The Supreme Court has held that an employee is bound by a union's settlement of his case in the grievance procedure, including a union decision to drop the matter. The employee cannot sue to enforce alleged contractual rights contrary to a settlement. The only exception to this rule is if the union's settlement violates its duty of fair representation (see Chapter 12). In that case, the employee is not bound by the union's decision and can sue the employer for breach of contract.

B. SUITS BETWEEN A UNION AND A MEMBER

Section 301 only applies to suits between an employer and a union or between unions. What if an employee wants to sue his union for violation of the union's by-laws or the union wants to sue a member for a by-law violation, perhaps failure to pay a fine? A union's by-laws are considered a contract between the union and the member (see Chapter 10). The union's by-laws, however, are an internal matter, not a contract between the union and the employer or between two un-

ions. The by-laws, therefore, are not an enforceable agreement under Section 301. Some internal union matters are regulated by the Labor Management Reporting and Disclosure Act (see Chapters 10 and 11). An employee may bring suit in federal court on those matters. However, many internal union matters, including the interpretation of the union's by-laws, are not covered by federal law. In those cases, a suit between a union and a member must be brought in state court applying state law. A suit over a union's violation of its duty of fair representation is considered to be based on the underlying collective bargaining agreement that has been violated. Thus, as an exception, a fair representation suit may be brought under Section 301 even though the suit may be between the member and his union.

C. JURISDICTIONAL AND PROCEDURAL REQUIREMENTS OF A SECTION 301 SUIT

There are very few limitations on the right to sue under Section 301. The basic requirement is that the union represent employees in an industry affecting commerce, basically the same broad jurisdictional standard as for the NLRB (see Chapter 1). Almost every business purchases goods or material either directly or indirectly from businesses in other states or sends goods across a state line. Thus, the commerce requirement is easily met. Only the smallest of employers are not covered under Section 301. Of course, Section 301 actions cannot be brought by or against employers or unions that are not covered by the Labor Management Relations Act. Thus, Section 301 does not apply to a collective bargaining agreement between a governmental agency and a public employee union.

1. Monetary and Geographic Requirements

Some federal statutes only permit federal court suits if a certain amount of money is involved or if the plaintiff and defendant live in different states (referred to as diversity jurisdiction). Suits not meeting these requirements can be brought only in the state courts. Many labor disputes, however, involve important issues even though the amount of money may not be great, and many labor disputes would affect commerce even though both the employer and the union are in the same state. Therefore, Congress provided in Section 301(b) that a suit to enforce contracts can be brought without regard to the amount in controversy and the citizenship (state of residency) of the parties.

2. Suits By or Against the Union as an Entity

Under Section 301(b) suits may be brought by or against the union as an entity. Before Section 301 was enacted, it was frequently necessary to sue union members directly and individually in order to enforce a collective bargaining agreement. This procedure was necessary because a union is an unincorporated association at common law (see Chapter 10) and cannot be sued as an entity. Congress wanted to make it easier to enforce collective bargaining agreements, and thus provided in Section 301 that a union can be sued as an entity. Section 301 also provides that any judgment against a union under Section 301 is enforceable only against union assets, not against individual members or their assets. Prior to Section 301, if an employer successfully sued individual union members for breach of contract, money owed on the judgment could be collected from each union member. The trade-off for permitting a union to be sued as an entity in federal courts, thus making it much easier to enforce contracts, was that any judgment entered could be collected only from union assets.

The Supreme Court has held that suits to enforce collective bargaining agreements can also be brought in the state courts. The state courts, however, must apply the federal law. In that way, uniformity of law, a primary goal of Section 301, is maintained. Through a legal procedure called *"removal,"* the defendant in a state suit to enforce a collective bargaining agreement can transfer the case to the federal courts. Many unions exercise their right to remove state court suits to the federal courts because they believe that federal judges are more familiar with the governing principles. The vast majority of suits are initially brought in federal courts.

3. Application of Federal Law to Section 301 Suits

In some federal court actions the parties are permitted to bring suit in federal court, but state law determines the parties' legal rights. For example, if two automobiles driven by residents of different states collide, a suit growing out of the accident may be brought in federal court if the damages exceed $10,000. But the law determining which driver was at fault is usually the law of the state where the accident occurred. There is no federal law determining liability. State laws covering liability may vary. This means that the laws a federal court apply may vary from case to case depending upon where the accident occurred.

Does state or federal law apply in a suit brought under Section 301? The Act itself does not say, but the Supreme Court has held that the courts are to apply federal law. This means that all federal courts apply the same principles discussed in this chapter regardless of where the court is located or the state where the dispute arose.

Although Section 301 provides for the enforcement of contracts, it contains no detailed guidelines for the courts to follow. Thus, the courts have had to develop the law as cases have arisen. The rules discussed in this chapter have been developed by the federal courts on a case by case basis. In effect, a federal common (judge-made) law on enforcement of labor contracts has developed. This is a unique situation. Usually, federal courts either apply detailed federal statutes or state law, but not federal common law principles.

There are few Section 301 matters not covered by federal law. The principal one is the Statute of Limitations. Section 301 does not say how long a party has to bring suit to enforce a contract. As a general principle, the federal courts apply state law to procedural matters not covered by federal law. Thus, the length of time for bringing suit under Section 301 equals the length of time that a suit for breach of contract may be brought in the state where the contract was made. The time varies widely from state to state and is one of the few instances in which rights under Section 301 vary according to location.

D. ENFORCEMENT OF AGREEMENTS TO ARBITRATE: THE STEELWORKERS TRILOGY

The great majority of all collective bargaining agreements provide for final and binding arbitration of disputes that arise under the contract. Arbitration has taken the place of court action to enforce contractual rights that would be brought under Section 301. Initially, following enactment of Section 301, it was unclear whether the section authorized the federal courts to enforce a contractual agreement to arbitrate. Under the law in many states, agreements to arbitrate were not enforceable. The state courts took the view that parties are free to go directly into court on a dispute even though they have agreed to arbitration. Many state courts still apply this rule in cases of commercial arbitration between businesses. Some employers argue that the federal courts should apply the state law principles and not enforce agreements to arbitrate in a collective bargaining agreement.

The Supreme Court resolved this issue in the *Lincoln Mills* decision.[1] The Court pointed to Sections 201(b) and 203(d) of the Labor Management Relations Act, which favor arbitration as the desirable method for the peaceful resolution of industrial disputes. The Court reasoned that since national labor policy favors arbitration to resolve industrial disputes, the courts should specifically enforce agreements to arbitrate. As a result of this decision, agreements to arbitrate are enforceable under Section 301 in the federal courts and state courts.

Although *Lincoln Mills* established that a grievance arbitration provision in a collective bargaining agreement can be enforced, many questions remained about the subjects covered by the duty to arbitrate and the scope of the court's power to enforce an arbitrator's award. The issues were resolved several years later in three landmark decisions issued at the same time known as the "Steelworkers Trilogy."

1. The Warrior and Gulf Navigation Case

The first case in the Trilogy was *United Steelworkers v. Warrior and Gulf Navigation Co.*[2]

[1] See legal principle 1.

[2] See legal principle 2

In that case, the employer had laid off almost half of the employees in a bargaining unit over a two-year period. This reduction was due in part to the employer's use of outside contractors to do maintenance work previously performed by bargaining unit employees. These outside contractors used the employer's supervisors to lay out the work and hired some of the laid-off employees back at reduced wages to perform the work. A number of employees filed a grievance over contracting work out in this manner. The collective bargaining agreement between the employer and the union unit provided for the arbitration of unresolved grievances, but it also contained a provision excluding from the arbitration process matters that were strictly a function of management.

The employer and union did not resolve the grievance and the union requested arbitration. The employer refused to arbitrate on the grounds that contracting out is a function of management and therefore not subject to arbitration. The union sued in federal district court under Section 301 to compel arbitration. The district court agreed with the employer's position that the use of outside contractors is a management function under the collective bargaining agreement. Also no specific clause of the contract prohibited subcontracting. The court refused to order arbitration because the contract was clear and there was nothing to arbitrate. The case was appealed to the appropriate court of appeals and then to the United States Supreme Court.

The Need for an Agreement to Arbitrate

The Supreme Court reversed the ruling of the lower courts and held that the matter of contracting out should be arbitrated. The court noted initially that arbitration is a matter of contract and that a party cannot be required to arbitrate any dispute that it has not

agreed to arbitrate. But, because national labor policy favors arbitration to resolve labor disputes, a court should only determine whether the party that refuses to arbitrate a grievance has agreed to arbitrate the matter in dispute. The Court stated that a party should be required to arbitrate a dispute if the collective bargaining agreement provides for arbitration, *unless it can be stated with positive assurance that the arbitration clause of the collective bargaining agreement does not apply to the particular dispute.* The Court emphasized that any doubts about whether the parties have agreed to arbitrate a particular matter should be resolved in favor of arbitration.

Applying these principles, the Court, in *Warrior and Gulf,* limited its inquiry to whether the employer had agreed to arbitrate the subcontracting dispute. The Court noted that the arbitration clause applied to any difference between the parties. The dispute over contracting out, the Court reasoned, was such a difference, and was therefore arbitrable.

Court Consideration of the Dispute's Merits

But what if, as the district court concluded, the employer had the contractual right to subcontract as it had? Should an employer be required to arbitrate a dispute when its actions were correct under the contract? The Supreme Court rejected this approach to determining arbitrability. The Court stressed that the courts are only to decide whether the parties have agreed to arbitrate the dispute, not consider the dispute's merits. Thus, the lower courts in *Warrior* had been wrong in deciding that contracting out was a function of management excluded from arbitration. That approach improperly interjected the courts into the merits of the dispute.

The Supreme Court strongly stressed the role of the arbitrator and that arbitration is not limited to the express terms of the agreement. Rather, the arbitrator may also consider the practices of the parties. The Court Stated:

> The labor arbitrator's source of law is not confined to the express provisions of the contract, as the industrial common law—the practices of the industry and the shop—is equally a part of the collective bargaining agreement although not expressed in it. The labor arbitrator is usually chosen because of the parties' confidence in his knowledge of the common law of the shop and their trust in his personal judgment to bring to bear considerations which are not expressed in the contract as criteria for judgment. The parties expect that his judgment of a particular grievance will reflect not only what the contract says but, insofar as the collective bargaining agreement permits, such factors as the effect upon productivity of a particular result, its consequence to the morale of the shop, his judgment whether tensions will be heightened or diminished. For the parties' objective in using the arbitration process is primarily to further their common goal of uninterrupted production under the agreement, to make the agreement serve specialized needs. The ablest judge cannot be expected to bring the same experience and competence to bear upon the determination of a grievance, because he cannot be similarly informed.

That a dispute is not arbitrable does not necessarily mean that a union has no recourse. If the union believes that the contract was violated, but the dispute is not arbitrable, the union can bring suit directly under Section 301 to enforce its contract rights. Also, the scope of the no-strike clause is generally the same as the scope of a contract's arbitration clause (see Chapter 6). Thus if a dispute is not arbitrable, the union can strike over the issue. It would take very clear contractual language for a no-strike clause to apply to a dispute that is not arbitrable.

2. The American Manufacturing Case

The second trilogy case is *United Steelworkers v. American Manufacturing Co.*[3] In that case, the collective bargaining agreement provided for arbitration of any disputes between the parties "as to the meaning, interpretation and application of the provisions of this agreement." The contract also reserved to management the power to suspend or discipline any employee for cause and provided that promotions would be made on the principle of seniority where ability and efficiency were equal. An employee who left work due to an occupational injury settled a claim for workmen's compensation benefits against the company on the basis of a 25 percent permanent partial disability. The union filed a grievance that the employee was entitled to return to his job by virtue of the seniority provisions in the collective bargaining agreement.

The company refused to arbitrate the grievance and the union brought suit in district court under Section 301 to compel arbitration. The district court held in the employer's favor. The court of appeals affirmed the decision on the grounds that the grievance was without merit and therefore not subject to arbitration. The Supreme Court reversed the lower courts. As in *Warrior and Gulf*, the Court stated that the courts have no business weighing the merits of a grievance in determining whether to order arbitration, but that their sole function is to determine whether the parties have agreed to arbitrate the matter. Since the parties in *American Manufacturing* had agreed to arbitrate any dispute arising under the contract, the Court ruled that the grievance should be arbitrated. The Court strongly stated:

> The function of the court is very limited when the parties have agreed to submit all

[3] See legal principle 2.

questions of contract interpretation to the arbitrator. It is then confined to ascertaining whether the party seeking arbitration is making a claim which on its face is governed by the contract. Whether the moving party is right or wrong is a question of contract interpretation for the arbitrator. In these circumstances the moving party should not be deprived of the arbitrator's judgment, when it was his judgment and all that it connotes that was bargained for.

The courts therefore have no business weighing the merits of the grievance considering whether there is equity in a particular claim, or determining whether there is particular language in the written instrument which will support the claim. The agreement is to submit all grievances to arbitration, not merely those the court will deem meritorious. The processing of even frivolous claims may have therapeutic values of which those who are not a part of the plant environment may be quite unaware.

The practical effect of the *Warrior and Gulf* and *American Manufacturing Company* decisions is that as long as a particular grievance is subject to arbitration, the courts will order that it be arbitrated, regardless of whether the grievance is obviously without merit or frivolous.

3. Enforcement of an Arbitrator's Award: The Enterprise Wheel Decision

Both *Warrior and Gulf* and *American Manufacturing* dealt with enforcement of agreements to arbitrate. The third case of the Steelworkers trilogy, *United Steelworkers v. Enterprise Wheel and Car Corp.*, pertained to the enforcement of an arbitrator's award.[4] In *Enterprise Wheel*, a group of employees staged a wildcat strike to protest an employee's discharge. The union advised the employees to return to work, but the employer refused to

4 See legal principle 2.

allow them back. The union filed a grievance. Although the collective bargaining agreement provided for binding arbitration of any differences over the meaning and application of the agreement, the employer refused to arbitrate. The union then successfully brought suit under Section 301 to compel arbitration. The arbitrator found that although the employees' conduct was improper, it did not justify discharge. The arbitrator concluded that the facts warranted, at most, a ten day suspension for each man. The collective bargaining agreement had expired after the employees' discharge, but before the arbitrator's decision; however, the union continued representing the workers at the plant. The arbitrator rejected the company's contention that expiration of the agreement barred reinstatement of the employees. He held that a contractual provision, that unjustly discharged employees would be reinstated with full compensation at their regular rate for the time lost, imposed an unconditional obligation on the employer. He awarded the employees reinstatement with back pay, minus the period of a ten day suspension and such sums as the employees received from interim employment.

The employer refused to comply with the arbitrator's award and the union brought suit under Section 301 in the district court to enforce it. The district court ordered the employer to comply, but the court of appeals reversed the decision. The appellate court held that the employees had no contractual right to reinstatement or to back pay for any time subsequent to the expiration of the contract. The Supreme Court reversed the court of appeals.

The Supreme Court stated that an arbitrator's decision must be enforced by the courts so long as it "draws its essence" from the collective bargaining agreement, even though the court may disagree with the decision. The

Court stated it was unclear whether the arbitrator in *Enterprise* had based his award, allowing back pay even though the collective bargaining agreement had expired, on an interpretation of federal labor law statutes or on the contract. The Court said the award would not be enforceable if the decision was based solely upon the law, but would be enforceable if it was based upon the arbitrator's interpretation of the contract. Moreover, the Court held that the award had to be enforced even though it was ambiguous. The Court stated:

[A]n arbitrator is confined to interpretation and application of the collective bargaining agreement; he does not sit to dispense his own brand of industrial justice. He may of course look for guidance from many sources, yet his award is legitimate only so long as it draws its essence from the collective bargaining agreement. When the arbitrator's words manifest an infidelity to its obligation, courts have no choice but to refuse enforcement of the award.

The opinion of the arbitrator in this case, as it bears upon the award of back pay beyond the date of the agreement's expiration and reinstatement is ambiguous. It may be read as based solely upon the arbitrator's view of the requirements of enacted legislation, which would mean that he exceeded the scope of his submission. Or it may be read as embodying a construction of the agreement itself, perhaps with the arbitrator looking to "the law" for help in determining the sense of the agreement. A mere ambiguity in the opinion accompanying an award, which permits the inference that the arbitrator may have exceeded his authority, is not a reason for refusing to enforce the award. Arbitrators have no obligation to the court to give their reasons for an award. To require opinions free of ambiguity may lead arbitrators to play it safe by writing no supporting opinions. This would be undesirable for a well-reasoned opinion tends to engender confidence in the integrity of the process and aids in clarifying the underlying agreement. Moreover, we see no reason to assume that this arbitrator has abused the trust the parties confided in him and has not stayed within the areas marked out for his consideration. It is not apparent that he went beyond the submission. The Court of Appeals opinion refusing to enforce the reinstatement and partial back pay portions of the award was not based upon any finding that the arbitrator did not premise his award on his construction of the contract. It merely disagreed with the arbitrator's construction of it.

The Supreme Court further stated:

As we . . . emphasized, the question of interpretation of the collective bargaining agreement is a question for the arbitrator. It is the arbitrator's construction which was bargained for; and so far as the arbitrator's decision concerns construction of the contract, the courts have no business overruling him because their interpretation of the contract is different from his.

Suppose a collective bargaining agreement provides that promotions are to be based on seniority provided the senior employee has sufficient ability for the job. The union grieves that the employer violated the collective bargaining agreement by promoting a junior employee. If the arbitrator sustains the grievance with no explanation and orders the company to assign the job to the senior employee, the award is enforceable. Applying *Enterprise Wheel*, a court will assume that the arbitrator based his decision on the contract and will order the employer to comply.

What if the arbitrator states that the employer had the contractual right to promote the junior employee, because the senior employee lacked the ability, but the arbitrator still orders the company to award the job to the senior employee on the grounds that the employee can learn the job? In that case, a court would probably not enforce the arbitrator's decision as the arbitrator would be erroneously dispensing his own brand of industrial justice rather than drawing the essence of his decision from the contract.

Suppose an employer discharges an employee for theft. The union grieves that the discharge was not for just cause under the contract. The arbitrator finds that the employee did, in fact, steal, but orders that the discharge be reduced to a suspension because of extenuating circumstances, such as that the employee was under severe emotional distress at the time. If the employer refuses to comply, a court will probably enforce the award because a determination as to just cause includes both the issues of whether the employee committed a particular offense and whether the penalty was appropriate to the act committed. An arbitrator is therefore only intrepreting the just cause provision of the contract if he reduces the penalty.

E. EXPIRATION OF THE DUTY TO ARBITRATE

As discussed above, the duty to arbitrate is a matter of contract. Logically, once the contract containing an arbitration clause expires, the duty to arbitrate expires as well. This means that there is generally no duty to arbitrate disputes that arise after a contract expires. There is a duty, however, to arbitrate disputes that arise while the contract is in effect, even if the grievance is not filed or the request to arbitrate is not made until after the contract's expiration.

In *Nolde v. Bakery Workers*, the Supreme Court held that, under some circumstances, there is a duty to arbitrate disputes that arise after the contract expires.[5] In that case the employer and the union were parties to a collective bargaining agreement that called for arbitration of any grievance. The contract provided for severance pay on termination of

employment for all employees having three or more years of active service. The contract was to remain in effect until July 21, 1973, and thereafter until such time as the parties entered into a new agreement or one of the parties terminated it.

The parties were unable to reach a new agreement by July and continued their negotiations until August. The contract remained in effect until August 27, when the union terminated it. On August 31, the employer closed the plant, thereby terminating all the employees. The employer paid the employees their accrued wages and vacation pay under the contract, but it refused to pay severance pay. The union filed a grievance for severance pay. The company refused to arbitrate the severance pay claim on the grounds that the issue of severance pay did not arise until after the collective bargaining agreement expired and the dispute was therefore not arbitrable.

The union brought suit under Section 301 to compel arbitration. The district court held that there was no duty to arbitrate, but the court of appeals reversed the district court. The Supreme Court affirmed the decision of the court of appeals that the dispute was arbitrable. It held that the parties' agreement over the severance pay issue was based on their differing interpretations of the contract provision. The union argued that the severance pay clause applied to a shutdown occurring after the contract expired, while the company argued that it was free to shut down the plant without paying severance pay after the expiration date. The Court stated that the dispute was arbitrable, even though the dispute arose after the contract's expiration because the issue was the continued application of the severance pay clause. There was, therefore, a dispute as to the contract's meaning and application that was arbitrable.

Note that the Supreme Court made no determination over the merits of the union's claim to severance pay based on the expired contract's clause. The Court concluded only that the dispute was arbitrable.

F. PROCEDURAL DEFENSES TO ARBITRATION

1. Late Grievances

Other than the defense that a matter is not covered by the arbitration clause, the most common employer defense against arbitration is that a particular grievance was not filed within the time limits specified in the collective bargaining agreement.

Suppose a collective bargaining agreement provides that a grievance on a discharge must be filed within five days of the discharge, but the employee does not file the grievance until seven days after his discharge. The employer refuses to arbitrate on the grounds that the grievance was untimely. The union brings a suit under Section 301 to compel arbitration. Sometimes an arbitrator will excuse the late filing of a grievance if the limits have not been enforced in the past, if the employer had actual notice in time even though no formal grievance was filed, or if there are other circumstances that would excuse the delay. Should a court order arbitration even though the grievance was late?

The Supreme Court has held that a court should order arbitration even though a grievance was filed late. The Court reasons that procedural defenses such as timeliness pertain to the merits of a grievance and accordingly should be decided by the arbitrator, not the court. Of course, a court order requiring arbitration of a late grievance does not mean that the union will prevail before the arbitrator. It is up to the arbitrator to decide whether the grievance was untimely, and if it was,

whether there are circumstances for which the time limits should not be applied.

Suppose that an arbitrator decides that a discharge grievance is untimely, but that the late filing is excusable. The arbitrator then orders an employee reinstated with back pay, but the employer refuses to comply with the award on the grounds that the arbitrator exceeded his authority. If the union files suit to enforce the award, will the court enforce the decision? A court reviews an arbitrator's decision on timeliness under the same standards for reviewing the arbitrator's interpretation of any other contract term. What if the arbitrator rules, for example, that the contractual time limit should not be applied because the parties have not strictly followed it in the past. The award, based on the arbitrator's conclusion that the parties did not intend for the time limits to be rigidly enforced, would draw its essence from the collective bargaining agreement. The courts, therefore, would enforce the award.

2. Equitable Defenses to Arbitration

Employers sometimes argue that there are reasons why it would be unfair (inequitable) to permit a union to arbitrate a grievance even though the time limits have not expired. These are called equitable defenses. For example, employers sometimes argue that a union has waited too long to process a case to arbitration and that the employer has been prejudiced by the delay, even though the time limits for filing a grievance have not expired.

For example, what if an employer subcontracts work and the union does not file a grievance? The employer subcontracts the same work again. This time the union files a grievance claiming that the subcontracting violates the collective bargaining agreement. The employer can argue that it is inequitable for the union to arbitrate the validity of the second subcontract after taking no action in the first case. He might argue that he had incurred extra expenses or entered into long-term subcontracts, which he would not have done if the union had protested the first time. In some cases, arbitrators have denied grievances based upon such equitable defenses, regardless of the contractual merits of the union's claim.

Who should decide whether there is an equitable defense barring arbitration? The Supreme Court has held that equitable defenses should be treated the same as procedural defenses. If the subject of a dispute is covered by the arbitration clause, the court must order arbitration regardless of possible equitable defenses. The arbitrator decides whether an equitable defense has merit, just as the arbitrator decides timeliness issues.

Employers sometimes argue that if a union breaches a contractual no-strike clause by engaging in a wildcat strike, the employer has the right to terminate the agreement in full. That means the employer can discharge the employees or change the contract's terms and that his actions cannot be arbitrated. The Supreme Court has held, however, that a breach of a no-strike clause does not relieve the employer of his duty to arbitrate. Of course, an arbitrator is free to consider what effect, if any, the union's breach of its no-strike clause has on the employer's contractual obligations.

G. EMPLOYER'S DUTY TO GRIEVE OVER A UNION BREACH OF CONTRACT

What happens if the union violates the contract? Can the employer sue the union for breach of contract or must the employer submit its claim to arbitration?

The Supreme Court has held that an employer must exhaust (complete) the grievance procedures including arbitration before filing suit, unless it is clear that the employer has no contractual right to file a grievance. Most contracts provide that a union or an employee may file a grievance, but say nothing about the employer's right to file a grievance. If the contract is silent, the employer is not required to arbitrate its claim before filing a suit against the union. If, however, the contract provides that the employer may file grievances or if the employer has filed grievances as a matter of past practice, the employer must arbitrate. Of course, if the union strikes in violation of a no-strike clause, the employer can file suit to enjoin the strike even though the contract provides for employer grievances. But if the employer seeks money damages, as well as an injunction, and the contract allows employer grievances, the employer must arbitrate the damage issues.

H. TRIPARTITE ARBITRATION

An arbitration hearing in which an employer and two unions participate is called tripartite arbitration. The usual arbitration hearing between the employer and a single union is called bilateral arbitration. What if an employer has contracts with two unions and each claims that certain work belongs to it under its agreement? If both contracts provide for arbitration, then both unions have the right to arbitrate their respective claims in a bilateral hearing. However, since arbitration is a matter of contract, neither union can be compelled to participate in a tripartite arbitration hearing unless the contract provides for it.

If an employer separately arbitrates each union's claim to the disputed work, the employer might end up with two conflicting

awards. Both unions might have their grievances sustained and be awarded the work.
What can the employer do? Can he refuse to
arbitrate with one union?

The Supreme Court decided in *Carey v.
Westinghouse* that an employer can be required to arbitrate with only one of the
competing unions despite the possible conflict.[6] The Court said that arbitration should
be ordered because the possibility that two
arbitrators' awards might conflict is speculative. The Court would not presume that the
awards would conflict or that the arbitrators
could not frame their awards to avoid conflict.
Also, the Court said that arbitration might
prove beneficial even if conflict did result because the arbitrators might still point out
ways of resolving the dispute.

Although a union can compel an employer
to proceed with bilateral arbitration under
Carey, there have been a few cases in which
the courts have ordered two unions involved
in a jurisdictional dispute with their employer
to arbitrate their claims in a tripartite arbitration proceeding provided both union contracts provide for arbitration. That is,
however, still an uncommon procedure.

I. ARBITRATION OF
SUCCESSORSHIP RIGHTS

Under the Supreme Court's *Burns Detective*
decision, a successor employer normally has
no obligation to assume the collective bargaining agreement of the prior employer (see
Chapter 5). The successor's only obligation is
to bargain with the incumbent union if and
when the former employees represented by
the union constitute a majority of the new
work force. If a successor employer voluntarily assumes the existing contract, he is bound
by the entire agreement, including the duty to

arbitrate. But if the employer does not assume the contract, does he have any obligations under the prior agreement?

In *John Wiley and Sons v. Livingston,* the
Supreme Court held that a successor employer is obligated to arbitrate the extent of
its obligations under a prior collective bargaining agreement.[7] In that case, a small publishing company merged into a larger
company and the small company ceased to
exist. The successor retained a majority of the
prior work force. The prior union brought
suit to compel arbitration as to the successor's
obligations under the prior contract. The
Court did not rule that the successor employer had any specific liability under the old
contract; it ruled only that the successor is obligated to arbitrate the question. Following
the usual rules, the Court did not consider the
merits of the union's claim.

Wiley was decided before the decision in
Burns Detective that a successor employer is
not bound by its predecessor's agreement. In
the *Howard Johnson* case, decided after *Burns,*
Howard Johnson purchased the assets of a
motel.[8] Howard Johnson continued to operate
the facility as a motel, but only nine out of
forty-five employees had worked for the
prior owner, who had employed fifty-three
employees. The Supreme Court held that
Howard Johnson was not required to arbitrate
the question of its liability under the prior
owner's collective bargaining agreement. The
Court noted that, in contrast to *Wiley*, the
prior motel company still existed even though
the motel in question had been sold to Howard Johnson. Also, Howard Johnson had not
kept the former employees. The Court also
reasoned that since the prior motel owner was
still in operation, the union can look to the
predecessor for contractual damages, if any,

---

[6] See legal principle 4.

[7] See legal principle 3.

[8] See legal principle 6.

growing out of the motel's sale to Howard Johnson. Apparently, the *Wiley* decision requiring arbitration can still apply if a predecessor employer has ceased all operations and the former employees are a majority of the successor employer's work force. However, since *Burns Detective* has established that a successor employer is not obligated to assume a prior contract, the practical usefulness of arbitration is questionable. A court might require a successor employer to arbitrate, but the arbitrator might decide, based on *Burns*, that the successor employer has no contractual obligations except those expressly assumed.

J. INTEREST ARBITRATION

The principles discussed here pertain to grievances arising under the terms of an existing collective bargaining agreement, called "grievance arbitration." There is another type of arbitration known as "interest arbitration." Interest arbitration is arbitration of unresolved bargaining issues on a new or amended agreement. An arbitrator determines the terms of the agreement rather than interpreting the agreement the parties have reached, as in grievance arbitration. A contract clause providing that the contract may be opened at midterm for the purpose of bargaining on wages, and that the matter should be submitted to arbitration if the parties are unable to reach mutual agreement on an increase, is an example of interest arbitration.

The NLRB has held that interest arbitration is a permissive, rather than a mandatory, subject of bargaining. (See Chapter 5 for a discussion of the distinction between mandatory and permissive subjects of bargaining.) Therefore, a party cannot bargain to impasse over a proposal for interest arbitra-

tion and a union cannot strike to obtain an interest arbitration clause.

Some early court decisions held that a provision requiring interest arbitration is not enforceable under Section 301. Those cases were decided, however, before the Steelworkers trilogy decisions discussed above. The cases since the *Trilogy* have held that a provision requiring interest arbitration is binding and enforceable under Section 301. However, an agreement to engage in interest arbitration must be expressly spelled out in the contract. A general arbitration clause requiring the arbitration of any dispute arising under the contract applies only to grievance arbitrations. Such a clause does not obligate the party to engage in interest arbitration of new or amended contract terms.

K. ARBITRATION AND THE NLRB

1. The Concurrent Role of the Board and the Arbitrator

Under Section 10(a) of the LMRA, the NLRB is empowered to prevent all unfair labor practices. This power cannot be affected by any agreement that the parties may have about adjusting their disputes.

A contract violation is not necessarily an unfair labor practice. At the time the Taft–Hartley Act was under consideration, a proposal was made to make the breach of a contract by either an employer or a union an unfair labor practice. The proposal was rejected and Section 301 was enacted instead. Thus, the Board has no jurisdiction to determine typical employer-union disputes as to a contract's meaning or application. However, the Board has held that the total repudiation of an agreement by either an employer or a union is an unfair labor practice in violation of the duty of good faith bargaining.

Although the Board does have general jurisdiction to enforce contracts, some specific contract breaches may also be unfair labor practices. If a union officer is discharged, the employer's action may violate the just cause provisions of the contract. The discharge may also be an unfair labor practice if it is in retaliation for the officer's union activities.

Although Section 10(a) establishes the Board's paramount authority, federal labor policy also favors the resolution of disputes through arbitration. The courts and the Board have developed principles balancing the Board's authority with the policy favoring arbitration.

The Supreme Court has held that an arbitrator has authority to resolve a contract dispute even though the facts may also allege an unfair labor practice. Thus, a court can order arbitration of a contract dispute that might also involve an unfair labor practice (such as a discharge of a union officer), applying the same principles that apply to any other case arising under a contract arbitration clause. On the other hand, the Board has authority to remedy unfair labor practices even though there may also be a contract violation. The Supreme Court held in *C & C Plywood* that the Board, not just the arbitrator, has authority to interpret a contract if that is necessary to determine whether an unfair labor practice has occurred (see Chapter 5).[9]

Often there is no conflict between a Board and an arbitrator's decision. Consider the case of the union officer who was discharged. An arbitrator might decide that the officer was not discharged for cause under the contract, even though the Board might conclude that the discharge was not an unfair labor practice. Do these decisions conflict? No, because the Board's decision that the employee was not discharged for union activity is not inconsistent with the arbitrator's decision that the discharge was not for cause. The Board's only concern is whether the discharge was for union activity. If the Board concludes that the discharge was not for union activity, it has no authority to determine whether the discharge was not for cause under the contract.

What if the arbitrator decides that the discharge was for cause, but the Board decides that the discharge was unlawful? Then the arbitrator and the Board's decision are inconsistent. Under Section 10(a), the Board's decision prevails and the employee would be reinstated.

2. The Spielberg Doctrine: Deferral to an Arbitrator's Award

It is in the interest of both the Board and the arbitration process that conflict between arbitrators and the Board be held to a minimum. Industrial peace is not furthered by the same matter being processed before both an arbitrator and the Board. The Board has developed two doctrines limiting the circumstances under which it will decide the merits of an unfair labor practice charge that may also be a contract violation subject to arbitration. The *Spielberg Doctrine*, governs the circumstances under which the Board will accept a prior arbitration award on an issue that may also be an unfair labor practice.[10] The *Collyer Doctrine* governs the circumstances under which the Board will require the parties to arbitrate a dispute before proceeding to the Board.[11]

The question of Board deferral to an arbitrator's award most frequently arises in cases in which an employee is allegedly discharged without just cause and in violation of Section 8(a)(3) for engaging in concerted activity. An-

[9] See legal principle 8.

[10] See legal principle. 7.

[11] See legal principle 8.

other frequent case is that in which an employer's action, such as subcontracting, allegedly violates the collective bargaining agreement and is also a unilateral change in working conditions violating Section 8(a)(5).

Suppose an employer discharges an employee for alleged drunkenness. The employee claims that other employees have not been discharged for drunkenness and that he was actually discharged for engaging in union activities. A grievance is filed and the matter is brought to arbitration. The arbitrator rules that the grievant was properly discharged for being drunk rather than for his union activities. The union then files an unfair labor practice charge with the Board, alleging that the employee was discharged in violation of the Act. Will the Board conduct a hearing on the unfair labor practice charge or will it accept the arbitrator's decision that the employee was discharged for drunkenness?

a. The Spielberg Requirements: The Fair Hearing Requirement

The *Spielberg Doctrine,* named after the principal case, establishes four requirements that must be met before the Board accepts an arbitrator's decision without a full retrial. First, the arbitration proceedings must be fair and regular so that the employee receives a fair hearing as he would before the Board. The Board will consider, for example, whether the grievant was present at the arbitration hearing and whether he was permitted to present evidence in his own behalf. The Board recognizes that most arbitration hearings are less formal than Board hearings. This informality in an arbitration proceeding is not grounds for refusing to defer so long as the hearing was fair. The Board will not defer to a decision if it is apparent that the union is so hostile to the employee-grievant that the employee's interests were not adequately repre-

sented. In that case, the Board will hold a hearing.

b. Binding Arbitration

Second, arbitration of the matter must be mandatory and binding on the parties. If arbitration is voluntary or if one of the parties is free to disregard the arbitrator's decision, the Board will not defer to the award, even if the proceedings were conducted properly.

c. Consistency With Board Policies

Third, the arbitrator's decision must not be repugnant to the Act. This means that the arbitrator's decision cannot be contrary to principles established by the Board, thus depriving an employee of rights guaranteed by the LMRA. Suppose that an employee is discharged for distributing literature on his own time in a nonwork area, a statutory right under the LMRA. If an arbitrator upholds the discharge, the Board will not accept the arbitrator's decision because it is repugnant to the employee's statutory right to distribute literature. The employee will receive a full evidentiary hearing before the Board.

The Board distinguishes between a possible factual error in an arbitrator's decision and an error on a governing legal principle. Suppose in the prior example the arbitrator finds that the employee has, in fact, distributed literature on company time in a work area. That is not a statutory right. If the arbitrator holds that there was just cause for discharge based on this factual determination, the Board will accept the arbitrator's award, provided that the other requirements for deferral (a fair hearing, etc.) are met. The arbitrator's factual determinations, even if an error, are not repugnant to the Act. If an arbitrator's factual decision, however, is clearly erroneous and thus deprives an employee of his statutory rights, the Board will not defer to the arbitrator's award.

d. Consideration of the Unfair Labor Practice Issues

Fourth, the *Spielberg Doctrine* requires that the arbitrator consider the unfair labor practice issue in making his decision. For example, what if an arbitrator's decision upholding an employee's discharge considers whether the employee was drunk on the job, but does not consider whether this alleged reason was a pretext for discharging the employee for his union activity? The Board will not accept the award. The arbitrator must consider both the contract and unfair labor practice issues. The Board will not assume that an arbitrator considered the unfair labor practice issues in reaching his decision; there must be an express finding by the arbitrator. Thus, if an arbitrator finds that a discharge was for cause without specifying his reasons, the Board will not defer to the award.

If all four *Spielberg* requirements are met, the Board will accept an arbitrator's award and not relitigate the same issues. If any of the factors are not met, the Board will not defer and will hold a hearing as in any other unfair labor practice case. Remember, there are only six months to file an unfair labor practice charge from the date of an unlawful occurrence. Filing a contract grievance does not stop the six month period from expiring. Thus, a union awaiting an arbitrator's decision on a grievance involving an unfair labor practice may have to file a Board charge before the six months are up so that a Board remedy will still be available if the arbitrator's decision is unfavorable and does not meet the *Spielberg* standards. The Board will usually defer action on the charge until after the arbitrator's decision is rendered. The union can then either withdraw the charge if

the arbitrator's decision is favorable, or the decision can be reviewed under the *Spielberg* standards.

3. Requiring Arbitration Before Board Proceedings: The Collyer Doctrine

The *Spielberg Doctrine* pertains to deferral to an arbitrator's award. But if the union does not request arbitration, but goes directly to the Board, should the Board proceed or require the parties to arbitrate their dispute? The Board's approach to this issue is known as the *Collyer Doctrine*.

In *Collyer*, the union alleged that an employer had made certain unilateral changes in wages and working conditions in violation of Section 8(a)(5). The employer argued that the contract and past practice authorized the changes so that there was no need to bargain with the union first. An employer has no duty to bargain before making unilateral changes the contract permits (see Chapter 5). Thus, an employer need not bargain before subcontracting work if the contract permits it. Whether an employer has violated Section 8(a)(5) in such cases depends upon whether the employer has the contractual right to act unilaterally. In *Collyer*, the Board held that if the determination of a Section 8(a)(5) violation depends upon interpreting the contract and the contract provides for arbitration, the Board will require the parties to arbitrate their dispute before proceeding to the Board.

Although *Collyer* entailed an alleged employer unilateral action violation of Section 8(a)(5), the Board quickly expanded the doctrine to cover virtually any case in which the actions that give rise to an unfair labor practice charge are also a contract violation subject to arbitration. Thus, if a union filed a charge that an employee was discharged for union activity in violation of Section 8(a)(1) and 8(a)(3), but the discharge might also have violated the contractual just cause provision, the Board required the union to arbitrate the dispute.

Following a change in Board membership, however, the Board reversed itself and returned to the original doctrine. Currently, the *Collyer Doctrine,* requiring deferral to arbitration, only applies to cases of alleged unilateral action violating Section 8(a)(5). The Board no longer defers charges pertaining to other sections of the Act, such as alleged discriminatory discharges.

4. Procedure in Cases Deferred to Arbitration

The Board's procedure in cases that still fall within the *Collyer Doctrine* is to make a preliminary determination on whether a charge may have merit. If the charge lacks merit, it is dismissed outright. Remember, even though the Board might conclude that there is no statutory violation, there might still be a contractual one. If the Board determines that a charge may have merit, it will defer the charge to arbitration, but retain jurisdiction while arbitration is proceeding. In that way, the six month limit for filing a charge does not expire. If the charging party is dissatisfied with the arbitrator's decision, it may request that the Board reassert jurisdiction. The Board will consider whether to accept the arbitrator's decision under the *Spielberg Doctrine.* If the *Spielberg* criteria are

met, the Board dismisses the unfair labor practice charge. If the criteria are not met, the Board reasserts its jurisdiction and considers the charge on the merits.

Remember that most cases involving the *Spielberg* or *Collyer* doctrines do not actually reach the Board. If an unfair labor practice charge is filed prior to arbitration the regional director decides whether the case falls within the *Collyer* doctrine or whether a complaint should be issued leading ultimately to a trial and a Board decision. Similarly, the regional director decides whether an arbitrator's decision meets the *Spielberg* standards or a complaint should be issued.

Current Exceptions to Collyer

There are few exceptions to the *Collyer* doctrine as presently applied. The most important is that the employer must be willing to arbitrate a dispute on the merits before the Board will defer it to arbitration. If a union files an unfair labor practice charge, and the employer maintains that the dispute is not arbitrable, the Board will not defer. Similarly, if a union files an untimely grievance and the employer raises a procedural defense, the Board does not defer to arbitration. If the employer delays arbitration proceedings, the Board reasserts jurisdiction and proceeds. Also, if an employer essentially has repudiated the agreement, the Board does not defer to arbitration.

Summary

This chapter considered the enforcement of collective bargaining agreements under Section 301 of the Labor Management Relations Act. Section 301 permits either an employer or a union to enforce the terms of a contract against the other. Individual employees may also bring suit under some circumstances.

Suits under Section 301 can be brought by or against the union as an entity in federal court. Suits to enforce contracts can also be brought in state courts, but the state courts must apply federal law so that uniformity in enforcing agreements, a prime goal of Section 301, is maintained. Employer suits against unions for damages and/or injunctive relief growing out of a strike and breach of contract are brought under Section 301.

The *Lincoln Mills* decision established that a grievance arbitration provision in a collective bargaining agreement can be enforced under Section 301, an important change from state law under which a party could take a matter to court notwithstanding an agreement to arbitrate. In the landmark "Steelworkers Trilogy," the court held that the parties should be required to arbitrate a dispute subject to arbitration under their contract unless it can be stated with positive assurance that the arbitration clause of the collective bargaining agreement does not apply to the particular dispute. Doubts are to be resolved in favor of arbitration and the courts cannot consider the merits of a dispute in determining its arbitrability. An arbitrator's decision must be enforced by a court so long as it draws its essence from the collective bargaining agreement even though the court may disagree with the arbitrator's decision.

Procedural or equitable defenses to arbitration pertain to the merits of a grievance and must be decided by the arbitrator, not by a court. Thus a court must order arbitration if a dispute is covered by the contract even though the grievance is filed late. The arbitrator decides whether the grievance is untimely or, if it is, whether there is some special circumstance for which the time limit should not be applied.

Before an employer can sue the union for breach of contract, the employer must first exhaust the contractual arbitration provisions unless it is clear that the employer has no contractual right to file a grievance.

An arbitrator has authority to resolve a contract dispute even though the facts may also allege an unfair labor practice. Under the *Spielberg* doctrine, the Board, to avoid conflict, will accept an arbitrator's decision meeting its standards rendered on an issue that may also be an unfair labor practice.

Under the *Collyer* doctrine, if the parties' contract provides for arbitration, the Board requires the parties to arbitrate cases that allege that an employer's unilateral action violates both Section 8(a)(5) and the contract. The Board no longer requires arbitration of charges alleging other violations of the Act such as an alleged discriminatory discharge. The Board reviews an arbitrator's decision in cases deferred to arbitration under the *Spielberg* standards.

Review Questions

1. Does Section 301 apply only to contracts between an employer and a union?

2. Can an employee sue his union for violation of the union's by-laws under Section 301?

3. Does Section 301 apply to a collective bargaining agreement between a governmental agency and a public employee union?

4. Is a dispute which arises after a contract has expired arbitrable?

5. Can an individual employee bring a suit to enforce his contract rights contrary to a union's settlement of his grievance?

6. How long does a party have to bring a suit under Section 301?

7. What is the federal standard for enforcing an agreement to arbitrate?

8. To what extent can the courts consider the merits of a dispute in determining its arbitrability?

9. What is the importance of the *Warrior and Gulf* decision?

10. Must a court enforce an arbitrator's decision that is clearly wrong?

11. Is an employer required to arbitrate a claim for damages growing out of a union's breach of a no-strike clause?

12. What is the difference between grievance and interest arbitration?

13. Which decision will prevail if there are any inconsistent decisions by an arbitrator and the NLRB over a matter which is both an alleged contract violation and an unfair labor practice?

14. Is there any advantage for a union to file an unfair labor practice charge over a matter that the Board will defer to arbitration anyway?

(Answers to review questions appear at end of book.)

Basic Legal Principles

1. Suits brought under Section 301 to enforce a collective bargaining agreement can be brought in federal or state court, but federal law governs in either court in determining the merits. Only the union as an entity is liable for damages against it. *Textile Workers Union v. Lincoln Mills*, 353 U.S. 448, 40 LRRM 2113 (1957); *Smith v. Evening News Assn.*, 371 U.S. 195, 51 LRRM 2646 (1962); *Atkinson v. Sinclair Refining Co.*, 370 U.S. 238, 50 LRRM 2433 (1962).

2. Under the Steelworkers Trilogy: (1) the function of a court is limited to determining whether the party seeking arbitration has a claim which, on its face, is governed by the contract, (2) doubts on the coverage of the arbitration clause should be resolved in favor of arbitration, (3) courts cannot consider the merits of a dispute in determining arbitrability, (4) an arbitrator's award must be enforced if it draws its essence from the collective bargaining agreement even though a court may disagree with the result. *Steelworkers v. Warrior & Gulf Navigation Co.*, 363 U.S. 574, 46 LRRM 2416 (1960); *Steelworkers v. American Manufacturing Co.*, 363 U.S. 564, 46 LRRM 2414 (1960); *United Steelworkers v. Enterprise Wheel & Car Corp.*, 363 U.S. 593, 46 LRRM 2423 (1960).

3. Courts determine whether a particular dispute is subject to arbitration, but procedural defenses, such as timeliness, are determined by the arbitrator. *John Wiley & Sons, Inc. v. Livingston,* 376 U.S. 543, 55 LRRM 2769 (1964).

4. A court may enforce an agreement to arbitrate, even though a contract violation is also an unfair labor practice, but the Board's decision prevails in case of conflict between a Board and arbitrator's decision. *Carey v. Westinghouse Electric Corp,* 375 U.S. 261, 55 LRRM 2042 (1964).

5. An employer can be required to arbitrate a work assignment dispute with only one of two competing unions although both claim the same work under their respective collective bargaining agreements. *Carey v. Westinghouse Electric Corp., supra.*

6. A successor employer may be required to arbitrate the extent to which the successor incurred any obligation under its predecessor's collective bargaining agreement. Since the *Burns Detective* decision, however, it is unlikely that the union would prevail on the merits of any such claim. Compare *John Wiley & Sons, Inc. v. Livingston, supra;* with *Howard Johnson Co. v. Hotel & Restaurant Employees Detroit Local Joint Board,* 417 U.S. 249, 86 LRRM 2449 (1974).

7. The Board will defer to an arbitrator's decision if (1) the statutory issues are presented and considered in arbitration, (2) the arbitration proceeding is fair and regular, (3) the arbitration proceeding is final and binding on both parties, (4) the award is not repugnant to the policies of the Act. *Spielberg Mfg. Co.,* 112 NLRB 1080, 36 LRRM 1152 (1955); *Machinists, District 15,* 231 NLRB No. 103, 96 LRRM 1625 (1977); *United Parcel Service, Inc.,* 232 NLRB No. 179, 96 LRRM 1288 (1977); *Filmation Associates, Inc.,* 227 NLRB No. 237, 94 LRRM 1470 (1977).

8. If the determination of a charge alleging a unilateral change violating Section 8(a)(5) depends upon the party's contract and the contract provides for arbitration, the Board will require the parties to arbitrate the dispute rather than proceeding directly to the Board. *Collyer Insulated Wire,* 192 NLRB No. 150, 77 LRRM 1931 (1971); *Columbus Foundries, Inc.,* 229 NLRB No. 14, 95 LRRM 1090 (1977); *Roy Robinson Chevrolet,* 228 NLRB No. 103, 94 LRRM 1474 (1977). See also. *NLRB v. C & C Plywood Corp.,* 385 U.S. 421, 64 LRRM 2065 (1967).

9. The duty to arbitrate expires upon the expiration of the agreement. However, disputes arising during the contract's term are arbitrable even though arbitration is not requested until after the contract expires. Arbitration may be required on disputes arising after expiration if the issue is the contract's continued application past the expiration date. *Nolde Bros. Inc. v. Bakery & Confectionery Workers Union, Local 358,* 430 U.S. 243, 94 LRRM 2753 (1977).

10. Employers may be required to exhaust contractual remedies before bringing suit against the union for breach of contract. A union's breach of the no-strike clause does not release the employer from its obligation to arbitrate. *Packinghouse Workers Local 721 v. Needham Packing Co.,* 376 U.S. 247, 55 LRRM 2580 (1964).

Bloch, "Labor Arbitration's Crossroads Revisited: The Role of the Arbitrator and the Response of the Courts," 47 *U. Cin. L. Rev.* 363 (1978).

Edwards, "Arbitration as an Alternative in Equal Employment Disputes," 33 *Arb. J.* 22 (1978).

Truesdale, "Is Spielberg Dead?", 31 *N.Y.U. Conf. Lab.* 61 (1978).

Recommended Reading

Chapter Ten

Union Membership and Union Security

*T*his chapter includes a discussion of the internal relationship between a union and its own members, including the nature of the legal relationship, the right to union membership, required union membership (union security agreements), and related matters.

A. THE UNION AS AN UNINCORPORATED ASSOCIATION

1. The Labor Union at Common Law

To understand the legal relationship between the union and its members, it is necessary to understand what a union is. Of course, a union is an organization that engages in collective bargaining, but there is a common law legal definition of a union that is important to understand. Common law is the law gradually developed over the years by judges through decisions handed down in individual cases, in contrast to statutory law passed by a legislative body, such as the *Labor Management Relations Act*. For example, most of the legal principles governing the right to own, buy, and sell real estate are based on the common law. In contrast, workmen's compensation law is statutory.

Under common law, a union is regarded as an unincorporated association, as is a partner-ship, another form of unincorporated association. A labor organization, as an unincorporated association, is simply a combination of members. It has no legal existence apart from its members. A corporation is different. It is a legal entity, legally separate from the stockholders. The officers or shareholders of a corporation may change, but the corporation continues to exist. A corporation sues and is sued in its corporate name. It is not necessary to sue the officers or the shareholders to enforce a corporation's legal obligations. In contrast, an unincorporated association cannot sue or be sued as an entity because it has no separate legal existence apart from its members. It is necessary to sue the individual members to enforce the association's legal obligations.

Because it is not practical to sue individually all the members of a large union, the law allows large unincorporated groups to sue or be sued as a class. A representative group, usually a union's officers, can file suit or can be sued on behalf of all the members as a class. The decision is binding on all members of the class as if they had been sued individually.

Under the common law, every member of a union was individually liable for a judgment rendered against the association in a class action. The personal assets of each and every union member could be attached to pay a judgment against a union. Of course there were limitations. Most states restricted property that could be seized to collect the judgment. In many cases employers with judgments against union members as a class found collection procedures so cumbersome that they either did not bother to collect or compromised their claim to avoid the problem.

2. The Union Under Federal Law

The legal status of a union has changed under federal law. Section 301 of the LMRA, pertaining to suits for the enforcement of contracts, specifically provides that a labor organization may sue or be sued as an entity in federal court, but a judgment against a union is only enforceable against the union's assets, not against individual union members (see Chapter 9).

Section 303, which pertains to private damage suits against unions for engaging in secondary boycotts (see Chapter 7), provides that the procedures of Section 301 are to be followed under Section 303, thus permitting a union to be sued as an entity under Section 303.

In addition to the specific statutory authority under Sections 301 and 303, the Supreme Court has held that unions may sue or be sued as an entity in the federal courts in any action involving application of a federal law to a union. For example, unions may be sued as an entity for alleged violations of the federal antitrust laws (see Chapter 8), even though these laws do not specifically authorize such suits.

3. The Continued Applicability of State Law to Unions

The common law rule that a union is an unincorporated association still has practical importance. Many union matters are not regulated by federal law. A union's right to own real estate involves continued application of the old common law rules. In most states an unincorporated association cannot hold real estate in its own name. How does a union own its hall? Technically, each union member can individually own a portion. But that is a practical impossibility. Every time a member left he would have to deed back his portion. To avoid these problems most unions establish a separate building corporation that owns the hall. Alternately, a union can establish a separate real estate trust and union members can serve as trustees to hold title to the union's property. Some states now permit unincorporated associations to own real estate in their own name so that these technicalities are no longer necessary.

Suppose a union member walking into a union hall trips and falls over a loose floorboard. The member may sue the union for negligence in failing to keep the hall in proper repair, just as he can sue a store if he trips and falls in it. The suit would be a state court common law action, not governed by federal law. The member cannot sue the union as an entity but must sue the union members individually or in a class action.

Some states still prohibit a union member from suing his fellow members for common law claims against the union. The courts have reasoned that since a union is an unincorporated association composed of the members, a member is in effect suing himself, a legal impossibility.

4. Federal Court Application of Common Law Rules

Sometimes the federal courts have a case that involves a union in which state rather than federal law applies. Suppose a union in one state contracts to purchase office equipment from a supplier in another state. A dispute arises and the union refuses to pay for the equipment. The federal courts have jurisdiction to decide cases in which the parties to a suit are from different states and the amount involved in the suit is $10,000 or more, even though there is no federal law involved. The federal court applies the relevant state law in deciding the case. This is called diversity jurisdiction. The out-of-state supplier can sue the union in federal court if $10,000 or more is involved. Although the suit is brought in the federal courts, the court applies state law in deciding the matter.

The federal courts still apply the old common law rule governing unions as unincorporated associations in diversity jurisdiction cases. Thus, the supplier in the example must bring suit against the union members as a class. The supplier cannot bring suit against the union as an entity as it could if a federal law were involved. There is a requirement in federal court diversity cases that there be complete diversity between the parties. That means that none of the defendants can reside in the same state as the plaintiff. What if a union located in New Jersey has members who live in both New York and New Jersey? A New York supplier cannot file a diversity suit in the federal courts against the New Jersey union on a state law claim because some of the defendant union members live in the same state as the plaintiff supplier. There

would not be complete diversity. So, the common law rule covering the union as an unincorporated association still applies and has importance today. Remember, these rules apply only to common law actions brought in federal courts. Suits based on federal labor laws can be brought directly against the union as an entity.

B. THE CONTRACTUAL RELATIONSHIP BETWEEN A UNION AND ITS MEMBERS

If a union is an unincorporated association composed of its membership, how are the rights and responsibilities of the members determined? The courts have traditionally held that the relationship between a union and its members is contractual. The union's constitution and by-laws are the contract. The individual, by becoming a union member, becomes contractually bound by the constitution and by-laws.

Suppose a union's by-laws provide that dues are $25 a month. If a member refuses to pay, can the union collect the dues in court, even though the member personally voted against the increase? Yes, because by becoming a union member, the member became contractually bound to pay the dues provided in the by-laws. Suppose the by-laws provide that if a member is sued for delinquent dues, the member must pay the union's attorneys fees for collecting the amount owed. Normally under our court system, each side in a suit must pay their own attorney fees unless a statute, (such as certain civil rights statutes) provides that the winning side is entitled to an attorney's fee from the loser. However, a union can collect its attorney's fee from the member who is being sued for delinquent dues because the member is contractually bound to pay the union's legal fees in accordance with the by-law provision.

The common law principle that a union member is bound by the constitution and by-laws as a contract has been modified to an extent by the *Labor Management Relations Act* and the *Labor Management Reporting and Disclosure Act*. These statutes guarantee members certain rights that the by-laws cannot change but still give unions great leeway in internal regulation through their constitution and by-laws (see Chapter 11).

If a union wants to enforce a by-law provision or collect a fine in court against a member, the suit must be filed in the state court because the union is enforcing its by-laws as a matter of state contract law. Since enforcing a by-law is a common law rather than a federal statutory right, the union has to file suit through its members as a class except in those few states that have adopted statutes permitting unions to file suit as an entity. The union officers can be named as the plaintiffs representing the entire membership.

C. THE RIGHT TO UNION MEMBERSHIP

Since a union was regarded as a private association at common law, the courts held that a union had the right to admit whomever it wished as members, the same as a fraternal organization or a social club. A union had no obligation to admit all employees to membership. Some unions excluded minorities from membership; others restricted membership to relatives or friends of members. Those practices were permitted by the courts on the theory that a union, as a private association, had the right to select its members. Those practices have, of course, ceased, both because the Civil Rights Act prohibits a union from excluding anyone from membership be-

cause of race, color, religion, sex, or national origin (see Chapter 13) and because unions recognize that all employees should be eligible for membership without discrimination.

Except to the extent that federal law prohibits discrimination in selecting members, unions still have the common law right as a private association to determine eligibility for membership. Congress recognized a union's right to establish its own membership requirements in LMRA Section 8(b)(1)(A), providing that nothing in that section should impair the right of a labor organization to prescribe its own rules with respect to the acquisition or retention of union membership. There are many reasons for which a union can still choose to exclude certain persons. Some international union constitutions prohibit a person from joining one local of the international if that person still owes a debt to another local. That is a valid restriction that a union has the right to impose as a private organization.

D. REQUIRED UNION MEMBERSHIP

1. Statutory Provisions on Union Security Clauses

Section 8(a)(3) permits a company and a union to negotiate an agreement requiring union membership as a condition of employment on or after the thirtieth day following the beginning of employment or the effective date of the contract, whichever comes later. Under Section 8(f), an agreement can require union membership in the construction industry after the seventh day of employment. Contract provisions requiring union membership are commonly called union security clauses. Section 8(a)(3) prohibits an employer from discharging an employee because of his membership or nonmembership in the union except if the employee has refused to pay uniformly required dues and initiation fees under a union security clause. Section 8(b)(2) prohibits a union from requesting an employee's discharge for nonmembership except for failure to tender the periodic dues and initiation fees required under a union security clause. Section 19, a health care amendment, establishes procedures under which an employee of a health care institution with religious objections to joining a union can pay the equivalent to the initiation fees and dues to charity.

2. Types of Union Security Clauses

Section 8(a)(3) specifically authorizes contracts requiring union membership after 30 days of employment. A 30-day provision is the most common form of union security clause, but it is not the only kind. There are three basic kinds of union security clauses: (1) the union shop clause, (2) the maintenance of membership clause, and (3) the agency shop clause. Although Section 8(a)(3) only expressly refers to the 30-day union shop agreement, the Supreme Court has held that the lesser varieties of union security, such as maintenance of membership or agency shop, are also permitted. Prior to the Taft-Hartley Act, which enacted Section 8(a)(3), closed shops were permitted. A closed shop provision, which Section 8(a)(3) abolished, required that an employee be a union member in order to be hired for a job.

A union shop clause is one that requires that an employee become a union member on or after 30 days of employment or after the seventh day in the construction industry. Of course, a collective bargaining agreement can provide for a longer employment period than the statutory minimum, but it cannot require

a shorter period. Remember that employees of health care facilities with religious objections to joining a union have the right to pay the equivalent of the initiation fees and dues to a charity instead.

Under a maintenance of membership clause, each employee who is a union member on the effective date of the contract must remain a member, but the initial decision to join is voluntary. Maintenance of membership clauses frequently contain an escape provision allowing an employee to resign his membership during a specified period before the contract's termination date. Membership is automatically renewed for anyone who does not resign during this period.

Sometimes a contract combines maintenance of membership and union shop provisions. A clause may state that employees already employed on the contract's effective date will not be required to join the union, but must remain members once they do join. All newly hired employees will be required to join the union after 30 days. This combination occurs most frequently when a union organizes a new employer and the employer objects to requiring "old and faithful employees" to join the union.

An agency shop is a contract provision under which employees do not have to join the union but are required to pay a service fee instead. That fee can be the same as the monthly dues. This type of provision is becoming especially popular among public employee unions in states that prohibit compulsory membership for governmental employees.

All forms of union security clauses must provide for the minimum applicable 30 or 7 day grace period.

Union Security and Probationary Periods

What if a collective bargaining agreement has a 90-day probationary period during which the employer can discharge employees without just cause? Can a union have a union security clause requiring employees to join the union in 30 days, even though the employee is still subject to discharge? Yes, because there is no necessary correlation between a probationary period and union membership. Although probationary employees may be subject to discharge, they are covered by other contractual provisions. A union has the duty to represent these employees whether or not they are union members. Thus, it is not unreasonable to require probationary employees to join. Some unions may, however, conclude, on balance, that it is too burdensome administratively to take in employees as members before their probationary period is over.

3. The Financial Core Member

Although Section 8(a)(3) refers to mandatory union membership, the Supreme Court held in *General Motors* that an employee cannot actually be required to join the union, but only to pay the initiation fees and monthly dues.[1] The Court reached this conclusion based upon the language of Sections 8(a)(3) and 8(b)(2) that an employee can only be discharged for failure to *tender* dues and initiation fees. The Court reasoned that if an employee is willing to tender his initiation fees and dues he cannot be discharged even though he refuses to become a full member. A person who pays the initiation fees and dues but refuses to become a full member is called a "financial core member." Contracts may legally use the typical union security clause language requiring membership, but only financial core membership can be enforced through discharge. The result is simi-

[1] See legal principle 3.

lar to an agency shop provision that only requires that an employee may pay a "service fee" equal to the amount of the union's initiation fees and dues.

Why would an employee want to pay the union's initiation fees and dues, but not become a full member? Remember, a union member is bound by the union's constitution and by-laws and he is subject to internal union discipline. But, an employee who simply pays the initiation fees and dues in order to keep his job, but does not formally join the union, is not bound by the union's by-laws and is not subject to discipline. Of course, employees who refuse to become formal members are covered by the collective bargaining agreement and have all contractual rights, but they have no right to participate in the union. Only full union members get to vote on the ratification of collective bargaining agreements. Only members get to vote for union officers or on union policies. Thus, the employee who refuses to become a full member keeps his job, but he gives up the right to control his working conditions that full membership offers.

4. The Definition of Dues

a. Assessments vs. Dues

What are union dues under Section 8(a)(3)? What if, for example, a union assesses all members a specified amount in addition to monthly dues to pay off the mortgage on the union hall? Must an employee pay union assessments in order to keep his job under a lawful union security clause?

Any employee who wishes to be a full union member enjoying all the privileges of membership must pay an assessment provided it is duly passed in accordance with the union's by-laws and also in accordance with Section 101(a)(3) of the Labor Management Reporting and Disclosure Act, which requires reasonable notice and a secret ballot in most instances. But the Board has held that an employee who is just a financial core member, only paying the minimum amount to keep his job, cannot be required to pay an assessment and cannot be discharged under the union security clause if he refuses to pay.

Definition of Dues. The NLRB defines dues as payments used to meet the union's general and current obligations. The payments must be regular, periodic, uniform, and not used for a special purpose. Payments to a special fund or for a special purpose, especially if the payments are for a limited time, are regarded as assessments. Payments to pay off the union's mortgage, the example given above, are an assessment because they are for a special purpose, not general operating expenses. As assessments are not dues, an employee cannot be required to pay an assessment as a condition of employment under Section 8(a)(3).

An employee who is a full union member and refuses to pay the assessment can be sued in court to collect the amount owed or internal union discipline can be imposed. The employee cannot be discharged, however, because the only grounds for discharge are failure to pay initiation fees or dues, but not assessments. If the member is expelled for refusing to pay the assessment, the employee is no longer required to pay union dues, but his employment cannot be affected. If an employee is not a union member at all, and thus not bound by the union's by-laws, an assessment cannot be collected.

The label a union places on a payment is not controlling as to its enforcement. The union may call a payment dues, but the payment may legally be classified as an assessment because it is used for a special purpose, etc. But, in contrast, a union may call a payment an assessment, but it may legally be classified as dues because it is used to meet current general obligations, etc. The actual purpose rather than the label controls. This means, for example, that if a payment the union refers to as an assessment is legally classified as dues, all employees may be required to pay it as a condition of continued employment under a union security clause.

b. Union Fines

A union fine is not classified as dues, thus, an employee cannot be discharged for failure to pay a fine. A member may be suspended or expelled, however, for failure to pay a fine and a fine can be collected in court (see Chapter 11). A union by-law that states that a fine is treated as dues is not enforceable.

5. Excessive or Discriminatory Dues

Section 8(b)(5) makes it an unfair labor practice for a union to require employees covered by a union security agreement to pay a membership fee in an amount that the Board finds excessive or discriminatory under all the circumstances. The section requires the Board to consider, among other relevant factors, the practices and customs of labor organizations in the particular industry and the wages currently paid to the affected employees.

There are very few reported cases involving Section 8(b)(5). This section does not prohibit classes of membership. Thus, a union that represents employees with different skills, in different industries, or at different pay levels, can divide its membership into classes or divisions. There can be different dues structures for each classification it represents. This arrangement would not violate Section 8(b)(5) as long as the union has a reasonable basis for the distinction.

6. Union Dues Rebates and Attendance Incentives

Section 8(b)(2)provides that required dues be uniform, and Section 101(a)(5) of the Labor Management Reporting and Disclosure Act (see Chapter 11) requires that a member have a hearing before being disciplined for any reason other than non-payment of dues. What if a union adopts a dues schedule under which dues are $20 a month, but are reduced to $15 a month if the member attends the union's monthly meeting? The reduction is an incentive to get members to the meeting. Is the reduction, in effect, a $5 fine on members who do not attend a weekly meeting? If so, it cannot be imposed without a hearing.

The courts have held that this kind of dues reduction is an incentive to attend meetings, not a fine for failure to attend. Similarly, courts have upheld union policies reducing dues if they are paid by a certain date early in the month. This is regarded as a legitimate incentive to get dues in early, not a fine against those who do pay late in the month. Also, since all members have an equal right to the reduction by meeting the uniformly applied requirements, the reduction does not violate the Section 8(b)(2) uniformity requirement. An employee who does not come to union meetings or pay his dues by the established cut-off date, may be required to pay the full amount. The employee may be discharged under the union security clause if he fails or refuses to pay.

7. Late Payment of Union Dues

A union by-law may provide that dues must be paid no later than the fifteenth day of the month. What if the employee's dues are not paid until the seventeenth day, two days late? The collective bargaining agreement contains a union security clause. Can the employee be discharged for such a slight violation? If the employee has signed a check-off form authorizing his employer to deduct his initiation fee and dues and forward them to the union, he cannot be discharged. The union is obligated to make sure the employer deducts the proper amount and forwards it to the union on time. But if the collective bargaining agreement does not provide for check-off, or if an employee has not signed a check-off form, the employee is obligated to get his dues in on time.

Any policy on discharging employees for late payment must be uniformly applied to all employees. If a union by-law or practice allows a grace period for late payments or permits an employee to pay a reinstatement fee to regain membership, all employees must have the same grace period or be permitted to regain membership in the same way. If the union makes exceptions in hardship cases (perhaps an employee has extra medical bills to pay), the hardship rules must be applied to all employees in the same situation. There are also certain notice requirements a union must meet before an employee can be discharged (see below).

If a union has been lax in enforcing a dues payment deadline, it cannot suddenly begin enforcing the rule strictly. The union must give employees fair notice of its intention. But if a union has a hard and fast rule requiring payment on time with no exceptions and no excuses, that rule can be enforced and an employee can be discharged for late payment in accordance with the union security clause of the collective bargaining agreement.

8. Effect of a Union's Rejection or Expulsion of an Employee on Continued Employment

a. Effect of Rejection

Suppose a collective bargaining agreement contains a union security clause. The employee applies for membership, but the union rejects the employee as a member for a valid nondiscriminatory purpose. If the union rejects an employee who is willing to join the union, as required by the union security clause, can the union then have the employee discharged for failure to be a member? No. The union cannot have it both ways. If the union rejects an employee for membership, the employee is not subject to discharge. The union would violate Section 8(b)(2) by requesting that an employee be discharged under those circumstances, and the employer would violate Section 8(a)(3) by discharging him. The employee would become a legal "free rider."

Section 8(a)(3) prohibits an employer from discriminating against (discharging) an employee for nonmembership in a labor orgainization pursuant to a union security agreement if the employer has reasonable grounds for believing membership is not available to the employee on the same terms and conditions generally applicable to other members or that the employee was denied membership for reasons other than the employee's failure to tender the uniformly required periodic dues and initiation fees.

The use of the word *tender* is significant. To tender means to offer the initiation fees and dues. Thus, if an employee offers to pay his initiation fees and dues, but the union rejects the employee and refuses to accept the dues, the employer cannot discharge the employee, because the tender was made. If the employee does not tender his dues and initiation fees, then he can be discharged. Of course, the law does not require meaningless acts. If a union has advised an employee that he will not be admitted, the employee does not even have to offer to pay and the employee cannot be discharged for failing to make the tender.

b. Effect of Expulsion

What if a union expels a member and the union's collective bargaining agreement has a union security clause? Can the union require that the employer discharge the employee? If a member is expelled for refusing to tender periodic dues and initiation fees, then he can be discharged upon the union's request, as expressly authorized by Section 8(a)(3). If an employee is expelled for any other reason, however, his employment cannot be affected. Failure to pay the periodic dues and initiation fees is the only ground for terminating an employee's employment under a union security clause. A union violates Section 8(b)(2) by requesting the discharge of an employee for any reason other than failure to pay the initiation fees and dues. The employer violates Section 8(a)(3) by that type of discharge.

Although the employee's employment cannot be affected, the expulsion can be valid as an internal union matter. The expelled member is not entitled to participate in union affairs. The employee is entitled to all collective bargaining benefits, however, including the right to have his grievances adjusted by the union.

Can a union require that an expelled member continue paying periodic dues, as a kind of service charge, since the employee still has all contractual benefits? No, if an employee is willing to be a full union member, but the union expels him (other than for failure to pay initiation fees and dues), the union security clause cannot be enforced. At that point the employee becomes a free rider.

9. Application of Union Security Clauses to Supervisors and Transferred Employees

A union cannot require that supervisors pay dues, although it is customary and not unlawful for first line supervisors to remain union members in many industries. Contracts frequently contain provisions permitting supervisors to return to the bargaining unit with full seniority. The Board has held that, in most cases, supervisors returning to the unit must be given the full 30 days grace period under Section 8(a)(3) to rejoin the union. However, in *A. O. Smith Corp.*, the Board upheld a contract clause requiring supervisors to rejoin the union immediately.[2] In that case, supervisors frequently shuttled back and forth from supervisory to bargaining unit positions. The Board stated that the critical factor in determining whether a supervisor may be required to pay union dues immediately is whether an employee who becomes a supervisor has a reasonable expectation that he may return soon to the bargaining unit. If an employee anticipates frequent transfer from employee status to supervisor, and back to employee, depending upon production factors, etc., then the union may require that the employee resume paying union dues immediately each time he returns to the bargaining unit. But, if an employee who becomes a supervisor does not have a reasonable expectation of returning frequently to the bargaining unit, the supervisor cannot be required to resume membership payments immediately upon return. The supervisor then is entitled

[2] See legal principle 4.

to the 30 day grace period afforded a new employee.

The Board has also held that a union can negotiate a clause in which employees transferred out of the unit to other work may continue to accrue seniority rights in the bargaining unit, provided the employee remains a union member and continues to pay dues while employed out of the unit. The Board reasons that the employee can be required to pay dues because the employee, by retaining his seniority rights, is receiving a benefit he would not otherwise be entitled to.

10. Effect of Contract Expiration on a Union Security Clause

Some contract provisions remain in effect as a condition of employment after a contract expires until bargaining impasse is reached (see Chapter 5). That is not true of a union security clause, which expires immediately unless the parties agree to extend the contract beyond its expiration date. This means that union members can resign from the union after a contract containing a union security clause has expired. In that way (as discussed in Chapter 11) employees who wish to do so can cross a union's picket line without being disciplined. However, if the union subsequently negotiates a contract containing a union security clause, the employees who resigned can be required to rejoin. They must pay the same reinitiation fee required of any other employee who resigns and returns. They cannot be charged a higher fee; that would violate the Section 8(b)(2) requirement that initiation fees and dues be uniformly required of all employees. What if the union refuses to take the employee back or requires that he pay a fine before being readmitted? Under those circumstances, the employee is not obligated to tender his initiation fees and dues and becomes a legal free rider.

11. Union Deauthorization Elections

A union deauthorization election (referred to as a UD election) nullifies the union security clause of a collective bargaining agreement. A union deauthorization election is sometimes confused with a union decertification election (an RD petition). The two are very different. A decertification election is one to revoke the representation rights of a union. A UD election is only to revoke the contractual union security clause. If a union loses a decertification petition, it no longer represents the employees. If the union loses a union deauthorization election, it still represents the employees, but the union security clause cannot be enforced. Decertification procedures are based on Section 9(c)(1)(A), whereas deauthorization procedures are based on Section 9(e)(1). The election procedures are those followed in all representation cases (see Chapters 1 and 2).

a. Majority Vote Requirement for Union Deauthorization

As in other representation matters, a union deauthorization petition must be supported by a 30 percent showing of interest of bargaining unit employees. A deauthorization election, however, is different in one respect. A representation or decertification election is determined by a majority of the eligible employees voting. But a deauthorization election requires a majority of all employees in the bargaining unit. Thus, if there are ten employees in the unit, six votes are needed to deauthorize the union security clause.

b. Dues Obligation During Deauthorization Proceedings

Questions sometimes arise about whether employees must continue to pay union dues while a UD petition is pending. The Board's view is that employees are obligated to continue paying dues until the Board certifies the results of a deauthorization election revoking the union security clause. The same rule applies to decertification petitions. The Board has held that a union may continue to enforce a union security clause after a decertification petition is filed until the results of the decertification petition are certified. This means that, if a union loses a decertification or deauthorization election but files objections to the election, the union can continue to enforce the union security clause until the objections are ruled on and the results certified.

E. ENFORCEMENT OF A UNION SECURITY CLAUSE

1. Notice of the Union Security Requirement

The most important point to remember in enforcing a union security clause is that responsibility for lawful enforcement lies completely with the union. The Board has held that a union is obligated to notify the employees that their collective bargaining agreement has a union security clause requiring union membership by a specific date and that the employee can be discharged if he fails to pay initiation fees and dues as required. The Board refers to this requirement as the union's fiduciary obligation. A fiduciary obligation is the obligation owed by a person in a position of trust and confidence. So, the Board has established a very high standard for unions to meet.

What if the employer tells the employees

when they are hired that they have to join the union at the specified time? Can the union later discharge an employee who fails to join as required by a union security clause? No. There are numerous Board cases that stress that an employer's notice to the employee is insufficient. If the union wants to enforce a union security clause, it must notify the employee of his obligation.

A union may prepare a letter welcoming each new employee, and informing him of his union obligations. Politely, but clearly, the union should make sure the employee understands he is subject to discharge if he does not join. This letter can be given to the employee directly by the shop steward or union officer or can be mailed to the employee's home. The union should keep a record so that, if necessary, the union can prove that an employee had notice. Unless the union can prove notice, an employee cannot be discharged for failure to comply with a union security clause.

A union has wide discretion in determining its dues policies. But the policy once determined must be applied equally to all employees and all employees must have notice of it. Thus, the union's notice to the employee must specifically tell the employee how much he is obligated to pay; the due date for payment; who and where to pay; installment payment procedures, if any; and grace periods for late payment, if available. The notice must also inform the employee of the availability of dues check-off and how to obtain check-off forms.

2. Notice of a Delinquency

If an employee, despite notice of the union security obligation, fails to join the union or subsequently falls behind in dues payments, the union must send him a discharge warning letter. This second notice must remind the employee of his union security obligation and tell him how much he owes; how the amount was determined; the months for which the dues are owed; and to whom, where, and by what final date the amounts must be paid. The employee must once again be reminded of the availability of installment payments and of dues check-off, if any. The employee must be given a reasonable time to pay the amounts owed. That, of course, depends on the amount. The notice must specifically tell the employee that unless the necessary payment is made by a certain date, or satisfactory arrangements are made for payment by a certain date, the employee will be discharged.

The Board has repeatedly emphasized that the union has a fiduciary duty to make sure that the employee has actual notice of his delinquency and possible discharge. If an employee is sent a letter there must be proof, such as a certified mail-return receipt form, that the letter was received. If an employee denies receiving the letter, the Board will not uphold the discharge in the absence of proof. The union can also personally hand the notice to the employee and have him initial a copy.

Remember that, although a union security clause may lawfully refer to joining the union and most employees, in fact, join, an employee's only obligation is to become a financial core member. An employee cannot be discharged if he refuses to join the union so long as he pays the initiation fees and dues in the same way required of other employees.

The Board will order an improperly discharged employee reinstated to his employment and the union will be required to pay the employee back pay for his lost work. Thus, there can be serious financial consequences if the union fails to meet the notice requirements.

3. Consequences of Late Notice

What if a union does not give an employee notice of his dues obligation until several months after he is hired? Can the union require the employee to pay the past due amounts or has the union forfeited that right? The Board applies a rule of reason in such cases. If a union fails to notify an employee for a reasonably short period of time, the union can give proper notice and can collect the amounts owed retroactively for the entire period. The union, of course, must give the employee reasonable time to make up the amount. There is no hard and fast rule on the period for which a union may retroactively collect dues. It depends on the facts and circumstances. Certainly the longer it waits, the harder it is for a union to justify retroactive payments.

What if the employee actually knows of his dues obligation because the employer or other bargaining unit employees tell him about it? That is not enough. The union has the duty to give notice, and notice from another source does not relieve it of the responsibility.

4. Strict Adherence to the Board's Standards

A discharge for failure to comply with a union security clause will be upheld if the union has fulfilled its duties of giving the employee notice of his union security obligation and notice of his delinquency. The union can even refuse an employee's offer to pay what he owes after the last date stated for payment in the notice provided that all employees are treated in the same fashion. Certainly, the requirements that a union must meet in order to discharge an employee under a union security clause are technical, but they are not too

difficult to meet. Unions get into problems when they attempt to short circuit the process. In the following Board decision, the union probably thought it was meeting its obligation by posting a notice in the plant that certain employees were delinquent. But the Board held that the union had violated its duty of actual notice.

Triple A. Machine Shop, Inc.
239 NLRB No. 69 (1978)
(Boilermakers Local Lodge No. 732)

Decision and Order*

On August 22, 1978, Administrative Law Judge James T. Baker issued the attached Decision in this proceeding. Thereafter, Respondent [the Union] and the General Counsel each filed exceptions and supporting briefs.

Pursuant to the provisions of Section 3(b) of the National Labor Relations Act, as amended, the National Labor Relations Board has delegated its authority in this proceeding to a three-member panel.

The Board has considered the record and the attached Decision in the light of the exceptions and briefs and has decided to affirm the rulings,[1] findings,[2] and conclusions of the Administrative Law Judge, and to adopt his recommended Order, as modified herein.[3]

Respondent [the union] and the Employer are parties to a collective-bargaining agreement which requires all employees to become members of Respondent. Since the contract does not provide for checkoff, Re-

* Some footnotes deleted.

[2] Respondent has excepted to certain credibility findings made by the Administrative Law Judge. It is the Board's established policy not to overrule an Administrative Law Judge's resolutions with respect to credibility unless the clear preponderance of all of the relevant evidence convinces us that the resolutions are incorrect. *Standard Dry Wall Products, Inc.*, 91 NLRB 544 (1950), enfd. 188 F.2d 362 (C.A. 3, 1951). We have carefully examined the record and find no basis for reversing his findings.

spondent requires all members to tender their monthly dues directly.[4] It considers members who have failed to tender dues for 2 or more months to be delinquent. Each month it posts at or near the timeclocks a notice listing such persons. The notices specify the amounts owed and the periods for which they are owed and grant the delinquents 10 days within which to pay the arrearages before the Union seeks their termination.

The Administrative Law Judge found that Respondent breached its fiduciary duty of fairness with respect to employees White, Fillingame, and Gizoni by seeking their termination without providing them with adequate prior notice of their delinquency and by failing to accord them reasonable opportunities to pay their arrearages. In so finding, the Administrative Law Judge rejected Respondent's contention that its notice postings constituted adequate notice to these members, since Respondent was aware that White was on military leave and that Fillingame and Gizoni were on layoff during the period of the posting. With respect to members Dunn and Talley, however, the Administrative Law Judge found that the notice posting constituted sufficient notice because both Dunn and Talley were employed at the plant during the period of the posting and because they admitted they were generally aware of their dues obligations and of the Union's practice of posting monthly a list of delinquent employees. Nevertheless, the Administrative Law Judge concluded that Respondent breached its fiduciary duty of fairness by failing to accord Dunn and Talley reasonable opportunities to pay their arrearages before seeking their termination.

Although we agree with the Administrative Law Judge that Respondent breached its fiduciary duty of fairness with respect to all five of the Charging Parties, we disagree with his finding that Respondent's posting

of a list of delinquent members at or near the timeclocks constituted, in and of itself, adequate notice to Dunn and Talley. The Board had consistently held that a union's fiduciary obligation to its members entails taking "the necessary steps to make certain that a reasonable employee will not fail to meet his membership obligations through ignorance or inadvertence but will do so only as a matter of conscious choice." *Conduction Corp.*, 183 NLRB 419, 426 (1970). In holding a labor organization to this standard we have required that it give the delinquent employee actual as opposed to constructive notice of his dues delinquency[5] and that it provide him with a reasonable opportunity to meet his obligations.[6]

In the instant case, however, the only effort by Respondent to notify Dunn, Talley, and other charging Parties was by posting a notice at or near the timeclocks. Apparently, Respondent was content to leave it to happenstance or to the factory "grape vine" to ensure that Dunn, Talley, and the others[7] received actual notice of their dues delinquency and their possible loss of employment. Under these circumstances, and in view of Dunn's and Talley's credited denials that they had seen the posted notice, we find Respondent breached its fiduciary duty not only by its treatment of Dunn and Talley after July 7, as found by the Administrative Law Judge, but also by the inadequacy of its initial notice procedure.[8]

Order

Pursuant to Section 10(c) of the National Labor Relations Act, as amended, the National Labor Relations Board adopts as its Order the recommended Order of the Administrative Law Judge, as modified below, and

---

[4] The Administrative Law Judge concluded that each of the five Charging Parties had actual notice of their obligations to pay monthly dues, both during periods of employment and during periods of layoff, because they had been provided, upon their initiation into membership, with packets of information which contained letters outlining these responsibilities.

[7] As found by the Administrative Law Judge the remaining Charging Parties were in no position to observe the posted notice inasmuch as they were either on layoff status or on temporary military leave.

[8] In passing, we note that a union could demonstrate that it has met its fiduciary duty to employees in several ways. Thus, for example the union could present credible evidence of personal notice to the employee or offer documentary proof such as a return receipt from a registered letter or certified mail.

hereby orders that the Respondent, its officers, agents, and representatives, shall take the action set forth in the said recommended Order, as so modified.

Appendix
Notice to Members

Posted by Order of the
National Labor Relations Board
An Agency of the United States
Government

WE WILL NOT fail to give reasonable advance notice to our members that they are about to become delinquent in their dues, and our notice to such members shall contain the following: (1) the amount of dues owed, (2) the months for which dues are owed or the method of calculating the pending dues delinquency, and (3) the last day upon which the specified amounts can be paid to the Union.

WE WILL NOT fail to carry out our fiduciary responsibility to our members by failing to give them reasonable notice of their dues delinquency which would authorize us to require the Company to terminate them under the union-security provision of our collective-bargaining agreement with the Company.

WE WILL NOT fail in our fiduciary responsibility to our members by implementing the union-security provision of our contract with the Company in an arbitrary and capricious way so as to lead to the termination of our members or their loss of employment, seniority, or other rights and privileges.

WE WILL NOT cause or attempt to cause Triple A Machine Shop, Inc., d/b/a Triple A South, or any other employer, to discriminate against Oscar Dunn, Roy Fillingame, Byron Gizoni, Raymond Talley and William White, or any other employee, in violation of Section 8(a)(3) of the Act.

WE WILL NOT in any other manner restrain or coerce employees in the exercise of rights guaranteed in Section 7 of the Act, except to the extent that such rights may be affected by our lawful application and implementation of an agreement requiring membership in a labor organization as a condition of employment.

WE WILL notify Triple A Machine Shop, Inc. d/b/a/ Triple A South, in writing, that we withdraw all our objections to the Company employing Oscar Dunn, Roy Fillingame, Byron Gizoni, Raymond Talley, and William White, and in the letter we shall request their full reinstatment and the restoration of their full seniority rights and other rights and privileges as though their employment or recall rights had never been interrupted.

WE WILL make Oscar Dunn, Roy Fillingame, Byron Gizoni, Raymond Talley, and William White whole for any loss of pay suffered by them because of the discrimination against them, plus interest.

WE WILL refund to employees Roy Fillingame and Byron Gizoni the reinstatement fees paid to us by them.

F. RIGHT TO WORK LAWS

So called "right to work" laws are authorized by Section 14(b) of the LMRA, providing: "Nothing in this Act shall be construed as authorizing the execution or application of agreements requiring membership in a labor organization as a condition of employment in any State or Territory in which such execution or application is prohibited by State or Territorial law."

Most right to work laws prohibit all forms of union security, but they do not have to. Under Section 14(b) a state may prohibit all forms of union security, or may permit some forms of union security, but prohibit others. At one time Indiana had a right to work law it has since repealed. The Indiana Supreme Court held that an agency shop was permissible under that law.

If an employee's home office is in a right to work state, but the employee works in another state having no such law, can that employee be required to join a union? The Board has held that the place where an employee works controls. Thus, an employee working in a state where union security clauses are permitted, even though he may have been hired in a right to work state, can be required to join a union, provided the collective bargaining agreement so requires.

An employee in a right to work state who formally joins a union is bound by the constitution and by-laws of the union, as is a member in any other state. If a member does not pay his dues, he can be expelled from membership, sued, or both in the state court for the amount owed. The employee cannot be discharged for not paying the dues because a right to work law prohibits conditioning employment upon the payment of union dues or initiation fees.

Under the duty of fair representation (see Chapter 12), a union must represent all employees fairly whether the employee is a union member or not. A union security clause insures that employees bear their fair share of the union's costs. In contrast, in right to work states, or under contracts that do not contain a union security clause, some employees are free riders on the coat tails of the other employees who do contribute. This is one of the strongest arguments against right to work laws.

G. CONTRACTUAL CHECK-OFF PROVISIONS

1. Termination and Renewal

Section 302(c)(4) permits an employee to sign a written statement authorizing the employer to deduct the employee's initiation fees and monthly dues from his wages and forward them to the union. This is commonly referred to as union dues check-off. An employer's agreement to check off initiation fees and dues as authorized (a contractual "check-off clause") is a mandatory subject of bargaining (see Chapter 5).

The check-off form can be irrevocable for up to a year or until the expiration date of the collective bargaining agreement, whichever occurs first. The form may provide for automatic renewal if the employee does not revoke the check-off within a specified period before its expiration. The Board has held that if the check-off form does not expressly provide for revocation, the check-off authorization is revocable at any time.

Recently the Board has held that a check-off authorization may lawfully remain in effect in the periods between collective bargaining agreements, or even after an employee has resigned from the union, if the form expressly so provides. Otherwise, the authorization remains in effect only during the contract's term. However, if a contract contains a union security clause and an employee signs a check-off card, the employee may revoke his check-off authorization at any time if the union security clause is deauthorized.

2. Consequences of Late Payment to the Union

What is the employee's status if he signs a check-off form, but the initiation fees and dues for some reason are not checked off? What if the employer deducts the proper amounts, but fails to forward them to the union? The courts and Board have held that signing a check-off form is equivalent to tendering dues. The employee is a member in good standing even if the funds are not forwarded to the union and cannot be discharged. It is the union's responsibility to insure compliance with the check-off provision. Section 401(e) of the Labor Management Reporting and Disclosure Act, which governs election procedures, specifically provides:

> No member whose dues have been withheld by his employer for payment to such organization pursuant to his voluntary authorization provided for in a collective bargaining agreement shall be declared ineligible to vote or be a candidate for office in such organization by reason of alleged delay or default in the payment of dues.

What if a union requires that a member be in good standing for a certain number of months before an election to hold office, defining good standing as having paid dues by the tenth day of each month? If an employee has executed a check-off form and the employer pays the union late, the employee will still be in good standing. On the other hand, if an employee has not executed a check-off form and pays his own dues late, he is bound by the by-law provision and will not be in good standing.

Remember, signing a check-off is voluntary. An employee has the right to pay his dues directly if he chooses. If an employee executes a check-off form, however, late payment is the union's responsibility. If the employee decides to pay himself, he is responsible for paying the proper person on time.

Employees sometimes confuse the check-off concept with union security clauses. A contract can have a check-off clause whether or not it contains a union security clause. Further, right to work states cannot prohibit check-off clauses because check-off is not a form of union security.

H. HIRING HALLS

Some people regard an exclusive hiring hall, in which all employees are referred to employment through the union, as a form of union security. It is not. An exclusive hiring hall has to serve everyone, whether a union member or not. The method of referral must be nondiscriminatory. The union cannot give preference to union members. A hiring hall may base referral preference on seniority determined by the number of years of employment in the industry or even on employment within the bargaining unit. Technically, such requirements do not favor union members because nonunion members may also have experience in the industry or in the bargaining unit. However, preference for referral cannot be based on years of union membership. Under Section 8(f), a hiring hall in the construction industry can base referral priority on length of service with a specific employer; with employers within a multiemployer association; or with employers who, although not association members, agree to be bound by the multiemployer contract while performing work within the union's geographical jurisdiction.

The Board has upheld a union's right to make the union steward the first referral to a new job site. The Board has held that this is a reasonable requirement to make sure the contract is complied with. The Board regards the requirement that a shop steward be referred to a job first as being similar to the right of an industrial union to require that shop stewards be given preference for work on a certain shift or on overtime to insure that someone is present to enforce the collective bargaining agreement. (See Chapter 4.)

Since hiring halls are not a form of union security, they cannot be regulated or prohibited in right to work states.

Summary   This chapter covered union membership and union security, focusing on the internal relationship between a union and its members. At common law, a union is an unincorporated association, simply a combination of its members. It has no legal existence apart from its members and cannot sue or be sued as an entity.

The LMRA Section 301 specifically provides that a labor organization may sue or be sued as an entity in federal courts to enforce a contract. The old common law rules still apply, however, on the many aspects of unions not governed by federal law.

The courts have traditionally held that the relationship between the union and its members is contractual. The constitution and by-laws of the union are the contract. A union that wants to enforce a by-law provision against a member must file such a suit as a class action in the state courts. Such a suit over an internal union matter is not governed by federal law.

Since a union was regarded as a private association at common law, the courts held that a union had the right to admit whomever it wished as a member, the same as any other fraternal organization or social club. That rule still basically applies except that unions can no longer exclude minorities from membership because of the Civil Rights Act.

Section 8(a)(3) permits a company and a union to negotiate an agreement requiring union membership as a condition of employment on or after the thirtieth day following the beginning of employment or the effective date of the contract, whichever comes later. Under Section 8(f) membership can be required after seven days in the construction industry. Although the statute refers to membership, an employee can only be required to be a "financial core member." A financial core member must pay the initiation fees and dues, but does not formally become a member, and is thus not subject to union discipline. Such an employee is entitled to the same representation and contract benefits as anyone else, but is not entitled to participate in internal union matters such as elections of union officers or voting on a contract. An employee can be required to pay initiation fees and dues, but not assessments. There is a distinction between the union's internal right to discipline and the right to have an employee discharged for nonmembership. The union can fine a member or even expel him from membership for violating the union's by-laws or policies. But an employee cannot be discharged except for failure to tender his initiation fees or dues.

If the union rejects an employee who is willing to be a full union member or expels an employee for any reason other than failure to tender initiation fees and dues, the union cannot require that the employee be discharged.

The critical point in enforcing a union security clause is that responsibility for proper enforcement lies completely with the union. The union has a fiduciary obligation to give employees detailed information of their obligation under a union security clause. Employees who are delinquent must be given a specific warning that they are delinquent and will be discharged. Union attempts to short circuit this procedure may result in an invalid discharge and a substantial back pay liability. But a union that establishes proper procedures and applies them uniformly can strictly enforce a union security clause.

Hiring halls and contractual check-off provisions are not forms of union security. They are permitted even if a contract does not have a union security clause and also in a right to work state. An exclusive hiring hall has to serve all employees, whether they are union members or not. The method of referral must be nondiscriminatory. However, the Board has upheld the right of unions to refer a union steward first to a new job site. This is a reasonable requirement to insure that the contract is lived up to.

Review Questions:

1. What is a union at common law?

2. Can a union be sued in its own name as an entity under the common law?

3. How did federal law change the method of suing a union for violations of federal statutes?

4. Can a money judgment against a union be collected against the individual members under Section 301 as is the case at common law?

5. How are the internal union rights and responsibilities of union members determined?

6. If a union rejects an employee who is willing to join the union as required by a union security clause, can the union have the employee discharged for failure to be a union member?

7. Can a union's dues check-off be irrevocable?

8. If a union expels a member, can the union require that the employee be discharged under a union security clause?

9. Can a union require that an expelled member continue paying periodic dues, as a kind of service charge, since the employee still has all contractual benefits?

10. Why would an employee be willing to pay the union's initiation fees and dues, but not want to become a full member?

11. Does a union security clause remain in effect as a condition of employment after the contract expires?

12. What can be done in a right to work state if a member does not pay his dues?

13. Can an exclusive hiring hall serve only union members?

14. Can an employee be discharged for late payment of union dues?

15. Who is responsible for the enforcement of a union security clause?

16. If an employee knows that he is delinquent in paying dues even though the union has failed to notify him, can the employee be discharged for nonpayment?

(Answers to review questions appear at end of book.)

1. A union may require an employer to discharge an employee covered by a union security clause for failure to tender the union's regular initiation fees or his periodic dues. However, the union has a fiduciary obligation to inform the employee of the delinquency prior to taking such action so that the employee may protect his job. *H. C. Macaulay Foundry Co. v NLRB*, 553 F.2d 1198, 95 LRRM 2581 (9th Cir. 1977); *John J. Roche & Co., Inc.*, 231 NLRB No. 180, 96 LRRM 1281 (1977).

Basic Legal Principles

2. A union cannot require an employer to discharge an employee covered by a union security agreement for failure to pay fines or assessments. Assessments are payments to a special fund or for a special purpose. *Painters Local 1627*, 233 NLRB No. 118, 97 LRRM 1010 (1977); *Longshoremen Local 13*, 228 NLRB No. 174, 96 LRRM 1450 (1977); *Pittsburgh Press Co.*, 241 NLRB No. 99, 100 LRRM 1542 (1979).

3. Only "financial core membership," not full membership, can be required under a union security clause. The union cannot hold financial core members to stricter payment requirements than full members. *NLRB v. General Motors Corp.*, 373 U.S. 734, 53 LRRM 2313 (1963). *Service Employees Local 680*, 232 NLRB No. 49, 97 LRRM 1186 (1977); *Hospital and Nursing Home Employees Local 113*, 228 NLRB No. 197, 96 LRRM 1422, *enforced*, 567 F.2d 831, 97 LRRM 2160 (8th Cir. 1977).

4. Supervisors returning to the bargaining unit are generally treated as "new employees" with 30 days to join the union for union security purposes. However, supervisors who shuttle between supervisory and bargaining unit positions may be required to rejoin the union immediately if there is a reasonable expectation when an individual becomes a supervisor that he might return to the unit. *Electrical Workers Local 399*, 200 NLRB 1050, 82 LRRM 1077 (1972), *enforced*, 499 F.2d 56, 86 LRRM 2826 (7th Cir. 1974); *A. O. Smith Corp.*, 227 NLRB No. 116, 94 LRRM 1115 (1977).

5. A union cannot discriminate between members and nonmembers in the operation of an exclusive hiring hall. However, preference based on length of service in the industry (not length of union membership) is lawful if the procedure is not discriminatorily applied. *Carpenters Local 1089*, 233 NLRB No. 47, 96 LRRM 1508 (1977); *Plumbers Local 630*, 222 NLRB No. 82, 91 LRRM 1224 (1976); *Carpenters District Council of Denver*, 222 NLRB No. 86, 91 LRRM 1178 (1976); *Plumbers Local 121*, 223 NLRB No.

193, 92 LRRM 1185 (1976); *Teamsters Local 83*, 243 NLRB No. 26, 101 LRRM 1508 (1979).

6. A union with an exclusive hiring hall can legally insist that the first employee referred to a job be a shop steward to insure compliance with the collective bargaining agreement. *Teamsters Local 959*, 239 NLRB No. 193, 100 LRRM 1160 (1979).

7. If the union rejects an employee as a member or expels him for any reason other than the failure to pay his initiation fees and dues, the union cannot request the employee's discharge for failure to be a member or pay dues. *H.C. Macaulay Foundry Co. v. NLRB*, 553 F.2d 1198, 95 LRRM 2581 (9th Cir. 1977); *Pen & Pencil Workers*, 91 NLRB No. 155, 26 LRRM 1583 (1950).

8. A union cannot request the discharge of an employee for non-payment of his initiation fees or dues unless the union first informs the delinquent employee in writing of his delinquency. The notice must state the amount owed, the months for which owed or the method of calculating the amount; the payment procedures, including reasonable time to pay; and the last day the employee can pay the amount owed before being discharged. *Boilermakers Local 732*, 239 NLRB No. 69, 99 LRRM 1706 (1978); *District 9, Machinists*, 237 NLRB No. 207, 99 LRRM 1133 (1978); *Teamsters Local 122*, 203 NLRB No. 157, 83 LRRM 1235, *enforced*, 509 F.2d 1160, 87 LRRM 3274 (1st Cir. 1974).

9. Check-off authorizations that do not expressly contain any limitation on their revocation are revocable at will. *Trico Products Corp.*, 238 NLRB No. 184, 99 LRRM 1473 (1978); *Cameron Iron Works, Inc.*, 235 NLRB No. 47, 97 LRRM 1516 (1978); *Luke Construction Co., Inc.*, 211 NLRB 602, 87 LRRM 1087 (1974). As an exception, a check-off authorization may remain in effect according to its terms between contracts or even after a member has resigned from the union. *Frito-Lay, Inc.*, 243 NLRB No. 16, 101 LRRM 1390 (1979); *Carpenters Council of San Diego*, 243 NLRB No. 17, 101 LRRM 1394 (1979).

10. A union security clause terminates automatically at the expiration of the collective bargaining agreement and members are thereafter free to resign from the union and cease paying dues until such time as a new contract is agreed to. *Trico Products Corp.*, 238 NLRB No. 184, 99 LRRM 1473 (1978); *Auto Workers Local 1756*, 240 NLRB No. 13, 100 LRRM 1208 (1979).

Recommended Reading   "Political Contributions and Tax-Exempt Status for Labor Organizations," 1974 *Wash. U.L.Q.* 139 (1974)

"Restrictions on the Right to Resign: Can a Member's Freedom to 'Escape the

Union Rule' Be Overcome By Union Boiler Plate?," 42 *Geo. Wash. L. Rev.* 397 (1974)

"Union Dues Checkoff as a Subject in Labor-Management Negotiations: Good Faith Bargaining and NLRB Remedies," 39 *Fordham L. Rev.* 299 (1970).

Gibson Wilhoit, III, "Can a State Right to Work Law Prohibit The Union Operated Hiring Hall?," 26 *Lab. L.J.* 301 (1975)

Chapter Eleven

Rights and Responsibilities of Union Members

The rights and responsibilities of union members to the union are governed by the Landrum–Griffin Act, formally the Labor–Management Reporting and Disclosure Act of 1959 (LMRDA). It is the basic federal legislation pertaining to individual rights of union members. The most important section of the law covering individual rights is Title I, entitled the "Bill of Rights of Members of Labor Organizations."

A. AN OVERVIEW OF THE "BILL OF RIGHTS" FOR UNION MEMBERS

Section 101(a)(1) of the LMRDA gives every union member equal rights. It states: "Every member of a labor organization shall have equal rights and privileges within such organization to nominate candidates, to vote in elections or referendums of the labor organization, to attend membership meetings, and to participate in the deliberations and voting upon the business of such meetings, subject to reasonable rules and regulations in such organization's constitution and by-laws."

1. Section 101(a)(1): The Meaning of Equal Rights

Section 101(a)(1) does not grant any specific rights, nor does it require that a union grant its members any specific rights. It simply requires that every member have an equal chance to exercise the rights established by the union's constitution and by-laws. Some candidates for union office have filed suits challenging union requirements for holding office such as attending a certain percentage of the union's meetings. They have alleged that, in violation of Section 101(a)(1), the restrictions deny members the equal right to nominate candidates of their choice. The courts have uniformly rejected these suits, holding that the equal rights provision of Section 101(a)(1) does not apply, because all members have an *equal right* to nominate those who are eligible. The result would be different if some members were barred from the nominations meeting; then, some members would have the right to nominate while others would have no right at all. That would violate Section 101(a)(1). Thus, the basic key to understanding Section 101(a)(1) is that the section does not establish rights, but only requires that if a right is established every member must enjoy it.

Section 101(a)(1) contains an exception that allows unions to establish reasonable rules and regulations on the exercise of membership equal rights. For example, a union can establish membership divisions. Matters such as a collective bargaining agreement covering the division employees can be voted on only by members of a division. That is a lawful, reasonable regulation, even though union members who were not members of that division are not permitted to vote.

2. Section 101(a)(3): Dues Increases

Section 101(a)(3) regulates the procedure for enacting or increasing union dues, initiation fees, and assessments. The most important requirements are that a dues increase must be passed by a *secret* vote and that there must be reasonable notice of the intention to vote. The notice must specifically state that a *vote* will be taken. A notice that dues will be the subject of a meeting that does not indicate that a vote will be taken is insufficient.

It is a common misconception that the only way a local union can increase its dues is by a vote of the local's members. That is incorrect. Under Section 101(a)(3)(B), local dues can be increased by action at an international convention or by a secret ballot referendum of the entire international membership.

Section 101(a)(4) governs a member's right to sue the union. A union cannot bar its members from suing it, but it can require a member to exhaust reasonable internal union remedies for up to, but not beyond, four months before filing suit. Section 101(a)(5) provides procedural safeguards to insure a fair hearing in internal union disciplinary proceedings. Sections 101(a)(4) and (5) are discussed fully below.

3. Section 101(b): The Primacy of the LMRDA Over the Union's By-Laws

Finally, Section 101(b) states: "Any provision of the constitution and by-laws of any labor organization which is inconsistent with the provisions of this section shall be of no force or effect." This is a very important section. Sometimes a union leader, if told that some particular union practice does not meet Landrum–Griffin requirements, replies that the practice is permitted by the union's constitution and by-laws. The answer to that is clear. The union's constitution and by-laws cannot conflict with the law's requirements. A union's constitution and by-laws are a contract and are binding on the members, except in those areas governed by federal law (see Chapter 10). In those areas (such as Landrum–Griffin Title I rights), the federal law prevails over inconsistent union provisions.

Section 102 deals with civil enforcement of Title I and establishes a member's right to file suit to enforce the Bill of Rights. Title I is unique. Most of the Landrum–Griffin Act is enforced by the Department of Labor, but Title I is enforced by individual members going directly to court, subject to internal exhaustion requirements under Section 101(a)(4) (see below).

Section 103, "Retention of Rights," insures that the law does not take away any rights. Thus, if a union's constitution and by-laws establish a higher standard of conduct on a specific matter than the law requires, the union cannot apply the lower legal standard; the higher union standard must prevail. Also, state laws continue to apply where applicable. A few states have detailed laws governing internal union activities and individual member rights. Union members may continue to exercise their rights under state law as well as Landrum–Griffin.

Under Section 104 every employee has a right to a copy of his collective bargaining agreement. Section 105 requires every labor organization to inform its members concerning the provisions of the LMRDA. These are simple requirements routinely complied with.

B. COVERAGE OF THE LABOR–MANAGEMENT REPORTING AND DISCLOSURE ACT

1. Definition of a Union Member

Who is covered by the law? Section 101(a) grants rights to every *member* of a labor organization. The limitation on rights to union members is different from the Labor Management Relations Act, which covers all "employees" (see Chapter 1). Thus, a bargaining unit employee who is not a union member has no rights under Landrum–Griffin. If the union's by-laws require a vote to ratify collective bargaining agreements, all union members in the bargaining unit have an equal right to vote on the contract, but nonmember employees have no such right under Landrum–Griffin.

Section 3(o) states: "Member, or member in good standing when used in reference to a labor organization, includes *any person who has fulfilled the requirements for membership* in such organization, and who neither has voluntarily withdrawn from membership nor has been expelled or suspended from membership after appropriate proceedings . . ." (emphasis added). Suppose a union requires that a person take an oath before becoming a member. Is it possible that a person can be a "member" covered by Landrum–Griffin even before

taking the oath if he meets all other union requirements? What if, for example, an employee has applied for membership and tendered his initiation fees, but has yet to attend the membership initiation ceremony? Section 3(o) defines a member as someone who has *fulfilled the requirements for membership.* The law does not require that the person be *admitted* to membership to be classified as a member. The important factor is whether the remaining requirements to become a formal member are simple administrative acts. An initiation ceremory is an administrative act. If an employee has been employed for 30 days and if he has fulfilled all the requirements for membership except to be formally initiated, the courts would probably say that the employee is a member for purposes of the rights guaranteed under Landrum–Griffin.

2. Arbitrary Denial of Admission

The definition of member is very carefully drafted. Its purpose is to prevent a union from arbitrarily denying membership to people who meet all the requirements. Historically, some unions restricted their *membership* to only a few of the employees they represented. Since only union members could vote, relatively few persons could control the destiny of many. The definition of member was intended to prevent these restrictions. Now if employees meet the requirements for membership but the union arbitrarily denies it, the employee is classified as a member under the LMRDA and entitled to the rights that the statute grants to members. He would have the same right as other members to vote on union contracts, for example. Note, however, that the Act does not regulate requirements for union membership—that is still an internal union matter.

There is a distinction between someone

who voluntarily chooses not to become a member and someone who is denied membership. The statutory definition is designed to provide membership rights to employees who seek membership but are arbitrarily denied it. If membership is open, but persons choose not to join, they are not entitled to the member rights the LMRDA protects.

3. Membership Votes for Admission

What if a union requires a membership vote before an applicant is admitted to membership? When is an applicant who has fulfilled all membership requirements except the vote considered a member under the LMRDA? Some courts have held that a person is not a member as defined in Section 3(o) until he is voted in. Thus, a person who is brought up for membership and rejected would not be classified as a member because all the requirements for membership would not have been met. However, if a union arbitrarily refused to bring a person's name up for consideration, the person would probably be classified as a member under the statute. This area of the law has not been fully developed by the courts. The definition of a member must be applied in light of the Act's intent to prevent a union from arbitrarily denying membership to people who meet the requirements and want to join and enjoy the benefits of membership.

4. Rights of Officers under the LMRDA

The rights of union officers under the LMRDA is an important recurring issue. Title I refers to membership rights, but does not refer to officer's rights or to the right to hold office. What if a union officer is removed from his office because he spoke out against a union policy approved by the union executive

board, but which he personally opposed? Section 101(a)(2) protects the right of members to free speech and Section 101(a)(5) requires that a member be given a hearing before being disciplined. Has an officer been "disciplined" if he is removed from his office in retaliation for expressing his views on a union matter? Have the officer's free speech rights been violated and is he entitled to a hearing before being removed from office?

a. Right to a Hearing Before Removal From Office

The courts that have considered these questions have held that Title I protects an officer's right to membership, but not necessarily the right to hold office. Most courts have reasoned that, since the right to hold office is not expressly protected by Title I, an officer does not have a right to a hearing before being removed from office. This rule may seem harsh at first, but there is actually strong logic supporting it. There are many reasons for which a union may have a legitimate need to remove an officer immediately. If an officer has been misappropriating union funds, the union would want to remove him right away ay. Hearings can go on for a long time; therefore, the courts have given greater weight to the union's need for prompt removal of an incompetent officer than to the need for a hearing.

b. Removal From Office as Discipline

Although all courts basically agree that the union's legitimate need to remove an officer immediately in some cases overrides the hearing requirements under Section 101(a)(5), most courts also agree that an officer retains the same Title I rights, such as free speech, as any other member. An officer cannot be disciplined for exercising those rights. Most courts also agree that removing a member from office in retaliation for exercising Title I rights is discipline. An officer removed in retaliation for exercising his free speech rights, for example, may file suit under LMRDA Section 102 authorizing civil suits for violations of Title I. The officer can seek reinstatement to office and monetary damages. But, the officer is not entitled to an internal union hearing before he is removed. The officer's only recourse is a direct civil suit if the removal is in retaliation for the officer's exercise of his Title I rights.

One important reservation must be stressed. While a majority of the courts apply the reasoning discussed above, not all courts agree. A minority of courts take the view that an officer is not protected at all under Title I. Under this approach, an officer can be removed for any reason so long as his membership rights, other than holding office, are not affected. These courts have reasoned that if an officer disagrees with union policy, he should resign from his position. Once he resigns, he has the same free speech rights as any other member to express his opinions. Of course, even the courts that do not protect the right to hold office under Title I would still protect the officer's rights as a member. Under this view, an officer cannot be suspended or expelled from membership in retaliation for opposing union policies even though he can be removed from office.

c. Removal of Appointed Officers

Although there have not been many decisions on the point, courts seem to make some distinction between removal of appointed or elected officers. Courts tend to give unions greater freedom in removing appointed officers on the theory that appointed officials must be loyal to the person appointing them. Also, some courts, applying the concept of insubordination, have reasoned that an officer

who refuses to carry out union policy may be removed from office. Thus, a business agent's right to argue against the business manager's policies may be protected under Title I. If the business agent goes even further, and either refuses to carry out the policy or tries to undermine it, he may have exceeded his free speech rights and his removal may be lawful. This is an area of Title I litigation on which the principles are still being developed.

Remember, the statutory right to remove an officer without a hearing is subject to any restrictions on removal or hearing requirements established under the union's constitution and by-laws. As discussed above, a union must follow its own constitution and by-laws if they establish a higher standard than the LMRDA, but it is bound by the Act's standards if the union's constitution and by-laws set a lower standard or are silent on a point. Thus, some union constitutions might not allow a business manager or president to remove another elected officer without a hearing (even though the LMRDA does permit it), but might authorize the removal of an appointed officer.

5. Election Procedures: Title I vs. Title IV

Other than establishing an equal right for all members to nominate and vote, Title I does not regulate internal union election procedures. Union elections are regulated by Title IV. Most of its provisions are administrative and it is a matter of reading the requirements and following them.

a. Major Provisions of Title IV

A local union must elect officers at least once every three years by secret ballot (Section 401(b)). The union must mail a notice of the election to each member to his last known home address at least 15 days before the election (Section 401(e)). A union, upon a candidate's request, must distribute the candidate's campaign literature to all union members in good standing at the candidate's expense. A candidate is entitled to inspect a list of persons required to be members pursuant to a union security clause once within the 30 days prior to the election. A union is prohibited from discriminating between candidates with respect to distribution of literature and the inspection of membership lists (Section 401(c)). Union funds cannot be used to promote anyone's candidacy (Section 401(g)). Section 401(e) requires that all members be given a reasonable opportunity to nominate candidates. Every member in good standing must be eligible to be a candidate and hold office subject to Section 504 (prohibiting certain persons from holding office) and reasonable uniformly imposed qualifications for office. The United States Department of Labor publishes a pamphlet entitled "Electing Union Officers," which covers nomination and election procedures in detail. This pamphlet is must reading for all candidates for union office and anyone who oversees an election.

b. Title IV as the Exclusive Remedy for Election Challenges

The courts have held that Title IV, not Title I, protects the right to run for office. Title IV is also the exclusive federal remedy for challenging election irregularities. Section 403 preserves a limited state court remedy to enforce a union's constitution and by-laws on elections before an election is held, but provides that Title IV is the exclusive remedy for challenging an election that has been held.

There are important procedural distinctions between Titles I and IV. An individual must bring his own suit to enforce rights guaranteed under Title I. In contrast, the Department of Labor enforces Title IV through individual complaints filed with it. The Department of Labor investigates the complaint and files suit if it determines that there is probable cause to believe that Title IV has been violated. The member cannot file suit directly on his own. However, if the Department of Labor files suit, the member is permitted to intervene in the case. Complaints under Title IV may challenge an election only after the election is held, not before. A federal court injunction cannot be used to prevent an election from being held.

Why did Congress structure the law so that an action challenging election irregularities can be brought only under Title IV after the election, but not under Title I beforehand? Congress preferred the risk of an improper election to the risks of delayed elections because it did not want elections to be delayed for years.

If a member were to get an injunction against an election, who would be the union officers in the meantime? Do the old officers hold over after their terms expire or not? No one can be sure. It might be years before a contested election was resolved in the courts. Congress wanted to avoid any instability that would hamper the legitimate operations of the union.

C. THE MEMBER'S RIGHT OF FREE SPEECH

1. The "Absolute" Free Speech Right

Suppose a union member accuses the union president of using union funds for personal use. The member, a political opponent of the president, makes the charge at the union meeting in the hope that it will arouse union opposition to the president. The charge is false and would constitute slander in court. Can the union president bring charges under the union's constitution against his opponent for attacking his character? Can the member be fined, suspended, or perhaps expelled for his slanderous remarks?

No, he cannot. Under LMRDA, Section 101(a)(2) a member has virtually an *absolute* right of free speech. The member's statements may be outrageous and totally unfounded; they might be considered as slanderous in a court action—that does not matter. Except for the narrow exceptions discussed below, a member has an absolute right to say whatever he wishes.

2. Common Law Remedies Against False Statements

Although a member cannot be disciplined by the union for what he says, a member who has been falsely accused may personally bring a civil suit for libel or slander. Libel is a written falsehood; slander is a spoken falsehood. Libel and slander are jointly referred to as defamation. However, the courts have treated a union officer as a "public figure" for the purpose of winning a defamation suit. The Supreme Court has held that if a false statement is made about a politician or "public figure," the public figure cannot successfully sue for defamation unless he proves not only that the statement was false, but also that the statement was malicious. Malice means that (1) a person knows a statement is false but makes it anyway; or (2) a person does not know whether a serious accusation is true or not, but makes the statement anyhow without trying to verify it (technically termed intentional disregard of the truth). These same two requirements apply to defamatory accusations against a union officer. Thus, if a union officer is defamed by a member, the officer must prove not only that the statement is false, but also that it is malicious.

Even if a statement is defamatory and made with malice, in which case the member might be subject to successful suit by the officer, the member still is not subject to internal union discipline. The statutory right to free speech applies even though the statements are defamatory.

3. Exceptions to Membership Free Speech

There are some exceptions to a member's free speech. Section 101(a)(2) has a proviso stating: "Provided, that nothing herein shall be construed to impair the right of a labor organization to adopt and enforce reasonable rules as to the responsibility of every member toward the organization as an institution and to his refraining from conduct that would interfere with the performance of its legal or contractual obligations."

a. Dual Unionism

The exception permitting a union to enforce reasonable rules on the responsibility of every member toward the organization applies to dual unionism. Dual unionism means supporting another union, such as advocating that the members leave their union and join another. A union can, for example, prohibit a member from standing up at a union meeting and urging everybody to join another union. Rules against dual unionism are reasonable rules covering responsibility of every member towards the organization as an institution.

The free speech exceptions are narrowly applied. If a member at a union meeting severely criticizes the union's operations, even without good reason, but does not advocate any other union in its place, the criticism is protected free speech. A union cannot prevent criticism on the grounds that it violates the member's responsibility to the organization as an institution. The law regards criticism as beneficial. A member can be stopped only if the member steps over the line from criticism to advocating another union.

There are some unexpected twists in the law on dual unionism. If a member files a decertification petition he is subject to union discipline. The NLRB has held, however, that a member can be expelled from the union as discipline for filing a decertification petition, but cannot be fined. Why the distinction? Isn't expulsion more severe than a fine? The reason for expulsion instead of a fine is to minimize the conflict between the individual's statutory right under the LMRA to file a decertification petition and the union's right to protect its existence as the employees' representative. If a member is so hostile that he seeks to decertify the union, the union should be able to protect itself by expelling that person. On the other hand, expelling the member, in context, is not a great penalty because obviously the person is not interested in the union. A monetary fine is, therefore, a greater penalty than expulsion. That is why, in resolving the conflicting interests of the union and the member, the Board has held that it is unlawful to expel a member for filing a certification petition, but not to fine him.

b. Interference With Legal or Contractual Obligations

The second exception to a members' free speech right is that a union can prevent conduct that interferes with the performance of its legal or contractual obligations. Under this exception, a union, for example, can discipline participants in a wildcat strike. If members engage in a wildcat strike, the union may be sued for breach of its no-strike clause. Thus, a union can prevent its members from interfering with the union's performance of its legal or contractual obligations by engag-

ing in a strike, a slowdown or other unlawful conduct. The union can prohibit discussion of illegal conduct at its meetings and can fine members for advocating or participating in such conduct.

Although the union has the right to discipline a member under the limited freedom of speech exceptions, the member is entitled to a hearing first under Section 101(a)(5) (Safeguards Against Improper Discipline). Even though a union can discipline members for activity such as dual unionism or advocating wildcat strikes, a hearing is necessary before a member can be disciplined for any reason except failure to pay dues. There are no other exceptions. A hearing is required regardless of how flagrant a violation may have been or how clear the evidence. Congress apparently did not require a hearing before disciplining a member for failure to pay dues because there is not a factual issue and discipline prevents a person from enjoying the benefits of union membership without paying for them pending a hearing.

D. UNION'S DISCIPLINARY AUTHORITY OVER ITS MEMBERS

1. Union's Authority to Establish Grounds for Discipline

At common law the union, as a private unincorporated association, had a virtually unlimited right to fine or discipline its members, subject only to whatever limitations on discipline or procedural requirements were established by its own constitution and by-laws. Under the "contract theory" (see Chapter 10), the constitution and by-laws formed a contract binding upon all the members.

Even under Landrum–Griffin, the union still retains broad authority over its members. A union cannot discipline a member without a hearing, except for nonpayment of dues. A union cannot discipline a member for exercising any of the rights protected under the Bill of Rights. Further, as discussed below, a union cannot discipline members for exercising rights protected under the Labor Management Relations Act. But, it cannot be overemphasized that these restrictions have limited scope. Congress intended for most discipline to remain solely an internal union matter. To a great extent, unions still have the right to decide what actions to prohibit and what discipline to impose.

The Supreme Court has held that a union has the right, through its trial board, to determine whether its constitution and by-laws have been violated. A court cannot substitute its judgment for the union's. The Supreme Court stated that if a member appeals his discipline to court, the court must uphold the union's decision on discipline as long as it is supported by some credible evidence. Also, the grounds for discipline do not have to be spelled out in detail in the union's constitution and by-laws. The Supreme Court's decision recognizes Congress' intent that unions regulate their own affairs. Of course, the courts will more closely scrutinize a union's actions that appear to impinge upon statutorily protected rights.

2. Discipline for Crossing a Picket Line

A recurring issue under Title I of the LMRDA is a union's right to discipline its members for crossing a picket line. Generally, unions have the right to fine or otherwise discipline union members for crossing a lawful authorized lawful picket line. (See Chapter 7 discussing permissible picketing and the right to honor picket lines, etc.). A member's duty to respect a picket line established by his own union is a responsibility of the member to the union, one of the exceptions to membership free speech.

Some argued that a union violated Section 8(b)(1)(A) of the LMRA by disciplining members who refused to join in the union's strike. It was argued that the discipline coerced the employees in the exercise of their right under Section 7 not to engage in concerted activity. In *Allis-Chalmers Mfg. Co.*, the Supreme Court rejected this argument.[1] It extensively reviewed the LMRA legislative history and concluded that Congress had not intended to interfere in the union's traditional power to maintain control and unity during a strike.

Although a union may fine a member who crosses its picket line, the Supreme Court and the NLRB have held, in a series of cases, that if a member resigns from the union, even after a strike has begun, the member cannot be disciplined for any strike conduct occurring after the effective date of the resignation. A resignation is generally effective at the time received. A member can resign at the beginning of a strike, cross the picket line, return to work, and be immune from union discipline. If the member crosses the picket line without resigning, and subsequently resigns, he can be disciplined for conduct occuring before the resignation is received by the union.

Some unions have tried to pass constitutional or by-law provisions that prohibit a member from resigning during or immediately before a strike. So far, the NLRB has found that the restrictions in the cases reaching it are an unreasonable limitation on an employee's right to refrain from union activities, and thus violate Sections 7 and 8(b)(1)(A) of the LMRA. Some of the Board decisions indicate, however, that a union, in principle, can lawfully restrict the right to resign if there is a reasonable period during which the mem-

[1] See legal principle 13.

bers are free to resign, including some time during the strike, and if the procedures are not cumbersome for those wishing to resign. Any such restriction would have to be carefully drafted based on the union's specific situation. One court of appeals, reversing the Board, upheld a union's constitutional provision prohibiting a member from resigning during a strike, or within 14 days preceding a strike, and crossing the union's picket line. The court upheld the union's fine of members who crossed its picket line in violation of the constitutional provision, even though the members had resigned from the union. Because of the conflict between the Board and the court, this issue may be resolved by the Supreme Court.

3. Discipline of Supervisors

Questions frequently arise about a union's right to fine supervisors who are union members. The law does not prohibit supervisors from remaining in a union if they wish. It is especially common in craft unions for supervisors to remain union members. The union, through its constitution and by-laws, need not allow supervisors to be members. Further, employers can require that supervisors resign from their union. The NLRB has held that an employer can lawfully discharge a supervisor who refuses to resign because a supervisor has no statutory right to engage in union activity.

a. Crossing the Union's Picket Line

If a supervisor is a union member, but continues to work during a strike, can the union discipline him for crossing the picket line and continuing to work? As is frequently the case in legal questions, it depends on the facts. If a supervisor crosses the line but only does supervisory work, he cannot be disciplined by the union. This rule is based on Section 8(b)(1) that makes it an unfair labor practice for a labor organization to restrain or coerce an employer in selecting his representative for the purpose of collective bargaining or the adjustment of grievances. The NLRB's view is that if a supervisor is just doing supervisory functions during a strike, he cannot be disciplined by the union for crossing the picket line. The discipline would have an intimidating effect on the supervisor and thus interfere in the employer's selection of his representative for bargaining or adjusting grievances in violation of Section 8(b)(1).

b. Doing Bargaining Unit Work During a Strike

In contrast, under the Supreme Court's decision in *Florida Power and Light,* a supervisor can be fined for doing bargaining unit work during a strike.[2] The Court reasoned that a supervisor doing bargaining unit work is not engaged in a supervisory or bargaining function. Discipline, therefore, does not interfere in the employer's selection of his bargaining representative.

The Board is currently split on the proper implementation of the *Florida Light* decision. The Board's three-member majority opinion is that a supervisor may be disciplined for crossing the union's picket line and doing "more than a minimal amount" of bargaining unit work. One member of the three is also of the opinion that supervisors may be fined for doing any bargaining unit work during a strike. The two dissenting members' opinion is that a supervisor can be fined only for doing more bargaining unit work during a strike than he did before the strike. Eventually, the Supreme Court may have to resolve this issue.

[2] See legal principle 11.

c. Supervisor Conduct in Administering the Collective Bargaining Agreement

Apart from a strike, what right does a union have to fine a supervisor member because of actions arising during the term of the collective bargaining agreement? Suppose a supervisor is a union member, but is responsible for giving the employer's answer to first-step grievances. The collective bargaining agreement provides that overtime must first be offered to the most senior employee. The supervisor, who is a union member, offers overtime work to an employee with lower seniority. He has violated the contract, but can he be disciplined? No, because the supervisor cannot be disciplined if he is acting in a bargaining capacity for his employer. Acting in a bargaining capacity includes administering and interpreting the contract (whether the supervisor is right or wrong) and resolving grievances.

4. Union Discipline to Maintain Production Limits

Suppose a union, to protect declining jobs, sets a production quota on the number of units that its members can produce in a day. The union also prohibits employees from working overtime. Can a union fine a member for failure to follow these restrictions? Under the Supreme Court's decision in *Scofield v. NLRB*, a union can maintain production quotas and enforce them through membership fines.[3] However, the quota cannot be inconsistent with terms of the collective bargaining agreement.

In *Scofield*, the contract provided for piece work. The union limited the number of units any employee-member could put out in a day. If the employee-member put out more

units, he was prohibited from collecting additional pay so there was no incentive to produce more. The union enforced the rule through fines. The Supreme Court held that the production restriction was lawful and could be enforced by a fine. The quota did not violate the collective bargaining agreement because the contract did not prohibit the employees from stopping production when they reached the point established by the union. Also, the union never refused to bargain with the company about the quota. Thus, the union was not compelling its members to engage in an unlawful conduct.

The Court noted that under LMRA Section 8(b)(1), a union is "free to enforce a properly adopted rule which reflects a legitimate union interest, impairs no policy Congress has imbedded in the labor laws, and is reasonably enforced against union members who are free to leave and escape the rule." The Court's reference to the member's freedom to leave the union is based upon the concept of the "financial core" member (see Chapter 10). The Court generally has stressed, in cases involving a union's right to fine members, that any member can avoid union discipline altogether, even if there is a union security clause in the collective bargaining agreement, by resigning from the union and becoming a financial core member.

Some contracts require mandatory overtime, while others make overtime voluntary. If overtime is voluntary under a contract, can a union enforce a union rule prohibiting employees from working overtime? Such a rule is probably lawful under the *Scofield* decision. The rule does not violate the collective bargaining agreement. In contrast, if the contract makes overtime mandatory, the union cannot enforce a rule against accepting overtime contrary to the agreement. That violates the union's duty of good faith bargaining (see Chapter 5).

[3] See legal principle 14.

5. Discipline for Filing an NLRB Charge

The Board has held that a member cannot be disciplined for filing a charge against the union with the NLRB. A member can be expelled for filing a decertification petition; however, the Board has held that a member has an absolute right to file an unfair labor practice charge against the union or to testify in Board proceedings against the union.

E. REQUIRED PROCEDURES FOR IMPOSING INTERNAL DISCIPLINE

The procedures that a union must follow in disciplining a member are listed in LMRDA Section 101(a)(5). The language is broad: "No member of any labor organization may be fined, suspended, expelled, or otherwise disciplined except for nonpayment of dues by such organization or by any officer thereof unless such member has been (a) served with written specific charges; (b) given a reasonable time to prepare his defense; (c) afforded to a full and fair hearing."

1. Written Specific Charges

The first requirement of Section 101(a)(5) is that a member be served with written *specific* charges. Suppose that a member violates a union by-law by crossing a primary picket line during a strike. Can the union simply serve the member with a charge that he violated the union's by-laws without stating the reasons? No, that would violate the requirement for a *specific* charge; the union must tell the member specifically what he did. The charge should state that the member violated the article by crossing the union's picket line and returning to work beginning on a certain day and continuing thereafter.

2. Reasonable Time to Prepare

Section 101(a)(5) requires that the member be given a reasonable time to prepare his defense. This is a very straightforward requirement. If a union serves notice on the member one day before the hearing day, the union is not giving reasonable time. Is two days reasonable, or two weeks? There is no definite answer. It depends on the nature of the charge, the availability of witnesses, and the complexities of the case.

3. A Full and Fair Hearing

Finally, Section 101(a)(5) requires that the member be afforded a full and fair hearing. A full and fair hearing does not require that a lawyer be present. The courts have held that, since discipline is fundamentally an internal union matter, union trial boards are properly composed of lay union members. The hearing need only meet basic due process requirements. Due process, in our democratic society, contains the common sense precepts that a defendant must be permitted to face his accuser, the decision must be based on evidence presented at the hearing, and the defendant must be permitted to cross-examine the witnesses and present evidence and witnesses in his own defense. Of course, a union's by-laws may go farther than minimum due process. They may allow a member to have a lawyer or be assisted by a fellow union member, even though the statute does not require it.

a. Composition of the Trial Board

As a matter of due process, a member who brings a charge should not sit on the trial board. Beyond that, however, any union member, as permitted by the by-laws, can be appointed a trial board member. The trial board determines the guilt or innocence and penalty for an accused member. There is no need for an independent outside person to be the judge. Frequently, the union executive board sits as the trial board. This is permissible, except that a board member who is personally involved in a matter should not sit as a board member in that case.

The only other restriction on the trial board membership is that the trial board cannot be stacked against the defendant member. A trial board composed of political opponents of the accused is highly suspect. Nor can the board be composed of persons who have prejudged the matter.

b. Applying the Rules of Evidence

Courts have fairly strict rules for court proceedings covering the type of evidence that can be admitted at a trial, the form evidence must take, and the weight it can be given. These rules do not apply to internal union procedures. If they did, union trial boards would be subject to continued second guessing by the courts. Remember, Congress intended for the unions to retain maximum control over their own internal procedures, subject to the specific restrictions of the Bill of Rights. That would not be possible if the courts expected a lay board to know and correctly apply the rules of evidence.

The Supreme Court has held that the courts must uphold a union's disciplinary decision if it is supported by some credible evidence. A court will not reverse a union's decision just because the trial was not conducted the way the court would have conducted it. The union's trial procedures only need to meet basic due process standards for a full and fair hearing.

The right to cross-examine witnesses and the right to confront your accusers are fundamental rights required to meet the full and fair hearing requirement of Section 101(a)(5). If a member is denied these rights, the discipline is set aside.

Except for these basic rights of fair notice, reasonable time to prepare, and a full and fair hearing, there are no other statutory requirements for discipline. This once again emphasizes how much leeway unions have in their internal disciplinary proceedings.

F. CONTROL OVER THE AMOUNT OF UNION FINES OF MEMBERS

The amount of a union's fine is not controlled by federal law. Some people had argued that an excessive fine against a union member for crossing the union's picket line and returning to work violates Section 8(b)(1)(A) because it coerces an employee in the exercise of his right to refrain from union activity. The Supreme Court rejected this argument in *NLRB v. Boeing Co.*[4] In *Boeing,* an employee crossed the union's picket line and returned to work without resigning from the union. He was subject to union discipline and fined $450. The union sued the member to collect the fine and the employee filed a charge with the NLRB alleging the fine was unreasonable. The Board dismissed the complaint and the employee appealed. The Supreme Court held that the NLRB had no authority to regulate the amount of a fine. The Court stated: "While 'unreasonable' fines may be more coercive than 'reasonable' fines, all fines are coercive to a greater or lesser degree. The underlying basis [is] not that reasonable fines were noncoercive under the language of Section 8(b)(1)(A) of the Act, but was instead that those provisions were

[4] See legal principle 15.

not intended by Congress to apply to the imposition by the union of fines not affecting the employer-employee relationship and not otherwise prohibited by the Act."

What did the Supreme Court mean when it said the Act did not apply to fines not affecting the employer-employee relationship? It meant that a member cannot be discharged for refusing to pay a fine. Discharging an employee for failure to pay a fine would violate LMRA Sections 8(a)(3) and 8(b)(2) (see Chapter 10). However, court action to enforce a fine does not violate the LMRA, provided, of course, that the fine was imposed for a lawful reason. (Remember, for example, a member cannot be fined for filing a decertification petition although the union can expel him.) A suit to enforce a fine would be brought in state court.

There are limits on the amount of a union fine. The Supreme Court stated in *Boeing* that the state court in which the suit is pending has authority to determine whether the fine is reasonable. The Supreme Court stated: "Issues as to the reasonableness or unreasonableness of such fines must be decided upon the basis of the law of contracts, voluntary associations, or such other principles of law as may be applied in a forum competent to ajudicate the issue. Under our holding, state courts will be wholly free to apply state law to such issues at the suit of either the union or the member fined."

G. MEMBERSHIP SUITS AGAINST UNIONS: THE EXHAUSTION REQUIREMENT

Members have the right under LMRDA, Section 102, to sue their union for violation of their Title I rights. However, most union constitutions restrict a member's right to sue the union. Unions customarily establish internal dispute procedures, including provisions for appealing an adverse local decision to the international president, the international executive board, and even to the international convention. The constitution usually requires a member to exhaust (complete) these internal remedies before filing suit. It can take many months, perhaps a year or more, to exhaust internal union remedies. Some unions do not even hold international conventions every year.

Section 101(a)(4) limits a union's right to restrict suits by members. The section provides that a member *may* be required to exhaust reasonable hearing procedures not to exceed four months within the union before instituting legal or administrative proceedings against the union or any of its officers. This is a compromise between the union's right to require use of internal procedures and the member's right against unreasonable delay.

1. Court Restrictions on the Exhaustion Requirement

The use of the word "may" in Section 101(a)(4) is significant. This means that the four month exhaustion requirement is discretionary with the courts. If a member files a suit before the period is up, a court can waive the requirement for good cause. The most common exception to the exhaustion requirement is if a member's appeal within the union would be futile. For example, if a union member files a charge against an action of the international president and the internal appeal is to the international president, the likelihood of the member succeeding within the union is very slim. So, a court in such a case will probably conclude it is futile to wait four months and will permit an immediate suit.

As another exception, courts have held

that a member does not have to exhaust internal union remedies if the member is clearly right in his claim. This exception may be applied if the member's claim pertains to a statutory right that clearly has been violated. Also, exhaustion may not be required if internal union remedies are unclear or inadequate. Although there are ways of avoiding the exhaustion requirement, a member is probably better off pursuing internal union remedies in most cases. The courts do not lightly disregard the exhaustion requirement. After all, federal labor policy strongly favors resolving union disputes within the union. Also, courts sometimes rule that they will not set aside disciplinary action based on grounds that the member had not raised with the union during the course of internal proceedings. This approach is in accord with the policy favoring internal resolution of disputes. Thus, a member who goes into court without even attempting to pursue internal remedies may be more limited in the arguments the court will consider. Finally, unions try to handle as many of their problems as possible internally. A member who has a union's best interests in mind, even though engaged in a dispute with it, might well consider exhausting internal remedies first in the hope that public litigation can be avoided.

2. NLRB Restrictions On Exhaustion

The four month exhaustion requirement does not apply at all to NLRB proceedings. The Board has held that a union member has the right to file an NLRB charge immediately without attempting to exhaust internal remedies. The Board bases this rule on LMRA Section 10(a), establishing the Board as the agency to prevent unfair labor practices and stating that the Board's authority cannot be affected by any other means of adjustment or prevention. As discussed above, a member cannot be disciplined in any way for filing an NLRB charge.

Summary   This chapter considered internal union matters primarily regulated by the Labor–Management Reporting and Disclosure Act, focusing on Section 101, known as the "Bill of Rights." One of the basic issues under the Act is the extent to which it protects officers. Some courts have held that Section 101 does not protect an officer's right to hold office and that an officer can be removed from his office for any reason. Other courts, representing the majority view, hold that an officer is protected in the right to hold office to the extent that an officer cannot be removed from office as discipline for exercising freedom of speech rights. However, even these courts take the position that an officer is not entitled to a hearing before being removed. Rather, if the removal is for an unlawful reason, the officer may sue for reinstatement to his position. The reason for this approach is that unions must be able to get rid of incompetent officers quickly without long, involved hearing procedures.

Removal of insubordinate officers is still a partially unresolved issue under the Act. Most courts allow removal of an officer who refuses to carry out instructions with which he disagrees or for disloyalty, but a union official probably cannot be removed for disagreeing with a policy so long as the officer carries it out.

In contrast to officers, members have a statutory right, with only narrow exceptions, to criticize an officer or union policy. Thus, the union can enforce a member's responsibility as a member to the organization (e.g., prohibit dual unionism). Also, members may be prohibited from encouraging actions, such as advocating wildcat strikes, that can interfere with the union's legal obligations.

Despite the statutory restrictions, most aspects of the relationship between a union and its members are still internal matters. So long as no federally protected rights are infringed, the union has broad authority to determine the actions for which it will impose discipline and the penalties. Similarly, the union decides whether its rules have been broken subject only to limited judicial review.

Discipline can be imposed only following a full and fair hearing with reasonable notice of the specific charge. No hearing is necessary to discipline a member for failure to pay dues. A fair hearing entails the right to present evidence in one's defense, confront one's accusers, and cross-examine them.

So long as fair procedures are followed and the discipline does not infringe on a federally protected right, federal law does not govern the amount of a fine. However, if a union sues in the state courts to enforce a fine, the member may raise the reasonableness of the fine as a defense.

1. What rights does Section 101(a)(1) of the Labor–Management Reporting and Disclosure Act (LMRDA) guarantee to union members? *Review Questions*

2. Must a person be formally admitted to union membership in order to be protected under the LMRDA?

3. Is an officer entitled to a hearing before being removed from union office?

4. Can a member be disciplined by the union for slandering a union officer at a meeting?

5. What grounds for discipline does the LMRDA permit?

6. Can the union discipline a supervisor who has remained a union member?

7. What are the statutory requirements for a hearing before discipline is imposed?

8. What are the basic due process requirements with which a union disciplinary hearing must comply?

9. How much may a union fine a member?

10. Must a union member exhaust internal union remedies before suing the union?

(Answers to review questions appear at end of book.)

Basic Legal
Principles

1. A person is considered to be a union member under the LMRDA if he has fulfilled all requirements for membership, even though he may not be formally admitted. In some cases, if a membership vote is required, a person will not be considered a member until voted in. *Axelrod v. Stoltz*, 391 F.2d 549, 67 LRRM 2764 (3rd Cir. 1968).

2. A union's constitution and by-laws may provide a member with more rights than the LMRDA requires, but a statutory violation cannot be excused or waived on the grounds that the union constitution and by-laws permitted the action taken. *Pignotti v. Sheet Metal Workers International Association*, 477 F.2d 825, 83 LRRM 2081 (8th Cir. 1973).

3. A member has an absolute right of free speech under the LMRDA except for the statutory exceptions for reasonable rules on the conduct of union meetings, the individual's responsibility to the union as an institution, and conduct interfering with the union's legal or contractual obligations. Free speech includes the right to make critical or even false statements about the union or its officers without discipline. *Hall v. Cole*, 412 U.S. 1, 83 LRRM 2177 (1973); *Salshandler v. Caputo*, 316 F.2d 445, 52 LRRM 2908 (2nd Cir. 1963); *Fulton Lodge No. 2, International Association of Machinists v. Nix*, 415 F.2d 212, 71 LRRM 3124 (5th Cir. 1969); *Giordani v. Upholsterers International Union*, 403 F.2d 85, 69 LRRM 2548 (2nd Cir. 1968); *King v. Grand Lodge International Association of Machinists*, 335 F.2d 340, 56 LRRM 2639 (9th Cir. 1964); *Wood v. Dennis*, 489 F.2d 849, 84 LRRM 2662 (7th Cir. 1973); *International Brotherhood of Boilermakers v. Rafferty*, 348 F.2d 307, 59 LRRM 2821 (9th Cir. 1965).

4. Except for the nonpayment of union initiation fees and dues, a member must be afforded a hearing before being disciplined, regardless of how clear the member's violation of a policy may be. *Figueroa v. National Maritime Union*, 342 F. 2d 400, 58 LRRM 2619 (2nd Cir. 1965).

5. Although Title I of the LMRDA requires that all members have an equal right to nominate officers, Title I does not regulate union election procedures or requirements for holding office. Election procedures are governed by Title IV of the Act as the exclusive remedy, which is administered by the Department of Labor. *Calhoon v. Harvey*, 379 US 134, 57 LRRM 2561 (1964); *Schonfeld v. Penza*, 477 F.2d 899, 83 LRRM 2020 (2nd Cir. 1973).

6. LMRDA Title I requires that members have an equal right to vote on matters on which the union's constitution and by-laws require a vote, but the law does not specify the matters on which a vote must be

taken. *Cleveland Orchestra Committee v. Cleveland Federation of Musicians*, 303 F.2d 229, 50 LRRM 2100 (6th Cir. 1962).

7. Application of the LMRDA's four month exhaustion requirement before a member may file suit against the union is discretionary with the courts. An immediate suit may be allowed for such reasons as: exhaustion is futile, the member's statutory rights have been clearly violated, or internal union remedies are unclear or inadequate. *NLRB v. Industrial Union of Marine and Shipbuilding Workers*, 391 U.S. 418, 68 LRRM 2257 (1968); *Detroy v. American Guild of Variety Artists*, 286 F.2d 75, 47 LRRM 2452 (2nd Cir. 1961); *Fruit and Vegetable Packers v. Morley*, 378 F.2d 738, 65 LRRM 2542 (9th Cir. 1967).

8. Except on statutorily protected rights, a union is free to determine the grounds for disciplining a member and the penalty. The union's decision as to whether a violation has occurred need only be supported by some credible evidence. *International Brotherhood of Boilermakers v. Hardeman*, 401 U.S. 233, 76 LRRM 2542 (1971); *Rosario v. ILGWU Local 10*, ———F.2d———, 101 LRRM 2958 (2nd Cir. 1979) (due process requires verbatim record of union disciplinary proceedings).

9. The majority rule is that a union officer can be removed from office without a hearing, but that removing a union officer in retaliation for the exercise of his rights as a member is unlawful discipline. *King v. Grand Lodge International Association of Machinists*, 335 F.2d 340, 56 LRRM 2639 (9th Cir. 1964); *Wood v. Dennis*, 489 F.2d 849, 84 LRRM 2662 (7th Cir. 1973). But see *Sheridan v. United Brotherhood of Carpenters and Joiners*, 306 F.2d 152, 50 LRRM 2637 (3rd Cir. 1962) (upholding removal of officer for any reason).

10. A member may be expelled from membership for filing a decertification petition with the NLRB, but he may not be fined or otherwise disciplined for such activity. *Tawas Tube Products, Inc.*, 151 NLRB No. 9, 58 LRRM 1330 (1965); *Molders Local 125*, 178 NLRB No. 25, 72 LRRM 1049 (1969). A member may not be expelled or disciplined in any way for filing an NLRB unfair labor practice charge against the union. *NLRB v. Industrial Union of Marine Workers*, 391 U.S. 418, 68 LRRM 2257 (1968).

11. A union may fine supervisors who are union members for crossing its picket line and doing bargaining unit work. *Florida Power and Light Company v. IBEW Local 641*, 417 U.S. 790, 86 LRRM 2689 (1974). The Board's majority opinion is that a supervisor may be fined for doing more than a mimimal amount of bargaining unit work during the strike. *Columbia ITU Union No. 101*, 242 NLRB No. 135, 101 LRRM 1312 (1979).

12. A union cannot fine a supervisor for matters pertaining to the supervisor's function as the employer's representative for bargaining, con-

tract administration, or grievance adjustments. *American Broadcasting Cos. Inc. v. Writers Guild,* 437 U.S. 411, 98 LRRM 2705 (1978).

13. A union may fine members for crossing its picket line unless they have effectively resigned from the union before crossing. *NLRB v. Allis-Chalmers Mfg. Co.,* 388 U.S. 175, 65 LRRM 2449 (1967); *NLRB v. Textile Workers Granite State Joint Board,* 409 U.S. 213, 81 LRRM 2853 (1972); *Booster Lodge 405, IAM v. NLRB,* 412 U.S. 84, 83 LRRM 2189 (1973). But see *NLRB v. Machinists Local 1327,* ———F.2d———, 101 LRRM 3097 (9th Cir., 1979) (upholding union restrictions on right to resign during a strike).

14. A union may fine members for violating union-imposed work restrictions so long as the rules do not otherwise violate the law or the collective bargaining agreement. *Scofield v. NLRB,* 394 U.S. 423, 70 LRRM 3105 (1969); *Orange County Carpenters,* 242 NLRB No. 75, 101 LRRM 1173 (1979).

15. So long as a fine of a member is for a lawful purpose, the amount of the fine is not regulated by federal law. *NLRB v. Boeing Co.,* 412 U.S. 67, 83 LRRM 2183 (1973).

Recommended Reading

Archer, "Allis-Chalmers Revealed: A Current View of a Union's Right to Fine Employees for Crossing a Picket Line," 7 *Ind. L. Rev.* 498 (1974)

Hornberger, "Title I of the Landrum–Griffin Act," 6 *Idaho L. Rev.* 77 (1969).

Naumoff, "Landrum–Griffin Regulation of Internal Union Affairs," 18 *Lab. L.J.* 387 (1967).

"Substantive and Procedural Due Process in Union Disciplinary Proceedings," 3 *U. San Francisco L. Rev.* 389 (1969).

Chapter Twelve

The Duty of Fair Representation

The duty of fair representation is becoming increasingly important to unions as they negotiate collective bargaining agreements, administer contracts, and resolve grievances. Almost every union member has heard of the duty of fair representation, but there are many misunderstandings about the doctrine.

A. THE DEVELOPMENT OF THE FAIR REPRESENTATION DOCTRINE

1. The Steele Decision

The fair representation doctrine began with *Steele,* a 1944 Supreme Court decision concerning racial discrimination by a union.[1] The union had been certified under the Railway Labor Act to represent a bargaining unit of railway firemen. A majority of the work force was white, but there was a substantial black minority. The union, however, excluded blacks from membership. The case predated the Civil Rights Act that prohibits race discrimination in membership. The union proposed contract changes that would have ultimately excluded all blacks from fireman positions. A black bargaining unit em-

ployee brought suit to have the agreement between the employer and the union voided.

The Supreme Court held that the union had to represent all employees in the bargaining unit fairly, even if they were not union members. The Railway Labor Act provides that a union is the exclusive bargaining representative of all employees in a bargaining unit. The Court said this right to exclusive representation imposed the duty to represent all employees fairly.

2. Early Developments Under the Labor Management Relations Act

Unions under the Labor Management Relations Act also have the right to exclusive representation (see Chapter 4). Accordingly, the Supreme Court held in *Ford Motor Company v. Huffman* (1953) that unions governed by the LMRA also have the duty to represent

---

[1] See legal principle 1.

all bargaining unit employees fairly.[2] In *Huffman*, the Court upheld the union's right to negotiate a seniority clause giving certain seniority preferences to veterans. In *Miranda Fuel* (1962), the NLRB ruled that a union's violation of its duty of fair representation is an unfair labor practice.[3] The Board reasoned that Section 7 of the Act guarantees employees the right to engage in collective bargaining, and that right includes the right to be represented fairly by the exclusive bargaining representative. Thus, the Board concluded that, by failing to represent all employees fairly, a union violates Section 8(b)(1)(A) (prohibiting interference with Section 7 rights).

3. Full Development of the Doctrine: The Vaca Decision

Although the fair representation doctrine began with the *Steele* decision, the doctrine was not fully developed until the Supreme Court's decision in *Vaca v. Sipes* (1967).[4] In *Vaca*, an employee had been discharged because of poor health. The employee claimed he was able to do his job and filed a grievance. The union processed the grievance through the prearbitration steps of the grievance procedure. At the union's expense, the employee went to a doctor for examination, but the examination was unfavorable. The union tried to convince the employer to give the employee light work, but the employer refused. The union then decided to drop the grievance.

The employee filed suit against the union in the state court, alleging that the union had arbitrarily and capriciously dropped his grievance. A jury awarded the employee

[2] See legal principle 1.

[3] See legal principle 2.

[4] See legal principle 4.

$10,000 in damages. The case was appealed to the state supreme court, which upheld the jury verdict. The state court reasoned that there was sufficient evidence for the jury to conclude that the employee was able to work and that the union had made the wrong decision in not arbitrating the grievance. The case was appealed to the United States Supreme Court.

The Supreme Court reversed the state court decision. The Court said that the actual issue in the case was whether the union had violated its duty of fair representation in dropping the employee's grievance. A union breaches its duty of fair representation if it represents an employee arbitrarily, discriminatorily, or in bad faith. Arbitrarily means making a decision without reason or at whim. The Supreme Court said the state court had incorrectly based the union's liability on whether the union was right or wrong in its decision. The Court indicated that it did not matter whether a union was right or wrong, only whether a union had acted arbitrarily, discriminatorily, or in bad faith in dropping a grievance. The Court concluded that the union had not acted arbitrarily and had met the fair representation standard in this case.

B. UNION DISCRETION TO ARBITRATE

The *Vaca* decision clearly establishes that a union does not have to take every grievance to arbitration. A union has the right to settle or to drop a grievance even though the grievance may have merit, so long as its decision does not violate the union's duty of fair representation. The Court stated:

A breach of the statutory duty of fair representation occurs only when a union's conduct toward a member of the collective bargaining unit is arbitrary, discriminatory, or in bad faith. There has been considerable debate over the extent of this duty in the context of a union's enforcement of the grievance and arbitration procedures in a collective bargaining agreement . . . . Some have suggested that every individual employee should have the right to have his grievance taken to arbitration. Others have urged that the Union be given substantial discretion to decide whether a grievance should be taken to arbitration, subject only to the duty to refrain from patently wrongful conduct such as racial discrimination or personal hostility.

Though we accept the proposition that a union may not arbitrarily ignore a meritorious grievance or process it in perfunctory fashion, we do not agree that the individual employee has an absolute right to have his grievance taken to arbitration regardless of the provisions of the applicable collective bargaining agreement. In providing for a grievance and arbitration procedure which gives the union discretion to supervise the grievance machinery and to invoke arbitration, the employer and the union contemplate that each will endeavor in good faith to settle grievances short of arbitration. Through this settlement process, frivolous grievances are ended prior to the most costly and time-consuming step in the grievance procedures. Moreover, both sides are assured that similar complaints will be treated consistently, and major problem areas in the interpretation of the collective bargaining contract can be isolated and perhaps resolved. And finally, the settlement process furthers the interest of the union as statutory agent and as coauthor of the bargaining agreement in representing the employees in the enforcement of that agreement . . . .

If a union's decision that a particular grievance lacks sufficient merit to justify arbitration would constitute a breach of the duty of fair representation because a judge or jury later found the grievance meritorious, the union's incentive to settle such grievances short of arbitration would be seriously reduced. The dampening effect on the entire grievance procedure of this reduction of the union's freedom to settle claims in good faith would surely be substantial.

Since the union's statutory duty of fair representation protects the individual employee from arbitrary abuses of the settlement device by providing him with recourse against both employer . . . and union, this severe limitation on the power to settle grievances is neither necessary nor desirable . . . .

C. PERFUNCTORY PROCESSING AS A VIOLATION OF FAIR REPRESENTATION: THE HINES DECISION

The basic standard for compliance with a union's duty of fair representation is that a union not act arbitrarily, discriminatorily, or in bad faith with a bargaining unit employee. However, the Supreme Court also indicated in *Vaca* that a union can violate the duty if it processes a grievance in a perfunctory manner. Perfunctory means acting in a superficial manner without care or interest. In *Vaca*, the union had thoroughly investigated the employee's grievance and had even sent the employee to another doctor for evaluation at the union's expense. Thus, the Court briefly noted that perfunctory treatment could be a violation but did not consider that aspect of the doctrine in detail because it was clearly inapplicable under the facts.

In *Hines v. Anchor Motor Freight Inc.*, the Court directly faced the perfunctory issue.[5] In *Hines*, the employer discovered that certain drivers had turned in expense vouchers for a motel room that, according to motel records, were higher than the amount the drivers had actually paid for the rooms. The employer, concluding that the drivers had pocketed the difference, discharged them. The drivers maintained that they had paid the full amount for the rooms. They told the union that the motel clerk must have altered the motel's

[5] See legal principle 3.

records and embezzled money from the motel. The union business agent told the drivers that he would check with the motel, but he never did. The union processed the drivers' case to arbitration. The drivers continued to maintain their innocence, but the arbitration board upheld the discharge.

The employees sued the union for breach of fair representation and the employer for breach of contract in the same suit, on the theory that their discharges had violated the just cause provision of the contract. During pretrial proceedings, the motel clerk admitted that he had stolen the money and that the drivers were innocent, as they had claimed. The employer argued that the arbitration board's decision was final and binding, even though the employees could now prove their innocence. The Supreme Court stated that normally an arbitrator's decision, right or wrong, is final and binding on the employees. However, the Court held that an arbitrator's decision is not binding on the employees if the union violates its duty of fair representation in processing the case. The Court concluded that the union had violated its duty because it had handled the grievances in a perfunctory manner by failing to check out the employees' defense that the motel clerk was guilty.

1. Perfunctory Processing vs. Mistake

The Supreme Court emphasized in *Hines* that the union had not violated its duty of fair representation just because the employees could prove their innocence. The *Vaca* decision had already established that a right—wrong test is not the basis for determining whether or not a union has violated its duty of fair representation.

Thus, the employees in *Hines* had to prove more than bad judgment or a poor investiga-

tion by the union. The court said that the grievance process could not be expected to be error free. The employees had to prove perfunctory treatment. What if the union had checked out the drivers' claims that the clerk was guilty by contacting the motel, but the clerk had not admitted his guilt? Then, the union's handling of the grievance would not have been perfunctory and the employees would have been bound by the arbitrator's decision.

The *Hines* case requires that a union investigate the merits when a grievance is filed; it cannot simply go through the motions. A union's decision whether to proceed, drop, or settle a grievance must be based on a consideration of the grievance's merits, and the advantages or disadvantages of proceeding. A grievance cannot be treated as a casual matter. So long as a union gives a grievance the consideration it deserves and does not deal arbitrarily, discriminatorily, or in bad faith with employees, the union's decision (right or wrong) does not violate the duty of fair representation.

2. Practical Steps to Avoid a Fair Representation Suit

A union should also keep employees informed on the status of their grievance. Some fair representation suits are filed just because the employee is unaware of the union's efforts in his behalf. Unions win most of these cases, but only after considerable time and expense. If a union drops a grievance, the employee should be advised of the union's decision and its reasons. The union should give the employee the opportunity to present additional evidence or arguments in his behalf. In this way, the union can avoid being accused of treating the grievance in an arbitrary or perfunctory way.

A union is not required to process a grievance every time an employee complains that his contract rights have been violated. The facts of a grievance or the contract's language may be such that the grievance is clearly without merit, or a prior grievance may have already raised and answered the same issue. However, a union that does not file a grievance because it apparently lacks merit runs the risk of being accused of perfunctory treatment. After all, the union in *Hines* may have thought it was a waste of time to check with the motel. In most cases, the better practice is to file a grievance for an employee, investigate the facts as necessary, and then withdraw the grievance with notice to the employee if it lacks merit.

D. UNION NEGLIGENCE AS A VIOLATION OF FAIR REPRESENTATION

The Supreme Court's decision in *Hines* as to the perfunctory processing of a grievance has raised questions whether a union violates its duty of fair representation if it handles a grievance negligently. Sometimes negligence and perfunctory treatment are very similar. For example, if a union business representative has an employee's grievance in ample time to meet contractual time limits, but forgets to file it until the time has expired, is the failure perfunctory consideration, negligence, or both? What if the business representative has a stack of grievances that must all be filed the same day? The representative intends to put a grievance in with the others with the same deadline, but he accidentally places the grievance with documents having no time limit and by the time the mistake is discovered, the time limit has expired. The representative may have been negligent, but he

probably has not been perfunctory. Has the union violated its duty of fair representation in this situation?

As of yet, there is no clear answer on negligence as a breach of fair representation. The Supreme Court said in *Hines* that mere errors in judgment are not a breach of the duty. Lower courts have also held that "inadequate representation" is not a breach of the duty if the union acts in good faith, etc. Fair representation is not based on the union's level of expertise; after all, poor representation may be better than no representation at all. However, one court of appeals has held that a union violates the duty of fair representation by inept handling of grievances. In that case, the union failed to notice a contract provision directly on point supporting an employee's grievance and the union withdrew a grievance it should have pursued.

A few lower court decisions have stated that negligence may be grounds for a fair representation violation, but the facts in those cases indicate that the unions had acted perfunctorily in processing a grievance.

If a union is not handling a grievance in a perfunctory manner, the commission of a negligent act probably does not violate the duty of fair representation. But if the negligent act is part of an overall pattern of perfunctory treatment, the union probably is liable. This issue may ultimately have to be resolved by the Supreme Court. In any event, a union should develop a system to keep track of all grievances.

E. APPLICATIONS OF THE FAIR REPRESENTATION DOCTRINE

The duty of fair representation applies to the negotiation and administration of the collective bargaining agreement, as well as to processing grievances.

1. Fair Representation in the Negotiation Process

A union that is negotiating a contract must make decisions that favor some bargaining unit employees over others. The union must decide whether to press for higher wages (helping younger workers) or for higher pension benefits (helping older workers). Should a union favor a strict seniority system or one that considers skill and ability? Which decision must a union make to comply with its duty of fair representation? Either decision may fulfill the union's duty. Remember, the duty of fair representation is not based on whether a union's decision is right or wrong, but only on whether the union acts arbitrarily, capriciously, discriminatorily, or in a perfunctory manner. Thus, so long as a union makes a considered choice, weighing the advantages and disadvantages and the relative impact, its duty is fulfilled.

2. Fair Representation During Contract Administration

The union's duty of fair representation also arises in the course of contract administration. The union must decide whether certain employer acts violate the contract. Unforeseen situations may arise, requiring contract changes or side agreements. Again, a union may make agreements with the employer that adversely affect certain employees as long as the union's decision is not arbitrary, discriminatory, bad faith, or made in a perfunctory manner.

Suppose an employer with two plants represented by the same union decides to combine the two facilities. After the employees from the closed plant are transferred to the remaining facility, the employer and the union meet to determine the relative seniority rights of the two merged work forces. Should the employees of the two work forces be dovetailed into a single seniority list or should the employees of the closed facility be placed at the bottom of the list? There are arguments favoring both approaches, but which alternative must the union support? Again, the union can favor either method so long as its decision is not arbitrary, etc. As long as the union's duty of fair representation is met, it does not matter that the decision is "wrong" or that there was a better method. The union's judgment cannot be the basis for a fair representation violation.

3. Acts Initiated by Union Hostility

The duty of fair representation occasionally arises in cases of outright union hostility against a particular employee. The union must separate its internal relationship with an individual as a union member from its relationship with him as a bargaining unit employee. Regardless of differences on internal union policies, a union cannot retaliate against an employee in employment. Thus, a union cannot treat an employee arbitrarily, discriminatorily, or in bad faith on the job because of an internal union dispute. The employee is entitled to the same treatment as any other bargaining unit employee. Thus, a union may violate its duty of fair representation if (for arbitrary, discriminatory, or bad faith reasons) it encourages an employer to discharge an employee, refuses to process the employee's grievances, or refers the employee to less desirable jobs.

The Board has held that a union cannot charge a nonunion employee for processing his grievances if other bargaining unit employees are not subject to the same charge. The charge would violate the union's duty of fair representation.

F. REMEDIES FOR A BREACH OF THE DUTY OF FAIR REPRESENTATION

1. NLRB and Judicial Remedies

An employee has two concurrent remedies for a union's breach of its duty of fair representation. First, he can file an unfair labor practice charge with the NLRB. Second, he can file suit under LMRA Section 301 against the union for violating its duty of fair representation and against the employer for breach of contract. (See Chapter 9 for discussion of Section 301 procedures.)

The NLRB applies the same criteria as the court, including the perfunctory treatment standard, in determining whether the union has breached its duty of fair representation. However, in contrast to some federal courts, the Board does not regard union negligence as a breach of its duty under the LMRA.

If the Board finds that a union has breached its duty, the Board may order the union to process a grievance through the grievance procedure, including arbitration if warranted, and permit the employee to be represented at the arbitration hearing by an attorney of his own choice at the union's expense. If an employee suffers lost pay because of an employer's action (such as a lost promotion or a discharge) and the employee's grievance over the action is time-barred because the union fails to process the grievance in accordance with its duty of fair representation, the Board may order the union to pay the employee back pay for the lost earnings.

G. PROCEDURAL REQUIREMENTS OF A FAIR REPRESENTATION SUIT

1. Exhausting Contractual Remedies

Ordinarily, an employee is required to exhaust all contractual remedies before filing suit under Section 301. Further, as the Supreme Court indicated in *Hines*, an employee is bound by a union's decision to withdraw or settle his grievance, or by an arbitrator's decision upholding the employer's action, and cannot successfully sue the employer unless the union violated its duty of fair representation in processing the matter. This means that an employee may lose his suit, even though his contract rights were violated, because the union did not violate its duty. The Supreme Court recognized that this rule means that some employees can lose out on meritorious claims, but felt that the need for finality in the decision-making process and the importance of employer–union discretion in resolving grievances outweigh that risk.

If a suit is filed, the court must decide two issues: first, whether the union has violated its duty of fair representation; and second, whether the employer's actions violate the collective bargaining agreement. If the court concludes that the union has not violated its duty of fair representation, the suit is dismissed because the employer has no liability unless the union violated its duty. If the court concludes that the union violated its duty, the court then decides whether the employer breached the contract. The employee can lose his suit even though the union has violated its duty because the court can conclude that the employer did not violate the contract notwithstanding the union's breach.

2. Exhausting Internal Union Remedies

Before filing suit, an employee must also exhaust available internal union remedies to appeal a union's decision to drop or settle a grievance. This requirement is in accord with the general judicial policy favoring internal resolution of disputes. In most cases, courts dismiss a suit if an employee has not at least attempted to exhaust internal remedies first. However, a member cannot be required to exhaust internal remedies for more than four months. (See chapter 11.)

If a union denies an employee's grievance, the union should notify the employee of its decision and its internal appeal procedures. If that is done, a court is more likely to dismiss an employee's suit filed without even attempting internal union relief.

3. Damages in a Fair Representation Suit

The *Vaca* decision also established the method of dividing damages between an employer and a union in a fair representation suit if the union is sued for violation of its fair representation duty, and the employer for breach of contract. The Supreme Court held that the employer is liable for the damage caused by the contractual violation, such as the lost wages for a discharge without just cause. The union is liable only for the additional damage caused by its processing in violation of its duty of fair representation.

In most cases, the employer is responsible for the greatest part of the damages because of its contract violation. The union is liable only for the additional delay caused by its actions.

In some instances, a union may have initiated the employer's contract violation. A union may improperly insist that an employee be discharged and the employer may comply with the request. If the union's request violates its duty of fair representation, the union bears primary responsibility for the damages.

If the court concludes that the employer has not violated the contract, the employee cannot collect damages against the union either, even if the union violated its duty of fair representation, because the union is liable only for the additional loss caused by the violation. If the employer has not violated the contract, there is no loss from the union's violation.

Punitive Damages

The Supreme Court held in *Electrical Workers v. Foust* that punitive damages cannot be awarded against a union that violates its duty of fair representation in processing a grievance.[6] An employee is only entitled to recover his actual losses caused by the breach. The court reasoned that the possibility of punitive damages would improperly curtail unions in their broad discretion needed to handle grievances and "thus disrupt the responsible decision making essential to peaceful labor relations."

Presumably, punitive damages, under the same reasoning, cannot be assessed against a union for acts growing out of the negotiation or administration of an agreement.

[6] See legal principle 5.

Summary

The duty of fair representation is derived from the authority of a union to be the exclusive representative of a bargaining unit. Since a union is the exclusive representative, with all the authority that implies, a union cannot act arbitrarily, discriminatorily, or in bad faith toward the employees it represents. Also, the union cannot treat its members in a perfunctory manner.

The union's duty of fair representation applies to the negotiation process, contract administration, and the grievance procedure. A union may properly make decisions favoring the interest of some employees over others as long as its decision does not violate its fair representation duty. Errors in judgment do not violate the duty of fair representation.

A union is not obligated to arbitrate all grievances. It may drop or settle a grievance so long as the decision is not arbitrary, discriminatory, in bad faith, or made in perfunctory manner. An employee is bound by the settlement or an adverse arbitrator's decision unless the union violated its duty of fair representation in processing the grievance.

The unanswered question in the area of fair representation is whether a union's negligent acts violate the duty. Perfunctory acts may violate the duty, and, in some cases, the line between perfunctory acts and negligent acts is very difficult to draw.

The duty of fair representation can be enforced by the Board in an unfair labor practice proceeding or by the courts in an action under Section 301 for breach of contract. The Board has held that a union's breach of duty constitutes an unfair labor practice under Section 8(b)(1)(A).

Suits under Section 301 are usually brought against the union for violation of its duty of fair representation and against the employer for breach of contract. If a court determines that the union breached its duty, an employee is not bound by a grievance settlement or even by an adverse arbitrator's decision. The court then determines whether the employer's actions violated the contract. Technically, it is possible for a union to have violated its duty of fair representation in handling a grievance, but for the employer not to have violated the contract.

The employee's damages in a Section 301 suit are apportioned between the employer and the union. The employer is liable for the damages caused by its breach of contract and the union is liable for any additional damages caused by its violation of the duty of fair representation. Damages in a fair representation case are limited to the employee's actual losses.

*Review
Questions*
1. What is the basis for imposing the duty of fair representation on a union?

2. What are the basic requirements for meeting the duty of fair representation?

3. Does a breach of the duty of fair representation violate the LMRA?

4. Is an employee bound by an arbitrator's decision upholding his discharge?

5. If a union drops a discharge grievance and the employee subsequently comes up with additional evidence proving that his discharge was not for just cause, can the employee successfully sue the employer for breach of contract?

6. Does federal or state law govern a court action for violation of the duty of fair representation?

7. Can a union lawfully negotiate a change in a contract's seniority system from one basing promotion strictly on seniority to one considering both seniority and ability?

8. Is a mere error in judgment a violation of the duty of fair representation?

9. Who is responsible for an employee's damages in a successful suit growing out of a union's violation of its fair representation duty and an employer's breach of contract?

10. Has a union violated its duty of fair representation if an employee handed a grievance to a union business representative in time, but the representative failed to file it with the employer until the contractual time limit for filing had expired?

(Answers to review questions appear at end of book.)

*Basic Legal
Principles*
1. A union's duty of fair representation under both the Railway Labor Act and the Labor Management Relations Act is derived from the union's right of exclusive representation under those statutes. *Steele v. Louisville & N.R.R.*, 323 U.S. 192, 15 LRRM 708 (1944); *Ford Motor Co. v. Huffman*, 345 U.S. 330, 31 LRRM 2548 (1948).

2. A union's failure to represent employees fairly is an unfair labor practice in violation of Section 8(b)(1)(A) and 8(b)(2) of the LMRA. *Miranda Fuel Co.*, 140 NLRB 181, 51 LRRM 1584 (1962); *Glass Bottle Blowers Assoc.*, 240 NLRB No. 29, 100 LRRM 1294 (1979).

3. In a suit under Section 301, an arbitrator's award sustaining a discharge may be set aside in an action against the employer for wrongful discharge only if the union breached its fair representation duty in the

arbitration proceedings. *Hines v. Anchor Motor Freight, Inc.* 424 U.S. 554, 91 LRRM 2481 (1976); *Hardee v. North Carolina Allstate Services, Inc.*, 537 F.2d 1255, 92 LRRM 3342 (4th Cir. 1976).

4. A breach of the union's statutory duty occurs if the union's actions or decisions are arbitrary, discriminatory, in bad faith, or perfunctory. As a general rule, mere errors in judgment are not a breach of the duty. *Vaca v. Sipes*, 386 U.S. 171, 64 LRRM 2369 (1967); *Hughes v. Teamsters Local 683*, 554 F.2d 365, 95 LRRM 2652 (1977); *Russom v. Sears, Roebuck & Co.*, 558 F.2d 439, 95 LRRM 2914 (8th Cir. 1977); *Teamsters Local 355*, 229 NLRB No. 186, 95 LRRM 1232 (1977). But see *Milstead v. Teamsters Local 957*, 580 F.2d 232, 99 LRRM 2150 (1978), (inept handling of a grievance may violate the union's duty of fair representation).

5. Damages against a union in a fair representation suit are limited to an employee's actual damages. Punitive damages cannot be awarded. *Electrical Workers v.Foust*,———U.S.———,101 LRRM 2365 (1979).

6. A union is not obligated to arbitrate a grievance that is filed so long as the union's decision not to proceed does not violate its duty of fair representation. *Vaca v. Sipes, supra; Hines v. Anchor Motor Freight, Inc., supra.*

7. A union may negotiate contract terms or enter into grievance settlements that favor some employees over others as long as the union's decisions are not arbitrary, discriminatory, in bad faith, or perfunctory. *Ford Motor Co. v. Huffman, supra; Humphrey v. Moore*, 375 U.S. 335, 55 LRRM 2031 (1964).

"Exhaustion of Internal Union Remedies as a Pre-Requisite To Section 301 Actions Against Labor Unions and Employers," 55 *Chi-Kent L. Rev.* 259 (1975)

Hill, "Union's Duty to Process Discrimination Claims," 32 *Arb. J.* 180 (1977)

Jacobs, "Fair Representation And Binding Arbitration," 28 *Lab. L.J.* 369 (1977)

"Union's Duty of Fair Representation—Fact or Fiction," 60 *Marq. L. Rev.* 1116 (1977)

Recommended Reading

Chapter Thirteen

Unions and Equal Employment Opportunity

Unions have been in the forefront of legislative efforts to eliminate discrimination and to support equal employment opportunity. Unions enforce the rights of employees to job equality by filing discrimination charges with the Equal Employment Opportunity Commission, negotiating contract clauses eliminating discriminatory practices, and arbitrating issues of job discrimination. Unions are classified as employers in relation to their own employees (secretaries, etc.), and thus have an obligation to comply with fair employment practices the same as any other employer. Unions are prohibited from discriminating in union membership. They also have a legal duty to insure that employees are not discriminated against on the job. A union may be joined as a defendant in a civil rights case with the employer if the employer engages in unlawful discrimination that the union either encourages or does not actively oppose. Unions that operate a hiring hall or apprenticeship programs are required to recruit, refer persons to employment, and operate their apprenticeship programs without discrimination.

Civil rights litigation has become so complex that a discussion of civil rights tends to emphasize "do's and don'ts" for avoiding litigation. The cases discussed in this chapter tend to emphasize the problems that remain rather than the progress that has been made. Although there may be disagreement on some issues within the labor movement, organized labor has been and continues to be fundamentally committed to the goal of equal employment opportunity.

A. AN OVERVIEW OF THE STATUTORY REMEDIES AGAINST DISCRIMINATION

1. Title VII, Civil Rights Act of 1964

a. Employers and Unions Covered Under the Act

Title VII of the Civil Rights Act of 1964, as amended in 1972, commonly referred to simply as Title VII (reproduced in the appendix), is the basic statute regulating equal employment opportunity. The other titles of the Act deal with equal rights in housing and education.

Section 701(b) defines the term "employer" as a person who employs at least fifteen employees in twenty or more calendar weeks of the current or preceding year. Section 701(a) broadly defines a person to include individuals, corporations, labor unions, partnerships, trusts, and governmental units, etc. Thus, essentially every form of business organization is covered by the Act. State and local governmental units are covered by the definition of employer, but federal governmental units are expressly excluded from coverage. Section 717, however, requires nondiscrimination in federal employment. This section provides for enforcement by the Civil Service Commission, but a Presidential Reorganization Order has reassigned this function to the Equal Employment Opportunity Commission (EEOC).

If an employer employs at least fifteen employees for more than twenty weeks in the year, the employer is subject to the Act for the balance of that year and the next year even if the work force falls below the fifteen employee minimum. The requirement that an employer have at least fifteen employees to be covered by Title VII is high compared to the Labor Management Relations Act. The NLRB asserts jurisdiction over employers who have only two employees. To hold down the number of cases, the Board, however, has also established monetary jurisdictional standards that an employer must meet before the Board will assert jurisdiction over the employer (see Chapter 1). The Equal Employment Opportunity Commission has no such requirement.

Note that under Section 701(b), only employers engaged in an industry affecting commerce are covered by the Act. This is the same broad statutory coverage the NLRB has under the LMRA (see Chapter 1).

Sections 701(d) and (e) establish the coverage of labor unions under Title VII. Basically, every union that operates a hiring hall, regardless of the number of members, is covered by the Act. All other unions having at least fifteen members are covered if they either are a certified bargaining agent under the National Labor Relations Act or the Railway Labor Act or if the union has been voluntarily recognized as the bargaining representative by an employer engaged in an industry affecting commerce even though the union is not certified.

If a union has more than fifteen members, but less than fifteen employees, is it subject to Title VII as an employer? Some unions have argued that a union should not be classified as an employer under the Act unless it has fifteen employees. However, the courts have held that a union is subject to Title VII regardless of the number of employees, if it has at least fifteen members.

Religious Discrimination. Section 701(j) is an important provision covering religious discrimination. It requires that an employer make reasonable accommodations to the employee's religious beliefs so long as there is no undue hardship to the employer's business (discussed more fully below). Section 702 exempts religious organizations from the Act, permitting them to hire persons of their faith to carry out the organization's activities. There is a related exemption under Section 703(e) permitting schools of a particular religion to employ employees of that religion.

B. Prohibited Discrimination

Section 703 is the heart of Title VII. Section 703(a) broadly prohibits an employer from discriminating on the basis of a person's race, color, religion, sex, or national origin. Section 703(b) prohibits discrimination by an employment agency.

Section 703(c) broadly prohibits discrimination by a union on the basis of race, color, religion, sex, or national origin in union membership or job referrals. A union is prohibited from limiting, segregating, or classifying its members, or applicants for membership, in any way that would deprive or affect a person's employment opportunities or employee status. Unions are prohibited from causing or attempting to cause an employer to discriminate against a person in violation of the Act.

Section 703(d) prohibits discrimination by employers, unions, or joint apprenticeship training programs in apprenticeship or other training programs.

Section 703 does not prohibit all types of discrimination; only discrimination based upon race, color, religion, sex, or national origin. Persons protected by the Act are referred to as members of a protected group or class. Persons discriminated against are referred to as discriminatees. An employer can lawfully discriminate against blonds or left-handed people because the law does not prohibit such discrimination. Section 703 does not prohibit age discrimination, but discrimination against people between 40 and 70 is prohibited by the Age Discrimination in Employment Act (discussed more fully below).

Bona Fide Occupational Qualifications (BFOQ).   Section 703(e) contains an exception permitting discrimination in religion, sex, or national origin if religion, sex, or national origin is a bona fide occupational qualification (BFOQ). This section, the subject of considerable litigation in sex discrimination, is considered more fully below. The Age Discrimination in Employment Act contains a similar exception. Section 703(e) does not list race as a BFOQ; thus, race can never be a bona fide occupational qualification.

Seniority and Testing.   Section 703(h) deals with the important issues of seniority and testing. This section permits the operation of a bona fide seniority system even though it results in different standards of compensation, different conditions, or privileges of employment between employees, as long as the differences are not the result of an intention to discriminate on the basis of race, sex, relig-

ion, or national origin. The section also permits the use of professionally developed ability tests that are "not designed, intended or used to discriminate." The relationship between seniority and the perpetuation of past discrimination, and the lawful use of tests under Section 703(h) are discussed below.

Section 703(j) provides that an employer is not required to grant preferential treatment because of an individual's race, color, religion, sex, national origin, or an imbalance in the work force. This section is important in reverse discrimination and affirmative action programs.

Section 704(a) protects persons against retaliation for opposing unlawful employment practices; for filing a charge with the EEOC; or for testifying, assisting, or participating in any manner in an investigation, procedure, or hearing under Title VII. Section 704(b) prohibits any advertisement for employment indicating a preference based on race, religion, national origin, or sex except where there is a BFOQ.

c. Establishment and Powers of the Equal Employment Opportunity Commission

Sections 705(a), 706, and 707 establish the Equal Employment Opportunity Commission and the procedures to enforce Title VII. The EEOC is composed of five members appointed by the President for five years, one member designated chairman by the President. The commission also has a general counsel appointed by the President for four years. The EEOC is organized into districts.

The role of the EEOC and its general counsel is very different from the role of the NLRB and its general counsel (see Chapter 1). Under the Labor Management Relations Act, the General Counsel of the NLRB prosecutes unfair labor practice cases before the Board. The Board decides whether the LMRA has been violated and issues appropriate remedial orders.

In contrast, the EEOC only investigates unlawful employment practice charges to determine whether there is reasonable cause to believe the Act has been violated. If the EEOC finds reasonable cause, it attempts to eliminate the practice by conciliation. There is no trial before the EEOC as there is before an administrative law judge in the case of the NLRB. If conciliation fails, either the EEOC, the attorney general, or the complaining party can bring suit in federal court to enforce Title VII rights. The EEOC's general counsel, through his legal staff, litigates cases for the EEOC and provides general legal assistance and advice to the agency. Currently, attorneys assigned to the EEOC's district offices assist the agency's investigators in determining whether unlawful employment practice charges have merit.

Under Section 706(e), an unlawful employment practice charge must be filed with the EEOC within 180 days of the discriminatory act.

d. Effect on State Laws

Under Section 708, state laws regulating employment discrimination remain in effect. State law, however, cannot permit an act prohibited by federal law. This provision has invalidated so-called "protective legislation," formerly adopted in many states, limiting the hours that women could work or even the jobs they could hold. Some states, however, have stronger laws against employment discrimination that those contained in Title VII. Under Section 708, an employer or union is bound by the higher state standard.

Sections 709 and 710 establish the investigatory powers of the EEOC. Section 709(c) permits the EEOC to establish, as it has done,

detailed recordkeeping requirements for employers and unions.

e. EEOC Procedural Guidelines

Section 713(a) permits the EEOC to establish procedural regulations. Some agencies are authorized to establish substantive regulations governing the conduct of people who are subject to the Act the agency administers. The Federal Communications Commission and the Security and Exchange Commission, for example, issue detailed substantive regulations. The EEOC was not given this authority; however, it does issue "guidelines" on what it regards as lawful or unlawful conduct under Title VII. There are detailed guidelines, for example, on testing as a means of employee selection, sex discrimination, and religious discrimination. Technically, these guidelines are only the EEOC's opinion on permissible conduct and they are not binding on a court, an employer or a union. However, the Supreme Court has held that the guidelines are still entitled to "great deference" in interpreting the Act. Further an employer or union may raise good faith reliance on an EEOC guideline or opinion as a defense in a suit against it under Title VII.

2. Other Remedies Against Employment Discrimination: The Civil Rights Acts of 1866 and 1871

Besides Title VII, two other statutes are important in enforcing equal employment: the Civil Rights Acts of 1866 and 1871. These laws, known as the Reconstruction Civil Rights Acts, were passed by Congress to give effect to the thirteenth and fourteenth Amendments of the Constitution that abolished slavery and provided equal protection of the laws for all citizens of the United

States. They are now contained in Volume 42 of the United States Code, Sections 1981 and 1983 (abbreviated 42 U.S.C. 1981 and 1983).

42 U.S.C. 1981 provides that all persons shall have the same right to make and enforce contracts and to full and equal benefit of all laws and proceedings for the security of persons and property as are enjoyed by white citizens. Section 1981 is a remedy against discrimination by private employers or unions. Section 1983 prohibits state and local governmental officials from depriving any person of any rights, privileges, or immunities secured by the Constitution and laws. Section 1983 is a remedy against discrimination by state and local governmental bodies.

Federal Contractor Compliance Programs.   In addition to the Civil Rights Acts, federal Executive Orders (issued by the President) prohibit employers with federal contracts from discriminating against their employees and require employers to adopt affirmative action programs for minority hiring. Detailed clauses prohibiting discrimination are part of standard government contracts. An employer may be barred from government contracts for failure to comply with these requirements. Each federal agency has an office responsible for insuring contractor compliance. The programs are centrally administered by the Department of Labor, Office of Contract Compliance.

The State and Local Fiscal Assistance Act prohibits governmental bodies that receive federal revenue sharing funds for their programs from engaging in discrimination in such programs based on race, color, national origin, sex, religion, age, and handicap. Other federal statutes prohibit discrimination against handicapped employees by federal contractors or in any program or activity receiving federal financial assistance.

B. THE BASIC CATEGORIES OF UNLAWFUL DISCRIMINATION: DISPARATE TREATMENT AND DISPARATE IMPACT

The courts have divided unlawful discriminatory conduct into two basic categories: disparate (different) treatment and disparate impact. Disparate treatment, as the name implies, means that an employer treats a person differently because of the person's race, national origin, sex, or religion. Disparate treatment is intentional discrimination. An employer's refusal to hire or promote an employee because of his race, etc., is an example of disparate treatment.

Disparate impact means that an employer engages in an employment practice or policy that has a greater adverse impact (effect) on the members of a protected group under Title VII than on other employees, regardless of the employer's intent. For example, an employer's requirement that a certain job be filled by a person with a college education would have a disparate impact on both blacks and women because fewer blacks and women have college educations than white males. Under some circumstances, this educational requirement might violate Title VII because of the consequences, even though the employer adopted the requirement in good faith.

1. Disparate Treatment Discrimination

The leading case pertaining to disparate treatment discrimination is *McDonnell Douglas Corp. v. Green.*[1] Employee Green, a black male and civil rights activist, worked as a mechanic until he was laid off in the course of a general reduction in the company's work force. While on layoff, Green engaged in protests that the general hiring practices of the

[1] See legal principle 1.

company were racially motivated. As part of this protest, Green and others illegally stalled their cars on the main roads leading to the company's plant to block access to the plant during the morning shift change. Shortly thereafter the company advertised for mechanics, a job for which Green was qualified. Green applied for the job, but was not reemployed because of the stall-in.

a. Proving a Prima-Facie Case of Disparate Treatment

Green filed a charge with the EEOC that the company had refused to hire him because of his race and his civil rights activities. The case ultimately reached the Supreme Court. There, the Court set down four factors that a person must prove to establish a "prima facie" case of discrimination based on disparate treatment. The term prima facie case means that the person bringing the suit (the plaintiff) has presented enough evidence at a trial for a court to conclude that the person was unlawfully discriminated against. The four factors that a plaintiff must prove are: (1) that the person belongs to a protected group under Title VII; (2) that the person applied for and was qualified for a job for which the employer was seeking applicants; (3) that despite being qualified, the person was rejected; and (4) that after the person was rejected, the position remained open and the employer continued to seek applicants from others with the rejected applicant's qualifications.

The Court held that Green had proven a prima facie case because: (1) he was black and therefore a member of a group protected under Title VII; (2) he was qualified for the job; (3) he was rejected despite being qualified; and (4) the company continued to seek persons with Green's abilities after Green was rejected.

b. Legitimate Employer Reasons for Rejecting the Individual

A person will not necessarily win his suit because he has proven a prima facie case of discrimination. Instead, the Supreme Court stated that the employer then has the burden "to articulate some legitimate, nondiscriminatory reason for [the person's] rejection." If the employer proves that the employment decision was based on a legitimate consideration, not an illegitimate one such as race, the employer may prevail in the suit. In *McDonnell Douglas,* the Court stated that Green's stall-in tactics would be a lawful reason for discharge refuting the prima facie case. The Supreme Court stated in a later case applying *McDonnell Douglas* that an employer does not have to prove that his hiring procedure is the best method to maximize the hiring of minority employees so long as the hiring decisions are based on legitimate nondiscriminatory considerations.

c. Employer Pretext for Discriminatory Actions

Even if the employer successfully articulates a legitimate nondiscriminatory reason for his actions, the case is not necessarily over. The Court stated in *McDonnell Douglas* that an employee can still prevail if he can prove that the employer's supposed lawful reason is a pretext, and that he in fact was discharged or otherwise treated in a disparate manner for discriminatory reasons. The Court indicated that Green might still prevail if he could prove that white employees engaged in misconduct comparable to his, but that the white employees were not discharged, or that the employer based Green's discharge on his legitimate civil rights activities. The Court stated that the manner in which Green had been treated in his prior period of employment and the employer's general policies and practices regarding minority employment could also be considered in determining whether the company's lawful reason (Green's stall-in) was a pretext for unlawful discrimination. Proving pretext under Title VII is very similar to proving pretext in cases of unlawful discharge for union activity under the Labor Management Relations Act. The NLRB often must decide whether an employee apparently discharged for a lawful reason (such as being drunk or asleep on the job) was in fact discharged for union activity, proven, for example, by the fact that other employees who had engaged in similar misconduct were not discharged.

Thus, determining whether an employer has unlawfully discriminated against a person by disparate treatment involves three shifting burdens of proof. The employee has the initial burden of proving a prima facie case under the four *McDonnell Douglas* criteria. If the employee established a prima facie case, the employer then has the burden of proving a nondiscriminatory reason for his actions. If the employer proves a nondiscriminatory reason, the burden is once again on the employee to prove that the reason given is a pretext for unlawful discrimination.

d. Application of the Basic Disparate Treatment Criteria

Although *McDonnell Douglas* involved alleged race discrimination, the same order and burden of proof are applied in all disparate treatment discrimination cases against a protected group including those based on religion, national origin, sex, and age. The principles apply not only to refusals to hire, as in *McDonnell Douglas*, but to any other alleged disparate treatment, such as discriminatory layoffs, the denial of a promotion, or a discharge.

The Supreme Court has indicated that al-though *McDonnell Douglas* establishes the basic procedural and proof requirements in disparate treatment discrimination cases, the four factors listed in that case are not to be applied rigidly or mechanically. The court said that the case's approach is simply a sensible orderly way to evaluate the evidence in a case.

For example, the fourth requirement stated in *McDonnell Douglas* is that a position remain open after the complaining party was rejected for it and that the employer continue to seek applicants of the complainant's qualifications after he or she was rejected. What if an employer withdraws a job without filling the position at all because the only qualified applicants were members of a minority group? Or what if an employer raises the qualifications for a job after discriminatorily rejecting a minority group member who met the original qualifications, in order to avoid meeting the requirement that the employer continue to seek applicants of the same qualifications as the rejected applicant? If the employer could not prove a legitimate reason for his actions, a court undoubtedly would find that the employer had violated Title VII under these circumstances, even though all the requirements for a prima facie case under *McDonnell Douglas* were not met.

2. Disparate Impact Discrimination

a. The Adverse Consequences Test

The basic principles in disparate impact discrimination cases were established by the Supreme Court in *Griggs v. Duke Power Co.*[2] In *Griggs,* the employer required that job applicants for any job other than basic labor be a high school graduate and have a satisfactory score on two professionally recognized gen-

[2] See legal principle 3.

eral aptitude tests. The tests did not measure the ability to learn or perform a particular job. These two job requirements had a disproportionate impact on blacks because a lower percentage of blacks than whites had a high school education and passed the tests. A suit was filed to have the requirements abolished. The employer argued that the high school graduation and test requirements were lawful because they were not adopted with an intent to discriminate. The employer also argued that the tests were lawful under Section 703(h) that permitted the used of professionally developed aptitude tests.

The Supreme Court held that both the high school graduation requirement and the tests violated Title VII. The Court stated that a specific intent to discriminate was not needed for conduct to violate Title VII, but that Congress required:

> [T]he removal of artificial, arbitrary, and unnecessary barriers to employment when the barriers operate invidiously to discriminate on the basis of racial or other impermissible classification.... The Act proscribes not only overt discrimination, but also practices that are fair in form, but discriminatory in operation.

The Court held that an employer must prove business necessity for an employment practice such as the high school graduation requirement, which operates to exclude blacks from employment. Title VII prohibits an employment practice that operates to exclude blacks or any other protected group if the practice is not related to job performance. The burden is on the employer to prove job relatedness.

The Court concluded in *Griggs* that neither the general intelligence tests nor the high school graduation requirement had a proven relationship to successful performance on the job. To the contrary, the evidence showed that employees hired before the company adopted these requirements performed satisfactorily even though they were not all high school graduates or had passed the test. The Court rejected the employer's argument that he acted in good faith, finding that Title VII was directed at the *consequences* of employment practices, not the motivation. The Court held that the provision of Section 703(h) permitting the use of professionally developed tests only applied if the test was job related.

Although *Griggs* involved testing and educational requirements, the case's principles have been applied to any employment practice or policy that has a disparate impact on a protected group. Courts have invalidated employer rules providing for the discharge of employees for excessive garnishments. These rules have had a disproportionate impact on blacks and employers have been unable to demonstrate business necessity for the rules. The employer's minor inconvenience in processing garnishments is insufficient to justify the adverse consequences. Similarly, employer blanket policies against hiring employees with arrest records have been invalidated under Title VII because of the disparate impact on blacks and because employers have been unable to prove the business necessity for the policy. That an employee has prior arrests has no relationship to the employee's ability to do assembly line work.

b. Order of Proof in Disparate Impact Cases

As in cases of disparate treatment, there is also a shifting burden of proof in impact discrimination cases. The plaintiff has the initial burden of proving that a practice or procedure has disparate impact. If there is disparate impact, the employer has the burden of proving businesss necessity and job relatedness for the practice. Even if the employer proves business necessity, however, the plaintiff can still prevail if he can prove that there is an alternative method that would satisfy the employer's legitimate needs without the undesirable adverse consequences on a protected group. The Supreme Court stated in *Griggs* that proof of an alternative method would indicate that the employer's purported business reason was a pretext for unlawful discrimination.

c. Perpetuation of Past Discrimination

Sometimes practices appear neutral on their face, but are in fact discriminatory because they perpetuate (prolong the effect of) past discrimination. An employer may establish a line of promotion with a number of steps from trainee to journeyman status in a particular classification and require that an employee work for a specified period in the lower classification before being promoted to the highest position. Normally, that is a permissible requirement. But, consider the situation in which an employer previously discriminatorily barred members of a protected group from the job classification. What if the employer ceases its discriminatory practices, but still requires the minority employees to work their way up each step of the classification in the specified time. Under those circumstances, requiring experience in the lower jobs first would perpetuate the prior discrimination because the victims of the discrimination (the discriminatees) might already have been in the top classification, but for the prior discrimination. The Supreme Court held in *Griggs* that practices that perpetuate past discrimination in this fashion violate Title VII because of their discriminatory impact.

d. Use of Statistics in Proving Disparate Impact

As in *Griggs*, the Supreme Court has frequently upheld the use of statistics to prove the disparate impact of an employment policy or practice by showing that a lower percentage of a protected group than the general population can meet a specific job requirement. A prima facie case of disparate impact discrimination can be proven by showing that a particular protected group makes up a significantly lower percentage of a company's work force than the general population in a given labor market.

The Court indicated in *McDonnell Douglas* that statistics on an employer's employment policies are also relevant in determining whether a particular act of apparent disparate treatment is part of an overall general pattern of discrimination. Statistics, of course, work both ways. An employee can use statistics as evidence of overall discriminatory conduct, from which a court can infer that the individual employee was also subjected to disparate treatment. An employer, however, can also use statistics of an overall proportionate work force to refute allegations that a particular employee was denied employment, or otherwise treated differently, because of race.

The Supreme Court has also cautioned that statistics are not irrefutable and that their usefulness varies from case to case. They can be rebutted by showing that there is an error in the statistics themselves, or that the statistics, while correct, are being used to make improper comparisons. For example, should an employer's minority work force percentage be compared with the minority group's percentage in the overall population of an entire metropolitan area or a more restricted geographical area? If a company is large, the company's minority group employment percentages might be compared with each group's percentage of an entire metropolitan area because the company draws its work force from the entire area. In contrast, if the employer is a small store that traditionally hires employees from the surrounding neighborhood, the metropolitan area figure would be meaningless.

An employer's percentages may also be meaningless in some cases unless they are compared to the percentage of a minority group that is qualified for the jobs in question. If a minority group member is denied employment in an unskilled job, general population figures are useful in determining whether the employer has discriminated. However, if the job in question is highly specialized, it might be necessary to compare an employer's minority group percentages with the percentage of the group that is qualified for the job.

What if an employer requires that employees pass a test that is not job related, but there is not a disproportionate impact on members of a protected group? The percentage of blacks in the work force, for example, may be the same as the percentage of blacks in the overall labor market; or the same percentage of black and white applicants may pass the test even though it is not job related. The purpose of Title VII is to prevent practices or policies that have adverse consequences on protected groups. Thus, if an employment policy or practice has no adverse consequences, the employer can retain the requirement. Job relatedness is a *defense* after the plaintiff establishes a prima facie case of discrimination by proving a disproportionate impact.

e. Testing Requirements and Disparate Impact

The use of tests in making employment decisions, whether for hiring, promotion, or

other purposes, has been a recurring issue under Title VII. Under Section 703(h), an ability test can be used if it is professionally developed and is not designed, intended, or used to discriminate. The Supreme Court indicated in *Griggs* that tests that have a disproportionate impact on a protected group must be job related to be lawful under Section 703(h).

Since 1966, the EEOC has periodically issued detailed guidelines for determining whether a test is job related. The Supreme Court has indicated the court should give great deference to these guidelines when determining whether a test with disparate impact violates Title VII. In *Albemarle Paper Co. v. Moody*, the Court relied heavily on the guidelines in ruling that the employer's tests for promotion to skilled jobs violated Title VII because of the disparate impact on black employees.[3] The Court upheld the guidelines' basic principle that a test must be predictive of success on a specific job in order to be job related. There must be a correlation between performance on the test and performance on the job.

The employer in *Albermarle* attempted to validate his test by comparing test results with employee performance on the higher level jobs in each skilled classification promotion series, not on the entry level positions in which employees would start. The Court upheld the EEOC guidelines position that tests should generally be validated by comparing test results with employee performance on a job at or near the entry level, unless the job progression structure and seniority system are such that new employees will probably progress to a higher level within a reasonable period of time in the great majority of cases. Jobs must be validated at or near the entry level if progress is not nearly automatic or if

[3] See legal principle 5.

the time span before promotion is such that the higher level job might change in the meantime or the employee's own potential for the higher job could be significantly changed. There was no evidence in *Albemarle* that employees progressed automatically or rapidly to the higher level jobs. Thus, the Court held the tests were invalid under Title VII because they improperly measured success at the higher level jobs rather than at the entry level.

For example, what if an employer is hiring clerks to do routine tabulations in an accounting department where the top job, the auditor classification, requires years of experience or a professional degree? If only a few employees ever advance to the top position, can an employer base his decision to hire someone for the clerk's position on a test that measures success as an auditor? No, because promotions from clerk to auditor are not automatic and there is a long time span involved during which either the auditor's job can change or the employee's ability can improve. A test can be used only if it measures success in the clerk's position. But if an employee applies for a trainee's job that has a six month probationary period after which the employee is classified as a journeyman, a test can probably be validated as job related if it measures success as a journeyman, not as a trainee.

f. The Bottom Line Concept: The Uniform Testing Guidelines

A major issue under Title VII is whether an employer has complied with Title VII if the proportion of protected group employees in the overall work force is representative although some aspects of the   employer's practices are discriminatory. What if an employer uses an employment test that proportionately fewer blacks pass, but the employer hires a higher percentage of the blacks who do pass so that the employer's overall work force is proportionate? If the test is not job related, some individual black applicants may have been discriminatorily denied employment under the *Griggs'* principles because of the test even though the employer ends up with a proportionate work force. Some persons have argued that any individual member of a protected group denied a job because of a test or any other employment practice that does not meet Title VII requirements has a claim under Title VII, even though the employer's overall work force is proportionate. On the other hand, employers argue that only the "bottom line" should matter and that employers should be judged on the overall impact of their employment policies, not on each individual component practice or policy. Thus, these employers argue, a proportionate work force should be sufficient to comply with Title VII even though a particular practice, such as a test, might have a disproportionate impact on a protected group.

In 1978, the Equal Employment Opportunity Commission, the Department of Labor, the Department of Justice, and the United States Civil Service Commission, the four agencies having primary federal responsibility in the civil rights field, adopted "Uniform Guidelines on Employee Selection Procedures." These guidelines pertain to the use of tests in making employment decisions. They are especially important because these agencies had previously disagreed among themselves on certain issues pertaining to tests. Remember, these Guidelines are not necessarily binding on either an employer or a union. They do, however, set forth the agencies' interpretation of the law and, under prior Supreme Court decisions, are entitled to a great deference by a court.

The Uniform Guidelines adopt the bottom line concept of testing. The Guidelines provide that the agencies will not require that employment tests be validated for job relatedness if the employer's overall selection procedures are such that the selection rate for any race, sex, or ethnic group is not less than four-fifths (80 percent) of the group with the highest selection rate. The agencies regard the four-fifths as a "rule of thumb" for determining whether an employer's practices have a disproportionate impact. For example, if an employer hires 90 percent of the white applicants for employment (the highest selection rate), the employer must hire at least 72 percent of all black applicants (80 percent of 90 percent) in order for the employer's "bottom line" results to indicate that the employer's overall selection processes do not have a disproportionate impact. If the selection rate for any protected group is less than 80 percent of the selection rate for the highest group, the agencies will find that the employer's employment practices have adverse consequences. In that event, each employment practice, including the test, must be validated for job relatedness. If, however, the four-fifths figure is reached, the agencies only look at the "bottom line" and do not require validation. The Guidelines do not require comparison of minority subgroups, such as white males versus black females.

The Uniform Guidelines emphasize that the agencies adopted the "bottom line" approach only as an administrative procedure because of the impracticality of policing each and every employer. The agencies, thus, decided to concentrate on employers where there is statistical evidence of possible discrimination under Title VII. That an employer meets the four-fifths rule of thumb does not necessarily mean that he is not discriminating. Thus, the Guidelines emphasize, an individual can still bring a discrimination charge against an employer meeting the four-fifths requirement if the employee can prove that he was discriminatorily denied employment based on a specific employment practice or policy, even though the employer's overall statistics meet the bottom line standard.

The Uniform Guidelines contain a number of exceptions under which the four-fifths rule would not apply. Thus, regardless of meeting the four-fifths requirement, an employer cannot engage in a practice that perpetuates past discrimination against current employees. Further, an employer cannot maintain an employment practice, such as maintaining a policy against hiring employees with an arrest record, that either the courts or an administrative agency have found is not job related under similar circumstances.

Validation Methods. The Uniform Guidelines continue the basic policy of the prior EEOC Guidelines that a test must be professionally validated to show a clear relationship between selection procedures and performance on the job. A selection procedure, however, must be validated only if it has a disparate impact. The Uniform Guidelines further require that an employer, as part of a validation study, investigate whether there are alternative selection procedures that would meet his legitimate needs, but that would have less adverse impact on a protected group.

A test can be validated in one of three ways. First, the test can correlate to performance on the job. Second, the test can correlate with success in an important element of the job (typing abilities for a secretary). Third, the test can be validated by demonstrating a correlation with an important trait needed for success on the job, such as traits needed for success as a salesperson.

The Uniform Guidelines contain standards and documentation requirements for validating tests using each of the three basic methods. The guidelines are technical and many pages long. Because there are detailed requirements and exceptions that a book of this nature cannot cover, the Uniform Guidelines themselves must be consulted to determine their application to a particular situation.

C. SPECIAL PROBLEMS OF SEX DISCRIMINATION

1. Sexual Stereotypes

Unlawful discrimination because of sex also generally falls into either the disparate treatment or disparate impact categories. Additionally, women have also faced the problem of sexual stereotyping under which employers assume that women are only suited for, or only want to do, certain work. The courts have uniformly held that an employer cannot reject a woman for a job because of a sexual stereotype. Under Title VII, each woman must be judged on her individual capability. Thus, an employer cannot assume that women are incapable of or do not wish to do heavy manual labor. There are women who have the physical strength and desire for such jobs. An employer, therefore, violates Title VII by limiting such jobs to men.

a. Height and Weight Restrictions

There has been considerable litigation over height and weight restrictions on jobs because of the disproportionate impact on women. Many such requirements have been invalidated under Title VII because employers have been unable to prove the need for an arbitrary cutoff on height or weight to do a particular job. Again, the basic principle of Title VII is that each applicant must be judged by her own ability to do a particular job, not by arbitrarily established standards.

b. Different Social or Moral Standards for Men and Women

An employer cannot limit jobs requiring travel to men on the assumption that married women do not want to travel or that a single woman traveling alone may create a poor image for the company, because the employer would be basing his decision on a stereotyped assumption about the work and social roles of women.

Similarly, women cannot be denied employment on the basis of different moral standards than those that apply to men. At one time, some employers would not hire a woman who had a child out of wedlock, but they would hire the father of such a child. These employers apparently assumed that the woman had lower moral standards than the man. Depending upon the job, employers may be able to consider moral and ethical standards in determining whether to hire a person, but the same standards must be applied to men and women. A hiring practice that considered an employee's moral or ethical standards, even if it did not discriminate on the basis of sex, could still violate Title VII under some circumstances if it had a disparate impact on a protected group and was not job related.

2. Grooming Standards

Grooming standards are an exception to the usual rule that an employer cannot apply different rules to men and women. The courts have upheld rules requiring short hair for male employees, but allowing women to have any length of hair. The courts have concluded that such rules do not deny employment opportunities and that hair length is "peripheral" (not of concern) to the Civil Rights Act. However, an employer must prove business necessity if a grooming standard, such as a rule forbidding afros, has a disproportionate impact on a particular race.

Although different grooming standards for men and women do not violate Title VII, disciplining an employee for failure to meet a particular grooming standard might still violate the just cause provisions of a collective bargaining agreement. For example, if an employer discharged an employee because of his hair length, an arbitrator might decide that the hair length rule was unreasonable, unless justified for safety or public relations reasons, and that the employee could not be disciplined for violating it.

3. Fringe Benefit Contributions for Men and Women

Many fringe benefit plans are funded solely by employer contributions. Other plans require that the employees contribute a percentage of their salary to a plan as well. Such plans are called contributory plans.

The Supreme Court held in *City of Los Angeles v. Manhart* that an employer cannot require women to pay a higher percentage than male employees as their share in a contributory plan.[4] Employers argued that women could be required to pay more into a pension plan than men because women live longer and would therefore receive greater pension benefits upon retirement. But the Supreme Court reasoned that Title VII requires that employees be treated as individuals and not have their rights determined by assumptions based on their sex as a group. The Court stated that since there is no way to determine whether a particular woman would live longer than a particular man, an individual woman cannot be required to pay more than a man. Therefore, an employer must contrib-

[4] See legal principle 8.

ute equal amounts to fringe benefit funds for men and women.

Although the *Manhart* case pertained to pension plans, the same reasoning applies to any fringe benefit plan. Thus, an employer cannot require either men or women to pay in more to a health and welfare plan on the assumption that employees of one sex, as a group, are absent or ill more often than the other.

The Supreme Court cautioned in *Manhart* that it was not requiring changes in the insurance industry. Insurance companies customarily pay lower monthly pension benefits to women than men, even though the same amount of money has been paid into a fund to provide pension benefits for them. Statistically, women live longer than men, and the lower monthly payments to women, who will have more retirement years, is statistically equal in value to the higher monthly payment for men who do not live as long. An employer must contribute equal amounts for men and women employees and cannot require women to contribute more themselves. However, an insurance company can still lawfully provide a lower monthly retirement benefit to a woman. An employer does not violate Title VII as long as he sets aside equal amounts for men and women employees, even if the men and women ultimately receive different benefits because of insurance industry practice.

4. The Equal Pay Act

In addition to Title VII, women employees are also protected by the Equal Pay Act, which requires an employer to pay women the same as a man for doing the same work. This Act predated Title VII and prohibits the once common practice of paying women less for doing the same job based on the theory that a married man needed a greater salary to support his family. This Act does not prohibit disparate treatment other than prohibiting paying women less for the same work.

Of course, Title VII also prohibits paying women less for performing the same job as a male employee. However, the Equal Pay Act is part of the Fair Labor Standards Act commonly known as the Wage-Hour Law. The Fair Labor Standards Act has a two-year limitations period for filing suit in court rather than the 180 days allowed under Title VII for filing a charge with the EEOC. Thus, it might be possible to remedy an equal pay violation under the Equal Pay Act after the time for filing a charge under Title VII has expired. Also, the Equal Pay Act permits an employee to collect not only the amount of back pay owed, but also an additional sum as damages equal to the amount of the pay owed. The amount is at the court's discretion. Thus, an employee may receive a greater back pay award under the Equal Pay Act than under Title VII. Sometimes a suit may be brought under both Title VII and the Equal Pay Act if both provisions have been violated. That can be done by filing a charge with the EEOC, waiting six months while the charge is processed (as discussed below), and then filing suit in federal court under both statutes. The Equal Pay Act provides for enforcement through the Department of Labor, but a Presidential Reorganization Order has transferred enforcement to the EEOC.

5. Bona Fide Occupational Requirements

An employer may use sex as an employment qualification if it is a BFOQ under Section 703(e), although the courts have emphasized that this is a narrow exception. Sex can be a BFOQ only if an employer has a reasonable factual basis for believing that all

or substantially all of the excluded group (women) would be unable to perform a job. There must be a reasonable necessary connection between the employee's sex and the job to be performed. A distinction based on a stereotyped assumption on male or female roles is not valid.

The Supreme Court upheld the State of Alabama's right to limit "contact" prison guards in an all male prison to men because the prisoners were poorly controlled and the women's sex might incite unrest and even attacks upon them. The Court emphasized, however, that its decision was narrowly based on the specific facts at that prison. In the same decision, the Court still held that Alabama's general height and weight requirements for prison guards were unlawfully discriminatory against women because the requirements excluded 44 percent of all women from consideration for prison guard positions.

That an employer's customers or other employees prefer or expect employees to be of a particular sex is not a lawful basis for limiting employment opportunities to that sex. Thus, the courts have held that airline cabin attendant positions cannot be limited to women. The primary purpose of attendants is passenger safety and there is no necessary connection between an employee's sex and the performance of these duties. That most airline passengers are male and might prefer female stewardesses is irrelevant.

6. State Protective Laws

State protective laws for women limited the right of women to work overtime or to engage in certain occupations. These laws originally had good motives. They were designed to protect the "weaker sex," but they were based on sexual stereotypes of a woman's role and work ability. The laws frequently worked against women because employers refused to hire them for certain jobs because of the restrictions.

The EEOC, with court approval, has held that the existence of a state protective law cannot justify an employer's refusal to hire or promote a woman to a certain position. Further, once a woman is hired, she is subject to the same working conditions as any other employee. Under Section 708, the provisions of Title VII prevail over the state legislation.

Once a female employee is hired, she is not entitled to any special privileges. If a job requires heavy lifting, she must do the lifting. If the job requires overtime, she must work the same as any other employee.

7. Pregnancy Benefits

Pregnancy benefits were a much debated issue under Title VII. The Supreme Court held in 1976 that Title VII did not prohibit an employer from excluding pregnancy benefits from a hospitalization plan. This decision raised many questions, such as whether pregnant women were entitled to sick leave if their pregnancy disabled them for work or whether pregnant women who went on pregnancy leave could continue to accumulate seniority under the same conditions as a male employee on sick leave.

These issues were resolved by the Pregnancy Disability Amendment to Title VII effective October 31, 1978. The pregnancy amendment broadened the definition of sex discrimination in Title VII to include discrimination on the basis of pregnancy, childbirth, or related medical conditions. Under this amendment, women disabled due to pregnancy must be treated the same as to their conditions of employment, including fringe benefits, as any other person disabled for work for any other reason. Thus, a woman

cannot be discharged because she is pregnant. A woman who is able to work, although pregnant, cannot be required to take sick leave at a certain time. A woman on leave due to her pregnancy can continue to accumulate seniority and is entitled to reinstatement under the same conditions as any other temporarily disabled employee.

A pregnant woman disabled for work is entitled to the same disability benefits as a worker disabled for any other reason. Hospitalization plans must cover the cost of hospitalization for pregnancy, childbirth, and related medical conditions. As an exception, however, the amendment states that employers are not required to pay health insurance benefits for abortion except where the life of the mother would be in danger if the fetus were carried to term or where "medical complications" have arisen from an abortion. An employer, however, can provide such benefits voluntarily or if a collective bargaining agreement requires them.

If an employer does not provide disability or paid sick leave to other employees, it does not need to for pregnant workers. The law as amended only requires the employer to treat pregnancy and childbirth the same as other disabilities under fringe benefit plants. An employer is not required to establish a disability program if it does not already have one.

An employer is not required to provide diability payments to a pregnant worker who asks for time off unless she is disabled for work because of her condition. Similarly, after a woman gives birth, she is entitled to benefits while she is disabled for work. If a woman is able to work, however, but chooses to stay off longer to be with her newborn child, she is not entitled to continued benefits while she voluntarily stays off work. A woman who wishes to remain off work longer than medically necessary is entitled to personal leave under the same conditions any other employee receives it.

D. RELIGIOUS AND AGE DISCRIMINATION

Whether an employee has been discriminated against because of religion or age is judged by the same standards generally applicable to racial or sex discrimination. An employee cannot be individually subjected to disparate treatment because of religion or age as determined under the *McDonnell Douglas v. Green* criteria. Also, an employer cannot adopt an employment practice or policy that discriminates because of its disparate impact on employees of a particular age or religion as determined under the *Griggs* standards.

The provisions of Title VII prohibiting religious discrimination and the Age Discrimination in Employment Act both contain exceptions permitting religion or age to be bona fide occupational qualifications. The courts use the same criteria in determining whether a person's religion or age is a BFOQ as they use for determining whether a person's sex is a BFOQ for a job. A job qualification cannot be based on a stereotyped assumption of appropriate jobs or the ability of persons of a particular age or religion. An employer must have a reasonable factual basis to believe that all or substantially all of a group is unable to perform a job before excluding them.

1. Religious Discrimination: The Reasonable Accommodation Test

The principal issue in religious discrimination arises under the provision of Section 701(j) requiring an employer to make reasonable accommodation to an employee's religious observances or practices that do not entail undue hardship on the employer's business. How far must an employer go in accommodating the religious beliefs of an employee? This issue was considered by the Supreme Court in *Trans World Airlines v. Hardison.*[5] Hardison was a member of a religious group whose Sabbath was from Friday night sundown to Saturday night sundown. Hardison refused to work on Saturdays. The collective bargaining agreement required that the lowest seniority employees do weekend work unless a higher seniority employee volunteered to work instead. Because of his low seniority date, Hardision was frequently required to work Saturday, but he refused because of his religious beliefs and was discharged. He filed a charge with the EEOC alleging that he had been discriminated against because of his religion and the case ultimately reached the Supreme Court.

Hardison argued that the religious accommodation provisions of Section 701(j) required that TWA either find a supervisor to do Hardison's work or else TWA should require another employee, whose religious beliefs did not prohibit Saturday work, to do the work instead. Hardison argued that another employee should be required to work even though that employee might have higher seniority and requiring the other employee to work would violate the contract's seniority provisions.

The Supreme Court rejected Hardison's argument. It held that an employer does not have to violate the terms of a contractual seniority clause in order to accommodate an employee's religious beliefs. TWA did not have to deny contractual shift or job preferences to some employees in order to accommodate the religious beliefs of another employee. The Court did emphasize, however, that the TWA seniority system was a

---

[5] See legal principle 9.

bona fide system that was not designed or intended to discriminate against employees because of their religious beliefs. If a seniority clause were designed to discriminate, its application would not be protected under Title VII.

The court stated in upholding the seniority provisions:

> [W]e do not believe that the duty to accommodate requires TWA to take steps inconsistent with the otherwise valid agreement. Collective bargaining, aimed at effecting workable and enforceable agreements between management and labor, lies at the core of our national labor policy, and seniority provisions are universally included in these contracts. Without a clear and express indication from Congress, we cannot agree with Hardison and the EEOC that an agreed upon seniority system must give way when necessary to accommodate religious observances.

As to Hardison's other arguments that TWA could have used supervisory personnel or could have offered employees premium pay to work on Saturday, the Court pointed out that both alternatives involved costs to TWA, either through lost efficiency in other jobs or in higher wages. The Court stated that requiring TWA to bear more than a *de minimis* cost to give Hardison Saturdays off would be an undue hardship under Section 701(j) that the company was not required to bear.

Thus, under the *Hardison* decision, an employer does not have to change its seniority system or compel an employee to work at a time when he would be off in order to accommodate the religious beliefs of another employee. Further, an employer does not have to make any work changes that would involve more than a *de minimis* expense to it. Of course, the *Hardison* opinion does not permit an employer to sit back and do nothing if an employee requests time off for religious reasons. In Hardison's case, no other employee

was available to fill Hardison's position without violating the contract's seniority clause or entailing extra cost to the company. Certainly, however, if another employee was available to do the work without extra cost, or if an employee's absence would not disrupt operations, or if two employees were willing to exchange shifts so that one of them could be off for religious observance, the employer would be obligated under Title VII to allow the employee time off.

2. Age Discrimination

The Age Discrimination in Employment Act (ADEA) prohibits discrimination on account of age against individuals who are at least forty years of age, but less than seventy. The Act applies to employers, unions, and employment agencies. The ADEA was originally enforced by the Department of Labor, but enforcement authority was transferred to the EEOC by a Presidential Reorganization Order effective July 1, 1979.

Essentially the ADEA prohibits the same discriminatory conduct because of a person's age that Title VII prohibits because of race, religion, national origin, or sex. Thus, the Act prohibits discrimination in hiring, discharge, and conditions of employment. Classifications based on age, which would deprive a person of employment opportunities or otherwise adversely affect his status as an employee, are prohibited. A union is prohibited from discriminating in membership and job referrals. Nor can a union classify its members by age in any way that deprives an individual of employment opportunities or adversely affects his status as an employee. The Department of Labor's position was that apprenticeship programs do not violate the ADEA by imposing age eligibility limitations on admission to apprenticeship training.

However, the EEOC has tentatively indicated it may not follow the Department of Labor's interpretation. Whether the EEOC will challenge age restrictions on admission to apprenticeship programs may not be known until the EEOC issues new regulations interpreting the ADEA and those regulations are challenged in Court.

Originally, the ADEA, as enacted in 1967, only applied up to age sixty-five, but the age limit was raised to age seventy in 1978. Thus, an employee cannot be required to retire before age seventy unless, of course, age is a BFOQ. As an exception, employees engaged in a bona fide executive or high policy making function, with retirement income of at least $27,000 per year, and tenured teachers at an institution of higher education, may still be retired at age sixty-five.

The original Act contained a provision under which an employee could be forced to retire before age sixty-five pursuant to a bona fide retirement plan. This provision was eliminated in the 1978 amendments when the age limit was raised to age seventy. Pension plans can no longer require that an employee retire before age seventy unless retirement at an earlier age is a BFOQ. Of course, the ADEA does not prohibit plans from permitting voluntary early retirement before age seventy.

ADEA Procedures

A charge alleging violations of the ADEA must be filed with the EEOC within 180 days of the alleged unlawful practice. A suit to enforce the ADEA can be filed in federal court either by the EEOC or the individual. But an individual must wait 60 days after filing a charge with the EEOC before filing suit on his own. This requirement is to afford time for conciliation.

If a state has a law prohibiting age discrimination, no suit can be filed unless the complaining party has filed a charge with the state agency and waits at least 60 days unless the state proceedings are terminated before the 60 days are up. If a state law prohibits age discrimination, the 180 day requirement for filing a charge under the ADEA is extended to 300 days after the alleged unlawful employment practice occurs, or within 30 days after the individual receives notice that the state proceedings have been terminated, whichever is earlier. However a person can proceed under the ADEA 60 days after filing a charge with the appropriate state agency even if state proceedings are not completed.

There was a question about whether an employee forfeits his right to relief under the ADEA if he fails to file a timely charge with the state agency. What if a state law requires that an age discrimination charge be filed within 90 days of an unlawful occurrence, but the employee does not file the charge until the one hundredth day, when the state agency is powerless to act? Can the employee still file a charge under the ADEA, which allows 180 days to file a charge, even though the ADEA requires that a charge be filed with the state agency?

The Supreme Court resolved this issue in a rather unique way. The Court held that the employee must file the charge with the state agency even though it is untimely. After waiting the required 60 days, even though the state agency may be powerless to act, the employee can then proceed with his case under the ADEA.

E. TITLE VII PROCESSING REQUIREMENTS AND SUIT PROCEDURES

1. Filing the Charge

Under Section 706(e), a charge must be filed with the EEOC within 180 days after the occurrence of an alleged discriminatory act violating Title VII. Under Section 706(b), a charge may be filed by or on behalf of a person claiming to be aggrieved (damaged by an unlawful act). This permits a union to file a charge on behalf of its members who may have been discriminated against. A charge may also be filed by a member of the Commission itself.

A charge is filed in one of the EEOC's district or subarea offices that have the necessary forms and can provide assistance. The EEOC must serve a notice of the charge on the charged party within ten days after filing.

Continuing Violations

The filing time for a charge may be longer that 180 days if it alleges a "continuing violation." A continuing violation, as the name indicates, is one that occurs over time rather than being a single isolated occurrence. For example, if a black employee receives lower wages or is forced to work under more difficult working conditions than white employees, those conditions are a continuing violation. If an employer has a promotion policy that has an adverse impact upon members of a protected group, and the policy is not justified by business necessity, the continued use of the policy is a continuing violation. However, decisions not to hire or promote a particular person or to discharge an employee are considered single occurrences. A charge must be filed within 180 days from the occurrence.

What if an employee is discriminatorily laid off, but does not file a charge with the EEOC over the layoff and is then recalled to work more than 180 days after the layoff? Can he still file a timely charge with the EEOC within 180 days after being recalled on the grounds that the earlier discriminatory layoff resulted in the employee being recalled later

or having lower seniority than he should have had? No, the charge must be filed within 180 days of the original occurrence or no action can be taken under Title VII regardless of the later consequences.

It is not always easy to determine whether a particular violation of Title VII should be classified by a court as a single occurrence or a continuing violation. Therefore, the best procedure is to file a charge within 180 days of the initial occurrence in every case.

2. Deferral to State Civil Rights Agencies

Under Section 706(c), if an alleged unfair employment practice occurs in a state that has both a law prohibiting the alleged practice and an agency to enforce the law, the charging party is required to file a charge with the state agency and wait 60 days before filing a charge with the EEOC. The EEOC, however, has adopted a procedure under which charges can be filed directly with it after which the EEOC defers the charge to the state agency. If the state agency has not resolved the matter within 60 days, the EEOC reasserts its own jurisdiction and proceeds. In some states, the state agency routinely waives its jurisdiction over cases deferred to it, and the EEOC reasserts jurisdiction immediately. These deferral procedures are handled as internal matters and the charging party may be unaware of them.

3. Investigation and Conciliation

Under Section 706(b), the EEOC investigates a charge filed with it to determine whether there is "reasonable cause" to believe that the statute has been violated. If the EEOC determines that there is not reasonable cause, the charge is dismissed and the charging party is so notified. That is not necessarily the end of the matter, however. Even though the EEOC has found no reasonable cause, the charging party still has the statutory right to file suit in federal court on his own against the parties named in the charge. This suit must be filed within 90 days from the date the charging party receives notice that the charge has been dismissed. This notice is referred to as a "right to sue letter."

If the EEOC finds reasonable cause to believe there is a violation, it must attempt to eliminate the practice by "conference, conciliation, and persuasion." The EEOC has recently modified this statutory procedure under its Rapid Charge Processing System. Under this system, the appropriate local EEOC office schedules a conference between the party filing the charge and the charged party as soon as possible after a charge is filed. The EEOC attempts to work out a quick resolution of the charge without any admission of liability by the charged party. If the EEOC is unable to resolve the charge in this informal manner, it will, as quickly as possible, make an initial determination on whether the charge lacks merit and should be dismissed, or whether the charge should be held for a full investigation on reasonable cause and formal conciliation efforts.

Section 706(b) provides that nothing said or done during or as part of conciliation procedures may be made public by the commission, its officers, or employees or used as evidence in any subsequent proceedings. Congress imposed this secrecy requirement so that attempts at conciliation would not be hampered by a party's fear that something said or done during conciliation would be used against it at a later trial. Congress wants conciliation, not court action, to be the primary method of resolving civil rights matters.

4. EEOC Authority to Broaden an Investigation

Most charges are filed by charging parties only in their own behalf. That is true even though the individual may be complaining of an act or an employment policy or procedure that also adversely affects other members of the same minority group. Although an individual may have filed a charge in his own behalf only, the EEOC has authority to broaden the charge to include the class (group) of persons who face the same discriminatory situation. For example, if an employee files a charge that a hiring test discriminated against him as a black, the EEOC can broaden the charge to include the class of all black employees. The EEOC can also broaden the charge to include unlawful acts or policies that the charging party did not allege as a violation so long as the additional acts are reasonably related to, or grow out of, the initial charge. Thus, if a person files a charge pertaining to an alleged discriminatory employment test, the EEOC may broaden the charge to include an employer's entire hiring policy. Courts permit such broadening on the theory that a charging party frequently does not know what his legal rights are or know all the facts of an occurrence at the time a charge is filed. The Courts reason it is, therefore, proper for the EEOC to broaden the charge as necessary to eliminate the underlying discrimination completely rather than just the single act that might have triggered the employee's charge.

Sometimes an employee will file a charge only against the employer, but the EEOC will encourage the employee to name the union as a charged party as well. That may be necessary because the remedy for an alleged discriminatory practice may require the employer to change an employment policy or practice contained in a collective bargaining agreement. If the union is not a party to the charge, it is not bound by any agreement the employer makes with the EEOC. Also, the EEOC's position, which the courts have approved, is that a union violates Title VII if it does not fairly represent minority group employees and does not actively seek to eliminate discriminatory practices against them.

5. EEOC vs. Private Suits Under Title VII

a. Authority to Bring Suit

If the EEOC determines that there is reasonable cause to believe that Title VII has been violated and conciliation fails, further proceedings depend upon whether the charge is against a private employer, a union, or a governmental agency subject to the Act.

If the charge is against a private party, the EEOC has authority to file suit itself in federal court against the charged party. If the EEOC decides not to file suit, it can notify the charging party that conciliation has failed and that the EEOC is not bringing suit, but that the charging party has the right to do so. The charging party then has the right to bring suit within 90 days after receiving the right to sue notice. If a charging party does not have an attorney, the Act permits a federal court to appoint one. If the charged party is a state or local or government body subject to the Act and conciliation fails, the EEOC refers the case to the United States Attorney General. The EEOC does not have authority to file suit against governmental agencies. The Attorney General's office decides whether to file suit on behalf of the United States in federal court against the governmental body. If the Attorney General decides not to file suit, he notifies the charged party of the right to sue within 90 days after receiving the notice.

The EEOC receives so many charges that it is not feasible for it or the Attorney General to file suit in most cases. These agencies, thus, try to select for suit the cases that will have the broadest national impact, such as those involving important legal issues or widespread (systematic) discrimination. In other cases, even though the charge has merit, the charging party most proceed on his own. Section 706(k) allows a court to award an attorney's fee to the prevailing party in a suit brought under Title VII; thus, in most cases, an employee with a meritorious claim has little difficulty in obtaining an attorney.

6. Time Requirements for Filing Suit

Requesting a Right to Sue Letter

Prior to the 1972 amendments, charging parties had to sit by helplessly while the EEOC processed their case until they finally received a right to sue letter notifying them that their charge had been dismissed or that conciliation efforts had failed. The charging party could take no action until the EEOC sent this letter. The 1972 amendments to Section 706(f)(1) permit a charging party to bring suit on its own 180 days after the charge has been filed with the EEOC by requesting a right to sue letter from the EEOC or the Attorney General if the charge is against a governmental agency. The charging party can request the right to sue letter even though the agency has not completed its investigation or conciliation efforts; thus, the charging party no longer must wait until the EEOC acts. The EEOC or the Attorney General, as appropriate, however, has the exclusive right to file suit during the first 180 days. The charging party cannot file suit on his own behalf during that period. If the agency does file suit, the charging party is permitted to intervene in the action. Similarly, if the charging party files a suit after 180 days, the EEOC or the Attorney General can intervene in the suit.

Remember, the 90-day statutory period for filing a suit under Title VII starts from the date the charging party receives a right to sue letter. Therefore, even though a charge has been filed for more than 180 days, the charging party should not request a right to sue letter unless the party is ready to file suit. In practice, attorneys will often prepare their case in advance. After the suit is prepared, the charging party will request a right to sue letter and the suit can be filed immediately after the letter is received without any difficulty.

During its early years especially, the EEOC committed many procedural errors in processing charges under the Act. Some defendants in civil rights cases urged that meritorious claims should be barred because of administrative error in enforcing the Act by the EEOC. The Supreme Court, however, held in *McDonnell Douglas Corp. v. Green*, that there are only two basic procedural requirements that the charging party must meet to file suit. First, the charging party must file a timely charge with the EEOC within 180 days of the alleged unlawful employment practice. Second, the charging party must file suit within 90 days after receiving the right to sue letter. So long as these two requirements are met, a court has jurisdiction over a suit despite what other procedural irregularities may have occurred. The courts have reasoned that charging parties, most of whom are initially not represented by attorneys, should not be held responsible for errors made by the EEOC.

7. Trial Procedures

If a suit is filed by either the charging party, the EEOC, or the Attorney General, the suit can include any unlawful practices rea-sonably related to or growing out of the charge. Also, even if the original charge is filed only by an individual for himself, the suit can be filed as a "class action" on behalf of the charging party and all other persons in the same situation. Class action suits can result in very broad remedies against the defendants, including revision of hiring and promotion policies and sizeable back pay awards.

Trial procedures can, of course, be very complex, expecially in class action suits against a large employer or Union. Most suits brought under Title VII follow the basic format established by *McDonnell Douglas v. Green* in cases of disparate treatment or *Griggs* in cases of disparate impact. It is customary, especially in complicated class action suits, to divide the trial into two portions. First, the court determines whether the defendant has engaged in unlawful discrimination. If the court concludes that the Act has been violated, a second hearing is held to determine the damages and the appropriate remedies.

F. REMEDIES UNDER TITLE VII

1. Broad Judicial Discretion in Framing Remedies

Under Section 706(g), if a court finds that the defendant has or is "intentionally" engaging in unlawful employment practices, the court can enjoin the defendants from engaging in those practices and "order such affirmative action as may be appropriate" including reinstating or hiring employees with or without back pay. The back pay liability cannot be longer than two years prior to the date the charge was filed. As with NLRB proceedings, interim earnings are deducted from the back pay. Also, a person who has lost work because of a discriminatory act must look for employment with reasonable diligence.

The requirement that a court find that a defendant has "intentionally" engaged in discrimination before ordering any remedy is of no practical significance. The word intentional has been given the broadest possible legal meaning. An act is intentional under Title VII if a party intends the logical or forseeable consequences of an act, even though the party acted in good faith. Thus, a court would find that an employer or union intentionally engaged in discrimination under Section 706(g) in any case in which a plaintiff proved a prima facie case of either disparate treatment or disparate impact.

The Supreme Court has stressed that Section 706(g) is intended to give the courts power to eliminate the past, present, and future effects of discrimination. Thus, the Court stated in *Franks v. Bowman Transportation Co. Inc.*:[6]

> Congress intended to prohibit all practices in whatever form which create inequality in employment opportunity due to discrimination on the basis of race, religion, sex, or national origin . . . [O]ne of the central purposes of Title VII is "to make persons whole for injuries suffered on account of unlawful employment discrimination.". . . To effectuate this "make-whole" objective, Congress in Section 706(g) vested broad equitable discretion in the Federal Courts to "order such affirmative action as may be appropriate, which may include, but is not limited to, reinstatement or hiring of employees, with or without back pay . . . , or any other relief as the Court deems appropriate." The legislative history supporting the 1972 Amendments of Section 706(g) of Title VII affirms the breadth of this discretion. "The provisions of [Section 706(g)] are intended to give the Courts wide discretion exercising their equitable powers to fashion the most complete relief possible. . . . The Act is intended to make the victims of un-

[6] See legal principle 12.

lawful employment discrimination whole and . . . the attainment of this objective . . . requires that persons aggrieved by the consequences and effects of the unlawful employment practice be, so far as possible, restored to a position where they would have been were it not for the unlawful discrimination.". . . This is emphatic confirmation that federal courts are empowered to fashion such relief as the particular circumstances of a case may require to effect restitution, making whole insofar as possible the victims of racial discrimination in hiring.

2. Back Pay as a Remedy

Section 706(g) indicates that a court has discretion in awarding victims of discrimination ("discriminatees") back pay. The Supreme Court, however, has held that since Title VII is a remedial statute designed to make discriminatees whole, back pay should normally be awarded by a court whenever it finds that a person has incurred lost pay because of a discriminatory act. The Supreme Court has stated that circumstances must be very unusual to deny back pay. Interim earnings are deducted from any back pay award.

a. Back Pay in Class Actions

Once discrimination is proven in a class action suit, there is a presumption that each member of the class was similarly discriminated against. Thus, if a class action is filed challenging hiring practices and a court concludes that the employer's practices violated the Act, there is a presumption that each individual member of the class who applied for and was denied employment was discriminated against. This means that each member of the class is presumably entitled to back pay. The employer has the burden of proving that a particular individual was not discriminated against and is thus not entitled to back pay. He also must prove that a particular person would not have been hired even if the company had not engaged in discriminatory hiring practices. Similarly, if a court finds that an employer engaged in discriminatory promotion policies, there is a presumption that each member of the class who was denied a promotion was discriminated against.

b. Back Pay for Non-Applicants

A person can be entitled to back pay even if he never applied for employment. The Supreme Court has held that such a person may be entitled to back pay if he can prove that he did not apply for a job because the employer's discriminatory practices made it clear that it would be futile to apply. The Court stressed, however, that a person who had never applied has a heavy burden of proving that he would have applied, but for the employer's discriminatory practices.

c. Back Pay against Unions

Although the primary burden of damages is usually on the employer, unions also have potential liability in cases in which they are a defendant. The union may be a defendant because it actively encouraged an employer to discriminate, or it violated its duty of fair representation by not actively opposing discriminatory practices. The union may also be a defendant if it has discriminated in the operation of a hiring hall or union membership. Section 706(g) specifically authorizes a court to require that back pay be paid by the employer, employment agency, or labor organization responsible for the unlawful employment practice. A union's back pay liability is usually slight if the employer is responsible for an unlawful employment practice and the union's only failure is not taking sufficient action to end the practice. However, a union faces greater potential lia-

bility if it actively encourages the employer's actions or is itself responsible for the unlawful conduct.

3. Injunctive and Affirmative Action Relief to Remedy Discrimination

a. Employer Affirmative Action

In virtually every case in which a court finds that there has been discrimination, it issues an injunction ordering that the discriminatory practices cease and reinstates or promotes the person discriminatorily denied employment, denied a promotion, or discharged. However, courts frequently order much broader remedies as required both to eliminate past discrimination and prevent future discrimination. Thus, courts may require that an affirmative action program be established to recruit and train minority members. Section 706(g) specifically authorizes a court to require such affirmative action as may be appropriate. The courts may require that a specified percentage of minority group members be hired or promoted or that a specified ratio of white to black employees be maintained until there is a proportionate work force.

If minority group members lack the background or training to be eligible for certain jobs, a court may require that special training programs be established. A court may require that minority group members who were previously discriminatorily denied higher paying jobs be processed through the training program and advanced from step to step as quickly as possible, rather than wait the usual number of years. The court may even require that these persons be paid "front pay" at the higher journeyman's rate before their training is completed.

A court can adjust an employee's seniority date to the employee's "rightful place" on a seniority list as if the employee had not been discriminated against.

b. Union Affirmative Action

A union can also be ordered to take affirmative action to recruit minority group members as union members if membership has been discriminatorily denied previously. If an apprenticeship program has discriminated against minority group members, the apprenticeship program may also be required to take affirmative action to recruit and train more minority group members. If a union has discriminated in the operation of a hiring hall, it may be required to give some minority group members preference in referrals to make up for past discrimination, to revise the referral system to prevent future discrimination, to refer a certain percentage of minority group members to jobs, or to maintain a specified referral ratio of minority group members to other union members.

The remedies mentioned here are merely examples of the courts' broad discretion. Each remedial order is tailored to the specific facts of the prior discrimination and the actions necessary to eliminate past and prevent future discrimination.

c. Remedies Displacing Current Employees

Can a court order that a discriminatee be placed in the job which he would have had, but for the discrimination, even if another employee must be removed from the position? This is a difficult problem. After all, the employee occupying the position did not cause the discrimination against the other employee. Is it right to remove this innocent employee from his job to remedy the discrimination against the other? The Supreme Court, although recognizing the difficulties, has indicated that it is proper, if necessary, to remove one employee in order to place a discriminatee in the job he would have held, but for the discrimination. The Court noted that the NLRB routinely orders that employees who have been discharged for union activities be reinstated to their former positions even though reinstatement may mean the discharge of the replacement. The Court also noted that seniority rights are subject to change, either due to statutory requirements or by negotiations between an employer and a union, subject, of course, to the union's duty of fair representation. The Court said there is no reason not to follow the same approach in awarding a job to an employee who was discriminatorily denied it in violation of Title VII.

Of course, a court may have some discretion to limit the impact of its remedy on innocent employees. For example, a court might order that discriminatees be placed in the appropriate jobs as vacancies occur, rather than replacing the present employees. The court might require the employer to pay the discriminatees at the higher rate until vacancies occur. Of course, a court's remedy cannot defeat the statutory purpose of Title VII to eliminate both past and future discrimination. Thus, whether a court can postpone a discriminatee's advancement to a higher position might depend upon the number of discriminatees entitled to higher positions and the number of job vacancies anticipated within a reasonable period of time. If necessary, a court can, and perhaps must, require that the discriminatees be placed in the appropriate positions immediately, even if it means that other employees must be removed.

4. Revision of a Seniority System as a Remedy

a. Discrimination After Title VII's Effective Date

In *Franks v. Bowman Transportation Co., Inc.,* the Supreme Court held that an individual who is discriminatorily denied employment is entitled to full seniority rights retroactively to the date he should have been hired. This is referred to as "rightful place seniority." The discriminatee is entitled to rightful place seniority even though it places the individual ahead of other innocent employees who were not responsible for the discrimination. The Court held that rightful place seniority should be granted routinely to discriminatees, just as they are routinely awarded back pay, unless there is an unusual adverse impact arising from facts and circumstances not generally found in Title VII cases. That is rare.

In *Franks,* the employer's discrimination took place after the effective date of Title VII. In *T.I.M.E.-D.C., Inc. v. United States,* the Supreme Court faced a situation in which discrimination had occurred both before and after the effective date of Title VII.[7] The employer had engaged in a pattern and practice of employment discrimination against blacks and Spanish-surnamed Americans in which only whites were employed in the higher paying over-the-road truck driver jobs. The minority group employees were limited to other lower paying jobs. An employee's seniority for purposes of benefits, such as vacations and pensions, was based on the date of hire with the company. An employee's seniority for competitive purposes, such as job bidding, layoff, and recall, however, was based upon service as an over-the-road truck driver. This system perpetuated the effects of prior discrimination because a

[7] See legal principle 4.

discriminatee who was finally hired as an over-the-road truck driver obviously would have less seniority than he would have had, but for the employer's prior discriminatory refusal to hire him. The union was a defendant in the suit, charged with having agreed with the employer to create and maintain this seniority system.

One of the primary issues in *T.I.M.E.-D.C., Inc.* was whether the seniority system had to be revised so it would not perpetuate the effects of the past discrimination against the black and the Spanish-surnamed employees.

The Supreme Court had a straight-forward remedy for the discrimination taking place after Title VII's effective date—employees who had been discriminated against after the effective date were entitled to full rightful place seniority under the *Franks v. Bowman* decision. These employees would simply be given the seniority date they would have had, but for the discrimination. They would have full competitive seniority rights without any need to revise the seniority system.

b. Discrimination before Title VII's Effective Date

For employees who were discriminated against before Title VII's effective date, the Supreme Court looked to the provisions of Section 703(h) under which a "bona fide" seniority or merit system is lawful under the Act so long as differences created by the system are not the result of an "intention to discriminate" because of race, color, religion, sex, or national origin. The Court, considering the legislative history of Section 703(h), concluded that the unmistakable purpose of the provision was that the routine application of a bona fide seniority system is not unlawful under Title VII. The Court concluded that Congress had intended for seniority rights accumulated before the effective date of Title VII to remain in effect even though the employer had engaged in discrimination prior to the passage of the Act and the system therefore perpetuated the effects of pre-Act discrimination. The Court stated:

> Accordingly, we hold that an otherwise neutral, legitimate seniority system does not become unlawful under Title VII simply because it may perpetuate pre-Act discrimination. Congress did not intend to make it illegal for employees with vested seniority rights to continue to exercise those rights, even at the expense of pre-Act discriminatees.

Thus, in *T.I.M.E.-D.C.* the Court ruled that the persons who suffered discrimination only before the effective date of Title VII were not entitled to any relief. Employees who suffered discrimination after the effective date were entitled to relief, in the form of rightful place seniority, back to the date of the discrimination against them, but no earlier than the effective date of Title VII. Since these employees would receive full seniority rights through the application of rightful place seniority, there was no need to revise the seniority system.

As an exception, the Supreme Court indicated that a seniority system could be revised, notwithstanding the provisions of Section 703(h), if the seniority system itself was racially discriminatory or had its inception in racial discrimination. If an employer maintained separate seniority lists for black and white employees before Title VII's effective date, the seniority system has its inception in racial discrimination and a court could revise such a system because it would not be bona fide under Section 703(h). On the other hand, if a seniority system, as in *T.I.M.E.-D.C.*, was not discriminatory in its inception, but is discriminatory in impact because of the employer's hiring policies, the seniority system

itself would not be revised. Employees who had been subjected to discrimination, however, would still get full relief through rightful place seniority.

5. Attorney's Fees to the Prevailing Party

Section 706(k) permits the court to award an attorney's fee to the prevailing party. Technically, this means that if the defendants win, the court can require that the plaintiff pay their attorney's fee. Obviously, most plaintiffs in a civil right action cannot afford to pay such fees and Section 706(k) can deter some employees from filing suit even though their claim has merit. To reduce this possibility, however, the courts have held that a prevailing defendant is entitled to an attorney's fee only if the plaintiff's claim is clearly frivolous and without merit. Thus, even an employee with a questionable claim who loses should not be required to pay the opposing party's attorney's fee.

G. THE RECONSTRUCTION CIVIL RIGHTS STATUTES

1. Coverage Under Sections 1981 and 1983

Besides proceeding under Title VII, a discriminatee may also file suit under the Reconstruction Civil Rights Statutes (42 U.S.C. 1981 and 1983). Section 1981 prohibits racial discrimination by a private (nongovernmental) employer or union, but it does not prohibit sex discrimination. Section 1983 prohibits discrimination by state or local governmental bodies. It prohibits both race and sex discrimination, but does not apply to federal agencies. Title VII is the exclusive remedy against sex discrimination by a private employer or union and against discrimination by federal agencies.

Sections 1981 and 1983 are enforced directly by the discriminatees by filing suit in federal court. The sections are separate independent remedies from Title VII. Thus, it is not necessary to file a charge with the EEOC and exhaust Title VII procedures before filing suit under Sections 1981 or 1983 as appropriate. One advantage of Sections 1981 or 1983 is that a suit can be filed much quicker after a discriminatory act occurs than under Title VII. Also, there is a longer statute of limitations period for filing suit under Sections 1981 or 1983 than the 180-day limit under Title VII for filing a charge with the EEOC. Because Sections 1981 and 1983 do not contain an express limitations period, federal courts apply the applicable limitations period of the state where the discrimination occurred for an offense comparable to employment discrimination. This period varies from state to state, but usually ranges from two to five years. Some states may have a longer or shorter period, but the period, in any event, would be longer than under Title VII. Thus, a discriminatee who has waited too long to file a charge under Title VII might still be able to proceed under 42 U.S.C. 1981 or 1983 if either section applies to the discrimination in question.

2. Remedies and Procedures

Sections 1981 and 1983 do not specify the remedies for a violation. The courts have generally held that an individual is entitled to the same remedies under these statutes as under Title VII. The prevailing party (plaintiff or defendant) is entitled to attorney's fee as under Title VII. One difference is that a court can award punitive damages under 42 U.S.C.

1981 or 1983 if an employer or union has engaged in willful discriminatory conduct. In contrast, a court can only award a discriminatee actual damages under Title VII. Also, the two year limitation on back pay under Title VII does not apply to Sections 1981 and 1983.

The most common procedure in civil rights litigation is for the discriminatee to file a timely charge with the EEOC, wait the required six months, request a right-to-sue letter from the EEOC, and then file suit under both Title VII and Sections 1981 or 1983 as appropriate. The limitations period for filing suit under either Sections 1981 or 1983 continues to run even after a charge has been filed under Title VII. Thus, in states where the time limitation for filing suit is relatively short, the discriminatee must be careful to file suit in time even though the EEOC charge is still being processed.

3. Plaintiff's Burden of Proof

In *Washington v. Davis*, the Supreme Court held that if a person brings suit under the Constitution against a federal agency, claiming that discriminatory practices by the federal agency violate the constitutional right to equal protection of the laws, he must prove that the alleged practice had a discriminatory *purpose*.[8] As previously discussed, discriminatory impact is sufficient to prove a violation of Title VII, but the Supreme Court has held that impact alone is insufficient to prove a constitutional violation. The Court said, however, that impact could be evidence of the purpose. Sections 1981 and 1983 implement the Thirteenth and Fourteenth Amendments. For this reason, some courts have now held that a person cannot prevail in a suit under either Sections 1981 or 1983 unless the party can prove

[8] See legal principle 14.

a discriminatory purpose rather than only disparate impact.

The discriminatory purpose requirement for a violation of Sections 1981 or 1983 has little effect on cases of individual discrimination based on disparate treatment because the disparate treatment in itself proves the discriminatory purpose. If proof of discriminatory purpose is required, however, Sections 1981 and 1983 will not apply to cases of disparate impact discrimination in which the courts, applying Title VII standards, have held that impact alone without regard to intent is sufficient for a violation. This higher burden of proof applies only to suits under Sections 1981 or 1983. Disparate impact alone is still sufficient to prove a case under Title VII.

H. THE ROLE OF ARBITRATION IN ELIMINATING DISCRIMINATION

There is often an overlap between an alleged civil rights violation and a contract violation. A collective bargaining agreement may expressly prohibit discrimination on account of race, religion, national origin, sex, or age. Or, a person may allege that he was discharged, denied a promotion, or otherwise denied a contractual benefit, because of race, etc.

1. Arbitration and Title VII as Concurrent Remedies

The Supreme Court has held that Title VII and arbitration are concurrent remedies. Thus, if an employer's discriminatory act violates both Title VII and a collective bargaining agreement, the discriminatee, the union, or both can file an EEOC charge and a grievance leading to arbitration.

The Supreme Court has held that filing a grievance does not toll the time for filing an EEOC charge. Rather the 180-day period for filing a charge begins on the day of the discriminatory act and continues to run while a grievance is being processed. Therefore, an employee or union may not be able to wait until the grievance–arbitration procedures are completed before filing a charge with the EEOC. In order to protect the individual's Title VII rights, the charge must be filed, even though the grievance–arbitration procedures may ultimately turn out in the employee's favor.

2. Weight Accorded an Arbitrator's Decision

If an arbitrator rules in the employee's favor within the six month period, there is no need to file a charge with the EEOC or to file suit under 42 U.S.C. 1981 or 1983. But what if the arbitrator rules against the employee, before the 180-day filing period has expired, or only provides partial relief to the employee? Perhaps the arbitrator orders the employer to rehire an employee, without requiring back pay, as a court would usually order. Can the union or the employee still file a charge with the EEOC and proceed under Title VII, or is the arbitrator's decision binding? In *Gardner-Denver*, the Supreme Court held that an employee can proceed under Title VII even though the employee lost in arbitration.[9] The Court held that an employee does not waive his rights under Title VII by arbitrating his claim first.

The NLRB often defers to an arbitrator's award, which meets its standards for deferral under the *Spielberg* decision, even though the Board might have reached a different result in the case (see Chapter 9). The Supreme Court,

[9] See legal principle 15.

however, held in *Gardner-Denver* that the federal courts should not defer to an arbitrator's award under Title VII and that an employee is entitled to a full court hearing. The Court stated that Congress intended for the federal courts to resolve discrimination cases, noting that an arbitrator's duty is to follow the contract, even though in some cases the contract might be in conflict with Title VII rights. Title VII also involves statutory issues to which courts are accustomed rather than contract rights or past practices that are the typical issues for arbitration.

The Supreme Court, however, did say that an arbitrator's award can be admitted into evidence and "accorded such weight as the court deems appropriate." In a famous footnote to its decision, the Court set down the factors a federal court should consider in determining the weight to give a prior arbitrator's decision in a civil rights matter. The Court said:

> We adopt no standards as to the weight to be accorded an arbitral decision, since this must be determined in the court's discretion with regard to the facts and circumstances of each case. Relevant factors include the existence of provisions in the collective-bargaining agreement that conform substantially with Title VII, the degree of procedural fairness in the arbitral forum, adequacy of the record with respect to the issue of discrimination, and the special competence of particular arbitrators. Where an arbitral determination gives full consideration to an employee's Title VII rights, a court may properly accord it great weight. This is especially true where the issue is solely one of fact, specifically addressed by the parties and decided by the arbitrator on the basis of an adequate record. But courts should ever be mindful that Congress, in enacting Title VII, thought it necessary to provide a judicial forum for the ultimate resolution of discriminatory employment claims. It is the duty of courts to assure the full availability of this forum.

Of course, an employee's grievance alleging discrimination should be evaluated and processed by a union in accordance with the duty of fair representation, the same as any other grievance. A union does not have to arbitrate a grievance that lacks merit just because it alleges discrimination.

I. THE NLRB'S ROLE IN ELIMINATING DISCRIMINATION

The NLRB also has an important role in enforcing the federal policy against discrimination. The Board has held that a union violates its duty of fair representation by treating employees arbitrarily, discriminatorily, or in bad faith because of their race, sex, or religion. The Board has held that a union cannot arbitrarily refuse to process an employee's grievance because it relates to a discrimination issue which the employee could take to the EEOC. Such a grievance must be processed and evaluated the same as any other grievance.

Certification Revocation as a Remedy Against Union Discrimination

The NLRB held in *Handy Andy* that it would revoke the certification of a union that engages in racial or sexual discrimination against bargaining unit employees.[10] Prior to *Handy Andy*, the Board had taken the position that it would refuse to certify a union that engaged in discrimination. Under the prior procedure, if a union won a representation election, the employer could file an objection to the election that the union discriminated against employees. The Board would not certify the union if the employer's objection had merit. Some employers filed meritless objec-

---

[10] See legal principle 16.

tions just to delay bargaining. The Board reversed that procedure in *Handy Andy*.

Under current procedures, the Board will certify a union regardless of its past record of discrimination. If a union discriminates against bargaining unit employees after being certified, either an employee or the employer can file an unfair labor practice charge against the union. The employer, however, must continue to recognize and bargain with the union while the charge is pending. Thus, an employer cannot file a meritless discrimination charge to avoid its bargaining obligation. If the Board finds that the union is engaging in discriminatory conduct, it can either order the union to take appropriate steps to remedy the situation or it can revoke the union's certification.

J. REVERSE DISCRIMINATION AND VOLUNTARY AFFIRMATIVE ACTION PROGRAMS

1. Reverse Discrimination.

In *McDonald v. Santa Fe Trail Transportation Company*, the Supreme Court held that Title VII and 42 U.S.C. 1981 prohibit reverse discrimination against white employees.[11] In that case, two white employees alleged that a black employee and the two white employees were jointly charged with stealing certain merchandise from a company shipment. The employer discharged the two white employees, but retained the black employee. The two white employees filed a grievance over their discharge, but the union did not pursue it to arbitration. The employees then filed charges with the EEOC. After receiving right to sue letters, the white employees filed a timely action against both the employer and the union in federal court under both Title VII and 42

U.S.C. 1981. The employees alleged that the union had failed to represent them properly because it had either not opposed or had joined in the employer's discriminatory discharge. The lower federal court dismissed the employees' suit. The Supreme Court reversed the lower federal courts and held that both Title VII and 42 U.S.C. 1981 prohibit discrimination against white persons as well as blacks. The Court did not consider the merits of the white employees' charges that they had been discriminated against, but held only that if the charges were true, the acts violated both Title VII and 42 U.S.C. 1981.

2. Affirmative Action Programs

The *McDonald* decision raised questions as to whether an employer, union, or both, can voluntarily adopt an affirmative action program to hire and train additional minority group employees. Some argue that such programs are reverse discrimination against those excluded from the program. The legality of affirmative action programs under Title VII, however, has been subsequently upheld by the Supreme Court in *Kaiser Aluminum Corporation v. Weber*.[12]

In *Kaiser*, the employer and union voluntarily adopted an affirmative action program to train black workers for the employers' craft work forces at each of its plants. The craft work forces were almost exclusively white. At the plant in question, less than 2 percent of the craft employees were black although blacks made up 39 percent of the available local work force. The affirmative action program required that at least 50 percent of craft trainees be black until the percentage of black skilled craft workers approximated the percentage of blacks in the local labor force.

Weber was denied admission to the craft

[11] See legal principle 14.

[12] See legal principle 17.

training program although he had greater seniority than one of the black employees who was admitted. He filed a charge under Title VII alleging that his rejection constituted unlawful reverse discrimination. The charge was processed under Title VII and ultimately reached the Supreme Court.

The Supreme Court upheld the legality of the affirmative action program and held that Weber's rejection did not constitute reverse discrimination. The Court noted that the employer–union plan was voluntarily adopted to eliminate traditional patterns of racial segregation. The Court extensively examined the legislative history of Title VII and concluded that one of the Act's primary purposes was to eliminate such traditional patterns as existed at the Kaiser plant. The Court noted that Section 703(j) provides that no employer can be *required* to grant preferential treatment to any person because of his race, color, religion, sex, or national origin, because of an imbalance that might exist in the work force for that group. The Court said, however, that although Section 703(j) did not "require" an employer to correct a racial imbalance, the Section did not prevent an employer, union, or both from voluntarily undertaking an affirmative effort to correct a racial imbalance. The Court concluded that Congress did not intend to forbid all voluntary race conscious affirmative action.

The Court's decision, narrowly based on the specific facts of the Kaiser affirmative action program, emphasized that it was merely holding that Title VII does not prevent all private voluntary race conscious affirmative action programs. It indicated that some affirmative action programs might result in impermissible discrimination, but held that the challenged Kaiser affirmative action plan fell on the permissible side of the line. The Court noted that Kaiser's plan did not require the discharge of white workers and their replacement by new black employees. Further, the plan did not create an absolute bar to the advancement of white employees because half of those trained in the program are white. Further, the plan was a temporary measure that would end as soon as the percentage of black skilled craft employees at the plant approximated the percentage of blacks in the local labor force.

Prior to the Court's decision in *Kaiser,* some had argued that an affirmative action program could be voluntarily adopted only if an employer, union, or both were facing a civil rights suit if they did not adopt a program or were potentially liable under Title VII because a disproportionate work force raised questions of disparate treatment or impact discrimination. The Supreme Court, however, did not rely on that argument for approving affirmative action programs; instead, it broadly approved the general right to establish voluntary programs. There will undoubtedly be further litigation on the scope of permissible or impermissible affirmative action program as approved in the *Kaiser* decision. It is clear, however, that such a program may be adopted voluntarily by an employer, union, or both even if the parties are not potentially liable under Title VII or do not face a lawsuit if they do not adopt such a program.

Summary   This chapter considered equal employment opportunity, focusing on Title VII of the Civil Rights Act of 1964. Title VII prohibits discrimination by employers and unions based on race, color, religion, sex, or national origin. Unions may find themselves on either side in civil rights litigation. They frequently process civil rights claims for their own members. Unions, however, are sometimes the defendants in such cases either because they have joined in or did not actively oppose an employer's discrimination or because the union itself discriminated in membership or job referrals. Unions are classified as employers under Title VII as to their own employees.

There are two basic categories of discrimination under Title VII: disparate treatment and disparate impact. Disparate treatment is intentional discrimination. Disparate impact pertains to the consequences of an act regardless of the intent. Under *McDonnell Douglas v. Green*, the charging party in a disparate treatment case must first prove a prima facie case of discriminatory intent. The employer can refute this case by proving that it had a legitimate nondiscriminatory reason for its actions. The burden then shifts to the charging party to prove that the employer's reason is a pretext for discriminatory action.

Under *Griggs v. Duke Power Company*, evidence of adverse consequences to a protected group is prima facie evidence of disparate impact discrimination. The employer may rebut this evidence by proving the business necessity for the employment practice or policy in question. A test can be used to select employees on grounds of business necessity if it is job related. If the employer successfully proves business necessity, the charging party can still prevail under Title VII if it proves there are alternate means meeting the employer's legitimate needs that do not have the same adverse consequences. Remember, there is no need to prove necessity for any employer policy or practice, regardless of how unreasonable or irrational it may seem to be, as long as it does not have adverse consequences on a protected group.

Current employment policies or practices that perpetuate past discrimination are generally unlawful under Title VII because of their disparate impact. The Supreme Court, however, has held that an employee is not entitled to retroactive seniority beyond the effective date of Title VII because of the provisions of Section 703(h) protecting the operation of a bona fide seniority system. A discriminatee, however, is entitled to rightful place seniority from the date of the discriminatory act as far back as the effective date of the Act.

The principal problem in sex discrimination is sexual stereotypes. An employer cannot simply assume that women are only suited for or wish to hold certain jobs. Nor can an employer establish job requirements that have an adverse impact on women unless the employer can prove the business necessity for the requirements. There is a narrow exception for bona fide occupational requirements, but the employer must prove a reasonable factual basis for concluding that all or substantially all women cannot do a specific job. Under Title VII as amended, pregnant employees must be treated the same as any other employee. If a woman is disabled during her pregnancy or following the birth of her child, she is entitled to the same benefits as any other disabled employee and must be covered by the employer's hospitalization plan if any.

An employer must make reasonable accommodations to the religious beliefs of its employees so long as there is no undue hardship to the employer's business. But an employer is not required to violate the seniority rights of other employees to accommodate an employee's religious requirements and is not required to incur more than a *de minimis* expense.

Actions under Title VII begin with the filing of a charge with the Equal Employment Opportunity Commission. A charge must be filed within 180 days of the alleged discriminatory act unless it is a continuing violation. The EEOC investigates to determine whether there is reasonable cause to believe the statute has been violated. If so, the EEOC attempts conciliation. If that fails, either the EEOC; the Attorney General, in the case of discrimination by a state or local governmental body; or the charging party may file suit to enforce the discriminatees' Title VII rights.

The charging party can file suit under Title VII even if the EEOC finds no reasonable cause to believe that the statute has been violated. Under the 1972 amendments, the charging party can request a right to sue letter from the EEOC if the agency has not acted within 180 days from the date the charge was filed. There are two basic jurisdictional requirements for filing a suit in federal court under Title VII: filing a timely charge with the EEOC and filing suit within 90 days from the date the charging party receives its right to sue letter. Even though the charge may have been filed by an individual, alleging a narrow violation, the suit can be brought as a class action that includes all persons subject to the same discrimination. The suit can also include additional discriminatory acts and practices reasonably related to but beyond those originally alleged in the charge.

A court's remedial power under Title VII is very broad. It can issue an injunction requiring that discriminatory practices cease and can require that corrective steps be taken, including affirmative action to prevent discrimination in the future. Except in very unusual circumstances courts must also award the discriminatees back pay and rightful place seniority to which they are entitled as a result of past discriminatory acts.

A federal court has a clear statutory right to require an employer, union, or both to take affirmative action to eliminate past and future discrimination. The Supreme Court has also upheld the right of employers and unions to establish affirmative action programs voluntarily.

In addition to Title VII, victims of discrimination can also bring suit under the Reconstruction Civil Rights Acts, 42 U.S.C. 1981 and 1983. Suits under these sections are independent remedies and can be brought directly in the federal courts without exhausting Title VII remedies. A higher burden of proof, however, a discriminatory purpose rather than just discriminatory consequences, may be required under these statutes than under Title VII. Section 1981 only applies to race discrimination by a private employer or union, while Section 1983 applies to both race and sex discrimination by a state or local governmental body.

An employee also has remedies against discrimination by a union under the LMRA if the union violates its duty of fair representation by discriminating against the employee because of race or sex. A union has a statutory obligation to fairly represent the interests of minority employees; if it fails to meet its obligation, its certification may be revoked in appropriate cases.

Finally, an employee may also arbitrate issues of discrimination arising under a collective bargaining agreement. An employee, however, is not required to arbitrate such cases and may proceed directly to the EEOC or into court under 42 U.S.C. 1981 and 1983 as appropriate. Arbitration and Title VII procedures are separate independent remedies. An employee is not bound by an unfavorable arbitrator's award and may proceed with a Title VII action even though an arbitrator has upheld an employer's action. The federal court will make an independent determination on whether Title VII rights have been violated, giving the arbitrator's award such consideration as the court deems warranted. Because arbitration and Title VII are separate remedies, the time limit for filing a charge with the EEOC continues to run while a grievance is being processed. Thus, an employee and union must be careful to file a charge on time with the EEOC even though they are fairly confident of a favorable arbitrator's award.

Review Questions

1. How many members must a union have to be covered by Title VII of the Civil Rights Act?

2. What groups are protected against discrimination by Title VII?

3. What are the two basic categories of unlawful discrimination?

4. Can an employer violate Title VII even if he proves a legitimate non-discriminatory reason for rejecting a protected group member for a job?

5. Can an employment practice violate Title VII even though the employer had no discriminatory intent in adopting the practice?

6. Must an employment practice (such as a test) be job related to be lawful under Title VII?

7. Can an employer's employment practices violate Title VII even if his overall work force has a proportionate number of protected group members?

8. Can an employer lawfully bar women from jobs requiring heavy lifting because the work would be too difficult for women to do?

9. How long a leave of absence must an employer allow a woman after she gives birth to a child?

10. Must an employer allow an employee off of work because of the employee's religious holiday?

11. At what age may an employer require an employee to retire involuntarily?

12. What are the basic requirements which must be met before an individual can file a federal court suit under Title VII?

13. Can an employee file suit under Title VII even though the EEOC does not find reasonable cause to believe the statute has been violated?

14. What remedies may a court require of an employer or union to eliminate unlawful discrimination?

15. Can a court require that one employee be removed from a job and replaced by another employee who has been the victim of discrimination?

16. Would a black employee who failed to file a timely charge against an employer, union, or both under Title VII have any other remedy against the alleged unlawful discrimination?

17. Can an employee proceed with a charge under Title VII even though an arbitrator has ruled against the employee on the discrimination issue?

18. How long does an employee have after receiving an unfavorable arbitrator's decision to file a timely charge under Title VII with the EEOC?

19. Will the NLRB certify a union with a past history of racial or sex discrimination against bargaining unit employees?

20. Can an employer and union voluntarily adopt an affirmative action program that prefers black or female employees for certain positions over other employees with higher seniority?

(Answers to review questions appear at end of book.)

Basic Legal Principles   1. An individual may establish a prima facie case of disparate treatment discrimination by proving: (1) that the person belongs to a protected group under Title VII; (2) that the person applied for and was qualified for a job for which the employer was seeking applicants; (3) that despite being qualified, the person was rejected; and (4) that after the person was rejected, the position remained open and the employer continued to seek applicants from persons of the rejected applicants' qualifications. *McDonnell Douglas v. Green*, 411 U.S. 792, 5 F.E.P. Cases 965 (1973). These criteria, however, only set the general framework for proving a prima facie case and are not to be followed mechanically. *Furnco Construction Corp. v. Waters,* 428 U.S. 567, 17 F.E.P. Cases 1062 (1978).

2. An employer may refute a prima facie case of disparate treatment discrimination by establishing a legitimate nondiscriminatory reason for the action taken. The employer, however, does not have to prove it used the best method to maximize hiring minority employees. *Furnco Construction Corp. v. Waters, supra,* note 1.

3. An employment policy that is neutral on its face may be unlawful under Title VII if it has a disparate impact on a protected group regardless of the employer's intent. *Griggs v. Duke Power Co.,* 401 U.S. 424, 3 F.E.P. Cases 175 (1971).

4. Current neutral employment practices which perpetuate past discrimination are unlawful under Title VII. *Griggs v. Duke Power Co., supra,* note 3. However, a bona fide seniority system is lawful under Title VII and does not have to be revised, even though it may perpetuate pre-Title VII discrimination, unless the seniority system had a discriminatory intent in its inception. *T.I.M.E.-D.C., Inc. v. United States,* 431 U.S. 324, 14 F.E.P. Cases 1514 (1977).

5. A test that has a disparate impact on a protected group is unlawful under Title VII unless it is job related and there is no alternative method of providing the employer with qualified employees with less disparate impact. *Albemarle Paper Co. v. Moody,* 422 U.S. 405, 10 F.E.P. Cases 1181 (1975).

6. Height and weight restrictions that have a disparate impact on women are unlawful under Title VII unless they are justified by business necessity. *Dothard v. Rawlinson,* 433 U.S. 321, 15 F.E.P. Cases 10 (1977).

7. An employer may violate Title VII by limiting jobs to employees of one sex because of a stereotyped assumption as to the appropriate jobs for men and women. Jobs may be lawfully restricted by sex only if sex is a bona fide occupational qualification, which means that all or substantially all of the excluded sex would be unable to perform the task. *Dothard v. Rawlinson, supra,* note 6; *Weeks v. Southern Bell Telephone and Telegraph Co.,* 408 F.2d 228, 1 F.E.P. Cases 656 (5th Cir. 1969).

8. An employer must contribute the same amounts to fringe benefit funds for individual male and female employees regardless of general assumptions about the life span or illness rate of men or women as a group. *City of Los Angeles v. Manhart,* 435 U.S. 702, 17 F.E.P. Cases 395 (1978).

9. An employer must make reasonable accommodation to the religious beliefs of its employees so long as there is no undue hardship to the employer's business. An employer is not required to violate the seniority provisions of a collective bargaining agreement or to incur more than *de*

minimis expense to accommodate an employee's religious beliefs. *Trans World Airlines v. Hardison*, 432 U.S. 63, 14 F.E.P. Cases 1697 (1977).

10. An individual alleging age discrimination must file a charge with the appropriate state agency, if any, before filing suit in federal court. But an employee can proceed with a federal court suit under the Age Discrimination in Employment Act after waiting the required 60 days even though the time for filing a charge with the state agency has already expired. *Oscar Mayer & Co. v. Evans*, 99 S. Ct. 2066, 19 F.E.P. Cases 1167 (1979).

11. The basic jurisdictional requirements for filing suit under Title VII are that a charge must be filed with the EEOC within 180 days of the initial occurrence of the alleged discriminatory act, unless the act is a continuing violation, and that the suit must be filed within 90 days after receiving the right to sue letter from the EEOC. *McDonnell Douglas v. Green*, *supra*, note 1. Acts such as a discriminatory refusal to hire an employee, an unlawful discharge, or the denial of a promotion are considered as single occurrences, rather than a continuing violation. *United Airlines v. Evans*, 431 U.S. 553, 14 F.E.P. Cases 1510 (1977).

12. Federal courts have broad power to remedy unlawful discrimination including orders to hire or reinstate employees, requiring back pay, and requiring such affirmative action programs as necessary to eliminate past and prohibit future discrimination. *Griggs v. Duke Power Co.*, *supra*, note 3; *Albemarle Paper Co. v. Moody*, *supra*, note 5; *Franks v. Bowman Transportation Co., Inc.*, 424 U.S. 747, 12 F.E.P. Cases 549 (1976); *T.I.M.E.-D.C., Inc. v. United States*, *supra*, note 4 (back pay for nonapplicants).

13. The courts have authority to award victims of discrimination back seniority to their "rightful place" on a seniority list even though this may mean that the discriminatees will replace other innocent employees. Back seniority, however, cannot be awarded prior to the effective date of Title VII. *Franks v. Bowman Transportation Co., Inc.*, *supra*, note 12; *T.I.M.E.-D.C., Inc. v. United States*, *supra*, note 4.

14. Title 42 United States Code Sections 1981 (prohibiting racial discrimination by a private employer, union, or both) and 1983 (prohibiting race or sex discrimination by state or local governmental bodies) are independent remedies against discrimination in addition to Title VII. Thus, an individual does not have to exhaust Title VII procedures before filing suit under either Sections 1981 or 1983 as appropriate, and can proceed under those sections even though the time for filing a charge under Title VII has expired. *McDonald v. Santa Fe Trail Transportation Co.*, 427 U.S. 273, 12 F.E.P. Cases 1577 (1976); *Johnson v. Railway Express Agency*, 421 U.S. 454, 10 F.E.P. Cases 817 (1975). A higher burden of proof, however, may be required under Sections 1981 and 1983 than under Title VII. *See Washington v. Davis*, 426 U.S. 229, 12 F.E.P. Cases 1415 (1976).

15. Arbitration is a separate independent remedy against discrimination in addition to Title VII. However, an employee is not required to exhaust contractual grievance procedures before proceeding under Title VII, and filing a grievance does not toll the time for filing a timely charge under Title VII. Courts do not defer to an arbitrator's award on a matter that may also violate Title VII. *Alexander v. Gardner-Denver Co.*, 415 U.S. 36, 7 F.E.P. Cases 81 (1974); *Electrical Workers Local 790 v. Robbins and Myers, Inc.*, 429 U.S. 229, 13 F.E.P. Cases 1813 (1976).

16. The National Labor Relations Board may revoke the certification of a union that engages in racial or sex discrimination against bargaining unit employees after it is certified. *Handy Andy, Inc.*, 228 NLRB No. 59, 94 LRRM 1354 (1977).

17. Title VII, and 42 U.S.C. 1981 and 1983 prohibit reverse discrimination against white employees. *McDonald v. Santa Fe Trail Transportation Co., supra,* note 14. However, an employer and a union may voluntarily adopt an affirmative action program to end traditional patterns of segregation even though such a program may grant preference to members of a protected group over other employees. *Kaiser Aluminum and Chemical Corp. v. Weber*, 99 S. Ct. 272, 20 F.E.P. Cases 1 (1979).

Recommended Readings

Blumrosen, "Individual Worker-Employer Arbitration Under Title VII," 31 *NYU Conf. Lab.* 329 (1978).

"Cost of Growing Old: Business Necessity And The Age Discrimination In Employment Act," 88 Yale *L.J.* 565 (1979).

"Employment Testing: The Aftermath of Griggs v. Duke Power Company," 72 *Colum. L. Rev.* 900 (1972).

"Disparate Impact and Disparate Treatment: The Prima Facie Case Under Title VII," 32 *Ark. L. Rev.* 571 (1978).

"Dothard v. Rawlinson: a Method of Analysis for Future BFOQ Cases," 16 *Urban L.J.* 361 (1979).

"Layoffs and Equal Employment: Retroactive Seniority As A Remedy Under Title VII," 10 *U.C.D.L. Rev.* 115 (1977).

"Seniority System Exemption In Title VII: International Brotherhood of Teamsters v. United States, and Seniority Systems Violations Under Title VII: A Requirement of Discriminatory Intent," 42 *Albany L. Rev.* 279 (1978) (discusses *T.I.M.E.-D.C.* Case).

Shober, "Differential Pass-Fail Rates In Employment Testing: Statistical Proof Under Title VII," 91 *Harv. L. Rev.* 793 (1978).

Wall, "Sex Discrimination and Employment," 128 *New L.J.* 179 (1978).

Chapter Fourteen

Federal-State Relationships in Labor Relations

Most aspects of the labor-management relationship and some aspects of the union-member relationship are subject to extensive federal regulation. Some matters, however, are not covered by federal law. Much of the relationship between unions and their members, which are governed by the union's constitution and by-laws, is enforced solely by state courts (see Chapters 10 and 11). Also, the states retain power to prohibit violent conduct in strikes. Some states even have comprehensive state statutes containing many of the same provisions found in the LMRA or the LMRDA.

If both federal and state agencies attempt to regulate labor relations, there is potential for conflict.

Acts may be lawful under federal law and unlawful under state law or vice versa. A federal and state statute might contain similar language, but the NLRB and the state agency might interpret the provisions differently or reach different factual conclusions. A balance of power has been drawn between federal and state regulation of labor relations based on two fundamental doctrines: preemption and primary jurisdiction. Preemption is the doctrine under which federal law preempts, or supersedes, state law. Primary jurisdiction is the doctrine used in determining whether particular conduct governed by federal law is regulated by the NLRB, the federal courts, or by both the courts and the Board.

A. THE PREEMPTION DOCTRINE

Congress has constitutional authority (U.S. Const. Art. I, Sec. 8) to regulate exclusively any conduct affecting commerce. This means that federal law may supersede (preempt) state law on the subject. Congress has discretion when it passes federal legislation under the commerce power to determine the extent to which the federal statute preempts or permits state regulation of the same subject. The constitutional basis of federal labor law legislation is the commerce power. Thus, Congress has the power to regulate exclusively all labor matters affecting commerce. The commerce power was previously discussed in Chapter 1 in relation to the jurisdiction of the National Labor Relations Board.

Sometimes, federal legislation contains a provision stating whether the law is to be the exclusive remedy, or whether, and to what extent, the states are free to regulate the same conduct. Section 103 of the LMRDA expressly provides that state remedies remain as to matters covered by Title I of that statute (The Bill of Rights). Section 603 of the

LMRDA provides that nothing in the Act limits the responsibility of a union under any other federal or state law except as expressly provided in the statute. LMRDA Section 403 is such an express limitation. It makes Title IV (election proceedings) the exclusive remedy for challenging an election. Under Section 708 of the Civil Rights Act of 1964, as amended, the Act does not preempt state law, except to the extent that state law requires or permits an act federal law prohibits. In contrast, Section 514(A) of the Employee Retirement Income Security Act (ERISA) provides that that Act supersedes state law except for state laws regulating insurance or securities.

To what extent did Congress intend for the LMRA to preempt state law over labor management relations? Unfortunately—in contrast to the other statutes indicated above—Congress did not expressly spell out the limits of permissible state regulation. Thus, the Supreme Court has had to define the limits on a case by case basis.

1. Arguably Protected or Prohibited Conduct

The basic rule governing state regulation of labor relations was established by the Supreme Court's 1959 decision in *San Diego Building Trades Council v. Garmon.*[1] In *Garmon*, a union engaged in picketing that was probably unlawful secondary activity under Section 8(b)(4). The employer brought suit for damages and an injunction in the California state courts. The California court held that the picketing violated California's state law and awarded the employer damages. The union appealed to the United States Supreme Court on the grounds that the conduct in question was preempted by federal law. The Court

[1] See legal principle 1.

held that the matter was preempted and that the state courts did not have jurisdiction.

Acts permitted by the LMRA are called protected acts. Acts that the statute makes an unfair labor practice are called prohibited acts. Primary picketing is protected, while secondary boycotts are prohibited. The Supreme Court recognized in *Garmon* that although the LMRA does not expressly provide for the preemption of state law, the Act was intended to establish uniform federal regulation. The Court, therefore, concluded that the LMRA preempts state law over matters regulated by the statute. The Court emphasized that preemption applied whether the union's conduct was lawful (protected) or unlawful (prohibited) under the federal law. The Court stated the guiding principle that is still applied, that:

> When it is clear or may fairly be assumed that the activities which a State purports to regulate are protected by Section 7 of the Taft-Hartley Act, or constitute an unfair labor practice under Section 8, due regard for the federal enactment requires that state jurisdiction must yield. To leave the States free to regulate conduct so plainly within the central aim of federal regulation involves too great a danger of conflict between power asserted by Congress and requirements imposed by state law. Nor has it mattered whether the States have acted through laws of broad general application rather than laws specifically directed towards the governance of industrial relations. Regardless of the mode adopted, to allow the States to control conduct which is the subject of national regulation would create potential frustration of national purposes . . . It is not for us to decide whether the National Labor Relations Board would have, or should have, decided these questions in the same manner. *When an activity is arguably subject to Section 7 or Section 8 of the Act, the States as well as the federal courts must defer to the exclusive competence of the National Labor Relations Board if the danger of state interference with national policy is to be averted.* (emphasis added).

Thus, under *Garmon*, if conduct is arguably protected or prohibited by the LMRA, federal law preempts. The NLRB has primary jurisdiction to enforce the provisions. State courts or state administrative agencies cannot act. Even if the state law is similar to the federal law, only federal law and procedures apply to conduct that is preempted. Even the federal courts may act only to review Board decisions or enter injunctions requested by the Board under Sections 10(j) or 10(l).

If the Board decides that an act is unlawful, should the states be permitted to assess penalties in addition to the NLRB's relief? What if, for example, the Board does not order any monetary relief in a case, but a state court could? The Supreme Court has held the states are powerless to act, even though the remedies might be different. Congress intended that the LMRA regulate not only the conduct, but the remedies as well.

Suppose a union engages in a handbill consumer boycott of a store continuing to sell products of a struck employer and truck drivers, seeing the handbilling, refuse to make deliveries to the store. A consumer boycott is lawful under Section 8(b)(4) only if it does not have the effect of stopping deliveries (see Chapter 7). The store owner cannot seek a state court injunction against the handbilling. Handbilling is either protected or prohibited by the Labor Management Relations Act depending upon whether the statutory requirements are met. Thus, the employer cannot obtain a state court injunction, but can only file a charge with the NLRB. The Board, but not the employer, can then seek injunctive relief against the boycott from the federal courts under Section 10(1).

2. Union Security Matters

Although *Garmon* pertains to state regulation of picketing, the principles apply to any conduct arguably protected or prohibited. Thus, in the Supreme Court's *Lockridge* decision, an employee sued a union for damages in an Idaho state court alleging that he had been wrongfully discharged under a union security clause pursuant to the union's request.[2] The employee maintained that he had paid his dues in time under the union's by-laws and should not have been discharged. The Idaho court awarded the employee over $32,000 in damages. The Supreme Court reversed the Idaho decision, holding that the action was preempted. The Court noted that LMRA Sections 8(a)(3) and 8(b)(2) regulate discharge of an employee under a union security clause. The Court stated that the union's conduct in requiring that the employee be discharged was either arguably protected or prohibited under the LMRA. Therefore, preemption applied. It did not matter that the state court might have afforded a different remedy than the NLRB.

B. FEDERAL COURT EXCEPTIONS TO THE BOARD'S PRIMARY JURISDICTION

The only exceptions to the NLRB's primary jurisdiction at the federal level are under LMRA Sections 301 and 303. Section 301 grants the federal courts jurisdiction to enforce collective bargaining agreements (see Chapter 9). Section 303 authorizes federal court damage suits arising out of unlawful secondary activity prohibited by Section 8(b)(4) (see Chapter 7). The Supreme Court has held that the federal courts have jurisdiction to enforce collective bargaining agreements, including awarding damages, even though an alleged breach of contract may also be an unfair labor practice. The courts also have jurisdiction under Section 301 to enforce

[2] See legal principle 7.

the union's duty of fair representation (see Chapter 12), although the Board has also held that a violation of the duty of fair representation is an unfair labor practice. These are areas of concurrent federal court-NLRB jurisdiction.

C. STATE COURT EXCEPTIONS TO THE PREEMPTION DOCTRINE

1. Violent Conduct

The primary exception to federal preemption is that the states still have jurisdiction over traditional areas of state concern that do not impede upon matters regulated by the LMRA. States have the authority to regulate violent conduct, including intimidation and picket line violence. States may even regulate peaceful picketing that interferes with people entering or leaving a struck facility. State courts can prohibit mass picketing at a plant during a strike and regulate threatened or actual destruction of property. These powers are retained as part of the state's traditional control over disturbance of the peace. State courts or state labor agencies as appropriate can enjoin such strike misconduct and award damages against unions that engage in it.

2. Regulation of Libel and Slander

State authority over libel and slander suits is another example of continued state jurisdiction over traditional areas of state concern. In *Linn v. United Plant Guard Workers*, a supervisor sued a union for damages because the union had allegedly made untrue statements about him during a union organizing campaign.[3] The union argued that the matter was

[3] See legal principle 2.

preempted because the statements were either arguably protected or prohibited under Board rules as to permissible election propaganda.

The Supreme Court refused to apply the preemption doctrine. The Court viewed the regulation of libel and slander (jointly referred to as defamation) as a traditional area of state concern. Also, the LMRA does not regulate libel and slander. However, the Court recognized the danger that a state court might assess damages for statements that the Board might find permissible campaign propaganda. Most states uphold a defamation suit if a statement is in fact untrue, even if the party making the statement thought it was true. A plaintiff does not have to prove malice. Good faith does not matter. Some state laws presume that a person is damaged by a defamatory statement and the victim is entitled to damages without proof of specific harm. To lessen the possibility that state courts will interfere with permissible campaign tactics, the Supreme Court held in *Linn* that a person can prevail in a defamation suit arising out of a labor relations matter only if he proves that a false statement was made with malice. This means that the person making the statement knew it was false or made a serious allegation without checking whether it was true or false—called reckless disregard of the truth. Also, the Court held that the plaintiff must prove actual damages to obtain a monetary award. Damages cannot be presumed. In this way, the Court hoped to balance the traditional state concern in prohibiting libel and slander against the federal interest in regulating labor relations.

D. INROADS INTO THE PREEMPTION DOCTRINE

In *Sears Roebuck & Company*, the Supreme Court slightly modified the preemption doctrine.[4] In *Sears,* the company had a dispute with a union because certain carpentry work was done by employees not dispatched from the union hall. The union established a peaceful picket line on sidewalks around the Sears store on Sears' property. Sears asked the union to remove the pickets to public property, but the union refused. The company then sought a state court injunction to require that the pickets remain on public property. Sears sought the injunction on the grounds that the union pickets were trespassing. The state court issued an injunction despite the union's argument that the dispute was preempted.

Under *Garmon,* the union's picket line at Sears may arguably have been protected or prohibited activity. The object of the picketing was unclear. The union argued that the purpose was to advertise the employer's substandard wages, which would be lawful primary activity. Arguably, the picketing might have been for recognition or to have the work reassigned to employees represented by the union. In that event, the picketing was prohibited activity.

The *Hudgens* decision on shopping center picketing (see Chapter 7) protects a union's right to enter private property in the course of some primary labor disputes. The Board must balance the ability of the union to publicize its dispute against the private property rights of the shopping center owner.

Although the union picket line at Sears arguably was either protected or prohibited activity, the Supreme Court still upheld the right of the state court to issue an injunction. The reasons for the Court's decision were twofold. First, the Court noted that control over trespassing is a traditional area of state concern, similar to the state's right to prevent violence or property damage, which are not

[4] See legal principle 4.

preempted. Second, and apparently more important, the Court emphasized that Sears did not have a means of bringing the trespassing issue before the NLRB. If Sears had filed a charge with the Board, the Board would only decide whether the picketing was primary or secondary. But if the Board held that the picketing was primary, the Board would not be concerned about the location. Thus, Sears could not obtain a NLRB order requiring the union to leave the property if the Board held the picketing was primary.

The Supreme Court pointed out that the union had the opportunity to present the issue directly to the Board. When Sears asked the union to leave the property, the union could have filed a charge with the Board against Sears alleging it had a statutory right, applying the *Hudgens* doctrine, to picket on Sears' property. The Board could have then decided the issue. However, the union did not exercise its right to go to the Board, but simply continued to picket. Thus, the Supreme Court reasoned that the only way that Sears could resolve the picketing issue was by a state court action.

The *Sears* decision does not mean that an employer may immediately seek a state court injunction whenever a union pickets on private property. The Supreme Court emphasized in its decision that a union must be given a fair opportunity to present the issue to the NLRB before the employer can seek a state court injunction. The employer must order the union to leave the employer's property and give the union a chance to file an unfair labor practice charge to determine its rights before the employer can seek an injunction. Also, the Court emphasized that *Sears* involved a situation in which it was unclear whether the union's actions were protected or prohibited. Thus, the preemption doctrine applies as before in situations in which the protected or prohibited status of the conduct is clear under the LMRA.

E. PREEMPTION OF CONDUCT NOT REGULATED BY FEDERAL LAW

Not all conduct arising during a labor–management dispute is regulated by federal law. Federal law does not prohibit unions from engaging in quickie strikes during bargaining in support of their bargaining demands (see Chapter 5). On the other hand, activities such as quickie strikes, sit-down strikes, or slowdowns, are not protected by federal law and employees may be discharged for such conduct.

The states may not be able to regulate certain conduct even though it is neither protected nor prohibited by federal law. The Supreme Court has held it is necessary to consider why Congress chose not to regulate the conduct. Congress might have intended for the conduct to be totally unregulated. In that case, the conduct cannot be regulated by the federal courts or by state courts or agencies. Or, Congress might have intended that the matter be left to the states because the conduct is not considered of federal concern.

The Supreme Court has consistently held that internal union matters not regulated by federal law are subject to state regulation because Congress has not intended for these matters to be totally unregulated. In contrast, the Supreme Court held in *Machinists Lodge 76 v. Wisconsin Employment Relations Commission* that a state cannot prohibit a union from ordering its members not to work any overtime in support of the union's bargaining demands.[5] This conduct is neither protected nor prohibited by federal law, and the Court held that Congress intended for the conduct to be

[5] See legal principle 3.

totally unregulated. Because the union's conduct was peaceful, it did not fall under the exception for traditional state regulation of violent conduct. Thus, union self-help activites, such as quickie strikes, are not subject to regulation by either federal or state law. Such activity is simply a test of economic strength between an employer and a union.

F. EMPLOYERS NOT SUBJECT TO THE BOARD'S JURISDICTION

The LMRA only applies to employers whose activities affect commerce. The operations of some very small employers may not affect commerce and are not subject to federal regulation. Preemption does not apply to these employers, they are subject to state law.

1. Failure to Meet Board Jurisdictional Standards

An employer whose business meets the statutory requirement of affecting commerce may still not meet the discretionary monetary standards the Board has established for asserting jurisdiction (see Chapter 1). Initially, the Supreme Court held that if an employer met the statutory standard of affecting commerce, but failed to meet the Board's discretionary standards, a dispute involving that employer was still preempted and not subject to state regulation. This meant that a dispute might not be regulated by either federal or state law creating a jurisdictional "no man's land."

To remedy the no man's land situation, in 1959, Congress enacted Section 14 (c) of the LMRA, which allows the states to take jurisdiction over a labor dispute if the Board declines jurisdiction over it. If an employer does not meet the Board's jurisdictional standards, a state can assert jurisdiction over the dispute and apply state law.

Although a few states have employment relations boards to regulate conduct that is not preempted, most do not. Most state laws are very outmoded. Because most disputes are preempted, the state courts have had very few cases in which to develop a comprehensive approach. Most state labor law is based on court decisions from the 1940s or early 1950s before the preemption doctrine was fully developed.

The 1974 Health Care Amendments further reduced the significance of state regulation. Nonprofit health care facilities were placed under the LMRA, thus preempting another area. Further, the Board at one time refused to assert jurisdiction over private colleges and universities and other nonprofit institutions. In recent years, the Board has changed its policy and asserted jurisdiction in these fields, thus further reducing the area subject to state regulation.

G.   SECTIONS 301, 303, AND FEDERAL ANTITRUST PREEMPTION OF STATE REGULATION

Sections 301 and 303 provide federal court remedies to enforce collective bargaining agreements and award damages for unlawful secondary activity. Both Sections 301 and 303 preempt state regulation over the matters covered by those statutes. State courts have jurisdiction over suits to enforce collective bargaining agreements, or for damages against secondary boycotts, but the state courts must apply the federal law (see Chapter 9). The Supreme Court has held that Sections 301 and 303 only permit an employer to collect actual damages, such as lost profits, growing out of a violation. Punitive damages are not permitted. Since state courts must apply the federal law, an employer can collect only actual damages even though the suit is brought in a state court. As an exception, the Supreme Court has held that Section 303 does not preempt state regulation over violent conduct occurring during a secondary boycott. Thus an employer can recover actual damages resulting from a secondary boycott under Section 303 and punitive damages under state law if there is violent conduct.

The Supreme Court has applied the same principles to the antitrust laws that it has applied to Sections 301 and 303. Thus, the federal antitrust laws (see Chapter 8) preempt state antitrust regulation of labor relations except to the extent that violent conduct is involved.

Summary   This chapter considered federal–state relationships in labor relations focusing on two fundamental concepts: the doctrines of preemption and primary jurisdiction. Preemption is the doctrine under which federal labor law preempts, or supersedes, state law. Primary jurisdiction is the doctrine determining whether particular conduct, preempted by federal law, is to be regulated by the NLRB, the courts, or by both the courts and the Board.

The Supreme Court has held that if conduct is arguably protected or prohibited by the LMRA, federal law preempts state law and state courts or administrative agencies cannot act. Further, the NLRB, as the agency established to administer the Act, has primary jurisdiction over the federal courts to enforce the provisions.

Preemption does not apply if an employer is not covered by the Act: if the employer's operations do not affect commerce or if the employer fails to meet the applicable Board monetary jurisdictional standards. The states may still regulate disputes outside the Board's jurisdiction.

The only exceptions to the NLRB's primary jurisdiction at the federal level are Section 301 (pertaining to the enforcement of contracts) and Section 303 (pertaining to damages growing out of secondary boycotts) of the LMRA. The federal courts and the NLRB have concurrent jurisdiction under Section 301 if a breach of contract is also an unfair labor practice and to enforce the duty of fair representation. Section 301 and Section 303 preempt state law over the matters these provisions regulate.

States, however, retain jurisdiction over traditional areas of state concern that do not impede upon actions regulated by the LMRA. States have authority to regulate violent conduct of any type, including picketing, and may even regulate peaceful picketing that interferes with entering or leaving a struck facility.

Libel and slander actions growing out of a labor dispute are also not preempted because the Court views defamation as a traditional area of state concern and the LMRA does not regulate it. To avoid conflict, however, the Court held that the party would have to prove malice before prevailing in a defamation suit.

Most internal union matters are still subject to state regulation. The LMRDA expressly provides for concurrent jurisdiction over most matters covered by that Act.

Sears Roebuck & Co. appears to have modified slightly the preemption doctrine. The Court upheld the right of a state court to enjoin a union from picketing in a private shopping center even though the union's dispute was either arguably protected or prohibited activity. The court emphasized that control over trespass is a traditional area of state concern, similar to the state's right to prevent violence or property damages that are not preempted. The Court also stressed that Sears did not have a means of bringing the trespass issue before the Board.

The *Sears* decision does not mean that an employer can seek a state court injunction whenever a union pickets on private property. A union must be given a fair opportunity to present the dispute to the NLRB before the employer can seek a state court injunction.

Congress has intended that certain acts, such as work slowdowns or quickie strikes, must be totally unregulated. Neither the federal nor the state agencies have jurisdiction to regulate such conduct as long as it is peaceful.

Review
Questions

1. What is the difference between the doctrines of preemption and primary jurisdiction?

2. What conduct does the LMRA preempt?

3. What conduct possibly subject to the LMRA can the state courts still regulate?

4. If the Board decides that an act is unlawful, can the states assess penalties in addition to the NLRB's relief?

5. If a union unlawfully pickets to encourage a total boycott of a store selling struck products, can the store owner obtain a state court injunction?

6. What are the exceptions to the NLRB's primary jurisdiction at the federal level?

7. If certain conduct is neither protected nor prohibited by federal law, are the states free to regulate it?

8. Are internal union matters subject to state regulation?

9. Can the states regulate any employers whose activities affect commerce?

10. Are libel suits preempted?

11. Can a state court assess punitive damages if a union engages in an unlawful secondary boycott?

12. Are suits to enforce collective bargaining agreements preempted?

(Answers to review questions appear at end of book.)

Basic Legal
Principles

1. Conduct that is arguably protected by LMRA Section 7 or prohibited by Section 8 is preempted by federal law and is subject to the primary jurisdiction of the NLRB. *San Diego Building Trades Council v. Garmon,* 359 U.S. 236, 43 LRRM 2838 (1959).

2. A defamatory statement during the course of a labor dispute can be the basis of a state court libel suit only if the statement was made with malice. *Linn v. Plant Guards,* 383 U.S. 53, 61 LRRM 2345 (1966).

3. Federal preemption applies to conduct, such as slowdowns, which Congress intended to be totally unregulated by either federal or state agencies, but "controlled by the free play of economic forces." *Machinists Lodge 76 v. Wisconsin Employment Relations Commission,* 427 U.S. 132, 92 LRRM 2881 (1976).

4. As an exception to preemption, state courts may be permitted to issue injunctions against pickets who are trespassing on private property, even if the picket's conduct is arguably protected or prohibited, if the

property owner is unable to present the issue of the picketing's validity to the NLRB, and the union fails to do so although having the opportunity. *Sears, Roebuck & Co. v. Carpenters,* 436 U.S. 180, 98 LRRM 2282 (1978).

5. States have the power to regulate conduct that is violent or causes or threatens to cause injury to persons or property. These are traditional areas of state concern that the Act does not preempt. *UAW v. Russell,* 356 U.S. 634, 42 LRRM 2142 (1958); *San Diego Building Trades Council v. Garmon, supra.*

6. State court jurisdiction is not preempted in cases in which a union member sues his union for intentional infliction of emotional distress (intimidation) that no reasonable person could be expected to endure because the conduct is similar to violent conduct traditionally regulated by the state. *Farmer v. Carpenters, Local 25,* 430 U.S. 290, 94 LRRM 2759 (1977).

7. Regulation of purely internal union affairs is not preempted. *Int'l. Asso. of Machinists v. Gonzales,* 356 U.S. 617, 42 LRRM 2135 (1958); *Motor Coach Employees v. Lockridge,* 403 U.S. 274, 77 LRRM 2501 (1974)

8. Federal and state courts have concurrent jurisdiction under Section 301 to enforce collective bargaining agreements, even though the conduct involved may also be arguably protected or prohibited by the Act. However, the state courts must apply federal law. *Textile Workers Union v. Lincoln Mills,* 353 U.S. 448, 40 LRRM 2113 (1957); *Vaca v. Sipes,* 386 U.S. 171, 64 LRRM 2369 (1967).

9. Section 303 preempts civil damage suits for secondary boycotts. Such suits may be brought in federal or state court, but federal law prevails in either court. *Teamsters Local 20 v. Morton,* 377 U.S. 252, 56 LRRM 2225 (1964).

10. The NLRB may seek a federal court injunction to prohibit a state court from improperly issuing an injunction against peaceful picketing in a preempted matter if the state court action is interfering with the Board's administration of the Act. *NLRB v. Nash-Finch Co.,* 404 U.S. 138, 78 LRRM 2967 (1971).

Recommended Reading

Benke, "Apparent Reformation of Garmon: Its Effect On the Federal Preemption of Concerted Trespassory Union Activity," 9 *U. To l. L. Rev.* 793 (1978)

"Federal Preemption Pension and Retirement Plans," 17 *Duquesne L. Rev.* 189 (1979)

"Preemption Doctrine: New York Balks," 29 *Syracuse L. Rev.* 62 (1978)

Answers to Review Questions

CHAPTER 1

FEDERAL REGULATION OF LABOR-MANAGEMENT REGULATIONS

1. The Norris–LaGuardia Act removed the jurisdiction of the federal judges to issue injunctions in labor disputes regardless of the strike's purpose. The law prevented judges from enjoining a strike because they did not approve of its goals or methods.

2. The Taft–Hartley Act was intended to strike what Congress regarded as a better balance between labor and management. The original NLRA established employee rights and restricted employer acts. Taft–Hartley also established union unfair labor practices.

3. The Board acts as a judge in unfair labor practice cases. It only hears cases in which a complaint has been filed alleging a violation of Section 8. The general counsel serves as the prosecutor. He, or more commonly the regional director acting on the general counsel's behalf, decides whether a charge filed with the agency has merit. If it does, a complaint is issued that may lead to a trial before an administrative law judge and ultimately to a Board decision. The NLRB also administers elections under Section 9, but the general counsel's authority is limited to the unfair labor practice portions of the Act.

4. In addition to the statutory jurisdic-tional requirements of affecting commerce, the Board has established additional mone-tary standards that an employer must meet before the Board will accept jurisdiction over a dispute even though the employer's opera-tions affect commerce.

5. The first step in an unfair labor prac-tice case is the filing of a charge. The Board has no self-enforcement powers. Therefore, even if an unfair labor practice has been com-mitted, the Board can take no action until someone files a charge with it.

6. Anyone can file a charge: an employer, an employee, or a union.

7. A charge must be filed within six months of the date of the alleged unfair labor practice. Sometimes a violation is a continu-ing act, so that a charge can be filed within six months from the last date the act was com-mitted. However, most charges must be filed within six months from the initial occurrence, such as the date of a discharge.

8. The purpose of a representation hear-ing is to resolve any disputed issues as to the appropriateness of a bargaining unit, the em-ployees to be included or excluded in the unit, and the election procedures.

9. The Board requires a 30 percent show of interest of employee support in the appro-priate bargaining unit before proceeding with a representation election. The showing of in-terest is usually made through signed recog-nition cards.

10. In most cases the regional director's decision must be appealed by filing a request for review. There are limited grounds for review and granting review is discretionary with the Board.

CHAPTER 2
THE COLLECTIVE BARGAINING UNIT

1. Community of interest refers to what employees have in common, such as skills, interrelated functions, common supervision, and the same working conditions. The more the employees have in common the more likely it is that the Board will find that they have a distinct community of interest and are an appropriate unit for bargaining.

2. Yes. In most cases a work force could be divided into a number of appropriate units. An election could be held in any of them. The unit does not have to be the best or most appropriate.

3. No. The Board has held that a bargaining unit must have a minimum of two employees because one person cannot engage in collective bargaining by himself. However, this rule does not prevent an employer from voluntarily recognizing a union as the representative for a single employee.

4. A professional employee performs work of a predominately intellectual nature that is not standardized. The work must require the use of discretion and independent judgment and knowledge of an advanced type in a field of science or learning customarily acquired in an institution of higher learning.

5. No. The function an employee performs, not a title, controls. If a person's job is crowd control, he is not a guard despite his title. Similarly, classification as a supervisor is based on duties, not a supervisory title.

6. Agricultural laborers, domestics in the service of a family or person in their home, people employed by a parent or spouse, independent contractors, and supervisors are excluded from the definition of employee.

7. An independent contractor is generally distinguished from an employee based on the amount of control the employer exercises over how a person works. The more control an employer exercises over the work, the more likely it is that the individual will be classified as an employee.

8. Yes. Authority to hire or fire are only two of the twelve separate factors under the Act by which a person may be classified as a supervisor. Even effective authority to recommend supervisory action is sufficient for classification as a supervisor.

9. Yes. Seasonal employees can be included in a bargaining unit of regular full-time employees if they have a reasonable expectation of returning each season. Similarly, probationary employees are included in a bargaining unit if they have a reasonable expectation of completing their probationary period and being permanently employed.

10. The contract bar doctrine establishes the periods for filing representation petitions during or at the termination of a collective bargaining agreement.

11. Unfair labor practice strikers are eligible to vote indefinitely as long as they do not obtain permanent employment elsewhere or are not discharged for strike misconduct.

12. The insulated period is the 60-day period before the termination of a contract when no representation petition may be filed so that the parties may bargain for a contract without interference. The open period is the 90-to-60 day period before expiration when a

timely petition may be filed. If no contract is agreed to during the insulated period, a petition may be timely filed again after the contract's expiration.

CHAPTER 3
UNION ORGANIZING RIGHTS
AND EMPLOYER RESPONSES

1. No. An employer has an absolute right to a Board-conducted election. But if the employer voluntarily verifies the union's majority status, he has waived his right to an election and must bargain with the union.

2. The two types are a single purpose card and a dual purpose card. The single purpose card states that its purpose is to authorize the union to represent the employee signing the card. The dual purpose card states it is for recognition and an election.

3. No. The Board requires clear evidence that a union represented a majority of the employees before it will order an employer to bargain with a union that has lost an election. Dual purpose cards are inadequate because the employee may have signed a card just to get an election, not because he supported the union.

4. Yes. A card cannot be more than a year old to be counted as part of the 30 percent "showing of interest" the Board requires. The Board will not accept undated cards.

5. The Board will not count a single purpose card in determining the union's majority status if the employee signing the card was told its only purpose was for an election.

6. Yes. Handing out recognition cards is considered to be oral solicitation, not distribution of literature. Oral solicitation can take place in working areas, but only on an employee's own time. Literature can be distributed in nonwork areas only.

7. Yes, but unions cannot restrict the offer of free membership to employees who sign recognition cards before the election. Free membership must be allowed for a reasonable time after the election as well as before.

8. No. An employer could discharge an employee for engaging in political activity in violation of a plant rule forbidding it. In contrast, an employer cannot discipline an employee for campaigning for a union in accordance with the Board's rules covering the time and place for such activity because it is a statutorily protected right.

9. Yes. The key factor is whether an employer's prediction of an adverse effect is of something within the employer's control. An employer's prediction of an effect outside of his control is permissible free speech under Section 8(c). An employer can control layoffs, so the statement would be unlawful.

10. An employer may give benefit increases during an election campaign if the benefit increase was planned before the election. But an employer cannot increase benefits that were not already planned. Similarly, an employer cannot refuse to give employees an increase they would have received, but for an election campaign.

11. Yes, because elections are judged on the totality of a party's conduct. Thus an isolated unfair labor practice (e.g., one unlawful threat in an otherwise proper employer campaign) might not be grounds for setting aside the election.

12. The union has five days after the election to file objections. To be grounds for setting aside an election, the misconduct must

occur after the union files its petition. The Board will not issue a bargaining order following an election based on employer unfair labor practices unless the election is also set aside based on timely objections. Thus, it is important to file objections on time.

CHAPTER 4
PROTECTION OF THE EMPLOYEE'S RIGHT TO UNION REPRESENTATION

1. Section 8(a)(1) protects concerted activity whether through a union, through informal groups, or through spontaneous employee protest.

2. Once a union is either lawfully recognized voluntarily or certified as a bargaining agent by the NLRB, the employer is prohibited from dealing with any other employee representative about wages, hours, or other terms and conditions of employment. That is the right of exclusive representation.

3. Intent can be proven from an employer's antiunion statements, from an employer's general antiunion animus, or from the foreseeable consequences of an employer's acts.

4. An employer has the free speech right under Section 8(c) to state a preference for one union over another. However, it is unlawful under Sections 8(a)(1) and (3) for an employer to couple statements favoring one union with threats of adverse consequences if the other union wins.

5. The purpose is twofold: first, to maintain arm's-length bargaining between the employer and the union; and, second, to prevent a union from becoming dependent on the employer's assistance and thus subject to employer pressure.

6. Ordinarily a steward cannot be disciplined for insubordinate remarks made during a grievance or bargaining session. However, a steward may be disciplined for threatening physical harm to an employer or for certain disparaging remarks made in the presence of other employees.

7. Yes, such clauses lawfully insure that there will be a steward present to enforce the contract under all working conditions.

8. Section 8(f) expressly allows pre-hire agreements in the construction industry. This exception was made because construction jobs are frequently of short duration and employers look to the construction unions for their employees.

9. Yes. An employee protesting a contract violation, even if it only affects himself, is engaged in concerted activity because he is protecting the right of all employees to have the contract followed.

10. The employee is entitled to a steward if the investigation is focused on the employee and the employee reasonably believes that he may be facing discipline.

11. The employer can either stop the meeting, offer to continue only if the employee waives his right to representation, or call in the shop steward and continue the investigation in the steward's presence.

12. The discharge may still be unlawful if the purported bona fide reason is a pretext or if the discharge is in part based on the employee's union activities.

CHAPTER 5
THE DUTY TO BARGAIN

1. The party desiring to terminate or modify a contract must serve a written notice upon the other party of the proposed termi-

nation or modification at least 60 days prior to the contract's expiration date and notify the Federal Mediation and Conciliation Service of the dispute within 30 days thereafter. The required notices must be sent respectively 90 and 60 days before a contract's expiration in the health care industry. The notices may be sent earlier than the required date.

2. Not necessarily. An employer is not obligated to agree to any specific contract term. However, failure to agree to a union security clause may be considered in evaluating an employer's overall good faith intent to reach an agreement.

3. No. If a union gives late notice, it must wait the required 60 to 30 day period after the notices were received. After that the union is free to strike.

4. If a union fails to meet contractual notice requirements to terminate the contract, the contract may renew itself in accordance with its terms. In that event, the employer has no duty to bargain during the renewal period. The union cannot strike if the contract as renewed contains a no-strike clause, even though the union may have met the statutory notice requirements. A contract is not extended for failure to give statutory notice, but only for failure to give contractual notice.

5. Yes. Normally there is a presumption that the incumbent union continues to have majority status at the termination of a contract. The employer can withdraw recognition only if he has a good faith doubt of the union's continued majority status based on objective considerations. The parties must cease bargaining for a new agreement if a timely representation petition is filed, but may continue to meet on routine contract administration and grievance matters.

6. An employer is a successor obligated to bargain with the incumbent union if the prior employees compose a majority of the successor's work force in the same industry.

7. No. A successor employer is not bound by the predecessor's contract and is free to negotiate his own agreement. The successor must, however, recognize the incumbent union even though the employer is not bound by the contract.

8. Yes. Normally a successor has no obligation to bargain with the incumbent union until after the successor has individually re-hired the present employees at the wages and working conditions unilaterally established. The union's continued majority is not proven until then. As an exception, the successor is required to bargain on initial terms, but not accept the prior contract, if he announces an intention to keep all former employees.

9. The Board can order an employer to sign a contract incorporating a term that the employer has agreed to. However, the Board has no authority to require any party to accept a term not agreed to, even if the party has been engaged in bad faith bargaining.

10. No. Bargaining for increased retirement benefits for employees who have already retired is a permissive subject of bargaining.

11. Yes. Pay for employees on the union's negotiating committee pertains to wages and is therefore a mandatory subject of bargaining.

12. The union is broadly entitled to any information relevant to administering the contract, insuring the employer's compliance, evaluating grievances, and processing grievances to arbitration. The employer may not be required to produce information to the union in a form that is unduly burdensome, or if, for proper cause, the data is confidential and denial is not unduly burdensome.

CHAPTER 6
STRIKES, STRIKER RIGHTS, AND LOCKOUTS

1. No. The right to strike has never been afforded an unqualified constitutional protection.

2. Section 13 of the LMRA protects the right to strike except as limited by the Act. The proviso to Section 8(b)(4)(B) protects the right to engage in a primary strike or primary picketing not otherwise unlawful. Section 502 protects the right to refuse work which is abnormally dangerous.

3. An unfair labor practice strike is a strike over an employer's unfair labor practice, such as the discharge of a union adherent because of union activity.

4. An economic strike is a strike over an economic issue, such as wages, fringe benefits, or working conditions.

5. An unfair labor practice striker cannot be replaced permanently and is entitled to reinstatement upon an unconditional offer to return to work. An economic striker can be permanently replaced. A replaced economic striker is not entitled to immediate reinstatement, but is entitled to recall as vacancies occur.

6. Economic strikers who have been permanently replaced are eligible to vote in a representation election held within 12 months of the commencement of the strike. Their replacements are also eligible. Unfair labor practice strikers and economic strikers who have not been replaced are entitled to vote indefinitely. Temporary replacements are ineligible to vote.

7. Strikers lose their right to reinstatement or recall if they find permanent employment elsewhere. There is a presumption that employment during a strike is only temporary. Employees who engage in serious misconduct during a strike can be lawfully discharged.

8. Neither unfair labor practice nor economic strikers are entitled to wages during a strike regardless of the reason, because they are withholding their services, unless the employer unlawfully rejects their unconditional offer to return to work.

9. A sympathy strike is one in which employees respect another union's picket line although not directly involved in the dispute.

10. Usually, no. A no-strike clause does not prohibit a sympathy strike unless the clause expressly so states or the bargaining history makes it clear the union waived the right to engage in a sympathy strike.

11. If it is necessary to continue operations, an employer can permanently replace, but not discipline, sympathy strikers who are respecting an economic strike picket line.

12. No. A no-strike clause normally only prohibits economic strikes. It does not prohibit strikes over serious unfair labor practices, sympathy strikes, or refusal to perform abnormally dangerous work.

13. The courts will imply a no-strike obligation if a contract contains an arbitration clause and the strike is over an arbitrable issue.

14. A court can award an employer damages for a union's breach of a contractual no-strike clause, and enjoin a strike over an arbitral issue provided that the employer is willing to arbitrate the dispute.

15. No. A federal court has no jurisdiction to enjoin a sympathy strike because it is not over an arbitrable dispute. However, if a sympathy strike does violate the contract, the employer may be able to collect damages even though the strike is not enjoinable.

CHAPTER 7
PICKETING AND RELATED ACTIVITY

1. There is a limited constitutional right to picket as a matter of free speech. However, picketing is a form of action, not just speech, and can therefore be regulated.

2. A primary picket is directed against the employer with whom the union has a dispute. A secondary picket line is directed against an employer other than the one with whom the union has its dispute.

3. No. Picketing employees have only the moral strength of their picket signs and their power of peaceful persuasion to prevent persons from crossing. An employer could obtain a state court injunction against mass picketing.

4. Section 8(b)(4) refers to the object of a dispute. From this, the courts have developed a distinction between the object of picketing and its effect. If the object is primary, (i.e., directed against the employer with whom the union has its dispute), the picketing is lawful even though there may be a secondary effect.

5. No. Picketing is unlawful if it has both a primary and secondary object. Picketing can, however, have a primary object with a secondary effect.

6. A union picketing at its own plant can have signs that simply state "on strike" without identifying the picketed employer. However, in the *Moore Dry Dock* secondary situs situation, the union must identify the employer with whom it has its dispute.

7. No. The picketing union must limit its picketing to the scheduled time as long as the primary employer keeps the schedule. The secondary employer can legally limit the picketing's impact in this manner.

8. Yes. An appeal to fellow employees is for mutual aid and protection, which is a primary object. The rules set forth in *Moore Dry Dock, Denver Building Trades*, and *General Electric* only apply to a union's appeal to employees of other employers.

9. Yes. A union's right to picket a struck product is not restricted by Section 8(b)(4), unless the object of the picketing is a total boycott of the employer handling the struck product as in the case of a "merged product."

10. No. Substandard picketing is primary picketing. It can lawfully have the effect (but not the object) of inducing other employees to honor a picket line.

11. The picketing may be unlawful if it has a recognition object and does not meet the requirements of Section 8(b)(7).

12. The employer may file a charge under Section 8(b)(4) and also file suit for damages under Section 303. Section 303 is the only section of the law that allows private damage suits to remedy an unfair labor practice.

CHAPTER 8
UNION REGULATION OF WORK AND THE ANTITRUST LAWS

1. Section 8(e) follows the general policy of Section 8(b)(4) limiting a labor dispute to the primary employer and the striking union.

2. The clause would be unlawful because it might permit employees to honor a secondary picket line. A picket line clause must be limited to primary picketing under Section 8(e).

3. No. A clause worded that broadly would violate Section 8(e). A struck work clause must be limited to a primary strike and

must permit two employers to maintain a normal business relationship during a strike.

4. Such clauses are unlawful under Section 8(e) because they go beyond the valid object of preserving unit work and have the secondary object of influencing the labor relations of a secondary employer.

5. No. A union standards clause permitting subcontracting only to an employer who maintains the equivalent total in wages, hours, and fringe benefits is lawful, but requiring a subcontractor to maintain exactly the same pay package has the secondary object of dictating the subcontractor's labor policies.

6. Yes. A contract clause in which an employer agrees that he will not sell his business except to someone who assumes the collective bargaining contract does not violate Section 8(e).

7. The construction industry proviso permits a construction union to negotiate a clause limiting the contracting and subcontracting of work to be done on the construction site to union contractors. Construction unions are subject to the same restrictions as any other union for off situs subcontracting clauses.

8. Yes, provided that a no-strike clause does not prohibit it. Self-help usually does not violate Section 8(e) because enforcing a valid work preservation clause is a primary object even though there may be a secondary effect on a subcontractor. As an exception, self-help may violate Section 8(e) if the contracting employer does not have the "right to control" the disputed work.

9. No. The Board has jurisdiction under Section 10(k) only if the Board has reasonable cause to believe that one of the competing unions has engaged in a coercive act violating Section 8(b)(4)(D). If the unions exert peace-

ful persuasion on the employer or request arbitration Section 8(b)(4)(D) is not violated and Section 10 (k) does not come into play.

10. The employer's assignment and preference are by far the most important factors.

11. Yes. Make work does not violate the Section 8(b)(6) "featherbedding" restrictions, and manning requirements are a mandatory bargaining subject.

12. Yes. Such a clause does not violate the antitrust laws if the union seeks the clause in the union's own self-interest and not in combination with any employers.

13. No. Multi-employer bargaining can violate the antitrust laws only if the union seeks to impose the same contract on other employers pursuant to an agreement with the multi-employer association to do so.

CHAPTER 9
ENFORCEMENT OF COLLECTIVE BARGAINING AGREEMENTS

1. No. Section 301 also applies to contracts between unions such as no-raiding pacts.

2. No. A union's by-laws are considered a contract between the union and the member. That is not one of the contracts enforceable under Section 301.

3. No. Section 301 actions cannot be brought by or against employers or unions not covered by the LMRA.

4. Usually a dispute arising after a collective bargaining agreement has expired is not arbitrable. However, the dispute would be arbitrable if the issue pertained to the continued application of a specific clause beyond the contract's expiration.

5. Generally an employee cannot sue to enforce alleged contract rights contrary to a settlement. The only exception is if the settlement is made in violation of the union's duty of fair representation.

6. The length of time to file a suit varies from state to state based on the time that the state allows to bring a suit for breach of contract.

7. A federal or state court must order arbitration if a collective bargaining agreement provides for arbitration unless it can be stated with positive assurance that the contract's arbitration clause does not apply to the particular dispute. Any doubts should be resolved in favor of arbitration.

8. The merits of a dispute are irrelevant and cannot be considered by a court in determining arbitrability.

9. *Warrior* emphasized that federal labor policy favors arbitration rather than litigation or strikes as a means of resolving industrial disputes. The decision affirmed the right of arbitrators to apply past practice as well as the express provisions of the contract. Finally, *Warrior* established that arbitration is a matter of contract and that the courts determine arbitrability.

10. Yes, whether a decision is right or wrong does not matter as long as the arbitrator based his decision on his interpretation of the contract.

11. The employer must exhaust the contractual provisions for arbitration before filing suit unless it is clear that the employer has no right to file grievances. Many contracts only permit union or employee grievances.

12. Grievance arbitration pertains to a dispute arising under an existing collective bargaining agreement. Interest arbitration is over new contract terms. The arbitrator determines the contents rather than interpreting the agreement the parties have reached.

13. Under LMRA Section 10(a), the Board's decision would prevail. However, under the *Spielberg* doctrine, the Board will sometimes defer to an arbitrator's award meeting its standards even though the Board might not have reached the same result.

14. Yes, if a union waits until after the arbitrator rules before filing a charge, the six month time limit for filing may have already passed. Also, if the union files a charge that the Board defers to arbitration, the arbitrator is more likely to face and determine the unfair labor practice issue.

CHAPTER 10
UNION MEMBERSHIP AND UNION SECURITY

1. At common law a union is an unincorporated association, a combination of its members with no separate legal existence.

2. In most states a union, as an unincorporated association, cannot sue or be sued in its own name as an entity. Large unincorporated groups, however, can sue or be sued as a class.

3. Federal labor law statutes (such as LMRA Sections 301 and 303) expressly permit a union to sue or be sued as an entity in federal court. The Supreme Court has further held that a union may be sued as an entity in a federal court for violation of any federal statute.

4. No. Section 301(b) provides that any money judgment against a union in federal court is enforceable only against the organization as an entity and against its assets and is

not enforceable against any individual member or his assets.

5. The relationship between the union and its members is contractual. The union's by-laws, as a contract, determine the members' rights and responsibilities.

6. No. If the union rejects an employee who is willing to tender his initiation fees and dues for membership, then the employee becomes a legal free rider.

7. A check-off form can be irrevocable for up to a year or until the expiration date of the collective bargaining agreement whichever occurs first. The form may provide for automatic renewal if the employee does not revoke the check-off within a specified period before its expiration.

8. If a member is expelled for refusal to tender his periodic dues and initiation fees he is properly subject to discharge upon the union's request under Section 8(a)(3). If an employee was expelled or denied membership for any other reason, however, his employment cannot be affected by his membership status.

9. No. If an employee is willing to be a full union member, but the union expels him for a valid reason (other than the failure to pay initiation fees and dues), the union security clause cannot be enforced against him. The employee becomes a free rider.

10. An employee who simply pays the initiation fees and dues in order to keep his job, but does not formally join the union is not bound by the union's by-laws and is not subject to discipline by the union.

11. No. The clause expires immediately unless the parties agree to keep the contract in effect. That means that union members usually have the right to resign from the union after the contract has expired.

12. An employee in a right-to-work state who formally joins the union is bound by the constitution and by-laws of the union the same as a member in any other state. If an employee does not pay his dues, he can be expelled from the membership, sued, or both in the state court for the amount owed.

13. No. An exclusive hiring hall must serve everyone, whether or not a union member. The method of referral must be nondiscriminatory.

14. If the employee has signed a check-off form he cannot be discharged because it is the union's obligation to make sure the employer deducts the proper amount and forwards it to the union. But if the collective bargaining agreement does not provide for check-off or if an employee has decided to pay directly on his own, the employee is obligated to get his dues in on time and can be discharged for being late provided the union has fulfilled its fiduciary notice requirements.

15. The responsibility for proper enforcement of a union security clause lies solely and completely with the union.

16. No. The union is responsible for notifying the member of his delinquency. The employee cannot be discharged if the union fails to give him personal notice, even though the employee is, in fact, aware of his delinquency.

CHAPTER 11
RIGHTS AND RESPONSIBILITIES OF UNION MEMBERS

1. Section 101(a)(1) does not guarantee any specific rights. Instead, it requires that whatever rights are established by a union's constitution or its by-laws be shared equally by all members.

2. No. The LMRDA defines a member as a person who has fulfilled the requirements for membership, although in some cases, that person may not have been formally admitted by the union.

3. No, an officer is not statutorily entitled to a hearing before removal. But some courts have held that an officer may sue the union for reinstatement to his office and for damages if he was removed in retaliation for the exercise of statutorily protected rights.

4. No, a member has a virtually unlimited right to say whatever he wants at a union meeting, even if his statements are untrue, subject only to reasonable rules to preserve order at the meeting. As *narrow* exceptions, a member may be prohibited from making comments contrary to the members' responsibility toward the union as an institution or that would interfere with the union's legal or contractual obligations.

5. The LMRDA does not specify the grounds for discipline. It only prohibits discipline for the exercise of statutorily protected rights and establishes minimum requirements for a hearing before discipline is imposed. Other than that, the grounds for discipline and the procedures are internal union matters. The Act does not require a hearing before disciplining a member for failure to pay the union's initiation fees or dues.

6. Yes, provided that the discipline does not impair the supervisor's functioning as his employer's representative for purposes of bargaining, contract administration, or grievance adjustments.

7. Under LMRDA Section 101(a)(5), the member must be served with written specific charges, given a reasonable time to prepare his defense, and afforded a full and fair hearing.

8. Due process requires that the accused member face his accuser, that the decision be based on evidence presented at the hearing, and that the accused be permitted to cross-examine the witnesses against him. A union need not follow the formal rules that a court would apply. The member is not entitled to have a lawyer present.

9. Federal law does not regulate the amount of a fine. The amount is purely an internal union matter and state law. Generally, a fine may be any amount that is reasonable under all the facts and circumstances.

10. LMRDA Section 101(a)(4) requires that a member exhaust reasonable internal appeal procedures for up to four months. However, application of this exhaustion requirement is discretionary with the courts. A court may not require exhaustion if it appears internal procedures would be futile or there is a clear statutory violation.

CHAPTER 12
THE DUTY OF FAIR REPRESENTATION

1. The duty of fair representation is implied from the union's right to exclusive representation under Section 9 of the LMRA.

2. A union meets its duty of fair representation as long as its decisions and actions are not arbitrary, discriminatory, in bad faith, or perfunctory.

3. Yes. There is no specific provision of the LMRA that makes a violation of the fair representation duty an unfair labor practice, but the Board has implied the duty under Sections 7 and 8(b)(1)(A).

4. Ordinarily an employee is bound by an arbitrator's decision unless the union has violated its duty of fair representation in

processing the employee's grievance to arbitration.

5. The employee cannot successfully sue the employer unless the union violated its duty of fair representation. The employee must prove that the union did not discover the evidence proving the employee's innocence because the union violated its duty of fair representation. If the employee cannot prove that the union violated its duty, it is irrelevant that the employee was in fact wrongly discharged.

6. Suits for violation of the union's duty of fair representation are governed by Section 301 of the LMRA. Federal law governs such suits whether they are filed in state or federal court.

7. Yes. A union can change the seniority system, even though the change favors one employee group over another, as long as the union's decision does not violate its duty of fair representation.

8. No. The duty of fair representation does not permit second guessing by either a court or the Board. Errors in judgment, or even the fact that a union made the wrong decision, do not violate the duty of fair representation.

9. Damages are apportioned between the employer and the union depending upon the respective responsibility of each for the employee's damages. Ordinarily, the employer is responsible for most of the damages, unless the union instigates the employer's action.

10. There is no clear answer at present. If the union fails to meet a contractual time limit because it perfunctorily processed the grievance, the union has violated its duty of fair representation. If, however, the union processed the grievance properly, but missed a deadline strictly because of negligence, there is probably no violation.

CHAPTER 13
UNIONS AND EQUAL EMPLOYMENT OPPORTUNITY

1. Usually a union must have fifteen or more members to be covered by Title VII. However, a union that maintains or operates a hiring hall is covered by the Act regardless of its size.

2. Title VII prohibits discrimination because of an individual's race, color, religion, sex, or national origin. A person discriminated against for any of these reasons is a member of a protected group. Thus, the Act prohibits reverse discrimination against white persons because of their race as well as discrimination against blacks. Title VII does not prohibit age discrimination, but age discrimination is prohibited by the Age Discrimination in Employment Act.

3. The two basic categories of unlawful discrimination are disparate treatment discrimination and disparate impact discrimination.

4. Yes, an employer may still violate Title VII, even if he proves a legitimate nondiscriminatory reason for rejecting a protected group member, if the person can prove that the reason given is a pretext, and that the person was in fact discriminatorily denied employment.

5. Yes, an employment practice having a disparate impact can violate Title VII regardless of the employer's intent. A practice having disparate impact is lawful under Title VII only if the employer proves business necessity and there are no alternatives available that can meet the employer's legitimate needs without the same disproportionate impact.

6. No, an employment practice does not have to be job related under Title VII unless it has a disproportionate impact on the mem-

bers of a protected group. So long as there is no disproportionate impact, an employer can set any job requirements he wishes, even if they are clearly not job related.

7. Yes, a specific employment practice can violate Title VII even though the employer's overall work force has a proportionate number of protected group employees. Federal agencies, at their discretion, might not take action against an employer whose overall employment practices result in a proportionate work force, but that does not prevent an individual from proving that he was discriminatorily denied employment in a specific case either because of disparate treatment or disparate impact discrimination.

8. No, barring women from heavy jobs is unlawful under Title VII because the bar is based upon a stereotyped assumption of a woman's role. A person can be barred from a job only if sex is a bona fide occupational qualification.

9. Title VII, as amended by the Pregnancy Disability Amendment, does not specify the number of months of leave an employer must allow a woman. Rather, an employer must allow a woman, disabled for work due to pregnancy or childbirth, the same number of months off it would allow a disabled male employee.

10. An employer must accommodate an employee's religious observances or practices that do not entail undue hardship on the employer's business. An employer is required to allow an employee off for a religious holiday subject to the undue hardship exception. An employer need not incur more than *de minimis* expense or infringe upon one employee's seniority rights to accommodate another employee's religious practices.

11. An employee cannot be required to retire before age seventy unless age is a bona

fide occupational qualification for a job. As an exception, certain high income executives and tenured professors at institutions of higher education may be required to retire at age sixty-five.

12. The basic requirements are that a timely charge must be filed with the EEOC within 180 days of the occurrence of the alleged unlawful employment practice and that the suit must be filed within 90 days after receiving notice of the right to sue from the EEOC. Also, an individual cannot request a right to sue notice from the EEOC until 180 days after the charge has been filed.

13. Yes. An employee may file suit under Title VII within 90 days after receiving a right to sue notice whether or not the EEOC found reasonable cause to believe the statute has been violated.

14. A federal court has broad discretion to impose whatever remedies are necessary to overcome the effect of past discrimination and bar future discrimination. The court's remedies include back pay, rightful place seniority, and affirmative action programs.

15. Yes, a court may require that a discriminatee be placed in a job currently held by another innocent employee if that action is necessary to remedy the discrimination that has occurred.

16. A black employee who fails to file a timely charge under Title VII could still file suit under 42 U.S.C. 1981 or 1983 as appropriate. These statutes are separate independent remedies from Title VII. A female employee who fails to file a timely charge under Title VII against either a private employer or union has no other remedy; however, she can still file suit under 42 U.S.C. 1983 against discrimination by a state or local governmental body employer.

17. Yes. An employee who has lost an ar-

bitration hearing can still proceed under Title VII and is entitled to a full hearing on the Title VII claim. A court is not bound by an arbitrator's decision on a Title VII issue. The court may give an arbitrator's award such weight as it deserves, keeping in mind that Congress intended for the courts to make the final decision on Title VII violations.

18. A charge must be filed under Title VII within 180 days after the *occurrence* of a discriminatory act, not after receiving the arbitrator's award. Filing a grievance does not toll the 180 day requirement. Thus, an employee may not be able to wait for the arbitrator's decision before filing a charge with the EEOC, or the 180 days may pass in the meantime.

19. The Board will certify a union that has engaged in past discrimination regardless of its past record, but it may revoke the certification of a union that engages in such discrimination after it is certified.

20. Title VII prohibits reverse discrimination against white or male employees. However, voluntary affirmative action programs adopted by an employer, union, or both to remedy traditional patterns of segregation are lawful under Title VII.

CHAPTER 14
FEDERAL-STATE RELATIONSHIPS IN LABOR RELATIONS

1. Preemption is the doctrine used to determine whether federal labor law supersedes state law on a certain matter. Primary jurisdiction is the doctrine used in determining whether a particular matter that is preempted by federal law is to be regulated by the NLRB, the courts, or both the courts and the Board.

2. The LMRA preempts conduct that is arguably protected or prohibited by the Act.

3. State courts can continue to regulate traditional areas of state concern that do not impede activities regulated by the LMRA, such as violent conduct or trespass.

4. No. The states are powerless to act even though the state remedies might be different. Congress intended for the LMRA to preempt not only the conduct, but the remedies as well.

5. No. Since the picketing is either protected or prohibited by the LMRA, the preemption doctrine applies. A state court cannot enjoin the picketing so long as it is peaceful.

6. The exceptions to the NLRB's primary jurisdiction are LMRA Section 301 (pertaining to enforcement of contracts) and Section 303 (pertaining to damage suits for secondary boycotts).

7. Not always. It is possible that Congress intended that conduct such as sit down strikes be totally unregulated by either state or federal agencies.

8. Yes. Most internal union matters are subject to extensive state regulation. The LMRDA expressly provides for continued state regulation over most matters covered by that statute.

9. Yes. The states can regulate employers whose activities affect commerce if the employer is not subject to the LMRA or if he fails to meet the Board's monetary standards.

10. No. Libel suits are not preempted, but the Supreme Court requires that a party prove malice in order to recover in a libel suit growing out of a labor dispute.

11. No. Section 303 preempts state regulation over secondary boycotts. Such suits can be filed in the state courts, but the states must apply federal law. Punitive damages are not allowed for peaceful secondary boycotts.

12. Yes. Suits to enforce contracts are governed by federal law even though such suits may be filed in the state courts. The NLRB and courts have concurrent jurisdiction over unfair labor practices that may also be contract violations.

Statutory Appendix

TAFT - HARTLEY ACT

Text of Labor Management Relations Act, 1947, as Amended by Public Laws 86–257, 1959,* and 93–360, 1974**

[Public Law 101—80th Congress]

DEFINITIONS

SEC. 2. When used in this Act—

(1) The term "person" includes one or more individuals, labor organizations, partnerships, associations, corporations, legal representatives, trustees, trustees in bankruptcy, or receivers.

(2) The term "employer" includes any person acting as an agent of an employer, directly or indirectly, but shall not include the United States or any wholly owned Government corporation, or any Federal Reserve Bank, or any State or political subdivision thereof,** or any person subject to the Railway Labor Act, as amended from time to time, or any labor organization (other than when acting as an employer), or anyone acting in the capacity of officer or agent of such labor organization.

(3) The term "employee" shall include any employee, and shall not be limited to the employees of a particular employer, unless the Act explicitly states otherwise, and shall include any individual whose work has ceased as a consequence of, or in connection with, any current labor dispute or because of any unfair labor practice, and who has not obtained any other regular and substantially equivalent employment, but shall not include any individual employed as an agricultural laborer, or in the domestic service of any family or person at his home, or any individual employed by his parent or spouse, or any individual having the status of an independent contractor, or any individual employed as a supervisor, or any individual employed by an employer subject to the Railway Labor Act, as amended from time to time, or by any other person who is not an employer as herein defined.

(4) The term "representatives" includes any individual or labor organization.

(5) The term "labor organization" means any organization of any kind, or any agency or employee representation committee or plan, in which employees participate and which exists for the purpose, in whole or in part, of dealing with employers concerning grievances, labor disputes, wages, rates of pay, hours of employment, or conditions of work.

**Pursuant to Public Law 93–360, 93d Cong., S. 3203, 88 Stat. 395, Sec. 2(2) is amended by deleting the phrase "or any corporation or association operating a hospital, if no part of the net earnings inures to the benefit of any private shareholder or individual,".

(6) The term "commerce" means trade, traffic, commerce, transportation, or communication among the several States, or between the District of Columbia or any Territory of the United States and any State or other Territory, or between any foreign country and any State, Territory, or the District of Columbia, or within the District of Columbia or any Territory, or between points in the same State but through any other State or any Territory or the District of Columbia or any foreign country.

(7) The term "affecting commerce" means in commerce, or burdening or obstructing commerce or the free flow of commerce, or having led or tending to lead to a labor dispute burdening or obstructing commerce or the free flow of commerce.

(8) The term "unfair labor practice" means any unfair labor practice listed in section 8.

(9) The term "labor dispute" includes any controversy concerning terms, tenure or conditions of employment, or concerning the association or representation of persons in negotiating, fixing, maintaining, changing, or seeking to arrange terms or conditions of employment, regardless of whether the disputants stand in the proximate relation of employer and employee.

(10) The term "National Labor Relations Board" means the National Labor Relations Board provided for in section 3 of this Act.

(11) The term "supervisor" means any individual having authority, in the interest of the employer, to hire, transfer, suspend, lay off, recall, promote, discharge, assign, reward, or discipline other employees, or responsibly to direct them, or to adjust their grievances, or effectively to recommend such action, if in connection with the foregoing the exercise of such authority is not of a merely routine or clerical nature, but requires the use of independent judgment.

(12) The term "professional employee" means—

(a) any employee engaged in work (i) predominantly intellectual and varied in character as opposed to routine mental, manual, mechanical, or physical work; (ii) involving the consistent exercise of discretion and judgment in its performance; (iii) of such a character that the output produced or the result accomplished cannot be standardized in relation to a given period of time; (iv) requiring knowledge of an advanced type in a field of science or learning customarily acquired by a prolonged course of specialized intellectual instruction and study in an institution of higher learning or a hospital, as distinguished from a general academic education or from an apprenticeship or from training in the performance of routine mental, manual, or physical processes; or

(b) any employee, who (i) has completed the courses of specialized intellectual instruction and study described in clause (iv) of paragraph (a), and (ii) is performing related work under the supervision of a professional person to qualify himself to become a professional employee as defined in paragraph (a).

(13) In determining whether any person is acting as an "agent" of another person so as to make such other person responsible for his acts, the question of whether the specific acts performed were actually authorized or subsequently ratified shall not be controlling.

**(14) The term "health care institution" shall include any hospital, convalescent

---

**Pursuant to Public Law 93–360. 93d Cong.. S. 3203. 88 Stat. 395. Sec. 2 is amended by adding subsection 14.

hospital, health maintenance organization, health clinic, nursing home, extended care facility, or other institution devoted to the care of sick, infirm, or aged person.

NATIONAL LABOR RELATIONS BOARD

SEC. 3. (a) The National Labor Relations Board (hereinafter called the "Board") created by this Act prior to its amendment by the Labor Management Relations Act, 1947, is hereby continued as an agency of the United States, except that the Board shall consist of five instead of three members, appointed by the President by and with the advice and consent of the Senate. Of the two additional members so provided for, one shall be appointed for a term of five years and the other for a term of two years. Their successors, and the successors of the other members, shall be appointed for terms of five years each, excepting that any individual chosen to fill a vacancy shall be appointed only for the unexpired term of the member whom he shall succeed. The President shall designate one member to serve as Chairman of the Board. Any member of the Board may be removed by the President, upon notice and hearing, for neglect of duty or malfeasance in office, but for no other cause.

(b) The Board is authorized to delegate to any group of three of more members any or all of the powers which it may itself exercise. The Board is also authorized to delegate to its regional directors its powers under section 9 to determine the unit appropriate for the purpose of collective bargaining, to investigate and provide for hearings, and determine whether a question of representation exists, and to direct an election or take a secret ballot under subsection (c) or (e) of section 9 and certify the results thereof, except that upon the filing of a request therefor with the Board by any interested person, the Board may review any action of a regional director delegated to him under this paragraph, but such a review shall not, unless specifically ordered by the Board, operate as a stay of any action taken by the regional director. A vacancy in the Board shall not impair the right of the remaining members to exercise all of the powers of the Board, and three members of the Board shall, at all times, constitute a quorum of the Board, except that two members shall constitute a quorum of any group designated pursuant to the first sentence hereof. The Board shall have an official seal which shall be judicially noticed.

(c) The Board shall at the close of each fiscal year make a report in writing to Congress and to the President stating in detail the cases it has heard, the decisions it has rendered, the names, salaries, and duties of all employees and officers in the employ or under the supervision of the Board, and an account of all moneys it has disbursed.

(d) There shall be a General Counsel of the Board who shall be appointed by the President, by and with the advice and consent of the Senate, for a term of four years. The General Counsel of the Board shall exercise general supervision over all attorneys employed by the Board (other than trial examiners and legal assistants to Board members) and over the officers and employees in the regional offices. He shall have final authority, on behalf of the Board, in respect of the investigation of charges and issuance of complaints under section 10, and in respect of the prosecution of such complaints before the Board, and shall have such other duties as the Board may prescribe or as may be provided by law. In case of a vacancy in the office of the General Counsel the President is authorized to designate the officer or employee who shall act as General Counsel during such vacancy, but no person or persons so designated shall so act (1) for more than forty days when the Congress is in session unless a nomination to fill such vacancy shall have been submitted to the Senate, or (2) after the adjournment *sine die* of the session of the Senate in which such nomination was submitted.

SEC. 4. (a) Each member of the Board and the General Counsel of the Board shall receive a salary of $12,000* a year, shall be eligible for reappointment, and shall not engage in any other business, vocation, or employment. The Board shall appoint an executive secretary, and such attorneys, examiners, and regional directors, and such other employees as it may from time to time find necessary for the proper performance of its duties. The Board may not employ any attorneys for the purpose of reviewing transcripts of hearings or preparing drafts of opinions except that any attorney employed for assignment as a legal assistant to any Board member may for such Board member review such transcripts and prepare such drafts. No trial examiner's report shall be reviewed, either before or after its publication, by any person other than a member of the Board or his legal assistant, and no trial examiner shall advise or consult with the Board with respect to exceptions taken to his findings, rulings, or recommendations. The Board may establish or utilize such regional, local, or other agencies, and utilize such voluntary and uncompensated services, as may from time to time be needed. Attorneys appointed under this section may, at the direction of the Board, appear for and represent the Board in any case in court. Nothing in this Act shall be construed to authorize the Board to appoint individuals for the purpose of conciliation or mediation, or for economic analysis.

RIGHTS OF EMPLOYEES

SEC. 7. Employees shall have the right to self-organization, to form, join, or assist labor organizations, to bargain collectively through representatives of their own choosing, and to engage in other concerted activities for the purpose of collective bargaining or other mutual aid or protection, and shall also have the right to refrain from any or all of such activities except to the extent that such right may be affected by an agreement requiring membership in a labor organization as a condition of employment as authorized in section 8(a)(3).

UNFAIR LABOR PRACTICES

SEC. 8. (a) It shall be an unfair labor practice for an employer—

(1) to interfere with, restrain, or coerce employees in the exercise of the rights guaranteed in section 7;

(2) to dominate or interfere with the formation or administration of any labor organization or contribute financial or other support to it: *Provided,* That subject to rules and regulations made and published by the Board pursuant to section 6, an employer shall not be prohibited from permitting employees to confer with him during working hours without loss of time or pay;

(3) by discrimination in regard to hire or tenure of employment or any term or condition of employment to encourage or discourage membership in any labor organization: *Provided,* That nothing in this Act, or in any other statute of the United States, shall preclude an employer from making an agreement with a labor organization (not established, maintained, or assisted by any action defined in section 8(a) of this Act as an unfair labor practice) to require as a condition of employment membership therein on or after the thirtieth day following the beginning of such employment or the effective date of such agreement,

---

*Pursuant to Public Law 90–206, 90th Cong., 81 Stat. 644, approved Dec. 16, 1967, and in accordance with Sec. 225(f)(ii) thereof, effective in 1969, the salary of the Chairman of the Board shall be $40,000 per year and the salaries of the General Counsel and each Board member shall be $38,000 per year.

whichever is the later, (i) if such labor organization is the representative of the employees as provided in section 9(a), in the appropriate collective-bargaining unit covered by such agreement when made, and (ii) unless following an election held as provided in section 9(e) within one year preceding the effective date of such agreement, the Board shall have certified that at least a majority of the employees eligible to vote in such election have voted to rescind the authority of such labor organization to make such an agreement: *Provided further,* That no employer shall justify any discrimination against an employee for non-membership in a labor organization (A) if he has reasonable grounds for believing that such membership was not available to the employee on the same terms and conditions generally applicable to other members, or (B) if he has reasonable grounds for believing that membership was denied or terminated for reasons other than the failure of the employee to tender the periodic dues and the initiation fees uniformly required as a condition of acquiring or retaining membership;

(4) to discharge or otherwise discriminate against an employee because he has filed charges or given testimony under this Act;

(5) to refuse to bargain collectively with the representatives of his employees, subject to the provisions of section 9(a).

(b) It shall be an unfair labor practice for a labor organization or its agents—

(1) to restrain or coerce (A) employees in the exercise of the rights guaranteed in section 7: *Provided,* That this paragraph shall not impair the right of a labor organization to prescribe its own rules with respect to the acquisition or retention of membership therein; or (B) an employer in the selection of his representatives for the purposes of collective bargaining or the adjustment of grievances;

(2) to cause or attempt to cause an employer to discriminate against an employee in violation of subsection (a)(3) or to discriminate against an employee with respect to whom membership in such organization has been denied or terminated on some ground other than his failure to tender the periodic dues and the initiation fees uniformly required as a condition of acquiring or retaining membership;

(3) to refuse to bargain collectively with an employer, provided it is the representative of his employees subject to the provisions of section 9(a);

(4) (i) to engage in, or to induce or encourage any individual employed by any person engaged in commerce or in an industry affecting commerce to engage in, a strike or a refusal in the course of his employment to use, manufacture, process, transport, or otherwise handle or work on any goods, articles, materials, or commodities or to perform any services; or (ii) to threaten, coerce, or restrain any person engaged in commerce or in an industry affecting commerce, where in either case an object thereof is:

(A) forcing or requiring any employer or self-employed person to join any labor or employer organization or to enter into any agreement which is prohibited by section 8(e);

(B) forcing or requiring any person to cease using, selling, handling, transporting, or otherwise dealing in the products of any other producer, processor, or manufacturer, or to cease doing business with any other person, or forcing or requiring any other employer to recognize or bargain with a labor organization as the representative of his employees unless such labor organization has been certified as the representative of such employees under the provisions of section 9: *Provided,* That nothing contained in this clause (B) shall be construed to make unlawful, where not otherwise unlawful, any primary strike or primary picketing;

(C) forcing or requiring any employer to recognize or bargain with a particular labor organization as the representative of his employees if another labor organization has been certified as the representative of such employees under the provisions of section 9;

(D) forcing or requiring any employer to assign particular work to employees in a particular labor organization or in a particular trade, craft, or class rather than to employees in another labor organization or in another trade, craft, or class, unless such employer is failing to conform to an order or certification of the Board determining the bargaining representative for employees performing such work:

Provided, That nothing contained in this subsection (b) shall be construed to make unlawful a refusal by any person to enter upon the premises of any employer (other than his own employer), if the employees of such employer are engaged in a strike ratified or approved by a representative of such employees whom such employer is required to recognize under this Act: *Provided further,* That for the purposes of this paragraph (4) only, nothing contained in such paragraph shall be construed to prohibit publicity, other than picketing, for the purpose of truthfully advising the public, including consumers and members of a labor organization, that a product or products are produced by an employer with whom the labor organization has a primary dispute and are distributed by another employer, as long as such publicity does not have an effect of inducing any individual employed by any person other than the primary employer in the course of his employment to refuse to pick up, deliver, or transport any goods, or not to perform any services, at the establishment of the employer engaged in such distribution;

(5) to require of employees covered by an agreement authorized under subsection (a)(3) the payment, as a condition precedent to becoming a member of such organization, of a fee in an amount which the Board finds excessive or discriminatory under all the circumstances. In making such a finding, the Board shall consider, among other relevant factors, the practices and customs of labor organizations in the particular industry, and the wages currently paid to the employees affected;

(6) to cause or attempt to cause an employer to pay or deliver or agree to pay or deliver any money or other thing of value, in the nature of an exaction, for services which are not performed or not to be performed; and

(7) to picket or cause to be picketed, or threaten to picket or cause to be picketed, any employer where an object thereof is forcing or requiring an employer to recognize or bargain with a labor organization as the representative of his employees, or forcing or requiring the employees of an employer to accept or select such labor organization as their collective bargaining representative, unless such labor organization is currently certified as the representative of such employees:

(A) where the employer has lawfully recognized in accordance with this Act any other labor organization and a question concerning representation may not appropriately be raised under section 9(c) of this Act,

(B) where within the preceding twelve months a valid election under section 9(c) of this Act has been conducted, or

(C) where such picketing has been conducted without a petition under section 9(c) being filed within a reasonable period of time not to exceed thirty days from the commencement of such picketing: *Provided,* That when such a petition has been filed the Board shall forthwith, without regard to the provisions of section 9(c)(1) or the absence of a showing of a substantial interest on the part of the labor organization, direct an election in such unit as the Board finds to be appropriate and shall certify the results thereof: *Provided further,* That nothing in this subparagraph (C) shall be construed to prohibit any picketing or other publicity for the purpose of truthfully advising the public (including consumers) that an employer does not employ members of, or have a contract with, a labor organization, unless an effect of such picketing is to induce any individual employed by any other person in the course of his employment, not to pick up, deliver or transport any goods or not to perform any services.

Nothing in this paragraph (7) shall be construed to permit any act which would otherwise be an unfair labor practice under this section 8(b).

(c) The expressing of any views, argument, or opinion, or the dissemination thereof, whether in written, printed, graphic, or visual form, shall not constitute or be evidence of an unfair labor practice under any of the provisions of this Act, if such expression contains no threat of reprisal or force or promise of benefit.

(d) For the purposes of this section, to bargain collectively is the performance of the mutual obligation of the employer and the representative of the employees to meet at reasonable times and confer in good faith with respect to wages, hours, and other terms and conditions of employment, or the negotiation of an agreement, or any question arising thereunder, and the execution of a written contract incorporating any agreement reached if requested by either party, but such obligation does not compel either party to agree to a proposal or require the making of a concession: *Provided,* That where there is in effect a collective-bargaining contract covering employees in an industry affecting commerce, the duty to bargain collectively shall also mean that no party to such contract shall terminate or modify such contract, unless the party desiring such termination or modification—

(1) serves a written notice upon the other party to the contract of the proposed termination or modification sixty days prior to the expiration date thereof, or in the event such contract contains no expiration date, sixty days prior to the time it is proposed to make such termination or modification;

(2) offers to meet and confer with the other party for the purpose of negotiating a new contract or a contract containing the proposed modifications;

(3) notifies the Federal Mediation and Conciliation Service within thirty days after such notice of the existence of a dispute, and simultaneously therewith notifies any State or Territorial agency established to mediate and conciliate disputes within the State or Territory where the dispute occurred, provided no agreement has been reached by that time; and

(4) continues in full force and effect, without resorting to strike or lockout, all the terms and conditions of the existing contract for a period of sixty days after such notice is given or until the expiration date of such contract, whichever occurs later:

The duties imposed upon employers, employees, and labor organizations by paragraphs (2), (3), and (4) shall become inapplicable upon an intervening certification of the Board, under which the labor organization or individual, which is a party to the contract, has been superseded as or ceased to be the representative of the employees subject to the provisions of section 9(a), and the duties so imposed shall not be construed as requiring either party to discuss or agree to any modification of the terms and conditions contained in a contract for a fixed period, if such modification is to become effective before such terms and conditions can be reopened under the provisions of the contract. **Any employee who engages in a** strike within ****any notice period specified in this subsection ****, or who engages in any strike within the appropriate period specified in subsection (g) of this section shall lose his status as an employee of the employer engaged in the particular labor dispute, for the purposes of sections 8, 9, and 10 of this Act, as amended, but such loss of status for such employee shall terminate if and when he is reemployed by such employer. ****Whenever the collective bargaining involves employees of a health care** institution, the provisions of this section 8(d) shall be modified as follows:

(A) The notice of section 8(d)(1) shall be ninety days; the notice of section 8(d)(3) shall be sixty days; and the contract period of section 8(d)(4) shall be ninety days;

(B) Where the bargaining is for an initial agreement following certification or recognition, at least thirty days' notice of the existence of a dispute shall be given by the labor organization to the agencies set forth in section 8(d)(3).

(C) After notice is given to the Federal Mediation and Conciliation Service under either clause (A) or (B) of this sentence, the Service shall promptly communicate with the parties and use its best efforts, by mediation and conciliation, to bring them to agreement. The parties shall participate fully and promptly in such meetings as may be undertaken by the Service for the purpose of aiding in a settlement of the dispute.

(e) It shall be an unfair labor practice for any labor organization and any employer to enter into any contract or agreement, express or implied, whereby such employer ceases or refrains or agrees to cease or refrain from handling, using, selling, transporting or otherwise dealing in any of the products of any other employer, or to cease doing business with any other person, and any contract or agreement entered into heretofore or hereafter containing such an agreement shall be to such extent unenforceable and void: *Provided,* That nothing in this subsection (e) shall apply to an agreement between a labor organization and an employer in the construction industry relating to the contracting or subcontracting of work to be done at the site of the construction, alteration, painting, or repair of a building, structure, or other work: *Provided further,* That for the purposes of this subsection (e) and section 8(b)(4) (B) the terms "any employer", "any person engaged in commerce or in industry affecting commerce", and "any person" when used in relation to the terms "any other producer, processor, or manufacturer", "any other employer", or "any other person" shall not include persons in the relation of a jobber, manufacturer, contractor, or subcontractor working on the goods or premises of the jobber or manufacturer or performing parts of an integrated process of production in the apparel and clothing industry: *Provided further,* That nothing in this Act shall prohibit the enforcement of any agreement which is within the foregoing exception.

(f) It shall not be an unfair labor practice under subsections (a) and (b) of this section for an employer engaged primarily in the building and construction industry to make an agreement covering employees engaged (or who, upon their employment, will be engaged) in the building and construction industry with a labor organization of which building and construction employees are members (not established, maintained, or assisted by any action defined in section 8(a) of this Act as an unfair labor

---

**Pursuant to Public Law 93–360, 93d Cong., S. 3203, 88 Stat. 396, the last sentence of Sec. 8(d) is amended by striking the words "the sixty day" and inserting the words "any notice" and by inserting before the words "shall lose" the phrase ", or who engages in any strike within the appropriate period specified in subsection (g) of this section." In addition, the end of paragraph Sec. 8(d) is amended by adding a new sentence "Whenever the collective bargaining . . . aiding in a settlement of the dispute."

practice) because (1) the majority status of such labor organization has not been established under the provisions of section 9 of this Act prior to the making of such agreement, or (2) such agreement requires as a condition of employment, membership in such labor organization after the seventh day following the beginning of such employment or the effective date of the agreement, whichever is later, or (3) such agreement requires the employer to notify such labor organization of opportunities for employment with such employer, or gives such labor organization an opportunity to refer qualified applicants for such employment, or (4) such agreement specifies minimum training or experience qualifications for employment or provides for priority in opportunities for employment based upon length of service with such employer, in the industry or in the particular geographical area: *Provided,* That nothing in this subsection shall set aside the final proviso to section 8(a)(3) of this Act: *Provided further,* That any agreement which would be invalid, but for clause (1) of this subsection, shall not be a bar to a petition filed pursuant to section 9(c) or 9(e).*

**(g) A labor organization before engaging in any strike, picketing, or other concerted refusal to work at any health care institution shall, not less than ten days prior to such action, notify the institution in writing and the Federal Mediation and Conciliation Service of that intention, except that in the case of bargaining for an initial agreement following certification or recognition the notice required by this subsection shall not be given until the expiration of the period specified in clause (B) of the last sentence of section 8(d) of this Act. The notice shall state the date and time that such action will commence. The notice, once given, may be extended by the written agreement of both parties.

REPRESENTATIVES AND ELECTIONS

SEC. 9. (a) Representatives designated or selected for the purposes of collective bargaining by the majority of the employees in a unit appropriate for such purposes, shall be the exclusive representatives of all the employees in such unit for the purposes of collective bargaining in respect to rates of pay, wages, hours of employment, or other conditions of employment: *Provided,* That any individual employee or a group of employees shall have the right at any time to present grievances to their employer and to have such grievances adjusted, without the intervention of the bargaining representative, as long as the adjustment is not inconsistent with the terms of a collective-bargaining contract or agreement then in effect: *Provided further,* That the bargaining representative has been given opportunity to be present at such adjustment.

(b) The Board shall decide in each case whether, in order to assure to employees the fullest freedom in exercising the rights guaranteed by this Act, the unit appropriate for the purposes of collective bargaining shall be the employer unit, craft unit, plant unit, or subdivision thereof: *Provided,* That the Board shall not (1) decide that any unit is appropriate for such purposes if such unit includes both professional employees and employees who are not professional employees

---

*Sec. 8(f) is inserted in the Act by subsec. (a) of Sec. 705 of Public Law 86–257. Sec. 705(b) provides:

Nothing contained in the amendment made by subsection (a) shall be construed as authorizing the execution or application of agreements requiring membership in a labor organization as a condition of employment in any State or Territory in which such execution or application is prohibited by State or Territorial law.

**Pursuant to Public Law 93–360, 93d Cong., S. 3203, 88 Stat. 396, Sec. 8 is amended by adding subsection (g).

unless a majority of such professional employees vote for inclusion in such unit; or (2) decide that any craft unit is inappropriate for such purposes on the ground that a different unit has been established by a prior Board determination, unless a majority of the employees in the proposed craft unit vote against separate representation or (3) decide that any unit is appropriate for such purposes if it includes, together with other employees, any individual employed as a guard to enforce against employees and other persons rules to protect property of the employer or to protect the safety of persons on the employer's premises; but no labor organization shall be certified as the representative of employees in a bargaining unit of guards if such organization admits to membership, or is affiliated directly or indirectly with an organization which admits to membership, employees other than guards.

(c)(1) Wherever a petition shall have been filed, in accordance with such regulations as may be prescribed by the Board—

(A) by an employee or group of employees or any individual or labor organization acting in their behalf alleging that a substantial number of employees (i) wish to be represented for collective bargaining and that their employer declines to recognize their representative as the representative defined in section 9(a), or (ii) assert that the individual or labor organization, which has been certified or is being currently recognized by their employer as the bargaining representative, is no longer a representative as defined in section 9(a); or

(B) by an employer, alleging that one or more individuals or labor organizations have presented to him a claim to be recognized as the representative defined in section 9(a);

the Board shall investigate such petition and if it has reasonable cause to believe that a question of representation affecting commerce exists shall provide for an appropriate hearing upon due notice. Such hearing may be conducted by an officer or employee of the regional office, who shall not make any recommendations with respect thereto. If the Board finds upon the record of such hearing that such a question of representation exists, it shall direct an election by secret ballot and shall certify the results thereof.

(2) In determining whether or not a question of representation affecting commerce exists, the same regulations and rules of decision shall apply irrespective of the identity of the persons filing the petition or the kind of relief sought and in no case shall the Board deny a labor organization a place on the ballot by reason of an order with respect to such labor organization or its predecessor not issued in conformity with section 10(c).

(3) No election shall be directed in any bargaining unit or any subdivision within which, in the preceding twelve-month period, a valid election shall have been held. Employees engaged in an economic strike who are not entitled to reinstatement shall be eligible to vote under such regulations as the Board shall find are consistent with the purposes and provisions of this Act in any election conducted within twelve months after the commencement of the strike. In any election where none of the choices on the ballot receives a majority, a run-off shall be conducted, the ballot providing for a selection between the two choices receiving the largest and second largest number of valid votes cast in the election.

(4) Nothing in this section shall be construed to prohibit the waiving of hearings by stipulation for the purpose of a consent election in conformity with regulations and rules of decision of the Board.

(5) In determining whether a unit is appropriate for the purposes specified in subsection (b) the extent to which the employees have organized shall not be controlling.

(d) Whenever an order of the Board made pursuant to section 10(c) is based in whole or in part upon facts certified following an investigation pursuant to subsection (c) of this section and there is a petition for the enforcement or review of such order, such certification and the record of such investigation shall be included in the transcript of the entire record required to be filed under section 10(e) or 10(f), and thereupon the decree of the court enforcing, modifying, or setting aside in whole or in part the order of the Board shall be made and entered upon the pleadings, testimony, and proceedings set forth in such transcript.

(e)(1) Upon the filing with the Board, by 30 per centum or more of the employees in a bargaining unit covered by an agreement between their employer and a labor organization made pursuant to section 8(a)(3), of a petition alleging they desire that such authority be rescinded, the Board shall take a secret ballot of the employees in such unit and certify the results thereof to such labor organization and to the employer.

(2) No election shall be conducted pursuant to this subsection in any bargaining unit or any subdivision within which, in the preceding twelve-month period, a valid election shall have been held.

PREVENTION OF UNFAIR LABOR PRACTICES

SEC. 10. (a) The Board is empowered, as hereinafter provided, to prevent any person from engaging in any unfair labor practice (listed in section 8) affecting commerce. This power shall not be affected by any other means of adjustment or prevention that has been or may be established by agreement, law, or otherwise: *Provided,* That the Board is empowered by agreement with any agency of any State or Territory to cede to such agency jurisdiction over any cases in any industry (other than mining, manufacturing, communications, and transportation except where predominantly local in character) even though such cases may involve labor disputes affecting commerce, unless the provision of the State or Territorial statute applicable to the determination of such cases by such agency is inconsistent with the corresponding provision of this Act or has received a construction inconsistent therewith.

(b) Whenever it is charged that any person has engaged in or is engaging in any such unfair labor practice, the Board, or any agent or agency designated by the Board for such purposes, shall have power to issue and cause to be served upon such person a complaint stating the charges in that respect, and containing a notice of hearing before the Board or a member thereof, or before a designated agent or agency, at a place therein fixed, not less than five days after the serving of said complaint: *Provided,* That no complaint shall issue based upon any unfair labor practice occurring more than six months prior to the filing of the charge with the Board and the service of a copy thereof upon the person against whom such charge is made, unless the person aggrieved thereby was prevented from filing such charge by reason of service in the armed forces, in which event the six-month period shall be computed from the day of his discharge. Any such complaint may be amended by the member, agent, or agency conducting the hearing or the Board in its discretion at any time prior to the issuance of an order based thereon. The person so complained of shall have the right to file an answer to the original or amended complaint and to appear in person or otherwise and give testimony at the place and time fixed in the complaint. In the discretion of the member, agent, or agency conducting the hearing or the Board, any other person may be allowed to intervene in the said proceeding and to present testimony. Any such proceeding shall, so far as practicable, be conducted in accordance with the rules of evidence applicable in the district courts of the United States under the rules of civil procedure for the district courts of the United States, adopted by the Supreme Court of the United States pursuant to the Act of June 19, 1934 (U. S. C., title 28, secs. 723–B, 723–C).

(c) The testimony taken by such member, agent, or agency or the Board shall be reduced to writing and filed with the Board. Thereafter, in its discretion, the Board upon notice may take further testimony or hear argument. If upon the preponderance of the testimony taken the Board shall be of the opinion that any person named in the complaint has engaged in or is engaging in any such unfair labor practice, then the Board shall state its findings of fact and shall issue and cause to be served on such person an order requiring such person to cease and desist from such unfair labor practice, and to take such affirmative action including reinstatement of employees with or without back pay, as will effectuate the policies of this Act: *Provided,* That where an order directs reinstatement of an employee, back pay may be required of the employer or labor organization, as the case may be, responsible for the discrimination suffered by him: *And provided further,* That in determining whether a complaint shall issue alleging a violation of section 8(a)(1) or section 8(a)(2), and in deciding such cases, the same regulations and rules of decision shall apply irrespective of whether or not the labor organization affected is affiliated with a labor organization national or international in scope. Such order may further require such person to make reports from time to time showing the extent to which it has complied with the order. If upon the preponderance of the testimony taken the Board shall not be of the opinion that the person named in the complaint has engaged in or is engaging in any such unfair labor practice, then the Board shall state its findings of fact and shall issue an order dismissing the said complaint. No order of the Board shall require the reinstatement of any individual as an employee who has been suspended or discharged, or the payment to him of any back pay, if such individual was suspended or discharged for cause. In case the evidence is presented before a member of the Board, or before an examiner or examiners thereof, such member, or such examiner or examiners, as the case may be, shall issue and cause to be served on the parties to the proceeding a proposed report, together with a recommended order, which shall be filed with the Board, and if no exceptions are filed within twenty days after service thereof upon such parties, or within such further period as the Board may authorize, such recommended order shall become the order of the Board and become effective as therein prescribed.

(d) Until the record in a case shall have been filed in a court, as hereinafter provided, the Board may at any time, upon reasonable notice and in such manner as it shall deem proper, modify or set aside, in whole or in part, any finding or order made or issued by it.

(e) The Board shall have power to petition any court of appeals of the United States, or if all the courts of appeals to which application may be made are in vacation, any district court of the United States, within any circuit or district, respectively, wherein the unfair labor practice in question occurred or wherein such person resides or transacts business, for the enforcement of such order and for appropriate temporary relief or restraining order, and shall file in the court the record in the proceedings, as provided in section 2112 of title 28, United States Code. Upon the filing of such petition, the court shall cause notice thereof to be served upon such person, and thereupon shall have jurisdiction of the proceeding and of the question determined therein, and shall have power to grant such temporary relief or restraining order as it deems just and proper, and to make and enter a decree enforcing, modifying, and enforcing as so modified, or setting aside in whole or in part the order of the Board. No objection that has not been urged before the Board, its member, agent, or agency, shall be considered by the court, unless the failure or neglect to urge such objection shall be excused because of extraordinary circumstances. The findings of the Board with respect to questions of fact if supported by substantial evidence on the record considered as a whole shall be conclusive. If either party shall apply to the court for leave to adduce additional evidence and shall show to the satisfaction of the court that such additional evidence is material and that there were reasonable grounds for the failure to adduce such evidence in the hearing before the Board, its member, agent, or agency, the court may order such additional evidence to be taken before the Board, its member, agent, or agency, and to be made a part of the record. The Board may modify its findings as to the facts, or make new findings, by reason of additional evidence so taken and filed, and it shall file such modified or new findings, which findings with respect to questions of fact if supported by substantial evidence on the record considered as a whole shall be conclusive, and shall file its recommendations, if any, for the modification or setting aside of its original order. Upon the filing of the record with it the jurisdiction of the court shall be exclusive and its judgment and decree shall be final, except that the same shall be subject to review by the appropriate United States court of appeals if application was made to the district court as hereinabove provided, and by the Supreme Court of the United States upon writ of certiorari or certification as provided in section 1254 of title 28.

(f) Any person aggrieved by a final order of the Board granting or denying in whole or in part the relief sought may obtain a review of such order in any circuit court of appeals of the United States in the circuit wherein the unfair labor practice in question was alleged to have been engaged in or wherein such person resides or transacts business, or in the United States Court of Appeals for the District of Columbia, by filing in such court a written petition praying that the order of the Board be modified or set aside. A copy of such petition shall be forthwith transmitted by the clerk of the court to the Board, and thereupon the aggrieved party shall file in the court the record in the proceeding, certified by the Board, as provided in section 2112 of title 28, United States Code. Upon the filing of such petition, the court shall proceed in the same manner as in the case of an application by the Board under subsection (e) of this section, and shall have the same jurisdiction to grant to the Board such temporary relief or restraining order as it deems just and proper, and in like manner to make and enter a decree enforcing, modifying, and enforcing as so modified, or setting aside in whole or in part the order of the Board; the findings of the Board with respect to questions of fact if supported by substantial evidence on the record considered as a whole shall in like manner be conclusive.

(g) The commencement of proceedings under subsection (e) or (f) of this section shall not, unless specifically ordered by the court, operate as a stay of the Board's order.

(h) When granting appropriate temporary relief or a restraining order, or making and entering a decree enforcing, modifying, and enforcing as so modified, or setting aside in whole or in part an order of the Board, as provided in this section, the jurisdiction of courts sitting in equity shall not be limited by the Act entitled "An Act to amend the Judicial Code and to define and limit the jurisdiction of courts sitting in equity, and for other purposes," approved March 23, 1932 (U.S.C., Supp. VII, title 29, secs. 101–115).

(i) Petitions filed under this Act shall be heard expeditiously, and if possible within ten days after they have been docketed.

(j) The Board shall have power, upon issuance of a complaint as provided in subsection (b) charging that any person has engaged in or is engaging in an unfair labor practice, to petition any district court of the United States (including the District Court of the United States for the District of Columbia), within any district wherein the unfair labor practice in question is alleged to have occurred or wherein such person resides or transacts business, for appropriate temporary relief or restraining order. Upon the filing of any such petition the court shall cause notice thereof to be served upon such person, and thereupon shall have jurisdiction to grant to the Board such temporary relief or restraining order as it deems just and proper.

(k) Whenever it is charged that any person has engaged in an unfair labor practice within the meaning of paragraph (4)(D) of section 8(b), the Board is empowered and directed to hear and determine the dispute out of which such unfair labor practice shall have arisen, unless, within ten days after notice that such charge has been filed, the parties to such dispute submit to the Board satisfactory evidence that they have adjusted, or agreed upon methods for the voluntary adjustment of, the dispute. Upon compliance by the parties to the dispute with the decision of the Board or upon such voluntary adjustment of the dispute, such charge shall be dismissed.

(l) Whenever it is charged that any person has engaged in an unfair labor practice within the meaning of paragraph (4) (A), (B), or (C) of section 8(b), or section 8(e) or section 8(b)(7), the preliminary investigation of such charge shall be made forthwith and given priority over all other cases except cases of like character in the office where it is filed or to which it is referred. If, after such investigation, the officer or regional attorney to whom the matter may be referred has reasonable cause to believe such charge is true and that a complaint should issue, he shall, on behalf of the Board, petition any district court of the United States (including the District Court of the United States for the District of Columbia) within any district where the unfair labor practice in question has occurred, is alleged to have occurred, or wherein such person resides or transacts business, for appropriate injunctive relief pending the final adjudication of the Board with respect to such matter. Upon the filing of any such petition the district court shall have jurisdiction to grant such injunctive relief or temporary restraining order as it deems just and proper, notwithstanding any other provision of law: *Provided further,* That no temporary restraining order shall be issued without notice unless a petition alleges that substantial and irreparable injury to the charging party will be unavoidable and such temporary restraining order shall be effective for no longer than five days and will become void at the expiration of such period: *Provided further,* That such officer or regional attorney shall not apply for any restraining order under section 8(b)(7) if a charge against the employer under section 8(a)(2) has been filed and after the preliminary investigation, he has reasonable cause to believe that such charge is true and that a complaint should issue. Upon filing of any such petition the courts shall cause notice thereof to be served upon any person involved in the charge and such person, including the charging party, shall be given an opportunity to appear by counsel and present any relevant testimony: *Provided further,* That for the purposes of this subsection district courts shall be deemed to have jurisdiction of a labor organization (1) in the district in which such organization maintains its principal office, or (2) in any district in which its duly authorized officers or agents are engaged in promoting or protecting the interests of employee members. The service of legal process upon such officer or agent shall constitute service upon the labor organization and make such organizations a party to the suit. In situations where such relief is appropriate the procedure specified herein shall apply to charges with respect to section 8(b)(4)(D).

(m) Whenever it is charged that any person has engaged in an unfair labor practice within the meaning of subsection (a)(3) or (b)(2) of section 8, such charge shall be given priority over all other cases except cases of like character in the office where it is filed or to which it is referred and cases given priority under subsection (1).

LIMITATIONS

SEC. 13. Nothing in this Act, except as specifically provided for herein, shall be construed so as either to interfere with or impede or diminish in any way the right to strike, or to affect the limitations or qualifications on that right.

SEC. 14. (a) Nothing herein shall prohibit any individual employed as a supervisor from becoming or remaining a member of a labor organization, but no employer subject to this Act shall be compelled to deem individuals defined herein as supervisors as employees for the purpose of any law, either national or local, relating to collective bargaining.

(b) Nothing in this Act shall be construed as authorizing the execution or application of agreements requiring membership in a labor organization as a condition of employment in any State or Territory in which such execution or application is prohibited by State or Territorial law.

(c)(1) The Board, in its discretion, may, by rule of decision or by published rules adopted pursuant to the Administrative Procedure Act, decline to assert jurisdiction over any labor dispute involving any class or category of employers, where, in the opinion of the Board, the effect of such labor dispute on commerce is not sufficiently substantial to warrant the exercise of its jurisdiction: *Provided,* That the Board shall not decline to assert jurisdiction over any labor dispute over which it would assert jurisdiction under the standards prevailing upon August 1, 1959.

(2) Nothing in this Act shall be deemed to prevent or bar any agency or the courts of any State or Territory (including the Commonwealth of Puerto Rico, Guam, and the Virgin Islands), from assuming and asserting jurisdiction over labor disputes over which the Board declines, pursuant to paragraph (1) of this subsection, to assert jurisdiction.

SEC. 15. Wherever the application of the provisions of section 272 of chapter 10 of the Act entitled "An Act to establish a uniform system of bankruptcy throughout the United States," approved July 1, 1898, and Acts amendatory thereof and supplementary thereto (U.S.C., title 11, sec. 672), conflicts with the application of the provisions of this Act, this Act shall prevail: *Provided,* That in any situation where the provisions of this Act cannot be validly enforced, the provisions of such other Acts shall remain in full force and effect.

**INDIVIDUALS WITH RELIGIOUS CONVICTIONS

SEC. 19. Any employee of a health care institution who is a member of and adheres to established and traditional tenets or teachings of a bona fide religion, body, or sect which has historically held conscientious objections to joining or financially supporting labor organizations shall not be required to join or financially support any labor organization as a condition of employment; except that such employee may be required, in lieu of periodic dues and initiation fees, to pay sums equal to such dues and initiation fees to a nonreligious charitable fund exempt from taxation under section 501(c)(3) of the Internal Revenue Code, chosen by such employee from a list of at

---

**Pursuant to Public Law 93–360, 93d Cong., S. 3203, 88 Stat. 397, the National Labor Relations Act is amended by adding Sec. 19.

least three such funds, designated in a contract between such institution and a labor organization, or if the contract fails to designate such funds, then to any such fund chosen by the employee.

TITLE II—CONCILIATION OF LABOR DISPUTES IN INDUSTRIES AFFECTING COMMERCE; NATIONAL EMERGENCIES

SEC. 201. That it is the policy of the United States that—

(a) sound and stable industrial peace and the advancement of the general welfare, health, and safety of the Nation and of the best interest of employers and employees can most satisfactorily be secured by the settlement of issues between employers and employees through the processes of conference and collective bargaining between employers and the representatives of their employees;

(b) the settlement of issues between employers and employees through collective bargaining may be advanced by making available full and adequate governmental facilities for conciliation, mediation, and voluntary arbitration to aid and encourage employers and the representatives of their employees to reach and maintain agreements concerning rates of pay, hours, and working conditions, and to make all reasonable efforts to settle their differences by mutual agreement reached through conferences and collective bargaining or by such methods as may be provided for in any applicable agreement for the settlement of disputes; and

(c) certain controversies which arise between parties to collective-bargaining agreements may be avoided or minimized by making available full and adequate governmental facilities for furnishing assistance to employers and the representatives of their employees in formulating for inclusion within such agreements provision for adequate notice of any proposed changes in the terms of such agreements, for the final adjustment of grievances or questions regarding the application or interpretation of such agreements, and other provisions designed to prevent the subsequent arising of such controversies.

SEC. 202. (a) There is hereby created an independent agency to be known as the Federal Mediation and Conciliation Service (herein referred to as the "Service," except that for sixty days after the date of the enactment of this Act such term shall refer to the Conciliation Service of the Department of Labor). The Service shall be under the direction of a Federal Mediation and Conciliation Director (hereinafter referred to as the "Director"), who shall be appointed by the President by and with the advice and consent of the Senate. The Director shall receive compensation at the rate of $12,000* per annum. The Director shall not engage in any other business, vocation, or employment.

FUNCTIONS OF THE SERVICE

SEC. 203. (a) It shall be the duty of the Service, in order to prevent or minimize interruptions of the free flow of commerce growing out of labor disputes to assist parties to labor disputes in industries affecting commerce to settle such disputes through conciliation and mediation.

---

*Pursuant to Public Law 90–206, 90th Cong., 81 Stat. 644, approved Dec. 16, 1967, and in accordance with Sec. 225(f)(ii) thereof, effective in 1969, the salary of the Director shall be $40,000 per year.

(d) Final adjustment by a method agreed upon by the parties is hereby declared to be the desirable method for settlement of grievance disputes arising over the application or interpretation of an existing collective-bargaining agreement. The Service is directed to make its conciliation and mediation services available in the settlement of such grievance disputes only as a last resort and in exceptional cases.

NATIONAL EMERGENCIES

SEC. 206. Whenever in the opinion of the President of the United States, a threatened or actual strike or lock-out affecting an entire industry or a substantial part thereof engaged in trade, commerce, transportation, transmission, or communication among the several States or with foreign nations, or engaged in the production of goods for commerce, will, if permitted to occur or to continue, imperil the national health or safety, he may appoint a board of inquiry to inquire into the issues involved in the dispute and to make a written report to him within such time as he shall prescribe. Such report shall include a statement of the facts with respect to the dispute, including each party's statement of its position but shall not contain any recommendations. The President shall file a copy of such report with the Service and shall make its contents available to the public.

SEC. 208. (a) Upon receiving a report from a board of inquiry the President may direct the Attorney General to petition any district court of the United States having jurisdiction of the parties to enjoin such strike or lock-out or the continuing thereof, and if the court finds that such threatened or actual strike or lock-out—

(i) affects an entire industry or a substantial part thereof engaged in trade, commerce, transportation, transmission, or communication among the several States or with foreign nations, or engaged in the production of goods for commerce; and

(ii) if permitted to occur or to continue, will imperil the national health or safety, it shall have jurisdiction to enjoin any such strike or lock-out, or the continuing thereof, and to make such other orders as may be appropriate.

SEC. 209. (a) Whenever a district court has issued an order under section 208 enjoining acts or practices which imperil or threaten to imperil the national health or safety, it shall be the duty of the parties to the labor dispute giving rise to such order to make every effort to adjust and settle their differences, with the assistance of the Service created by this Act. Neither party shall be under any duty to accept, in whole or in part, any proposal of settlement made by the Service.

(b) Upon the issuance of such order, the President shall reconvene the board of inquiry which has previously reported with respect to the dispute. At the end of a sixty-day period (unless the dispute has been settled by that time), the board of inquiry shall report to the President the current position of the parties and the efforts which has been made for settlement, and shall include a statement by each party of its position and a statement of the employer's last offer of settlement. The President shall make such report available to the public. The National Labor Relations Board, within the succeeding fifteen days, shall take a secret ballot of the employees of each employer involved in the dispute on the question of whether they wish to accept the final offer of settlement made by their employer as stated by him and shall certify the results thereof to the Attorney General within five days thereafter.

SEC. 210. Upon the certification of the results of such ballot or upon a settlement being reached, whichever happens sooner, the Attorney General shall move the court to discharge the injunction, which motion shall then be granted and the injunction discharged. When such motion is granted, the President shall submit to the Congress a full and comprehensive report of the proceedings, including the findings of the board of inquiry and the ballot taken by the National Labor Relations Board, together with such recommendations as he may see fit to make for consideration and appropriate action.

**CONCILIATION OF LABOR DISPUTES IN THE HEALTH CARE INDUSTRY

SEC. 213. (a) If, in the opinion of the Director of the Federal Mediation and Conciliation Service a threatened or actual strike or lockout affecting a health care institution will, if permitted to occur or to continue, substantially interrupt the delivery of health care in the locality concerned, the Director may further assist in the resolution of the impasse by establishing within 30 days after the notice to the Federal Mediation and Conciliation Service under clause (A) of the last sentence of section 8(d) (which is required by clause (3) of such section 8(d)), or within 10 days after the notice under clause (B), an impartial Board of Inquiry to investigate the issues involved in the dispute and to make a written report thereon to the parties within fifteen (15) days after the establishment of such a Board. The written report shall contain the findings of fact together with the Board's recommendations for settling the dispute, with the objective of achieving a prompt, peaceful and just settlement of the dispute. Each such Board shall be composed of such number of individuals as the Director may deem desirable. No member appointed under this section shall have any interest or involvement in the health care institutions or the employee organizations involved in the dispute.

(c) After the establishment of a board under subsection (a) of this section and for 15 days after any such board has issued its report, no change in the status quo in effect prior to the expiration of the contract in the case of negotiations for a contract renewal, or in effect prior to the time of the impasse in the case of an initial bargaining negotiation, except by agreement, shall be made by the parties to the controversy.

TITLE III

SUITS BY AND AGAINST LABOR ORGANIZATIONS

SEC. 301. (a) Suits for violation of contracts between an employer and a labor organization representing employees in an industry affecting commerce as defined in this Act, or between any such labor organizations, may be brought in any district court of the United States having jurisdiction of the parties, without respect to the amount in controversy or without regard to the citizenship of the parties.

(b) Any labor organization which represents employees in an industry affecting commerce as defined in this Act and any employer whose activities affect commerce as defined in this Act shall be bound by the acts of its agents. Any such labor organization may sue or be sued as an entity and in behalf of the employees whom it represents in the courts of the United States. Any money judgment against a labor organization in a district court of the United States shall be enforceable only against the organization as an entity and against its assets, and shall not be enforceable against any individual member or his assets.

**Pursuant to Public Law 93–360, 93d Cong., S. 3203, 88 Stat. 396–397, Title II of the Labor Management Relations Act, 1947, is amended by adding Sec. 213.

(c) For the purposes of actions and proceedings by or against labor organizations in the district courts of the United States, district courts shall be deemed to have jurisdiction of a labor organization (1) in the district in which such organization maintains its principal offices, or (2) in any district in which its duly authorized officers or agents are engaged in representing or acting for employee members.

(d) The service of summons, subpena, or other legal process of any court of the United States upon an officer or agent of a labor organization, in his capacity as such, shall constitute service upon the labor organization.

(e) For the purposes of this section, in determining whether any person is acting as an "agent" of another person so as to make such other person responsible for his acts, the question of whether the specific acts performed were actually authorized or subsequently ratified shall not be controlling.

RESTRICTIONS ON PAYMENTS TO EMPLOYEE REPRESENTATIVES

SEC. 302. (a) It shall be unlawful for any employer or association of employers or any person who acts as a labor relations expert, adviser, or consultant to an employer or who acts in the interest of an employer to pay, lend, or deliver, or agree to pay, lend, or deliver, any money or other thing of value—

(1) to any representative of any of his employees who are employed in an industry affecting commerce; or

(2) to any labor organization, or any officer or employee thereof, which represents, seeks to represent, or would admit to membership, any of the employees of such employer who are employed in an industry affecting commerce; or

(3) to any employee or group or committee of employees of such employer employed in an industry affecting commerce in excess of their normal compensation for the purpose of causing such employee or group or committee directly or indirectly to influence any other employees in the exercise of the right to organize and bargain collectively through representatives of their own choosing; or

(4) to any officer or employee of a labor organization engaged in an industry affecting commerce with intent to influence him in respect to any of his actions, decisions, or duties as a representative of employees or as such officer or employee of such labor organization.

(b)(1) It shall be unlawful for any person to request, demand, receive, or accept, or agree to receive or accept, any payment, loan, or delivery of any money or other thing of value prohibited by subsection (a).

(2) It shall be unlawful for any labor organization, or for any person acting as an officer, agent, representative, or employee of such labor organization, to demand or accept from the operator of any motor vehicle (as defined in part II of the Interstate Commerce Act) employed in the transportation of property in commerce, or the employer of any such operator, any money or other thing of value payable to such organization or to an officer, agent, representative or employee thereof as a fee or charge for the unloading, or the connection with the unloading, of the cargo of such vehicle: *Provided,* That nothing in this paragraph shall be construed to make unlawful any payment by an employer to any of his employees as compensation for their services as employees.

(c) The provisions of this section shall not be applicable (1) in respect to any money or other thing of value payable by an employer to any of his employees whose established duties include acting openly for such employer in matters of labor relations or personnel administration or to any representative of his employees, or to any officer or employee of a labor organization, who is also an employee or former employee of such employer, as compensation for, or by reason of, his service as an employee of such employer; (2) with respect to the payment or delivery of any money or other thing of value in satisfaction of a judgment of any court or a decision or award of an arbitrator or impartial chairman or in compromise, adjustment, settlement, or release of any claim, complaint, grievance, or dispute in the absence of fraud or duress; (3) with respect to the sale or purchase of an article or commodity at the prevailing market price in the regular course of business; (4) with respect to money deducted from the wages of employees in payment of membership dues in a labor organization: *Provided,* That the employer has received from each employee, on whose account such deductions are made, a written assignment which shall not be irrevocable for a period of more than one year, or beyond the termination date of the applicable collective agreement, whichever occurs sooner; (5) with respect to money or other thing of value paid to a trust fund established by such representative, for the sole and exclusive benefit of the employees of such employer, and their families and dependents (or of such employees, families, and dependents jointly with the employees of other employers making similar payments, and their families and dependents): *Provided,* That (A) such payments are held in trust for the purpose of paying, either from principal or income or both, for the benefit of employees, their families and dependents, for medical or hospital care, pensions on retirement or death of employees, compensation for injuries or illness resulting from occupational activity or insurance to provide any of the foregoing, or unemployment benefits or life insurance, disability and sickness insurance, or accident insurance; (B) the detailed basis on which such payments are to be made is specified in a written agreement with the employer, and employees and employers are equally represented in the administration of such fund, together with such neutral persons as the representatives of the employers and the representatives of employees may agree upon and in the event the employer and employee groups deadlock on the administration of such fund and there are no neutral persons empowered to break such deadlock, such agreement provides that the two groups shall agree on an impartial umpire to decide such dispute, or in event of their failure to agree within a reasonable length of time, an impartial umpire to decide such dispute shall, on petition of either group, be appointed by the district court of the United States for the district where the trust fund has its principal office, and shall also contain provisions for an annual audit of the trust fund, a statement of the results of which shall be available for inspection by interested persons at the principal office of the trust fund and at such other places as may be designated in such written agreement; and (C) such payments as are intended to be used for the purpose of providing pensions or annuities for employees are made to a separate trust which provides that the funds held therein cannot be used for any purpose other than paying such pensions or annuities; (6) with respect to money or other thing of value paid by any employer to a trust fund established by such representative for the purpose of pooled vacation, holiday, severance or similar benefits, or defraying costs of apprenticeship or other training program: *Provided,* That the requirements of clause (B) of the proviso to clause (5) of this subsection shall apply to such trust funds; or (7) with respect to money or other thing of value paid by any employer to a pooled or individual trust fund established by such representative for the purpose of (A) scholarships for the benefit of employees, their families, and dependents for study at educational institutions, or (B) child care centers for preschool and school age dependents of employees: *Provided,* That no labor organization or employer shall be required to bargain on the establishment of any such trust fund, and refusal to do so shall not constitute an unfair labor practice: *Provided further,* That the requirements of clause (B) of the proviso to clause (5) of this subsection shall apply to such trust funds*; or (8) with respect to money or any other thing of value paid by any employer to a trust fund established by such representative for the purpose of defraying the costs of legal services for employees, their families, and dependents for counsel or plan of their choice: *Provided,* That the requirements of clause (B) of the proviso to clause (5) of this subsection shall apply to such trust funds: *Provided further,* That no such legal services shall be furnished: (A) to initiate any proceeding directed (i) against any such employer or its officers or agents except in workman's compensation cases, or (ii) against such labor organization, or its parent or subordinate bodies, or their officers or agents, or (iii) against any other employer or labor organization, or their officers or agents, in any matter arising under the National Labor Relations Act, as amended, or this Act; and (B) in any proceeding where a labor organization would be prohibited from defraying the costs of legal services by the provisions of the Labor-Management Reporting and Disclosure Act of 1959.

(d) Any person who willfully violates any of the provisions of this section shall, upon conviction thereof, be guilty of a misdemeanor and be subject to a fine of not more than $10,000 or to imprisonment for not more than one year, or both.

(e) The district courts of the United States and the United States courts of the Territories and possessions shall have jurisdiction, for cause shown, and subject to the provisions of section 17 (relating to notice to opposite party) of the Act entitled "An Act to supplement existing laws against unlawful restraints and monopolies, and for other purposes," approved October 15, 1914, as amended (U.S.C., title 28, sec. 381), to restrain violations of this section, without regard to the provisions of sections 6 and 20 of such Act of October 15, 1914, as amended (U.S.C., title 15, sec. 17, and title 29, sec. 52), and the provisions of the Act entitled "An Act to amend the Judicial Code and to define and limit the jurisdiction of courts sitting in equity, and for other purposes," approved March 23, 1932 (U.S.C., title 29, secs. 101–115).

(f) This section shall not apply to any contract in force on the date of enactment of this Act, until the expiration of such contract, or until July 1, 1948, whichever first occurs.

(g) Compliance with the restrictions contained in subsection (c)(5)(B) upon contributions to trust funds, otherwise lawful, shall not be applicable to contributions to such trust funds established by collective agreement prior to January 1, 1946, nor shall subsection (c)(5)(A) be construed as prohibiting contributions to such trust funds if prior to January 1, 1947, such funds contained provisions for pooled vacation benefits.

BOYCOTTS AND OTHER UNLAWFUL COMBINATIONS

SEC. 303. (a) It shall be unlawful, for the purpose of this section only, in an industry or activity affecting commerce, for any labor organization to engage in any activity or conduct defined as an unfair labor practice in section 8(b)(4) of the National Labor Relations Act, as amended.

(b) Whoever shall be injured in his business or property by reason of any violation of subsection (a) may sue therefore in any district court of the United States subject to the limitations and provisions of section 301 hereof without respect to the amount in controversy, or in any other court having jurisdiction of

---

*Sec. 302(c)(7) has been added by Public Law 91-86, 91st Cong., S. 2068, 83 Stat. 133, approved Oct. 14, 1969: Sec. 302(c)(8) was added by Public Law 93-95, 93d Cong., S. 1423, 87 Stat. 314-315, approved Aug. 15, 1973.

the parties, and shall recover the damages by him sustained and the cost of the suit.

RESTRICTION ON POLITICAL CONTRIBUTIONS

SEC. 304. Section 313 of the Federal Corrupt Practices Act, 1925 (U.S.C., 1940 edition, title 2, sec. 251; Supp. V, title 50, App., sec. 1509), as amended, is amended to read as follows:

SEC. 313. It is unlawful for any national bank, or any corporation organized by authority of any law of Congress to make a contribution or expenditure in connection with any election to any political office, or in connection with any primary election or political convention or caucus held to select candidates for any political office, or for any corporation whatever, or any labor organization to make a contribution or expenditure in connection with any election at which Presidential and Vice Presidential electors or a Senator or Representative in, or a Delegate or Resident Commissioner to Congress are to be voted for, or in connection with any primary election or political convention or caucus held to select candidates for any of the foregoing offices, or for any candidate, political committee, or other person to accept or receive any contribution prohibited by this section. Every corporation or labor organization which makes any contribution or expenditure in violation of this section shall be fined not more than $5,000; and every officer or director of any corporation, or officer of any labor organization, who consents to any contribution or expenditure by the corporation or labor organization, as the case may be, in violation of this section shall be fined not more than $1,000 or imprisoned for not more than one year, or both. For the purposes of this section "labor organization" means any organization of any kind, or any agency or employee representation committee or plan, in which employees participate and which exists for the purpose, in whole or in part, of dealing with employers concerning grievances, labor disputes, wages, rates of pay, hours of employment, or conditions of work.

TITLE V

DEFINITIONS

SEC. 501. When used in this Act—

(1) The term "industry affecting commerce" means any industry or activity in commerce or in which a labor dispute would burden or obstruct commerce or tend to burden or obstruct commerce or the free flow of commerce.

(2) The term "strike" includes any strike or other concerted stoppage of work by employees (including a stoppage by reason of the expiration of a collective-bargaining agreement) and any concerted slow-down or other concerted interruption of operations by employees.

(3) The terms "commerce," "labor disputes," "employer," "employee," "labor organization," "representative," "person," and "supervisor" shall have the same meaning as when used in the National Labor Relations Act as amended by this Act.

SAVING PROVISION

SEC. 502. Nothing in this Act shall be construed to require an individual employee to render labor or service without his consent, nor shall anything in this Act be construed to make the quitting of his labor by an individual employee an illegal act; nor shall any court issue any process to compel the performance by an individual employee of such labor or service, without his consent; nor shall the quitting of labor by an employee or employees in good faith because of abnormally dangerous conditions for work at the place of employment of such employee or employees be deemed a strike under this Act.

Labor-Management Reporting and Disclosure Act of 1959, As Amended

[Revised text [1] showing in bold face new or amended language provided by Public Law 89—216, as enacted September 29, 1965, 79 Stat. 888]

Definitions

73 Stat. 520.

(29 U.S.C. 402)

SEC. 3. For the purposes of titles I, II, III, IV, V (except section 505), and VI of this Act—

(a) "Commerce" means trade, traffic, commerce, transportation, transmission, or communication among the several States or between any State and any place outside thereof.

(b) "State" includes any State of the United States, the District of Columbia, Puerto Rico, the Virgin Islands, American Samoa, Guam, Wake Island, the Canal Zone, and Outer Continental Shelf lands defined in the Outer Continental Shelf Lands Act (43 U.S.C. 1331–1343).

67 Stat. 462.

(c) "Industry affecting commerce" means any activity, business, or industry in commerce or in which a labor dispute would hinder or obstruct commerce or the free flow of commerce and includes any activity or industry "affecting commerce" within the meaning of the Labor Management Relations Act, 1947, as amended, or the Railway Labor Act, as amended.

(d) "Person" includes one or more individuals, labor organizations, partnerships, associations, corporations, legal representatives, mutual companies, joint-stock companies, trusts, unincorporated organizations, trustees, trustees in bankruptcy, or receivers.

(e) "Employer" means any employer or any group or association of employers engaged in an industry affecting commerce (1) which is, with respect to employees engaged in an industry affecting commerce, an employer within the meaning of any law of the United States relating to the employment of any employees or (2) which may deal with any labor organization concerning grievances, labor disputes, wages, rates of pay, hours of employment, or conditions of work, and includes any person acting directly or indirectly as an employer or as an agent of an employer in relation to an employee but does not include the United States or any corporation wholly owned by the Government of the United States or any State or political subdivision thereof.

(f) "Employee" means any individual employed by an employer, and includes any individual whose work has ceased as a consequence of, or in connection with, any current labor dispute or because of any unfair labor practice or because of exclusion or expulsion from a labor organization in any manner or for any reason inconsistent with the requirements of this Act.

(g) "Labor dispute" includes any controversy concerning terms, tenure, or conditions of employment, or concerning the association or representation of persons in negotiating, fixing, maintaining, changing, or seeking to arrange terms or conditions of employment, regardless of whether the disputants stand in the proximate relation of employer and employee.

(h) "Trusteeship" means any receivership, trusteeship, or other method of supervision or control whereby a labor organization suspends the autonomy otherwise available to a subordinate body under its constitution or bylaws.

(i) "Labor organization" means a labor organization engaged in an industry affecting commerce and includes any organization of any kind, any agency, or employee representation committee, group, association, or plan so engaged in which employees participate and which exists for the purpose, in whole or in part, of dealing with employers concerning grievances, labor disputes, wages, rates of pay, hours, or other terms or conditions of employment, and any conference, general committee, joint or system board, or joint council so engaged which is subordinate to a national or international labor organization, other than a State or local central body.

73 Stat. 521.

(j) A labor organization shall be deemed to be engaged in an industry affecting commerce if it—

61 Stat. 136;
29 U.S.C. 167.
44 Stat. 577;
45 U.S.C. 151.

(1) is the certified representative of employees under the provisions of the National Labor Relations Act, as amended, or the Railway Labor Act, as amended; or

(2) although not certified, is a national or international labor organization or a local labor organization recognized or acting as the representative of employees of an employer or employers engaged in an industry affecting commerce; or

(3) has chartered a local labor organization or subsidiary body which is representing or actively seeking to represent employees of employers within the meaning of paragraph (1) or (2); or

(4) has been chartered by a labor organization representing or actively seeking to represent employees within the meaning of paragraph (1) or (2) as the local or subordinate body through which such employees may enjoy membership or become affiliated with such labor organization; or

(5) is a conference, general committee, joint or system board, or joint council, subordinate to a national or international labor organization, which includes a labor organization engaged in an industry affecting commerce within the meaning of any of the preceding paragraphs of this subsection, other than a State or local central body.

(k) "Secret ballot" means the expression by ballot, voting machine, or otherwise, but in no event by proxy, of a choice with respect to any election or vote taken upon any matter, which is cast in such a manner that the person expressing such choice cannot be identified with the choice expressed.

(l) "Trust in which a labor organization is interested" means a trust or other fund or organization (1) which was created or established by a labor organization, or one or more of the trustees or one or more members of the governing body of which is selected or appointed by a labor organization, and (2) a primary purpose of which is to provide benefits for the members of such labor organization or their beneficiaries.

(m) "Labor relations consultant" means any person who, for compensation, advises or represents an employer, employer organization, or labor organization concerning employee organizing, concerted activities, or collective bargaining activities.

(n) "Officer" means any constitutional officer, any person authorized to perform the functions of president, vice president, secretary, treasurer, or other executive functions of a labor organization, and any member of its executive board or similar governing body.

(o) "Member" or "member in good standing", when used in reference to a labor organization, includes any person who has fulfilled the requirements for membership in such organization, and who neither has voluntarily withdrawn from membership nor has been expelled or suspended from membership after appropriate proceedings consistent with lawful provisions of the constitution and bylaws of such organization.

(p) "Secretary" means the Secretary of Labor.

(q) "Officer, agent, shop steward, or other representative", when used with respect to a labor organization, includes elected officials and key administrative personnel, whether elected or appointed (such as business agents, heads of departments or major units, and organizers who exercise substantial independent authority), but does not include salaried nonsupervisory professional staff, stenographic, and service personnel.

(r) "District court of the United States" means a United States district court 73 Stat. 522 and a United States court of any place subject to the jurisdiction of the United States.

TITLE I—BILL OF RIGHTS OF MEMBERS OF LABOR ORGANI-ZATIONS

Bill of Rights
(29 U.S.C. 411)

SEC. 101. (a)(1) EQUAL RIGHTS.—Every member of a labor organization shall have equal rights and privileges within such organization to nominate candidates, to vote in elections or referendums of the labor organization, to attend membership meetings and to participate in the deliberations and voting upon the business of such meetings, subject to reasonable rules and regulations in such organization's constitution and bylaws.

(2) FREEDOM OF SPEECH AND ASSEMBLY.—Every member of any labor organization shall have the right to meet and assemble freely with other members; and to express any views, arguments, or opinions; and to express at meetings of the labor organization his views, upon candidates in an election of the labor organization or upon any business properly before the meeting, subject to the organization's established and reasonable rules pertaining to the conduct of meetings: *Provided,* That nothing herein shall be construed to impair the right of a labor organization to adopt and enforce reasonable rules as to the responsibility of every member toward the organization as an institution and to his refraining from conduct that would interfere with its performance of its legal or contractual obligations.

(3) DUES, INITIATION FEES, AND ASSESSMENTS.—Except in the case of a federation of national or international labor organizations, the rates of dues and initiation fees payable by members of any labor organization in effect on the date of enactment of this Act shall not be increased, and no general or special assessment shall be levied upon such members, except—

(A) in the case of a local organization, (i) by majority vote by secret ballot of the members in good standing voting at a general or special membership meeting, after reasonable notice of the intention to vote upon such question, or (ii) by majority vote of the members in good standing voting in a membership referendum conducted by secret ballot; or

(B) in the case of a labor organization, other than a local labor organization or a federation of national or international labor organizations, (i) by majority vote of the delegates voting at a regular convention, or at a special convention of such labor organization held upon not less than thirty days' written notice to the principal office of each local or constituent labor organization entitled to such notice, or (ii) by majority vote of the members in good standing of such labor organization voting in a membership referendum conducted by secret ballot, or (iii) by majority vote of the members of the executive board or similar governing body of such labor organization, pursuant to express authority contained in the constitution and bylaws of such labor organization: *Provided,* That such action on the part of the executive board or similar governing body shall be effective only until the next regular convention of such labor organization.

(4) PROTECTION OF THE RIGHT TO SUE.—No labor organization shall limit the right of any member thereof to institute an action in any court, or in a proceeding before any administrative agency, irrespective of whether or not the labor organization or its officers are named as defendants or respondents in such action or proceeding, or the right of any member of a labor organization to appear as a witness in any judicial, administrative, or legislative proceeding, or to petition any legislature or to communicate with any legislator: *Provided,* That any such member may be required to exhaust reasonable hearing procedures (but not to exceed a four-month lapse of time) within such organization, before instituting legal or administrative proceedings against such organizations or any officer thereof: *And provided further,* That no interested employer or employer association shall directly or indirectly finance, encourage, or participate in, except as a party, any such action, proceeding, appearance, or petition.

73 Stat. 523.

(5) SAFEGUARDS AGAINST IMPROPER DISCIPLINARY ACTION.—No member of any labor organization may be fined, suspended, expelled, or otherwise disciplined except for nonpayment of dues by such organization or by any officer thereof unless such member has been (A) served with written specific charges; (B) given a reasonable time to prepare his defense; (C) afforded a full and fair hearing.

(b) Any provision of the constitution and bylaws of any labor organization which is inconsistent with the provisions of this section shall be of no force or effect.

Civil Enforcement
(29 U.S.C. 412)

SEC. 102. Any person whose rights secured by the provisions of this title have been infringed by any violation of this title may bring a civil action in a district court of the United States for such relief (including injunctions) as may be appropriate. Any such action against a labor organization shall be brought in the district court of the United States for the district where the alleged violation occurred, or where the principal office of such labor organization is located.

Retention of Existing Rights
(29 U.S.C. 413)

SEC. 103. Nothing contained in this title shall limit the rights and remedies of any member of a labor organization under any State or Federal law or before any court or other tribunal, or under the constitution and bylaws of any labor organization.

Right to Copies of Collective Bargaining Agreements
(29 U.S.C. 414)

SEC. 104. It shall be the duty of the secretary or corresponding principal officer of each labor organization, in the case of a local labor organization, to forward a copy of each collective bargaining agreement made by such labor organization with any employer to any employee who requests such a copy and whose rights as such employee are directly affected by such agreement, and in the case of a labor organization other than a local labor organization, to forward a copy of any such agreement to each constituent unit which has members directly affected by such agreement; and such officer shall maintain at the principal office of the labor organization of which he is an officer copies of any such agreement made or received by such labor organization, which copies shall be available for inspection by any member or by any employee whose rights are affected by such agreement. The provisions of section 210 shall be applicable in the enforcement of this section.

Information as to Act
(29 U.S.C. 415)

Sec. 105. Every labor organization shall inform its members concerning the provisions of this Act.

TITLE II—REPORTING BY LABOR ORGANIZATIONS, OFFICERS AND EMPLOYEES OF LABOR ORGANIZATIONS, AND EMPLOYERS

73 Stat. 524.

Report of Labor Organizations
(29 U.S.C. 431)

Sec. 201. (a) Every labor organization shall adopt a constitution and bylaws and shall file a copy thereof with the Secretary, together with a report, signed by its president and secretary or corresponding principal officers, containing the following information—

(1) the name of the labor organization, its mailing address, and any other address at which it maintains its principal office or at which it keeps the records referred to in this title;

(2) the name and title of each of its officers;

(3) the initiation fee or fees required from a new or transferred member and fees for work permits required by the reporting labor organization;

(4) the regular dues or fees of other periodic payments required to remain a member of the reporting labor organization; and

(5) detailed statements, or references to specific provisions of documents filed under this subsection which contain such statements, showing the provisions made and procedures followed with respect to each of the following: (A) qualifications for or restrictions on membership, (B) levying of assessments, (C) participation in insurance or other benefit plans, (D) authorization for disbursement of funds of the labor organization, (E) audit of financial transactions of the labor organization, (F) the calling of regular and special meetings, (G) the selection of officers and stewards and of any representatives to other bodies composed of labor organizations' representatives, with a specific statement of the manner in which each officer was elected, appointed, or otherwise selected, (H) discipline or removal of officers or agents for breaches of their trust, (I) imposition of fines, suspensions, and expulsions of members, including the grounds for such action and any provision made for notice, hearing, judgment on the evidence, and appeal procedures, (J) authorization for bargaining demands, (K) ratification of contract terms, (L) authorization for strikes, and (M) issuance of work permits. Any change in the information required by this subsection shall be reported to the Secretary at the time the reporting labor organization files with the Secretary the annual financial report required by subsection (b).

(b) Every labor organization shall file annually with the Secretary a financial report signed by its president and treasurer or corresponding principal officers containing the following information in such detail as may be necessary accurately to disclose its financial condition and operations for its preceding fiscal year—

(1) assets and liabilities at the beginning and end of the fiscal year;

(2) receipts of any kind and the sources thereof;

(3) salary, allowances, and other direct or indirect disbursements (including reimbursed expenses) to each officer and also to each employee who, during such fiscal year, received more than $10,000 in the aggregate from such labor organization and any other labor organization affiliated with it or with which it is affiliated, or which is affiliated with the same national or international labor organization;

(4) direct and indirect loans made to any officer, employee, or member, which aggregated more than $250 during the fiscal year, together with a statement of the purpose, security, if any, and arrangements for repayment;

73 Stat. 525.

(5) direct and indirect loans to any business enterprise, together with a statement of the purpose, security, if any, and arrangements for repayment; and

(6) other disbursements made by it including the purposes thereof; all in such categories as the Secretary may prescribe.

(c) Every labor organization required to submit a report under this title shall make available the information required to be contained in such report to all of its members, and every such labor organization and its officers shall be under a duty enforceable at the suit of any member of such organization in any State court of competent jurisdiction or in the district court of the United States for the district in which such labor organization maintains its principal office, to permit such member for just cause to examine any books, records, and accounts necessary to verify such report. The court in such action may, in its discretion, in addition to any judgment awarded to the plaintiff or plaintiffs, allow a reasonable attorney's fee to be paid by the defendant, and costs of the action.

61 Stat. 143;
29 U.S.C. 159.

(d) Subsections (f), (g), and (h) of section 9 of the National Labor Relations Act, as amended, are hereby repealed.

29 U.S.C. 158.

(e) Clause (i) of section 8(a)(3) of the National Labor Relations Act, as amended, is amended by striking out the following: "and has at the time the agreement was made or within the preceding twelve months received from the Board a notice of compliance with sections 9 (f), (g), (h)".

Report of Officers and Employees of Labor Organizations [deleted]
(29 U.S.C. 432)

Reports Made Public Information
(29 U.S.C. 435)

SEC. 205. (a)[2] The contents of the reports and documents filed with the Secretary pursuant to sections 201, 202, **203, and 211** shall be public information, and the Secretary may publish any information and data which he obtains pursuant to the provisions of this title. The Secretary may use the information and data for statistical and research purposes, and compile and publish such studies, analyses, reports, and surveys based thereon as he may deem appropriate.

---

[2] Prior to amendment by section 2(a) of Public Law 89-216, the first sentence of section 205(a) read as follows: "Sec. 205. (a) The contents of the reports and documents filed with the Secretary pursuant to sections 201, 202, and 203 shall be public information, and the Secretary may publish any information and data which he obtains pursuant to the provisions of this title."

Retention of Records
(29 U.S.C. 436)

SEC. 206. Every person required to file any report under this title shall maintain records on the matters required to be reported which will provide in sufficient detail the necessary basic information and data from which the documents filed with the Secretary may be verified, explained or clarified, and checked for accuracy and completeness, and shall include vouchers, worksheets, receipts, and applicable resolutions, and shall keep such records available for examination for a period of not less than five years after the filing of the documents based on the information which they contain.

Criminal Provisions
(29 U.S.C. 439)

SEC. 209. (a) Any person who willfully violates this title shall be fined not more than $10,000 or imprisoned for not more than one year, or both.

(b) Any person who makes a false statement or representation of a material fact, knowing it to be false, or who knowingly fails to disclose a material fact, in any document, report, or other information required under the provisions of this title shall be fined not more than $10,000 or imprisoned for not more than one year, or both.

(c) Any person who willfully makes a false entry in or willfully conceals, withholds, or destroys any books, records, reports, or statements required to be kept by any provision of this title shall be fined not more than $10,000 or imprisoned for not more than one year, or both. | 73 Stat. 530.

(d) Each individual required to sign reports under sections 201 and 203 shall be personally responsible for the filing of such reports and for any statement contained therein which he knows to be false.

Civil Enforcement
(29 U.S.C. 440)

SEC. 210. Whenever it shall appear that any person has violated or is about to violate any of the provisions of this title, the Secretary may bring a civil action for such relief (including injunctions) as may be appropriate. Any such action may be brought in the district court of the United States where the violation occurred or, at the option of the parties, in the United States District Court for the District of Columbia.

TITLE III—TRUSTEESHIPS

Purposes for Which a Trusteeship May Be Established
(29 U.S.C. 462)

73 Stat. 531.

SEC. 302. Trusteeships shall be established and administered by a labor organization over a subordinate body only in accordance with the constitution and bylaws of the organization which has assumed trusteeship over the subordinate body and for the purpose of correcting corruption or financial malpractice, assuring the performance of collective bargaining agreements or other duties of a bargaining representative, restoring democratic procedures, or otherwise carrying out the legitimate objects of such labor organization.

Unlawful Acts Relating to Labor Organization Under Trusteeship
(29 U.S.C. 463)

Sec. 303. (a) During any period when a subordinate body of a labor organization is in trusteeship, it shall be unlawful (1) to count the vote of delegates from such body in any convention or election of officers of the labor organization unless the delegates have been chosen by secret ballot in an election in which all the members in good standing of such subordinate body were eligible to participate or (2) to transfer to such organization any current receipts or other funds of the subordinate body except the normal per capita tax and assessments payable by subordinate bodies not in trusteeship: *Provided*, That nothing herein contained shall prevent the distribution of the assets of a labor organization in accordance with its constitution and bylaws upon the bona fide dissolution thereof.

(b) Any person who willfully violates this section shall be fined not more than $10,000 or imprisoned for not more than one year, or both.

Enforcement
(29 U.S.C. 464)

Sec. 304. (a) Upon the written complaint of any member or subordinate body of a labor organization alleging that such organization has violated the provisions of this title (except section 301) the Secretary shall investigate the complaint and if the Secretary finds probable cause to believe that such violation has occurred and has not been remedied he shall, without disclosing the identity of the complainant, bring a civil action in any district court of the United States having jurisdiction of the labor organization for such relief (including injunctions) as may be appropriate. Any member or subordinate body of a labor organization affected by any violation of this title (except section 301) may bring a civil action in any district court of the United States having jurisdiction of the labor organization for such relief (including injunctions) as may be appropriate.

(b) For the purpose of actions under this section, district courts of the United States shall be deemed to have jurisdiction of a labor organization (1) in the district in which the principal office of such labor organization is located, or (2) in any district in which its duly authorized officers or agents are engaged in conducting the affairs of the trusteeship.

(c) In any proceeding pursuant to this section a trusteeship established by a labor organization in conformity with the procedural requirements of its constitution and bylaws and authorized or ratified after a fair hearing either before the executive board or before such other body as may be provided in accordance with its constitution or bylaws shall be presumed valid for a period of eighteen months from the date of its establishment and shall not be subject to attack during such period except upon clear and convincing proof that the trusteeship was not established or maintained in good faith for a purpose allowable under section 302. After the expiration of eighteen months the trusteeship shall be presumed invalid in any such proceeding and its discontinuance shall be decreed unless the labor organization shall show by clear and convincing proof that the continuation of the trusteeship is necessary for a purpose allowable under section 302. In the latter event the court may dismiss the complaint or retain jurisdiction of the cause on such conditions and for such period as it deems appropriate.

73 Stat. 532.

Complaint by Secretary
(29 U.S.C. 466)

Sec. 306. The rights and remedies provided by this title shall be in addition to any and all other rights and remedies at law or in equity: *Provided*, That upon the filing of a complaint by the Secretary the jurisdiction of the district court over such trusteeship shall be exclusive and the final judgment shall be res judicata.

TITLE IV—ELECTIONS

Terms of Office; Election Procedures
(29 U.S.C. 481)

SEC. 401. (a) Every national or international labor organization, except a federation of national or international labor organizations, shall elect its officers not less often than once every five years either by secret ballot among the members in good standing or at a convention of delegates chosen by secret ballot.

(b) Every local labor organization shall elect its officers not less often than once every three years by secret ballot among the members in good standing.

(c) Every national or international labor organization, except a federation of national or international labor organizations, and every local labor organization, and its officers, shall be under a duty, enforceable at the suit of any bona fide candidate for office in such labor organization in the district court of the United States in which such labor organization maintains its principal office, to comply with all reasonable requests of any candidate to distribute by mail or otherwise at the candidate's expense campaign literature in aid of such person's candidacy to all members in good standing of such labor organization and to refrain from discrimination in favor of or against any candidate with respect to the use of lists of members, and whenever such labor organizations or its officers authorize the distribution by mail or otherwise to members of campaign literature on behalf of any candidate or of the labor organization itself with reference to such election, similar distribution at the request of any other bona fide candidate shall be made by such labor organization and its officers, with equal treatment as to the expense of such distribution. Every bona fide candidate shall have the right, once within 30 days prior to an election of a labor organization in which he is a candidate, to inspect a list containing the names and last known addresses of all members of the labor organization who are subject to a collective bargaining agreement requiring membership therein as a condition of employment, which list shall be maintained and kept at the principal office of such labor organization by a designated official thereof. Adequate safeguards to insure a fair election shall be provided, including the right of any candidate to have an observer at the polls and at the counting of the ballots.

(d) Officers of intermediate bodies, such as general committees, system boards, joint boards, or joint councils, shall be elected not less often than once every four years by secret ballot among the members in good standing or by labor organization officers representative of such members who have been elected by secret ballot. 73 Stat. 533.

(e) In any election required by this section which is to be held by secret ballot a reasonable opportunity shall be given for the nomination of candidates and every member in good standing shall be eligible to be a candidate and to hold office (subject to section 504 and to reasonable qualifications uniformly imposed) and shall have the right to vote for or otherwise support the candidate or candidates of his choice, without being subject to penalty, discipline, or improper interference or reprisal of any kind by such organization or any member thereof. Not less than fifteen days prior to the election notice thereof shall be mailed to each member at his last known home address. Each member in good standing shall be entitled to one vote. No member whose dues have been withheld by his employer for payment to such organization pursuant to his voluntary authorization provided for in a collective bargaining agreement shall be declared ineligible to vote or be a candidate for office in such organization by reason of alleged delay or default in the payment of dues. The votes cast by members of each local labor organization shall be counted, and the results published, separately. The election officials designated in the constitution and bylaws or the secretary, if no other official is designated, shall preserve for one year the ballots and all other records pertaining to the election. The election shall be conducted in accordance with the constitution and bylaws of such organization insofar as they are not inconsistent with the provisions of this title.

(f) When officers are chosen by a convention of delegates elected by secret ballot, the convention shall be conducted in accordance with the constitution and bylaws of the labor organization insofar as they are not inconsistent with the provisions of this title. The officials designated in the constitution and bylaws or the secretary, if no other is designated, shall preserve for one year the credentials of the delegates and all minutes and other records of the convention pertaining to the election of officers.

(g) No moneys received by any labor organization by way of dues, assessment, or similar levy, and no moneys of an employer shall be contributed or applied to promote the candidacy of any person in an election subject to the provisions of this title. Such moneys of a labor organization may be utilized for notices, factual statements of issues not involving candidates, and other expenses necessary for the holding of an election.

(h) If the Secretary, upon application of any member of a local labor organization, finds after hearing in accordance with the Administrative Procedure Act that the constitution and bylaws of such labor organization do not provide an adequate procedure for the removal of an elected officer guilty of serious misconduct, such officer may be removed, for cause shown and after notice and hearing, by the members in good standing voting in a secret ballot conducted by the officers of such labor organization in accordance with its constitution and bylaws insofar as they are not inconsistent with the provisions of this title.

(i) The Secretary shall promulgate rules and regulations prescribing mimimum standards and procedures for determining the adequacy of the removal procedures to which reference is made in subsection (h).

73 Stat. 534.

Enforcement
(29 U.S.C. 482)

SEC. 402. (a) A member of a labor organization—
    (1) who has exhausted the remedies available under the constitution and bylaws of such organization and of any parent body, or
    (2) who has invoked such available remedies without obtaining a final decision within three calendar months after their invocation,
may file a complaint with the Secretary within one calendar month thereafter alleging the violation of any provision of section 401 (including violation of the constitution and bylaws of the labor organization pertaining to the election and removal of officers). The challenged election shall be presumed valid pending a final decision thereon (as hereinafter provided) and in the interim the affairs of the organization shall be conducted by the officers elected or in such other manner as its constitution and bylaws may provide.

(b) The Secretary shall investigate such complaint and, if he finds probable cause to believe that a violation of this title has occurred and has not been remedied, he shall, within sixty days after the filing of such complaint, bring a civil action against the labor organization as an entity in the district court of the

the United States in which such labor organization maintains its principal office to set aside the invalid election, if any, and to direct the conduct of an election or hearing and vote upon the removal of officers under the supervision of the Secretary and in accordance with the provisions of this title and such rules and regulations as the Secretary may prescribe. The court shall have power to take such action as it deems proper to preserve the assets of the labor organization.

(c) If, upon a preponderance of the evidence after a trial upon the merits, the court finds—

(1) that an election has not been held within the time prescribed by section 401, or

(2) that the violation of section 401 may have affected the outcome of an election,

the court shall declare the election, if any, to be void and direct the conduct of a new election under supervision of the Secretary and, so far as lawful and practicable, in conformity with the constitution and bylaws of the labor organization. The Secretary shall promptly certify to the court the names of the persons elected, and the court shall thereupon enter a decree declaring such persons to be the officers of the labor oganization. If the proceeding is for the removal of officers pursuant to subsection (h) of section 401, the Secretary shall certify the results of the vote and the court shall enter a decree declaring whether such persons have been removed as officers of the labor organization.

(d) An order directing an election, dismissing a complaint, or designating elected officers of a labor organization shall be appealable in the same manner as the final judgment in a civil action, but an order directing an election shall not be stayed pending appeal.

Application of Other Laws
(29 U.S.C. 483)

Sec. 403. No labor organization shall be required by law to conduct elections of officers with greater frequency or in a different form or manner than is required by its own constitution or bylaws, except as otherwise provided by this title. Existing rights and remedies to enforce the constitution and bylaws of a labor organization with respect to elections prior to the conduct thereof shall not be affected by the provisions of this title. The remedy provided by this title for challenging an election already conducted shall be exclusive.

TITLE V—SAFEGUARDS FOR LABOR ORGANIZATIONS

Fiduciary Responsibility of Officers of Labor Organizations
(29 U.S.C. 501)

Sec. 501. (a) The officers, agents, shop stewards, and other representatives of a labor organization occupy positions of trust in relation to such organization and its members as a group. It is, therefore, the duty of each such person, taking into account the special problems and functions of a labor organization, to hold its money and property solely for the benefit of the organization and its members and to manage, invest, and expend the same in accordance with its constitution and bylaws and any resolutions of the governing bodies adopted thereunder, to refrain from dealing with such organization as an adverse party or in behalf of an adverse party in any matter connected with his duties and from holding or acquiring any pecuniary or personal interest which conflicts with the interests of such organization, and to account to the organization for any profit received by him in whatever capacity in connection with transactions conducted by him or under his direction on behalf of the organization. A general exculpatory provision in the constitution and bylaws of such a labor organization or a general exculpatory resolution of a governing body purporting to relieve any such person of liability for breach of the duties declared by this section shall be void as against public policy.

(b) When any officer, agent, shop steward, or representative of any labor organization is alleged to have violated the duties declared in subsection (a) and the labor organization or its governing board or officers refuse or fail to sue or recover damages or secure an accounting or other appropriate relief within a reasonable time after being requested to do so by any member of the labor organization, such member may sue such officer, agent, shop steward, or representative in any district court of the United States or in any State court of competent jurisdiction to recover damages or secure an accounting or other appropriate relief for the benefit of the labor organization. No such proceeding shall be brought except upon leave of the court obtained upon verified application and for good cause shown which application may be made ex parte. The trial judge may allot a reasonable part of the recovery in any action under this subsection to pay the fees of counsel prosecuting the suit at the instance of the member of the labor organization and to compensate such member for any expenses necessarily paid or incurred by him in connection with the litigation.

73 Stat. 536.

(c) Any person who embezzles, steals, or unlawfully and willfully abstracts or converts to his own use, or the use of another, any of the moneys, funds, securities, property, or other assets of a labor organization of which he is an officer, or by which he is employed, directly or indirectly, shall be fined not more than $10,000 or imprisoned for not more than five years, or both.

Making of Loans; Payment of Fines
(29 U.S.C. 503)

SEC. 503. (a) No labor organization shall make directly or indirectly any loan or loans to any officer or employee of such organization which results in a total indebtedness on the part of such officer or employee to the labor organization in excess of $2,000.

(b) No labor organization or employer shall directly or indirectly pay the fine of any officer or employee convicted of any willful violation of this Act.

(c) Any person who willfully violates this section shall be fined not more than $5,000 or imprisoned for not more than one year, or both.

Prohibition Against Certain Persons Holding Office
(29 U.S.C. 504)

SEC. 504. (a) No person who is or has been a member of the Communist Party [8] or who has been convicted of, or served any part of a prison term resulting from his conviction of, robbery, bribery, extortion, embezzlement, grand larceny, burglary, arson, violation of narcotics laws, murder, rape, assault with intent to

---

[8] The U.S. Supreme Court, on June 7, 1965, held unconstitutional as a bill of attainder the section 504 provision which imposes criminal sanctions on Communist Party members for holding union office (*U.S. v. Brown*, 381 U.S. 437, 85 S. Ct. 1707).

kill, assault which inflicts grievous bodily injury, or a violation of title II or III of 73 Stat. 537. this Act, or conspiracy to commit any such crimes, shall serve—

(1) as an officer, director, trustee, member of any executive board or similar governing body, business agent, manager, organizer, or other employee (other than as an employee performing exclusively clerical or custodial duties) of any labor organization, or

(2) as a labor relations consultant to a person engaged in an industry or activity affecting commerce, or as an officer, director, agent, or employee (other than as an employee performing exclusively clerical or custodial duties) of any group or association of employers dealing with any labor organization, during or for five years after the termination of his membership in the Communist Party,[8] or for five years after such conviction or after the end of such imprisonment, unless prior to the end of such five-year period, in the case of a person so convicted or imprisoned, (A) his citizenship rights, having been revoked as a result of such conviction, have been fully restored, or (B) the Board of Parole of the United States Department of Justice determines that such person's service in any capacity referred to in clause (1) or (2) would not be contrary to the purposes of this Act. Prior to making any such determination the Board shall hold an administrative hearing and shall give notice of such proceeding by certified mail to the State, county, and Federal prosecuting officials in the jurisdiction or jurisdictions in which such person was convicted. The Board's determination in any such proceeding shall be final. No labor organization or officer thereof shall knowingly permit any person to assume or hold any office or paid position in violation of this subsection.

(b) Any person who willfully violates this section shall be fined not more than $10,000 or imprisoned for not more than one year, or both.

(c) For the purposes of this section, any person shall be deemed to have been "convicted" and under the disability of "conviction" from the date of the judgment of the trial court or the date of the final sustaining of such judgment on appeal, whichever is the later event, regardless of whether such conviction occurred before or after the date of enactment of this Act.

Extortionate Picketing
(29 U.S.C. 522)

SEC. 602. (a) It shall be unlawful to carry on picketing on or about the premises of any employer for the purpose of, or as part of any conspiracy or in furtherance of any plan or purpose for, the personal profit or enrichment of any individual (except a bona fide increase in wages or other employee benefits) by taking or obtaining any money or other thing of value from such employer against his will or with his consent.

(b) Any person who willfully violates this section shall be fined not more than $10,000 or imprisoned not more than twenty years, or both.

Retention of Rights Under Other Federal and State Laws
73 Stat. 540.
(29 U.S.C. 523)

SEC. 603. (a) Except as explicitly provided to the contrary, nothing in this Act shall reduce or limit the responsibilities of any labor organization or any officer, agent, shop steward, or other representative of a labor organization, or of any trust in which a labor organization is interested, under any other Federal law or under the laws of any State, and, except as explicitly provided to the contrary, nothing in this Act shall take away any right or bar any remedy to which members of a labor organization are entitled under such other Federal law or law of any State.

(b) Nothing contained in titles I, II, III, IV, V, or VI of this Act shall be construed to supersede or impair or otherwise affect the provisions of the Railway Labor Act, as amended, or any of the obligations, rights, benefits, privileges, or immunities of any carrier, employee, organization, representative, or person subject thereto; nor shall anything contained in said titles (except section 505) of this Act be construed to confer any rights, privileges, immunities, or defenses upon employers, or to impair or otherwise affect the rights of any person under the National Labor Relations Act, as amended.

44 Stat. 577;
45 U.S.C. 151.

61 Stat. 136;
29 U.S.C. 167.

Effect on State Laws
(29 U.S.C. 524)

SEC. 604. Nothing in this Act shall be construed to impair or diminish the authority of any State to enact and enforce general criminal laws with respect to robbery, bribery, extortion, embezzlement, grand larceny, burglary, arson, violation of narcotics laws, murder, rape, assault with intent to kill, or assault which inflicts grievous bodily injury, or conspiracy to commit any of such crimes.

Criminal Contempt
(29 U.S.C. 528)

SEC. 608. No person shall be punished for any criminal contempt allegedly committed outside the immediate presence of the court in connection with any civil action prosecuted by the Secretary or any other person in any court of the United States under the provisions of this Act unless the facts constituting such criminal contempt are established by the verdict of the jury in a proceeding in the district court of the United States, which jury shall be chosen and empaneled in the manner prescribed by the law governing trial juries in criminal prosecutions in the district courts of the United States.

Prohibition on Certain Discipline by Labor Organization
(29 U.S.C. 529)

SEC. 609. It shall be unlawful for any labor organization, or any officer, agent, shop steward, or other representative of a labor organization, or any employee thereof to fine, suspend, expel, or otherwise discipline any of its members for exercising any right to which he is entitled under the provisions of this Act. The provisions of section 102 shall be applicable in the enforcement of this section.

Deprivation of Rights Under Act by Violence
(29 U.S.C. 530)

SEC. 610. It shall be unlawful for any person through the use of force or violence, or threat of the use of force or violence, to restrain, coerce, or intimidate, or attempt to restrain, coerce, or intimidate any member of a labor organization for the purpose of interfering with or preventing the exercise of any right to which he is entitled under the provisions of this Act. Any person who willfully violates this section shall be fined not more than $1,000 or imprisoned for not more than one year, or both.

CIVIL RIGHTS ACT OF 1964 AS AMENDED

TITLE VII—EQUAL EMPLOYMENT OPPORTUNITY [1]

DEFINITIONS

Sec. 701. For the purposes of this title—

(a) The term "person" includes one or more individuals, *governments, governmental agencies, political subdivisions,* labor unions, partnerships, associations, corporations, legal representatives, mutual companies, joint-stock companies, trusts, unincorporated organizations, trustees, trustees in bankruptcy, or receivers.

(b) The term "employer" means a person engaged in an industry affecting commerce who has *fifteen* or more employees for each working day in each of twenty or more calendar weeks in the current or preceding calendar year, and any agent of such a person, but such term does not include (1) the United States, a corporation wholly owned by the Government of the United States, an Indian tribe, or *any department or agency of the District of Columbia subject by statute to procedures of the competitive service (as defined in section 2102 of title 5 of the United States Code),* or (2) a bona fide private membership club (other than a labor organization) which is exempt from taxation under section 501(c) of the Internal Revenue Code of 1954, *except that during the first year after the date of enactment of the Equal Employment Opportunity Act of 1972,* persons having fewer than *twenty-five* employees (and their agents) shall not be considered *employers.*

(c) The term "employment agency" means any person regularly undertaking with or without compensation to procure employees for an employer or to procure for employees opportunities to work for an employer and includes an agent of such a person.

(d) The term "labor organization" means a labor organization engaged in an industry affecting commerce, and any agent of such an organization, and includes any organization of any kind, any agency, or employee representation committee, group, association, or plan so engaged in which employees participate and which exists for the

---

[1] Includes 1972 amendments made by P.L. 92–261 printed in italic.

purpose, in whole or in part, of dealing with employers concerning grievances, labor disputes, wages, rates of pay, hours, or other terms or conditions of employment, and any conference, general committee, joint or system board, or joint council so engaged which is subordinate to a national or international labor organization.

(e) A labor organization shall be deemed to be engaged in an industry affecting commerce if (1) it maintains or operates a hiring hall or hiring office which procures employees for an employer or procures for employees opportunities to work for an employer, or (2) the number of its members (or, where it is a labor organization composed of other labor organizations or their representatives, if the aggregate number of the members of such other labor organization) is (A) *twenty-five* or more during the first year after the *date of enactment of the Equal Employment Opportunity Act of 1972, or (B) fifteen* or more thereafter, and such labor organization—

(1) is the certified representative of employees under the provisions of the National Labor Relations Act, as amended, or the Railway Labor Act, as amended;

(2) although not certified, is a national or international labor organization or a local labor organization recognized or acting as the representative of employees of an employer or employers engaged in an industry affecting commerce; or

(3) has chartered a local labor organization or subsidiary body which is representing or actively seeking to represent employees of employers within the meaning of paragraph (1) or (2); or

(4) has been chartered by a labor organization representing or actively seeking to represent employees within the meaning of paragraph (1) or (2) as the local or subordinate body through which such employees may enjoy membership or become affiliated with such labor organization; or

(5) is a conference, general committee, joint or system board, or joint council subordinate to a national or international labor organization, which includes a labor organization engaged in an industry affecting commerce within the meaning of any of the preceding paragraphs of this subsection.

(f) The term "employee" means an individual employed by an employer, *except that the term 'employee' shall not include any person elected to public office in any State or political subdivision of any State by the qualified voters thereof, or any person chosen by such officer to be on such officer's personal staff, or an appointee on the policymaking level or an immediate adviser with respect to the exercise of the constitutional or legal powers of the office. The exemption set forth in the preceding sentence shall not include employees subject to the civil service laws of a State government, governmental agency or political subdivision.*

(g) The term "commerce" means trade, traffic, commerce, transportation, transmission, or communication among the several States; or between a State and any place outside thereof; or within the District of Columbia, or a possession of the United States; or between points in the same State but through a point outside thereof.

(h) The term "industry affecting commerce" means any activity, business, or industry in commerce or in which a labor dispute would hinder or obstruct commerce or the free flow of commerce and includes any activity or industry "affecting commerce" within the meaning of the Labor-Management Reporting and Disclosure Act of 1959, *and further includes any governmental industry, business, or activity.*

(i) The term "State" includes a State of the United States, the District of Columbia, Puerto Rico, the Virgin Islands, American Samoa, Guam, Wake Island, the Canal Zone, and Outer Continental Shelf lands defined in the Outer Continental Shelf Lands Act.

(j) The term "religion" includes all aspects of religious observance and practice, as well as belief, unless an employer demonstrates that he is unable to reasonably accommodate to an employee's or prospective employee's, religious observance or practice without undue hardship on the conduct of the employer's business.

EXEMPTION

Sec. 702. This title shall not apply to an employer with respect to the employment of aliens outside any State, or to a religious corporation, association, *educational institution,* or society with respect to the employment of individuals of a particular religion to perform work connected with the carrying on by such corporation, association, *educational institution,* or society of its *activities.*

DISCRIMINATION BECAUSE OF RACE, COLOR, RELIGION, SEX, OR NATIONAL ORIGIN

Sec. 703. (a) It shall be an unlawful employment practice for an employer—

(1) to fail or refuse to hire or to discharge any individual, or otherwise to discriminate against any individual with respect to his compensation, terms, conditions, or privileges of employment, because of such individual's race, color, religion, sex, or national origin; or

(2) to limit, segregate, or classify his employees *or applicants for employment* in any way which would deprive or tend to deprive any individual of employment opportunities or otherwise adversely affect his status as an employee, because of such individual's race, color, religion, sex, or national origin.

(b) It shall be an unlawful employment practice for an employment agency to fail or refuse to refer for employment, or otherwise to discriminate against, any individual because of his race, color, religion, sex, or national origin, or to classify or refer for employment any individual on the basis of his race, color, religion, sex, or national origin.

(c) It shall be an unlawful employment practice for a labor organization—

(1) to exclude or to expel from its membership, or otherwise to discriminate against, any individual because of his race, color, religion, sex, or national origin;

(2) to limit, segregate, or classify its membership, *or applicants for membership* or to classify or fail or refuse to refer for employment any individual, in any way which would deprive or tend to deprive any individual of employment opportunities, or would limit such employment opportunities or otherwise adversely affect his status as an employee or as an applicant for employment, because of such individual's race, color, religion, sex, or national origin; or

(3) to cause or attempt to cause an employer to discriminate against an individual in violation of this section.

(d) It shall be an unlawful employment practice for any employer, labor organization, or joint labor-management committee controlling apprenticeship or other training or retraining, including on-the-job training programs to discriminate against any individual because of his race, color, religion, sex, or national origin in admission to, or employment in, any program established to provide apprenticeship or other training.

(e) Notwithstanding any other provision of this title, (1) it shall not be an unlawful employment practice for an employer to hire and employ employees, for an employment agency to classify, or refer for employment any individual, for a labor organization to classify its membership or to classify or refer for employment any individual, or for an employer, labor organization, or joint labor-management committee controlling apprenticeship or other training or retraining programs to admit or employ any individual in any such program, on the basis of his religion, sex, or national origin in those certain instances where religion, sex, or national origin is a bona fide occupational qualification reasonably necessary to the normal operation of that particular business or enterprise, and (2) it shall not be an unlawful employment practice for a school, college, university, or other educational institution or institution of learning to hire and employ employees of a particular religion if such school, college, university, or other educational institution or institution of learning is, in whole or in substantial part, owned, supported, controlled, or managed by a particular religion or by a particular religious corporation, association, or society, or if the curriculum of such school, college, university, or other educational institution or institution of learning is directed toward the propagation of a particular religion.

(f) As used in this title, the phrase "unlawful employment practice" shall not be deemed to include any action or measure taken by an employer, labor organization, joint labor-management committee, or employment agency with respect to an individual who is a member of the Communist Party of the United States or of any other organization required to register as a Communist-action or Communist-front organization by final order of the Subversive Activities Control Board pursuant to the Subversive Activities Control Act of 1950.

(g) Notwithstanding any other provision of this title, it shall not be an unlawful employment practice for an employer to fail or refuse to hire and employ any individual for any position, for an employer to discharge any individual from any position, or for an employment agency to fail or refuse to refer any individual for employment in any position, or for a labor organization to fail or refuse to refer any individual for employment in any position, if—

(1) the occupancy of such position, or access to the premises in or upon which any part of the duties of such position is performed or is to be performed, is subject to any requirement imposed in the interest of the national security of the United States under any security program in effect pursuant to or administered under any statute of the United States or any Executive order of the President; and

(2) such individual has not fulfilled or has ceased to fulfill that requirement.

(h) Notwithstanding any other provision of this title, it shall not be an unlawful employment practice for an employer to apply different standards of compensation, or different terms, conditions, or privileges of employment pursuant to a bona fide seniority or merit system, or a system which measures earnings by quantity or quality of production or to employees who work in different locations, provided that such differences are not the result of an intention to discriminate because of race, color, religion, sex, or national origin, nor shall it be an unlawful employment practice for an employer to give and to act upon the results of any professionally developed ability test provided that such test, its administration or action upon the results is not designed, intended or used to discriminate because of race, color, religion, sex or national origin. It shall not be an unlawful employment practice under this title for any employer to differentiate upon the basis of sex in determining the amount of the wages or compensation paid or to be paid to employees of such employer if such differentiation is authorized by the provisions of section 6(d) of the Fair Labor Standards Act of 1938, as amended (29 U.S.C. 206(d)).

(i) Nothing contained in this title shall apply to any business or enterprise on or near an Indian reservation with respect to any publicly announced employment practice of such business or enterprise under which a preferential treatment is given to any individual because he is an Indian living on or near a reservation.

(j) Nothing contained in this title shall be interpreted to require any employer, employment agency, labor organization, or joint labor-management committee subject to this title to grant preferential treatment to any individual or to any group because of the race, color, religion, sex, or national origin of such individual or group on account of an imbalance which may exist with respect to the total number or percentage of persons of any race, color, religion, sex, or national origin employed by any employer, referred or classified for employment by any employment agency or labor organization, admitted to membership or classified by any labor organization, or admitted to, or employed in, any apprenticeship or other training program, in comparison with the total number or percentage of persons of such race, color, religion, sex, or national origin in any community, State, section, or other area, or in the available work force in any community, State, section, or other area.

OTHER UNLAWFUL EMPLOYMENT PRACTICES

SEC. 704. (a) It shall be an unlawful employment practice for an employer to discriminate against any of his employees or applicants for employment, for an employment agency, *or joint labor-management committee controlling apprenticeship or other training or retraining, including on-the-job training programs,* to discriminate against any individual, or for a labor organization to discriminate against any member thereof or applicant for membership, because he has opposed any practice made an unlawful employment practice by this title, or because he has made a charge, testified, assisted, or participated in any manner in an investigation, proceeding, or hearing under this title.

(b) It shall be an unlawful employment practice for an employer, labor organization, employment *agency, or joint labor-management committee controlling apprenticeship or other training or retraining, in-*

cluding on-the-job training programs, to print or publish or cause to be printed or published any notice or advertisement relating to employment by such an employer or membership in or any classification or referral for employment by such a labor organization, or relating to any classification or referral for employment by such an employment *agency, or relating to admission to, or employment in, any program established to provide apprenticeship or other training by such a joint labor-management committee* indicating any preference, limitation, specification, or discrimination, based on race, color, religion, sex, or national origin, except that such a notice or advertisement may indicate a preference, limitation, specification, or discrimination based on religion, sex, or national origin when religion, sex, or national origin is a bona fide occupational qualification for employment.

EQUAL EMPLOYMENT OPPORTUNITY COMMISSION

SEC. 705. (a) There is hereby created a Commission to be known as the Equal Employment Opportunity Commission, which shall be composed of five members, not more than three of whom shall be members of the same political party. *Members of the Commission shall be appointed by the President by and with the advice and consent of the Senate for a term of five years. Any individual chosen to fill a vacancy shall be appointed only for the unexpired term of the member whom he shall succeed, and all members of the Commission shall continue to serve until their successors are appointed and qualified, except that no such member of the Commission shall continue to serve (1) for more than sixty days when the Congress is in session unless a nomination to fill such vacancy shall have been submitted to the Senate, or (2) after the adjournment sine die of the session of the Senate in which such nomination was submitted.* The President shall designate one member to serve as Chairman of the Commission, and one member to serve as Vice Chairman. The Chairman shall be responsible on behalf of the Commission for the administrative operations of the Commission, and *except as provided in subsection (b),* shall appoint, in accordance with the *provisions of title 5, United States Code, governing appointments in the competitive service, such officers, agents, attorneys, hearing examiners, and employees as he deems necessary to assist it in the performance of its functions and to fix their compensation in accordance with the provisions of chapter 51 and subchapter III of chapter 53 of title 5, United States Code, relating to classification and General Schedule pay rates: Provided, That assignment, removal, and compensation of hearing examiners shall be in accordance with sections 3105, 3344, 5362, and 7521 of title 5, United States Code.*

(b)(1) There shall be a General Counsel of the Commission appointed by the President, by and with the advice and consent of the Senate, for a term of four years. The General Counsel shall have responsibility for the conduct of litigation as provided in sections 706 and 707 of this title. The General Counsel shall have such other duties as the Commission may prescribe or as may be provided by law and shall concur with the Chairman of the Commission on the appointment and supervision of regional attorneys. The General Counsel of the Commission on the effective date of this Act shall continue in such position and perform the functions specified in this subsection until a successor is appointed and qualified.

PREVENTION OF UNLAWFUL EMPLOYMENT PRACTICES

SEC. 706. (*a*) *The Commission is empowered, as hereinafter provided, to prevent any person from engaging in any unlawful employment practice as set forth in section 703 or 704 of this title.*

(*b*) Whenever *a charge is filed by or on behalf of a* person claiming to be aggrieved, or by a member of the Commission, *alleging* that an employer, employment agency, labor *organization, or joint labor-management committee controlling apprenticeship or other training or retraining, including on-the-job training programs*, has engaged in an unlawful employment practice, the Commission shall *serve a notice of the charge (including the date, place and circumstances of the alleged unlawful employment practice)* on such employer, employment agency, labor *organization, or joint labor-management committee* (hereinafter referred to as the "respondent") *within ten days, and shall make an investigation thereof. Charges shall be in writing under oath or affirmation and shall contain such information and be in such form as the Commission requires. Charges* shall not be made public by the Commission. If the Commission *determines* after such investigation that there is *not* reasonable cause to believe that the charge is true, *it shall dismiss the charge and promptly notify the person claiming to be aggrieved and the respondent of its action. In determining whether reasonable cause exists, the Commission shall accord substantial weight to final findings and orders made by State or local authorities in proceedings commenced under State or local law pursuant to the requirements of subsections (c) and (d). If the Commission determines after such investigation that there is reasonable cause to believe that the charge is true,* the Commission shall endeavor to eliminate any such alleged unlawful employment practice by informal methods of conference, conciliation, and persuasion. Nothing said or done during and as a part of such *informal* endeavors may be made public by the *Commission, its officers or employees, or used as evidence in a subsequent proceeding* without the written consent of the *persons concerned.* Any *person who makes* public information in violation of this subsection shall be fined not more than $1,000 or imprisoned *for* not more than one *year, or both. The Commission shall make its determination on reasonable cause as promptly as possible and, so far as practicable, not later than one hundred and twenty days from the filing of the charge or, where applicable under subsection (c) or (d) from the date upon which the Commission is authorized to take action with respect to the charge.*

(*c*) In the case of an alleged unlawful employment practice occurring in a State, or political subdivision of a State, which has a State or local law prohibiting the unlawful employment practice alleged and establishing or authorizing a State or local authority to grant or seek relief from such practice or to institute criminal proceedings with respect thereto upon receiving notice thereof, no charge may be filed under subsection (a) by the person aggrieved before the expiration of sixty days after proceedings have been commenced under the State or local law, unless such proceedings have been earlier terminated, provided that such sixty-day period shall be extended to one hundred and twenty days during the first year after the effective date of such State or local law. If any requirement for the commencement of such proceedings is imposed by a State or local authority other than a requirement of the filing of a written and signed statement of the facts upon which the proceeding is based, the proceeding shall be deemed to have been commenced for the purposes of this subsection at the time such statement is sent by registered mail to the appropriate State or local authority.

(d) In the case of any charge filed by a member of the Commission alleging an unlawful employment practice occurring in a State or political subdivision of a State which has a State or local law prohibiting the practice alleged and establishing or authorizing a State or local authority to grant or seek relief from such practice or to institute criminal proceedings with respect thereto upon receiving notice thereof, the Commission shall, before taking any action with respect to such charge, notify the appropriate State or local officials and, upon request, afford them a reasonable time, but not less than sixty days (provided that such sixty-day period shall be extended to one hundred and twenty days during the first year after the effective *date* of such State or local law), unless a shorter period is requested, to act under such State or local law to remedy the practice alleged.

(e) A charge under *this section* shall be filed within *one hundred and eighty* days after the alleged unlawful employment practice *occurred and notice of the charge (including the date, place and circumstances of the alleged unlawful employment practice) shall be served upon the person against whom such charge is made within ten days thereafter,* except that in *a* case of an unlawful employment practice with respect to which the person aggrieved has *initially instituted proceedings with a State or local agency with authority to grant or seek relief from such practice or to institute criminal proceedings with respect thereto upon receiving notice thereof,* such charge shall be filed by *or on behalf of* the person aggrieved within *three hundred* days after the alleged unlawful employment practice occurred, or within thirty days after receiving notice that the State or local agency has terminated the proceedings under the State or local law, whichever is earlier, and a copy of such charge shall be filed by the Commission with the State or local agency.

(f)(1) If within thirty days after a charge is filed with the Commission or within thirty days after expiration of any period of reference under subsection (c) or (d), the Commission has been unable to *secure from the respondent a conciliation agreement acceptable to the Commission,* the Commission *may bring a civil action against any respondent not a government, governmental agency, or political subdivision named in the charge. In the case of a respondent which is a government, governmental agency, or political subdivision, if the Commission has been unable to secure from the respondent a conciliation agreement acceptable to the Commission, the Commission shall take no further action and shall refer the case to the Attorney General who may bring a civil action against such respondent in the appropriate United States district court. The person or persons aggrieved shall have the right to intervene in a civil action brought by the Commission or the Attorney General in a case involving a government, governmental agency, or political subdivision. If a charge filed with the Commission pursuant to subsection (b) is dismissed by the Commission, or if within one hundred and eighty days from the filing of such charge or the expiration of any period of reference under subsection (c) or (d), whichever is later, the Commission has not filed a civil action under this section or the Attorney General has notified a civil action in a case involving a government, governmental agency, or political subdivision, or the Commission has not entered into a conciliation agreement to which the person aggrieved is a party, the Commission, or the Attorney General in a case involving a government, governmental agency, or political subdivision, shall so notify the person aggrieved and within ninety days after the giving of such notice a civil action may* be brought against the respondent named in the charge (A) by the person claiming to be aggrieved, or (B) if such charge was filed by a member of the Commission, by any person whom the charge alleges was aggrieved by the alleged unlawful employment practice. Upon application by the complainant and in such circumstances as the court may deem just, the court may appoint an attorney for such complainant and may authorize the commencement of the action without the payment of fees, costs, or security. Upon timely application, the court may, in its discretion, permit the *Commission*, or the Attorney General in a case involving a government, governmental agency, or political subdivision, to intervene in such civil action *upon certification* that the case is of general public importance. Upon request, the court may, in its discretion, stay further proceedings for not more than sixty days pending the termination of State or local proceedings described in subsections (*c*) *or* (*d*) *of this section or further* efforts of the Commission to obtain voluntary compliance.

(2) Whenever a charge is filed with the Commission and the Commission concludes on the basis of a preliminary investigation that prompt judicial action is necessary to carry out the purposes of this Act, the Commission, or the Attorney General in a case involving a government, governmental agency, or political subdivision, may bring an action for appropriate temporary or preliminary relief pending final disposition of such charge. Any temporary restraining order or other order granting preliminary or temporary relief shall be issued in accordance with rule 65 of the Federal Rules of Civil Procedure. It shall be the duty of a court having jurisdiction over proceedings under this section to assign cases for hearing at the earliest practicable date and to cause such cases to be in every way expedited.

(3) Each United States district court and each United States court of a place subject to the jurisdiction of the United States shall have jurisdiction of actions brought under this title. Such an action may be brought in any judicial district in the State in which the unlawful employment practice is alleged to have been committed, in the judicial district in which the employment records relevant to such practice are maintained and administered, or in the judicial district in which the aggrieved person would have worked but for the alleged unlawful employment practice, but if the respondent is not found within any such district, such an action may be brought within the judicial district in which the respondent has his principal office. For purposes of sections 1404 and 1406 of title 28 of the United States Code, the judicial district in which the respondent has his principal office shall in all cases be considered a district in which the action might have been brought.

(4) It shall be the duty of the chief judge of the district (or in his absence, the acting chief judge) in which the case is pending immediately to designate a judge in such district to hear and determine the case. In the event that no judge in the district is available to hear and determine the case, the chief judge of the district, or the acting chief judge, as the

case may be, shall certify this fact to the chief judge of the circuit (or in his absence, the acting chief judge) who shall then designate a district or circuit judge of the circuit to hear and determine the case.

(5) It shall be the duty of the judge designated pursuant to this subsection to assign the case for hearing at the earliest practicable date and to cause the case to be in every way expedited. If such judge has not scheduled the case for trial within one hundred and twenty days after issue has been joined, that judge may appoint a master pursuant to rule 53 of the Federal Rules of Civil Procedure.

(g) If the court finds that the respondent has intentionally engaged in or is intentionally engaging in an unlawful employment practice charged in the complaint, the court may enjoin the respondent from engaging in such unlawful employment practice, and order such affirmative action as may be appropriate, which may include, but is not limited to, reinstatement or hiring of employees, with or without back pay (payable by the employer, employment agency, or labor organization, as the case may be, responsible for the unlawful employment practice), or any other equitable relief as the court deems appropriate. Back pay liability shall not accrue from a date more than two years prior to the filing of a charge with the Commission. Interim earnings or amounts earnable with reasonable diligence by the person or persons discriminated against shall operate to reduce the back pay otherwise allowable. No order of the court shall require the admission or reinstatement of an individual as a member of a union, or the hiring, reinstatement, or promotion of an individual as an employee, or the payment to him of any back pay, if such individual was refused admission, suspended, or expelled, or was refused employment or advancement or was suspended or discharged for any reason other than discrimination on account of race, color, religion, sex, or national origin or in violation of section 704(a).

(h) The provisions of the Act entitled "An Act to amend the Judicial Code and to define and limit the jurisdiction of courts sitting in equity, and for other purposes," approved March 23, 1932 (29 U.S.C. 101–115), shall not apply with respect to civil actions brought under this section.

(i) In any case in which an employer, employment agency, or labor organization fails to comply with an order of a court issued in a civil action brought under *this section*, the Commission may commence proceedings to compel compliance with such order.

(j) Any civil action brought under *this section* and any proceedings brought under subsection (i) shall be subject to appeal as provided in sections 1291 and 1292, title 28, United States Code.

(k) In any action or proceeding under this title the court, in its discretion, may allow the prevailing party, other than the Commission or the United States, a reasonable attorney's fee as part of the costs, and the Commission and the United States shall be liable for costs the same as a private person.

EFFECT ON STATE LAWS

Sec. 708. Nothing in this title shall be deemed to exempt or relieve any person from any liability, duty, penalty, or punishment provided by any present or future law of any State or political subdivision of a State, other than any such law which purports to require or permit the doing of any act which would be an unlawful employment practice under this title.

SEC. 712. Nothing contained in this title shall be construed to repeal or modify any Federal, State, territorial, or local law creating special rights or preference for veterans.

SEC. 713. (a) The Commission shall have authority from time to time to issue, amend, or rescind suitable procedural regulations to carry out the provisions of this title. Regulations issued under the section shall be in conformity with the standards and limitations of the Administrative Procedure Act.

(b) In any action or proceeding based on any alleged unlawful employment practice, no person shall be subject to any liability or punishment for or on account of (1) the commission by such person of an unlawful employment practice if he pleads and proves that the act or omission complained of was in good faith, in conformity with, and in reliance on any written interpretation or opinion of the Commission, or (2) the failure of such person to publish and file any information required by any provision of this title if he pleads and proves that he failed to publish and file such information in good faith, in conformity with the instructions of the Commission issued under this title regarding the filing of such information. Such a defense, if established, shall be a bar to the action or proceeding, notwithstanding that (A) after such act or omission, such interpretation or opinion is modified or rescinded or is determined by judicial authority to be invalid or of no legal effect, or (B) after publishing or filing the description and annual reports, such publication or filing is determined by judicial authority not to be in conformity with the requirements of this title.

Index